Lafayette

LAFAYETTE.

Lafayette, in his uniform as a French brigadier general and maréchal de camp, in 1782, from an engraving by Adèle Ethiou of the painting at Versailles. (*From the author's collection.*)

Lafayette

Harlow Giles Unger

John Wiley & Sons, Inc.

Library of Congress Cataloging-in-Publication Data:

Unger, Harlow G., date.
    Lafayette / Harlow Giles Unger.
       p. cm.
    Includes bibliographical references and index.
    ISBN 0-471-39432-7 (cloth : alk. paper)
    1. Lafayette, Marie Joseph Paul Yves Roch Gilbert Du Motier, marquis de,
1757–1834. 2. Generals—United States—Biography. 3. United States. Army—
Biography. 4. Generals—France—Biography. 5. Statesmen—France—Biography.
6. United States—History—Revolution, 1775–1783—Participation, French.
7. United States—History—Revolution, 1775–1783—Biography. I. Title.

E207.L2 U45 2002
944.04′092—dc21
[B]
                                                                    2002071327

10 9 8 7 6 5 4 3

To my dear friends
André and Eva Mandel

To my brother
Roger H. Unger, M.D.

and
To my son
Richard C. Unger

The happiness of America is intimately connected with the happiness of all mankind; She is destined to become the safe and venerable asylum of virtue, of honesty, of tolerance, and of peaceful liberty.

Lafayette, June 7, 1777

Contents

Illustrations

Maps

Illustrations

Acknowledgments

The Lafayette family, Michel and Geneviève Aubert La Fayette, were exceptionally generous in welcoming me to their beautiful Château de Vollore* in the Auvergne, where they not only shared their collection of Lafayette memorabilia and documents but stood ready to serve as consultants at every stage in the development of this book. Also of great help were the curatorial staff at the Château de Chavaniac, Lafayette's birthplace and childhood home.

Of all those who helped me with this book, however, my deepest thanks must go to my dear friends of more than forty-five years, André and Eva Mandel, to whom I have dedicated this book. For two years, they willingly helped me in my research, translating archaic language, hunting for hard-to-find, out-of-print books, photographs, and documents, locating Lafayette descendants, and driving me over hundreds of miles of dusty roads in the Auvergne—at times through driving rain—on the trail of Lafayette and his family.

In the United States, my wonderful friend and literary agent, Edward Knappman, was, as always, kind and generous with his wise counsel and his help in locating a number of hard-to-find, out-of-print works that proved essential for this book—and in sharing his wisdom. The always gracious Louise Jones, the librarian at the Yale Club of New York City, was also helpful, as were Peter Jaffe, of the rare books department of Argosy Book Store in New York, my former editor, Randi Ladenheim Gil, and Sibylle Kazeroid, an excellent proofreader. Economist Jonathan Falk was also most generous in contributing his time and extensive knowledge. Finally, my deepest thanks, as always, to my editor and friend, Hana Lane, for her constant guidance and wise counsel in every phase of this book.

---

*The Château de Vollore, in Courpière, is the site of *Les Concerts de Vollore*, an annual music festival held in July. Although the château is still the home of the Lafayette family, its Lafayette Memorial room is open to the public, along with an art gallery, conference rooms, and guest suites.

Chronology

1757   September 6. Gilbert du Motier de La Fayette born in Chavaniac, France.
1759   Father killed in Battle of Minden.
1768   L moves to Paris.
1770   Mother dies.
1771   Enrolls in Black Musketeers at the Palace of Versailles.
1774   Marries Marie-Adrienne-Françoise de Noailles.
1775   Joins Noailles regiment at Metz; enrolls in Freemasons; daughter Henriette born.
1776   Enlists in American Continental army as major general.
1777   Sails for America; joins Washington's staff; wounded at Battle of Brandywine; Battle of Saratoga; routs Hessians at Gloucester; assigned command of Canada invasion; helps expose Conway Cabal; daughter Anastasie born; Henriette dies.
1778   Valley Forge; negotiates treaty with Indians; Battle of Barren Hill; Battle of Monmouth; d'Estaing's French fleet arrives; Battle of Newport.
1779   L returns to France; wins French support for American Revolution; birth of son, George-Washington Lafayette.
1780   L returns to America; Rochambeau arrives with French fleet, 4,000 French troops; treason of Benedict Arnold; hanging of Major André.
1781   L's Virginia campaign; traps Cornwallis; French fleet blocks Cornwallis escape by sea; siege of Yorktown; Cornwallis surrender.
1782   L returns to France; awarded Cross of Saint-Louis; becomes maréchal de camp; daughter Virginie born.

1783   Treaty of Paris ends Revolutionary War; Britain recognizes American independence.

1784   L's farewell tour of United States; forges treaty between Indians and Americans; last visit with Washington; Congress names him ambassador without portfolio in Europe; Jefferson replaces Franklin in France.

1785   L returns to France; visits Frederick the Great; buys plantation in French Guyana to free slaves; negotiates trade deals for U.S. whale oil, books, paper, agricultural products.

1786   Louis XVI convenes Assembly of Notables; L demands sweeping economic and social reforms under constitutional monarchy.

1787   First French provincial assemblies meet; L elected to Auvergne assembly; votes to curb royal spending; Americans ratify Constitution.

1788   King strips L of marshal's rank; second Assembly of Notables.

1789   King convenes Estates General; conversion to National Assembly; first U.S. Congress convenes; Washington elected first U.S. president; Lafayette, Jefferson write "First Declaration of Rights of Man for Europe"; French mob storms Bastille; L organizes National Guard; mob attacks Versailles; L saves royal family.

1790   Radicals seize French Assembly, abolish aristocracy, nationalize lands and Roman Catholic Church; Jacobins mutiny in army; L organizes huge *Fête de la Fédération* to unite nation.

1791   Royal family flees Paris, captured and confined to palace; Assembly approves constitution; L resigns, returns to Chavaniac; L ordered to war against Austrians.

1792   King vetoes Jacobin decrees; mob invades Assembly and Palace; L demands arrest of Jacobins; Jacobins overthrow monarchy, imprison royal family, and order L's arrest for treason; he flees France; Prussian king orders him imprisoned in Wesel, then Magdeburg.

1793   Jacobins execute King Louis XVI in January, Queen Marie-Antoinette in October; Adrienne Lafayette arrested; Robespierre begins the Terror, sends thousands to guillotine without trial.

1794   L transferred to Austrian prison at Olmütz; his wife, Adrienne Lafayette, transferred to Paris prison; Adrienne's sister, mother, and grandmother guillotined; Robespierre overthrown, dies on guillotine; the Terror ends.

1795   New constitution creates republican government under five-man directory, bicameral legislature; American ambassador James Monroe wins Adrienne's release; she sends son, George-Washington to America to his godfather, President George Washington; Adrienne and daughters join L in Olmütz prison.

1797   American officials and Napoléon win release of "Prisoners of Olmütz"; family moves to exile in Denmark; Anastasie marries.

1798   George-Washington Lafayette returns from America; family moves to Holland. Adrienne goes to Paris to recover family properties.

1799   Napoléon seizes power; L returns to France; retires as gentleman farmer at Château de La Grange; Washington dies.

1802   George-Washington Lafayette marries.

1803   L fractures hip; Virginie marries.

1807   Adrienne dies; is buried in Picpus cemetery in Paris, near graves of murdered mother, grandmother, and sister.

1814   Napoléon abdicates; First Restoration; Napoléon's "Hundred Days" of republican rule; L resumes political career, is elected to National Assembly; Napoléon's Waterloo; Coalition armies occupy France; Louis XVIII begins Second Restoration; L leads liberal opposition to king in Assembly.

1821   L backs conspiracy of Charbonniers to overthrow king.

1823   L defeated for reelection to Assembly.

1824–   Congress invites L as "the Nation's Guest" for triumphal thirteen-
1825   month tour of United States; lays cornerstone of Bunker Hill monument.

1827   L reelected to French Assembly; provides aid to rebels in Poland, Italy, Greece, elsewhere.

1830   King dissolves Assembly; suspends free press; riots break out; L takes command of National Guard, leads "Three Glorious Days" of July Revolution; king abdicates; L rejects presidency, seats Louis-Philippe on throne as constitutional monarch; king rescinds rights agreement; L resigns.

1831   L reelected to Chamber of Deputies; leads liberal opposition to king.

1832   L leads funeral cortège for General Lamarque; Parisians riot; king crushes insurrection, seizes authoritarian powers.

1834 L makes last speech to Chamber of Deputies, assails Louis-Philippe's government. Dies in Paris on May 20, is buried beside Adrienne at Picpus beneath soil from Bunker Hill.

1917 July 4. General Pershing's aide plants American flag over L's grave: "Lafayette, we are here."

Preface

"Pronounce him one of the first men of his age, and you have yet not done him justice. . . . Turn back your eyes upon the records of time . . . and where, among the race of merely mortal men, shall one be found, who, as the benefactor of his kind, shall claim to take precedence of Lafayette?"[1]

With those words to Congress in 1834, John Quincy Adams plunged America into deep and universal mourning. Lafayette was dead, and Americans mourned as they had never mourned before, not even when Washington had died, thirty-five years earlier. For no one in the history of the nation had ever given of themselves as generously or as freely as "Our Marquis." Lafayette was the last of the world's gallant knights, galloping out of Arthurian romance, across the pages of history, to rid the world of evil. Of all the Founding Fathers—the heroes and leaders of the Revolutionary War—only Lafayette commanded the unanimous acclaim and veneration of Americans. For only he came with no links to any state or region; only he belonged to the entire nation; and only he, among all who pledged their lives, fortunes, and sacred honor, sought no economic or political gain. He asked no recompense but the right to serve America and liberty, and, when Americans lost him, they knew that they and the world would never see his kind again—a hero among heroes.

An intimate and friend of world leaders over seventy years of earth-shaking social, political, and economic change, Lafayette led three revolutions that changed the course of world history and became the world's foremost champion of individual liberty, abolition, religious tolerance, gender equality, universal suffrage, and free trade. He was arguably the wealthiest aristocrat in France, with close ties to the king, the royal family, and the entire court; his wife's family was equally wealthy and well-placed. He

xvii

and his family danced at Marie-Antoinette's balls, hunted with the king, and glutted themselves at palace banquets in Versailles. Lafayette turned his back on it all—indeed, fled, from incomparable luxury—to wade through South Carolina swamps, freeze at Valley Forge, and ride through the stifling southern heat of Virginia—as an unpaid volunteer, fighting and bleeding for liberty, in a land not his own, for a people not his own. Even the most selfless of his fellow Founding Fathers in America had some personal interests at stake. George Washington also refused compensation for his military service, but admitted that his initial motive for battling the British was his distaste for taxes: "They have no right to put their hands in my pockets," Washington complained.

Lafayette had no such motives when he came to America in 1777. Only nineteen, he all but immediately proved himself a brave, brilliant soldier and field commander, admired and adored by his troops and fellow commanders. And when the American Revolution seemed lost, he sailed back to France to win the most stunning and paradoxical diplomatic victory in world history—coaxing Europe's oldest, most despotic monarchy into making common cause with rebels to overthrow a fellow monarch. Returning with a huge French armada and thousands of French troops, Lafayette helped lead a brilliant military campaign in Virginia that climaxed with Britain's defeat at Yorktown and earned him world acclaim as "the Conqueror of Cornwallis."

Lafayette's triumph in America, however, turned to tragedy in France when he tried to introduce American liberty to his native land and took command of the French Revolution. In releasing the French from their chains of despotism, he unwittingly unleashed a horde of beasts who plunged France and Europe into decades of unimaginable savagery and world war. The despots of Europe—and the French themselves—punished him and his family horribly, sending him, his wife, Adrienne, and their two daughters to dungeon prisons and exile, and some of his wife's family to the guillotine. America's James Monroe saved the surviving family members, winning Adrienne's release and helping Lafayette's fourteen-year-old son escape to America and the safety of George Washington's home in Mount Vernon. Ultimately, it was the courage of Lafayette's brilliant, adoring wife who saved his name and some remnants of the family fortune.

Lafayette lived in two worlds, and his story is the story of both during the most critical period in Western political history. Born in the Old World, his spirit belonged to the New, and the revolutions he led in each changed the course of both: one spawned American democracy; the other became the uterine vessel for genocidal political ideologies—communism, fascism, and Nazism.

Lafayette was an intimate of the New World's heroes and an enemy of the Old World's villains. The savage Robespierre condemned him to death for treason, but Washington loved him "as if he were my own son," and he called Washington "my adoptive father." Jefferson, Madison, Monroe, Quincy Adams, Alexander Hamilton, Nathanael Greene, Henry Knox, Anthony Wayne, and Benjamin Franklin were trusted friends. Schooled at Versailles with the future Louis XVIII and Charles X, he mingled as easily with Louis XVI and Marie-Antoinette, with Frederick the Great and William Pitt, as he did with his troops on America's battlefields, where he won veneration as "the soldier's friend."

Over the years, grateful Americans have named more than 600 villages, towns, cities and counties, mountains, lakes, and rivers, educational institutions, and other landmarks for the great French knight who helped win their liberty. Ironically, not a single community in France has ever acknowledged his existence in this way. The isolated mountain hamlet of Chavaniac hyphenated his name to its own only after American philanthropists bought and restored the château where he was born, converting it into a museum and a source of income for surrounding communities. Paris named a street and a small square for him, and a department store took his name to identify its location on that street—not to celebrate him. To this day, many in France call him traitor—especially radicals at opposite ends of the political spectrum—royalists, Bonapartists, and fascists on the right; socialists, communists, and anarchists on the left. For such extremists, Lafayette's American-style republican self-government represents a threat to the absolute power they still seek—and the profits that power would put in their pockets.

The pervasive French distrust of Lafayette and the American ideals he took to Europe have colored not only many French biographies of Lafayette but also the works of American biographers who relied too much on their French predecessors instead of original documents. That reliance is easy to understand because there is so much original material available that most biographers simply cannot or will not read it all, and much of it is written in an older French that many Americans mistranslate so badly that they obscure or alter its meaning. Lafayette lived an extraordinarily long life for his era—seventy-seven years—and participated in some of the most cataclysmic events in modern history: the American

Revolution, the French Revolution of 1789, the abdication of Napoléon and the restoration of the French monarchy, and the French Revolution of 1830. He "reigned" over France twice in his life and personally enthroned a French monarch. Not only did Lafayette compile his own voluminous memoirs, but both the French government and American Congress commissioned enormous compilations of every document each nation produced during the American Revolutionary War. The results were two massive works: five volumes, *quarto,* by Henri Doniol—*Histoire de la Participation de la France à l'Etablissement des Etats-Unis d'Amérique*—and six volumes, *octavo,* small type, by Francis Wharton—*The Revolutionary Diplomatic Correspondence of the United States.* Added to these two overwhelming works—and Lafayette's own six-volume memoirs—are the endless multi-volume biographies, autobiographies, diaries, and collections of letters and personal papers of those who knew him intimately: Washington, Adams, Hamilton, Jefferson, Madison, Monroe, Gouverneur Morris, to name just a few whose works color the portrait of this complex man. In France, his doctor, his friends, his comrades in arms, political colleagues, enemies, and a host of others who knew him wrote biographies and autobiographies that portray their impressions of Lafayette. There is also the small jewel of a volume by his wife and his daughter— written in their prison cells—that details the tenderness, love, and devotion he lavished on his family. To this library must be added the countless eighteenth- and nineteenth-century histories and the political, social, and economic analyses written in France, England, and the United States.

Beyond the enormous mass of published books are thousands of pages of his correspondence, essays, and pronouncements, collected at various institutions in France and America—in the Library of Congress, the libraries at Cornell University and the University of Chicago, the New York Public Library, the archives of the French Foreign Ministry in Paris, the Bibliothèque Historique de la Ville de Paris, the Bibliothèque de l'Institut de France, the Bibliothèque Nationale, the Château de Vollore, and the Château de Chavaniac, Lafayette's birthplace in Auvergne, in central France. Without a pilgrimage to difficult-to-reach places that helped shape his life, it is impossible to understand this complex aristocrat.

University of North Carolina professor of history Lloyd Kramer maintains that Lafayette's modern biographers have made "cultural assumptions about human behavior [that] transform him into a psychological case that John Quincy Adams [an intimate of Lafayette's for fifty years!] would not recognize. Indeed, the 'Lafayette' that Adams described has more or less disappeared from history." I believe that other intimates of Lafayette—Washington, Franklin, Jefferson, Madison, Monroe, and others—would be as hard put as Adams to recognize the descriptions of Lafayette that range from "naive," in some biographies, to "glory-thirsty," in others.[2]

For Professor Kramer, these "generalizations . . . became questionable" while he "pursued the peculiar activity of a historian."[3] They were even more questionable for me, as a former journalist, pursuing the peculiar activity of a biographer. Like Professor Kramer, I have read all of Lafayette's correspondence and the correspondence of others to him or to others about him—Washington, Jefferson, Madison, Adams, Franklin . . . and on and on. There is no need to *interpret* Lafayette's personality, motivations, sentiments, maturity, or effects and influences on others— no need to *imagine* what he may have thought or what his motives *may* have been; no need for this imaginative interpretation or for psychological evaluation.

Everything about the man—everything he said and thought, along with his motives—is on paper, in writing, on hundreds of thousands of pages. An early (1930) bibliography listing all the works written by and about Lafayette at that time runs more than 225 pages. There is no need for guesswork—only legwork, objectivity, and a willingness to let Lafayette tell his own story and let those who knew him speak for themselves—without cynical interruptions and specious interpretations. The man *was* what he and those who knew him best say he was. Everything he wrote about himself and the events in which he participated is consistent with what Washington, Adams, Jefferson, Madison, Monroe, Morris, and many others wrote about him and those same events; together, his own writings and those of his contemporaries paint a clear, unambiguous portrait of Lafayette that needs no interpretation by later biographers who never knew the man.

John Stuart Mill, the English philosopher and economist who began a close friendship with Lafayette in 1820, characterized him this way:

His was not the influence of genius, nor even of talents; it was the influence of a heroic character: it was the influence of one who, in every situation,

and throughout a long life, had done and suffered everything which opportunity had presented itself of doing and suffering for the right. . . .

   Honour be to his name, while the records of human worth shall be preserved among us! It will be long ere we see his equal, long ere there shall
rise such a union of character and circumstances as shall enable any other
human being to live such a life.[4]

As Professor Kramer points out, some nineteenth-century historians
may well have been too romantic, but too many twentieth-century historians were so cynical that they not only distorted history, they so discolored the portraits of historic figures as to make them unrecognizable.
Lafayette was a splendid man—brimming with passions and compassion,
but tempered with a marvelous, self-deprecating sense of humor. He was,
for example, balding noticeably when he reached an Indian outpost in
the wilds of upper New York in 1784, and he calmed his wife's anxieties
by noting that "I cannot lose what I do not have." His passions included
a love of adventure, liberty, and the rights of man; loyalty to friends and
devotion to his wife and family. The compassionate Lafayette reached
out to the oppressed, the downtrodden, the helpless—even buying an
entire plantation in French Guyana for one purpose: to educate and free
its slaves. Recent biographers, in my opinion, have deprived Americans
and, indeed, the world, of essential knowledge about our nation by
diminishing his importance and relegating him to the shadows of history—with, I might add, too many of our nation's many other heroes. I
hope this biography will help restore him to his rightful place as one of
the great leaders in American history. It was he who assured our independence and justifiably earned the title of "hero" in the hearts and
minds of America's leaders and, indeed, all Americans—during the Revolutionary War and for more than a half-century thereafter—and they
were not wrong in their beliefs. He was a giant among the Founding
Fathers of our nation. He was "Our Marquis."

   At the end of Lafayette's visit to America in 1824, President John
Quincy Adams told him, "We shall look upon you always as belonging to
us, during the whole of our life, as belonging to our children after us. You
are ours by more than patriotic self-devotion with which you flew to the
aid of our fathers at the crisis of our fate; ours by that unshaken gratitude
for your services which is a precious portion of our inheritance; ours by
that tie of love, stronger than death, which has linked your name for
endless ages of time with the name of Washington. . . . Speaking in the

name of the whole people of the United States, and at a loss only for language to give utterance to that feeling of attachment with which the heart of the nation beats as the heart of one man, I bid you a reluctant and affectionate farewell."[5]

"God bless you, Sir," Lafayette replied, "and all who surround you. God bless the American people, each of their states and the federal government. Accept this patriotic farewell of a heart that will overflow with gratitude until the moment it ceases to beat."[6]

Lafayette

Part One

The Best of Times

1

The Young Knight

THERE WAS A TIME when heroes walked the earth: Alexander, Hercules, Hector, and Lysander. In America, their names were Washington, Greene, Hancock . . . and . . .

. . . Lafayette—Gilbert du Motier, marquis de Lafayette.

Lafayette was the New World's first—and the Old World's last—great and gallant knight of old, sprung from Arthurian romances, in quest of honor and glory, atop his great white steed, charging through history, sword flashing, poised for attack. His warrior roots reached back across the centuries to the year 1000, when Pons Motier emerged from the mists of the Middle Ages as lord of Villa Faya—one of the small, crumbling demesnes the Romans had long ago abandoned in the forbiddingly cold, black hills of central France. Pons Motier de Villa Faya, or de La Fayette,[1] as the name devolved, sired a race of swordsmen. In 1250, they rode with Saint Louis in the Sixth Crusade and seized the Crown of Thorns from Moslem infidels. A century later, Gilbert de La Fayette II repelled England's Black Prince Edward at Poitiers, in the Hundred Years' War. In 1428, the legendary Gilbert III, maréchal de France, attacked British lines alongside Joan of Arc at Orléans, scattering the enemy and saving the French throne for Charles VII.[2]

"It was natural that I grew up hearing many tales of war and glory in a family so closely tied to memories and sorrows associated with war," Lafayette wrote.[3] Indeed, from the moment he first walked and talked, his doting grandmother filled his mind, heart, and soul with wondrous tales of brave knights whose heralded mantle he would one day wear, whose honor he would have to defend, whose spilled blood he would have to avenge. His grandfather fell wounded three times, fighting for France against England;

The Château de Chavaniac, in Auvergne, where Lafayette was born (in the second-floor room, just above the hedge, in the right tower) and where he spent the first eleven years of his life. (*Roger-Viollet, Paris.*)

and his father, a twenty-five-year-old grenadier colonel, died in a hail of British cannon fire in the battle of Minden in Prussia and orphaned his only child when the boy was two.

Lafayette was born on September 6, 1757, in the same tower bedroom where his father had been born, in the Château de Chavaniac, a Spartan, fortresslike, stone château, built over the ruins of an old castle about one hundred miles south of the ancient Villa Faya. He was baptized in the parish church down the hill as "the very high and very mighty lord Monseigneur Marie-Joseph-Paul-Yves-Roch-Gilbert du Motier de La Fayette, legitimate son of the very high and very mighty lord Monseigneur Michel-Louis-Christophe-Roch-Gilbert du Motier, marquis de La Fayette, baron de Vissac, lord of Saint-Romain and other places and of the very high and very mighty lady Madame Marie-Louise-Julie de La Rivière."[4]

"It's not my fault," Lafayette quipped in his autobiography. "I was baptized like a Spaniard, with the name of every conceivable saint who might offer me more protection in battle. . . . So large a proportion of fathers and sons were killed on the field of battle that the family's misfortunes in war became a kind of proverb throughout the province."[5] Indeed, had Lafayette

Left: Lafayette's father, Gilbert du Motier IV, marquis de La Fayette, was killed by British cannon fire when his son was two years old. Right: Lafayette's mother, Julie de La Rivière de La Fayette, was heiress to an old and powerful Breton family with ties to the royal family's inner circle. (*From the author's collection.*)

knights not married and hurriedly sired offspring before leaving for battle, the family would have died out centuries earlier.

As assiduous as they were in procreating prior to battle, Lafayette's ancestors were even more careful to marry daughters of lords with properties that extended the family's demesne. By the time Lafayette was born, the family fiefdom stretched thirty-five miles across the Auvergne in central France and seventy-five miles north to south.[6] Lafayette's father expanded family holdings and influence beyond the Auvergne by marrying the beautiful Marie-Louise-Julie de La Rivière, heiress of an ancient line of powerful nobles, with vast properties in Brittany and ties to the *noblesse de la robe*, the royal family's inner circle of courtiers. Her grandfather, the famed general, comte de La Rivière, commanded the Mousquetaires du Roi, the king's personal horse guard known as "the Black Musketeers."[7]

The death of Lafayette's father drove his distraught wife for solace from her father and grandfather in Paris. She left young Lafayette in Chavaniac with his grandmother and a maiden aunt, whose unbridled love gave him free rein to romp about the château grounds, his unruly red hair flailing, his wooden sword slashing at imaginary British villains lurking behind the corner towers. Peasant boys too young to work the fields cheerfully followed their seigneur into battle or on parade down the narrow, crooked street of their tiny hamlet. Chavaniac was a patchwork of small stone houses that leaned against each other for support along the slope beneath the Lafayette manor. Most had apiaries and clusters of fruit trees in the rear and sometimes a few sheep or a tethered goat. The pace of daily life seldom exceeded the slow, rumbling cadence of a passing oxcart. The Lafayette château stood—and still stands—above the hamlet, on one of many small, forested hills in what was once a boiling sea of lava that poured from nearby volcanoes in the *chaîne des puys*, or chain of cones. Extinct for two million years, the *chaîne* and its valley rested peacefully until 52 B.C., when Caesar's legions marched into Gaul—and the fearsome Gallic chieftain Vercingetorix[8] made his epic stand that covered the plain with Roman blood and halted the advance.

"I cannot tell you whether I am a Gaul or a Frank," Lafayette wrote, "but I hope I am a Gaul. . . . I would much rather have been Vercingetorix defending the mountains of Auvergne."[9]

Whether Gaul or Frank,[10] Lafayette was an exceptionally beautiful little boy, who combined the features of his handsome parents with the goodness of his grandmother and the irrepressible spirit of a feudal knight. Feudalism still reigned in rural France when Lafayette was a boy. Peasants owned no land and had few rights. Rents and taxes left them crushed by poverty and hunger—rents to the landlord to live on the land they tilled, and taxes on what was left of their meager earnings for harvesting his crops. In a nation of twenty million, the wealthiest half-million—the nobility and the clergy—were exempt from taxes, while the poorest fifteen million not only paid the most taxes but slaved under the dreaded corvée—a day's forced labor each week to maintain public roads. Taxes so depleted peasant earnings that most fed their families from gleanings.

"Every class must share equal responsibility to preserve order in an efficient monarchy," a Paris magistrate explained. "The clergy provides instruction, religious services and solace; the nobility counsels the sovereign and sheds its blood to defend the state; and the lowest class, which cannot render such distinguished services, fulfills its responsibility to the state with taxes, hard work and labor."[11]

The death of his father in battle in 1779 left the management of Chavaniac in the hands of Lafayette's grandmother, "a woman . . . of the highest character, respected throughout the province" and universally "venerated" for her kindness and generosity.[12] Hers was an islet of liberty in a sea of feudal oppression. She invited her peasants to hunt in her forests and extracted only enough foodstuffs from her lands to meet her family's needs, then gave the rest to the villagers. Her wise, frugal management left them with enough food to nourish themselves and their families—and a surplus to sell at market, to profit from their labors. "Village heads traveled twenty leagues from

The six-year-old Lafayette with his widowed aunt, Charlotte, and a portrait of her daughter. (*From the author's collection.*)

every direction to consult her,"[13] according to her neighbors. In contrast to angry, perennially oppressed peasants elsewhere, Auvergnats cheered and merrily doffed their hats whenever their handsome little marquis rode by with his aunt or generous grandmother. He, in turn, grew up with deep affection for the adoring peasantry. He loved the land, fields, and forests; he loved the people, trusted them, and respected them.

When he was five, Lafayette's widowed aunt, Charlotte, came to live at Chavaniac with her six-year-old daughter, Marie de Guèrin, who became a sister to him. Lafayette's grandmother hired a cheerful tutor, Abbé Fayon,[14] who taught the children their letters and numbers and lightened his lessons with tales of "Vercingetorix defending our mountains" and Lafayette knights riding through French history. "From the time I was eight, I longed for glory," Lafayette recalled in his memoirs. "I remember nothing of my childhood more than my fervor for tales of glory and my plans to travel the world in quest of fame."[15]

He did not wait long. When he was ten, the monstrous Beast of Gévaudan invaded the region, ravaging livestock. Hysterical—and drunken—peasants claimed it was a hyena that had slaughtered 122 women and children. The ten-year-old knight snatched his father's musket from its wall mounts and charged into the forest, "my heart beating with excitement, to slay this hyena."[16] With the cries of his terrified tutor and aunts echoing across the hillside, the intrepid young knight led his loyal troop of boys to find the beast's den. "I am Lord of this village," he protested to his grandmother afterwards. "It is up to me to defend it."[17] To his deep disappointment, a hunter found the beast first and killed what was only a larger-than-average wolf that had inspired larger-than-average exaggerations of its outrages.

When Lafayette was eleven, his mother took him from the rustic life he loved to Paris, to live with her and her grandfather, the powerful comte de La Rivière, at the sumptuous Palais du Luxembourg,[18] built for King Henri IV's queen, Marie de Médicis. Determined to raise his only heir to the highest ranks at court, the comte inscribed Lafayette's name on the list of future Musketeers and, in the interim, enrolled the boy in the prestigious Collège du Plessis,[19] a private school for young knights, where Lafayette abandoned his comfortable country clothes for a military uniform, a scabbard and sword, and a carefully coiffed powdered wig.[20]

The stiff dress, however, belied the new curriculum that illuminated student minds. To the classics, the Age of Enlightenment added works of the philosophes—Newton, Locke, Montesquieu, Voltaire, and others—who inspired a revolution in men's minds long before it spread to the streets. Montesquieu challenged the divine right of kings, Abbé Raynal demanded popular rule, and Voltaire proclaimed the rights of man. The philosophes reinforced Lafayette's own ideas of justice, and, when his teacher described an intelligent horse as one that obeyed at the sight of the rider's whip, he contradicted him: "I described the perfect horse as one which, at the sight of the whip, had the sense to throw his rider to the ground before he could be whipped. . . . Monsieur Binet had a good sense of humor and smiled instead of getting angry."[21]

In a tragic coincidence, Lafayette's mother and great-grandfather died within weeks of each other in the spring of 1770; they left him—at twelve—one of the richest aristocrats in France. To his vast estates in the Auvergne he now added his mother's huge properties in Brittany—and an annual income of 120,000 *livres*, or about $1.2 million in today's currency.[22] "Burning with desire to be in uniform," he entered the Black Musketeers at the Palace of Versailles, as a second lieutenant. Selected for their decorative value on horseback rather than any combat skills, the musketeers were the tallest, most handsome, most charming young men. By the time he turned thirteen in September, Lafayette had evolved into just such a young man and began training at the royal riding school at Versailles with the king's three grandsons—the comte d'Artois, who was Lafayette's age, and the count's older brothers, the comte de Provence and the dauphin, or crown prince. Each would eventually inherit the French throne.

Lafayette, at eleven in school uniform and powdered wig, combined all the beauty of his handsome parents with the goodness of his grandmother and the spirit of a young feudal knight. (*From the author's collection.*)

As a Black Musketeer, Lafayette rode in the daily palace ceremony, with a musketeer chosen each day to trot up to the king to receive royal orders and high-trot back to the musketeer commander. "The King told me that all was well and that he had no orders," Lafayette wrote of his first encounter with Louis XV. "I returned to my commanding officer to repeat words he heard repeated three hundred sixty-five days a year."[23]

Just before Lafayette's fifteenth birthday, the powerful brigadier general of the King's Armies, Jean-Paul-François de Noailles, the duc d'Ayen, picked him from among the musketeers to marry his second daughter, Adrienne, then only twelve years old. The duke's selection enraged his wife, the duchess. She refused to permit her daughter to marry at so young an age, without a semblance of womanly maturity, before she completed her education—or the Lafayette boy, for that matter, completed his. The quarrel over Adrienne's marriage raged for weeks, spilling into every fashionable and unfashionable Paris salon. The Noailles were among the oldest, wealthiest, proudest members of the French nobility—"more powerful than the House of Bourbon,"[24] according to some. They counted bishops, cardinals, field marshals, admirals, diplomats, and cabinet ministers among their forebears. The family patriarch, the duc de Noailles, was a near-legendary military figure who commanded the historic regiment of dragoons, Les Dragons de Noailles,[25] inherited by the family, generation after generation.[26] His friendship with

Left: Lafayette's future father-in-law, the duc d'Ayen, had no sons of his own and turned to the Black Musketeers for the most handsome, wealthiest, and most socially eligible men to marry his daughters and provide him with grandsons. Right: The duchesse d'Ayen, Lafayette's future mother-in-law, objected to her twelve-year-old daughter, Adrienne, marrying the fourteen-year-old Lafayette and insisted that both complete their education first. (*From the author's collection.*)

the king extended beneath the royal bedsheets into the arms of a mistress they shared. To be near his king, Noailles maintained small palaces adjacent to each of the king's two large ones at Versailles and Paris. Unable to live in both at the same time, he lived at Versailles, and let his son the duc d'Ayen live with his family at the Paris mansion near the older, seldom used Tuileries Palace.[27]

But the duchesse d'Ayen came from an equally powerful family; her father had been one of France's greatest jurists and chancellor of France. When, therefore, the duke and duchess disagreed, neither ceded quickly. "You don't know my wife," complained the duc d'Ayen. "No matter how bitterly she argues, she'll apologize like a rueful little girl if you show her she is wrong, but she will never budge if she doesn't see it."[28]

At the heart of the conflict lay the duchess's deep fear of separation from her children. She had lost her firstborn, and when her second, a little girl, fell gravely ill, she was distraught. "My mother thought she would go out of her mind with grief," Adrienne wrote later, "but heaven restored her daughter's health. A year later [November 2, 1759], I was born and we two became the center of her life, although she bore three more daughters."[29] But the duke wanted a son and heir to bear the family name, and he waited impatiently as his wife gave him nothing but girls. Convinced he would never have sons of his own, he searched the realm for the most eligible young noblemen to marry his daughters and give him grandsons to assume the family arms. He chose two from the king's musketeers: Louis de Noailles, a young cousin, five months older than Lafayette, would marry the oldest d'Ayen daughter, Louise, and perpetuate the family name; Lafayette would marry his second-oldest daughter, Adrienne, and unite two of the nation's most distinguished ancestries and family fortunes.

The duchesse d'Ayen was incensed by the prospects of her oldest daughter marrying a cousin and her twelve-year-old "baby" marrying a fourteen-year-old soldier. "My sister and I had no idea what was going on," Adrienne recalled in her memoirs. "My mother and father were constantly quarreling—and refused to tell us why." To restore peace, d'Ayen promised "to defer the marriage for two years and assured my mother that I would live at home with my husband during the first years of marriage. In the meantime, he would personally see to it that Lafayette finished his education." When the duchesse met the young officer, Adrienne wrote, "she cherished him ever after as the most beloved of sons. I cannot describe our joy at the reconciliation between our parents."[30]

Adrienne's father and Lafayette's uncle drew up the marriage contract. Romantic marriages were all but unheard of in European aristocracy; the bride and groom had no say in the contract or marriage and often did not meet until their wedding. After weeks of tangled offers and counter offers, Adrienne's father agreed to provide a dowry of 200,000 livres (about $2 million in today's currency).

"The two marriages were arranged," Adrienne wrote, "but only on condition that no one was to mention them to my sister before a year had passed and to me before eighteen months. My mother agreed that Monsieur de Noailles and Monsieur de Lafayette would meet us haphazardly from time to time, either at my mother's home or on walks. But my mother did not want us to be distracted from our education."[31]

Although her mother never spoke Lafayette's name as a potential mate, Adrienne fell irretrievably in love with him, conquered by the knightly image he worked hard to project in his musketeer's uniform. While others found him awkward, shy, or out of place, Adrienne found him irresistible. "What joy it was for me to learn, after more than a year, that my mother already looked at him as her son. . . . I was only fourteen years old."[32]

In February 1773, fifteen-year-old Lafayette moved into the Noailles mansion at Versailles, where Adrienne's grandfather enrolled him and the young vicomte de Noailles in the prestigious Académie de Versailles,[33] a school for princes of the blood and sons of the king's courtiers and ministers. The duc and duchesse d'Ayen embraced him as a son. He was, after all, a

Left: Sixteen-year-old Lafayette, at the time of his marriage, in his lieutenant's uniform of the Dragons de Noailles. Right: Fourteen-year-old Adrienne de Noailles at the time of her marriage to Lafayette. (*From the author's collection.*)

sweet and exceptionally handsome boy, if not yet terribly clever, and he eagerly reciprocated their love, basking for the first time in his life in the warmth of a large family, complete with mother, father, and a bevy of happy, chattering little sisters, one of whom—doll-like in appearance and dress—was to be his wife. The young knight saw her as more child than woman and treated her with appropriate kindness, but without a hint of romantic inclination. She, on the other hand, all but swooned at his every glance.

On March 14, 1774, a year after Lafayette had joined their family, the duc de Noailles and the duc and duchesse d'Ayen presented their future son-in-law at court. Because Lafayette's bloodlines tied him to the *noblesse de la robe*, King Louis XV himself signed the marriage contract, as did his three grandsons—the future kings Louis XVI, Louis XVIII, and Charles X. With the king's blessing, Marie-Adrienne-Françoise de Noailles married Gilbert du Motier de La Fayette, on Monday, April 11, 1774, in a quiet ceremony in the chapel of the Hôtel de Noailles, the bride's family mansion in Paris. The archbishop of Paris presided, and only the immediate families witnessed the ceremony—thirty-one aunts, uncles, sisters, and other relatives of the bride and nine relatives of the groom. With his vows, Lafayette acquired the mantle of the most celebrated family of France to wear with those of his own distinguished ancestors. As a wedding gift, the duc de Noailles promised the young man a captain's rank and command of a company in the Noailles Dragoons when he turned eighteen.

In contrast to the simple wedding ceremony, the reception saw the royal family, members of the court, and Europe's most illustrious aristocrats

1ᵉʳ Service

17 Domans, un grand surtout et 2 girandoles.

8 POTS D'OUILLE

2 à la jambe de bois; — 2 de ris au coulis d'écrevisses; — 1 d'une purée verte; — 1 de santé au naturel; — 2 de vermicelle.

12 POTAGES

1 de bisque de pigeons garnis de crêtes; — 2 à la reine garnis d'issues d'agneau; — 1 de caneton aux navets; — 2 de pigeons aux œufs garnis de chicons; — 2 de santé aux petits oignons et laitue; — 2 de bisque d'écrevisse; — 1 de poulet aux œufs et pointes d'asperges; — 1 de tortue.

2 GRANDES ENTRÉES POUR LES 2 BOUTS

1 de quartier de veau à la reine; — 1 d'un alloyau.

26 MOYENNES ENTRÉES

1 de brochet à la Civita Veschia; — 1 de truites à la Périgord; — 2 de dindons gras, sauce à la carpe; — 2 de poulardes de pain aux mousserons; — 2 de pâtés dressés de lapereaux; — 2 de têtes de veaux à l'agneau; — 2 de gigots de moutons à l'eau; — 2 de noix de veau à l'oseille; — 2 de canetons aux petits pois; — 2 de pigeons aux œufs en fantaisie; — 2 de filets de bœuf à l'indienne; — 2 de grenadins; — 2 de terrines de viande mêlée; — 2 autres terrines à la bavaroise.

30 HORS-D'ŒUVRE

4 de petits pâtés à l'espagnole; — 4 de baraquilles; — 4 de bouillants; — 4 de petits pâtés en blanc; — 2 de marinade de poulets gras; — 2 de pigeons au soleil; — 2 de surprise; — 2 de petits gâteaux de veau; — 2 de pigeons à la régence; — 2 romains; — 2 de côtelettes de veau aux fines herbes.

2ᵉ Service

20 ASSIETTES D'HUÎTRES

10 ASSIETTES DE RAVES ET RADICES

10 ENTRÉES POUR RELEVER LES 8 POTS A OUILLE
ET LES ENTRÉES DES 2 BOUTS

1 d'une épaule à la piémontaise; — 2 de soles au vin de Champagne; — 2 de quartiers de chevreuil une poivrade; — 2 de poularde nouvelle à la Chia; — 2 de canetons de Rouen à l'échalotte; — 2 de princesse.

30 PETITES ENTRÉES POUR RELEVER LES 30 HORS-D'ŒUVRE

2 de poulets gras à l'italienne aux mousserons; — 2 de brezoles à l'italienne; — 2 de filets de mouton aux épinards; — 2 de tourterelles en laurier; — 2 de perche à la hollandaise; — 2 de filet de sole; — 2 de pigeons au gratin; — 2 de saumons en friardeaux; — 2 d'anguilles à la bavaroise; — 2 de poulets et canetons; — 2 de pigeons à la d'Huxelles; — 2 de filets de mouton aux laitues; — 2 de pain de perdrix; — 2 devants d'agneaux en friandeaux; — 2 de filets de lapereaux à l'italienne.

22 GRANDES ENTREMETS FROIDS

1 d'un pâté de dindon en hérisson; — 1 d'un pâté de jambon; — 1 de gâteaux de Compiègne; — 2 de croquants en dôme; — 2 de hures de sanglier; — 2 de gâteaux de lièvre; — 2 de cochon de lait à l'allemande; — 2 de marbres; — 2 de gâteaux de Savoie; — 2 de beignets en pavot; — 2 de mortadelle; — 2 de jambon à la broche.

16 MOYENS ENTREMETS FROIDS

2 de buissons d'écrevisses; — 2 de bonnets de Turquie; — 2 de tourtes à la glace; — 2 de crème veloutée; — 2 de petits pains aux pistaches; — 2 de petits gâteaux d'amandes; — 2 de langues fourrées de Saint-Germain; — 2 d'asperges à l'huile.

30 PLATS DE RÔT

2 de marcassins; — 2 d'agneaux; — 2 de poules de Caux; — 2 de dindons gras; — 2 de tourterelles; — 2 de canetons de Rouen; — 2 de dindons; — 2 de campines; — 2 de lapereaux; — 2 de poulets aux œufs; — 2 de rameaux; — 2 de poulets à la reine; — 2 de pigeons en ortolans; — 2 de pigeons aux œufs.

30 SALADES
8 ASSIETTES DE BIGARRADES
8 SAUCES

46 ENTREMETS CHAUDS POUR RELEVER LES SALADES ET SAUCES

2 de morilles; — 2 de mousserons; — 2 de petits pois; — 2 d'artichauts à l'estoufade; — 2 de palais de bœuf au gratin; — 2 d'oreilles de veau frites; — 2 d'animelles; — 2 d'amourettes; — 2 de crêtes et petits œufs; — 2 de champignons à l'italienne; — 2 d'écrevisses à la Sainte-Menehould; — 2 de grosses truites à l'huile; — 2 d'omelettes fourrées; — 1 de grenadines en peaux d'Espagne; — 2 d'asperges aux petits pois; — 2 de concombres en mateloté; — 2 de foies gras en crépine; — 2 de canapé; — 2 d'œufs à la Lombardie; — 2 d'huîtres en coquille; — 2 de truffes; — 2 d'écrevisses à l'italienne; — 2 de rôties au jambon.

Menu of the wedding dinner following Lafayette's marriage to Adrienne de Noailles, on April 11, 1774. (*Château Chavaniac Lafayette.*)

and diplomats flock to the Noailles mansion for a Rabelaisian feast of more than one hundred platters of appetizers and hors d'oeuvres, twelve soups, eight stews, two dozen kinds of meat pies, thirty salads, and thirty platters of roasted meats—baby boar, venison, game birds, lamb, chickens, turkeys, ducks, pigeons, and the like—with a half side of veal and beef at either end of the long buffet table for carvers to slice and serve to the gargantuan gathering. Forty-six desserts ended the meal, before the two newlyweds shyly slipped away for the night—she to her apartment, he to his, both still pure in body and spirit. For the moment, her mother refused to permit the consummation of their marriage, and a few days later Lafayette and his brother-in-law, Louis, vicomte de Noailles, rode off to Metz, in northeastern France, for summer training as future company commanders in the Noailles Regiment.

A month after Lafayette's wedding, King Louis XV—"Louis the Beloved"—died, and his oldest grandson, barely twenty, assumed the throne as Louis XVI. His beautiful young wife, Marie-Antoinette, the youngest daughter of Austrian Empress Maria Theresa and Emperor Francis I, became queen of France. Only nineteen, Marie-Antoinette had chafed in the austere Versailles atmosphere for four years. Her husband, fat and taciturn, had no interest in society or sex. He loved nothing more than the solitude of a quiet room, a comfortable chair, and a history book or maps to study. Because of a disability that made arousal difficult, he was content to let his boisterous, high-strung queen enjoy herself in her own apartments—and in the royal treasury. After the old king's death, the queen began planning a nonstop frenzy of sumptuous masked balls, banquets, and theater galas. When the social season began in September, she filled her boudoirs and ballrooms with the brightest, wittiest, most charming young noblemen and women of Paris and Versailles—an elite *société de la cour* that included Lafayette and his wife and Adrienne's older sister, Louise, and her erudite husband, the vicomte de Noailles. From the first, Lafayette felt ill at ease. The high-pitched cacophony of giggled inanities left the country boy from Chavaniac dazed—at times, even morose—staring silently into space, while those around him convulsed hysterically at witty comments about the latest fashions in men's wigs.

"Lafayette always seemed distant . . . with a cold, solemn look—as if he were timid or embarrassed," wrote the comte de Ségur, a friend from the Académie de Versailles and military camp. "He was very tall and broad shouldered, but seemed awkward, danced badly and spoke little. But that distant stare, which contrasted so sharply with the light-hearted arrogance and showy loquaciousness of the people of his age, concealed a fiery spirit, a strong character and a warm soul."[34]

The queen's haughty behavior and harsh Austrian accent did not help. "It was impossible to see anything but the Queen," commented British author Horace Walpole about the weekly balls. "She is a statue of beauty when standing or sitting; grace itself when she moves. She was dressed in silver, scattered over with laurier-roses . . . diamonds and feathers."[35] As Lafayette danced the obligatory quadrille with her one evening, "he proved so clumsy and so awkward," Ségur reported, "that the queen laughed at him"[36]—a public humiliation that left him eager to shun palace society.

"What can I say about my entrance into the world of manners?" he explained in his memoirs. "The favor I enjoyed among the young nobility was short-lived, because of the unfavorable impression created by my silence. I listened and observed but my awkward country manners—and a certain self-respect—made it impossible for me to adapt entirely to the required graces of the court."[37]

Lafayette's distaste for court life did not improve with the continued insistence of his parents-in-law that he and his wife live in separate apartments, unable to consummate their marriage. At the urging of Noailles and Ségur, he found relief in "two romances with celebrated beauties, in which my will played more of a role than my heart." Neither lasted long: "Jealousy smashed the first one before it even got started, and, in the second, I was less interested in conquering her than triumphing over my rival."[38] Crest-fallen after his flirtations with adultery, Lafayette breached the sanctity of his wife's apartment and "never again stopped trying to demonstrate my firm, tender love for the woman I had the good fortune to marry." In the spring of 1775, not long after he returned to military camp, Adrienne wrote that she was pregnant with their first child.

When Adrienne's letter arrived, the shots at Lexington were echoing across Lafayette's camp at Metz. Hundreds of officers lined up each day to volunteer in the American Revolution and avenge the French army's humiliation by the British in the Seven Years' War, a dozen years earlier. Lafayette fell victim to the frenzy after his commanding general, Charles-François, comte de Broglie, a grand master Freemason, invited Lafayette, Noailles, and Ségur to "see the light" by joining the Masonic military lodge. Nowhere in the political and intellectual darkness of Europe's autocratic monarchies did the Age of Enlightenment shine brighter than in France's Masonic lodges, where the American Revolution represented a struggle by Freemasons like Washington and Franklin for Masonic principles and man's right to life, liberty, and property.[39] Lafayette embraced his new fraternity with all his heart. The orphaned country boy with no brothers had found an entire brotherhood—each a brother to him and he a brother to each. De Broglie invited Lafayette and other Freemasons to dine with the duke of Gloucester, the younger brother of English king George III. An outspoken foe of his brother's policies in the American colonies, Gloucester fired Lafayette's chivalric—and, now, Masonic—imagination with descriptions of Americans as "a people fighting for liberty."

"Such a glorious cause," wrote Lafayette, "had never before rallied the attention of mankind. Oppressors and oppressed would receive a powerful lesson; the great work would be accomplished or the rights of humanity would fall beneath its ruin. The destiny of France and that of her rival [England] would be decided at the same moment. . . . I gave my heart to the Americans and thought of nothing else but raising my banner and adding my colors to theirs."[40]

A month later, Lafayette turned eighteen, received his captaincy and command in the Noailles Dragoons, and returned to Paris to his wife, who gave birth to their first child, Henriette, on December 15. A few days later, Lafayette, Noailles, and Ségur joined a Masonic lodge in Paris,[41] where Lafayette fell under the thrall of the famed Abbé Guillaume Raynal. Raynal had discarded Jesuit robes to rail against kings, priests, and slave owners in tedious diatribes that had few readers—until the French government banned them.[42] Overnight, he became the toast of Paris Masonic lodges and intellectual salons, where he assailed "barbaric" colonialism and demanded an end to slavery. He condemned the Roman Catholic Church for "destroying

Lafayette at eighteeen, in his captain's uniform of the Dragons de Noailles. (*Réunion des Musées Nationaux*.)

all principles of justice" and called for religious tolerance and an end to despotism. "Liberty is the fruition of the enactment of the rights of man," he proclaimed. "People have a right to be sovereign." He called for international free trade, with "all ports open to all ships, without customs, without barriers, without formalities of any kind."[43] Asked whom he considered the greatest writer of the eighteenth century, Lafayette replied without hesitation: "The Jesuit Raynal!"

Convinced that the American Revolution embodied all the principles he believed in, Lafayette told Noailles and Ségur he would go to America to fight for liberty. He found them as eager as he, and the three musketeers pledged to sail together, fight together, and, if necessary, die together.

2

The Quest

IN MARCH 1776, the British evacuation of Boston provoked paroxysms of joy in France. Parisians poured into the streets to sing, dance, and celebrate the defeat of their ancient enemy—and laugh uncontrollably at the improbable humiliation of the world's most powerful professional army by bands of ill-clad farmers and woodsmen with hunting muskets hiding behind trees.

With America preparing to declare independence, Congress sent Silas Deane, a naive Connecticut lawyer and merchant, to seek French aid. During a secret two-hour meeting with Louis XVI's foreign minister, Charles Gravier, comte de Vergennes, Deane convinced the French minister that America had ample men to bear arms but lacked the arms, ammunition, and money to defeat Britain—and ships to protect her ports. Although the bankrupt French economy could not afford another war, Vergennes saw indirect intervention in the American war as a relatively low-cost opportunity to exact revenge against England and restore French power in North America—without firing a shot. By surreptitiously filling American military needs and assuring victory in some of the rebel colonies, France would bind herself to the Americans and replace England as principal trading partner and protector. "The power of England will diminish and ours will increase accordingly," Vergennes told the king. "Her commerce will suffer an irreparable loss while ours will increase; it is very probable that . . . we may be able to recover part of the possessions that the English seized from us in America, such as . . . Canada."[1]

Vergennes proposed establishing a private trading company with secret government financing to trade surplus French arms from the Seven Years' War for American products such as tobacco, cotton, lumber, and whale oil

17

Louis XVI's minister of foreign affairs, Charles Gravier, comte de Vergennes, plotted to undermine British power by providing surreptitious French financial and military aid to the American Revolution. (*Réunion des Musées Nationaux.*)

that would normally flow to Britain. "This exchange of traffic," Vergennes explained, "could be made without the government appearing involved in any way." To provide Americans with a fleet, the trading company would ship goods to the West Indies on merchantmen that the Americans could buy and refit with cannons "without our appearing as parties to the transaction."[2] In the months that followed, the French trading company lured Deane into paying six million livres for surplus French arms, ammunition, and war materiel worth only two million, and, according to Lafayette, "when the English ambassador inquired at our court in Versailles, Vergennes denied all knowledge and made a show of chasing American privateers from French ports."[3]

Not long after the Americans declared independence, British and Hessian forces routed George Washington's Patriots on Long Island and in New York, killing 1,500 Americans and capturing more than 1,000 others, including generals John Sullivan and William Alexander, Lord Stirling. The rout left Congress disillusioned with Washington's leadership and his high command, and Deane again turned for help to the wily Vergennes, who saw an opportunity to expand the scope of his ambitions in America. France had surplus officers as well as materiel. If they assumed command of the American army, a victory over Britain might allow them to convert some of England's American colonies into French puppet states and begin rebuilding the French empire in North America. Vergennes urged Deane to commission top-ranking French officers for the American army and replace Washington with a French generalissimo—a military dictator, or *stathoudérat* ("stateholder"),[4] with sweeping political as well as military powers.

The king opposed the plan at first, fearing it could provoke war with England, which France could not afford, but Vergennes argued that "France has the right to influence all great affairs. Her king is comparable to a supreme judge and is entitled to regard his throne as a tribunal established by Providence. England is the natural enemy of France. . . . The invariable and most cherished purpose in her politics has been, if not the destruction of France, at least her overthrow, her humiliation, and her ruin. . . . All means to reduce the power and greatness of England . . . are just, legitimate, and even necessary, provided they are efficient."[5]

The twenty-year-old French king was still too inexperienced to resist Vergennes's compelling arguments. Vergennes proposed General de Broglie, Lafayette's commander at Metz, as commander in chief for the American army, and, in early November, de Broglie came to Paris to meet with Deane. With him, he brought his top aide, "Baron" Johann de Kalb, a gigantic Prussian-born major, who had been to America and spoke fluent English, but was decidedly not a baron and had never been one. The son of a Prussian peasant, with no chance for advancement as a commoner in the Prussian army, he had enlisted in the French army at twenty-two, dubbed himself "baron," and tied his fortunes to de Broglie's ambitions.

"A military and political leader is wanted," de Broglie explained to Deane, through Kalb, "a man fitted to carry the weight of authority in the colonies, to unite its parties, to assign to each his place, to attract a large number of persons of all classes and carry them along with him; not courtiers, but brave, efficient, and well educated officers, who confide in their superior, and repose implicit faith in him."[6] De Broglie suggested sending Kalb to America with a staff of officers to explain the advantages to Congress. Deane agreed and sent an immediate report to Philadelphia: "Count Broglie, who commanded the army of France in the last [Seven Years'] war, did me the honor to call on me twice yesterday with an officer who served as his quartermaster general [Kalb] in the last war and . . . is desirous of engaging in the service of the United States of North America. I can by no means let slip an opportunity of engaging a person of so much experience,

The general of the French army at Metz, the comte de Broglie, plotted to replace George Washington as commander of America's Continental army and become military dictator in the United States. Unwittingly, Lafayette foiled the scheme. (*Réunion des Musées Nationaux.*)

and who is by every one recommended as one of the bravest and most skillful officers in the kingdom. . . .

"I submit one thought to you," he continued. "If you could engage a great general of the highest character in Europe, such for instance as . . . Marshal Broglie or others of equal rank, to take the lead of your armies . . . it would give a character and credit to your military, and strike perhaps a greater panic in our enemies. I only suggest the thought, and leave you to confer with the Baron de Kalb on the subject at large."[7]

In early December, Kalb gave Deane a list of sixteen officers. Lafayette's name was not among them. At Kalb's insistence, Deane enrolled the officers at enormously inflated salaries and ranks that placed them above most American officers in the Continental army. He appointed the fifty-year-old "baron" a major general, a rank second only to that of Washington himself. "It is a universal custom in Europe to allow something extra," he explained to Congress. "Men cannot be engaged to quit their native country and friends to hazard life . . . in a cause which is not their own."[8]

A few days after Deane commissioned de Broglie's officers, de Broglie commandeered two French frigates to take his prospective junta to Philadelphia. He gave Kalb special instructions for meeting with congressional lead-

"Baron" Johann de Kalb was the son of a Prussian peasant, and with no chance for advancement as a commoner in the Prussian army, he dubbed himself "baron" and enlisted as an officer in the French army. (*Réunion des Musées Nationaux.*)

ers: "The main point of the mission with which you have been entrusted will therefore consist in explaining . . . the absolute necessity of the choice of . . . a generalissimo."[9]

When Lafayette learned that de Broglie was sending officers to fight in America, he and his friends Noailles and Ségur eagerly volunteered—without the slightest notion that they had stumbled onto a fragile, complex plot to replace the American military command with a French military junta. De Broglie did not want loose-tongued young idealists undermining his scheme and tried discouraging them. "I witnessed your father's death at the Battle of Minden," he told Lafayette, "and I will not be accessory to the ruin of the only remaining branch of your family."[10] Lafayette protested, however, and, rather than risk Lafayette's exposing the expedition, de Broglie sent the young men with Kalb to see Deane. Deane's aide, William Charmichael, greeted them—the first American Lafayette had ever met. Both Charmichael and Deane seemed taken aback by their youth and inexperience, but they identified themselves as brother Masons, and Lafayette convinced him of the advantages of enlisting members of such illustrious families. "I spoke more of my ardour in the cause than of my experience," Lafayette recalled in his memoirs, "and I dwelt much upon the effect my departure would excite in France."[11]

Although all three boys were minors, only Noailles and Ségur needed family permission to enlist. The orphan Lafayette had no family, and, with an annual income of now nearly 150,000 livres from his estates—about $1.5 million in today's currency—he was free financially to do as he pleased. On December 7, 1776, Deane amended the list of de Broglie's officers to include "M. de la Fayette, Major-general," who signed the enlistment papers with this addendum of conditions:

> On the conditions here explained I offer myself, and promise to depart when and how Mr. Deane shall judge proper, to serve the United States with all possible zeal, without any pension or particular allowance, reserving to myself the liberty of returning to Europe when my family or my king shall recall me.
> Done at Paris this 7th day of December, 1776.
> The Marquis de la Fayette.[12]

Although elated, Deane feared Congress would question the enlistment of a nineteen-year-old major general who had yet to fire a shot in battle and could not even speak English to the troops he would command. He sent Congress a lengthy explanation: "The desire which the Marquis de la Fayette shows of serving among the troops of the United States of North America, and the interest which he takes in the justice of their cause, make him wish to distinguish himself in this war, and to render himself as useful as he possibly can. . . . His high birth, his alliances, the great dignities which his family hold at this court, his considerable estates in this realm, his personal merit, his reputation, his disinterestedness, and, above all, his zeal for the liberty of our provinces, are such as have only been able to engage me to promise him the rank of major-general in the name of the United States."[13]

Kalb and de Broglie's other officers were at the port of Le Havre boarding their frigates for America when Noailles and Ségur asked their families for permission to go to America—and unwittingly set off an international scandal that all but undermined foreign minister Vergennes's efforts to avoid provoking war with Britain. It was one thing for obscure soldiers of fortune such as Kalb to seek adventure across the sea, but quite another matter for three king's musketeers—three noblemen from France's oldest, most powerful families—to enlist in a rebellion against a fellow monarch with whom France was at peace. Although many young knights and their ladies applauded their daring, the British ambassador lodged a strong protest, threatening to break diplomatic relations and send the British fleet to blockade French ports.

Vergennes was furious at Lafayette's impetuous, impolitic plan; the prime minister, comte de Maurepas, called it "a hostile act that would most assuredly be against the wishes of the king"[14] and moved to appease Britain by closing French ports to American ships and banning the sale of war materiel to America. Vergennes forbade the departure of de Broglie's ships, and the minister of war ordered the arrest "with plenty of publicity and severity" of any French soldiers who claimed that the French government had ordered them to go to America. Unconvinced of French sincerity, the British blockaded French ports to curtail shipments to America. De Broglie recalled Kalb and his officers to Paris, and Vergennes ended the clandestine French aid to America. Deane feared he would have to return to America in disgrace.

On the rue Saint-Honoré in Paris, the duc d'Ayen was outraged by the embarrassment his sons-in-law had caused the family; he was particularly furious at Lafayette for considering abandoning his responsibilities as husband and as father of a newborn. To calm the duc's rage, Lafayette agreed to go to London with his cousin for a three-week visit to the marquis de Noailles, the duc d'Ayen's uncle, who had just assumed the ambassadorship to Britain.

Lafayette remained obsessed with his American quest, however, and met secretly with de Broglie to propose buying his own ship and financing the expedition to America himself. Ambitious for Washington's job, de Broglie gleefully agreed and sent an army procurement officer to purchase a cargo ship in Bordeaux, in southwestern France, far from the prying eyes of British spies at Le Havre. "Our young Marquis does not despair," de Broglie told Kalb. "He still has the greatest desire to go."[15]

Lafayette rushed to Deane's quarters on the place Louis XV (now place de la Concorde) to break the news: "Until now, sir," declared America's youngest major general, "you have only seen my zeal for your cause. I shall now purchase a ship to carry your officers; we must feel confidence in the future, and it is especially in the hour of danger that I wish to share your fortune."[16]

Carnival Week in February found Adrienne de La Fayette pregnant with her second child, and the demands of family and palace life seemed to capture Lafayette's every waking moment. He made a show of joining the throng of young nobles who trailed Queen Marie-Antoinette to an endless succession of costume balls, dinners, and dances that seldom ended before dawn. On Shrove Tuesday, February 11, Lafayette learned that de Broglie's envoy in Bordeaux had purchased a cargo ship, the *Victoire*, with a crew of thirty and two cannons on deck. That afternoon, Lafayette signed a note to cover the deposit and went off to celebrate the climactic event of Carnival Week—the Queen's Ball, where the queen would lead revelers in dance until sunrise the next morning.[17]

The following Sunday, February 17, 1777, Lafayette left for London, unable to speak a word of English, but, as the French ambassador's great-nephew by marriage and a member of the powerful Noailles family, he nonetheless became the center of attention in the highest ranks of London society. Ambassador Noailles presented him to King George III; he was guest of honor at a ball given by Lord George Germaine, British Secretary for the Colonies; and he chatted nonchalantly at the opera with General Sir Henry Clinton, one of the commanders in the epic British victories at Bunker Hill and Long Island.

Lafayette recalled his impudence in his memoirs: "A youth of nineteen may be, perhaps, too fond of playing a trick upon the king he is going to fight with. But, while I concealed my intentions, I openly avowed my sentiments; I often defended the Americans; I rejoiced at their success at Trenton; and my spirit of opposition obtained for me an invitation to breakfast with Lord Shelbourne[18] [leader of parliamentary opposition to British policy in the American colonies]."[19]

After two weeks, he grew impatient with bowing and smiling repeatedly to people he did not understand and believed he should hate. Consumed by fantasies of his quest, he invented an excuse to return to Paris, leaving his embarrassed uncle to explain why his nephew would not appear at the galas that London society had prepared for him. But instead of returning to his wife and child at the Noailles mansion, Lafayette went into hiding at Kalb's house in Chaillot, outside Paris, because he feared that if he returned home, his powerful father-in-law—a brigadier general—would order him to rejoin his military regiment at Metz and make departure for America nothing less than desertion from the French military. Lafayette assured both Kalb and de Broglie, however, that he had received his father-in-law's and his wife's blessings for the expedition and was simply avoiding public embarrassment for the Noailles family. Kalb ordered officers from the original Le Havre expedition to leave surreptitiously for Bordeaux by night, and on the evening of March 16, Kalb and Lafayette rode out to join them, with Lafayette abandoning his pregnant wife and infant child without a word, let alone an embrace. He was, after all, still an adolescent in an arranged marriage to a child-wife living in the bosom of her family. Like many young soldiers, he had yet to develop intimate emotional ties to his wife after so many long periods away from her during his military training at Metz.

The following morning, Lafayette's father-in-law, the duc d'Ayen, received this letter:

> You will be astonished, my dear papa, at what I have to say to you. . . .
> I have found a unique opportunity to distinguish myself and learn my [sol-
> dier's] trade; I am a general officer in the army of the United States
> of America. My zeal for their cause and my sincerity have won their

confidence. I shall embark in a vessel that I have myself purchased and chartered. My traveling companions are the Baron de Kalb, a very distinguished officer, brigadier in the [French] King's service, and, like me, a major-general in the United States army; and some excellent officers who want to share in my daring enterprise. I am overjoyed at having found such a glorious opportunity . . . this will not be a long trip, every day people take far longer trips just for pleasure, and, besides, I hope to return more worthy of all those who are kind enough to miss me.

Your affectionate son, Lafayette.[20]

The duc d'Ayen was furious, his wife heartbroken. "She was worried about the effect it would have on me," Adrienne de Lafayette recalled in her memoirs, "and alarmed about the . . . dangers the son [in-law] she cherished so much would have to face so far away from home. She brought the painful news of his cruel departure to me herself and tried to console me, while shedding the best possible light on Monsieur de Lafayette—his affection for me, his superior mind and character. . . . She had no knowledge of great quests or glory, but predicted two years before everyone else that Lafayette would achieve both."[21]

While his wife consoled their daughter, the raging duc d'Ayen rode to Versailles to urge the king to track down the rebellious adolescent runaway and prevent his leaving for America. Word of Lafayette's flight reached the palace—and the British embassy—before the duc d'Ayen. Vergennes was as furious as the duke. Even if it did not provoke war, Lafayette's departure would embarrass the government and compromise the French ambassador in London, a Noailles who had introduced Lafayette to King George only a few days earlier. By facing the British king, knowing he was about to battle the king's men, Lafayette had directly insulted a monarch with whom His Most Christian Majesty Louis XVI was at peace. King Louis issued a statement expressing shock and forbidding all French officers from serving in English colonies. He ordered all who arrive in the Americas to battle the English, "notably Monsieur le marquis de la Fayette, to leave immediately and return to France."[22] Vergennes announced that the king had issued a lettre de cachet, or peremptory arrest order, for Lafayette, but whether he did or not remains one of the mysteries of eighteenth-century court intrigue.

Lafayette and Kalb rode three days to Bordeaux, with the king's soldiers in hot pursuit, bearing the mysterious lettre de cachet—and an order to report to barracks in Marseilles and await further instructions from the king. As word of Lafayette's flight spread across France, young people hailed the intrepid young knight and his reckless disregard of danger. In Paris, his friends—especially the ladies—cheered for him, cried for him, prayed for him, adored him. Young knights longed to ride beside him; although he had not yet unsheathed his saber or fired a shot, his quest evolved into a popular melodrama, with audiences cheering the hero Lafayette and spewing catcalls at his antagonists. English ambassador Lord Stormont reported to his government, "The ladies reproach the parents [in-law] of M. de Lafayette for having tried to stop such a noble enterprise. One of the ladies even declared, 'If the duc d'Ayen thwarts his son-in-law in such a project, he should not expect to marry the rest of his daughters.'"[23]

When Lafayette and Kalb reached Bordeaux, word of his adventure—and the arrest order—had not yet arrived. The soldiers had apparently lost his trail. One by one, de Broglie's officers registered on the *Victoire*, with Lafayette disguising his identity by using his patronymic name, Gilbert du Motier, to which he added "Chevalier de Chavaillac," "knight of Chavaillac," an older spelling of Chavaniac. As the ship prepared for departure, however, a surge of guilt provoked his sending an urgent note to a cousin in Paris to learn how Adrienne and her family had reacted. A week later, his cousin's reply described the emotional turmoil his departure had caused his family and the political turmoil it had caused at court. He enclosed messages from the family.

"The letters from my family were terrible," Lafayette recalled. "They forbade my going to America, warned of the lettre de cachet and of the consequences of the anathema, the laws of the realm and the authority and anger of the government. They reminded me of the grief I was causing my pregnant, loving wife."[24] With favorable winds blowing, however, Lafayette decided to ignore his family's pleas and follow his life's dream by ordering the *Victoire* to set sail.

As the ship slipped away from shore, the boy soldier grew increasingly agitated and confessed to Kalb that he had not had his family's approval to go to America—that he had not even told his wife he was leaving. Kalb was furious at him for jeopardizing the venture. "If he had not been aboard the ship and under way," Kalb wrote to his wife, "I think he would have gone home and, in my opinion, it would have been the right thing to do."[25]

By noon the next day, the ship crossed into Spanish waters, beyond the reach of French soldiers and arrest warrants, and anchored at Los Passajes, a small port near San Sebastiàn. At dinner that evening in San Sebastiàn, Lafayette could no longer contain his agitation. Kalb demanded that he make a decision either to follow his family's wishes and cancel the expedition or carry it out and accept the consequences.

"I have just had dinner with the marquis in Saint-Sebastiàn," Kalb wrote his wife later that evening. "At this moment, he has abandoned his trip to America and recanted his lust for war. He has left for Bordeaux and from there he wants to go to Paris. . . . I do not think he will return, and I advised him to sell the ship . . . for certainly neither M. Maurepas nor the duc d'Ayen will permit him to rejoin us. It is certain that this folly will cost him dearly. But if it be said that he has done a foolish thing, it may be answered that he acted from the most honorable motives and that he can hold up his head before all high-minded men."[26] Kalb wanted to sail to America with the other officers, but the ship belonged to Lafayette and they had no choice but to await the young man's further orders.

After riding up the Spanish and French coasts, with only a brief rest at Saint-Jean de Luz—and a flirtation with an innkeeper's daughter—Lafayette arrived in Bordeaux on April 3. No troops awaited to arrest him; no lettre de cachet. The local military commander ordered Lafayette to report to Marseilles military headquarters and await further orders. The young knight wrote to Prime Minister Maurepas at Versailles pleading for a revocation of the king's order not to go to America.

In Paris, Lafayette's father-in-law demanded that Deane write to General George Washington to revoke Lafayette's commission and send him home to France. Eager to restore good relations with his French hosts, Deane agreed, writing to Washington that Lafayette's trip to America was "without the approbation or knowledge of the king, is disagreeable and that His Majesty expects that you will not permit him to take any command under you."[27] Deane tried to repair the ruptured pipeline of French aid to America by justifying his enlistment of Lafayette in a letter to Vergennes: "To gain a most gallant and amiable young Nobleman to espouse our cause," he pleaded, "and to give to the world a specimen of his native and hereditary bravery, surely cannot be deemed criminal. I have nothing to add . . . except that I rely on the Comte de Broglio [sic] to explain any and every part of my conduct in this affair."[28] A few days later, he wrote to Vergennes again: "I have felt much . . . for the delicate honor of the Marquis, least some report injurious to him should be spread, in either country; no country need be ashamed of him, and I am sure he will one day justify to the world, that my early prejudice in his favor were well founded."[29]

As agitated as Deane may have been, the marquis de Noailles in London was more so, fearing his nephew's action would provoke a premature end to his illustrious diplomatic career and a century of Noailles family influence at Versailles. He sent a letter of apology to French prime minister Maurepas. "I was extremely shocked," he wrote, "to learn . . . that M. de la Fayette had left for America. Fortunately, his age may excuse his thoughtlessness. This is the only consolation left to me in the chagrin I feel for so inconsiderate an action. . . . He concealed his intentions from his traveling companion, from me, and from everybody. . . . Why, Monsieur le Comte, should incidents that are independent of political affairs, damage my reputation?" The distraught marquis begged the prime minister, as well as foreign minister Vergennes, to inform King George of "my zeal in the foreign service."[30]

When word of Lafayette's return to France reached Paris, the British ambassador exulted that "Lafayette's expedition has been a short one indeed."[31] Deane was equally pleased—especially when the duc d'Ayen asked him not to send his embarrassing letter to Washington recalling Lafayette. Vergennes and Maurepas were both relieved, as was the marquis de Noailles in London. "You must know by now," Vergennes wrote to Noailles, "that . . . by the greatest good luck, the project has not been completed. No one would ever suspect you of being either an accomplice or of having any confidential information about the project, and I am certain you will be judged in that light in [England] as you are judged here."[32]

A few days later, a British naval vessel stopped a French cargo ship and captured three French officers and two sergeants on their way to America. When they asked for repatriation, Vergennes tried to heal relations with Britain with this public reply: "Having left France without permission to serve the Americans, the representative of the [French] king cannot involve himself in their situation."[33]

Only the scheming comte de Broglie fumed over Lafayette's return to France and the delay in sending his officers to America to prepare his ascension to generalissimo. De Broglie dispatched a young officer to steer Lafayette back to his ship by convincing him that the king had never actually issued a lettre de cachet—that the government had publicly remonstrated against him to appease the duc d'Ayen. The officer insisted that every one in Paris—except the duc d'Ayen—had cheered Lafayette's grand adventure. Lafayette desperately wanted to believe de Broglie's envoy—and finally did, after the officer reminded him of de Broglie's close ties to Vergennes and suggested that Prime Minister Maurepas's failure to answer Lafayette's earlier letter was an obvious indication of government approval for his expedition. Lafayette embraced the idea in a second letter to the prime minister, saying he concluded that Maurepas's "silence was a tacit order" to proceed to America.[34]

The Bordeaux commandant, however, was having none of it, and threatened to arrest Lafayette if he did not report to Marseilles. Lafayette pretended to comply and rode off in an eastbound coach, with Bordeaux officers following. While the coachman stopped to change horses at a post house, Lafayette disguised himself as a courier, took a horse, and galloped off toward the Spanish border. The officers soon noticed his absence and picked up his trail. When he reached Saint-Jean de Luz, the innkeeper's daughter saw through his disguise, "but at a signal from me, and, out of loyalty, she sent my pursuers in the wrong direction."[35]

On April 20, 1777, the *Victoire* sailed from Las Passajes for America with the nineteen-year-old Major General de la Fayette aboard, in quest of glory and honor but unwittingly leading an expedition to replace the American military high command with a French military junta and just as unwittingly undermining French government policy of avoiding war with Britain. On board with him were Kalb, in quest of colonial power for de Broglie, and the twelve French officers in de Broglie's high command.

Far from the glamorous adventure Lafayette had anticipated, the voyage proved a personal horror for the young French knight—as it was for many ocean travelers. Even the finest, calmest day at sea confined passengers to never-ending boredom in tiny wooden cubbies below decks, with little to eat but hard biscuits, salt pork, and fish—and nothing to do but ponder the possibility that if the trip lasted too long, the ship would run out of food and fresh water. On most crossings, passengers and crew went on short rations before the ship was midway to its destination. Still other dangers awaited over the horizon: privateers and pirates, ready to attack, maim, enslave, imprison, or kill innocents. And waves—the ever-present waves—clawing at the boat, toying with it sadistically, tossing, turning, and dropping it fiercely, so that it pitched and rolled and sickened almost every passenger on board. Sometimes the capricious craft slammed a passenger into oblivion against a bulkhead or sent him sliding along the deck into the sea, but always, it made everyone sick; terribly sick—and most especially Lafayette, who suffered relentlessly for more than a week, until he gradually acquired his sea legs and enough equilibrium for his life aboard ship to settle into a routine. He relieved the ensuing boredom by learning some English from Kalb and studying military tactics from books he had brought.

For more than a month, Lafayette postponed writing to the pregnant wife he had so abruptly deserted without a word. On May 30, he finally faced the responsibility of trying to justify the unjustifiable:

"*A bord de la Victoire*," he headed the letter: "Aboard the *Victoire*."

"It is from far away that I write you, sweetheart, and to this cruel separation is added the still more dreadful uncertainty of the time when I shall hear from you again. . . . Have you forgiven me? . . . Your grief, that of my friends, Henriette [their baby]—it all came into my mind with rightful vividness, and for an instant I felt that I had nothing to say in defense of what I was about to do. If you knew what I have suffered, what weary days I have passed fleeing everything I love best in the world! Must I yet learn, besides all this, that you refuse to forgive me? Indeed, my sweetheart, in that event I should be too unhappy."

Lest she think he was enjoying himself, he described the discomforts of the voyage: "One day follows another, and, what is worse, they are all alike. Nothing but sky and nothing but water; and tomorrow it will be just the same." He rambled on, almost incoherently, until shame overcame him, and he abandoned his hypocrisy for a week. A week later, on June 7, he picked up his plume to resume his adolescent lamentations of the hardships afflicting him at sea: "I am still out upon this dreary plain, which is beyond comparison the most dismal place that one can be in. I try to console myself a little by thinking of you and of our friends at home, and I picture to myself the joy . . . when I come home, when I rush in unexpectedly to take you into my arms—and perhaps I shall find you with your children." He tried to justify his desertion: "While defending the liberty I adore—of my own free will, as a friend, offering my services to this most interesting republic, I bring with me nothing but my heart and good will, with no personal ambitions to fulfill, no selfish interests to serve, working only for my own glory and for the happiness [of the American republic]. I hope that, for my sake, you will become a good American, for that feeling is worthy of every noble heart. The happiness of America is intimately connected with the happiness of all mankind; she is destined to become the safe and venerable asylum of virtue, of honesty, of tolerance, and of peaceful liberty." He put down his letter. The crow's nest had spotted birds, and he went topside. Later, after dinner, he resumed: "We have begun today to see certain kinds of birds which indicate that land is near. The hope of arriving there is sweet. . . . Adieu. Night obliges me to stop, for I have lately forbidden the use of lights about the ship . . . but with my fingers directed a little by the impulses of my heart, I have no need of lights to tell you that I love you and shall love you all my life."[36]

It would be mid-August—two months later—before his wife would receive these first words from her husband in the six months since he abandoned her in February.

On June 12, 1777, Lafayette's ship neared Charleston and encountered an American man-of-war that warned of two British frigates blockading the entrance to Charleston Bay. The *Victoire* sailed northward, and the next afternoon, fifty-four days after leaving Los Passajes, reached the South Carolina coast, sixty miles north of Charleston. It anchored near North Island at the entrance to Georgetown Bay.[37]

Lafayette had arrived.

3

First Blood

AT TWO IN THE AFTERNOON on Friday, June 13, 1777, seven sailors rowed Lafayette, Kalb, and four other officers in the jolly boat of the *Victoire* along the shore of North Island off the coast of South Carolina, seeking a pilot to guide the ship through the narrow mouth of the bay to safe harbor. Finding no sign of life, they continued rowing, stepping ashore occasionally, only to confirm the absence of civilization before reboarding and resuming their labor. It was ten o'clock at night before they reached the northern tip of the island and found some unintelligible black slaves combing for oysters. When the outgoing tide left the jolly boat mired in mud, Lafayette and the others climbed into the oyster boat—a crude, hand hewn, flat-bottomed craft. The slaves rowed them along the shore until a beam of light from their master's house flickered through the tall marsh grasses. It was midnight when they stumbled ashore.

"When I felt American soil under my feet for the first time that night," Lafayette wrote later, "my first words were an oath to conquer or die for America's cause."[1]

As Lafayette and the others sloshed their way across the marsh toward the light, dogs sounded a fierce alarm of yelps and barks, and, fearing a party of marauders from British privateers, a harsh voice demanded that the men identify themselves. Kalb answered that they were French officers seeking a pilot for their ship and a place to spend the night. As candlelight blossomed in each window, the doors opened and Major Benjamin Huger, one of the state's major rice growers, offered what Lafayette described as "a cordial welcome and generous hospitality" at his plantation home.[2] After inviting Lafayette and his party to spend the night, he told them Georgetown Bay

31

was too shallow for the *Victoire*, and promised to find a pilot to steer her to Charleston the next morning. He urged Lafayette to ride overland to Charleston, to avoid possible capture by the British at sea.

"I retired to rest that night," Lafayette recalled, "rejoicing that I had at last attained the haven of my dreams and had safely landed in America beyond the reach of my pursuers. The next morning was beautiful. Everything around me was new to me, the room, the bed draped in delicate mosquito curtains, the black servants who came to me quietly to ask my commands, the strange new beauty of the landscape outside my windows, the luxuriant vegetation—all combined to produce a magical effect and fill me with indescribable sensations."[3] Lafayette had never before seen or slept in a home built entirely of wood or lifted a wooden sash window; French homes were stone, with windows that opened like doors. He had never tasted corn bread or sweet potatoes.

In France, equally indescribable sensations—all of them unpleasant— were overwhelming the Noailles family, who feared Lafayette had been lost at sea—not an uncommon fate for transatlantic voyagers. Adrienne was frantic: "My mother spent all her time trying to console me."[4] French prime minister Maurepas sent a note of consolation to Ambassador Noailles in London. "I am truly distressed for you and your family. . . . I had the honor of seeing the Maréchal [Adrienne's grandfather, the Ambassador's brother] yesterday, and he seemed to me to be as distressed as I know you are. Neither you nor your family have any reason for self-reproach, and the king in no way holds you responsible for the behavior of a young man whose head had been turned."[5]

Foreign Minister Vergennes was even more distressed. Lafayette's impetuous departure risked exposing his policy of clandestine help for America. The British navy and British privateers were stopping every French ship they spotted to try to capture Lafayette. As it was, they captured so many other French officers bound for America that Vergennes feared war was inevitable. He sought help from Spain, whose king had a *pacte de famille* with his nephew the French king: war against one meant war against both. "If one examines . . . where things stand between France and England," Vergennes wrote to the Spanish foreign minister, "should we not anticipate that open warfare will . . . break out in a few months and [should we not] consider immediately the measures we should undertake advantageously?"[6]

If Lafayette's adventure plunged Versailles in gloom, it had the opposite effect in the salons and streets of Paris, where the flames of patriotism burned high and bright, stoked by fiery anti-British editorials. Across the city—across France—the young knight's daring quest inspired hundreds of young officers of every nationality to travel across Europe to queue outside Deane's door in Paris. The arrival of the celebrated Benjamin Franklin as unofficial ambassador to France added to the frenzy. Crowds gathered outside his house in Passy, west of Paris, to catch a glimpse of the legendary philosopher-scientist and cheer his every move.

"All Europe is for us," Franklin and Deane exulted in a letter to Congress, "and it is a very general opinion that if we succeed in establishing our liberties, we shall, as soon as peace is restored, receive an immense addition of numbers and wealth from Europe, by the families who will come over to participate in our privileges, and bring their estates with them. Tyranny is so generally established in the rest of the world, that the prospect of an asylum in America, for those who love liberty, gives general joy, and our cause is esteemed. . . . The desire that military officers here, of all ranks, have of going to the service of the United States is so general and so strong as to be quite amazing. We are hourly fatigued with their applications and offers."[7]

In Philadelphia, Congress had grown even more fatigued with the applications of foreign officers, and Washington was outraged. In an angry letter to Congress, he protested "the distress I am . . . laid under by the application of French officers for commission in our service. This evil . . . is a growing one . . . they are coming in swarms from old France and the Islands. . . . They seldom bring more than a commission and a passport, which, we know, may belong to a bad as well as a good officer. Their ignorance of our language and their inability to recruit men are insurmountable obstacles to their being ingrafted into our Continental battalions; for our officers, who have raised their men, and have served through the war upon pay that has hitherto not borne their expenses, would be disgusted if foreigners were put over their heads."[8] When Congress failed to act, Washington sent another angry note to Richard Henry Lee, his friend and fellow Virginian, asking "what Congress expects I am to do with the many foreigners they have at different times promoted to the rank of field officers. . . . These men have no attachment nor ties to the country . . . and are ignorant of the language they are to receive and give orders in . . . and our officers think it exceedingly hard . . . to have strangers put over them, whose merit perhaps is not equal to their own, but whose effrontery will take no denial." Washington told Lee he was "disgusted" by the practice of "giving rank to people of no reputation or service."[9]

Washington's second letter had its desired effect; Congress stopped granting military commissions to foreigners unless Washington himself requested it. Franklin and Deane, however, asked Congress to make an exception for Lafayette. Duped by de Broglie into believing that the French government had tacitly approved the Lafayette mission, Franklin and Deane exaggerated its importance:

> The Marquis de La Fayette, a young nobleman of great family connections here and great wealth is gone to America in a ship of his own, accompanied by some officers of distinction, in order to serve in our armies. He is exceedingly beloved and everybody's good wishes attend him; we can not

but hope he may meet with such a reception as will make the country and his expedition agreeable to him . . . we are satisfied that the civilities and respect that may be shown him will be serviceable to our affairs here, as pleasing not only to his powerful relations and to the court but to the whole French nation. He has left a beautiful young wife big with child and for her sake particularly we hope that his bravery and ardent desire to distinguish himself will be a little restrained by the General's [Washington's] prudence, so as not to permit his being hazarded much, but on some important occasion.[10]

The morning after Lafayette's arrival at Major Huger's rice plantation, Huger sent a pilot to guide the *Victoire* to Charleston Bay, while Lafayette and his party set off by horseback over seventy-five miles of sands, swamps, and trackless woods. Three days later, wrote one of Lafayette's officers, "we arrived looking like beggars and brigands. People mocked us when we said we were French officers here to defend their liberty. Even the large number of French who had preceded us to Charles-Town called us adventurers."[11] But the following day, Lafayette's ship "sailed into port triumphantly, and their attitude turned full circle. Everyone welcomed us everywhere. The French outcasts who had been first to mock us paid homage obsequiously to the Marquis de la Fayette and sought to enlist in his expedition. . . . The city's leading citizens opened their arms to us and entertained us . . . for eight days of feasts and gala celebrations. They showed the marquis all the honors due a marshal of France and protector of liberty."[12]

The city's leading citizens were Freemasons, and they embraced the young Frenchman as a brother when he identified himself at the tavern that served as the Masonic lodge. Almost every American town and city had one. South Carolina assembly president John Rutledge and General William Moultrie, the heroic leader who had successfully repelled the British assault on Charleston, embraced their French "brother" and opened their homes to him.[13]

"This beautiful city is worthy of its inhabitants," Lafayette wrote ecstatically, "and everything bespoke comfort and even luxury. Without even knowing me, Governor Rutledge . . . eagerly received me with the utmost kindness and attention. They showed me the new works that Moultrie had defended so well."[14] Moved by Moultrie's heroism, Lafayette gave his brother Mason the funds to dress, arm, and equip one hundred men. By the end of his stay in Charleston, the city's welcome left him so enamored of Americans and their ways that when he wrote to Adrienne the words "we republicans" flowed in the ink from his quill as easily as his signature:

A simplicity of manners, a desire to please, the love of country and of liberty . . . are to be found everywhere. The richest man and the poorest are upon the same social level, and, although there are some great fortunes in this country, I defy one to discover the least difference in the bearing of one man to another. The city is one of the most attractive, the best built, and inhabited by the most agreeable people, that I have ever seen. The American women are very beautiful, unaffected in manner, and charmingly and neatly dressed. . . . What delights me most is that all citizens are brothers. There are no poor people in America, not even what may be called peasants. Every man has his own property, and each has the same rights with the greatest land-owner in the country. . . . As for me, I have been welcomed in the most agreeable manner by everybody here. I have just this moment returned from a grand dinner that lasted five hours, given by a gentleman of this city in my honor. . . . We drank many healths and I spoke very bad English, which language, by the way, I am beginning now to use a little.[15]

As an afterthought, he remembered to ask, "Do you still love me? My heart always answers, yes: I trust it does not deceive me. . . . Embrace my Henriette most tenderly; should I add, embrace our children? Those poor children have a wanderer father, but he is, at heart, a good, honest man, a good father who loves his children very much, and a good husband as well, for he loves his wife with all his heart. . . . Adieu, then, my dearest love; I must leave off for want of time and paper; and if I do not repeat ten thousand times that I love you, it is not from want of affection, but from having the vanity to hope that I have already convinced you of it. The night is far advanced, the heat intense, and I am devoured by gnats covering me with big bites; but the best of countries, as you can see, has their inconveniences. Adieu, my love, adieu."[16] Adrienne did not receive his first letters to her until August 1. By then, she seemed uncertain about her own feelings for the husband who had sired her two children and abandoned her without an adieu, let alone a tender embrace. "My mother did everything to demonstrate from his letters how tenderly he felt towards me," Adrienne recalled.[17]

Lafayette outfitted his company with a train of splendid carriages and horses, and, on June 25, he rode out of town with Kalb and five other officers on the road to glory in Philadelphia. They did not get far. "Four days later our carriages were reduced to splinters," one of the officers wrote in his diary. "Several of the horses were old and unsteady and were either worn out or lame. We had to buy others along the road. . . . We had to leave part of our luggage behind, and part of it was stolen. We traveled a great part of the way on foot, often sleeping in the woods, almost dead with hunger, exhausted by the heat, several of us suffering from fever and dysentery."[18]

In contrast to his discouraged companions, Lafayette remained in high spirits and good humor. "I have experienced no ill effects," he wrote to his wife. "The farther I advance north, the better pleased I am with the country and its people. They refuse me no kindness or attention, even though most hardly know who I am."[19]

Their journey took them seven hundred miles through the "abominable heat" of both the Carolinas, then northward through Virginia, Maryland, and Delaware. The trek left some of the officers so disheartened they discussed quitting and returning to France, but Lafayette remained enraptured. He had spent his childhood battling brambles and thorns with his wooden sword in the woods at Chavaniac and knew which berries, plants, and mushrooms in the wild were edible. Compared to the horrors he had suffered at sea, the woods, fields, and streams of America offered a wonderland of new sights, sounds, and tastes. "Vast forests and immense rivers combined to give the country an appearance of youth and majesty," he wrote. "I studied the language and the customs of the inhabitants . . . observed new productions of nature and new methods of cultivation."[20]

After more than three weeks, Lafayette's suffering little troop reached Annapolis, with Lafayette exhilarated and gaining strength with each step. One of the officers, Chevalier Du Buysson, wrote that "Lafayette's enthusiasm was inspiring."[21] But Lafayette carefully disguised his joy in letters to his wife: "O! if you only knew how much I sigh to see you, how much I suffer at being separated from you, and all that my heart has been called on to endure. . . . I scarcely dare think of the time of your confinement, and yet I think of it every moment of the day. I cannot dwell upon it without the most dreadful anxiety. I am, indeed, unfortunate, at being so distant from you; even if you did not love me, you ought to pity me."[22] Adrienne was in no mood to pity her husband; she was in the agonies of giving birth to their second child, daughter Anastasie. After five months, she had yet to receive any word of her husband, and more weeks would elapse before his letters would arrive.

After thirty-two days, Lafayette and his bedraggled party reached Philadelphia on July 27, 1777, "in a more pitiable condition even than when we first came into Charleston," according to Du Buysson. After "brushing ourselves up a little," they went to the Pennsylvania State House, where Congress was sitting. When they presented Deane's letters of recommendation and commissions to the doorkeeper, he barred the way. Congressman James Lovell of Massachusetts, the chairman on foreign applications, heard the ruckus and went out to meet them, but after reading their commissions, brusquely dismissed them. "It seems that French officers have a great fancy to enter our service without being invited," he snarled. "It is true we were in need of officers last year, but now we have experienced men and plenty of them."[23]

Lafayette was crestfallen; Kalb, humiliated; the rest of the party, stunned to despair. "We didn't know what to think," said Chevalier Du Buysson.

"We tried to think of the possible reasons for such an insulting rebuff."[24] As it turned out, Lafayette and his friends could not have arrived at a worse time. Congress was in a foul mood: the Revolution seemed lost. General John Burgoyne's army had swept down from Canada to the foot of Lake Champlain and captured Fort Ticonderoga—hitherto thought impregnable. Two days later, they captured two more Patriot strongholds, at Mount Defiance and Mount Independence, where they seized substantial stores of Patriot arms and ammunition. Meanwhile, a force of loyalists and Indians was moving eastward from Lake Ontario to join Burgoyne, while General Henry Clinton was leading troops northward along the Hudson River. Still worse, Admiral Sir William Howe and a four-hundred-ship armada had set sail from New York toward the Patriot capital at Philadelphia, with 20,000 troops on board.

As if the war did not provide enough gloom, French adventurers were still tramping into town, badgering members of Congress for the high ranks and salaries that Silas Deane had promised them in Paris. Their arrogance, incompetence, and deceit had earned them nothing but scorn and hatred. Washington called them men of "unbounded pride and ambition;"[25] Major General Nathanael Greene called them "so many spies in our camp."[26] Just before Lafayette arrived, Philippe Trouson du Coudray "presented himself before Congress with lordly airs, implying that he had been a brigadier general in France, a counselor to the French ministry, to princes and dukes . . . demanding the rank of major general and commander in chief of the American artillery . . . and," Du Buysson noted, "demanding payment of 300,000 livres [$3 million current value] for his services."[27] Three of Washington's generals—Nathanael Greene, Henry Knox, and John Sullivan—threatened to resign until an investigation unmasked Du Coudray as the commoner son of a wine merchant and a former artillery brigade chief, not a brigadier general of noble birth. Du Coudray drowned accidentally in the Schuylkill River near Philadelphia a month later, and the committee moved to recall Silas Deane for granting commissions to unqualified applicants.

When, therefore, Lafayette showed up, Congress was in no mood to consider any more of Deane's commissions. Undeterred—and unwilling to return to France humiliated—Lafayette sent his own petition to Congress, addressing it to President John Hancock and inscribing the unmistakable triangle of dots—∴—that symbolized Hancock's own Masonic brotherhood. "After the sacrifices I have made in this cause," Lafayette wrote, "I have the right to exact two favours: one is, to serve at my own expense—the other is, to serve at first as a volunteer." Like Hancock and other signers of the Declaration of Independence, Lafayette pledged his life, his fortune, and his sacred honor to American independence.

With British troops about to storm Philadelphia, Congress was all but bankrupt and in desperate need of money and military aid. As president of Congress, Hancock was in charge of military procurement, and he believed that Lafayette's name, wealth, and ties to the French court might serve the American cause. He sent New York congressman William Duer to interview the young Frenchman and confirm his Masonic affiliation. Duer was a well educated, English-born financier and merchant who spoke fluent French. "He . . . was more polite and adroit, and . . . made some sort of apology to Lafayette," Chevalier Du Buysson wrote in his diary. "He had orders to sound him out. He spoke to him in private."[28] In a second interview, Duer and Lafayette worked out the terms of his commission: he would receive no pay or other compensation; his rank was strictly honorary, and he would receive no command or even the promise of one; moreover, the date of his commission would be July 31 to preclude his gaining even nominal seniority over any officers of the same rank. Lafayette agreed, and, on July 31, 1777, Congress passed a resolution:

"Whereas the Marquis de La Fayette, out of his great zeal to the cause of liberty, in which the United States are engaged, has left his family and connections, and at his own expence come over to offer his services to the United States without pension or particular allowance, and is anxious to risque his life in our cause—Resolved, That his service be accepted, and that in consideration of his zeal, illustrious family and connections he have the rank and commission of Major General in the Army of the United States."[29] Two hours later, Lafayette, still only nineteen, received the resolution and the sash of an American major general.

In granting Lafayette's commission, however, Congress rejected out of hand the applications by Kalb and the other de Broglie plotters, saying they lacked command of English and had misunderstood Deane. All pleaded with Lafayette to intercede on their behalf, saying they had no money to get home. Reasoning that no self-respecting major general could do without personal aides, he hired at his own expense the two youngest officers—Jean-Joseph Sourbader de Gimat and Chevalier Morel de La Colombe, both twenty-two years old. He promised the others he would petition Congress on their behalf.

On August 4, Patriot lookouts spotted Howe's fleet off the Delaware capes in southern New Jersey, south of Philadelphia. Washington rode to the capital the following day to confer with Congress. At a dinner for him and his aides that evening, the Continental army's newest major general caught his first glimpse of the leader he described as "this great man." From earliest childhood, fictional Arthurian heroes had peopled Lafayette's imagination; now, for the first time, one of them strode into his life. Washington stood as all heroes stood—"exactly what one would wish," according to Thomas Jefferson, "his deportment easy, erect, noble; the best horseman of his age, and

George Washington, the commander in chief of the Continental army, welcomed Lafayette to America as a brother Mason and invited him to live at his headquarters. Lafayette admired "the majesty of his face." (*Library of Congress.*)

the most graceful figure that could be seen on horseback."[30] One of Washington's servants was more emotional: "So tall, so straight! and . . . with such an air! Ah, sire, he was like no one else!"[31]

For Lafayette, the six-foot, four-inch-tall Washington was the embodiment of the ethereal warrior father who had haunted his imagination since infancy—statuesque, with the powerful build of a great cavalier, magnificently uniformed—more royal than any European monarch in his fine powdered wig. "Although he was surrounded by officers and private citizens," wrote the reverent Lafayette, "it was impossible not to recognize the majesty of his face and his countenance. The affable and noble manners and the dignity with which he addressed those about him were equally distinguished."[32]

Washington believed that Freemasonry provided him with "true brothers in all parts of the world,"[33] and, at evening's end, he drew "brother Lafayette" aside to express his good will towards the boy. Lafayette looked so young, so vulnerable. Washington complimented him for his "zeal and sacrifices in coming to America . . . in the most friendly manner, he invited me to reside in his house. I would have the happiness of living in the general quarters of the commander-in-chief as a member of his military family,

which offer I accepted with the same sincerity with which it was made."
With an uncharacteristic smile, Washington warned that "he could not
promise the luxuries of a king's court, but now that Lafayette had become an
American soldier, he would undoubtedly adapt with good grace to the hardships of life in a republican army."[34]

Lafayette spent the next few days equipping himself and his aides for
camp. He bought a carriage, a team of horses, and all the necessary arms,
equipment, and clothing he would need. He emerged as the most magnificent-
looking knight in the American army—indeed, the only one. He lacked
only a suit of shining armor. Before going off to war, the elated nineteen-
year-old sent a touching, almost childlike, letter of thanks in broken English
to "The honorable Mr. Hancock president of Congress" for making a reality
of his lifelong dream of emulating his warrior ancestors:

> the 13 august 1777
>
> Sir
>
> I beg you will receive yourself and present to Congress my thanks for the
> Commission of Major General in the Army of the United States of Amer-
> ica which I have been honor'd with in their name the feelings of my heart,
> long before it became my duty, engaged me in the love of the America
> cause. I now only consider'd it as the cause of Honor; Virtue, and univer-
> sal Happiness, but felt myself empressed with the warmest affection for a
> Nation who exhibited by their resistance so fine an example of Justice and
> Courage to the Universe.
>
> I schall [sic] neglect nothing on my part to justify the confidence which
> the Congress of the United States has been pleased to repose in me as my
> highest ambition has ever been to do every thing only for the best of the
> cause in which I am engaged. I wish to serve near the person of General
> Washington till such time as he may think proper to entrust me with a
> division of the Army.

Remembering the plight of his companions on the *Victoire* and convinced he now had at least some influence as a major general, Lafayette
added another paragraph:

> it is now as an american that I'll mention every day to congress the officers
> who came over with me, whose interests are for me as my own, and the
> consideration which they deserve by their merits their ranks, their state
> and reputation in France.
>
> I am sir with the sentiments which every good american owe to you.
>
> Your most obedient
> servant the mqis de lafayette.[35]

Congress ignored his appeal for his companions, and Lafayette reached into his own pocket to help them pay for their passage home. Just as he had unwittingly furthered de Broglie's plot by paying their way to America, Lafayette now just as unwittingly ended the plot by trying to pay their way back. Two days later, he rode off to war, accompanied by his handsomely uniformed squires, but leaving Kalb and the other de Broglie plotters fuming in Philadelphia over their humiliating rejection.

When Lafayette reached the American camp north of Philadelphia, the realities of George Washington's army seemed incongruous with the young knight's vision of King Arthur's knights in armor. "About eleven thousand men, ill armed, and still worse clothed, presented a strange spectacle," wrote the chastened young major general. "Their clothes were motley looking, discolored, and many were almost naked. The best dressed wore *hunting shirts*, large gray linen shirts used in the Carolinas."[36]

Washington responded to Lafayette's evident disappointment. "I suppose we ought to be embarrassed," said the commander in chief, "to show ourselves to an officer who has just left the French forces."

"I have come here to learn, *mon général*," said the young man, snapping to attention smartly, "not to teach." It was a humble answer that contrasted with the arrogance of other French officers Washington had encountered and one that the commander in chief obviously appreciated. "Those simple words," Lafayette recalled, "established the first bonds of mutual confidence and devotion that united two friends."[37]

Despite misgivings about the overdressed Frenchman and his aides, Washington graciously invited Lafayette to attend a council of war the next morning, August 21, 1777—an invitation that saved the young man the embarrassment of appearing to hold a sinecure. The army was encamped about five miles northwest of Philadelphia, between Germantown and the Schuylkill River, awaiting word of the destination of the British fleet. Initial fears that it would turn into Delaware Bay and attack Philadelphia had proved unfounded after it continued sailing southward, and Washington's council of war agreed the British fleet was on its way to attack Charleston. Although his poor English prevented Lafayette from participating in the discussion, he signed the minutes below Washington's name, alongside the names of the other majors general—Nathanael Greene and William Alexander Lord Stirling[38]—but above brigadiers general Henry Knox, Anthony Wayne, John Peter Gabriel Muhlenberg, and Thomas Conway, as well as Washington's twenty-two-year-old secretary, Lieutenant Colonel Alexander Hamilton.

The following morning, near pandemonium engulfed the encampment after a courier galloped in with an urgent dispatch from President Hancock: instead of continuing to Charleston, Admiral Howe's fleet had turned into Chesapeake Bay and was sailing northward. He had bypassed Delaware Bay to avoid Patriot fortifications along the narrow Delaware River and chosen the longer route along the unfortified shores of Chesapeake Bay. He would land at Head of Elk (now Elkton, Maryland) at the head of the bay, about sixty miles south of Philadelphia, and march northward to attack the capital. Washington ordered his army to prepare to march, and, on Sunday, August 24, he led his troops to Philadelphia, to display their colors to Congress and raise the city's morale. "The army is to march in one column through the city," read his general order. "The drums and fifes of each brigade are to be collected in the centre of it, and a tune for the quick-step played, but with such moderation that the men may step to it with ease."[39]

The tall, handsome Washington "shone" at the head of the parade, according to Lafayette, who rode alongside in his sparkling new uniform, his sword slapping smartly at his boot. Behind them, "with green sprigs in their hats, stepping to the lively music of the fife and drum before all the citizens of the city, the continentals made quite a show of it, despite their shabby clothes."[40]

Kalb and de Broglie's other officers watched Lafayette ride off to war without them and despaired bitterly of ever participating in the Revolution, let alone commanding the American army. In his outrage against de Broglie and Deane, one of the French officers went to Congress and exposed de Broglie's plot to become generalissimo.[41] Equally infuriated, "Baron" de Kalb sent Congress an angry letter threatening to expose Deane's recruitment activities in France if Congress did not confirm his commission or compensate him for the "very considerable expense I have been put to after arriving here. I do not think that either my name, my services, or my person are proper objects to be trifled with or laughed at. I cannot tell you, sir, how deeply I feel the injury done to me. . . . I should be sorry to be compelled to carry my case against Mr. Deane or his successors for damages. And such an action would injure his credit and negotiations, and those of the state at court."[42] Kalb argued that he alone in the Lafayette group was fluent in English, had negotiated his contract in English, and could not possibly have misunderstood Deane's intentions.

Kalb's threat of a public lawsuit was not an idle one. He was furious at the prospects of humiliation he faced in France for having failed his patron, the comte de Broglie. Indeed, a return to France would end his military career. He was, after all, a peasant's son. Soldiering was all he knew, and congressional confirmation of his commission in the American army was his only chance to continue that trade.

Kalb's letter had the desired effect. Congress feared that if Kalb exposed French complicity in the American Revolution, France would end her support rather than risk war with Britain. Congress resolved that "thanks be given to the baron de Kalb . . . and the officers . . . for their zeal in passing over to America to offer their services to these United States, and that their expences to this Continent and their return to France be paid."[43] The resolution assailed Silas Deane, saying he had "no authority" to commission the officers. A few days later, the French officers took their money and the funds Lafayette had given them and left for various ports to book passage back to France or the French West Indies. Kalb had no sooner left with his money than he received word that Congress had relented and issued him the major general's commission that Deane had promised him. Congress did not want to risk his returning to France and damaging American interests there. With the other French officers gone, however, it was too late for him to revive the de Broglie plot, and he wrote to his former commander:

"I beg you, Monsieur le Comte, to be persuaded of the respect and deference that at all times and in all places I have for your orders and for your wishes; that I have done all that lay in my power; that if I have not done better it is not my fault." He declared it "impossible to succeed in the grand project . . . it would be regarded as a crying injustice against Washington and an outrage on the country."[44]

Washington, Lafayette, and the Continental army halted for the night at Chester, about twenty miles south of Philadelphia. The following day as they pushed southward, the British army at Head of Elk marched north to Brandywine Creek, the last natural barrier to the American capital. Washington's forces stretched out along the opposite bank on the Philadelphia side. On September 11, the two sides opened fire at Chadd's Ford. Throughout the day, the battle raged with ever greater intensity. Washington badly miscalculated the strength and intentions of his enemy and concentrated his firepower at the center of the lines. Meanwhile, British general Lord Cornwallis quietly slipped away to the northwest with a second force of 8,000 British and Hessians. He crossed the Brandywine at its narrowest point, far from the battle at Chadd's Ford, looped around and behind the Patriot army's right flank, under Major General John Sullivan, and threatened to encircle Washington's entire army. Paralyzing British fire swept across Sullivan's troops from three sides—south, west, and north. As he had on Long Island, Sullivan faced the humiliation of surrender. Like most Patriot generals, he had no formal military training. He was a New Hampshire lawyer whose social rank had given him a seat in Congress and, in turn, an appointment as a general.

When word of the Cornwallis attack arrived, Lafayette was standing idly at Washington's side and begged permission to help Sullivan defend the right flank. In no mood to argue, Washington agreed, and Lafayette leaped onto his horse and, with his two "squires," Gimat and La Colombe, following gallantly, charged into his—and their—first battle.

"By the time [we] arrived, the enemy had crossed the ford," Lafayette recalled. "Sullivan's troops had barely enough time to form a line in front of

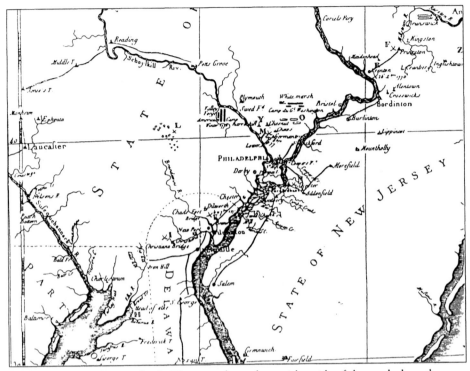

The Battle of Brandywine Creek. The crossed swords on either side of the creek show the placement of the British (left) and American forces (right), and the circular dotted line shows the path Cornwallis hoped to follow to cut Washington's retreat to Chester. (*From the author's collection.*)

a thin wood. The Hessians advanced, rested their rifles on a fence, aimed and sent off a cloud of fire to cover the advancing British troops. Lord Cornwallis's troops advanced in perfect order across the field, his first line firing cannons and muskets; the Americans fired a murderous barrage of musket-fire, but the entire right and left side buckled; the generals and officers fell towards the center of the line, where Lafayette and Lord Stirling were [fighting] alongside 800 men, brilliantly commanded by [General] Conway. By sheering off the two wings, the British troops could concentrate all their fire on the center of our line, although their advance across an open field cost them many men."[45]

The blistering fire and inexorable British advance sent the American soldiers fleeing in panic. Lafayette tried to halt their retreat. He reared his horse into the air, wheeled to the right, to the left, galloping back and forth to block the fleeing troops. Finally, he jumped off and grabbed at men's shoulders and arms, ordering them to turn about, stand and fight—a major general in full uniform; a madman refusing to face defeat. At six feet one inch, he was taller than they, a knight in battle, commanding his men to hold against the enemy—much as the legendary maréchal de France Gilbert de La Fayette III had held against the same British enemy with Joan of Arc at Orléans. Startled by a major general's presence among them in battle, the Americans halted their retreat, rallied around him, and took the enemy's charge. Stirling formed his brigade on a slight rise behind Lafayette and gave the French knight and his men covering fire, but the sheer number of British troops finally overwhelmed them. With his troops falling dead or wounded about him, Lafayette ordered them to fall back beside Sullivan's and Stirling's men, and, together, they stood their ground until the British were within twenty yards and forced them to flee to the safety of the woods behind. It was then that Gimat looked down and saw blood seeping from Lafayette's boot. In the noise and excitement of rallying the troops, a musket ball had passed through the calf of his left leg and transformed the glory of his Arthurian quest into the painful reality of soldiering. About him lay the dead and dying men and boys, many younger than he, their tatters soaked in blood, sweat, and dirt. Some begged for help, others called to God; some cried out for their mothers, and others just muttered incomprehensibly and sobbed.

Gimat and La Colombe lifted the wounded Lafayette onto his horse, and they joined the sad, general retreat eastward toward Chester. Aware of the disaster, General Nathanael Greene moved from Chadd's Ford to cover the retreat, opening his lines to let the waves of bewildered militiamen—mostly farm boys and woodsmen—escape the murderous Redcoat fire. In the confusion, Lafayette tried to rejoin Washington, but loss of blood left him so weak that he had to stop to have his wound bandaged and only barely escaped capture.

"Fugitives, cannon, and baggage crowded in complete disorder on the road to Chester," Lafayette recalled. "Meanwhile, Chadd's Ford was captured, the cannons seized, and the road to Chester became the common retreat of the whole army. In the midst of that dreadful confusion, and during the darkness of the night, it was impossible to recover."[46]

At Chester, twelve miles from the battlefield, Lafayette approached the entrance to a bridge and, despite searing pain in his leg, turned his horse and blocked the disorderly retreat of troops, ordering them to halt and reform their lines before allowing them to cross. "Some degree of order was re-established," he reported, when Washington and the other generals arrived to relieve him. Washington ordered a surgeon to dress Lafayette's wound, and Stirling's French-speaking aide, Captain James Monroe of Virginia, helped him to nearby Birmingham Church, where he lay on a makeshift litter, while Monroe commiserated with him and attended his needs. About seven months younger than Lafayette, Monroe had suffered a wound the previous year at Trenton. With Gimat and La Colombe, Monroe spent the night befriending the wounded Frenchman, displaying his French and talking of his venerated mentor, Mr. Jefferson, the author of the Declaration of Independence. The following day, as Washington prepared to march his army back to Germantown, his surgeon loaded Lafayette onto a boat for transport upstream along the Delaware to Philadelphia to be tended properly. "Treat him as if he were my son," Lafayette heard the commander in chief tell the surgeon.[47]

4

Boy General

WORD OF LAFAYETTE'S WOUND—and even rumors of his death—echoed through the gilded halls of Versailles and great Parisian mansions. In the Hôtel de Noailles, Lafayette's doting mother-in-law, the duchesse d'Ayen, almost collapsed, but, according to Adrienne de Lafayette, "She found a way to conceal the rumors of his death from me by taking me far from Paris."[1] Weeks later, a letter finally arrived that allowed the Noailles family to resume their normal routines:

"I must begin by telling you that I am perfectly well," Lafayette wrote in uncharacteristically subdued fashion to Adrienne, "because I must end by telling you that we fought a difficult battle last night, and that we were not the strongest. Our Americans, after having stood their ground for some time, ended at length by being routed; while I was trying to rally the troops, the gentlemen of England did me the honor of shooting me, which hurt my leg a little, but it is nothing, my sweetheart; the ball touched neither a bone nor a nerve, and I will have to stay in bed for only a little while, which has left me in a bad mood. I hope, sweetheart, that you won't be anxious; you should not be: I shall be hors de combat for some time, and you can be sure that I will take good care of myself. This defeat, I fear, will have harsh consequences for America."[2]

It was midnight before Washington began his report to John Hancock, the president of Congress. The Americans had lost about 1,000 men— almost 10 percent of the Continental army; the British only 576. Washington mentioned Lafayette's participation and injury. Had he not arrived when he did and rallied the fleeing American soldiers, the British might have surrounded, captured, or annihilated Sullivan's right flank and possibly the entire

47

Patriot force. "Notwithstanding the misfortune of the day," the commander in chief reported, "I am happy to find the troops in good spirits, and I hope another time we shall compensate for the losses now sustained."[3]

Lafayette left Brandywine battlefield a hero. He was a hero to the men on the line—a soldier's general, who had quit his horse to fight beside them. And he was an unlikely hero to Sullivan, from New Hampshire, where savage raids and depredations during the French and Indian war had left deep hatred for Indians and their Gallic allies.

Brandywine also gave Washington a new appreciation for his young charge, who, he realized, was like himself in so many ways. Washington had been orphaned as a child—at eleven, not two, but nonetheless fatherless during impressionable boyhood years. Like Lafayette, Washington was one of his nation's wealthiest men, with nearly eight thousand acres, huge wheat and tobacco crops, lumber mills, fisheries, a cloth manufactury, and about one hundred slaves. He was an aggressive land speculator with sixty thousand acres in the western Virginia and Ohio wilderness, awaiting what he believed would be the inevitable tide of westward migration. Largely self-taught after his father's death, he had studied self-help manuals, geographies, histories and biographies of great soldiers, and, like Lafayette, had refused pay for his service in the Revolutionary War. He began soldiering in 1754, as a lieutenant colonel with General Edward Braddock, commander in chief of British forces in North America, in a campaign to seize Fort Duquesne, in the Ohio country. About eight miles from the fort, a French and Indian ambush mortally wounded Braddock, and, as Lafayette would do at Brandywine, Washington assumed command and turned a rout into an orderly retreat, leading survivors across one hundred miles of wilderness to safety. Rewarded with command of the Virginia militia, he defended Virginia's frontier for three years and relished danger as much as Lafayette. He said he found "something charming in the sound . . . [when he] heard the bullets whistle."[4]

A week after Brandywine, Congress fled Philadelphia to a new, temporary capital in Lancaster, Pennsylvania, about eighty-five miles to the west. Lafayette continued up the Delaware River to Bristol, where South Carolina congressman Henry Laurens interrupted his journey to Lancaster to take the wounded Frenchman to the Moravian Community, which had converted the Single Brethren's House into a hospital. Laurens's son, Lieutenant Colonel John Laurens, was about Lafayette's age and, like Alexander Hamilton, one of Washington's trusted young aides. The long ride produced a warm friendship between the elder Laurens and the Frenchman, who sent Laurens a letter of deep, albeit convoluted, thanks:

Dear Sir

Troublesome it will be to you for ever to have been so Kind with me. . . . My leg is about in the same state and without your kindness would be in a very bad one. For my heart he is full of all the sentiments of gratitude and affection which I have the honor to be with Dear Sir Your most obedient servant

The Mquis de Lafayette[5]

On September 26, Howe's army marched into Philadelphia and sent a 9,000-man force north to Germantown. With the British poised to sweep across Pennsylvania, Congress distanced itself still farther by moving to York, about 110 miles west of Philadelphia. Rather than await a British attack, Washington made a bold move on the night of October 3, sending two separate columns along what seemed to be parallel roads to Germantown for a two-pronged attack on the British. One of the roads, however, followed a long, serpentine course, and the column on the straighter, shorter road penetrated the streets of Germantown before its twin column arrived. Faced with an impenetrable wall of British fire and no support from the second column, the Patriots retreated just as a dense fog enveloped the area, and they ran into their own second column, which mistook them for enemy soldiers. Caught between Patriot fire and British fire, the trapped column lost 700 men, with 400 more taken prisoner. The British lost 534 soldiers.

In Bethlehem, the wounded poured into the Moravian hospital, where Lafayette lay bedridden, suffering intense pain from his wound and "even more intensely from the boredom of inactivity. The good Moravian brothers," he wrote, "bewailed my passion for war, but, while listening to their sermons, I was making plans to set Europe and Asia aflame."[6] Determined to avenge the losses at Brandywine and Germantown, Lafayette began a bold campaign to influence French policy—a risky decision for an officer who had disobeyed the king's orders and remained officially out of favor at court. He fired a barrage of letters to French leaders urging a military and commercial alliance with America and all-out war with Britain. He wrote to Foreign Minister Vergennes and Prime Minister Maurepas urging immediate strikes against British forces in the Caribbean, Canada, India, and the China Sea. Maurepas dismissed the proposals, scoffing that if Lafayette had his way, he would "sell all the furniture at Versailles to underwrite the American cause."[7]

Far from alienating the court, however, Lafayette's descriptions of the American military situation and reports of his intimate ties to Washington, Hancock, Laurens, and other American leaders convinced Vergennes that the marquis had achieved considerable standing in America and could play a key role in cementing military, diplomatic, and commercial ties between the two nations—perhaps even assuming the role Vergennes had intended for de Broglie as French *stathoudérat* of a puppet American state. In any case, the collapse of the de Broglie plot left Vergennes with little choice: Lafayette was the only high-level French officer with direct ties to top American military and political authorities.

On October 1, Lafayette finally wrote to reassure his wife, telling her to be "perfectly at ease about my wound . . . the surgeons are astonished at how quickly it is healing . . . all the faculty in America are at my service. . . . I have a friend, who asked them to ensure my being well attended; that friend is General Washington. . . . His friendship has made me a happy man in this country. When he sent his best surgeon to me, he told him to take charge of me as if I were his son, because he loved me with the same affection. When he learned I wanted to rejoin the army too soon, he wrote the warmest of letters urging me to concentrate on getting well first."[8]

Lafayette urged Adrienne to adopt the role of the "wife of an American general officer. . . . The enemies of America may tell you, 'They were beaten' or 'Philadelphia is taken, the American capital, the boulevard of liberty.' Leave politely, and say, 'You are imbeciles.' "[9]

The disasters at Brandywine and Germantown plunged Congress into despair, and some angry members lashed out at Washington, demanding his replacement. A few ambitious generals agreed. Brigadier General Thomas Conway, a boastful Irish mercenary who had served thirty years in the French army before coming to America, wrote to Congress disparaging Lord Stirling's conduct at Brandywine. He sent a similar letter to Major General Horatio Gates, the equally ambitious English-born commander of the Northern Continental Army in Albany, New York, and no friend of Washington. Conway disparaged Washington and urged Gates to find a way to take Washington's place as commander in chief. Washington detested Conway, who had anointed himself comte Thomas de Conway. "It is a maxim with him to leave no service of his untold," Washington said of Conway.[10]

The Conway Cabal, as it came to be called, gained momentum after Gates's army encircled the entire 5,700-man British army in the north. British commander general John Burgoyne, one of the victorious commanders at Bunker Hill, had no choice but to surrender under the humiliating "Convention of Saratoga." His troops laid down their arms, pledged never to fight in America again, then marched back toward Boston past Bunker Hill to an internment camp near Cambridge—to languish there until an exchange of prisoners would permit their return to England.

Although Gates sent immediate word of his victory to his wife in Virginia, he pointedly neglected to inform Washington, who sent him a sharp letter of rebuke that forced Gates to apologize.

The victory at Saratoga electrified the world—Europeans as well as Americans. Patriot morale soared. Believing victory near, if not at hand, Congress put aside interstate disputes to approve the Articles of Confederation and Perpetual Union. In Europe, political leaders routinely spoke of "the new nation," while monarchs shuddered at the epochal character of Saratoga: an army of farmers and woodsmen with no military training had humiliated a well-disciplined, accomplished professional army; a peasant rebellion had crushed the military might of a divinely ordained, absolute monarch.

Almost every European newspaper embellished the British-Hessian humiliation, with many even inventing other imaginary American victories and British disasters. Lafayette's ceaseless flow of letters to his family and friends at court elevated the conflict to an Arthurian romance. With Frenchmen following his every move, his legend took on a life of its own: the *Gazette d'Amsterdam* reported that Lafayette had all but single-handedly sent a 2,000-man British regiment at Brandywine retreating in confusion.[11] Voltaire and others wrote of him; street minstrels sang ballads of the brave young knight forsaking fortune, friends, and family to fight for liberty; young French noblemen sought to fight beside him and queued outside Franklin's residence to plead for the right to fight for American liberty. Even English parents could not resist reading tales of the Legend of Lafayette to their children. And, after much posturing, Lafayette's reluctant father-in-law, the duc d'Ayen, at last put aside his anger at the young man to express pride in his accomplishments. "The very persons who had blamed him most for his bold enterprise now applauded him," wrote Lafayette's friend, the comte de Ségur. "The court showed itself almost proud of him and all the young men envied him. Thus, public opinion, turning more and more toward war, made it inevitable and dragged a government too weak to resist in the same direction."[12]

Lafayette laughed at the furor he had provoked. "By quitting France in such a scandalous fashion," he wrote, "I actually served the [American] revolution."

After Saratoga, it was clear that no British army would ever conquer the American interior, where, far from coastal ships and sources of supply, it would face desperate men defending their families, homes, and lands. But it was just as clear that American Patriots—even with clandestine French aid—would be unable to expel the British from major coastal cities and clear American waters of British warships without a massive, well-trained land force and a powerful fleet, which only the French could provide.

The widespread public acclaim for Lafayette and the American struggle, however, emboldened Vergennes to push King Louis XVI closer to war, using as a lure the immeasurable wealth awaiting the nation that dominated trade with the new nation. War was simply an investment to assure that wealth. England, too, however, now realized the economic folly of a rupture with America, and Lord North sent an offer of reconciliation to Franklin and Deane in Paris, while Parliament appointed commissioners to try to negotiate peace with Congress.

In Bethlehem, Pennsylvania, the Saratoga victory sent Lafayette leaping from his sickbed, although his "hurted foot," as he put it to Henry Laurens, was still unhealed and oozing—indeed, too painful for him to wear his boot. He believed Saratoga to be a prelude to an American strike against New York and the final, climactic battle of the war. He not only wanted to participate, he believed he was ready to command. He wrote to Washington, pleading, "with all the confidence of a son, of a friend" for command of a division. "Consider, if you please, that Europe and particularly France is looking upon me—that I want to do some thing by myself, and justify that love of glory which I let be known to the world in making those sacrifices which have appeared so surprising, some say foolish. Do not you think that this want is right?"[13]

After four days had passed without a response, Lafayette purchased a horse and rode off—his aide Gimat trailing "in my shadow"—to rejoin Washington at headquarters at Whitemarsh, almost in the jaws of the enemy at Germantown. He wrote to his wife to calm her fears. Like many soldiers at war, alone with men, he was falling deeper in love with the image he conjured of a wife he had abandoned before he ever got to know her. For the first time in his letters to her, he used the familiar, loving *tu*, instead of the formal *vous*:

> Do not worry about me; all the hard blows are over; all we face are some small skirmishes at most; I am as safe in this camp as I would be in the middle of Paris. If I could measure happiness by the joy of serving here, by the friendship of the army and its men, by the loving friendship and mutual confidence of the most respected and most admirable men, by the affection of Americans—all these could sustain my happiness, I would need nothing else. But my heart is far from easy. How you would pity me if you knew how much my heart suffers without you and loves you. . . . Have I two children? have I another infant to share my tender love with my dearest Henriette? Kiss my dear little girl a thousand times for me; embrace them both tenderly. . . . I trust they will know one day how well I love them. . . . Will you, too, always love me, my sweetheart? I dare to hope so . . . Adieu, adieu! How sweet it would be to kiss you now, to tell you myself: I love you more than I have ever loved—and will as long as I live.[14]

When Lafayette reached Whitemarsh, Howe's forces had seized Patriot forts along the Delaware, and the British navy could sail upriver to Philadelphia and beyond with impunity. British forces under Cornwallis prepared to create a huge, British-controlled zone from New York, along the Atlantic coast past the mouths of Delaware and Chesapeake Bays. Washington ordered General Nathanael Greene to determine the strength of the Cornwallis force and the likelihood of disrupting his scheme. Washington knew his untrained, outmanned army could not defeat Cornwallis in conventional battlefield confrontation, but he was working out a new strategy of unconventional warfare that American Indians had used successfully

Major General Nathanael Greene, seen here in a portrait by
Charles Willson Peale, entrusted Lafayette with the first battle-
field command in his young life, near Gloucester, New Jersey.
(*Library of Congress.*)

against him and Braddock in the west. Instead of direct engagement, he
would harass the British, with snipers moving about to ambush foraging parties, with quick, hit-and-run strikes that would cost the enemy 20, 30, or 40
troops in each skirmish, with few, if any, American losses. They would wage
a war of attrition that would cede the ground to the British after each engagement but ultimately cost them the war. Washington recognized that it
would take patience and many years, but he knew he would win, because
the British had never fought such a war and were as unprepared and
untrained for it as Americans were for conventional warfare.

Still limping badly, Lafayette eagerly volunteered to join Greene, who
had taken a strong liking to the young Frenchman—especially after seeing
Lafayette's courage at Brandywine. Though separated by fifteen years, they
enjoyed each other immensely. Greene was a prosperous Rhode Island farmer,

merchant, and manufacturer and a brilliant autodidact, who had taught himself Latin, higher mathematics, and military history and strategy, and learned French from his wife. His mastery of military logistics had made him Washington's most able and trusted associate. Greene and Lafayette eagerly fed on each other's intellectual provender and became close friends on the ride to Jersey. "He is one of the sweetest-tempered young gentlemen," Greene wrote to his wife; "he has left a young wife and a fine fortune . . . to come and engage in the cause of liberty—this is a noble enthusiasm."[15]

Greene and Lafayette crossed the Delaware into New Jersey, landing north of the Cornwallis force at Gloucester, opposite Philadelphia. In the first battlefield command of his life, Lafayette led four hundred riflemen toward Gloucester to reconnoiter, carefully posting pickets in the woods on either side of his trail, to prevent the enemy from circling behind and cutting off his retreat. To his aides' distress, Lafayette himself crept within firing range of British sentries at Gloucester to reconnoiter. After estimating the size of the Cornwallis force, he returned to his troops and led an assault on a forward post of about four hundred Hessians. Caught unprepared, the Hessians fled, with the Patriots chasing and firing at them furiously. Lafayette and his men pursued for about a mile, killing, wounding, or capturing at least sixty, before Cornwallis sent grenadiers to cover the Hessian retreat with rifle fire. Lafayette withdrew his men under cover of nightfall and rejoined Greene's camp with but one dead and five wounded. His men hailed his courage and leadership, and Greene sent an enthusiastic report to Washington: "The Marquis, with about four hundred militia and the rifle corps, attacked the enemy's picket last evening, killed about twenty and wounded as many more, and took about twenty prisoners. The Marquis is charmed with the spirited behavior of the militia and rifle corps. . . . The Marquis is determined to be in the way of danger."[16]

Lafayette was ecstatic with the success of his first command and wrote straightaway to Washington as he would have to his own warrior father. "I wish," he ended his letter, "that this little success of ours may please you, though a very trifling one . . . it will be a great pleasure for me to find myself again with you." And he signed it "With the most tender affection and highest respect."[17]

Lafayette's triumph so delighted Washington that he reversed his previous stand against foreign commanders in the American army and urged Congress to grant Lafayette a command. "There are now some vacant divisions in the army, to one of which he may be appointed, if it should be the pleasure of Congress," he wrote to Henry Laurens, who had succeeded John Hancock as president of Congress. "I am convinced he possesses a large share of that military ardor, which generally characterizes the nobility of his country."[18]

On December 1, Congress resolved "that General Washington be informed, it is highly agreeable . . . that the Marquis de La Fayette be appointed to the command of a division in the Continental Army."[19] Three days later, Washington offered Lafayette command of any division he chose, and he chose the Virginians from the commander in chief's own state. On the same day, he received word from France of the birth of his second child, Anastasie.

A military leader at last, Lafayette poured his pride into a letter to his father-in-law, the duc d'Ayen. Only slightly tinged with humility, the letter painted a portrait that his father-in-law could hang proudly in the gallery of great Noailles and Lafayette warriors. Designed, on the one hand, to heal the wounds he had inflicted on his family by running away to America, it was also a curriculum vitae that Lafayette knew his father-in-law would cite to obtain a court appointment for Lafayette in the ministry or military after the war. He wrote:

It is impossible to be more agreeably situated than I. The members [of Congress] I know overwhelm me with kindness and attention. The new president, Mr. Laurens, is one of the most respected men in America and is my particular friend. As to the army, I have made friends with everyone, with proof of such friendships forthcoming almost every day. . . . The task I am performing here . . . will improve my knowledge exceedingly. The major-general [in the American army] is the equivalent of the lieutenant-general and the field-marshal [in the French army] in the most important functions, and, as such, I can apply both my talents and experience. . . . I read, I study, I examine, I listen, I reflect, and I try to develop a reasonable, common-sense opinion. I do not talk too much—to avoid saying foolish things—nor risk acting in a foolhardy way. I do nothing to abuse the confidence with which the Americans have entrusted me.[20]

There was no better way for Lafayette to appeal to an old field marshal and confidant of the king than with tales of battle (and his wound, of course) at Brandywine, Chester, Germantown, Gloucester, and Saratoga. Lafayette concluded that America's advantage over Britain lay in "the superiority of General Washington. . . . Our general is a man formed, in truth, for this revolution, which could not have been accomplished without him. I see him more intimately than any other man, and I see that he is worthy of the adoration of his country. His warm friendship for me, and his complete confidence in me in all things military and political, large and small, put me in a position to share everything he has to do, all the problems he has to solve and all the obstacles he has to overcome. Every day, I learn to admire more his magnificent character and soul. . . . I spent the entire summer at

General Washington's quarters, where I felt as if I were a friend of twenty years' standing."

Lafayette urged his father-in-law to influence the French court to provide more aid to the United States. "America is most impatiently expecting us to declare for her, and France will one day, I hope, decide to humble the pride of England. This hope, and the measures which America appears determined to pursue, give me great hopes for the glorious establishment of her independence. We are not, I confess, as strong as I expected, but we are strong enough to fight; we shall do so, I believe, with considerable success; and with the help of France, we shall win the cause I so cherish because it is just, because it honors humanity, because it is in the interest of my nation, and because my American friends and I are deeply committed to it."

Lafayette ended his letter impressively—and shrewdly: "This letter will be given to you by the celebrated [John] Adams, whose name you undoubtedly know. . . . He wished me to give him letters of introduction in France, especially [to] you. May I hope that you will have the goodness to receive him in a kindly manner."[21]

With Adams ready to sail for France, Lafayette wrote hurriedly to Adrienne on the birth of Anastasie: "I have never been as happy in my life as the moment when the news arrived . . . I love you with unspeakable tenderness, I love you more than ever, and I hope we shall be happy the rest of our lives together." Knowing that the duc d'Ayen would be disappointed at her not bearing grandsons, Lafayette added tenderly, "What pleasure it will give me to embrace my two poor little girls. You do not believe me so hard hearted, and at the same time so ridiculous as to suppose that the sex of our new infant can have diminished in any way my joy at its birth. . . . I kiss each of our daughters a thousand times; tell them their father loves them madly, as he loves their wonderful mother. Believe me, I shall not lose a moment rejoining you as soon as I can. Adieu, adieu I kiss you ten million times." There was no way for him to know that his older daughter, Henriette, had died two months earlier.

Lafayette finished by expressing the hope that "Mr. Adams will tell you a lot about my dear and charming friend, the great and respected Gnl. Washington."[22]

Adams was on his way to replace Silas Deane in Paris and negotiate peace with Britain. Eager to befriend this new figure in French-American relations, Lafayette entrusted him with his letters to Adrienne and her father and offered Adams his family's hospitality: "I must beg your pardon, sir, for making myself free enough to recommend you to some friends of mine in France; but as I do not believe you have many acquaintances in that country, I thought it would not be disagreeable to you if I would desire Madame de la Fayette . . . to introduce you to some of my other friends. . . .

Such is the desire of a friend to your country and the noble cause we are fighting for. I wish you a pleasant and safe voyage, and with the highest esteem and greatest affection for a man to whom the hearts of every lover of liberty will be indebted forever."[23]

Before sailing, the often grumpy Adams acknowledged Lafayette's letter with uncharacteristic warmth. "I am happy in this opportunity to convey intelligence from you to your friends, and think myself greatly honored and obliged by your politeness and attention to me, a favor which makes me regret the more my misfortune in not having had the honor heretofore of a more particular acquaintance with a nobleman who has endeared his name and character to every honest American. . . . [I] Shall at all times be happy to hear of your welfare, and to have an opportunity of rendering you any service in my power."[24]

As Adams sailed from Boston harbor, a British envoy arrived in Paris to discuss reconciliation with Deane, Franklin, and Arthur Lee, a Virginia lawyer who had been Congress's representative in London and now joined the others as a third negotiator. After Franklin warned Vergennes that "Britain would be making some propositions of accommodation," Vergennes acted to disrupt the negotiations before they could begin by approving Lafayette's proposal for an alliance with America. In a letter to Congress, Franklin reported that "his majesty was determined, to acknowledge our independence, and make a treaty with us of amity and commerce. . . . Besides his real good will to us and our cause, it was manifestly the interest of France that the power of England should be diminished by our separation from it. . . . There is every appearance of approaching war . . . we obtained a promise of an additional aid of three millions of livres, which we shall receive in January. Spain, we are told, will give an equal sum."[25]

Although winter's first snows forced an end to skirmishing, Lafayette's successful attack at Gloucester provided unexpected benefits by fooling Howe into believing the main Patriot camp had been left undermanned and vulnerable to attack. As he would throughout the war, Washington used a simple but brilliant scheme to confuse enemy commanders about his military strength. Always beset by attrition, Washington himself never knew how many troops he would have at any given time. Deserters were legion, and those who did not desert had contracts to serve for specific periods of only thirty, sixty, or ninety days. Most went home at the end of their terms—sometimes in the middle of battle, if planting or harvest seasons beckoned. Washington, however, deceived the enemy by setting up large numbers of tents, many of them empty, when he wanted the enemy to believe he had a large force, and a small number, with a dozen or more men crammed in each, when he wanted to send the opposite message. So when Howe attacked what he thought was a small encampment at Whitemarsh, the tents disgorged three times the expected number of troops and sent the British retreating double-time to the safety and warmth of winter quarters in Germantown and Philadelphia.

Washington led his army to safer ground for the winter, on a wooded plateau about ten miles west of Whitemarsh, with a clear, elevated view of the British in the east. To the north, the plateau sloped down to the Schuylkill River, near a particularly wide ford for quick, easy withdrawal. On the bank of nearby Valley Creek stood the forge that gave the area its name.

As the snow fell, Lafayette watched Washington's exhausted troops set to work "artfully felling trees. I saw a small city of wooden huts emerge."[26] Arranged in a grid, with parallel streets and avenues, the huts each measured sixteen feet by fourteen feet and housed either twelve soldiers or two, four, or six officers, depending on rank. As a major general, Lafayette had a hut to himself. He acknowledged that he could have bought a warm furnished home nearby, but preferred to adopt "American clothes, habits and food, to appear more simple, frugal and austere than the Americans themselves . . . and embrace privation and fatigue."[27] He used his own funds to buy his Virginians shoes and clothes and earned a reputation as "the soldier's friend."

"I don't know whether General Howe will visit our little city," Lafayette wrote cheerfully to Adrienne, "but if he does, we will try to accord him the appropriate honors."[28]

The huts withstood the harsh winter winds only slightly better than tents. Before the year ended, one of the worst winters in memory reduced the camp to unimaginable squalor. "Our position was untenable," Lafayette recalled. "The soldiers lived in misery; they lacked for clothes, hats, shirts, shoes; their legs and feet black from frostbite—we often had to amputate. . . . The army often went whole days without provisions, and the patient endurance of soldiers and officers was a miracle which each moment served to renew. Their misery prevented new enlistments; it was impossible to recruit. The sacred fire of liberty burned on, however. . . . Which is why . . . the strength of that army never ceased being a mystery; even congress seemed unaware of it."[29]

In Philadelphia, Howe and his officers commandeered some of the city's most elegant homes and hosted lavish dinners and dances. Major John André, General Henry Clinton's handsome, twenty-seven-year-old adjutant, settled into Benjamin Franklin's home to profit from Franklin's huge library. A confirmed bibliophile and accomplished wit, he was also a skilled artist, whose quick hand sketched flattering likenesses of loyalist ladies on their programs at officers' balls.

Not far away, the discomforts of Valley Forge made Lafayette long for home. The wife he had never really known grew vividly inviting in his imagination. "Do you not think we shall be old enough to live in our own house when I return—to live there happily together, receive our friends. . . . I like to dream of building castles of happiness and joy; you always share them with me, my sweetheart, and once we are together again, nothing shall ever separate us or keep us from the happiness of our love for each other. Adieu, my heart; I wish I could make my dream come true today. . . . Adieu, Adieu; love me always, and never forget the unhappy exile who thinks of you always with ever increasing love."[30]

Washington sponsored Lafayette's induction into the military lodge of the American Masons, forging closer ties between the two men and between Lafayette and other American officers. The Frenchman eagerly embraced them as "brothers," regardless of rank, and they quickly fell victim to his disarmingly open, boyish enthusiasm, courage, and idealism. Of all the foreign soldiers and officers in the American army with claims to titles, Lafayette was the only person legitimately entitled to one by birth in one land and by zeal in another. His fellow officers dubbed him "Our Marquis," and, by winter's end, every Patriot soldier and, soon after, every Patriot in America called him "Our Marquis," a title he retained for the rest of his life.

5

An American Winter

IN THE WINTER OF 1777, Lafayette's hopes for America sank into a mire of misery at Valley Forge. While Tory Loyalists wallowed in superabundance in British-held New York and Philadelphia, Washington tried unsuccessfully to provision his starving army with continental dollars, the paper money that Congress was printing. The enemy, however, printed and distributed enough forged dollars to render continental dollars all but worthless.[1]

As word of the wretchedness at Valley Forge reached York, supporters of the Conway Cabal pressed Congress to replace Washington as supreme commander with a board of war headed by General Gates, the hero of Saratoga. Saratoga had been America's only military victory since the beginning of the war, and like other cabalists, Gates argued that Washington's strategy had failed; that he had been too timid, had lost too many battles, and had surrendered Philadelphia, the American capital, without firing a shot.

"The Tories fomented all these dissensions," according to Lafayette. "Greene, Hamilton, and Knox, his best friends, were slandered."[2]

Although Congress did not remove Washington as commander of the Continental army, it did establish the new Board of War, which represented a new layer of command between him and Congress, to determine war policies and grand strategy. Congress named Gates to head the board and make strategy decisions. To dilute Washington's authority still further, Congress appointed Conway inspector general, to report to the board and advise on all military promotions. "They speak of Conway as a man sent by heaven for the liberty and happiness of America," Lafayette grumbled. "He told so to them and they are fools enough to believe it."[3]

Devastated by the wounds Congress inflicted on his idol, Lafayette reassured Washington of his loyalty:

I don't need to tell you that I am sorry for all that has happened. . . . When I was in Europe I thought that here almost every man was a lover of liberty, and would rather die free than live a slave. You can conceive my astonishment when I saw that toryism was as openly professed as whiggism: however, at that time I believed that all good Americans were united together. . . . I wish you could know, as well as myself, what difference there is between you and any other man . . . you would see very plainly that if you were lost for America, there is nobody who could keep the army and the revolution for six months. . . . There are open dissensions in Congress, parties who hate one another as much as the common enemy; stupid men, who, without knowing a single word about war, undertake to judge you, to make ridiculous comparisons; they are infatuated with Gates . . . and believe that attacking is the only thing necessary to conquer . . . perhaps secret friends to the British Government, who want to push you . . . to some rash enterprise upon the lines or against a much stronger army.

He called Conway "cunning" and pledged, "I am now fixed to your fate, and I shall follow it and sustain it as well by my sword as by all means in my power."[4] Washington replied immediately:

My Dear Marquis,—Your favour of yesterday conveyed to me fresh proof of that friendship and attachment, which I have happily experienced since the first of our acquaintance, and for which I entertain sentiments of the purest affection. It will ever constitute part of my happiness to know that I stand well in your opinion; because I am satisfied that you can have no views to answer by throwing out false colours, and that you possess a mind too exalted to condescend to low arts and intrigues to acquire a reputation. Happy, thrice happy, would it have been for this army and the cause we are embarked in, if the same generous spirit had pervaded all the actors in it. But one gentleman [Gates], whose name you have mentioned, had, I am confident, far different views; his ambition and great desire of being puffed off, as one of the first officers of the age, could only be equaled by the means which he used to obtain them . . . he became my inveterate enemy; and he has, I am persuaded, practiced every art to do me an enjury [sic]. . . . The fatal tendency of disunion is so obvious . . . but we must not, in so great a test, expect to meet with nothing but sunshine. I have no doubt that everything happens for the best, that we shall triumph over our misfortunes, and, in the end, be happy; when, my dear marquis, if you will give me your company in Virginia, we will laugh at our past difficulty and the folly of others.[5]

Washington's letter gave Lafayette a new understanding of the American Revolution. Far from the Arthurian confrontation he had envisioned between good and evil—between forces of liberty and tyranny—he now saw that the Revolution "bore the stamp of a civil war. . . . Partisan passions divided provinces, towns, and families; it was not uncommon to see brothers, each serving as officers in the opposing armies, meet in their father's home and fall on their arms to fight each other."[6]

Touched deeply by Washington's letter, Lafayette protested to Henry Laurens, the president of Congress—as did Lieutenant Colonel John Laurens, the president's son. With Lafayette and Alexander Hamilton, John Laurens was one of Washington's little family of young aides de camp, whom he treated as sons and mentored in the arts of war, leadership, and diplomacy. Washington not only enjoyed the young, he inherently trusted them—and they adored him for it and gave him unqualified loyalty. The death of his own commander in the Ohio wilderness had forced him to assume command as a young man, and he eagerly surrounded himself with and trained a cadre of young officers to succeed him and other older leaders such as Nathanael Greene, should he or they fall. Although Laurens had a loving father of his own, the twenty-one-year-old Hamilton, like Lafayette, was a foreigner in a foreign land. Born in Nevis, in the Leeward Islands, he, too, had lost his father and mother at a young age and had found in Washington the caring father he had lacked as a child. Washington saw the boys as the sons he never had, who enthusiastically emulated their adoptive father and became ideal officers—brave, trustworthy, professional, with warm, fraternal ties to each other.

Together, they organized a letter-writing campaign to Congress by Valley Forge officers. Lafayette defended Washington's refusal to engage the enemy in conventional warfare: "We have at our head a great judge, a man [in] whom America and principally the army is to have a confidence as extended as the love he derives from them, and when he will think proper to fight, then I shall believe always that we have good reason for it."[7] Greene, Knox, and Hamilton also wrote to Congress on behalf of their commander—as did the peasant major general, "Baron" de Kalb, of all people. Although he had come to America to undermine Washington, he now sent Laurens a passionate defense of his American commander: "I think him the only proper person by his natural and acquired capacity, his bravery, good sense, uprightness and honesty, to keep up the spirits of the army and people. . . . I look upon him as the sole defender of his country's cause."[8]

Although Lafayette had consoled Adrienne with hints of his possible return to France, his commander's plight forced him to be more forthright—and blunt:

I have chosen to stay rather than enjoy the happiness of being with you. . . . All my feelings impelled me to go; but honor counseled me to stay here. . . . My presence is more necessary to the American cause at this moment than you may imagine; many foreigners who have failed to obtain commissions, or whose ambitious schemes after having obtained them could not be countenanced, have entered into powerful conspiracies. . . . General Washington would be really unhappy if I were to suggest my going away. . . . He knows he has in me a loyal friend to whom he may open his heart and who will always tell him the truth. Not a day passes that he does not hold a long conversation with me. . . . This is not the time for me to talk of going away.[9]

Adrienne accepted her husband's decision with equanimity. The tales of his riding alongside Washington in Philadelphia, of his heroics at Brandywine and his wound, of his generalship at Gloucester—all had elevated him to legendary status in Europe, and Adrienne had resolved to accept her role as a general's wife and patiently await her hero's return from battle.

Fearing that the Valley Forge protests to Congress would undermine their new authority, Gates and Conway plotted to topple Lafayette from his pedestal by exploiting his lust for glory and his nation's hatred for England: they asked Congress to sanction a midwinter invasion of Canada, led by Lafayette. Both knew the invasion was doomed from the start, but with France watching Lafayette's every move, and with the honor of his nation at stake, he would have to accept the appointment. They assured Congress that the recapture of "New France" by the French hero would cement America's alliance with France, yield massive French aid and, ultimately, ensure victory over Britain. Congress agreed.

In a direct insult to Washington, the Board of War appointed Lafayette commander in chief of the Northern Army of the United States—a rank equal to Washington's and subject only to Congress and the Board of War for his orders. It named Conway his second in command and chief advisor and ordered Lafayette to report immediately to York.

Lafayette responded angrily, saying he "would never accept any command independent of the general, and that the title of aide de camp to Washington was preferable to any other that might be offered to me."[10] Though wounded by the congressional assault on his command, Washington urged Lafayette to report to York, saying, "I prefer it being for you rather than any other person."[11]

Lafayette obeyed, but, sensing sinister motives for the expedition, he used his prerogatives as a new "commander in chief" to list conditions for his service. On the advice of Washington, Lafayette asked the Board of War to provide specific, written details of the invasion plan, including the size of his force. He insisted on appointing his own officers, and, in the most startling of his demands, he said he "would only accept the command on condition of remaining subordinate to General Washington . . . as an officer detached from him." He demanded that Congress and the Board of War issue all orders to him through Washington and that he would respond in kind.

Despite the obvious slap at Gates and Conway, President Laurens and the Board of War had to accept Lafayette's conditions or risk seeing the French hero return home in a huff and undermine French relations with America. He was, after all, a volunteer, who could leave whenever he wanted. Lafayette replaced Conway's cabalists with twenty loyal French officers, including his aides-de-camp, Gimat and La Colombe, who now became American officers in their own right. Joining them was a young French engineer, Captain Pierre Charles L'Enfant, who would later plan the new nation's capital city by the Potomac River.[12] In a brilliant political move to undermine the cabal, Lafayette appointed the Washington loyalist Kalb as second in command over Conway to prevent Conway's assuming command if he, Lafayette, should die in action. Gates pretended to ignore Lafayette's insults and invited him to his home to toast the success of the expedition. When it was Lafayette's turn to raise his glass, he stood and proposed the health of "*our* general George Washington." They had little choice, Lafayette wrote, but to stand and raise their glasses, "reddening with shame."[13]

As Lafayette had demanded, Gates and the Board of War sent written orders calling for an "irruption into Canada." After reaching the Canadian border, Lafayette was to lead the force to St. Johns or Montreal and invite Canadians "to join the Army of the United States." If, according to the orders, he found "a general disinclination . . . to join the American standard," he was to destroy all British military installations and ships and "retire" to Saratoga.

"If, on the contrary, the Canadians are ardently desirous of assisting to establish the Freedom, and Independence of America, you will inform them . . . to send delegates, to represent their State in the Congress of the United States, and to conform, in all political respects, to the Union, and Confederation, established in them." The "principal object of this expedition," however, was to take possession of Montreal and "all the Arms, Ammunition, and Warlike Stores, together with all the linnens, woolens and Indian goods that may be found."[14]

The Board promised 2,500 troops. Quartermaster General Thomas Mifflin—a Philadelphia merchant who was one of Washington's most vitriolic critics—pledged "Ammunition, Provisions, Stores and as many carriages as may be requisite for the intended service. . . . The proper officers are now providing Forage, at the general and particular places of rendezvous [near Albany, New York]."[15] Although Lafayette had misgivings about an expedition to Canada in the dead of winter, Gates assured him that a winter attack would catch the British unprepared.

Still fearful that Gates had plotted his doom, Lafayette sent Gates another letter, with a copy to Laurens, placing full responsibility for the expedition on Gates's shoulders: "I schould [*sic*] be in a terrible concern about my means of succeeding and the immensity of things which I must be provided for, had I not the greatest confidence in your friendship and your good care of my reputation as well as the public interest. This project is yours, Sir, therefore you must make it succeed. If I had not depended so much on you I would not have undertaken the operation."[16]

Lafayette's demand for detailed instructions from the Board of War proved prescient, although his sense of doom did not prevent his boasting to Adrienne and the duc d'Ayen of "the confidence with which I have been honoured by America. Canada is oppressed by the English; the whole of that immense country is in the power of the enemy. . . . I am to repair thither with the title of General of the Northern Army, at the head of three thousand men. . . . The idea of rendering the whole of New France free, and of delivering her from a heavy yoke, is too glorious for me to allow myself to dwell upon it."[17]

Lafayette left York on February 3, 1778, in terrible winter weather that only grew worse as he headed north, sometimes on horseback, sometimes in a sleigh. "I go on very slowly," he wrote to Washington, "sometimes drenched by rain, sometimes covered by snow, and not entertaining many handsome thoughts about the projected incursion into Canada."[18] After ten days, he reached Albany and discovered, "I have been deceived by the board of War."[19] There were no troops; no money to pay any troops; no arms, ammunition, or other supplies; neither the area commanders nor the commissary at Albany that was to supply the expedition knew that Gates had approved it. "General Schuyler, General Lincoln and General Arnold, had written, before my arrival, to General Conway, in the most expressive terms, that . . . there was no possibility to begin now, an enterprise into Canada," Lafayette wrote to Washington. "I have consulted everybody, and everybody answers me that it would be madness to undertake this operation."[20]

With the eyes of France upon him—for he knew his father-in-law would show his letter at court—the Gates deception was not only a deep humiliation, it was a deep personal wound that cut through the trust and affection that he felt for Americans and that he assumed they felt for him. He fired off an angry letter to Henry Laurens, describing the

hell of blunders, madness, and deception I am involved in. . . .What is your opinion, Sir, about my present situation? Do you think it is a very pleasant one? How schall I do to get of [off] from a precipice where I embarked myself out of my love for your country, my desire of distinguishing myself in doing good to America, and that so false opinion that there was in all the board of war. . . . My situation is such that I am reduced to wish to have never put the foot in America or thought of an american war. All the continent knows where I am, what I am sent for. . . . The world has theyr eyes fixed upon me. . . . Men will have right to laugh at me, and I'l be almost ashamed to appear before some. . . . No, Sir, this expedition will certainly reflect a little upon my reputation, at least for having been too confident in men who did not deserve it, but it will reflect much more upon the authors of such blunders. I'l publish the whole history, I'l publish my instructions *with notes* [his italics] through the world, and I'l loose [lose] rather the honor of twenty Gates and twenty boards of war, than to let my own reputation be hurted in the least thing.[21]

After venting his anger to Laurens, Lafayette turned to the only father he had ever known. "Why am I so far from you," he wrote Washington plaintively, "and what business had the board of War to hurry me through the ice and snow without knowing what I should do, neither what they were doing themselves?

"Your excellency may judge that I am very distressed by this disappointment. My being appointed to the command of the expedition is known through the continent, it will be soon known in Europe. . . . I am afraid it will reflect on my reputation, and I shall be laughed at."[22] Washington sent Lafayette a paternal letter of consolation:

I . . . hasten to dispel those fears respecting your reputation, which are excited only by an uncommon degree of sensibility. You seem to apprehend that censure, proportioned to the disappointed expectations of the world, will fall on you in consequence of the failure of the Canadian expedition. But, in the first place, it will be no disadvantage to you to have it known in Europe that you had received so manifest a proof of the good opinion and confidence of congress as an important detached command; and I am persuaded that every one will applaud your prudence in renouncing a project, in pursuing which you would vainly have attempted physical impossibilities. . . .

However sensibly your ardour for glory may make you feel this disappointment, you may be assured that your character stands as fair as ever it did.[23]

After demanding new instructions from the Board of War, Lafayette and his officers settled into a military camp outside Albany, where he found twelve hundred troops living in near anarchy, "naked even for a summer's campaign," their pay far in arrears, and the commissary all but bare. Lafayette acted quickly to prevent a coup by Conway by isolating him with paperwork assignments. "I fancy (between us)," he wrote to Washington, "that the actual scheme is to have me out . . . and General Conway in chief, under the immediate direction of General Gates. How they will bring it [about] I do not know, but you may be sure something of that kind will appear. . . . I should be very happy if you were here to give me some advice, but I have nobody to consult with."[24]

Washington, however, had problems of his own. As vile as Valley Forge had been in early February when Lafayette had left, conditions were far worse a month later. Desertions, disease, exposure to subzero temperatures, starvation, and thirst—for there were no springs on the plateau above Valley Creek—had reduced Washington's 11,000-man Continental army to about 5,000. Many froze to death, despite Washington's pleas for supplies to the sinister Quartermaster General Mifflin, and those who survived were too weak to fight. "Two thousand eight hundred and ninety were unfit for duty, 'being barefoot and otherwise naked,'" according to Washington.[25]

Although wary of Conway, Lafayette found the camp near Albany an ideal opportunity to perfect his mastery of the art of military training and organization. He devised a range of training procedures to restore order, discipline, and morale, dividing his army into twenty troops of sixty men each and placing each of his officers in command of one troop to train and drill. He ordered all troops on regular parade, and, perched majestically on his horse, he reviewed them and saluted each troop as its pennant passed before him. He studied and learned the basics of military procurement and quartermaster operations, although he had to use his own funds to buy clothing for the troops. In the end, he mastered all aspects of running a small army.

On March 11, Lafayette lost patience and fired off a second letter to the Board of War, challenging Gates: "I expect with the greater impatience letters from Congress and the Board of War where I'l be acquainted of what I am to do. I hope the good intentions of the honorable Board in my favor could be employed in a better occasion—indeed, Sir, there has been good deal of deception and neglect in that affair."[26]

A few days later, General Philip Schuyler, one of the commissioners Congress had appointed to negotiate with local Indian tribes, asked Lafayette's help in establishing an alliance with the Indians. Showered by British bribes for a decade, they had fought with Burgoyne's army at Saratoga and proved relentless in their barbarities against American settlers. But they had once been French allies who had fought the British expansion westward into their territory, and most Indian leaders still held the French in high esteem. Schuyler hoped that Lafayette's lofty position in the French court might help win the Indians to the colonist side. Together with Schuyler and the other Indian commissioners, Lafayette traveled by sleigh forty miles northwest to Johnson's Town (now Johnstown), New York, where the Six Nations—Senecas, Cayugas, Oneidas, Onondagas, Mohawks, and Tuscaroras—had gathered by the Mohawk River.

"Five hundred, men, women and children attended the convention," Lafayette reported, "streaked with multi-colored paint and feathers, their ears cut open, jewels dangling from their noses, their half-naked bodies tattooed and painted with a variety of designs. The old men smoked and talked about politics intelligently. When the drunkenness of rum did not distract them . . . their goal was a balance of power."[27]

Flattered by the presence of the world-renowned French nobleman, they were overwhelmed by the ease and evident joy with which the exquisitely dressed major general mingled with them, distributing little mirrors, rum, brandy, and handsome French gold coins—*louis d'or.* Unlike his American comrades, Lafayette embraced the European myth that Rousseau helped create of the noble savage and his simpler, utopian existence. Lafayette won the Indians over entirely and, at his urging, they agreed to make peace with the colonists. "Their kinship with the French," Lafayette reported to President Laurens, "mixed with their kinship with French louis d'or induced the Indians to promise to follow my recommendations."[28] They ended the convention by signing a treaty with the colonists—and adopting Lafayette as Kayewla, the name of one of their ancient, legendary warriors.

When Lafayette returned to Albany, he found letters from both Gates and Laurens. Gates enclosed a resolution of Congress suspending the expedition to Canada and thanking Lafayette for his "high sense of prudence, activity and zeal."[29] Laurens sent Lafayette a personal note assuring him that the praise in the Congressional resolution was "genuine, not merely complimentary."[30]

Gates indicated that the Board of War would transfer Lafayette and Kalb back to Washington's command at Valley Forge and leave Conway in charge of the Northern Army. Although Lafayette was elated that Congress had salvaged his reputation, the prospect of Conway's promotion left him determined to crush the Gates-Conway cabal. He wrote a fierce letter to Congress warning that "if I am recalled to leave this command in the hands of a gentleman . . . who is not above me neither by birth neither by his relations or influence in the world, who has not had any more particular occasion of distinguishing himself than I have had . . . I will look upon myself as not only ill used but very near being affronted—and such will be the sentiment of all those of my nation and Europe whose opinion is dear to me. . . . How do you think it will look? How can I agree to it?"[31] A week later, Lafayette issued another warning, implying that he had far more influence over French military and diplomatic affairs than he actually did, but his letter intimidated Laurens and Congress enough to overrule Gates and order

Conway transferred to an insignificant post at Peekskill, New York. They then asked Lafayette and Kalb to rejoin Washington and apologized to Lafayette with an expression of "esteem and regard."[32]

Before Lafayette left Albany, the last vestiges of the Conway Cabal collapsed when Quartermaster General Mifflin resigned after accusations of embezzlement produced evidence that he had exacerbated the Valley Forge sufferings by diverting purchases for the troops to his own warehouses and selling them in local markets. Mifflin's transfer and Conway's exile to a Hudson River backwater humiliated Gates and the Board of War. Gates resigned and returned to the Northern Army in Albany, and Congress restored Washington to supreme command. He immediately appointed Nathanael Greene as quartermaster general. A trusted friend, Greene was a brilliant business manager; as a young man, he and his brothers had inherited their father's prosperous farming enterprise, which included a flour mill, a sawmill, an ironworks, a wharf, and a warehouse. By the time he left to take command of the Rhode Island Militia at the beginning of the Revolution, they had expanded it into Rhode Island's most prosperous merchant house. Greene recovered most of the supplies that Mifflin had bought but never delivered to Valley Forge. Helped by the arrival of spring, the famine and other discomforts at Valley Forge gradually abated.

On April 22, 1778, Conway offered—and this time Congress accepted—his resignation. When, on July 4, the embittered cabalist slandered Washington, General John Cadwalader, a fierce Washington loyalist, challenged the Irishman to a duel and wounded him badly. Thinking he was about to die, Conway sent Washington a letter of apology. Although he recovered from his wound, he left North America in disgrace.[33]

Lafayette rejoined Washington at Valley Forge and resumed command of the Virginia division. He found an utterly different camp from the one he had left two months earlier. Greene had the camp overflowing with supplies—cattle, vegetables, water, and rum—and enough uniforms and shoes to clothe twice the number of men encamped there. A new inspector general from Germany, "Baron" von Steuben, had the men marching in step and drilling like a crack European elite guard, their arms snapping confidently, their tough bronzed faces radiating invincibility. Steuben was another of the shadowy foreign soldiers who had added titles to their names and convinced Franklin and Deane they had the skills and pedigree to win the war for America. Although little else was known of him, Steuben had indeed been a Prussian army captain (though never a baron), who had acquired a thorough knowledge of legendary Prussian training and drilling methods. Until he and Greene took over their respective commands, Continental army troops had relied on courage alone to fight professional soldiers who were better fed, clothed, trained, and armed. To their courage, Greene now added food, clothes, arms, and ammunition, while Steuben added training, discipline, and pride. The men improved their own living quarters, and, when Lafayette returned, they had converted their primitive huts into relatively comfortable living quarters. Indeed, many officers' wives, including Martha Washington and French-speaking Caty Greene, had joined their husbands—although the presence of the women made Lafayette long for Adrienne: "I love you more than ever, my sweetheart"—"*mon cher coeur.*"[34]

The collapse of the Conway Cabal emasculated the Board of War and left Washington the unquestioned commander in chief of the American military. At the same time, the Articles of Confederation combined with chronic absenteeism to render Congress so impotent that Washington had little choice but to expand his role into the political sphere. Surrounded by a cadre of loyal, experienced, and effective officers of every rank—some of them former merchants and bankers in civilian life—he appointed a provisional "cabinet," which included, among others, Quartermaster General Nathanael Greene and General Henry Knox, who commanded the Continental Army artillery. The brilliant young Alexander Hamilton remained his personal secretary, but assumed functions as a presidential chief of staff, screening visitors and organizing the general's day.

Washington gave Lafayette responsibility for "foreign affairs," and Lafayette did not disappoint him. Lafayette sent a stream of letters to Versailles and Paris, urging everyone he knew of influence to support America. "In every word, I did everything to draw our two peoples closer together," Lafayette recalled in his memoirs.[35] A week later, as Tory handbills reported Lord North's efforts to negotiate a reconciliation with Congress, Lafayette warned President Laurens of North's "black schemes. He ca'nt [sic] *fight us out* but hopes to *negotiate us out* of our rights." Echoing Washington's words, Lafayette insisted, "If he [North] sincerely wishes peace . . . let him withdraw his troops and treat afterwards." Congress agreed, unanimously resolving not to deal with North's envoys until the British forces either withdrew their forces or acknowledged American independence.

Lafayette also relieved Washington of the task of examining petitions from the hordes of foreigners seeking commissions. Rather than trying to integrate non-English-speaking officers into American divisions, he organized them into several "corps of strangers"—his literal translation of the French *corps d'étrangers.*[36] Many were outstanding cavalrymen who gave the Continental army several battalions of European professionals to counter Britain's Hessians. Lafayette appointed the marquis de La Rouërie, a shipmate from the *Victoire,* to lead an all-French cavalry, and he coaxed Count Casimir Pulaski, the Polish Patriot who had fought at Brandywine and Germantown, to organize other foreign soldiers into a mixed corps of cavalry and light infantry.[37]

With the cavalry in sure hands, Lafayette turned to training his own division, spending his own money to clothe and arm them and using Steuben's techniques to drill and train them for the summer campaign. What made his training remarkable—and bonded his troops to him—was his habit of questioning them respectfully about their previous campaigns and the tactics they had found most effective. For a major general—a European nobleman at that—to converse and consult with his men astonished them. He later claimed that American soldiers had been "my teachers"[38]—that he learned more from them than they from him. His lessons would serve him well. As one of Washington's most trusted aides and fourth-ranking general at Valley Forge—after Washington, Greene, and Lord Stirling—he commanded enormous influence. When others urged Washington to attack Philadelphia and liberate the nation's capital, Lafayette opposed the move, warning it would leave the city "in ashes" and cost the army one-third of its men. His opinion meshed perfectly with Washington's overall strategy of avoiding conventional battlefield confrontations with Howe's larger, professional forces. Steuben agreed, and Washington decided to watch the enemy from the safety of Valley Forge and postpone action until time, place, and circumstance favored the American army.

On May 1, Simeon Deane, Silas Deane's brother, rode into Washington's headquarters with a letter from Franklin and Deane in Paris. Lafayette's letters had helped win French recognition of American independence. "We have now the great satisfaction of acquainting you and the Congress," Franklin and Deane exulted, "that the Treaties with France are at length completed and signed. The first is a treaty of amity and commerce . . . the other is a treaty of alliance, in which it is stipulated that in case England declares war against France . . . we should then make common cause of it and join our forces and councils, etc. The great aim of this treaty is declared to be 'to establish the liberty, sovereignty, and independency, absolute and unlimited, of the United States, as well in matters of government as commerce;' and this is guarantied to us by France. . . . The preparations for war are carried on with immense activity and it is soon expected."[39]

After signing the treaty, Franklin, Deane, and Adams were officially presented to the king and the royal family and, according to Lafayette's memoirs, "all but ran to the young Madame de Lafayette, who was at Versailles, to demonstrate publicly how indebted they felt to Lafayette for the wonderful turn of events their affairs had taken."[40]

Tears streamed down Lafayette's cheeks as he heard Washington read the Franklin-Deane letter to his officers. Overcome by emotion, he gripped the commander in chief and embraced him[41]—perhaps a first for the usually austere Virginian, but certainly not the last. Lafayette sent Henry Laurens a letter of congratulations, but reminded the president that "I am myself fit to receive as well as to offer congratulations in this happy circumstance. If you remember, Sir, in which moment, in which sentiment, I left my country, you will easily conceive how surprised, how pleased I must be to see our noble cause arise at such a period of glory and success." He sent Laurens his wishes "for the happiness of mankind, the prosperity of freedom, and the glory of what they call in France, my *new country—America.*"[42]

As the army at Valley Forge burst into spontaneous celebration, Lafayette's own joy abruptly turned into grief when he opened a second letter that Deane had brought from Paris: Lafayette's daughter Henriette had died. The cheering troops about him knew nothing of his loss, and he refused to say or do anything to diminish their joy. They built a huge bonfire, and, after putting on a white scarf, the symbol of Bourbon France, he disguised his grief and led a march of French officers before the cheering American soldiers.

"How horrible is our separation!" Lafayette wrote to his wife late that night. "I never before felt the cruelty of separation so deeply. My heart suffers doubly, from my own sorrow and from my inability to share yours. The time it took before I learned of it has also increased my misery. . . . The loss of our poor child is almost always on my mind. The news came right after the news of the treaty, and, with my heart torn by pain, I had to participate in the public joy."[43]

On May 6, Washington issued a general order: "It having pleased the Almighty Ruler of the Universe to defend the cause of the United American States, and finally to raise us up a powerful friend among the princes of the earth, to establish our liberty and independency upon a lasting foundation; it becomes us to set apart a day for gratefully acknowledging the divine goodness and celebrating the important event, which we owe to his divine interposition." He proclaimed an official day of "public celebration," beginning with morning religious services and followed by "military parades, marchings, the firings of cannon and musketry." According to those present, "The appearance was brilliant and the effect imposing. The ceremony . . . was closed with an entertainment, Patriotic toasts, music, and other demonstrations of joy."[44]

Lafayette commanded the left division in the parade, Stirling the right, and Kalb the second line; "several times," wrote one officer, "the cannons discharged thirteen rounds." Steuben's training produced a snap and precision in the entire army—and precision to the traditional *feu de joie,* or "fire of joy," in which each member of a long line of musketeers fires a single shot, in rapid succession, to produce a long, continuous, and thunderous sound. Washington responded accordingly: "The Commander-in-Chief takes great pleasure in acquainting the army that its conduct yesterday afforded him the highest satisfaction. The exactness and order with which all its movements were formed, is a pleasing evidence of the progress it has made in military improvement, and of the perfection to which it may arrive by a continuance of that laudable zeal which now so happily prevails."[45]

Philadelphia's Robert Morris expressed the feelings of Congress by congratulating Washington and asserting, "Our independence is undoubtedly secured; our country must be free."[46]

A few days after King Louis XVI signed the treaty with the Americans, the French court notified the English government that it had recognized American independence and "the right of the American people to govern themselves." When Lafayette read the message, he noted wryly, "That is a noble concept that we will have to remind them about someday."[47]

6

The Alliance

"DURING THE WINTER OF 1778," Adrienne de Lafayette recalled, "my mother grew obsessed with news about Lafayette. The alliance of France with the United States had filled her with joy, and, although she had been totally unaccustomed to following political events, she now studied them intensely."[1]

The treaty filled Americans with joy as well. Coupled with fine spring weather, the enthusiasm provoked a stream of new volunteers to Valley Forge. A band of fifty Iroquois startled the camp one day: they had come as volunteers to serve the warrior Kayewla. As Washington's "foreign affairs minister," Lafayette had not forgotten to inform his Indian friends in upper New York of the alliance with France, in the hope that they would help the Americans and end their depredations against settlers.

By mid-May, Washington's little army had swelled to more than 13,000. With only 10,000 British troops in Philadelphia, Congress pressed Washington to attack, and he called a council of war. To heal the wounds of the Conway Cabal, he graciously invited the humbled cabalist generals Gates, Mifflin, and Major General Charles Lee to join Greene, Lafayette, Kalb, Stirling, Steuben, and Knox, who were all staunchly loyal to Washington. Lee was the second-highest-ranking general in the Continental army after Washington. English-born and unrelated to the Lees of Virginia, he had enlisted in the British army at twenty and spent nearly three decades as a career soldier before joining the Patriots. He was outspoken in his dislike of Washington, who reciprocated the feeling with equal passion. The British had captured Lee the previous December, but released him in a prisoner exchange, and by right of rank, if not trust, he returned to the army and took his seat at the council of war.

"After a full and unreserved discussion," Washington wrote, "it was the unanimous opinion of the council, that the line of conduct . . . best suited to promote the interests and safety of the United States, was to remain on the defensive and wait events, and not attempt any offensive operation against the enemy. . . . [it] was agreed that to take Philadelphia by storm was impracticable, and that thirty thousand men would be requisite for a blockade."[2]

The prospects of French intervention, however, forced the British from an offensive to a defensive strategy that would concentrate their land and naval forces in New York. In mid-May, they prepared to evacuate Philadelphia before the French fleet could block Delaware Bay and the sea lanes to New York. Washington sent Lafayette with an elite corps of light infantry and cavalry to watch British movements, determine their plan of evacuation, "and fall upon the rear of the enemy in the act of withdrawing. This will be a matter of no small difficulty," he warned Lafayette, "and will require the greatest caution and prudence in the execution. . . . Remember, that your detachment is a very valuable one, and that any accident happening to it would be a very severe blow to this army. . . . No attempt should be made, nor anything risked, without the greatest prospect of success, and with every reasonable advantage. . . . In general, I would observe that a stationary post is inadvisable, as it gives the enemy an opportunity of knowing your situation, and concerting plans successfully against you."[3]

Lafayette left Valley Forge on May 18, 1778, with the largest force he had ever commanded—some 2,200 men and five cannons, and his invaluable little company of reverent Iroquois warriors as scouts. After marching a dozen miles along the north bank of the Schuylkill, Lafayette reached Barren Hill, about midway between Valley Forge and Philadelphia—and immediately ignored the advice of his mentor by setting up a stationary post at the summit. To Lafayette's eye, Barren Hill seemed an all but impregnable crest with a commanding view of Germantown and the approaches to Philadelphia. A sheer rock cliff to the river protected his right, and he lined his five cannons in front to repel any attack from Philadelphia. Behind him lay a clear avenue of retreat, down a gentle slope back toward Valley Forge. Only his left flank was vulnerable, with but a few stone houses and a small wood to shield him, and he ordered a 600-man militia to patrol the area. He sent his cavalry and Indian scouts two miles forward to guard the approaches from Philadelphia and a band of spies into the city to reconnoiter British troop movements. One of the spies was a turncoat who delivered word of Lafayette's position to the British—just as General William Howe was packing to return to England after retiring as commander of English forces in America. He gleefully postponed his departure for the chance to ambush and capture the arrogant young marquis and take him back to Britain as a prize. Howe predicted that after English laughter at Lafayette's humiliation subsided, the marquis would disappear from the pages of history.

Howe left nothing to chance. He gathered more than three-fourths of his army—8,000 British and Hessians, equipped with fifteen pieces of artillery—and marched to Barren Hill during the night. "The English generals were so confident of success that they sent invitations to the ladies of Philadelphia to dine with Lafayette the following night," Lafayette recalled in his memoirs, "and his brother the admiral outfitted a special frigate" to carry Howe and Lafayette back to England together. Admiral Howe rode in an elegant carriage in the rear to watch his brother's entertainment at Barren Hill.[4]

By dawn on May 20, a sea of redcoats all but surrounded the Patriot camp, engulfing every road and even the sloping escape route back to Valley Forge. Lafayette's "very valuable" detachment seemed to have little choice but surrender or face massacre. Recalling Indian tactics his soldiers had described, Lafayette sent small flying squads scurrying to different parts of the surrounding woods to dart through the trees in one direction, fire a few rounds at the British, and then withdraw quickly and shift to another position to issue another round—appearing, disappearing, and reappearing—and giving the impression that a larger force was attacking. Shots came from everywhere. "In every direction the British looked," Lafayette recounted, "they saw nothing but the heads of false columns popping out among the trees and screens of shrubbery, then disappearing. At one point, fifty savages, our [Iroquois] friends in war paint, suddenly came face to face with fifty English cavalrymen; the war cries of each side so caught the other by surprise that they both fled with equal speed in opposite directions."[5]

While British officers lost time chasing imaginary columns, Lafayette regained the advantage, ordering his main force to file quietly down a steep narrow road along the side of the cliff to a ford on the Schuylkill River below. When he saw that they had crossed safely, he called in his snipers, one squad at a time, and, taking up the rear with the last of his men, he marched them down to the river and crossed without losing a single man. Lafayette regrouped his men to withstand a British assault, but the British generals in the woods above "fell to quarreling," as their troops kept running into each other in the frantic, undisciplined hunt for Lafayette's "false heads. . . . When the two British lines met," according to Lafayette, "they were on the point of attacking each other, for there was no longer anyone between them."[6]

"Howe was astonished," Lafayette laughed. "The whole British army, of which half had marched forty miles, retreated without a single captive. . . . The English returned to Philadelphia much fatigued and ashamed, and were laughed at for their ill success."[7] The expedition humiliated Howe and the other British generals; one general narrowly escaped court-martial. Lafayette and his force climbed back up Barren Hill to continue their reconnaissance for another three days before returning to Valley Forge, where news awaited that a large French fleet, with 4,000 troops, would reach Delaware Bay by early July.

On May 8, Sir Henry Clinton, with whom Lafayette had chatted amiably at the king's reception at St. James Palace in London, replaced Howe as British commander in chief. On June 18, he began evacuating Philadelphia, sending 3,000 men to New York by ship, while the rest began trekking overland through New Jersey. With their artillery, military equipment, and baggage train of 1,500 carriages stretching twelve miles, the slow-moving columns provided just the sort of inviting target Washington had sought to prove the efficacy of the unconventional warfare of harassment instead of direct confrontation. He called another council of war. Charles Lee, the former English army officer, proclaimed himself "passionately opposed" to such tactics. His experience with the British army swayed all but four of Washington's most loyal generals: Greene, Lafayette, "Mad" Anthony Wayne, and John Cadwalader, all of them veterans of Brandywine. Washington compromised by postponing any decision for forty-eight hours and simply following the slow-moving British into central New Jersey to see if conditions and terrain offered opportunities to attack.

A week of heavy rains, searing summer heat, and suffocating humidity slowed the huge British convoy to a mere six miles a day, and, on June 26, the exhausted Redcoats encamped at Monmouth Courthouse (now Freehold, New Jersey), with the Patriots less than twenty miles behind, in Cranbury. Again, Washington called his generals together. Lafayette recalled the meeting: "Lee very eloquently argued that we should provide a *pont d'or* [a "golden bridge," or face-saving way out] for the enemy to reach New York; that British negotiators were discussing possible reconciliation with Congressional leaders; that the British army had never been as disciplined and as strong."[8]

Again, all but Lafayette, Greene, Wayne, and Cadwalader agreed with Lee. Lafayette argued that "it would be disgraceful for the army command and humiliating for our troops to permit [the British] to travel the length of New Jersey with impunity; that we could attack their rear guard without risk."[9] When asked his opinion, the impetuous Anthony Wayne replied: "Fight, sir," and Lafayette, Greene, and Cadwalader, who had dispatched the plotter Conway in a duel, all echoed his cry: "Fight, sir."[10]

Washington decided to fight. Two small forces of 1,000 men each were stalking the British, and Washington ordered a 4,000-man brigade to join them and attack the enemy rear guard. If the attack succeeded, Washington's main army would join the battle; if the British proved too powerful, the main army would cover an orderly retreat by the forward brigade. By protocol, Washington placed Lee in command, but the Englishman refused it contemptuously, calling it a passport to disaster and disgrace. Washington turned it over to the next-highest-ranking combat officer, Lafayette, who eagerly accepted. The French knight rode off to anticipated glory with Wayne, his second in command.

By evening he had encamped just five miles from the British, when Charles Lee suddenly appeared at his tent. He had changed his mind about commanding the assault, but Washington had refused to unseat Lafayette without the Frenchman's consent. "My future and my honor are at stake," Lee pleaded with Lafayette. "I place them in your hands. I know you are too generous to cause me to lose either." The crafty old soldier knew his young adversary's intractable sense of chivalry, and, with Lafayette's consent, Lee took command.

Early that evening, Washington surveyed the English forces, then rode into Lee's camp and ordered a dawn attack. But at dawn the next day, when Lafayette, Wayne, and the other generals asked Lee for instructions, he claimed he lacked adequate intelligence and urged them to stand down. Seeing the army immobile, Washington again sent Lee orders to attack, but Lee gave his generals conflicting orders. The result was chaos: one company moved forward, another veered left, a third veered right. British commanders saw the disorder and sent their forces charging toward the disorganized Patriot lines, all but encircling Lafayette's company. Intuiting what had happened, "Mad" Anthony Wayne, true to his sobriquet, ordered an insanely impetuous charge that forced the British to retreat long enough to allow both his and Lafayette's forces to retreat and escape capture.

Finally, as if to prove his point about British superiority, Lee ordered a mass withdrawal of Patriot forces. Outraged, Washington galloped forward to Lee and shouted angrily, "What is the meaning of this?" After issuing a public reprimand, Washington relieved Lee of command and, suspecting he was a British spy, ordered him to the rear.[11]

Washington assumed command himself and, with Wayne as his second, reformed the lines, with Lord Stirling commanding the left wing, Greene the right, and Lafayette the second line, on a rise reinforced by cannons aimed at oncoming British troops in the ravine below. With cannon blasts blazing overhead, Washington led a huge infantry frontal attack. Great horseman that he was, Washington charged heroically, atop his huge horse, through shot and shell, calling to his men, inspiring them to follow. He was magnificent. With a surge of energy, the Patriots repelled a cavalry charge led by General Clinton himself and sent British forces reeling back toward Monmouth Court House.

"General Washington was never greater in battle than in this action," Lafayette recalled. "His presence stopped the retreat; his strategy secured the victory. His stately appearance on horseback, his calm, dignified courage, tinged only slightly by the anger caused by the unfortunate incident in the morning, provoked a wave of enthusiasm among the troops. Wayne distinguished himself; Greene and the brave Stirling led the first line forward in the most excellent fashion."[12]

Before Washington could seal his victory and destroy the British force, darkness set in, and the exhausted commander in chief spread a mantle on the ground beneath a tree, where, according to Lafayette's memoirs, Washington and his adoptive French son lay side by side to rest for the night, "talking about the conduct of Lee."[13] Later, in the dead of night, Clinton deprived Washington of victory by quietly leading his army away to Sandy Hook, a spit of land on the Jersey shore at the entrance to New York Bay, where transports took them to New York. Although the battle was indecisive—each side suffered about 300 dead—the Americans claimed victory: they had forced British evacuation of Philadelphia and New Jersey. Patriot forces now controlled a huge swath of territory in the middle-Atlantic states, stretching down the west shore of the Hudson River in New York, through New Jersey into Pennsylvania, Delaware, and Maryland.

Had Lee not ordered the initial retreat at Monmouth Court House, the Patriots might well have destroyed a significant part of the British army. The next morning, Lafayette recalled later, Lee sent Washington "a very improper, impudent and insubordinate letter of protest . . . and was placed under arrest."[14] Recognizing his error in having replaced the aggressive Lafayette with the defeatist Lee, Washington ordered Lee court-martialed for "disobedience of orders in not attacking the enemy . . . misbehaviour before the enemy . . . making an *unnecessary, disorderly* and *shameful retreat* . . . [and] disrespect to the Commander in Chief."[15] With Wayne and Lafayette testifying against him, a court-martial found Lee guilty and relieved him of all command for one year. He spent the time writing abusive letters to Washington. Colonel John Laurens challenged Lee to a duel—and wounded him. Before Lee could resume his career, Congress dismissed him from the army, and he died in disgrace in Philadelphia in 1782. Evidence later surfaced that while a prisoner of the British, Lee had plotted with British general William Howe to defeat Washington's army.

A few days after the Battle of Monmouth, the victorious American army gathered near Brunswick (now New Brunswick) on July 4, to celebrate the second anniversary of American independence. Adding to the festivities was the news that a French fleet under General-Vice-Admiral Charles-Henri, comte d'Estaing, had sailed into Delaware Bay near Philadelphia, with twelve ships of the line, five frigates, and an invasion force of 4,000 men.[16]

The French could not have made a worse choice to lead their first expeditionary force of the alliance. The fifty-five-year-old d'Estaing was a soldier—and a brave one—but he was no sailor and had never commanded a fleet or even been to sea. But he had been a close, lifelong friend of King Louis XV, and Louis XVI had chosen him over all the senior naval officers to lead the great fleet that would avenge his grandfather's loss of Canada and restore French glory.

D'Estaing's original mission was to trap the British fleet in Delaware Bay, while Washington cut off the British army's retreat northward, but the French leader lost time chasing British privateers and arrived three days after the British had evacuated Philadelphia and sailed for New York. Washington sent d'Estaing up the New Jersey coast to Sandy Hook to trap the British fleet in New York Bay and the British army on New York Island (now Manhattan). Washington, meanwhile, marched his army northward to Paramus, New Jersey, across the Hudson River from New York, to attack from the west while d'Estaing sailed in from the south. But d'Estaing's ships drew too much water to cross the sandbars into the bay, and, as the British fleet bobbed tantalizingly in the water beyond cannon range, a discouraged d'Estaing admitted he would have to abandon his American mission. "It is terrible to be within sight of your object," he fretted, "and yet to be unable to attain it."[17]

Washington had an alternative strategy for d'Estaing, however: a joint attack with American forces on the 6,000-man British fortification at Newport, Rhode Island, to rid New England of the last British troops. D'Estaing's fleet could attack from the sea, while an American army under General John Sullivan attacked from the north. Washington sent Lafayette and 2,000 Continentals to link up with Sullivan's 3,000-man army north of Newport and 6,000 militiamen from Boston under the command of Massachusetts governor John Hancock. Washington named Lafayette field commander under the overall strategic command of Sullivan. The two had worked well together at Brandywine, and Lafayette was the only commander who knew both languages well enough to coordinate the forces of the two nations.

By the time d'Estaing reached the waters off Rhode Island, however, his enthusiasm for the American Revolution had given way to pessimism. Already chastened by bad timing at Delaware Bay and bad planning at New York, he was ready to sail home. Weeks at sea under short rations had killed many of his marines and left the rest too weak to fight. Moreover, his cautious eye saw nothing but a design for disaster on the navigation charts. Three narrow arms of the sea reached into Narragansett Bay and wrapped themselves around two islands—desolate little Conanicut Island and the larger Rhode Island, with Newport near its southern tip. Rhode Island was—and is—indeed an island in Narragansett Bay, while the mainland that embraces the bay was called the Providence Plantations.* To clear the waters of British ships, d'Estaing would have to send a lone frigate into each waterway, where it would have little room to maneuver and could easily be trapped if a British fleet approached from the sea. D'Estaing needed to strike swiftly, before the British commander could send to New York for help, but Sullivan ordered him to wait until Hancock's troops arrived from Boston.

From the first, d'Estaing and Sullivan despised each other. It did not help that neither spoke the other's language. A rough-hewn New Hampshire lawyer and virulent Francophobe, the quick-tempered Sullivan was unused to European niceties of military protocol, and his gruff, direct tone offended the elegant count. Lafayette stepped in to mediate—only to have d'Estaing express "political anxiety about receiving a French officer who had violated the king's orders not to leave for America." After much discussion, Lafayette calmed d'Estaing by vowing that "he had come to fight the English to learn to serve his master [the French king]." D'Estaing finally accepted the young man's word, and, in his report to the French naval minister, the admiral concluded that "no one is in a better position than this young general officer to become an additional bond of unity between France and America."[18]

As his next task, Lafayette set about restoring cordiality, if not amity, between the French and American commanders, rowing back and forth from ship to shore to ship and back again. Lafayette told Sullivan that the admiral's haughtiness stemmed from "his wants of every kind, provisions, water, etc."—an explanation that Sullivan set to remedy. With Sullivan's animosity subdued, Lafayette poured balm on the admiral's sores. "General Sullivan," Lafayette pledged, "has sent in every direction to collect provisions . . . and orders have been given to bake biscuits at several different places. . . . You will also receive several boats loaded with barrels of water." Once reprovisioned, d'Estaing ordered his frigates to sprint through the narrow channels. With cannons ablaze and marines firing from the top rails, the French captured, burned, or rammed every British vessel they could find, including one frigate and two corvettes.[19] Three other British frigates were left ablaze and sinking—set afire by the British themselves to prevent their capture.

---

*Although universally known as Rhode Island, the state's legal name remains Rhode Island and the Providence Plantations, and that is the name that appears on all official state documents, including state bonds.

The rest of the Newport campaign proved far less successful, however. Although Sullivan and d'Estaing agreed on a joint assault on Newport, Sullivan suddenly attacked without notifying d'Estaing. The admiral and his officers were furious over what they perceived as an insulting breach of protocol. Sullivan scoffed, calling d'Estaing "unduly sensitive and punctilious."[20] Colonel John Laurens echoed his commander's words: "The French officers sounded like women disputing precedence in a country dance, instead of men engaged in pursuing the common interest of two great nations."[21]

The dispute quickly became moot, though, when a cry from a crow's nest heralded the approach of thirty-six enemy sail on the horizon. As d'Estaing had feared, the British had sent to New York for help, and Admiral Howe had responded. D'Estaing ordered his frigates to rejoin the ships of the line at sea. They maneuvered throughout the night in the tight channels, and, by morning, they lay in position offshore to repel the British attack. Then the winds shifted, and, seeing an opportunity to attack and destroy Howe's fleet, d'Estaing sailed out to sea "in the most beautiful weather in the world," according to Lafayette, "and in sight of both the English and American armies. I never was so proud as I was that day."[22]

With the approach of d'Estaing's powerful fleet, Howe's ships turned toward New York, with the French in pursuit under full canvas. The chase continued all day and night and most of the next day, with the French closing in by the hour. At the end of the second day, Howe had no choice but to come about and engage, but, before the titanic battle could begin, the sea began churning angrily. Violent waves and winds gripped both fleets and sent their ships tossing in the air, spinning them in different directions, out of control, rolling and pitching violently, ripping sails and snapping masts like twigs. The gale roared relentlessly throughout the night. By morning both fleets lay crippled, barely able to steer, let alone battle. D'Estaing's flagship had lost its masts and rudder and bobbed about helplessly. A second man-of-war had lost two of its three masts, and a third was out of sight, either beyond the horizon or at the bottom of the sea. A British ship of the line tried to sink the crippled French ships, but the bigger French guns held it off, and the British abandoned the attack and limped off to safety in New York.

D'Estaing regrouped the ships he could find and sailed slowly back to Rhode Island, his flagship in tow. Although his officers urged that they sail to Boston for repairs, d'Estaing insisted on fulfilling his pledge to Sullivan to return. When he arrived, however, he found an alarming shrinkage in Sullivan's force. Many troops had deserted after the French fleet sailed away, and the British garrison had turned the full fury of its artillery on the depleted American land force. The unholy storm that followed put thousands more soldiers to flight, and still others left for home to harvest their fields, after their fifteen-day enlistment periods ended. Hancock's 6,000-man Massachusetts militia shrank to a mere 1,000, and, seeing the expedition against Newport all but lost, he too left the muck of the rain-drenched battlefield and returned to Boston.

Because of his fleet's weakened condition, d'Estaing dared not reenter the narrow channels around Rhode Island. "The same operation which came near being disastrous to us when we had our full strength," d'Estaing explained, "would have been all the more imprudent to undertake now."[23]

Sullivan was outraged. He sent Lafayette and Greene to d'Estaing's flagship to urge a new joint attack on Newport. "If we fail in our negotiation," quipped the Francophile Greene, "at least we shall get a good dinner."[24] As it turned out, they failed on both counts: Greene got so seasick he could not eat, and Lafayette was unable to budge the admiral from his position, despite arguments that nearby Providence was as equipped as Boston to refit and reprovision the fleet. D'Estaing offered to evacuate American troops before sailing to Boston, and, when Sullivan rejected the offer, the French fleet sailed away, with its admiral planning to urge his friend the king to end military aid to the uncooperative, unappreciative Americans.

"At the departure of the vessels," Lafayette wrote, "anger spread among the militiamen: their hopes had been shattered, their time wasted and they were now in a difficult position strategically. Their discontent became contagious. The people of Boston spoke of closing the port to the French fleet; the generals drew up a protest, which [I] refused to sign. Carried away by passion, Sullivan charged the French admiral with responsibility for the 'ruinous consequences which would result to this army [by] abandoning the harbor at Newport.' He called d'Estaing's departure 'derogatory to the honor of France, contrary to the intention of His Most Christian Majesty and the interest of his nation, and destructive in the highest degree to the welfare of the United States of America, and highly injurious to the alliance formed between the two nations.'"[25] To compound the diplomatic damage, Sullivan issued a general order to the army disavowing the alliance with France and saying that the French departure "will prove America able to procure with her own arms that which her allies refused to assist her in obtaining."[26]

Sullivan's outbursts were not only undiplomatic, they were blatantly untrue, indeed absurd. If nothing else, the disaster at Newport proved that America's ill-equipped amateur soldiers were incapable of evicting the British army from the United States by themselves. Without massive French military and naval intervention—and financial help—the American Revolution was doomed.

Seeing that the alliance he had worked so hard to create was about to collapse, Lafayette lashed out at Sullivan, accusing him of undermining the revolution by insulting d'Estaing, the French navy, and France herself.

The two almost drew swords before their aides separated them. Desperate to save the alliance, Lafayette sent a courier with an angry dispatch to Washington describing the efforts of the French fleet and condemning Sullivan's "ungenerous sentiments." Sullivan, he said, dealt with d'Estaing as "one would be ashamed to treat the most inveterate enemies. . . . I wish, my dear general, you could know as well as myself, how desirous the Count d'Estaing is to . . . help your success, and to serve the cause of America.

"I earnestly beg you will recommend to the several chief persons of Boston to do everything they can to put the French fleet in a situation for sailing soon. . . . I am afraid the Count d'Estaing will have felt to the quick the behaviour of the people on this occasion. You cannot conceive how distressed he was."[27] After receiving a similar report from Nathanael Greene, Washington acted immediately to repair the diplomatic havoc Sullivan had wreaked—first, with a letter of consolation to Lafayette and a plea for his understanding and help:

> I feel for you and for our good and great allies the French. I feel myself hurt, also, at every illiberal and unthinking reflection which may have been cast upon the Count d'Estaing, or the fleet under his command; and, lastly, I feel for my country. Let me entreat you, therefore, my dear marquis, to take no exception at unmeaning expressions, uttered, perhaps, without consideration . . . but, in a free and republican government, you cannot restrain the voice of the multitude; every man will speak as he thinks, or, more properly, without thinking. . . . Let me beseech you . . . to afford a healing hand to the wound that, unintentionally has been made. . . . I, your friend, have no doubt but you will use your utmost endeavours to restore harmony, that the honour, the glory, and mutual interest of the two countries may be promoted and cemented in the firmest manner.[28]

Aware that the war was lost without the French, Washington apologized to d'Estaing:

> The adverse element, which robbed you of your prize, can never deprive you of the glory due to you. Though your success has not been equal to your expectations, yet you have the satisfaction of reflecting, that you have rendered essential services to the common cause.
>
> I exceedingly lament, that, in addition to our misfortunes, there has been the least suspension of harmony and good understanding between the generals of allied nations.[29]

Congress supported Washington with a resolution declaring that d'Estaing "hath behaved as a brave and wise officer, and that his excellency and the officers and men under his command have rendered every benefit to these states . . . and are fully entitled to the regards of the friends of America."[30]

Washington dispatched an urgent plea to John Hancock in Boston to ensure a warm welcome to the French fleet and its speedy refitting. He sent a stern reprimand—and a lesson in good manners—to Sullivan:

> The disagreement between the army under your command and the fleet has given me very singular uneasiness: the continent at large is concerned in our cordiality, and it should be kept up. . . . In our conduct towards them we should remember that they are people old in war, very strict in military etiquette. . . . Permit me to recommend, in the most particular manner, the cultivation of harmony and good agreement, and your endeavours to destroy that ill-humour which may have got into the officers. It is of the greatest importance, also, that the soldiers and the people should know nothing of the misunderstanding. . . . I have no doubt but you will do all in your power to forward the repair of the count's fleet, and render it fit for service.[31]

Washington also turned to the coolheaded Rhode Island veteran Nathanael Greene: "I depend much on your aid and influence to conciliate that animosity which I plainly perceive, by a letter from the marquis, subsists between the American officers and the French in our service. . . . The marquis speaks kindly of a letter from you to him on the subject; he will therefore take any advice coming from you in a friendly light."[32] Greene replied that Lafayette had done "everything to prevail upon the Admiral to cooperate with us that man could do. . . . General Sullivan very imprudently issued something like a censure in general orders. Indeed it was a general censure. It opened the mouths of the army in very clamourous strains."[33]

Greene responded with a gracious letter of apology to d'Estaing:

> I could not have been more shocked by the style and contents of the letter General Sullivan wrote to you; the more I think about it, the more surprised I become. I am convinced his heart did not dictate it. I have often heard him speak of Your Excellency in the most respectful terms—not just of your skills, but your conduct and your scrupulous attention to your duties. The words in his letter are so different from his normal words that I do not know what to attribute it to except the excitement of the moment. . . . I beg your excellency not to judge other American generals by the tone of his letter. I can assure you with the greatest sincerity of the respect and veneration that your reputation has inspired in them; permit me to add that no one feels this more deeply than I.[34]

At Washington's goading, other American military leaders, including Gates, the hero at Saratoga, wrote to d'Estaing complimenting his heroism and making it clear they all disagreed with Sullivan. Sullivan, in turn, responded to Washington's reprimand with an apology to both Washington and Lafayette for his "struggles of passion," and, after effecting a reconciliation, he asked Lafayette to ride to Boston to salve d'Estaing's wounds with a letter of apology and to meet with Massachusetts governor John Hancock and other Boston officials to ensure quick refitting of the French fleet.

Elated by the prospects of a rapprochement, Lafayette rode all night, covering the seventy miles to Boston in seven hours. The storm-damaged French fleet had limped into port the previous evening, before Hancock had received Washington's appeal. Memories of the French and Indian War remained fresh in the minds of most men of Massachusetts, and Sullivan's accusations against the French admiral turned Boston's hatred of the French into outright rage. When d'Estaing's fleet put into port, shipfitters—even the unemployed—claimed they had too much work to repair French ships, and that refitting would take months or years. They reinforced their assertions by assaulting French sailors—and killing one officer—who dared step ashore.

When Lafayette arrived in Boston, he met with Hancock and obtained his promise to refit the French fleet and restore relations with French leaders. Hancock lived up to his word. An extremely popular leader and first governor of Massachusetts, Hancock had been Boston's leading merchant and shipbuilder before the war, and he interceded with the city's shipfitters to repair the French fleet. Then, in a symbolic gesture that all Boston witnessed, Hancock rode to harborside in his resplendent coach to invite d'Estaing and Lafayette to a formal dinner at Hancock House, his magnificent mansion atop Beacon Hill. Dressed in purple velvet as brilliant as that of any European aristocrat, he came aboard to deliver the invitations personally. Lafayette introduced him to the admiral, then offered his own hand in a warm Masonic handshake with the former president of Congress, who had signed his major general's commission in Philadelphia only a year earlier.

Later that day, Hancock sent his magnificent coach to bring his renowned French guests to Beacon Hill to dine with Boston's leading citizens in the glittering banquet hall at Hancock House. A servant stood behind each chair to serve guests individually. The settings displayed the finest china, crystal, and silver, and Hancock's cellar provided French wines as fine as any the count had ever savored. Hancock climaxed the evening by presenting d'Estaing with a magnificent portrait of Washington. "I never saw a man so glad at possessing his sweetheart's picture," Lafayette wrote Washington, "as the admiral was to receive yours." D'Estaing ordered his guns to fire a royal salute as the portrait was hoisted aboard his flagship. He hung it above the mantel in his cabin, framed with laurel wreaths.[35]

The following day, Lafayette rode back to rejoin Sullivan's depleted force, which had retreated to the northern part of Rhode Island and, as darkness fell, began floating quietly across to the mainland by flatboat. By eleven, when the breathless Lafayette arrived, all but a rearguard of less than 1,000 men had slipped across. "He was sensibly mortified that he was out of action,"[36] Sullivan reported. Despite his fatigue, Lafayette insisted on crossing to take command of the rear guard and was on the last boat to leave the island, three hours later, at 2:00 A.M. "He returned in time enough to bring off the pickets . . . not a man was left behind, nor the smallest article lost."[37] It would be daybreak before the British discovered the retreat and claimed victory, but it was a hollow victory that left the Americans with far more political and military advantages.

The Battle of Newport cost each side about 250 lives and left the British in firm control of the islands of Narragansett Bay. But the arrival of the French fleet in America had forced the British to evacuate Philadelphia and concentrate much of their northern army in New York, effectively abandoning the middle colonies and opening Delaware and Chesapeake Bays to American navigation. The Americans also controlled most parts of New England, except for the isolated island outpost at Newport. The Battle of Newport also substantiated Washington's conviction that America's citizen soldiers were no match for the British army in conventional warfare.

With the 1778 campaign at an end, Lafayette watched his men leave for home, and he longed to do the same. To his delight, a letter from his father-in-law—the first since he had left France a year earlier—arrived to break the lonely boredom of his tent. It was a letter of forgiveness and encouragement, and it assured Lafayette that he was welcome to return. Filled with thoughts of home, Lafayette wrote to his wife: "If anything could lessen my pleasure in writing to you, my sweetheart, it would be the cruel thought that I must write you from a corner of America where everyone I love is two thousand leagues from me. But I have reason to hope that this will not be for long and that the moment of our reunion is not far off. . . . Oh, my sweetheart, when shall I be near you; when shall I be able to hold you in my arms and kiss you a hundred, a thousand times? . . . Cover [Anastasie] with kisses; teach her to love me. . . . Adieu, adieu; we shall not be apart very long."[38]

Late in September, Lafayette and Greene returned to Boston, where Hancock was still soothing d'Estaing's injured feelings and courting him to the American cause. Indeed, he and d'Estaing had become fast friends; night after night, the Harvard-educated Hancock and his wife, Dolly, held lavish dinner parties for the admiral and his officers, with virtually every officer in the fleet getting his turn to breakfast, dine, or sup at Hancock House. One morning, Hancock, who spoke French well, invited thirty officers for breakfast, "but the Count brought up almost all the officers of his fleet, mid-shipmen included," Dolly Hancock later recalled. Count d'Estaing sheep-ishly told her he would make it up to her, and, according to her biographer, asked her to visit the fleet, "and bring all her friends with her; and true enough she did . . . for she went down and carried a party of five hundred."[39]

When Lafayette and Greene arrived in Boston, Hancock invited them to a sumptuous reception at Faneuil Hall for the admiral, his officers, and about five hundred of the leading citizens of Boston and surrounding com-munities. With Hancock presiding, thirteen-gun salutes accompanied suc-cessive toasts to the United States and the king of France. It was the finest affair ever held on American soil, according to Abigail Adams.

Lafayette spent the days that followed in pleasant, informal excursions with d'Estaing—a fellow Auvergnat and, it turned out, a distant cousin. (Because they married only members of their own class, most French aristo-crats were cousins of one sort or another.) With Lafayette sermonizing about America's greatness, they toured Boston and the surrounding countryside, including Harvard College and the camp where Burgoyne's Saratoga army still languished, awaiting repatriation as hostages of Congress until the British recognized American independence.

With the annual winter hiatus in the war and no battles to fight, Lafa-yette's restless imagination conjured up a variety of chimerical adventures to lead against Britain—in Canada, the British West Indies, and virtually every English possession in the world, including England herself. Lafayette and d'Estaing worked out specific plans for winter and spring campaigns. Lafa-yette would ask Congress for 2,000 American troops to sail with d'Estaing's fleet to attack the British West Indies in January. In the spring, d'Estaing would return north, sail up the St. Lawrence to Quebec, where Lafayette would lead a combined Franco-American invasion force of 6,000 French marines and his 2,000 Continentals. Lafayette sent details to all his influen-tial friends—Vergennes at Versailles, of course, and Washington, whom he also asked for a leave of absence to join the West Indies expedition.

Washington approved Lafayette's taking leave, but urged his French general to do so at home in France with his wife and child and forget the Canadian and West Indies expeditions. "Friendship induces me to tell you that I do not conceive that the prospect of such an operation is so favourable at this time," Washington wrote. He said the invasion of Canada would require an enormous French army that Americans would resent on their soil as much as they resented the British army. Washington thanked his disciple for his "endeavors to cherish harmony among the officers of the allied powers" and assured him that "the sentiments of affection and attach-ment, which breath so conspicuously in all your letters to me . . . afford me abundant cause to rejoice at the happiness of my acquaintance with you.

Your love of liberty, the just sense you entertain of this valuable blessing, and your noble and disinterested exertions in the cause of it, added to the innate goodness of your heart, conspire to render you dear to me; and I think myself happy in being linked with you in bonds of friendship." In urging Lafayette to go home, he added an invitation to Lafayette and his "fair lady" to return to visit Mount Vernon, "when the war is ended, if she could be prevailed upon to quit for a few months, the gaieties and splendor of a court, for the rural amusements of an humble cottage." He signed his letter with "sincerity and affection,"[40] reminding him also to apply for official leave to Congress, which had issued his original commission.

Lafayette spent three weeks in Philadelphia, charming and winning the friendships of congressmen of every political persuasion—New York's witty Gouverneur Morris, a staunch friend and supporter of Washington; Virginia's Richard Henry Lee, who had been an equally staunch supporter of Gates; and even the irascible Samuel Adams of Massachusetts, who supported no one but himself. All were as eager to meet Lafayette as he was to meet them. Many were Freemasons who embraced him and called him brother. It was his signal personal gift to appear a disinterested friend of America and of liberty and, at each encounter, to win the awe and admiration of members of every political faction. He had been through much, had conducted himself heroically, had fought, bled, and risked death for *their* country, and asked nothing in return but their respect and friendship. His skill in winning both proved remarkable.

French ambassador Gérard wrote to French foreign minister Vergennes: "I cannot refrain from saying that the prudent, courageous and amiable conduct of the Marquis de Lafayette has made him the idol of the Congress, the army and the people of America. They all hold a high opinion of his military talents. You know how little inclined I am to adulation, but I would be less than just if I did not send you these universally acclaimed testimonials. . . . The Americans strongly want him to return with the troops which the king may send."[41]

Although Lafayette failed to win congressional support for his Caribbean venture, many congressmen lusted for Canada as a fourteenth member of the American confederation—especially the aggressive admirers of Gates. Lafayette convinced them that British retention of Canada would pose an ever-present military threat on the northern United States border. Unlike Washington, Congress agreed and approved his "Plan for Reducing the province of Canada" the following spring. It appointed him American liaison to the court at Versailles, ordered an American frigate, aptly named *Alliance*, to take him back to France, and it instructed Benjamin Franklin, the new minister plenipotentiary to France—the first American ambassador to any country—to "cause an elegant sword, with proper devices to be made, and presented in the name of the United States to the Marquis de Lafayette."[42]

On October 21, Congress resolved, "That the Marquis de Lafayette, major-general in the service of the United States have leave to go to France, and that he return at such time as shall be most convenient to him." It offered its thanks "for your zeal . . . and for the disinterested services you have rendered to the United States of America" and sent a formal letter to the king of France:

> To our great, faithful, and beloved friend and ally, Louis the Sixteenth, king of France and Navarre:—
> The Marquis de Lafayette having obtained our leave to return to his native country, we could not suffer him to depart without testifying our deep sense of his zeal, courage, and attachment. We have advanced him to the rank of major-general in our armies, which, as well by his prudent conduct, he has manifestly merited. We recommend this young nobleman to your majesty's notice, as one whom we know to be wise in council, gallant in the field, and patient under the hardships of war.[43]

Lafayette was deeply moved—not only by the genuine appreciation Congress had displayed but by their unsolicited effort to ensure his receiving an appropriate—and forgiving—welcome at Versailles.

Lafayette went to Boston to coordinate the Canadian campaign with d'Estaing before returning home. Traveling on horseback through torrents of rain, he fell ill—as much from the torrents of wine and rum as from the rain. Every town along his route celebrated his arrival and departure, and he collapsed when he reached Fishkill, midway between New York and Albany, and about eight miles from Washington's camp. As he had at Brandywine, Washington sent his own physician, Dr. John Cochran, to care for the young Frenchman. Lafayette was convinced he was dying: "[I was] Suffering from a raging fever and violent head-ache," he recalled. "General Washington came every day to inquire . . . and showed the most tender and paternal anxiety."[44]

Newspapers across the nation reported the impending death of "Our Marquis," but, after three weeks, just as the nation prepared to mourn his passing, "nature added the alarming though salutary remedy of a [four-hour] hemorrhage . . . [and my] life was no longer in danger."[45] As he recovered, he and Washington once again discussed the Canadian expedition, with Washington pointing out that any shift of American forces to Canada would loosen the noose around British encampments in Rhode Island and New York and allow them to break out. Moreover, it would change the complexion of the war: instead of fighting for independence, Americans would be aggressors, expanding beyond their borders and further alienating Tory loyalists at home. Although he did not want to hurt the young man's sensitive feelings about France, Washington feared France as much as England.

"France," he wrote to Congress, "[is] the most powerful monarchy in Europe by land, able now to dispute the empire of the sea with Great Britain, and, if joined by Spain, I may say, certainly superior, possessed by New Orleans on our right, Canada on our left, and seconded by the numerous tribes of Indians in our rear . . . so generally friendly to her. . . . It is much to be apprehended [that France would] have in her power to give laws to these states . . . it is a maxim founded on the universal experience of mankind," he told Congress, "that no nation is to be trusted farther than it is bound by its interests."[46]

In Boston, d'Estaing underscored Washington's fears by issuing a "Declaration in the king's name to all former Frenchman of North America" that pledged French recovery of Canada from the English. "You were born French," he said, "you have never ceased to be French."[47]

On December 2, Lafayette left Fishkill, but not before he and Washington took "tender and painful leave of each other."[48] While Lafayette waited for his frigate in Boston, Washington went to Philadelphia and convinced Congress to abandon the Canadian project. In Versailles, French foreign minister Vergennes also vetoed the expedition. French expenditures in America had already exceeded expectations. In addition to the costs of d'Estaing's foray, France had loaned the Continental Congress 42 million livres—equivalent to $420 million today—and Congress had no hard currency to repay it. Recapturing Canada would spread French military and naval resources so thin as to render her vulnerable to British attack in the West Indies.

With the Canadian project abandoned, d'Estaing left for the French West Indies and reopened American waters to British depredation. As if to underscore the folly of Sullivan's alienation of the French, a British flotilla sent its marines storming ashore in Georgia and captured Savannah. Fearing a similar assault on Boston, Congress ordered the army to escort Burgoyne and his 4,000 English and Hessian troops on a seven-hundred-mile trek to internment near Charlottesville, Virginia, too far to rise up in support of a British invasion.

Early in January 1779, Lafayette prepared to sail for France. "Adieu, my dear Marquis," Washington wrote. "My best wishes will ever attend you. . . . There is no need of fresh proofs to convince you of my affection for you personally, or of the high opinion I entertain of your military talents and merit. . . . May you have a safe and agreeable passage, and a happy meeting with your lady and friends!"[49]

Emotion got the better of Lafayette as he wrote his farewell to Washington:

> To hear from you, my most respected friend, will be the greatest happiness I can feel. The longer the letters you write, the more blessed with satisfaction I shall think myself.
>
> Be so kind, my dear general, as to present my best respects to your lady. . . . I hope you will quietly enjoy the pleasure of being with Mrs. Washington, without any disturbance from the enemy, till I join you again. . . . Farewell, my most beloved general; it is not without emotion that I bid you this last adieu, before so long a separation. Don't forget an absent friend, and believe me for ever and ever, with the highest respect and tenderest affection.[50]

On January 11, 1779, the *Alliance* weighed anchor, and the teary-eyed twenty-one-year-old could not help scribbling another last note to his beloved adoptive father. "The sails are just going to be hoisted, my dear General, and I have but time to take my last leave of you. . . . Farewell, my dear general; I hope your French friend will ever be dear to you; I hope I shall soon see you again, and tell you myself with what emotion I now leave the coast you inhabit, and with what affection and respect I am for ever, my dear general, your respected and sincere friend."[51]

7

$Return\ to\ Royal\ Favor$

THE EARTH ITSELF seemed to collapse beneath Lafayette's frigate as it struggled through the dangerous winter passage across the north Atlantic. A savage storm near Newfoundland ripped off its main topmast and, as the *Alliance* rolled and pitched out of control, huge waves sent their foamy tongues darting into the ship's companionways.

"During the long dark night, the ship was in imminent danger of sinking," Lafayette recalled, "but an even greater danger awaited only two hundred leagues [500 miles] from France. To encourage crew uprisings on American ships, His British Majesty had issued a proclamation promising them the value of every *rebel* ship they brought into English ports—an eventuality only possible by massacring officers and those who opposed the mutiny."[1]

The *Alliance* had a mixed crew—some Americans, but mostly French volunteers eager to return home and English deserters who hoped, eventually, to sneak home to England after landing in France. Once under way, the English deserters hungered for the profits they could pocket by seizing the ship and its famous French passenger and sailing directly to England to claim a lavish bounty for the ship and offer Lafayette to the king in exchange for full pardons.

"The cry of *Sail!* was to be raised at four in the morning," Lafayette recounted, "and when the passengers and officers came on deck, four cannon, loaded with grape shot . . . were to blow them to pieces."[2] One of the mutineers, however, reported the plot, and an hour before the scheduled mutiny, Lafayette led a team of forty officers and passengers to the crew's quarters, sliced the hammock cords of the four sleeping ringleaders, and, when they dropped to the floor, bound them and clapped them into irons.

93

Before the day was out, thirty-eight crewmen were in irons, and the ship sailed safely to France, putting into Brest, on the western tip of Brittany, ten days later, on February 6, 1779.

Nearly twenty-two months had elapsed since Lafayette had set foot on his native soil. He had left a fugitive, subject to immediate arrest for defying the king's orders. Now, the king's cannons roared their welcome to the heroic knight. After recovering his land legs, Lafayette rode to Versailles to seek the king's pardon and present a raft of letters and documents from Congress to Prime Minister Maurepas, Foreign Minister Vergennes, and to the king himself. He arrived at two in the morning—too late to breach the palace gates, but not too late to appear, unannounced, at a ball at his cousin's stately mansion, a few steps away. The handsome uniform of an American major general caused a stir. At first, they did not recognize him. He was a boy when he left; he now returned looking far older—and somewhat balder—than his twenty-one years. After a few moments of disbelief, applause broke out, then loud cheers. "I had left as rebel and fugitive," he exulted, "and returned in triumph as an idol."[3]

He looked about the ballroom for his wife, but in his absence she had foregone most social life and remained at home with her mother in the Noailles mansion in Paris. "He had arrived at the very moment no one expected," Adrienne recalled. "My mother tried to prepare me for his arrival herself. I will not even try to paint a picture of the joy we shared at that moment."[4]

The next morning, Lafayette went to the palace to see Maurepas, Vergennes, and, he hoped, the king. The two ministers gave him careful, extended, respectful audiences. He was, after all, the reigning French authority on all things American, a close personal friend of the legendary George Washington, a confidante of America's national political and military leaders, a major general and distinguished soldier in the American army, and as much an official emissary of the United States Congress as Benjamin Franklin himself. And, of course, he remained a French officer and nobleman, whose marriage had united two of France's most distinguished families.

"At my arrival, I had the honor to be consulted by all the ministers, and, what was even better," Lafayette recalled coyly, "to be kissed by all the ladies of the court. The kisses ended the next day, but I retained the confidence of the [king's] cabinet."[5]

At the end of the first day's discussions, only the matter of the king's arrest warrant remained unsettled. Assistant ministers, their assistants, and their assistants' assistants shuffled hurriedly back and forth all day between the king's apartments and the ministerial chambers, breathlessly whispering in each other's ears, passing notes back and forth. Finally, the king's word arrived: he refused to grant Lafayette an audience and ordered him pun-

Charles Willson Peale's realistic portrait of the prematurely balding Lafayette. Though he was only twenty-two, the rigors of camp life at Valley Forge and other Revolutionary War posts had aged him visibly. Unlike European artists, Peale did not idealize his subjects. (*From the author's collection.*)

ished. "I was interrogated, complimented, and exiled," Lafayette explained, "but to Paris. Instead of honoring me with a cell in the Bastille, as some of the king's advisors proposed, the king chose the precincts of the Hôtel de Noailles as my prison for the next week."[6]

Before he left the palace, the queen sent word of her desire to see him, although she could not do so officially. A minister's assistant arranged for Lafayette to walk across the courtyard as her carriage drove by, allowing her to stop briefly to extend her hand. He then went to his own carriage for the trip home to his lavish "prison" on the rue Saint-Honoré. His wife, still childlike at nineteen, all but fainted in his arms as she and her family welcomed him home. He was still her knight, and he played his role as gallantly in the salon and bedroom as he had on the battlefield.

The most illustrious men and women of Paris threw themselves at his feet during his week of "house arrest," but, at the end of each evening's entertainment, Adrienne had her husband to herself for the first time in nearly two years. Unlike wives in most arranged marriages of feudal France, Adrienne loved her husband completely. "My joy is impossible to describe," she wrote to Lafayette's aging aunts at Chavaniac. "Monsieur de La Fayette has come back to me as modest and as charming as when he went away. . . . For the moment, he is in disgrace with the king and is forbidden to show himself in public. God has preserved, in the midst of tremendous dangers, the most lovable person in all the world. . . . When I reflect on my good fortune at being his wife, I am truly grateful to God."[7]

Paris society—and, indeed, his wife and her family—discovered a new Lafayette. The awkward country manners and clumsiness that once provoked Queen Marie-Antoinette's disdainful laughter had vanished. No longer timid or embarrassed, Lafayette stood tall and proud, and chatted easily, even brilliantly, displaying what one French journalist would later describe as "a sensitive and polished intelligence . . . a lively unaffected power of describing the famous persons he had met."[8] His house arrest did not interfere with his diplomatic mission. Benjamin Franklin rode into Paris from Passy and John Adams from Auteuil to see him, and they agreed to work together to promote a French attack in North America.

"A strong Armament of Ships of the Line, with five thousand Troops," Adams wrote Lafayette by way of confirmation the next morning, "directed against Halifax, Rhode-Island or New York, must infallibly succeed—So it must against the Floridas—So it must against Canada, or any one of the West India Islands. . . . The French have a great advantage in carrying on this kind of War. . . . I should be happy to have further Conversations with you, Sir, upon those Subjects."[9]

Although the queen could not pay her respects during his house arrest, she did arrange for his promotion in the French army from reserve captain to *mestre de camp*, or colonel, in the cavalry. He was "given"—that is, allowed to purchase—command of a regiment of the king's dragoons, at the hefty price of 80,000 livres, or $800,000 in today's dollars.[10]

During his house arrest, he and his powerful in-laws—the duc d'Ayen and the duke's father, the duc de Noailles—carefully composed the requisite letter of apology and obeisance to the king, along with a plea for forgiveness. It was a masterpiece of feudal diplomacy:

> The misfortune of having displeased Your Majesty has saddened me so painfully that, rather than try to excuse myself, I shall try to explain the motives that inspired my misdeeds. My love for my country, my desire to see her enemies humiliated, and political feelings that the recent treaty would seem to justify, those, Sire, are the reasons that made me decide to help the American cause.
>
> When I received Your Majesty's orders, I attributed them to the tender concerns of my family rather than to any considerations of our nation's policies towards England. The emotions of my heart overcame my reason. . . . I would not dare, Sire, to try to justify an act of disobedience of which you disapprove and for which I must repent . . . but it is important for my own peace that Your Majesty attribute to its true motives the conduct which has disgraced me in your eyes. The nature of my wrongs makes me hope

The king of France, Louis XVI, seen here in his formal robes
of state, "exiled" Lafayette to a week at his in-laws' palatial
mansion in Paris for having disobeyed royal orders not to go
to America. After the symbolic punishment ended, the king
welcomed Lafayette to Versailles with honors. (*Réunion des
Musées Nationaux.*)

that I may expunge them. It is to Your Majesty's goodness that I shall owe
the happiness of absolving myself by whatever means you deign to serve
you, in whatever country and in whatever way possible. I am with the most
profound Respect, Sire, your Majesty's humble and obedient servant and
loyal subject.[11]

A few days later, the king received Lafayette, officially ended his house
arrest with a *réprimande douce,* and began several hours of questioning his
former riding-school companion about America, its people, and the progress of
the war. Before dismissing his new colonel of cavalry, the king complimented
Lafayette on his successes in America and on the glory he had earned for his

name and for France. Lafayette's return to Paris society was now complete. The king invited him on hunts through Marly Forest; his entrance into the salons of Paris drew swoons; his appearance at the theater, opera, and other public places invariably provoked thunderous ovations. At the Comédie Française, the great theater founded by Louis XIV for Molière, Lafayette's appearance one evening provoked additional words on stage to acknowledge his presence: "Behold this youthful courtier . . . his mind and soul inflamed. . . ."[12] The audience roared its approval.

"I enjoyed both the favors of the court of Versailles and celebrity status in Paris society," Lafayette recalled with delight. "They spoke well of me in all circles . . . I had everything I had always wanted—public acclaim and the affection of those I love. In the midst of all the excitement surrounding my arrival, however, I never lost sight of our revolution, whose success was still very much in doubt. . . . Accustomed to seeing matters of great import sustained by slender means in America, I said to myself that the price of one evening's dinner in Paris would have resupplied the United States army; as Monsieur Maurepas suggested, I would have gladly stripped Versailles of its furnishings to have clothed those men."[13]

In the weeks that followed, Lafayette shuttled back and forth between Paris, Versailles, and Franklin's embassy and home in Passy, where the venerable doctor conspired with the young Frenchman to develop a myriad of schemes to attack Britain and weaken her hold on the United States. He was now statesman and strategist—and sensitive to the changing moods at Versailles. By early spring, Lafayette recognized that Versailles was losing interest in promoting American independence. The French motive for supporting the American Revolution was to weaken Britain and replace her as the world's dominant commercial and military power. But the Revolution was going badly; the French military effort at Newport had failed, and French financial aid to the Americans was bankrupting the treasury. French ministers now agreed that a quicker, less costly way to weaken Britain was to abandon expensive adventures in faraway North America and strike directly at Britain, a mere twenty miles away across the Channel. Lafayette, Franklin, and Adams did not disagree; a French assault on Britain might force her to recall forces from the United States to protect her own shores and give Washington's Continental army enough of a military advantage to win the war.

With Franklin's help, Lafayette devised a plan to raid coastal cities in Britain and Ireland. Franklin had spent eighteen years in Britain as agent for three American colonies and knew the physical as well as the economic terrain. "I admire much the activity of your genius," Franklin told Lafayette. "It is certain that the coasts of England and Scotland are extremely open and defenseless. There are also many rich towns near the sea which four or five thousand men landing unexpectedly might easily surprise and destroy or exact from them a heavy contribution, taking a part in ready money and hostages for the rest . . . forty-eight millions of livres might be demanded of Bristol for the town and shipping; twelve millions of livres from Bath; forty-eight millions from Liverpool; six millions for Lancaster, and twelve millions from Whitehaven."[14]

In the spring of 1779, Lafayette became "the key link" between the United States and France. "I enjoyed the confidence of both countries and both governments," he explained. "I used the favor I had won at court and in French society to serve the American cause, to obtain every kind of help."[15]

His proposal to raid the British and Irish coasts answered the needs of both France and the United States, and, at Franklin's suggestion, he met with John Paul Jones, the notorious coastal raider, whose exploits against the British had earned him a captain's commission in the Continental navy. In April, the French government provided five ships and pledged a force of 2,000 raiders. "As this is understood to be an American expedition under the Congress' commission and colours," Franklin wrote to Jones, "the Marquis, who is a major-general in that service, has of course the step in point of rank, and he must have the command of the land forces, which are committed by the king to his care." Concerned that the Scottish-born Jones, a freebooting sea captain ten years older than Lafayette, might resent the young Frenchman, Franklin warned, "I am persuaded, that, whatever authority his rank in strictness give him, he will not have the least desire to interfere with you. There is honour enough to be got for both of you." To prevent repetition of the Sullivan-d'Estaing conflict at Newport, the wise old doctor also warned Jones that "there is not only a junction of land and sea forces, but there is also a junction of Frenchmen and Americans, which increases the difficulty of maintaining a good understanding. A cool, prudent, conduct in the chiefs is, therefore, the more necessary."[16]

To forestall any misunderstanding, Lafayette reached out to the proud Scotsman: "Be certain, my dear sir, that I shall be happy to divide with you whatever share of glory may await us." Jones replied, "Where men of fine feeling are concerned there is seldom misunderstanding." He pledged not to give Lafayette "a moment's pain by any part of my conduct."[17]

By mid-May, Jones and his fleet were ready to sail and awaited only the arrival of Lafayette's troops at Lorient, a major port on the south coast of Brittany. An unusually long personal letter from George Washington buoyed Lafayette's spirits. He described a British effort "to surprise the post at Elizabethtown [New Jersey]; but failing therein, and finding themselves closely pressed . . . they retreated precipitately through a marsh waist-deep in mud, after abandoning all their plunder." Washington clearly missed the companionship of his young friend. As long as the war continued, he wrote, "I shall not despair of sharing fresh toils and dangers with you in America; but if [peace] succeeds, I can entertain little hope, that the rural amusements of an infant world, or the contracted stage of an American theatre, can withdraw your attention and services from the gaieties of a court, and the active part you will more than probably be called to share in the administration of your government. The soldier will then be transformed into the statesman, and your employment in this new walk of life will afford you no time to revisit this continent, or think of the friends who lament your absence.

"The American troops are again in huts," Washington continued, "but in a more agreeable and fertile country, than they were in last winter at Valley Forge; and they are better clad and more healthy, than they have ever been since the formation of the army. Mrs. Washington is now with me, and makes a cordial tender of her regards to you . . . we respectively wish to have them conveyed to your amiable lady." Then, as if he had lifted a great weight from his shoulders, Washington ended his letter, "I have now complied with your request in writing a long letter, and I shall only add, that, with the purest sentiments of attachments, and the warmest friendship and regard, I am, my dear Marquis, your most affectionate and obliged, & c.

"P.S. All the other officers of my staff unite most cordially in offering you their sincere compliments."

Before Washington could dispatch his letter, two of Lafayette's letters arrived, and he added a second, uncharacteristically emotional postscript: "I must again thank you, my dear friend, for the numerous sentiments of affection which breath so conspicuously in your last farewell, and to assure you that I shall always retain a warm and grateful remembrance of it."[18]

To Lafayette's consternation, what he called "the economy and timidity of French ministers" suddenly annulled plans to raid the English coast. The government ordered him to take command of his regiment of King's Dragoons, in Saintes—about as far from Jones's fleet as he could go—in southwestern France, twenty miles inland from the Bay of Biscay. Lafayette was distraught. The transfer seemed to signal the end of French support for the American Revolution and his role as France's link to America. He saw his new post as nothing less than exile from the seat of government—and from his wife, his family, and the public eye. His departure devastated Adrienne, who was pregnant again and, as before, faced the birth of her child far from her husband.

Lafayette wrote to Jones: "I am only to tell you, my good friend, how sorry I feel not to be a witness of your success, ability and glory . . . nothing could please me more than the pleasure of having again something of the kind to undertake with such an officer as Captain Jones."[19] Jones was as distraught as Lafayette and demanded an explanation from Versailles. Instead, he received orders of his own to sail his little fleet southward into the Bay of Biscay and help chase the enemy's vessels from the area.

What neither Jones nor Lafayette could know was that far from abandoning the Lafayette plan to raid the English coast, the French government was planning to expand it to a full-scale invasion. Lafayette's cunning old friend the comte de Broglie and his brother the maréchal were already massing troops along the Normandy coast, but the French fleet was too small to clear the English Channel of British ships and permit the invasion force to cross unmolested. Vergennes convinced Spain to declare war on England and send an armada to complement the French fleet, and once the Spanish fleet arrived, the combined armada of more than one hundred ships would clear the channel.

When Lafayette learned that his "exile" was part of a broader plan, he whipped his regiment into shape and unsheathed his indefatigable pen to press for a key role in the landings. "Don't forget," he wrote to Vergennes, "that I love the trade of war passionately, that I consider myself born especially to play that game, that I have been spoiled for two years by the habit of having been in command and of winning great confidence. . . . After all that, Monsieur le Comte . . . judge whether I have the right to be the first to reach that shore and the first to plant the French flag in the heart of that insolent nation."[20]

Lafayette grew restless waiting for a reply. He wrote two enormous letters—more tomes than letters: one to Congress, the other to George Washington. He missed America and disarmed members of Congress by writing of his "unabounded affection and gratitude which I shall ever feel for them. So deeply are those sentiments engravn on my heart, that I every day lament the distance which separates me from them, and that nothing was ever so warmly and passionately wished for, as to return again to that country of which I shall ever consider myself as a citizen; there is no pleasure to be enjoyed which could equal this, of finding myself among that free and liberal nation, by whose affection and confidence I am so highly honored; to fight again with those brother soldiers of mine." He promised that "the affairs of America I shall ever look upon as my first business whilst I am in Europe. . . . If congress believe that my influence may serve them . . . I beg they will direct such orders to me." He went on to describe the military and political situation in France, before changing the tone of his letter to that of someone writing a personal note to close friends or relatives. He recounted his reunion with his wife and family in France: "Happy, in the sight of my friends and family, after I was, by your attentive goodness, safely brought to my native shore, I met there with such an honourable reception, with such kind sentiments, as by far exceeded any wishes I durst have conceived . . . and to the letter congress was pleased to write on my account, I owe the many favours the king has conferred on me . . . every thing I could have wished, I have received on account of your kind recommendations."[21]

In an even longer letter to Washington, he touched on the increasing disputes between the American states. "For God's sake," he pleaded, "prevent their loudly disputing together. Nothing hurts so much the interest and reputation of America as to hear of their intestine quarrels." Most of his tome was a deeply personal letter, however—from a son to his father:

> I ardently wish I might be near you. . . . Be so kind, my dear general, as to present my best respects to your lady, and tell her how happy I should feel to present them myself to her at her own house. I have a wife, my dear general, who is in love with you, and her affection for you seems to me to be so well justified that I cannot oppose myself to that sentiment of hers. She begs you will receive her compliments and make them acceptable to Mrs. Washington. I hope, my dear general, you will come to see us in Europe. . . . All Europe wants to see you so much, my dear general, that you cannot refuse them that pleasure. . . . I beg you will present my best compliments to your family, and remind them of my tender affection for them all. Be so kind, also, to present my compliments to the general officers, to all the officers of the army, to every one, from the first major-general to the last soldier.
>
> I earnestly entreat you, my dear general, to let me hear from you. Write me how you do, how things are going on. . . . Adieu, my dear general.[22]

The following morning he added a postscript: "I have just received, my dear general, an express from court, with orders to repair immediately to Versailles. There I am to meet M. le Comte de Vaux, Lieutenant-General, who is appointed to the command of troops intended for an expedition. . . . The necessity of setting off immediately prevents my writing to General Greene, to the gentlemen of your family, and other friends of mine in the army. . . . Farewell, my dear general, and let our mutual affection last forever."[23]

The government appointed Lafayette to the command staff of a 30,000-man army that would invade Britain as soon as the Spanish armada arrived. He was to go ashore with the vanguard of grenadiers, await his regiment of dragoons, and lead them into battle.

He spent the next ten days riding back and forth along the twelve-mile route between Versailles and Paris—his daylight hours at the palace with ministers and generals, his evenings with his wife, his family, and often with Benjamin Franklin. Franklin invited Lafayette and his wife to be guests of honor at an Independence Day celebration at his embassy-home in Passy, where he planned to unveil a portrait of Washington. By July 4, however,

Lafayette had left for Le Havre, and Adrienne, still nineteen, emerged from the shadows of her family—and her own shyness—to assume the role of statesman's wife. "Imagine Kindliness and Love and Virtue in one person met," wrote a poet who attended the ceremony.[24]

At Le Havre, Lafayette and the French army scanned the horizon impatiently for the French-Spanish armada under French admiral comte d'Orvilliers. When no sails came into sight after a month, Lafayette grew skeptical about the enterprise. With his "blood in fermentation," he wrote to Vergennes to state the obvious: "We hear nothing of M. d'Orvilliers." Lafayette longed for action, and, in the double negatives that typified French diplomatic language, he told the foreign minister that "if my presence would be less useless [in America] than it is here, I would be willing to go over on an American frigate, which I will take on my own authority, with the justification of rejoining the army in which I served." The impatient Lafayette then made a proposal—indeed, *the* proposal—that would determine the fate of the American Revolution. In one of the most important documents in the history of the American Revolution, he urged the French government to send a massive naval and military force to the United States for the campaign of 1780, to "restore vigor to the American army" and end the Revolutionary War decisively.[25]

The French-Spanish armada did not reach the entrance to the English Channel until mid-August, six weeks late, its crews decimated by smallpox. Wind, fog, and storms had combined with administrative incompetence to strip the expedition of any element of surprise. A few French ships tried blockading the British port of Plymouth, but a huge storm blew them out of the Channel, and when they returned, a small, swift British flotilla blocked their passage. When the French moved to engage the British, the fleet British boats all but flew away along a broad, endless, circular route that left them maddeningly out of reach of the big French guns. Days passed, with the French ships lumbering through the waves in vain pursuit of the speedy British boats, while Lafayette and the French army sat helplessly on the French coast awaiting a decisive naval victory that would permit them to cross the channel and invade.

While France and England waited, Benjamin Franklin's grandson showed up at Lafayette's headquarters with the magnificent sword Congress had asked Franklin to have made as a gift from the United States. Franklin had hired "the best artists in Paris," and their work proved remarkable—extraordinary—with a gold handle and intricately carved mottoes, coats of arms, and engraved scenes from four of the battles in which Lafayette had participated in America. On one side of the blade, an engraving showed a young warrior, Lafayette, dealing a death blow to the British lion; on the other, America, released from her chains, hands the young warrior an olive branch.

Franklin was sick and could not present it to Lafayette himself, but sent this note with his grandson: "Sir,—The Congress, sensible of your merit towards the United States, but unable to reward it, determined to present you with a sword, as a small mark of their grateful acknowledgment . . . of your bravery and conduct . . . the sense we have of your worth, and our obligations to you."[26]

Lafayette and Franklin's grandson became fast friends, with the latter intent on serving as Lafayette's aide in the invasion of Britain. Lafayette agreed, but, before young Franklin could even suit up for battle, the approach of the dangerous September storm season forced the exhausted French navy to abandon its hopeless, humiliating chase and put into safe harbor on the French coast. The French invasion ended without a single French soldier setting foot on British shores or firing a shot.

"To grieve in silence is the role that I have assigned myself," Lafayette wrote to Vergennes, before sending a plaintiff letter to his hero in America. "How unhappy I am to find myself so far from you," he wrote to Washington. He described his "sorrow" in not fulfilling "the hope I entertained of being here more useful to the United States. . . . Oh! my dear general, how happy I should be to embrace you again!" He signed the letter with "such affection as is above all expressions any language may furnish."[27]

The channel campaign did not end without at least one success. To the humiliation of French naval commanders, however, it was the work of freebooter John Paul Jones, who had refitted a decrepit French ship, crammed forty-two guns on deck, and renamed it *Bonhomme Richard*, to honor Benjamin Franklin, the pseudonymous author of *Poor Richard's Almanac*. Accompanied by another American ship and two French ships, he attacked the forty-four-gun *Serapis* off the east coast of England. After the British got the best of Jones in early exchanges, they demanded his surrender—to which he replied, "I have not yet begun to fight."[28] American marksmen in the rigging then strafed the deck of the *Serapis*, and, after a grenade touched off a powder explosion on the gun deck, the mainmast toppled and left her no choice but surrender. With the *Bonhomme Richard* in flames and about to sink, Jones transferred his 237-man crew, half of them casualties, onto the *Serapis* and sailed it to France, reaching port on October 6.

While Lafayette cheered and the French naval command pouted over Jones's success, French admiral d'Estaing's fleet returned to the American coast, determined to avenge his dismal performance at Newport the previous year. Over the summer, he had captured St. Vincent and St. Lucia from the British and sailed north to dislodge them from Savannah, Georgia, and open French trade routes to America. While 1,400 American troops under General Lincoln approached from the land, d'Estaing's fleet besieged the city from the mouth of the Savannah River. D'Estaing grew impatient with the progress of the siege, however, and landed his marines prematurely. He lost

Cartoon of French admiral d'Estaing in the English press, following his humiliating attempt to defeat the British at Savannah, Georgia, at the end of 1779. (*Réunion des Musées Nationaux.*)

700 men, including the heroic Polish Patriot, Pulaski. After suffering a wound himself, he escaped to his ship and ordered the fleet to sail away, once again abandoning Americans on shore as he had done in Newport. His sally left British and loyalist forces more firmly in control of the South than before and made him the subject of satiric cartoons in the American and English press for months thereafter. Unlike Sullivan at Newport, General Lincoln rushed to d'Estaing's defense, writing to Congress that the French leader had displayed "bravery in personally leading his men ashore, fearlessly leading them into the fray, and spilling his blood for us."[29]

Upset by d'Estaing's repeated failure to coordinate battle plans with American forces, Lafayette sought to counter growing anti-French feelings in America by bringing to fruition his original scheme to lead a huge French expeditionary force across the Atlantic the following spring. A letter from George Washington, written before the Savannah disaster, only served to increase his resolve. In one of his longest, most beautiful, and most emotional letters, Washington told Lafayette:

> My dear friend, let me congratulate you on your new, honourable, and pleasing appointment in the army . . . which I shall accompany with an assurance that none can do it with more warmth of affection, or sincere

joy, than myself. Your forward zeal in the cause of liberty; your singular attachment to this infant world; your ardent and persevering efforts, not only in America, but since your return to France, to serve the United States; your polite attention to Americans, and your strict uniform friendship for me, have ripened first impressions of esteem and attachment which I imbibed for you into such perfect love and gratitude, as neither time nor absence can impair. This will warrant my assurance that, whether in the character of an officer at the head of a corps of gallant Frenchmen . . . whether as a major-general, commanding a division of the American army; or whether, after our swords and spears have given place to ploughshare and pruning-hook, I see you as a private gentleman, a friend and companion, I shall welcome you with all the warmth of friendship to Columbia's shores; and, in the latter case, to my rural cottage, where homely fare and a cordial reception shall be substituted for delicacies and costly living. This, from past experience, I know you can submit to; and if the lovely partner of your happiness will consent to participate with us in such rural entertainment and amusements, I can undertake, in behalf of Mrs. Washington, that she will do everything in her power to make Virginia agreeable to the Marchioness. My inclination and endeavors to do this cannot be doubted, when I assure you that I love everybody that is dear to you, and, consequently, participate in the pleasure you feel in the prospect of again becoming a parent; and do most sincerely congratulate you and your lady on this fresh pledge she is about to give you of her love.[30]

Washington, who seldom wrote letters longer than a single page, went on and on, page after page, recounting every detail of the entire summer's campaign. And then the usually restrained commander in chief unleashed a brand of humor and playfulness he seldom displayed:

But to conclude—you requested from me a long letter. I have given you one. But methinks, my dear Marquis, I hear you say there is reason in all things—and this is too long. I am clearly in sentiment with you & will have mercy on you in my next. But at present must pray your patience a while longer, till I can make a tender of my most respectful compliments to the Marchioness. Tell her (if you have not made a mistake, & offered your *own love* instead of *hers* to me) that I have a heart susceptible of the tenderest passion, & that it is already so strongly impressed with the most favourable ideas of her, that she must be cautious of putting love's torch to it; as you must be in fanning the flame. But here again methinks I hear you say, I am not apprehensive of danger—my wife is young—you are growing old & the Atlantic is between you. All this is true, but you know my good friend that no distance can keep *anxious* lovers long asunder, and that the wonders of former ages may be revived in this. But alas! Will you not remark that amidst all the wonders recorded in holy writ no instance can be produced where a young woman from *real inclination* has preferred an old man. This is much against me that I shall not be able *I fear* to contest the prize with you. Yet, under the encouragement you have given me I shall enter the list for so inestimable a jewell.

I will not reverse the scene, & inform you, that Mrs. Washington . . . often in her letters to me, enquired if I had heard from you, and will be much pleased at hearing that you are well, & happy. In her name (as she is not here) I thank you for your polite attention to her—and shall speak her sense of honor conferred on her by the Marchioness.

When I look back to the length of this letter I am so much astonished & frightened at it myself, that I have not the courage to give it a careful reading for the purpose of correction. You must therefore receive it with all its imperfections—accompanied with this assurance that though there may be many incorrections in the letter, there is not a single defect in the friendship of my dear Marquis, Yr. most obedt. & affecte. servt.

G. Washington.[31]

As he gave his letter for Lafayette to the French ambassador to send to France, Washington said, "I do not know a nobler, finer soul, and I love him as my own son."[32]

Washington's loving letter arrived on Christmas Eve, as Adrienne was giving birth to their third child. To Lafayette's joy—and that of both the Marquis de Noailles and the duc d'Ayen—the new arrival was a boy, the first of his generation to survive in either the Lafayette or Noailles families. "Accept my congratulations, Monsieur le Marquis," Adrienne wrote rather icily to her husband at his army camp. "They are entirely sincere and heart-felt. America will put up illuminations, and I believe Paris should do the same. The number of those who resemble you is so rare that an increase in their number will be of public benefit." She opined that, with the birth of her son, her grandfather, the maréchal de Noailles, could no longer complain that "we only give him daughters." Although she offered sarcastic recognition of her husband's many responsibilities in the military, she scolded him for not being with her and their newborn. "The [joys] of paternity are so sweet, surrender yourself to them, you will find only goodness in them."[33] Lafayette got the message and rushed to her side. They agreed to name their son George Washington. Excited and so flustered that he lost his command of English, he wrote to Franklin to send the news to America as quickly as possible.

Paris 24h. December at
two o'clock in the morning

Dear Sir

I don't loose time in informing You that Mde. de Lafayette is happily deliver'd of a son, and too much depend on your friendship not to be certain that you will be pleas'd with the intelligence. The Boy shall be call'd *George,* and you will easely gess that he bears that Name as a tribute of Respect and love for my dear friend Gal. Washington.[34]

Although the baby's full name at baptism grew to Georges-Louis-Gilbert-Washington du Motier, marquis de La Fayette, the younger Lafayette would always call himself and be called George-Washington Lafayette, and his American namesake happily became his caring godfather.

After the Christmas season, neither the love of his wife nor the joys of paternity could restrain Lafayette's passion to do battle for his adopted country and adoptive father. He rained letters on the palace at Versailles, visited incessantly, alone, or with Franklin or Adams, offering plan after plan to send arms, ships, clothing, financial aid, and huge military expeditions to assure American victory and bring England to her knees. By late January, his ubiquitous presence, enthusiasm, confidence, and disinterested patriotism—his willingness to sacrifice his own fortune, if necessary—convinced Prime Minister Maurepas and other cabinet ministers that the expedition would succeed. By then, Lafayette had perfected his skills as a diplomat. He cited confidential reports from "Lieutenant Colonel Hamilton, who, with the full confidence of his general, my prudent friend [Washington], has sent me his opinions, which he knew I would not misinterpret." After reminding Maurepas of the recent French humiliations, he offered the prime minister a solution: "The miscarriage of our great preparations in Europe, the defeat at Savannah . . . are events that will affect the credibility of France and the credit of America. . . . Only by forcing the enemy to concentrate its forces in New York can we prevent total ruin of [American] trade, devastation of coastal cities by British squadrons, a *very dangerous expansion* of British control in the southern states." Hinting at Maurepas's worst fear—that the British would ultimately overrun the French West Indies—Lafayette proposed sending a fleet of "six ships of 64 and 50 guns, 8,000 tons of transport ships . . . four full-strength battalions [about 4,000 men] to which their grenadiers would be attached. . . . I will tell you frankly that we are losing precious time, and that military preparations should already have begun. They must arrive early in spring, and what would be effective in May will not have the same effect if we delay its execution. We have to count on a two months crossing and, therefore, we must be ready to leave at the end of February, we must write to America in two weeks, and I would like to see active preparations begin in four days."[35]

To avoid conflicts between French and American commanders, he told Vergennes, "I think it would be best to give me the corps." He said his commission "is not only a military and political, but also a social matter. . . . The corps must consider itself a division of [the American] army; its commander must abjure all pretensions [and] think of himself an American major-general, and execute, in all respects, the orders of General Washington."[36]

Maurepas, Vergennes, and the other ministers approved Lafayette's plan, even pledging 6,000 instead of 4,000 troops, and agreeing to send clothing and 15,000 muskets to the American army. Maurepas and Vergennes opened discussions with Franklin for new loans to the United States. Only the proposal that Lafayette command the force himself met with rejection. Both ministers agreed that veteran French officers with higher ranks and more battle experience would resent the appointment, and they named the veteran Jean-Baptiste-Donatien de Vimeur, comte de Rochambeau, to lead the force. A major general for nineteen years, the fifty-five-year-old soldier had fought in the Seven Years' War and was a brigadier general before Lafayette was born. To avoid misunderstandings between American and French forces, the ministers agreed to place Rochambeau under Washington's orders, although they promoted him to lieutenant general, a rank that did not exist in the American army, and placed him above all American officers except Washington. Similarly, the minister of the navy agreed to place the French fleet under Washington's orders. To exploit Lafayette's popularity, the ministry ordered him to sail to America on March 5, in advance of the expedition. "M. le Marquis de la Fayette," said his orders, "will hasten to join General Washington, to whom he will announce under the bond of secrecy that the king, who desires to give the United States a new proof of his affection and of his interest in their welfare, has decided to send . . . six ships of the line and six thousand infantrymen early in spring."[37]

Lafayette was to rejoin Washington, resume his command as an American major general, and serve as liaison between Washington and Rochambeau. Ironically, in adopting Lafayette's recommendation that Rochambeau report to Washington, the French government gave Washington his first independent authority over a major fighting force. Henceforth, he would no longer have to obtain congressional approval to move his forces and choose his battleground. The independence of command that Lafayette obtained for him in France would prove a key to victory.

John Adams wrote ecstatically to Henry Laurens in Congress: "There is armament preparing with the greatest expedition . . . and to consist of eight or ten ships of the line and frigates . . . with several thousand men; all numbers are mentioned from six to ten thousand. . . . Thus, the French are likely to be drawn into the American seas in sufficient force, where they have great advantages in carrying out the war."[38]

On February 29, Lafayette resumed his role as an American major general, and, dressed in his blue, white, and gold uniform, rode to Versailles to take formal leave of his monarch, King Louis XVI, and of Queen Marie-Antoinette. It was a far different departure from the furtive one three years earlier; he would now sail on the king's frigate, with the monarch's blessing and the queen's confidence in his success.

His work done, Lafayette stopped in Passy to see Franklin before returning to Paris. In but a year, he had re-established his position at home as a loyal subject and officer of the king; he had acquired a position at court as a skilled negotiator and diplomat; he had shaped government policy and military strategy; he had assumed command of the king's dragoons; and he had paved the way for Franklin to obtain additional French loans to the bankrupt American government. Franklin sent a letter of warm recommendation to Washington, citing Lafayette's "modesty" and "zeal for the honour of our country, his activity in our affairs here, and his firm attachment to our cause and to you."[39] And to Congress, Franklin wrote, "The Marquis de La Fayette, who during his residence in France has been extremely zealous in supporting our cause on all occasions, returns again to fight for it. He is infinitely esteemed and beloved here, and I am persuaded will do everything in his power to merit a continuance of the same affection from America."[40] Franklin recognized that without Lafayette he would never have obtained the French financial and military aid to save the revolution.

Lafayette spent his last few days in France in the warm intimacy of his wife and babies. He drew closer to Adrienne than ever before, even giving her power of attorney—unusual for a woman—to direct his financial affairs and ordering the stewards of his huge estate to accept Adrienne's decisions as his own. Lafayette dismayed the steward of his banking affairs by demanding 120,000 livres—about $1.2 million in today's currency—to equip an entire American division. The steward warned the marquis he was purchasing glory at the expense of his fortune, but Lafayette replied that glory was beyond price, and Adrienne agreed.[41]

On Monday, March 6, Lafayette separated himself from Adrienne's embrace and left Paris for the port of Rochefort, to sail to America. The separation devastated Adrienne, who took two weeks to recover. "The grief my mother experienced," daughter Virginie wrote later, "was far worse than when he had left her the first time. The enchanting moments they had spent together, coupled with anxieties for his safety, intensified her sadness. She was nineteen by then, and her sensitivities had matured and deepened; she had developed a deeper, more serious trust, intimately tied to his beliefs and ambitions; her heart embraced his judgment."[42]

As Adrienne's love intensified, Lafayette's heart beat reciprocally. All but devastated by her despondency at their separation, he wrote to her later that morning: "I have stopped here, sweetheart, to tell you how sad I am at leaving you, how much I love you, how much my happiness depends on you, and how moved I am by your anguish over my leaving. Oh, my dearest sweetheart, well though I thought I knew my feelings for you, I could never have imagined that leaving you would hurt me so or that our parting would prove so cruel! Love me, take care of yourself, and believe that I love you to distraction."[43]

On April 27, the frigate *Hermione* reached Marblehead, Massachusetts, and an excited young major general jumped ashore to scribble a quick message and shout for a courier to carry it overland at a gallop: "Here I am, my dear general, and, in the midst of the joy I feel in finding myself again one of your loving soldiers, I take but the time to tell you that I came from France on board a frigate which the king gave me for my passage. I have affairs of the utmost importance which I should at first communicate to you alone. In case my letter finds you anywhere this side of Philadelphia, I beg you will wait for me, and do assure you a great public good may be derived from it. To-morrow we go up to the town, and the day after I shall set off in my usual way to join my beloved and respected friend and general.

"Adieu, my dear general; you will easily know the hand of your young soldier."[44]

8

The Traitor and the Spy

MARTHA AND GEORGE WASHINGTON fluttered and flittered and fussed about the house like nervous schoolgirls awaiting their first suitor's knock at the door. They had spent a miserable winter—the coldest in memory—in Morristown, New Jersey, but spring sunshine held their house there in its warm embrace when a courier galloped to the door with the joyful news that "our Marquis has returned" to America.

"My Dear Marquis," Washington wrote excitedly. "Your welcome favour of the 27th came to my hands yesterday. I received it with all the joy that sincerest friendship would dictate, and with that impatience which an ardent desire to see you could not fail to inspire. I am sorry I do not know your route through the State of New York, that I might with certainty send a small party of horse, all I have at this place, to meet and escort you safely through the Tory settlements. At all events, Major Gibbs will go as far as Compton, where the roads unite, to meet you. . . . I most sincerely congratulate you on your safe arrival in America, and shall embrace you with all the warmth of an affectionate friend, when you come to head-quarters, where a bed is prepared for you. Adieu till we meet."[1]

Lafayette's return was the first good news the Washingtons—and other Patriot leaders—had received in months. The winter of 1780 had crushed the resolve of the American army and its hopes for success in the Revolution. Howling blizzards had whipped the winter quarters at Morristown, ripping tents from their stakes and all but smothering the soldiers beneath blankets of snow. "The snow on the ground is about two feet deep and the weather extremely cold," lamented Dr. James Thacher, a Massachusetts surgeon who had served with the Continental army since Bunker Hill. "The

112

soldiers are destitute of both tents and blankets and some of them are actually barefoot and almost naked."[2] Making matters worse was the refusal of pro-British loyalists to proffer food and other provisions to the army. Even Patriot farmers rejected the worthless paper currency—the "Continentals"— that Congress printed. After shortages shrank troop rations to one-eighth their daily needs, Quartermaster General Nathanael Greene bemoaned, "Poor fellows! They exhibit a picture truly distressing—more than half-naked and two-thirds starved. A country overflowing with plenty are now suffering an Army, employed for the defence of everything that is dear and valuable, to perish for want of food." At Greene's request, Washington pleaded for food and clothing from New Jersey authorities, writing that his soldiers were "without bread or meat . . . almost perishing for want . . . eating every kind of horse food but hay."[3] Many turned to plunder to survive; others simply deserted.

On February 1, 1780, the British fleet had laid siege to Charleston, South Carolina, while a 14,000-man British army surrounded the city by land. Washington was helpless to respond. Desertions had reduced his army in New Jersey to 6,000 troops, of whom little more than half were fit for duty, and even they were too ill-clothed and weakened by hunger and cold to go to Charleston. "The patience of the soldiery, who have endured every degree of conceivable hardship," Washington explained to Congress, "is on the point of being exhausted. . . . Drained and weakened as we already are . . . it will be impossible if not impracticable to recover; the country [is] exhausted, the people dispirited."[4]

But there was little Congress could do to relieve the army's plight. Congress was bankrupt, it had no power to tax, and the paper money it printed was worthless. Only the states could ease the nation's plight by mutual cooperation, but they were virtually independent nations, often as hostile to each other as they were to Britain.

Lafayette's arrival, therefore, brought the first ray of hope to the gloom that had enveloped America for months. No one knew his mission, but to every American, soldier and civilian alike, as well as to the Washingtons, he was a knight in shining armor from the chivalric past, come to save the nation. He glowed with enthusiasm, courage, and love of country; his was a unifying presence whose aura enveloped and bound them in common cause.

The *Hermione* fired the customary thirteen-gun salute to the United States as it sailed into Boston Harbor, and the harbor fort boomed its thirteen-gun response, arousing the entire city. Before boarding the ship at Marblehead, the pilot had sent advance notice of Lafayette's coming, and, when the guns announced his arrival, church bells pealed their welcome across the city. As the *Hermione* crossed the harbor and eased along the slip at Hancock Wharf, Governor John Hancock and Congressman Samuel Adams stood with the city's most prominent citizens and highest-ranking army officers to greet him, along with a huge crowd and several bands.

"I am embarrassed to describe the details of my arrival in Boston," Lafayette wrote to Adrienne, "because relating the acts of recognition they gave me may seem pompous. They welcomed me with cannon shots and a cheering crowd surrounded me as I stepped ashore. They escorted me in triumph to [Governor Hancock's] house. . . . A deputation asked that I appear at the State House, and I tried to remember my English during the hour I was there."[5] That evening, a huge, happy crowd gathered at Hancock House on the crest of Beacon Hill, where Lafayette spent his first night. On the Common below, joyous celebrants set off fireworks, lit a huge bonfire, and exploded in cheers that drew him onto the balcony to address them. The celebration lasted until midnight, only to begin again the following day, the first of four consecutive days of celebration and banqueting.

On May 2, when he prepared to leave, "All the people gathered in front of the house to await my departure," he wrote to Adrienne, "and there was no expression of love and affection that the crowd did not give me as they escorted me out of the city. Everywhere I've been, cannons have greeted my arrival and my departure; the principal citizens ride alongside on horseback to escort me; in short, sweetheart, my reception here is greater than anything I can describe."[6]

On May 10, he reached Morristown with an escorting cavalcade of cheering officers and soldiers, among them his beaming friend, Lieutenant Colonel Alexander Hamilton. Washington's "eyes filled with tears of joy . . . a certain proof of a truly paternal love."[7]

"After the first pleasure of meeting was over, General Washington and I retired into a private room to talk over the state of affairs. The condition of the army was very bad; there was no money, it had become impossible to recruit troops; in short, some special news was needed to re-energize the different States and the army. It was then that I told the commander-in-chief what had been arranged [in Versailles] and the help he could now expect."[8]

After an afternoon and evening in private together, the two spent the next three days plotting strategy with Washington's top commanders, all of them visibly elated at the prospects of a huge French force joining their withered army. At Washington's suggestion, Lafayette and his friend Hamilton spent a half day planning details for receiving the French—French flags on shore to signal it was safe to land; medical teams to treat troops beset by scurvy, dysentery, and other diseases after the long sea voyage; and a chain of express riders to relay messages from Washington's headquarters to the French camp. They also used some of Lafayette's cash to establish a network of spies behind British lines.

Washington recognized that the French force by itself would not ensure the revolution's success if the states did not provide troops, arms, and other supplies to rebuild the Continental army. Although Congress could not raise an army or levy taxes, its members were influential state leaders who, if Lafayette could convince them, might persuade their state governors and legislatures to act. Without such action, Washington wrote to Congress, "it will be impossible for us to undertake the intended cooperation [with the French army] with any reasonable prospect of success . . . the succor designed for our benefit will prove a serious misfortune. . . . The court of France has done so much for us, that we must make a decisive effort on our part."[9]

Knowing the affection members of Congress felt for Lafayette, Washington sent the young man to deliver his message in Philadelphia. As Washington had anticipated, Congress gave Lafayette an enthusiastic reception and a unanimous resolution welcoming his return to America. But it refused to respond to Washington's requests for aid—and paid dearly for its refusal when British troops swarmed into Charleston and captured General Lincoln and his entire 5,000-man army. It was the worst American defeat of the war—made more so by the pointed humiliation of Lincoln and his troops after the surrender. Instead of permitting the Americans to parade with honor at surrender, the British ordered them to stack their arms silently and choose either imprisonment or parole under a pledge to take no further part in the war and return to their homes as loyal British subjects.

Worse news followed. In mid-June, 1780, Horatio Gates, the so-called hero of Saratoga, took command of the Southern Department and, against the advice of baron de Kalb, sent 3,000 untrained Patriot troops to Camden, South Carolina, to face Lord Cornwallis's legendary British cavalry. The British sliced through the American lines and sent the Patriots fleeing in panic—except for Kalb's contingent of infantrymen on the right flank. At Gates's insistence, Kalb ordered his men to hold fast. Infuriated by their audacity at refusing the option to withdraw, Colonel Banastre Tarleton ordered horse troops to slaughter the stubborn Americans. The ensuing massacre left nearly 900 Patriots dead. Among the last to fall was the gigantic Kalb, Lafayette's old friend. After his wounded horse collapsed beneath him, Kalb slashed wildly at the piercing thrusts of British bayonets until, finally, a series of blows to the head by enemy rifle butts sent the great soldier of fortune to his knees. A few more stabs assured his end in the South Carolina muck. Kalb had come to America plotting Washington's overthrow and met his end loyally defending him.

The slaughter did not end, however. The savage Tarleton saw terror as the surest strategy for ending the American uprising and ordered the massacre of hundreds more American soldiers, even as they attempted to surrender. About 1,000 others escaped death only by surrendering to the more chivalrous Cornwallis. In fashioning the most brutal and disheartening engagement of the war, Tarleton stripped Horatio Gates of his aura of invincibility and showed the South the consequences of resisting British rule.

With the 8,000-man Cornwallis army in firm control of South Carolina and Georgia, and Gates limping northward into North Carolina, Sir Henry Clinton sailed his 6,000 troops back to New York in anticipation of an attack by the French armada. To further bolster British defenses, Clinton ordered the 6,000-man force at Newport to abandon Rhode Island and regroup in New York.

At Washington's urging, and with Alexander Hamilton at his side to edit his prose and spelling, Lafayette began cashing in some of the goodwill he had accumulated among state leaders to persuade them to provide more troops and supplies. He sent an emotional appeal to James Bowdoin of Massachusetts, saying, "I love America, and I love our cause."[10] To Samuel Adams, who had greeted him so enthusiastically in Boston, he wrote that "all Europe have theyr Eyes upon us . . . I would feel most unhappy and distress'd was I to tell the people that are coming over full of ardour and Sanguine hopes, that we have no army to cooperate with them, No provisions to feed the few soldiers who are left & c. & c. But I hope, My dear Sir, it will not be the Case, and More particularly depending on the Exertions of your State, *I know Mr. Samuel Adams's influence* and popularity will be as heretofore Employ'd to the Salvation and glory of America."[11]

The following day, he sent much the same message to Joseph Reed, the president of the Pennsylvania Supreme Executive Council—in effect, the governor of that state:

> These people are coming, my good friend, full of ardour and sanguine hopes. . . . The world is looking on us. . . . It is from me, on the moment of their arrival, that the French generals expect intelligence. . . . Shall I be obliged to confess our inability, and what shall be my feelings on the occasion, not only as an American and American soldier, but also as one that has highly boasted in Europe of the spirit, the virtue, the resources of America. . . .
>
> We have men, my dear sir, we have provisions, we have everything that is wanted, provided the country is awakened and its resources are brought forth. That, you know, can't be done by Congress, and unless the States take the whole matter upon themselves, we are lost. You will, both as a soldier and a politician, easily foresee that the crisis is . . . a decisive one, and that if proper exertions are made, we may expect everything good.[12]

Then it was the turn of New York governor George Clinton, who was unrelated to British general Henry Clinton: "How unhappy I shall be," Lafayette wrote to Clinton, "for to me they will look for an answer, I am obliged to confess to the people who are coming in sanguine hopes . . . to all the world, to confess the inability of America."[13]

The letters had immediate and dramatic effects, with all recipients assuring him—and Washington—they would provide arms, ammunition, clothing, and food, and draft enough soldiers to double the Continental army to 15,000 men. In Philadelphia, Joseph Reed's wife, Esther, organized a fund to clothe soldiers, to which Lafayette sent one hundred livres—equivalent to about $1,000 in today's currency—as a contribution in Adrienne's name, saying she was "heartly [sic] wishing for a personal acquaintance with the ladies of America" and that she "would feel particularly happy to be admitted among them on the present occasion."[14]

On July 10, 1780, the French fleet sailed into Newport—and immediately dashed American hopes for victory that summer. The French government failed to fulfill its pledges to Franklin and Lafayette: the fleet was smaller than expected and would not give the Americans the necessary superiority to attack New York or Charleston. The French had not sent the daring John Paul Jones to raid British coastal shipping—or the promised arms and ammunition (and clothing) for the American army. Instead of 6,000 troops, Admiral Rochambeau brought only 5,000, of whom 2,000 were ill and unfit for service. With 1,300 sailors equally sick and unfit, another French military expedition had obviously deteriorated into a costly and useless adventure. The American Revolution once again seemed doomed.

Washington sent Lafayette up to Newport to see Rochambeau and Chevalier de Ternay, the admiral of the French fleet. "As a general officer," Washington wrote of Lafayette, "I have the greatest confidence in him; as a friend he is perfectly acquainted with my sentiments and opinions; he knows all the circumstances of our army and the country at large; all the information he gives and all the propositions he makes, I entreat you will consider as coming from me."[15]

Lafayette left for Newport on July 20, stopping in Hartford, Connecticut, to elicit promises of men, money, and ammunition from Governor Jonathan Trumbull. Lafayette's mission at Newport proved far less successful—despite a joyful reunion with his brother-in-law, the vicomte de Noailles, and other young officers he had known in Metz.

The meeting with Rochambeau and de Ternay, however, was disastrous, with the French leaders announcing they would not engage the British until the king sent another division of French troops and additional ships to give the French clear superiority over the British at sea. Lafayette was furious. He argued for immediate action, pointing out that American militiamen only served for three months and that the main Continental army would lose most draftees by the end of the year. "From an intimate knowledge of our situation," he insisted, "I assure you, Sirs . . . it is important for us to act during the present campaign, that all the troops which you may expect from France next year, as well as all the projects with which you flatter yourselves, will never repair the fatal consequences of our inaction. Without American resources, all foreign assistance will accomplish nothing in this country. . . . I think it important to profit from those moments when you can get cooperation here; without it, you can do nothing for the common cause."[16]

Rochambeau, whose own son was older than Lafayette, was incensed by what he interpreted as a lecture and, still worse, a rebuke from a young subordinate. In France, Lafayette would have faced certain court-martial for addressing a superior officer with such frankness. The French commander demanded an interview with Washington, then sent this curt response to Lafayette: "As to your observation, my dear marquis, that the position of the French at Rhode Island is of no use to the Americans, I reply:—

"First, That I never heard it had been injurious to them.

"Second, That it would be well to reflect that the position of the French corps may have had something to do with Clinton's . . . [having] been obliged to confine himself to Long Island and New York; that, in short, while the French fleet is guarded here by an assembled and a superior naval force, your American shores are undisturbed, your privateers are making considerable prizes, and your maritime commerce enjoys perfect liberty. It appears to me, that, in so comfortable a situation, it is easy to await patiently the naval and land forces that the king assured me should be sent."[17] He thereupon refused any further discussions with Lafayette, insisting that he would await all further orders from "our generalissimo [Washington], and I entreat him to grant the admiral and myself an interview."[18]

Rochambeau's response stunned Lafayette. Having devoted himself for three years to cementing American relations with France, he had, in a brief moment, unwittingly threatened those relations by being too American. He had adopted the informal, easy-going, and frank—above all, frank—approach of Sullivan and other Continental Army commanders, from whom Washington expected honest battlefield appraisals. French commanders expected obsequious praise from subordinates, never criticism—no matter how high the cost in human lives. Jolted by Rochambeau's reply, Lafayette acted swiftly to repair the damage.

Calling up every resource of old-world diplomacy, he swallowed his pride and asked Rochambeau and de Ternay to "permit me . . . to accuse myself of having explained my own meaning in a very awkward manner." He pointed out, however, that Washington "had given me full powers to explain to you our situation. . . . All that I said to you, gentlemen . . . was from the reiterated orders of General Washington."[19] Lafayette then wrote a

The comte de Rochambeau, commander in chief of the French armies of North America, arrived with a fleet and landing forces smaller than the French government had promised and inadequate for engaging the British successfully. (*Réunion des Musées Nationaux.*)

personal letter to Rochambeau: "Permit me to address myself to you with the frankness born of the warm affection I have felt, and endeavoured to show you, from my earliest youth. Although your letter expresses your usual kindness for me . . . my feelings were deeply hurt by the unfavourable way you interpreted my letter. . . . If in that letter I have offended or displeased you; if, for example, you disapprove of that written account which General Washington asked for, and which I thought I ought to submit to you, I give you my word of honor that I thought I was doing a very simple thing; so simple, indeed, that I should have considered I was wronging you by not doing it." Lafayette said that Americans had become skeptical that any additional forces would arrive from France, and that newspapers were mocking the idle French force.

"If I have offended you, I ask your pardon, for two reasons; first, because I am sincerely attached to you; and secondly, because it is my earnest wish to do everything I can to please you here."[20]

Although Rochambeau was adamant in his refusal to deal with anyone but Washington, he did forgive Lafayette—in unusually warm terms that bespoke his recognition of Lafayette's stature in both the United States and

France. Moreover, Rochambeau, as much as Lafayette, was eager to avoid any rift in relations between the two countries—especially over so inconsequential a matter.

> Permit an old father, my dear marquis, to reply to you as he would to a son whom he loves tenderly and whom he holds in infinite esteem. You know me well enough to know that, at my age, when I have formed a resolution based on military reasons and the interests of the nation, I will never change my mind because of some momentary excitement or emotions. . . . Be ever convinced of my sincere affection, and that if I pointed out to you very gently what displeased me in your last dispatch, I felt at the time convinced that the warmth of your heart and soul had somewhat overheated your enthusiasm and sagacity of your judgment. Keep the last for the council chamber and reserve all of the first for the hour of action. It is still the old father Rochambeau who is speaking to his dear son Lafayette, whom he loves and will ever love and esteem until his last breath.[21]

Both men put aside—and quickly forgot—their differences and got on with the business of the Revolution. Washington bowed to French sensitivities and military tradition and agreed to deal directly with Rochambeau, and he deferred to Rochambeau's inclination to remain in Rhode Island until reinforcements arrived from France. In fact, thirty British vessels had blockaded the French port of Brest and ended any possibility of French reinforcements, while another thirteen British frigates and ships of the line sailed into New York, to make that port all but impregnable.

Without French support to launch a major offensive, Washington reorganized his forces, shifting to a defensive posture. He put the heroic general Benedict Arnold in charge of the quiet northern fortifications at West Point, an important defensive position, but far from any likely battle activity. After his daring capture of Fort Ticonderoga in 1775, Arnold suffered a crippling wound in the disastrous American assault on Quebec the following year, and his injuries left him reluctant to assume any more battlefield commands. As a result, Washington gave Lafayette command of the Light Division, a unit more likely to see battlefield action as an advanced element of the Continental army, encamped nearly fifty miles south on the west bank of the Hudson River, opposite New York.

Lafayette's division was an elite corps of about 2,000 light infantry,[22] made up of carefully selected companies from the New Hampshire, New York, Connecticut, Massachusetts, and Pennsylvania lines. He clothed them in handsome uniforms he had bought in France, along with swords, cockades, and epaulets for officers, and distinctive patches and red and black plumes for every soldier. Steuben-style drills each day transformed them into the snappiest, most distinctive unit in the northern army, renowned for their unmatched esprit de corps. Divided into two companies, under Generals Enoch Poor and Edward Hand, the Light Division had four cannon and 100 riflemen and included among its officers Lafayette's former aide Colonel Jean-Joseph Gimat and a young Virginia major, Henry Lee, who commanded the 300-man Light Horse Corps. They carried their own pennants that Lafayette had had fabricated in France, bearing the Latin motto *Ultimo Ratio*—"the final reckoning." Although the motto was new to Americans, Louis XIV had embossed all his cannons with the words *Ultimo Ratio Regum*, "the king's final reckoning," to inspire fear in the enemies of France. Lafayette bought himself an appropriate horse "of a perfect whiteness and the greatest beauty" for a knight to lead and inspire his men in battle. He was breathtaking atop his horse, leading his proud, handsomely equipped division—truly, the legendary knight of old he had always imagined himself. "They were the pride of his heart," said Dr. James Thacher, "and he was the idol of their regard."[23]

Lafayette would later recall proudly that "the affection between the members of that corps and its leader became legendary in the American army. Like the traveler who brings home presents from distant lands for family and friends, [I] had returned from France with a costly collection of ornaments for my soldiers, swords for officers and their junior officers, and banners for the battalions. This troop of chosen men, well drilled and disciplined, were easily recognized by their red and black plumes."[24]

By the end of August, however, he and they had seen no action. Like two boxers, the English and Patriot forces bobbed, weaved, and feinted in various directions, but, in the end, they stayed put. None of the supplies France had promised arrived, however, and the American army's condition deteriorated. Moreover, Congress had been unable to persuade all the states to contribute men, arms, or supplies. Congress grew so discouraged by its impotence that it talked of dissolving and ceding all authority to Washington—in effect, giving him dictatorial powers to impress soldiers and confiscate supplies and specie.

On September 17, 1780, Washington took matters into his own hands and set out by coach for Hartford, Connecticut, to meet Rochambeau. With him were Lafayette, Hamilton, Brigadier General Henry Knox, commander of artillery, a handful of aides, and a cavalry escort. The next day, they stopped to lunch with General Arnold, near West Point. Lafayette and Arnold had met—and liked each other—two years earlier at the time of the abortive Canadian invasion. After lunch, Arnold ferried Washington and the others across the Hudson before returning to his command. Washington promised to stop at West Point on his return to inspect the fortifications and dine with Arnold and his wife, the Philadelphia socialite Peggy Shippen.

Three days later, the Washington party reached Hartford, to booming cannons—thirteen rounds—and the cheers of the staunchly Patriot citizenry. Washington, Lafayette, Rochambeau, de Ternay, and French ambassador La Luzerne spent the next two days in private meetings, with Lafayette translating for Washington. By the end of the second day, they issued an unusual document, written in French, in two columns, with the left-hand column representing Rochambeau's point of view, paragraph by paragraph. Washington's answers to each point appeared in the right-hand column:

Ideas submitted to his Excellency General Washington by M. le Comte de Rochambeau and M. le Chevalier de Ternay.	Answers of General Washington
* * *	* * *
7th. The result of all these considerations is, the indispensable necessity of reinforcing the fleet and the army which are here, with ships, with men, and with money.	7th. The situation of America makes it absolutely necessary that the allies should give their vigorous support, and that His Most Christian Majesty should add to our many other obligations and to the many other proofs of his generous interest, that of assisting the United States of America by sending them more ships, more men, and more money.
Signed, Cte De Rochambeau. Le Chr De Ternay.	Signed, G. Washington.[25]

The discussions produced such complete agreement—especially on the failure of French strategists at Versailles to estimate British strength correctly—that there was no need to translate the document into English. "There was perfect understanding between the Americans and French, who seem entirely satisfied with the generalissimo [Washington]," Lafayette wrote to Adrienne after the conference. "I do not know when the troops of the two nations will be combined under his orders, but I am sure they will work together in complete harmony."[26]

Rochambeau, de Ternay, La Luzerne, and Washington agreed the Americans would need a land force of no less than 30,000 troops—10,000 of them French—to dislodge the British from New York, and a powerful fleet of no less than thirty ships of the line. La Luzerne pledged to send the agreement to Versailles with his recommendation that the French court adopt and act on it. Both the French and American commanders would keep their forces in their current positions until they received a response.

On the morning of September 25, Washington and Lafayette left for West Point to inspect the towering greystone fortress on the bluffs above the

Hudson River. As they approached, they sent word to General and Mrs. Arnold of their imminent arrival and to expect them for lunch. Lafayette described the events that followed in a letter he wrote from West Point that evening to the French Ambassador:

> When I left you yesterday morning, Monsieur le Chevalier, to come here to lunch with General Arnold, we were far from foreseeing the event I shall now describe to you. . . . West Point was sold, and it was sold by Arnold! The same who had covered himself with glory and signal services to his country recently signed a despicable pact with the enemy, and, but for our chance arrival at midday and a series of chance events that led to the fall of the adjutant-general of the British army into the hands of some [Patriot] farmers . . . West Point and the North River would probably have now been in the hands of the enemy. . . . The plan was to come up suddenly before West Point and to present all the appearance of an attack. Arnold intended to say that he had been surprised by a superior force.[27]

What Lafayette could not know was that Arnold had accepted £6,315 (about $50,000 in today's currency) from British general Henry Clinton to commit treason. Without adding the obvious—that he, Washington, and Hamilton would also have been in enemy hands—Lafayette described the rest of the day's harrowing events:

> When we left Fishkill yesterday, we were preceded by one of my aides-de-camp and General Knox's aide, who found General and Mrs. Arnold at table and who sat down to breakfast with them. During that time two letters were brought to General Arnold telling of the capture of a spy. He ordered a horse saddled, went to his wife's room and told her that he was done for, and he ordered his aide-de-camp to tell Washington that he had gone to [the village of] West Point and would return in an hour.
>
> On our arrival here, we crossed the river and went to examine the works. You can imagine our surprise when, on our return, we learned that the arrested spy was Major [John] André, adjutant-general of the English army; and that among the papers found on his person were a copy of an important council of war, the strength of the garrison and works, and observations on the means of attack and defense, all written in General Arnold's hand.
>
> We chased after Arnold, but he escaped in a boat to the English frigate *Vulture*, and, since no one suspected he was fleeing, none of the sentries thought to stop him. Colonel Hamilton, who chased after him, received soon after, under a flag of truce, a letter from Arnold to the general [Washington] giving no details to justify his treason, and an insolent letter from the English commander Robertson demanding release of the adjutant general, who had only acted with permission of General Arnold.
>
> The first concern of the general [Washington] has been to assemble at West Point the troops that Arnold had dispersed, under various pretexts [to

American general Benedict
Arnold, previously a hero,
turned traitor by accepting the
equivalent of $50,000 in current
dollars to deliver the plans of
the West Point fortifications to
the British. (*Library of Congress.*)

facilitate British capture of the fort]. We have remained here to supervise
security of the fort. . . . We have summoned additional Continental Army
troops, and since Arnold might convince Clinton to make a sudden attack,
the army has been ordered to march on a moment's notice.[28]

Arnold's treason hurt Lafayette deeply, violating every principle of
knightly chivalry that had been the foundation of his life. "I cannot describe
to you, M. le Chevalier, to what degree I am astounded by this piece of
news," Lafayette went on:

> In the course of a revolution such as ours it is natural that a few traitors
> should be found, and every conflict which resembles a civil war . . . must
> necessarily bring to light some great virtues and some great crimes. Our
> struggles have brought forward some heroes . . . [and] some great scoun-
> drels. . . . But that an Arnold, a man who . . . had given proof of talent, of
> Patriotism, and, especially, of the most brilliant courage, should at once
> destroy his very existence and should sell his country to the tyrants whom

he had fought against with glory . . . confounds and distresses me . . . humiliates me to a degree that I cannot express. I would give anything in the world if Arnold had not shared our labors with us, and if this man, whom it still pains me to call a scoundrel, had not shed his blood for the American cause. My knowledge of his personal courage led me to expect that he would decide to blow his brains out.[29]

After discovering Arnold's treason, Washington summoned Wayne and his troops to man the West Point fortifications, and he put Nathanael Greene in command. Before taking his new post, Greene convened a court-martial in the Congregational Church in Tappan, New York, on September 29, appointing Lafayette, Henry Knox, Lord Stirling, and eleven other major generals and brigadier generals to decide André's fate. They were unanimous: captured using a false name, in civilian clothes, André had acted as a spy and had no recourse to treatment as a prisoner of war. They condemned the winsome young man to death, despite pleas from locals to spare him. At noon, on October 2, 1780, they hanged him from a gibbet atop a thickly wooded hill and buried his body there, several hundred yards from the church and the sacred ground where Patriot soldiers lay buried. He was twenty-nine years old.[30]

"He was an interesting man," Lafayette wrote to Adrienne, "the confidant and friend of General Clinton; he conducted himself in such a frank, noble and honorable way that, during the three days we imprisoned him, I was foolish enough to develop a real liking for him. In strongly voting to sentence him to the gallows, I could not help regret what happened to him."[31]

9

Ride to Glory

THE HANGING OF MAJOR ANDRÉ was the most exciting event of the
1780 campaign—indeed, the only event in the Northern Department. A
few days later, Lafayette's insatiable lust for action sent him stalking the
perimeter of British positions around New York and yielded a plan for a
lightning strike at British positions on Staten Island with "Light-Horse
Harry" Lee.[1]

"We found all [Lafayette's] troops in order of battle on the heights," a
French officer recounted, "and himself at their head, expressing by his air
and countenance, that he was happier in receiving me there, than at his
estate in Auvergne. The confidence and attachment of the troops, are for
him invaluable possessions, well acquired riches, of which nobody can deprive him."[2]

A new and inexperienced quartermaster general had replaced the resourceful Nathanael Greene, however, and sent only three small craft to
carry Lafayette's Light Division across the narrow channel from Elizabethtown, New Jersey. Infuriated, Lafayette canceled the attack and led his
troops back to camp.

Fearful that inaction in the north and the Gates debacle in South Carolina would discourage further French aid to America, Lafayette pleaded
with Washington for a major strike—to end the 1780 campaign with a
Patriot victory to shore up American morale and renew the French government's faith in the American Revolution. He suggested attacking a Hessian
fort on the northern end of New York Island.

"Any enterprise will please the people of this country," he told Washington, "and shew them that when we have men we do not lie still. . . . The

French court have often complained to me of the inactivity of the American army. . . . They have often told me, your friends leave us now to fight their battles, and do no more risk themselves: it is . . . of the greatest political importance to let them know, that, on our side, we are ready to co-operate."[3]

Washington argued, "It is impossible to desire more ardently than I do to terminate the campaign by a happy stroke; but we must consult our means rather than our wishes. . . . We are to lament that there has been a misapprehension of our circumstances in Europe; but to endeavour to recover our reputation, we should take care that we do not injure it more . . . it would be imprudent to throw an army of ten thousand men upon an island against nine thousand, exclusive of seamen and militia."[4]

Although Washington planned no further activity in the north until French reinforcements arrived, he acted to salvage the debacle in the Southern Department by replacing the discredited Gates with Nathanael Greene. Greene set out immediately for North Carolina, taking with him Lieutenant Colonel "Light-Horse Harry" Lee's flying corps of horse and foot soldiers—Lee's Legion, as they were called—and General Daniel Morgan and his renowned Morgan's Raiders, who had been the victors at Saratoga. Although Horatio Gates took credit for the victory, he had sat miles away while Morgan's Raiders hid behind the trees and in the branches above as Burgoyne's unsuspecting regulars entered the forest into the murderous ambush of sniper fire that had forced their surrender. Humiliated British officers denigrated Morgan's sharpshooters as cowards for not "standing up like men to fight" in traditional battle array, but the sniper emerged from Saratoga as the Continental army's most effective new weapon.[5]

Rather than idle in northern winter quarters, Lafayette asked to join Greene. Noailles and Lafayette's officer friends at Newport were equally restless and took leave to visit his camp near Preakness, New Jersey (now Paterson), and they, too, sought to fight alongside Greene. Washington graciously entertained the dazzling array of young nobles at his table and took them to visit the West Point fortifications—but denied their requests to join Greene.

Gates's mismanagement in the south had left Greene with a mere 2,300 fighting men, and he needed troops more than officers. Those who had survived Camden were unorthodox bands of irregulars led by an eerie, unsmiling little man called the Swamp Fox—Francis Marion. Cornwallis and Tarleton had tried to crush Marion's force, but soon learned to dread him. Marion invented a new type of unorthodox battle strategy, later called guerrilla warfare: ambushing British patrols with sniper fire, then melting away into dense forests and swamps or dissolving into the local population, only to re-form and strike again; never seizing territory; only stalking, striking, slaying, and vanishing.[6] Marion avoided roads and trails; he swam his horses across deep streams to avoid the visibility of fords, and when currents were too swift, his men laid blankets across wooden bridges to deaden the sound of their horses' hooves. Using fear as well as fire to scourge Cornwallis's army, Marion sent confederates into marketplaces and taverns to whisper rumors of his omnipresence and readiness to strike. When the British responded to rumors by shifting troops from one post to strengthen another, the Swamp Fox invariably struck the weaker position.

Greene, Morgan, and Lee were quick to embrace Marion's amazingly effective strategy, which allowed a weaker force to dominate a far stronger one. With no place for traditional strategy, Greene rejected the requests of Lafayette's French officer friends to come south, although he did so in the most tactful terms in a letter to Lafayette:

> Was you to arrive, you would find a few rag[g]ed, half starved troops, in the wilderness, destitute of every thing necessary for either the comfort or convenience of soldiers: altogether without discipline, and so addicted to plundering that the utmost exertions of their officers cannot restrain them. Indeed my dear Sir the Department is in a deplorable situation; nor have I a prospect of its mending. The Country is laid waste and the Inhabitants plunder and destroy one another with little less than savage fury. We live from hand to mouth, and have nothing to subsist on but what we collect with armed parties. In this situation I believe you will agree with me, there is nothing inviting this way; especially when I assure you our whole force now fit for duty . . . dont amount to 800 men. I have made a small detachment under General Morgan . . . I give this the name of a flying army; and while its numbers are so small, and the enemy so much superior, it must literally be so.[7]

Without winter action, Lafayette took leave and went to Philadelphia, where he introduced his brother-in-law and the other French officers to Philadelphia society and guided them across the sites of his battlefield heroics at Brandywine and Barren Hill. By night they dined and danced; by day they discussed political theory with influential American political leaders and thinkers. Benjamin Franklin's American Philosophical Society elected Lafayette its first foreign member.[8]

"What is still remarkable for a young man [Lafayette's] age," wrote one of his French companions, "is the influence, the consideration he has acquired in the political, as well as military sector. I do not fear contradiction when I say, that private letters from him have frequently produced more effect upon some states than the strongest exhortations of the Congress. On seeing him, one is at a loss which most to admire, that so young a man as he should have given such eminent proofs of his talents, or that a man so tried, should give hopes of so long a career of glory."[9]

By late December, Congress had grown as anxious as Lafayette that the French might deny Rochambeau and Washington further military and naval support. Earlier in the year, the former president of Congress, Henry Laurens, had sailed to France to try to obtain such support, but the British had captured him at sea and imprisoned him for treason in the Tower of London.[10] Congress asked Lafayette to complete Laurens's mission, and, to add to its impact, the comte de Rochambeau agreed to send his son, the vicomte de Rochambeau, as his personal envoy. Lafayette refused to abandon Washington and the army again, however, and Congress sent Washington's trusted aide, Colonel John Laurens, Henry Laurens's son. Lafayette nonetheless provided strong logistical support to the mission with one of his most effective weapons: a barrage of letters to people in high places, with incontrovertible evidence that an American victory was not only possible, but ultimately in the best interests of France. He wrote to the foreign minister, to the minister of war, to Admiral d'Estaing, and to all his own, highly placed friends and relatives such as the comte de Ségur and his father-in-law, the duc d'Ayen.

Lafayette asked for money in a twelve-page letter to the marquis de Castries, his cousin, who had just been appointed minister of the navy. "Our Continental soldiers are excellent; our recruits are almost all men who have had more experience with gunfire than three quarters of the soldiers of Europe; our regular troops, as brave as any others, are more hardened, more patient, more acclimated. . . . Immense sums would be necessary to bring the same number of Frenchmen to . . . America, and they would cost very much more to maintain. . . . For the same sum we could have double the number of American regulars."[11] An even longer tome to Foreign Minister Vergennes explained the long inactivity of French and American forces: "With a naval inferiority," he declared, "it is impossible to make war in America. . . . It is physically impossible that we should carry on an offensive without ships. . . . Pecuniary succors and a naval superiority are the two most essential points. . . . Nothing of any importance has been sent us. . . . It is necessary to clothe the American army, it requires arms, and, to be able to besiege places, a great augmentation of powder."[12]

In the last of his letters, Lafayette wrote to Adrienne, to introduce Laurens. "The person who will deliver this to you, my sweetheart, is a man I care for very much and to whom I would like you to extend the warmest friendship. He is the son of president Laurens, who has just settled into the Tower of London. . . . General Washington is very fond of him; and of all the Americans whom I have sent to see you, he is the one I most particularly wish you to receive in the friendliest way. If I were in France, he should live entirely at my house, and I would introduce him to all my friends . . . and do everything in my power to assure his meeting people and spending time profitably at Versailles."[13] After three days of letter writing, Lafayette was too focused on American affairs to broach personal matters. He railed over Benedict Arnold's having "become an English general in Virginia, with a corps, which appears well pleased to serve under his orders; There is no accounting for taste."[14]

In subtle terms with which she had become familiar, he sent her information he expected her to disseminate in Paris salons and at court. "The Americans continue to show me the greatest kindness; there is no proof of affection and confidence which I do not receive each day from the army and nation. I am serving here in the most agreeable manner possible. At every campaign I command a separate flying corps, made up of chosen troops; I have developed a friendship with them that comes only after long periods of shared dangers, hardships, good and bad luck."[15]

Only in the final paragraph did Lafayette mention family matters. "Kiss our children a thousand times and a thousand times again for me; although a vagabond, their father does not feel less affectionate toward them or fail to keep them constantly in his thoughts. . . . My heart looks only to the moment when we may hold and caress them together."[16]

As winter wore on, the previous year's short rations and troop mutinies reached near-epidemic proportions. Unpaid for more than a year, with no money for food or other personal needs, 2,500 of Anthony Wayne's Pennsylvanians killed two officers and wounded several others before marching off to Philadelphia to confront Congress. Ultimately, the men won their back pay, additional clothing, and redress of other grievances, but half quit the service. Two weeks later, the New Jersey line mutinied, but by then Washington had lost patience with mutineers and ordered 600 West Point troops to crush the revolt. The West Pointers struck by surprise, overwhelmed and disarmed the mutineers, restored the officers to their command, and executed two ringleaders.

The disheartening mutinies and mass desertions combined with Benedict Arnold's invasion of Virginia to sink American spirits. Adding to Patriot pessimism was national insolvency. Congress had no money—not a sou left to spend and a national debt of nearly $200 million, which the states refused to cover with their own hoards of cash. There was little point printing more paper money: "Continentals" were worthless. Without money to pay or arm the Continental army, Congress began to debate sending a commission to negotiate terms of peace and reconciliation with England.

Late in January, however, the dismal pall over the nation lifted slightly. An excited courier arrived at Washington's headquarters: Greene's guerrillas—or, more accurately, Morgan's Raiders and Lee's Legion—had scored a stunning victory over the vaunted Colonel Banastre Tarleton, the barbaric cavalry leader at the battle of Camden. Morgan had lured the overconfident

British commander into what seemed a conventional confrontation with a line of retreating American infantry at the opposite end of a South Carolina meadow called Cowpens. As Tarleton's colossal thoroughbreds thundered across toward the terrified American troops, Morgan unleashed his infantry-men and horsemen from the surrounding forest and shrubs on Tarleton's flanks. "We made a sort of half circuit at full speed [and] came upon the rear of the British line, shouting and charging like madmen," reported one American officer. "We were in among them with the bayonets."[17] The British force panicked, their horses rearing and spinning, hooves flying, riders hurled to the ground, stumbling to their feet hysterically, and fleeing in all directions. Professionals all in traditional warfare, none had experienced guerrilla tactics. Some—the perpetrators of the Camden massacre—dropped their rifles and fell on their faces, their arms spread-eagled on the ground as they sobbed for mercy. Morgan reduced Tarleton's fearsome, thousand-man force as a factor in the campaign, killing 329 and capturing 600, at a cost of fewer than 75 American lives. "Not a man was killed, wounded or even insulted after he surrendered," Morgan boasted to Greene.[18]

Infuriated at the humiliation, Cornwallis pursued Morgan into North Carolina, where the American raider linked up with the main body of Greene's force and retreated northward into Virginia. But news of the victory sent spirits soaring at Washington's camp on the Hudson, and the commander in chief decided the time had come to act. With British forces scattered across the south in partial disarray, Washington ordered Lafayette to lead his Light Division to Virginia to join Baron von Steuben's Virginia militia in a strike at Benedict Arnold's force near Portsmouth. While Greene engaged Cornwallis in North Carolina, Lafayette and Steuben were to surround Arnold and pin him against the shore, where a French squadron would block his escape by water and force his surrender.

Washington ordered Lafayette to hang Arnold if he captured him: "You are to do no act whatever with Arnold that directly or by implication may skreen him from the punishment due to his treason and desertion, which if he should fall into your hands, you will execute in the most summary way."[19] Recognizing the enormous political consequences of the venture, Lafayette attacked his assignment with demonic energy. The vision of a French aristocrat-turned-American-republican capturing and executing an American republican-turned-British-aristocrat provoked devilish laughs as he pictured the effects on Patriot morale in America and on public sensibilities in England and France.

To disguise Lafayette's destination, Washington sent a small company to Elizabethtown, New Jersey, to set up an array of empty tents that deceived the British into believing Lafayette was planning another attack on Staten Island. As they reinforced their position, Lafayette and his men slipped to the south unseen, and, within a week, they were one hundred miles away in Trenton, New Jersey, with Lafayette charming, coaxing, and, when necessary, ordering his men to ignore fatigue and march still farther. He used the same tactics with farmers, townsmen, and local officials along the way to get food and shelter for his men. He was indefatigable—and remarkable—often riding miles ahead at full gallop to prepare the next town, then doubling back to smarten up his weary, footsore troops for a confident, heads-held-high march into town, with him in the lead, atop his great white horse, winning cheers and hospitality instead of sullen looks and locked doors.

He allowed his men two days' rest in Trenton while he rode ahead to Philadelphia, where he commandeered several hundred men from General Wayne's Pennsylvania line, along with twelve heavy cannon and six smaller ones. He obtained medicines, tools, and fifteen hundred pairs of shoes from the quartermaster general; he coaxed Congress into giving his men a month's pay in Pennsylvania currency to buy rum and other personal provisions; and he convinced French ambassador La Luzerne to give him French supplies of flour and salt pork.

At dawn on March 1, Lafayette's weary little army of twelve hundred gladly boarded boats for a restful float down the Delaware River from Trenton, past Philadelphia to Wilmington, Delaware. From there, they marched eighteen miles over two days to Head of Elk, Maryland, where they expected that a French naval squadron would sail them down Chesapeake Bay to Virginia. But to everyone's dismay, the French were nowhere in sight. A British flotilla had intercepted them, and the ensuing engagement had sent the French sailing back to Newport to lick their wounds.

No less determined to capture Arnold, Lafayette sent a message to Washington to send a second, stronger French fleet directly to Portsmouth, while he found alternative means to get his men to Virginia to rendezvous with Steuben. He then rode off to Baltimore to coax the city's merchants to give him transport vessels to take his men to Virginia. As other American cities had done, Baltimore eagerly embraced and fêted the renowned French knight. Now a consummate diplomat, he shook every hand, smiled, pleaded and cajoled—and soon had Baltimore's merchants bidding against each other to equip his excursion. They gave him boats, guns, ammunition, wagons, horses, oxen, fodder, medicine, clothing, bread, meat, stoves . . . and on and on—along with enough cash to pay his men and buy more supplies en route.

It was all for naught.

Lafayette's men sailed only sixty miles down Chesapeake Bay before a British flotilla forced them to put into Annapolis, on the west shore of Chesapeake Bay. Still undiscouraged, the marquis took a reconnoitering party of thirty troops to chart an overland route to Virginia, but when he reached Steuben's camp at Yorktown, the British fleet had attacked the second French squadron as it tried to enter Chesapeake Bay and sent it fleeing back to Newport. The reversal, he reportd to Washington, "destroys every prospect of an operation against Arnold,"[20] and Washington ordered Lafayette to return to Annapolis and lead his men back to the main Continental army encampment in New York.

Lafayette was furious at what he called the arrogance of French military and political leaders who had repeatedly sent smaller fleets and fewer troops to battle Britain, believing, as Vergennes had put it to the king, that France was "established by Providence" and destined by "right to influence all great affairs."[21] In America, at least, Providence had left the French with nothing better than a military stalemate in the north and a series of humiliating setbacks at sea. "Had the French fleet come in Arnold was ours," Lafayette wrote dejectedly to his friend Alexander Hamilton. "The more certain it was, the greater my disappointment has been."[22]

As Lafayette prepared to return to Annapolis, Steuben showed him a plan for trapping Cornwallis's army in North Carolina. Cornwallis had scored a pyrrhic victory over Greene at Guilford Courthouse, but lost nearly one-third of his men and had retreated to his coastal base at Wilmington. Steuben suggested moving his men in from the west while Lafayette's troops marched from the north and Greene's troops marched from the south to encircle the British. Lafayette agreed, and Steuben sent his plan to Washington for approval, while Lafayette returned to Annapolis.

Finding no new orders when he reached Annapolis, Lafayette assumed that Washington had rejected the Steuben plan. Lafayette ordered his men to begin the long trek back to New York. Singing songs of home and dreaming of reunions with their families, they marched happily for two days back to Head of Elk—only to find a courier waiting with new orders from Washington, apparently adopting Steuben's strategy for trapping Cornwallis. Lafayette was to make an about-face and march to Virginia to assume command of the state's military operations, under the overall southern command of Greene: "Your being already three hundred miles advanced, which is nearly half way," Washington wrote, "the detachment under your command should proceed and join the southern army . . . to reinforce General Greene as speedily as possible."[23]

The orders stunned Lafayette. The useless, monthlong encampment at Annapolis and the march back to Head of Elk had exhausted troop supplies; Baltimore merchants were unlikely to reprovision a force that had consumed a month's worth of supplies idling comfortably on the banks of Chesapeake Bay. The new orders so outraged his troops that many mutinied. Instead of returning home, they now faced another trek—this time without adequate supplies—over the same ground they had traveled senselessly from Head of

Elk to Annapolis and back again. Most were northerners unused to the south's oppressive summer heat and choking humidity—and the inevitable outbreaks of yellow fever. Lafayette himself was all but ready to mutiny, believing he was being relegated to the Virginia backwater while the Continental army in the north prepared for the decisive battle against the British in New York. He wrote to Washington hinting at his own disappointment and asking for a delay in "the execution of superior orders" because of "the Great want of Monney, Baggage, Cloathing, Under which Both officers and Men are Suffering. . . . I write to the Board of War for to get Some Shoes and other parts of Cloathing."[24]

Infuriated and frustrated by the accumulated failures of his expedition, Lafayette vented his anger on what he deemed the source of those failures: the French government, which had failed to live up to its promises to provide adequate aid to the Americans. In a letter designed to embarrass French political leaders, he wrote to French ambassador La Luzerne in Philadelphia: "We have neither money, nor clothes, nor shoes, nor shirts, and in a few days we will be reduced to eating green peaches; our feet are torn for want of shoes and our hands are covered with scabs for want of linens; when I say 'we' I mean it in every sense, for my own baggage has been stolen."[25]

As Lafayette knew he would, La Luzerne sent his frightening description to Versailles, and Foreign Minister Vergennes responded to Lafayette: "The tableau you painted of the condition of the Americans is truly distressing, and we believe . . . it necessary to give them additional help. You can tell General Washington that the King has decided to guarantee a credit of 10 million *tournois* [equivalent to $100 million in today's currency], on which the United States may now draw through Holland [banks]." Vergennes promised to send clothing, but said nothing of the arms and provisions he had pledged to the Americans—or the additional ships and 10,000 troops Rochambeau had demanded. In fact, Vergennes had decided against sending more French troops to America, concluding that the more Frenchmen he sent to fight, the less incentive Americans would have to risk their own lives in battle. He did, however, pledge help from a huge French fleet, then on its way to defend the French West Indies. "M. le Comte de Grasse, who commands our fleet in the Antilles, has been ordered to send part of his fleet to the coast of North America sometime before next winter," Vergennes told Lafayette, "or to detach a portion of it to sweep the coast and to co-operate in any undertaking which may be projected by the French and American generals."[26]

Despite Lafayette's plea for time to resupply his men, Washington refused to change his orders, and, fearful that his letter might fall into the hands of spies, he could not tell his young friend that, far from depriving him of a role in the decisive campaign against the British, he was giving him a key role. For the decisive campaign was not, as Washington took pains to indicate to the British, to be against General Clinton's force in New York. It was to be in the South, and Washington told no one—not Rochambeau, not Greene, not Lafayette, not even Steuben, whose own plan had suggested the new strategy. Washington's moves and apparent preparations along the Hudson River north and west of New York were a feint to draw as many British troops into New York as possible. As he later explained in a letter to his friend, lexicographer Noah Webster, his strategy was "to misguide & bewilder Sir Henry Clinton in regard to the real object by fictitious communications, as well as by making deceptive provision of Ovens, Forage & boats in his neighborhood. . . . Nor were less pains taken to deceive our own Army."[27]

In fact, Washington's plan was simple: a multipronged attack, with Lafayette striking from the west, Steuben from the southwest, and Greene from the south, to force Cornwallis to the coast, where a French fleet would sail in from the east to block escape by sea. The combined armies of Washington and Rochambeau would then sweep down from the north to strike the decisive blow. It was important to move swiftly, however, before Cornwallis linked up with Arnold's force at Portsmouth and moved inland against Richmond, the primary arms and munitions depot of southern Patriots.

To soothe Lafayette's evident disappointment with his southern assignment, Washington sent his nephew, George Augustine Washington, to serve as Lafayette's aide and deliver a letter with Washington's sympathies for the plight of the troops—and a flattering reaffirmation of his affection for and faith in his French friend:

"You must endeavour to get Shoes," Washington conceded, "before you can move, from Philada. . . . The difficulties which you will experience on the score of provisions and transportation would have been common to any other Body of Troops. They will I know be great, but I depend much upon your assiduity and activity. . . .

"I shall be glad to hear from you—the time of your setting out from Elk, your prospects of getting on and the temper of the Troops, and above all I shall ever be happy in knowing that you are well and that every thing contributes to your happiness and satisfaction."[28] Washington promised to reinforce Lafayette's army by sending his trusted friend, "Mad" Anthony Wayne, and the eight hundred Pennsylvanians who had not mutinied. Greene made the southern campaign more attractive by asking Lafayette to move against Arnold at Portsmouth, while he, Greene, moved against Cornwallis in the Carolinas. Adding one more enticement was the presence of British major general William Phillips, who had arrived with reinforcements for Arnold. Twenty-two years earlier, Phillips had commanded the battery that killed Lafayette's father at the Battle of Minden in Prussia, during the Seven Years' War.

On April 10, Lafayette issued the order he knew his men would dread—
to make an about-face and return southward toward Baltimore. They began
deserting: eight troops, the first day; eleven more the second; nine the day
after, as they approached the Susquehanna River. "Nothing can make me
more unhappy than the incessant desertion of our best, finest and most experienced soldiers," he wrote to Washington, warning that "they will be still
more reduced by the disorders of that unwholesome climate [in the South]."
Lafayette discovered three Tory spies among his men and ordered one of
them hanged, and, after crossing the Susquehanna, he began arresting
deserters. "These men say that they like better one hundred lashes than a
journey to southward . . . if this disposition lasts, I am afraid we will be
reduced lower than I dare expect."[29]

Once across the wild Susquehanna, however, the prospect of a difficult
recrossing discouraged desertions. As Lafayette put it, "I am anxious to have
rivers, other countrys, and every kind of barrier to stop the inclination of
the men to return home. . . . I wish we might soon come near the enemy,
which is the only means of putting a stop to that spirit of desertion."[30]

After the crossing, two more soldiers deserted, but were caught, and, as
Lafayette reported to Washington, "one . . . has been hanged to-day, and the
other (being an excellent soldier), will be forgiven, but dismissed from the
corps."[31] After the hanging, Lafayette's chivalric instincts—and the evident
cruelty of the soldiers' plight—got the better of him. He issued a general
order appealing to their honor as men and soldiers, their loyalty to country,
and their loyalty to him personally. "I endeavoured to throw a kind of
infamy upon desertion, and to improve every particular affection of theirs,"[32]
he explained to Washington. "[I] issued an order declaring that [I] was setting out for a difficult and dangerous expedition; that [I] hoped that the soldiers would not abandon [me], but that whoever wished to go away might do
so instantly. . . . From that hour all desertions ceased, and not one man
would leave; this feeling was so strong that an under officer, who was prevented by a diseased leg from following the detachment, hired, at his
expense, a cart rather than separate from it."[33]

Cheered by the response of his soldiers, he rode to Baltimore and obtained a personal credit of 2,000 livres from the city's merchants (equivalent
to $20,000 in today's currency) to buy his men shoes, hats, and enough linen
and other types of cloth to dress everyone. Invited to the inevitable ball in
his honor, he appealed to the ladies to make shirts for his men from the
linen he purchased. "The ladies will make up the shirts," he reported to
Washington, "and the overalls will be made by the detachment, so that our
soldiers have a chance of being a little more comfortable."[34]

A grateful Washington replied that he had been "extremely rejoiced to
learn, that the spirit of discontent had so entirely subsided. . . . The mea-

sures you had taken to obtain, on your own credit, a supply of clothing and necessaries for the detachment, must entitle you to all their gratitude and affection; and will, at the same time that it endears your name, if possible, still more to this country, be an everlasting monument of your ardent zeal and attachment to its cause, and the establishment of its independence. For my own part, my dear Marquis, although I stood in need of no new proofs of your exertions and sacrifices in the cause of America, I will confess to you, that I shall not be able to express the pleasing sensations I have experienced at your unparalleled and repeated instances of generosity and zeal for the service on every occasion. . . . With every sentiment of affection & esteem, I am . . ."[35]

Lafayette's concern for his men and his enormous personal investment in their welfare cemented their unquestioning loyalty and allowed him to lead them on a series of forced marches to Virginia, where he hoped to surprise Arnold and Phillips—to hang the first for treason and shoot the second to avenge his father's death. What Lafayette could not know as he left Baltimore was that he was initiating an historic campaign that would crown him, Washington, and Rochambeau with glory and create a new, independent nation.

"When the history of that country shall have become the history of antiquity," wrote the eloquent nineteenth-century French historian Henri Doniol, "school children will be taught, as the generations now passing away are taught the memorable events of Greece or of Rome, to repeat the actions that took place in the campaign which began in the South against the English army. . . .

"Rarely have such privation and suffering, such Patriotic firmness and courageous determination, been united, in any soldiers with the same display of intelligent resolution, of native ability, of devotion upon the part of the leaders, to win for a feeble little army of liberation the glory of driving back an enemy, well equipped, vigorous, and formidable, with whom it contended for its native land."[36]

10

"The Play Is Over"

ON APRIL 20, 1781, Lafayette decided he could not afford to wait for Wayne's reinforcements and set off with his 1,000-man division on a forced march of more than 150 grueling miles from Baltimore to Richmond, Virginia. He arrived there in less than ten days, having devised an ingenious method to speed troops southward without exhausting them. He ordered half the men to ride in wagons, while the other half marched for an hour; marchers and riders then switched places for an hour, giving each group an hour's rest for every hour on foot. He left the slower-moving heavy equipment and artillery behind, to follow as fast as possible. The technique, along with their new clothes and Lafayette's constant encouragement, kept the men fresh and their spirits high, and got them to Richmond fit and ready for action.

"Richmond was filled with munitions warehouses," Lafayette explained. "Its pillage would have proved fatal. [We] marched there so rapidly that, when General Phillips neared Richmond and learned that [we] had arrived the night before, he would not believe it."[1]

Lafayette did not arrive too soon. A combined force of 2,500 British regulars under Phillips and Arnold had moved up the James River and captured Petersburg, twenty-five miles south of Richmond, from Steuben's ineffectual band of 1,000 Virginia militiamen. Steuben had requested—and Governor Thomas Jefferson had promised—additional men, supplies, and horses, but they never arrived. "We can only be answerable for the orders we give," Jefferson explained feebly, "and not for the execution. If they are disobeyed from obstinacy of spirit or want of coercion in the laws, it is not our fault."[2]

In fact, Jefferson and Virginia were unprepared for war. Despite Patrick Henry's fiery liberty-or-death orations, few Virginians—including Henry—were willing to fight, let alone die, in a revolution over taxes that affected but a handful of wealthy property owners, and neither Henry nor Jefferson ever went into battle, despite their lofty language extolling liberty and independence. Desperate for more troops and supplies, Lafayette went to his first face-to-face meeting with the great Jefferson, a six-foot-tall, freckle-faced redhead like himself. Nearly fifteen years older, he was easily the most cultured American Lafayette had ever met—much as the young Monroe had described at Brandywine. Jefferson was fluent in Latin and Greek—and he spoke French, cruelly adulterated, however, by a curious Scottish accent absorbed from a Scottish tutor during his youth, before he attended the College of William and Mary.

Lafayette and Jefferson grasped each other's hand eagerly, warmly, held it long, and searched each other's face, recognizing the historic significance if not the impact of their meeting: two brilliant, towering figures on the world's stage; one, the world's most illustrious warrior, a knight who rode with kings but fought for liberty; the other, one of the world's most illustrious political philosophers, author of a document that created a new nation and form of governance; both knowing that, directly and indirectly, together and individually, they were reshaping the world, its governments and nations, and the human condition for centuries to come. They took to each other immediately and plunged into wide-ranging discussions: hunting and farming (both were born country boys); music; literature; the Greek and Roman republics; the French philosophes; Locke's *Rights of Man*, and Jefferson's appropriation of its thesis in the Declaration of Independence. Jefferson cited Locke, Sir Isaac Newton, and Sir Francis Bacon as his "trinity of immortals."[3]

When Lafayette asked the governor for troops and supplies, however, he discovered, to his chagrin, that Jeffersonian democracy endowed individuals with the right not to take up arms to defend liberty. As the embarrassed governor admitted, "I shall candidly acknowledge that it is not in my power to do anything. . . . Mild laws, a people not used to war and prompt obedience, a want of provisions of war and means of procuring them render our efforts often ineffectual."[4] Lafayette understood for the first time the limitations—and dangers—of republican government, unfettered by constitutional guidelines.

Believing Richmond defenseless, the British crossed the James River to attack on the morning of April 30—only to run into an all-enveloping rain of fire and musket balls from the heights above. Lafayette had spread his troops across a wide swath on the embankment before the city and ordered a staccato of rapid fire that Phillips interpreted as a defensive force far greater than it actually was. As he had done at Barren Hill, Lafayette kept his men scampering from one position to another between shots, so that every two shots each soldier fired seemed to come from two soldiers.

"The leaving of my artillery appears a strange whim," Lafayette recalled, "but had I waited for it, Richmond would have been lost. General Phillips told one of his officers how astonished he was at our celerity . . . as he was going to give the signal to attack, he reconnoitred our position . . . [and] flew into a violent passion, and swore vengeance against me and the corps I had brought with me."[5]

With Lafayette's "army" commanding the heights of Richmond, the British believed the city was impregnable, and they retreated across the James to Petersburg to await reinforcements from Cornwallis in North Carolina. The following day, Lafayette proclaimed victory to his cheering troops and sent them on parade in full uniform to celebrate the first Patriot triumph of the Virginia campaign: Lafayette had saved Richmond and its precious stores of Patriot arms. Two days later, his artillery and supplies arrived, but without Wayne and his 800 Pennsylvanians or any word of their whereabouts. Lafayette spent the next few days developing a grand strategy for the southern campaign—and organizing a network of spies to infiltrate British forces and determine their strategy. He purposely recruited slaves, whom the British had courted with promises of freedom for stealing their masters' horses and delivering them to British cavalrymen.

"The military scene in Virginia was soon to become more interesting," Lafayette wrote. "General Greene had marched [southeasterly] . . . to attack [British] posts in South Carolina while Lord Cornwallis was in North Carolina. Cornwallis . . . burnt his wagons, tents, and other heavy equipment to enable him to move more quickly; he then advanced rapidly [northward] toward Petersburg and made Virginia the principal seat of war."

On May 8, Lafayette crossed the James and marched to Petersburg to lay partial siege to the city and harass the British. To exact revenge from the officer who had fired the cannon shot that killed his father, Lafayette sent a cannonball crashing through General Phillips's headquarters, but it was too late. Phillips had died of a fever before Lafayette could claim his blood.

Phillips's death left Benedict Arnold in command of British forces in Virginia, and he sent Lafayette a message requesting an exchange of prisoners. Lafayette sent it back unanswered, although he told the British courier that "shou'd any other officer have written to me I wou'd have been happy to receive their Letters."[6]

"A correspondence with Arnold," Lafayette explained, "is so very repugnant to my feelings that I can never conquer them so far as to answer his letters . . . and I can not submit to such a . . . rascal."[7] Lafayette later gloated that his refusal "placed Arnold in an awkward situation with his own army."[8] Washington was as pleased as Lafayette. "Your conduct upon every occasion meets my approbation," he wrote, "but in none more than in your refusing to hold a correspondence with Arnold."[9]

Lafayette's rebuff so angered Arnold that he threatened to ship his American prisoners to the West Indies. When Lafayette sent lower-ranking officers to arrange the exchange, Arnold is said to have asked one of them, "What do you think the Americans would do with me if they should succeed in making me a prisoner?" One of the American officers replied, "We should cut off the leg which was wounded in the country's service, and we should hang the rest of you."[10]

With no word from Wayne, and Cornwallis approaching to reinforce Arnold's camp at Petersburg, Lafayette pulled back across the James River to the north bank, eight miles below Richmond. He wrote to Brigadier General George Weeden, who was raising a militia in Fredericksburg, and ordered him to come south immediately. The situation, he warned, was "precarious and with the handful of men I have, there is no chance of resisting the combined armies unless I am speedily and powerfully reinforced. . . . Riflemen and cavalry, or at least mounted infantry, are particularly wanting. No time ought to be lost, as the danger is pressing and it will soon be too late to have it in our power to make a becoming resistance."[11]

Lafayette could not understand Wayne's inexplicable delay and his failure even to send word of his whereabouts. He sent a courier galloping north: "Where this letter will meet you, I am not able to ascertain," he pleaded, "but ardently wish it may be near this place where your presence is absolutely necessary. . . . I request, my dear Sir, you will let me hear from you. . . . I am extremely anxious to know if your aid will come in time . . . without your detachment we are too weak for a proper resistance."[12]

On May 20, Cornwallis linked his force to Arnold's, but disdainfully ordered the traitor to leave. On June 1, Arnold returned to his patron, General Clinton, in New York, escaping capture by Lafayette and frustrating still another of the French knight's quests.

As 1,800 more British troops arrived from New York to reinforce Cornwallis's army, Lafayette at last heard from Wayne: he had not yet even left York, Pennsylvania. "I shall certainly take up my line of March the 23rd," he pledged, but offered no reasons for his delay. "Would to God I was with you now as I fear a change of circumstance previous to our junction."[13] Wayne's letter seemed to seal Lafayette's doom, promising to turn what might have been victory into a senseless, bloody end to his American journey. Facing an overwhelmingly superior force of more than 7,000 troops, Lafayette pulled back to the heights of Richmond to defend the munitions depots—and fired a barrage of letters for help. Steuben replied that he had "only 500 men altogether . . . I am of the opinion that my 500 men, and even if it were 1,000, together with those you have, would not prevent Cornwallis from advancing or going wherever he pleases."[14] Weedon replied that he had been unable to raise a militia in Fredericksburg. Governor Jefferson sent him a batch of useless warrants to impress horses. Alone, with fewer than 1,000 men, Lafayette knew he faced certain massacre—for he would never surrender. In a melancholy letter to Washington, he lamented, "I am not strong enough even to get beaten. Untill the Pennsylvanians arrive we are next to nothing in point of opposition to so large a force."[15]

Faced with inevitable defeat and death, he wrote a last, darkly light-hearted letter to his friend Hamilton:

> I have been long complaining that I had nothing to do; and want of employment was an objection I had to my going to the southward. But for the present, my dear friend, my complaint is quite of an opposite nature; and I have so many arrangements to make, so many difficulties to combat, so many enemies to deal with, that I am just that much of a general as will make me a historian of misfortunes and nail my name upon the ruins of what good folks are pleased to call the army of Virginia. We have nine hundred Continentals. Their infantry is near five to one; their cavalry ten to one. . . . Come here, my dear friend . . . I want your advice and exertions. If you grant my request, you will vastly oblige,
>
> Your friend,
> Lafayette.[16]

Washington, of course, was distraught over Lafayette's plight, but too far away to send aid, and, knowing that British spies would see everything he wrote, he could not even comfort Lafayette without revealing his own new master strategy and Lafayette's key role in it. "As you have no cypher by which I can write you in safety," he explained, "and my letter has been frequently intercepted of late I restrain myself from mentioning many matters I wish to communicate to you." Fully aware of Lafayette's dream—of his obsession—to fight in the final, decisive battle against Britain, Washington hoped Lafayette would understand his meaning when he wrote cryptically, "It would be unnecessary for you to be here at present, and I am sure you would not wish to leave your charge while you are so near an enemy." For the benefit of the spies he knew would intercept his message, Washington went on to announce his plans for a decisive assault on New York.

"I have just returned from Weathersfield," he continued, knowing that Lafayette—and the British spies—would realize that he had met with Rochambeau. "Upon a full consideration of our affairs in every point of view—an attempt upon New York with its present Garrison . . . was deemed preferable to a Southern operation as we had not the command of the water.

The reasons which induced this determination were the danger to be apprehended from the approaching [summer] Heats—the inevitable dissipation & loss of Men by so long a March—and the difficulty of transportation. . . . The French Troops are to March this way as soon as certain circumstances will admit."[17]

Washington had indeed met with Rochambeau and discussed attacking New York, but the master strategy Washington had worked out in his own mind was exactly the opposite: he had no intention of attacking well-rested, well-fed British troops sitting behind impregnable fortress walls on New York Island. The armies of Cornwallis were far more vulnerable after months of endless marching and debilitating battles in the Carolina swamps and forests, without adequate food or rest. A key element of Washington's Southern Strategy, however, was to exhaust Cornwallis by keeping him on the move, and he entreated Lafayette "not to hazard . . . a General Action unless you have grounds to do it on. No *rational person* will condemn you for *not fighting* with the odds against you and while so much is depending on it. But all will censure a rash step if it is not attended with success."[18]

Another key element of Washington's Southern Strategy was "command of the water," however, and Washington asked the French commander to speed the arrival of the armada from the French West Indies, along with added troops and enough money for Congress to pay the American army and prevent desertions.

"I must not conceal from you, sir," Rochambeau pleaded with Admiral de Grasse, "that these people are at the end of their means; that Washington will not have half the troops he counted upon . . . that M. de la Fayette has not one thousand regular soldiers with the militia to defend Virginia."[19] Coming from a friend and fellow commander, Rochambeau's letter moved de Grasse to immediate action. "I have learned with great chagrin of the distressing situation upon the continent, and of the need for prompt assistance," he replied, pledging that, once he succeeded in sweeping British ships from the waters off the French West Indies—perhaps by mid-August— he would send twenty-nine warships to America, with a force of 3,000 troops, including 100 artillerymen and 100 dragoons, ten cannon, and a supply of siege guns and mortars. He promised to bring 1.2 million livres (about $12 million) in cash for the American troops.

Puzzled but obsessively loyal to his "beloved general," Lafayette obeyed Washington's suggestions. In the days that followed, he and his men moved almost all the munitions from the Richmond depots to hiding places in the foothills west of the city. On May 26, Cornwallis and his force crossed the James River toward Richmond, with the terrifying Colonel Banastre Tarleton and a new 800-man cavalry leading the way. Lafayette had but forty horsemen to fend off Tarleton's "birds of prey,"[20] which flew across

Lord Cornwallis set out to capture Lafayette by sending his overwhelmingly superior force against Lafayette's light infantry at Richmond. "The boy cannot escape me," Cornwallis boasted. (*Library of Congress.*)

the countryside astride a thundering herd of colossal thoroughbreds—"the best horses in Virginia," according to Lafayette. Almost all had been stolen by Negro slaves from their masters and delivered to the British in exchange for freedom.

"I shall now proceed to dislodge La Fayette from Richmond," Cornwallis wrote to General Sir Henry Clinton in New York, "and with my light troops destroy any magazines or stores in the neighbourhood, which may have been collected for his use or for General Greene's army."[21] Like Howe at Barren Hill, Cornwallis was intent on capturing Lafayette, to carry him back to England in chains—a symbol of France, whose humiliation would crush French enthusiasm for the American Revolution. All but drooling contemptuously, Cornwallis crossed the James River proclaiming, "The boy cannot escape me."[22]

Lafayette anticipated Cornwallis's attack, however, and prepared evasive action to prevent capture of his little force by the swifter, more powerful

English army: "Public stores and private property being removed from Richmond," he wrote to Washington, "this place is a less important object. I don't believe it would be prudent to expose the troops for the sake of a few houses, which are empty; but I am wavering between two inconveniences. Were I to fight a battle, I should be cut to pieces, the militia dispersed, and the arms lost. Were I to decline fighting, the country would think itself given up. I am therefore determined to skirmish, but not to engage too far, and particularly to take care against their immense and excellent body of horse, whom the militia fear as they would so many wild beasts."[23]

After saving the last of the munitions, Lafayette ordered the evacuation of Richmond. On May 15, Governor Jefferson and the General Assembly fled westward to Charlottesville, and ten days later, Lafayette led his men out of the city on the beginning of a long and circuitous route northward, hoping for linkage with Wayne and his Pennsylvanians.

In Europe, the fall of Richmond produced jubilation in London and consternation at Versailles—as well as at the Noailles mansion in Paris. "During the Virginia campaign," his wife recalled, "the only news we received came from the newspapers. Monsieur de Lafayette had no time or means to write, and the newspapers painted a picture of desperation . . . in alarming circumstances." At the time, young George-Washington Lafayette "nearly died teething" and left Adrienne "weakened by anxieties."[24]

Lafayette's strategy of evasive action took his men along the high ground, in thick brush and heavily forested slopes, felling trees behind them to slow Cornwallis's pursuit and destroying bridges after crossing each of the myriad creeks and streams that wove through the Virginia hills and valleys. A handful of snipers covered the retreat, emerging suddenly from treetops and bushes to surprise the British vanguard with a spray of fire that stalled the enemy column just long enough for Lafayette's band to distance itself tantalizingly out of reach of its pursuers. With every advance, sniper fire cost Cornwallis a few more Redcoats—two here, three there, four . . . gradually but painfully eroding and demoralizing the British troops. As Lafayette explained, "The Americans retreated in such a manner that the front guard of the enemy arrived on the spot just as they quitted it, and, without running any risk themselves, they retarded as much as possible the enemy progress."[25]

Tarleton's thoroughbreds, however, were swift and powerful and often outflanked Lafayette's men. "Hasten to our aid," Lafayette wrote desperately to Wayne, warning that "should we be overtaken before you arrive we will soon vanish. . . . The other day . . . Tarleton surprised a party of militia and took about 30 or 40, some of whom were cut very barbarously."[26]

Tarleton's cavalry streaked across the landscape in ghostly fashion, appearing on the right flank one day, on the left the next, charging from the rear, then the front. Lafayette had no choice but to change course toward the forested western foothills, where Tarleton's cavalry would be less effective. He pleaded with Wayne to "leave your Baggage behind and come by forced marches."[27]

Lafayette received encouragement from Greene, along with descriptions of Marion's and Morgan's successful guerrilla tactics in South Carolina.[28] Indeed, Greene had recaptured Camden and the central part of South Carolina and pushed British forces toward the coast. Lafayette used some of Greene's tactics to refine his own to a fine art. He detached small groups of riflemen to pounce on enemy flanks, bobbing and weaving in the trees and shrubbery, out of reach of Tarleton's mounted swordsmen, raining shots from every direction before melting into the surrounding landscape and returning to their main body. They were few in number, but their speed and rapid fire gave the impression of being a much larger force. They won no battles, but, as Greene had done, they exhausted the Redcoats, who marched in full uniform through the stifling, soggy southern heat. Upright in traditional battle stance, the British were unprepared for multidirectional fire from unseen enemies behind bushes and trees.

Tarleton's cavalry was equally ineffective in the thick shrubs and forests, although they succeeded in terrorizing the civilian population on the flatlands, laying waste plantations, sacking and burning like Vandals of old. Far from helping the British cause, Tarleton's depredations harried Loyalists and Patriots alike, and many of both fled to Lafayette's camp, bent on retaliating against Tarleton by joining the Patriot cause.

Lafayette's little army moved swiftly, day and night, fearing armed loyalists and renegade slaves as much as the pursuing Redcoats. By June 5, Lafayette and his men had widened the distance between themselves and the British to about thirty-five miles and were in sight of the Rappahannock River when the British vanguard came to an abrupt halt: Wayne's force had arrived and encamped on the other bank.

As Lafayette's exhausted little army stood in tatters cheering and crying, Wayne's Pennsylvanians transported boatloads of supplies across the river, and within a few days, they had replenished, reclothed, and rearmed the entire force. Wayne brought oral instructions from Washington to Lafayette explaining the Southern Strategy for the first time.

Recognizing the impossibility of capturing Lafayette and his strengthened American force, Cornwallis changed tactics and ordered Tarleton to veer westward to Charlottesville, where the remnants of Burgoyne's 5,700-man army of British and Hessian soldiers captured at Saratoga were interned. If, as he fully anticipated, they rushed to rejoin their British comrades, they would double the British force in Virginia. Cornwallis also ordered Tarleton to capture Governor Jefferson, who was presiding over the Virginia Assembly. Like Lafayette, Jefferson was a symbolic figure, "the author" of the revolution, whose capture would undermine the spirit of the rebellion as much as the capture of Lafayette.

In less than two days, Tarleton's cavalrymen flew across fifty miles of Virginia landscape and burst into Charlottesville, capturing seven members of the Assembly before they could rise from their desks. Governor Jefferson was at his aerie at Monticello with John Tyler and Benjamin Harrison and just managed to flee after Patrick Henry galloped to the door to warn of Tarleton's approach. Although Tarleton's troops drained Jefferson's legendary wine cellar, to his credit, he ordered them out of the house before they could do any damage. Cornwallis, however, was so furious at losing Jefferson that he went to Monticello and, according to one English historian, "plundered and pilfered like a bandit," taking Jefferson's plate and silver for his home in England, burning his barns and fields, slaughtering his livestock, and carrying away thirty slaves, who later died in a smallpox epidemic that swept through the British camp.[29]

Cornwallis met even more frustration at the Hessian and British prisoner-of-war camp. In the two years after their long march from Boston, they had transformed the barren hilltop into an almost idyllic community of pleasant little homes, with hundreds of gardens and small droves of cows and sheep grazing along the nearby slopes. Most had formed close friendships in Charlottesville; some had married American women; the musically and intellectually gifted met regularly at Monticello, where, with Jefferson bowing his beloved violin, they made music together and discussed philosophy, history, and science. Baron de Geismer, a Hessian general and particularly talented violinist, formed an intimate friendship with the Sage of Monticello—as did Baron Jean Louis de Unger, a scientist with a vast knowledge of philosophy.[30]

Almost all the internees refused to return to battle against their American hosts, and Cornwallis marched away in disgust to resume his duel with Lafayette. Although Tarleton had captured one thousand muskets and four hundred barrels of gunpowder in Charlottesville, the new supplies did not last long. As he had done earlier with Greene in South Carolina, Cornwallis underestimated the dangers of fighting a smaller, inferior force on its home ground. Once again, he had moved too far inland into enemy territory and overextended his line of supplies from the succors of the British fleet. With his men exhausted from the stifling heat and humidity, he had little choice but to begin a retreat to the sea. Although Lafayette's snipers peppered his rear guard, dwindling supplies left the British unable to retaliate.

"The enemy have been so kind as to retire before us," Lafayette wrote to Washington. "Twice I gave them a chance of fighting (taking care not to engage further than I pleased), but they continued their retrograde motions. Our numbers are, I think, exaggerated to them and our seeming boldness confirms the opinion. . . . Adieu, my dear General; I do not know but what we will in our turn become the pursuing enemy."[31]

By June 22, Lafayette's force had returned to the outskirts of Richmond, where Weeden arrived with nearly 1,000 militiamen and Steuben added another 650 troops. As volunteers from plantations pillaged by Tarleton swarmed into camp, Lafayette's army swelled to more than 5,000 men— 2,000 of them crack Continentals and 3,000 militiamen, the so-called citizen soldiers. Although still too small for a head-to-head engagement with Cornwallis's 7,000 regulars, Lafayette's force was large enough to harass British flanks and seriously cripple the rear guard. Lafayette sent small squads darting through surrounding landscape, sniping first on one flank, then the other, pouncing on foraging parties and outposts, and always giving the impression that his force was larger than it was. The British hunter became the hunted.

With every step beyond Richmond, Lafayette grew bolder and more aggressive, forcing Cornwallis to retreat southeast, onto the Virginia cape, between the York and James Rivers. Lafayette sent patrols to roam the opposite banks conspicuously enough to dissuade the British from leaving the cape, while his vanguard struck incessantly at the British rear and forced them toward Chesapeake Bay. "Washington having finally adopted the project of uniting the land and sea forces against the army of Cornwallis," Lafayette explained, "we manoeuvred to prevent [the] enemy from withdrawing when he became conscious of his dangers."[32]

In the north, Rochambeau's army had left Rhode Island and linked up with Washington's for what Sir Henry Clinton believed would be a massive assault on New York—as did the French and American armies. As Washington knew they would, Clinton's spies had intercepted Washington's letter to Lafayette detailing his intention to attack New York. To reinforce Clinton's belief in the veracity of the letter, Washington sent wagon trains and artillery rumbling up and down the Hudson shore opposite New York and raised an enormous encampment of tents—almost all of them empty, of course—in Elizabethtown, New Jersey, across the narrow waterway from Staten Island. "[Washington] had determined . . . to give out and cause it to be believed, that New York was the point of attack at which he aimed with all the force and means that could be collected," explained Washington's friend, the historian Jared Sparks.[33]

The attack began—or seemed to begin—on July 1, when General Benjamin Lincoln, who had been paroled by the British after his capture at Charleston, sailed into the Harlem River and seized the high ground at Kingsbridge (now the Bronx), opposite the northern end of New York Island. Washington and Rochambeau each moved enough troops southward for Lincoln to attack several enemy outposts and force their retreat across

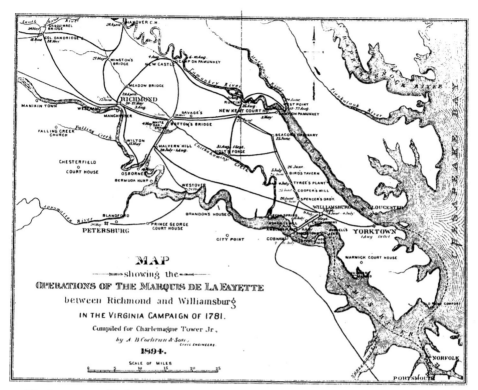

The last stages of Lafayette's campaign against Cornwallis, on the Virginia cape between the James and York Rivers, with Richmond, top left, and Yorktown, center right. (*From the author's collection.*)

the Harlem to New York. Believing he faced attack by the combined American and French armies, Clinton sent urgent orders to Cornwallis to lead his army to Portsmouth, Virginia, and await transport to sail north to help defend New York.

As Washington feigned his attack on New York, Lafayette's army celebrated the fifth anniversary of the Declaration of Independence outside Williamsburg, with what he described as ostentatious maneuvers and parades "almost in the face of the enemy."[34] Flushed with pride, Lafayette wrote Washington, "These three battalions are the best troops that ever took the field. My confidence in them is unblended. They are far superior to any British troops, and none will ever venture to meet them at equal numbers . . . their presence here, I must confess, has saved this State."[35] Lafayette had good reason to be proud. In less than twelve weeks, he had led a small band of soldiers—at times, less than 1,000—on a grueling campaign from Baltimore and freed almost the entire state of Virginia from British control.

In but five weeks, he had chased the British army—7,000 strong—from the outskirts of Fredericksburg, Charlottesville, and Richmond without even confronting Cornwallis in traditional battle. His tiny band of marksmen had so harassed the British that they could not safely occupy the ground they conquered. He had so outmaneuvered the vaunted British general that Cornwallis had little choice but to retreat with his entire army to a humiliatingly defensive position at Williamsburg, facing Lafayette's marksmen in front and on both flanks—and a watery grave in Chesapeake Bay to his rear. Lafayette was not yet twenty-four years old.

"I had the honour to command an army and oppose Lord Cornwallis," Lafayette wrote to Washington. "When incomparably inferior to him, fortune was pleased to preserve us; when equal in numbers, though not in quality of troops, we have also been pretty lucky. Cornwallis had the disgrace of a retreat and this State being recovered, government properly re-established."[36] For American Patriots, the Virginia campaign, according to Rochambeau's chaplain, made the word *marquis* "a beloved symbol which rouses their admiration and gratitude."[37]

The following day, Cornwallis abandoned Williamsburg and marched his army to the causeway to James Island, where river boats were to take them to Portsmouth and the ocean transports to New York. Lafayette hoped to exact a steep price for their evacuation by attacking the British rear guard, but a spy warned Cornwallis, and he hid several thousand men in the forest while the rest of his army marched across the causeway with the baggage train. Lafayette sent the intrepid Wayne to attack the British rear with a force of 500 infantrymen, two cavalry squads, 150 riflemen, and three pieces of artillery. As what seemed to be the Redcoat rear guard decoyed Wayne's men onto the causeway, Cornwallis sprang his trap, ordering his men in the forest to encircle the Patriots. Surrounded and outnumbered almost four to one, "Mad" Anthony Wayne, always true to his sobriquet, ordered his men to charge the enemy encirclement, but the British had too much firepower, and, Wayne reported later, "all on our side became a scene of confusion." Recognizing what had happened, Lafayette called to his Continentals to break the British stranglehold from the rear and give Wayne an alley of retreat. Lafayette led the charge through the enemy line to Wayne. Artillery fire staggered his magnificent white horse, which fell mortally wounded beneath him. He managed to reach Wayne on foot, and together they regrouped the trapped men and guided most of them through the hail of British fire to the safety of the Continental army line. "Not a man in the whole detachment was more exposed," Wayne said of Lafayette.[38] Lafayette's attack cost Cornwallis the lives of four sergeants and twenty-four infantrymen; seventeen officers and ninety-four soldiers were listed as wounded or missing.[39]

When news of the engagement and the accident to Lafayette reached Washington, he reacted like most worried fathers: "I have heard a thousand vague reports of your situation," he wrote to Lafayette, "but none of them satisfactory . . . my anxiety to hear from you is increased by my sincere regard for you and by the interest I take in every thing which concerns you. Believe me to be most Affectionately Yours."[40]

When Lafayette's official report reached him, Washington's tone changed to that of a proud father and commander in chief: "Be assured, my dear Marquis," Washington wrote, "your conduct meets my warmest approbation, as it must that of everybody. Should it ever be said, that my attachment to you betrayed me into partiality, you have only to appeal to facts to betray any such charge."[41] In an official order, Lafayette credited the "gallantry and talent" of his men for the successful outcome of the engagement.[42]

The day after the battle, Cornwallis and his army abandoned Jamestown and James Island to Lafayette and went "under protection of their works at Portsmouth,"[43] the last British stronghold in Virginia.

Three weeks after General Lincoln had encamped at Kingsbridge, neither Washington's nor Rochambeau's armies moved a step closer to New York. Aware of de Grasse's presence in the West Indies, Clinton concluded that Lincoln's assault had indeed been a feint; that New York remained secure enough to countermand his previous order to Cornwallis to come to New York. He sent Cornwallis new orders, to defend his position and build fortifications to protect the British fleet in Hampton Roads, the huge estuary where the James River estuary empties into Chesapeake Bay (see map on page 149). Deeming Hampton Roads too wide to protect, Cornwallis ordered the fleet into the narrow, more defensible York River estuary, where he began building fortifications on either side—at Yorktown on the south bank, and Gloucester, its twin town, across the river. His strategy would rank among the most brilliantly conceived designs for self-destruction in British military history and ensured the beginning of the decline of the British empire.

As Cornwallis built his fortifications, Lafayette established a ring of entrenched artillery positions about Yorktown to prevent a Cornwallis breakout by land, and he sent scouts to reconnoiter enemy positions along the coast. He sent one soldier from the Jersey line into the enemy camp to pretend he was a Patriot deserter and enroll in the British army. "His mission was to give advice of the movements of the enemy, and deceive them as the projects and resources of the Americans," Lafayette explained.[44] Lafayette relayed regular espionage reports to Washington, along with careful details of enemy movements, with descriptions of the surrounding geography. He was nothing if not thorough—obsessively so.

"The light infantry, the guards, the 80th regiment, and the Queen's rangers, are, it is said, destined for New York."[45]

"There are in Hampton-road thirty transport ships full of troops, most of them red coats. There are eight or ten brigs which have cavalry on board."[46]

"York is surrounded by the river and a morass, the entrance is but narrow. There is . . . a commanding hill, which, if occupied by the enemy, would much extend their works."[47]

"The greater part of the enemy are at York. . . . They have a forty-four gun ship; frigates and vessels are scattered lower down. . . . Lord Cornwallis must be attacked with pretty great apparatus.

"I hope you will come yourself to Virginia, and that . . . I will have, at least, the satisfaction of beholding you myself at the head of the combined armies. . . . Adieu, my dear general; I heartily thank you for having ordered me to remain in Virginia and to your goodness to me I am owing the most beautifull prospect that I may ever behold."[48]

For several weeks, Cornwallis feigned strategic breakouts, first toward the Carolinas, then toward northern Virginia, then actually embarking part of his army and sailing up Chesapeake Bay toward Baltimore, before returning to Yorktown. Lafayette dutifully reported each movement and countered accordingly, moving troops south, then north, then back to his original position on the cape just above Yorktown. His constant reports to Washington left him little time to write Adrienne. "If the naval superiority which we are expecting should arrive," he scribbled quickly, "I shall rejoice at the campaign closing. . . . *Maybe it will end in a very favorable way.*" He asked her to "kiss Anastasie and George a thousand times. . . . Adieu, my Sweetheart, I cannot find words to tell you how much I love you, but I will be happy when I have the chance to try in person."[49]

Early in August, de Grasse set sail from the West Indies. Washington dispatched a courier to Lafayette with orders "to prevent, if possible, the retreat of Cornwallis towards Carolina." Lafayette tightened his ring of artillery around Yorktown and sent Washington a confident reply: "Should a French fleet now come in Hampton Roads, the British army would, I think, be ours."[50]

As he waited for de Grasse's fleet, Lafayette shored up his military encirclement of Yorktown and laid in supplies for the Washington and Rochambeau armies. An expert on quartermastering since Albany, he badgered every governor for more manpower and materials, obtaining pledges of 500 militiamen from Maryland, 400 from Virginia, 600 from Pennsylvania. Virginia rebuffed his requests for supplies. "This state," he told Washington, "has a large quantity of beef—of corn—some flour—very little rum. . . . Had we anything like Monney matters would go on very well."[51]

Day after day, Lafayette complained about the "want of clothing of every sort, arms, ammunition, hospital stores, and horse accoutrements." He warned Washington that "heavy artillery and every thing relative to a siege from the cannon to the tool, is not to be found. . . . I May add medicines and hospital stores."[52]

Lafayette sent more spies into the Cornwallis camp, including some runaway slaves to whom he promised freedom for their services; some became personal aides to Cornwallis himself. He deployed Wayne's Pennsylvanians on the opposite, south bank of the James River to assure Patriot control of navigation and sent his old friend and former aide de camp Colonel Gimat, by then commander of a Continental army battalion of light infantry, to Cape Henry at the entrance to Chesapeake Bay, to await the arrival of de Grasse with dispatches, battle plans, and pilots.

On August 19, the combined American and French armies in the north—about 2,500 Americans and 4,000 Frenchmen—broke camp in New York. Leaving a few Patriot troops to continue the charade at the empty tents near Staten Island, Washington and Rochambeau hurried their forces southward through New Jersey, reaching Philadelphia on August 30—just as de Grasse's huge fleet loomed on the horizon near the entrance of Chesapeake Bay. As soon as Clinton discovered Washington's ruse, he ordered an expeditionary force to sail south to support Cornwallis—but it was too late.

With Wayne's troops protecting the south bank of the James River, de Grasse sailed into Hampton Roads and up to James Island and landed arms, ammunition, and other stores to replenish Lafayette's army—and 3,000 French troops to augment his firepower. For the first time in his career, Lafayette realized his cherished dream of commanding a combined force of French and American troops in war.

Wayne described the scene: "We lay about two hours on our ground expecting every moment to see a glorious sight; at last a number of large boats appeared with about three thousand French troops on board, and also three large armed vessels to cover the troops landing.

"The troops landed on our opposite side, on James Island, and . . . spread an universal joy amongst our officers and soldiers. Never did I behold a more beautiful and agreeable sight."[53]

That evening, Wayne was crossing the James to Lafayette's camp when an overanxious sentinel fired and wounded him slightly in the thigh with buckshot. He brushed it off nonchalantly, and, intent on showing the world why his troops called him "mad," he casually "took a walk to take a view of the French troops, who make a very fine soldierly appearance, they being all very tall men, their uniform is white coats turned up with blue, their underclothes are white."[54]

As Lafayette took command of the troops on land, other ships in the de Grasse fleet anchored at the mouth of the York River and bottled up the fleet of British frigates. Cornwallis's ill-conceived strategy had made the allied

Admiral de Grasse sailed into Chesapeake Bay with a huge armada that blocked Cornwallis's escape by water and landed 3,000 French troops to strengthen Lafayette's land forces. (*Réunion des Musées Nationaux.*)

mission all too simple. "The English army found itself enclosed on every side, and no possible means of escape was left to Lord Cornwallis," Lafayette related. On September 4, Lafayette tightened the noose around Cornwallis, and de Grasse, eager to return to the West Indies as quickly as possible, urged him to strike the final blow. Lafayette refused. In the Arthurian legend he envisioned, only his warrior father, George Washington, would lead American forces to victory, with Lafayette at his side.

Lafayette told de Grasse that Washington's specific orders were only "to prevent his [Cornwallis's] escape by land." He said the Washington and Rochambeau armies would soon arrive and double allied forces to 18,000 men. Cornwallis would have no choice but surrender "to spare the lives of the soldiers, which a good general ought always to do."[55] De Grasse tried coaxing Lafayette with flattery, offering 1,800 more marines and sailors to support an immediate strike. "There, Monsieur le Marquis," de Grasse said. "I want to contribute everything I can to further your glory and assure your spending a winter of tranquillity. It would fulfill my greatest wish to be a witness and I send you my compliments in advance on your victories. With pleasure, I join your admirers."

Lafayette argued that an immediate assault would constitute a "murderous attack [and] shed a great deal of blood only to satisfy a vain lust for glory. The temptation was great," he admitted later, "but even if the attack had succeeded, it would necessarily have cost a great deal of blood. [I] would not sacrifice the soldiers entrusted to me to personal ambition . . . by waiting, the reduction of the army of Cornwallis was secured at little cost."[56]

Washington was grateful: "I have received with infinite satisfaction, My Dear Marquis, the information of the Arrival of the Count de Grasse. And have an additional pleasure in finding that your ideas on every occasion have been so consonant with my own, and that by your military dispositions & prudent measures you have anticipated all my wishes."[57] In a subsequent note, the usually austere commander in chief chortled, "I hope you will keep Lord Cornwallis safe, without Provisions or Forage until we arrive. Adieu."

Ironically, Lafayette's stubborn chivalry proved fortuitous for de Grasse. The day after he moved into the mouth of the York River, a British fleet of nineteen ships sent to rescue Cornwallis sailed into Chesapeake Bay to challenge the French fleet from the rear. Had de Grasse landed his marines and sailors as he had wanted, he would have left his ships defenseless. As it was, he wheeled his big ships about and turned their heavy cannons on the British attackers. The two fleets jockeyed about before moving out of the bay into open waters for more room to maneuver. Although the heavy French cannons and fierce winds crippled a few British frigates the first day, the duel continued for three more days, with each fleet parrying, thrusting, and shifting course, but gaining little advantage. Then, eleven more French ships from Newport sailed in unexpectedly. Vastly outnumbered, the British put about and fled to New York for reinforcements, leaving de Grasse in control of Chesapeake Bay and sealing the fate of Cornwallis and his army.

With an expanded fleet of forty ships, de Grasse left his biggest ships of the line guarding the entrance of Chesapeake Bay, while his frigates and transports sailed up the bay to Head of Elk to ferry the Washington and Rochambeau armies to Jamestown.

On September 14, Washington and Rochambeau rode into Williamsburg for an emotional reunion with Lafayette, as the combined allied force of more than 15,000 men marched before them. Washington went to see de Grasse on his flagship, Ville de Paris, and returned incensed. The French admiral was preparing to abandon the Yorktown campaign: a powerful British fleet was on its way from New York, and rather than risk his ships in American waters, de Grasse preferred returning to defend the French West Indies. With d'Estaing's earlier withdrawals in mind, Washington sent de Grasse a blunt warning: "Your Excellency's departure from the Chesapeake, by affording an opening for the succor of York, which the enemy would instantly avail themselves of, would be, not only the disgrace and loss of renouncing an enterprise, upon which the fairest expectations of the allies have been founded, after the most expensive preparations and uncommon exertions and fatigues, but perhaps the disbanding of the whole army for want of provisions."[58] At Washington's behest, Lafayette finally coaxed the French admiral to reconsider. De Grasse agreed to leave two ships of the line and three frigates to blockade Cornwallis at the mouth of the York River, while he led his thirty-five other ships to the entrance of Chesapeake Bay to engage the British.

On September 28, the allied army, about 9,000 American and 7,800 French troops, marched out of Williamsburg to lay siege to Yorktown. It was a surprisingly short campaign. They encamped two miles from town, the Americans on the right, the French on the left. Without firing a shot, the British troops evacuated their outer works, allowing the Allies to move heavy siege guns through the wooden palisades to shell the English second wall, three hundred yards away. On October 6, with Yorktown surrounded by land, the shelling began; by the end of the day, shells breached the center and left sections of the second wall, but the British held firm to two sections on the Allied right flank, where Lafayette's heralded Light Division poised for their last attack as a unit under their revered commander. No stranger to Arthurian legend or poetic justice, Washington ordered two brigades forward to reinforce Lafayette's unit: one led by Colonel Alexander Hamilton, the other by Colonel John Laurens, the son of the still-imprisoned former president of Congress. From his vantage atop his huge horse, Washington watched his three cherished young protégés march into history together, with what Lafayette described as "the tread of veterans, colors flying, drums beating."[59] Washington assigned Colonel Gimat, Lafayette's loyal former aide, to Laurens's division, and he ordered Dr. James Thacher to Lafayette's side in case any of the young men he had nurtured suffered injury.

As darkness fell on October 14, Lafayette led the charge; bayonets fixed, they stormed the breaches in the British fortifications, flinging themselves at the British defenders with "an ardor" that sent the Redcoats who survived fleeing in terror—and ensured Lafayette's place on the walls of Chavaniac among the portraits of the other great Lafayette warriors—Pons Motier and the rest.

"Colonel Gimat's battalion led the van, and was followed by that of Colonel Hamilton, who commanded the whole advanced corps," Lafayette reported to Washington, giving credit to everyone but himself. "At the same time a party of eighty men, under Colonel Laurens turned the redoubt. . . . Colonel Hamilton['s] well known talents and gallantry were on this occasion most conspicuous and serviceable. Our obligations to him, to Colonel Gimat, to Colonel Laurens, and to each and all the officers, are above

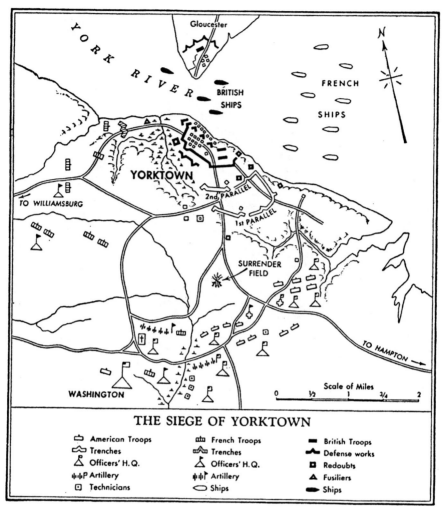

THE SIEGE OF YORKTOWN

🛝 American Troops	🎗 French Troops	▬ British Troops
🗘 Trenches	🎗 Trenches	▲ Defense works
⚖ Officers' H.Q.	⚖ Officers' H.Q.	▣ Redoubts
🎗P Artillery	🎗 Artillery	▲ Fusiliers
▣ Technicians	⬭ Ships	▬ Ships

The siege of Yorktown. Lafayette, Hamilton, and Laurens formed the front lines of Washington's Patriot army on the right flank, while Rochambeau's French forces formed the left flank. The starlike symbol in the center shows where the British surrendered. (From the author's collection.)

expression. . . . It adds greatly to the character of the troops, that, under the fire of the enemy, they displayed and took their ranks with perfect silence and order. Not one gun was fired . . . and, owing to the conduct of the Commanders and bravery of the men, the redoubt was stormed with an uncommon rapidity."[60]

As a storm of shells reduced Yorktown to rubble, Cornwallis made a vain counterattack the following day, but the Americans and French forced him to retreat to the York River, where a driving rain made escape by water

The British surrender at Yorktown. Too humiliated to appear, Cornwallis feigned illness and sent his adjutant, General Charles O'Hara, to surrender his sword. After Rochambeau ordered him to surrender it to Washington (at right, with black hat), Lafayette (at Washington's side, pointing) ordered him to surrender it to General Benjamin Lincoln, whom the British had humiliated at Charleston. (*Réunion des Musées Nationaux.*)

impossible. On October 17, 1781, Cornwallis sent a message to Washington under a flag of truce: "Sir,—I propose a cessation of hostilities for twenty-four hours, and that two officers may be appointed by each side . . . to settle terms for the surrender of the posts of York and Gloucester."[61]

Washington agreed; Cornwallis proposed that his troops surrender as prisoners of war, "with the customary honours" of marching out of their garrisons, to the beat of their drummers, colours aloft. Lafayette objected, citing the refusal of Cornwallis to grant General Lincoln the same courtesy at the surrender of Charleston. Washington named Colonel John Laurens, and Rochambeau appointed Lafayette's brother-in-law, the vicomte de Noailles, to carry Washington's terms of capitulation to Cornwallis: "The same honours will be granted to the surrendering army as were granted to the garrison of Charleston. . . . The garrison of York will march out to a place to be appointed in front of the posts, at two o'clock precisely, with shouldered arms, colours cased, and drums beating. . . . They are then to ground their arms and return to their encampments."[62]

On October 19, Cornwallis, Washington, Rochambeau, and de Grasse, among others, signed the articles of capitulation, but, feigning illness, Cornwallis refused to lead his troops to surrender, sending instead his adjutant, General Charles O'Hara, to suffer the humiliation of surrendering his sword. O'Hara sought to hand it to Rochambeau, but the French general rejected it, saying that American general Washington was sole commander-in-chief. With Lafayette at his side, Washington ordered O'Hara to surrender his sword to General Lincoln, who graciously returned it to him.

The American and French troops formed two lines, facing each other, and as the silent British troops marched between them to surrender, the Redcoats turned their faces toward the French line, by way of insult to the ragtag American rebels. Lafayette immediately ordered his drum major to strike up "Yankee Doodle," and, according to "Lighthorse Harry" Lee, "the band's blare made them turn their eyes" to their American conquerors. By the end of the day, Lee recounted, almost 8,000 British soldiers had laid down their arms and "became prisoners of Congress."[63] The officers were allowed to keep their sidearms; the rest of the men kept all their personal effects except items acquired by plunder. The British seamen who surrendered were turned over to de Grasse as prisoners of war.

The following day, Lafayette wrote to French prime minister Maurepas: "The play is over, Monsieur le Comte, the fifth act has just come to an end."[64]

11

Conqueror of Cornwallis

I have but a few minutes to give you some news, my sweetheart. The end
of the campaign was a brilliant one for the allied troops; I would have to
be difficult to please indeed, were I not completely satisfied with the close
of my Virginia campaign. You must have learned of all the difficulties Lord
Cornwallis' talents and superior forces gave me—the good luck we had in
regaining the ground we lost—and, finally, our drawing Lord Cornwallis
into the perfect position we needed to capture him; at the perfect moment,
our troops rushed in upon him. I count the moment when I commanded
the forces of three field marshals as among the happiest moments of my
life. I pity Lord Cornwallis, for whom I have the highest respect . . . and
having allowed myself the pleasure of repaying the incivilities of Charleston
at the capitulation, I do not intend carrying my vengeance any further.

My health is very good, and I suffered no injuries during our encounter. . . . Kiss our beloved children ten thousand times for me. Adieu, adieu.[1]

A FRIGATE CARRIED Lafayette's letter to Adrienne and his letters to each
of the king's ministers in only eighteen days—spectacular speed then. News
of the American victory at Yorktown produced consternation in England
but "great joy in all of France," according to Foreign Minister Vergennes,
who only four years earlier had sought to arrest the French knight before he
left for America. "Rest assured," he replied to Lafayette, "that your name is
now venerated. . . . I followed you step by step, Monsieur le Marquis, during
your entire campaign in Virginia. I would often have trembled for you if I
had not been so certain of your wisdom. It takes a great deal of skill to resist,
as you did for so long, despite a huge disparity of forces, a man as talented
in war as Lord Cornwallis. It was you who led him to his fatal end, when,
instead of his making you a prisoner of war as he had planned, you forced

him to become one himself. History offers few examples of such total success."[2] Vergennes added a sad note to his accolade, however: "I am replying, Monsieur le Marquis, for Monsieur le Comte de Maurepas. . . . It is not without great regret that you will learn of the loss we have suffered of this excellent man. You have lost a good friend; I can tell you that from personal knowledge; he confided his feelings for you to me, and I can assure you he would not differ with the good wishes I have already avowed to you." Lafayette had indeed lost a staunch friend at court. Fortunately, he had been meticulous in forming many other important friendships.

One of the most important was French minister of war marquis de Ségur, the father of his friend and fellow musketeer from Metz, the comte de Ségur. "You have led a most glorious campaign, Monsieur le Marquis," wrote the minister of war. "Our old warriors admire you; and the young ones, without the slightest taint of jealousy, want you as their model; your perfect conduct adds to the value of your virtues: the letter you honored me with is proof of that; I gave it to the King to read, and His Majesty was as pleased as I."[3]

As evidence of the king's pleasure, the marquis de Ségur enclosed an official proclamation:

> The king, sir, having been informed of the military talents of which you have given such multiplied proofs . . . has desired me to tell you, that the praises you have so justly merited . . . have fixed his attention, and that . . . you may depend on his future kindnesses. His Majesty, in order to give you a very particular and flattering mark of this, assigns you the rank of Maréchal de Camp [brigadier general] in his armies to take effect after the war in America has finished and you shall have terminated your services to the United States and reentered those of His Majesty. By this decision, you shall be considered a Maréchal de Camp effective October 19 . . . the date of the surrender of General Cornwallis after the siege of Yorck [sic].[4]

The king's proclamation raised Lafayette's rank in France to the nearest equivalent of his American rank and, in effect, completed the legend of his knighthood.

In the days and nights after the triumph at Yorktown, Washington, Lafayette, Knox, Lincoln, Rochambeau, the vicomte de Noailles, and other Freemasons and officers celebrated endlessly, continually toasting the United States, France, Washington, liberty, brotherhood, and each other at the tavern that served as Yorktown's Masonic lodge. Lafayette drew closer to Lincoln and Knox. Lafayette's insistence on avenging Charleston had touched Lincoln profoundly, and Knox asked Lafayette to be godfather to his son. Lafayette and the others visited Cornwallis several times: Cornwallis had been curious about Lafayette's tactics during the Virginia campaign, and the two men were cordial and respectful, if not friendly. Cornwallis was startled at Lafayette's tall, robust frame. In contrast to the brash youth Cornwallis had envisioned, "the boy" had aged—and balded—prematurely. Cornwallis complained that General Clinton in New York had betrayed him by pledging support that never arrived. In fact, Clinton had arrived off Chesapeake Bay with 7,000 troops on October 24, but Cornwallis had already surrendered, and Clinton returned to New York to avoid engaging the French fleet.

The victory at Yorktown did not seal American victory in the war, of course. Apart from New York, British garrisons still controlled three vital port cities—Wilmington, North Carolina; Charleston, South Carolina; and Savannah, Georgia. With part of Clinton's army still at sea, Washington urged de Grasse to support an immediate attack on New York, but de Grasse refused, saying he was overdue in the French West Indies. Lafayette proposed an alternative plan, asking Washington to send him to the Carolinas, to support Greene, who had encircled British forces in Charleston. The de Grasse fleet could leave immediately for the West Indies with Lafayette's 2,000-man Light Division and stop at Charleston Bay along the way, land Lafayette's troops, and besiege the city from the water while Greene and Lafayette stormed the city by land. Washington supported Lafayette's plan enthusiastically, but de Grasse again refused to cooperate. He said he had too few ships to transport an additional 2,000 men, and that in any event, the danger of autumn storms made navigation through the treacherous Carolina sandbars impractical.

With de Grasse out of the picture, and Lafayette's Light Division too exhausted to march overland, Washington ordered a fresh division to reinforce Greene, while he organized the rest of his army's long march north to encircle Clinton in New York. Rochambeau's army would remain in Virginia to anchor military gains in the south, while the army of Cornwallis was separated into three relatively impotent detachments and marched to prisoner-of-war encampments, each well away from the other two, in Winchester, Virginia; Fredericktown, Maryland; and Lancaster, Pennsylvania. With little action expected during the winter, Washington believed Lafayette could better serve the American Revolution by returning to France to obtain more naval support. "No land force can act decisively unless it is accompanied by a Maritime superiority," he said. "A constant Naval superiority would terminate the War speedily—without it, I do not know that it will ever be terminated honourably."[5]

At the end of October 1781, Lafayette said farewell to the men he had led for eight months, across mountains, fields, forests, and swamps, through icy rain, scorching sun, and smothering humidity. Day after day, he had encouraged and inspired them in battle, comforted and cajoled them in camp, imbued them with pride or shame. They were his men; he was their marquis.

"In the moment the Major General leaves this place," he called out to them through his tears, "he wishes once more to express his gratitude to the brave corps of light infantry who for nine months past have been companions of his fortunes. He will never forget that with them alone of regular troops, he had the good fortune to maneuver before an army which after its reduction is still six times superior to the regular forces he had at that time."[6] Although the rest of his address is missing, he wrote to his friend, the Reverend Samuel Cooper, in Boston that "never have my feelings been so delightfully gratified as they were . . . when the American light infantry . . . gallantly stormed a redoubt Sword in hand, and proved themselves equal in this business to the Grenadiers of the best troops in Europe."[7]

On November 1, Lafayette left Yorktown with his brother-in-law, the vicomte de Noailles, and other French officers who were returning to France with him. Baltimore hailed their arrival five days later, and James Madison greeted them on behalf of Congress in Philadelphia. After granting him official leave, Congress appointed him its official advisor to American diplomats abroad—in effect, America's first ambassador-at-large. Secretary of Foreign Affairs Robert Livingston instructed Franklin in Paris, Adams in The Hague, and John Jay in Madrid "to communicate and agree on everything with him."[8] Congress also assumed the 2,000-livre debt Lafayette had incurred with Baltimore merchants to clothe his Light Division—a generous gift from a bankrupt nation, but a mere pittance compared to the 165,952 livres—about $1.66 million in today's currency—that Lafayette had spent on the Revolution.

In still another display of affection, Congress sent an official letter of commendation to King Louis XVI. Addressed to America's "Great, Faithful and Beloved Friend and Ally," the letter thanked the French monarch effusively for his "generous support," and noted, "Major General the Marquis de la Fayette has in this campaign so greatly added to the reputation he had before acquired, that we are desirous to obtain for him, on our behalf, every notice in addition to that favourable Reception which his merits cannot fail to meet with from a generous and enlightened Sovereign; and in that view, we have directed our Minister Plenipotentiary to present the Marquis to Your Majesty."[9]

Always teary-eyed and flustered at such moments, Lafayette lost all command of English grammar and metaphors, replying, "My attachment to America, the sense of my obligations, and the new favors conferred upon me are so many everlasting ties that devote me to her. At every time, in every part of the world my hearts will be panting for opportunities to be employed in her service."[10]

On November 25, Livingston, Finance Secretary Robert Morris, and Washington met with Lafayette and instructed him to ask the French court for a new subsidy or loan of 10 million livres (about $100 million in today's currency), along with additional naval and military aid.

Congress assigned the frigate *Alliance* to carry Lafayette back to France, and, ten days later, Lafayette arrived in Boston with his friends to sail home. The people of Boston would have none of it: the bells of every church tolled his arrival, and, by the time he and the other French officers reached the town hall near Hancock Wharf, the entire population blocked their route with whoops and cheers and songs. John Hancock, Samuel Adams, Reverend Samuel Cooper, the French consul, and others welcomed them with speeches, then guided the heroes from one festivity to the next—for days on end. They visited every historic site in Boston, Lexington, Concord, and, of course, Charlestown, where an explosion of cheers greeted them on Bunker Hill as Lafayette pledged 25 livres—about $250 in modern money—to rebuild the Charlestown meeting house, which had burned during the battle. The endless celebrations provoked Noailles to write in broken English to an American friend, "I think [it] indeed more easy to take a British army than to have a frigate out of Boston harbour. Since my arrival in this town I have been running, speaking, disputing, and I don't believe we shall be able to go to sea."[11] A week passed before Boston finally let the *Alliance* sail.

> Adieu, my dear general, [Lafayette wrote to Washington]. I know your heart so well, that I am sure that no distance can alter your attachment to me. With the same candour, I assure you that my love, my respect, my gratitude for you, are above expression; that, at the moment of leaving you, I felt more than ever the strength of those friendly ties that for ever bind me to you, and that I anticipate the pleasure, the most wished for pleasure, to be again with you, and, by my zeal and services, to gratify the feelings of my respect and affection. Will you be pleased to present my compliments and respects to Mrs. Washington, and to remember me to General Knox and General Lincoln. Adieu, my dear general, your respectful and loving friend, &c.[12]

Ironically, Lafayette's ship slipped out of Boston harbor just as another ship sliced through Atlantic waters out of New York bay—carrying Benedict Arnold to exile in disgrace in Britain. Before leaving, Arnold compounded his crimes against his former compatriots by ordering troops to burn New London and the homes of former neighbors in Connecticut, where he had once been a simple apothecary who tended their ills.[13]

After twenty-four uneventful days at sea, Lafayette landed in Lorient, on the southern coast of Brittany on January 17, 1782, and, three days later, he burst through the doors of the Noailles mansion in Paris and swept his two children into his arms. When he finally set them down, he discovered they had "grown up so much and that I have grown a great deal older."[14] His wife was not home, but a crowd soon formed outside the mansion's great facade, as a cortege of gilded carriages approached.

"Everyone who was there at the time still remembers the enthusiasm that the return of Lafayette engendered," wrote Lafayette's daughter.[15] King Louis XVI and Queen Marie-Antoinette had been at the Hôtel de Ville— the city hall—for a gala celebration of the birth of their first son and heir to the throne. Throwing protocol aside, the queen rushed Adrienne into the royal carriage and took her to the Noailles mansion, where the great knight awaited in his American major general's uniform. "Marie-Antoinette congratulated him warmly on his victories and safe return," according to one witness. Then "she delivered his wife to him down the carriage steps to the cheers and applause" of the surrounding crowd. "Trembling and faint with joy, Adrienne fell into her Gilbert's arms, and he carried her into the house."[16]

Adrienne "was overwhelmed by the joy of having him with her again, of his returning home safely from so many terrible dangers. For many months after his return," according to her daughter, "she actually felt ill every time he left their room." Adrienne later confessed to her husband that during those first few months after his return, she often grew faint when he left the room, fearing he might return to war and that she would never see him again. "I tried to find ways to control my feelings so you wouldn't become annoyed with me," she told him. "How happy I was!"[17]

The day after his return, Lafayette went to Versailles to pay homage to the king and confer with the king's ministers. He found the entire court at his feet—as, indeed, he would find all France and all Europe. Crowds followed his carriage, cheering and applauding and crying out "*Vive Lafayette!*" Artists vied to paint his portrait; poets praised him in verse and song, comparing him to ancient Greek and Roman heroes; philosophers wrote pamphlets extolling him; performers in concert halls and at the opera acknowledged his presence; he and Adrienne were the center of attention and adulation at every court festivity and every salon in Paris.

"The reception I have met with from the nation at large, from the king and from my friends will I am sure be pleasing to you and has surpassed my utmost ambition," he wrote to Washington. The king heaped compliments on his new brigadier general and spoke of Washington "in terms of so high a confidence, regard, admiration, and affection that I cannot forbear mentioning it. I have been the other day invited . . . with all the maréchals of France where your health was drank with great veneration, and I was requested to present you with the homages of that body. All the young men of this court are soliciting a permission to go to America." As always, he ended

his letter on a personal note: "My Daughter and Your George are . . . in perfect health."[18]

Despite the social demands on his time, Lafayette happily renewed his
friendship with his Masonic brother Benjamin Franklin and set to work fulfilling his diplomatic mandate from Congress—much to the satisfaction of
the seventy-one-year-old Philadelphian, whose crippling arthritis had transformed the otherwise beautiful, ten-mile carriage ride to Versailles into pure
torture. The venerable doctor greeted Lafayette warmly, gazed with justifiable pride at the young man's uniform and sash of an American major general—and the handsome ceremonial sword Franklin had so lovingly helped
design as a gift from Congress two years earlier.

"We are on the most friendly and confidential footing with each other,"
Franklin assured Foreign Affairs Secretary Livingston, "and he is really very
serviceable to me in my applications for additional assistance. . . . The Marquis de la Fayette was, at his return hither received by all ranks with all possible distinction. He daily gains in the general esteem and affection and
promises to be a great man here."[19]

Washington renewed his request for Franklin and Lafayette to obtain
"further pecuniary aid" from France, along with "a decisive naval force upon
this Coast in the latter end of May or beginning of June [1782]—unlimited
in its stay and operations . . . to finish the War in the course of the next
campaign [summer, 1782] with the ruin of that People [the English]."[20]
Franklin had been trying to fulfill Washington's request for weeks and had
all but given up hope when Lafayette arrived and assured the venerable doctor that "the footing I am upon at this court enables me some times to go
greater lengths than could be done by a foreigner."[21] With Franklin's blessing, he eagerly assumed the role of American statesman in King Louis's court,
always wearing his American major general's uniform and sash to display his
fealty, and, with each visit, accumulating ever more skills in the art of
diplomacy and negotiation.

Franklin had sought a loan of only 6 million livres ($60 million in
today's currency); Lafayette asked for 12 million—and easily got the 6 million Franklin wanted. He asked for massive naval and military aid, pointing
out to Vergennes that while Yorktown had been an important victory, it had
not ended the war. Without a decisive new thrust by France, he told the
minister, "I think that the evacuation of New York and Charleston are as
remote a part of their future plans as the evacuation of London. To get them
out, they will have to be forced out. . . . Otherwise, you can be sure that
England is determined to play a waiting game, spreading despair, and they
will attempt at least one more military campaign."[22]

After Franklin thanked him for his efforts, Lafayette replied joyfully,
"Mr. Franklin cannot render his friend more happy than in employing of

him for the service of America, and he feels a particular pleasure in avoiding for the doctor the trouble of journeys to Versailles where his peculiar situation calls him two or three times a week."[23]

Late in February, the British House of Commons censured Prime Minister Lord North's American policies and voted against continuing the war. Subsequent instructions to begin peace negotiations obviated the need for France to invest in new military adventures in America. On March 20, North resigned after a dozen years in office, and, early in April, the British named Richard Oswald to begin preliminary peace talks with Vergennes and Franklin, although he quickly recognized he would have to deal with Lafayette as well. Lafayette insisted that before talks could begin, the British release former president of Congress Henry Laurens from the Tower of London, and they agreed, although he had to remain in London on parole. Learning that Laurens was penniless, Lafayette sent him a letter of credit for £500 and negotiated an exchange of Laurens for Lord Cornwallis, who was on parole in America.

Oswald accompanied Laurens across the channel to France, and preliminary peace talks appeared ready to proceed. At every meeting, however, Oswald did his best to undermine negotiations. "You will see," the comte de Ségur warned Lafayette, "that there are as many absurdities in [diplomatic] negotiations as in [military] campaigns. You are going to be more than ever revolted by English pride, absurd Spanish vanity, French inconsistency, and despotic ignorance. But the more obstacles you cross, the greater merit you will deserve."[24]

From the first, Oswald tried to divide the allied camp by meeting with Franklin, Lafayette, and Vergennes separately—warning Franklin not to trust the French and Vergennes not to trust the Americans. He sent an aide to The Hague with a separate proposal for John Adams, who already mistrusted the French. Lafayette reported the "insidious proposals" to Secretary Livingston, saying Vergennes had rebuffed Oswald with a curt comment that "France would never treat without her allies." Adams did the same, saying "nothing could be done but in concert with France."[25] Franklin refused to negotiate until England recognized American independence, but negotiations dragged on, with each new British proposal invariably falling short of full recognition.

"I see that the expectation of peace is a joke," Lafayette exploded at Oswald's aide one day, "and that you only amuse us without any real intention of treating."[26] Lafayette dutifully reported his pessimism to Secretary of State Livingston: "A good army in America will do more to bring peace than one can imagine. . . . The king of England is more irritated than humiliated, it is thus necessary to convince him firmly of the impossibility of conquering us. If this campaign is vigorous, it will certainly be the last."[27]

With negotiations stalled, the young knights of France again appeared at Franklin's house to enlist in the American army. "Our young lords all want to become Lafayettes," one newspaper commented.[28] His friend the comte de Ségur, who had just married into the Noailles family, at last got the chance to sail to America as Lafayette and the vicomte de Noailles had done. "Tell Lafayette," he wrote his wife after arriving in America, "that I am in a country where his name is everywhere and where everyone adores him."[29]

In addition to serving Franklin, Lafayette also served as liaison to the French court for John Adams, who was attempting to negotiate a loan from Holland, and for John Jay, who was in Spain trying in vain to win recognition of United States independence. Although allied with France against England, Spain had refused to help or even recognize the Americans, fearing the contagion of colonist rebellion would spread to its own colonies in the Americas. Spain also feared that an independent United States would inevitably expand westward into Spanish territory and demanded, as a price for recognition, American abandonment of all claims and navigation rights in the Mississippi Valley—terms that Jay vehemently rejected.

"I have a letter from Mr. Jay, whose negotiations are not advancing," Lafayette wrote to Livingston, "and it is the Spaniards' fault."[30] He complained to Vergennes that Spain's treatment of Jay was insulting. "When Mr. Jay addresses himself to the minister," Lafayette reported, "he is either much occupied or ill. . . . This want of health, time, or instructions has hitherto occasioned the neglect of all the memorials which have been presented by the Americans."[31]

When he was not tending to American interests, Lafayette attended a succession of court functions, dinners, and balls with Adrienne—many of them for visiting dignitaries who invariably insisted on meeting the legendary Lafayette—the Friend of Washington and Conqueror of Cornwallis. The king and queen named Adrienne one of the court's official escorts for the visiting heir to the Russian throne, the czarevitch Paul of Russia, and his wife. Marie-Antoinette crowned their visit to Versailles with a gala ball in the spectacular Hall of Mirrors. Enswathed in the sparkle of five thousand candles, the czarevitch honored Adrienne with his hand, while the queen honored Lafayette with hers, and the two couples stepped out onto the huge floor to dance the queen's favorite quadrille before the magnificent assembly. Lafayette was awkward no longer, and the queen no longer laughed. The evening was a triumph for both Lafayettes.

In May, Adams won Dutch recognition of American independence; Lafayette congratulated him and urged him to come to Paris to help break the impasse in the peace negotiations with Britain. "Mr Franklin is very desirous you would come here," Lafayette wrote to Adams, "and I am the more anxious for it."[32] Adams agreed to come after he finished negotiating a loan to the United States from the Dutch government. A few weeks later, however, the British ravaged the French fleet in the Caribbean and captured de Grasse. With unchallenged British control of American coastal waters, Oswald grew less enthusiastic about American independence, while Spain all but rejected the idea rather than risk the English fleet's disrupting her trade with her South and Central American colonies. With his mission to Spain all but ended, Jay decided he could be more useful in Paris helping Franklin further the peace talks with England.

During the summer recess that followed, Lafayette was able to attend to his personal affairs for the first time in years. With a third child on its way—"your God son will have a brother,"[33] he wrote to Washington gleefully—he decided it was time for him and Adrienne to have a home of their own. He bought a magnificent property at 183 rue de Bourbon (now the rue de Lille) for 200,000 livres—about $2 million in today's currency. Perched on the Left Bank of the river Seine near the Palais Bourbon,[34] it had a breathtaking view of the floral tapestries in the gardens of the Tuileries Palace across the river. From the upstairs windows, Adrienne could see the facade of the Hôtel de Noailles, the only home she had ever known until then. Lafayette spent another 100,000 livres to restore and remodel the house and 50,000 more to furnish and decorate with a curious mélange of ornate Louis XV pieces for the reception rooms and spartan American rustic furnishings in his office and several other rooms. American souvenirs and objets d'art sprouted incongruously—and conspicuously—amidst the gilded furnishings of the salons and corridors.

In September, Adrienne gave birth two months prematurely to her third surviving child—a little girl, whom the Lafayettes promptly named Marie-Antoinette-Virginie—a compromise name carefully—and gently—reached during Adrienne's difficult pregnancy. Both agreed to recognize her good friend the French queen. As for the name by which they would call their daughter, Adrienne was a devout Catholic, who favored a proper saint's name—Marie. Her husband, the staunch American patriot and Freemason, overruled his wife, insisting on an American name—Virginie. He explained his choice in a letter to Benjamin Franklin moments after her birth:

> Every child of mine that comes to light is a small addition to the number of American citizens. I have the pleasure to inform you that, tho' she was but seven months advanced, Mde. de Lafayette has this morning become mother of a daughter who however delicate in its beginning enjoys a perfect health, and I hope will soon grow equal to the heartiest children.
>
> This reminds me of our Noble Revolution, into which we were forced sooner than it ought to have been begun. But our strength came on very fast, and upon the whole I think we did *at least* as well as any other people.

They asked me what name my daughter is to have. I want to present her as an offering to my western country. And as their is'nt [sic] a good *Sainte* by the name of Virginie, I was thinking if it was not presuming too much to let her bear a name similar to that of one of the United States.

Never at a loss for a bon mot, Franklin apologized that "this cruel gout [arthritis]" had prevented his coming to Paris to visit. He assured Lafayette that

in the midst of my pain, the news of Madm. de la Fayette's safe delivery, and your acquisition of a daughter gives me pleasure. In naming your Children I think you do well to begin with the most antient State. And as we cannot have too many of so good a Race, I hope you & Mde. de la Fayette will go thro' the Thirteen. But as that may be in the common way too severe a Task for her delicate Frame, and Children of Seven Months may become as Strong as those of Nine, I concent to the Abridgement of Two Months for each; and I wish her to spend the Twenty-six Months so gained in perfect Ease, Health & Pleasure.

While you are proceeding, I hope our States will some of them new-name themselves. Miss Virginia, Miss Carolina, & Miss Georgiana will sound prettily enough for the Girls, but Massachusetts & Connecticut, are too harsh even for the Boys, unless they were to be Savages. That God may bless you in the Event of this Day as in every other, prays your affectionate Friend & Servant

B. Franklin

With peace still a distant dream in America, Lafayette pressed Vergennes to send another major naval and military force to America to force the British to grant American independence. France was financially unable and unwilling to mount such a force by itself, however, and the wily French minister coaxed Spain to join a huge joint expedition to further Spanish interests with a plan to dislodge the British from Gibraltar and then sail to the West Indies to capture Jamaica from the British for Spain. Only then would the armada sail to the United States to dislodge the British from Charleston and, ultimately, the rest of North America. The Spanish agreed, and the two Bourbon monarchies began assembling the greatest armada and invasion force in history—greater even than the Spanish Armada that faced Sir Francis Drake in 1588. The armada of 1782 would boast sixty-six ships of the line (the earlier Spanish Armada had forty) and transports for nearly 25,000 troops (the Spanish Armada carried 19,000).

Undeterred by the Admiral's previous defeats in American waters, Vergennes named d'Estaing commander in chief, and he, in turn, requested as his second in command and commander in chief of all land forces the marquis de Lafayette, Conqueror of Cornwallis, American major general, and maréchal de camp in the French king's armies. Vergennes agreed enthusiastically, and Lafayette, not yet twenty-six years old, immediately expanded the expedition's mission to include massive sea and land assaults against all of British North America. After sweeping the British from Jamaica and the United States, Lafayette would realize his long-standing ambition to avenge the 1763 loss of New France by seizing Canada from the English and delivering it to the United States as the "fourteenth state."

In explaining the expedition and his role in it to Washington, Lafayette wrote, "My personal opinion is that a victory is needed before any treaty can be concluded. . . . I will, however, keep my American uniform, and the outside as well as the inside of an American soldier. I will conduct matters and take commands as an officer borrowed from the United States . . . and will watch for the happy moment when I may join our beloved colours."[35] When, according to Lafayette, d'Estaing explained the enterprise to Spanish King Charles III and said that Lafayette would seize Jamaica for Spain, the old monarch cried out, "No! No! I do not want him there. He will turn it into a republic."[36]

As French troops streamed westward to the port of Brest, the prospects of a costly and possibly disastrous confrontation with the French and Spanish forced the British to negotiate peace with the United States in earnest. In the United States, the British withdrew their troops from South Carolina, but not before a series of nasty skirmishes claimed the life of young John Laurens. "Poor Laurens is no more," Washington wrote to Lafayette. "He fell in a trifling skirmish in South Carolina, attempting to prevent the Enemy from plundering the Country . . . offer a blessing in my name to your son, & my Godson. . . . Adieu my dear Marq. Believe me to be, what I really am, your sincere friend & most affectionate Humble Servt."[37]

By late November, the French armada was set to sail for Cadiz to join the Spanish fleet, and the British now pressed for reconciliation with the Americans, warning John Adams and John Jay that the French would seize control of the United States if they succeeded in dislodging the British. They pointed out that Rochambeau's 4,000-man army remained on the American mainland, and war-weary American soldiers were abandoning the Continental army in droves. If Lafayette's 25,000 troops dislodged the British in New York, the French would control the east coast from New York to Newport, Rhode Island, where Rochambeau's army was encamped. Neither Adams nor Jay had liked or trusted the French since their discovery of the de Broglie plot to become American generalissimo. "They are interested in separating us from Great Britain, and on that point we may, I believe, depend upon them," Jay concluded in a letter to Secretary Livingston, "but it is not in their interest that we should become a great and formidable people, and therefore they will not help us to become so."[38] Adams agreed that "they are not a moral people."[39]

As Lafayette boarded his ship for Cadiz, Adams and Jay signed preliminary articles of peace after Oswald convinced them that America and England shared a common heritage and interests and pledged on behalf of "His Britannic majesty" that the United States were "free, sovereign and independent States." Further, he pledged that the king, his heirs, and his successors would relinquish "all claims to the government, property, and territorial rights of the same, and every part thereof." It was a complete capitulation, provoked by the threat of the enormous French-Spanish armada.

On December 23, Lafayette arrived in Cadiz and, a week later, learned of the peace agreement between the United States and Britain. The agreement not only shattered his hopes of leading the greatest armada in western history, it ended his career as a major general in the American army. A month later, France and Spain signed preliminary articles of a general peace with England and disbanded the armada, bringing the French knight's American quest to an end.

Eager, nonetheless, to be first to deliver the news of peace to the United States, he induced d'Estaing to provide him with a swift cutter, appropriately named *Triomphe*, to take him to Philadelphia. Before he could board her, however, an urgent appeal for help arrived from William Carmichael, who had been Silas Deane's aide in Paris and was now John Jay's chargé d'affaires in Madrid. The Spanish court continued to refuse to see him or give any sign of recognizing American independence. Without such recognition, the withdrawal of British troops from the United States would open the way for Spanish forces in Florida to march northward into Georgia and the Carolinas. Remembering Carmichael as "the first American I ever knew,"[40] Lafayette canceled his American trip and went to Madrid for what he believed was a more urgent obligation on behalf of his adopted nation: to use his formidable personal influence to obtain Spanish recognition of United States independence and sovereignty—and establish precise boundaries with Spanish-held Florida and Louisiana.

Lafayette sent an aide to America on the *Triomphe*, with letters to Congress, to the president of Congress, to Secretary Livingston, to his friends Hamilton and Nathanael Greene, and, of course, to Washington. The letters mixed the expressions of his own joy with the congratulations of a former soldier and the maturing political thoughts of a young statesman.

"My dear General," he wrote to Washington:

> I rejoice at the blessings of a peace where our noble ends have been secured. Remember our Valley Forge times, and from a recollection of past dangers and labours, we still will be more pleased at our present comfortable situation. What a sense of pride and satisfaction I feel when I think of the times that have determined my engaging in the American cause! You,

my dear general, who truly can say you have done all this, what must your virtuous and good heart feel on the happy instant where the revolution you have made is now firmly established. I cannot but envy the happiness of my grand children when they will be about celebrating and worshipping your name—to have had one of their ancestors among your soldiers, to know he had the good fortune to be the friend of your heart will be the eternal honour in which they shall glory. . . . At the prospect of a peace, I had prepared to go to America. Had the Spaniards got common sense I could have dispensed with that cursed trip to Madrid. But I am called upon by a sense of my duty to America. I must go. . . . In the month of June, I will embark for America. Happy, ten times happy will I be in embracing my dear General, My father, My best friend.[41]

Emboldened by months of high-level policy negotiations for the United States, Lafayette went on to broach his many political and social concerns. He proposed a new constitution, asking Washington to induce the people of America "to strengthen their federal union. . . . I look upon it as a necessary measure. Depend upon it, my dear general, that European politics will be apt to create divisions among the states. Now is the time when the powers of Congress must be fixed, the boundaries determined—and Articles of Confederation revised . . . it is the finishing stroke that is wanting to the perfection of the temple of liberty."

Turning to military affairs, he asked, "As to the Army, my dear General, what will be its fate? Will part of the Army be kept together . . . so that in case of danger, we may be called upon from every quarter, and reunite in defense of a country which the army has so effectually, so heroically served."

Lafayette also broached the question of slavery, which he found incompatible with the Masonic beliefs he knew Washington shared:

Permit me to propose a plan to you which might become greatly beneficial to the black part of mankind. Let us unite in purchasing a small estate where we may try the experiment to free the Negroes, and use them only as tenants. Such an example as yours might render it a general practice, and if we succeed in America, I will chearfully devote a part of my time to render the method fashionable in the West Indies. If it be a wild scheme, I had rather be mad that way, than to be thought wise on the other tack.

Adieu, adieu my dear General. . . . My best, most affectionate respects wait upon Mrs. Washington. Now we are going to quarrell, for I must urge your returning with me to France. Her accompanying you there, is the best way I know of to compromise the matter, and so she will make Mde. de Lafayette and me perfectly happy. Adieu, once more, my dear general. With every sentiment of love and respect I am for ever your most devoted and affectionate friend.[42]

When Lafayette's letters arrived in Philadelphia with the first news of peace and independence, Congress and the rest of America hailed him—more than Franklin, Jay, or Adams—as the great peacemaker. Calling Lafayette "a zealous labourer in the cause of this country," Washington sent an eloquent letter addressing his protégé's concerns—and his own plans to retire from public life:

> We now stand an Independent People, and have yet to learn political tactics. We are placed among the Nations of the Earth, and have a character to establish: but how we shall acquit ourselves time must discover . . . we shall be guilty of many blunders . . . experience which is purchased at the price of difficulties and distress will alone convince us that the honor, power, & true interest of this country must be measured by a Continental Scale; & and that every departure therefrom weakens the Union, & may ultimately break the band, which holds us together. To avert these evils—to form a Constitution that will give consistency, stability & dignity to the Union; and sufficient powers to the great Council of the Nation . . . is a duty which is incumbent upon every man who wishes well to his country—and will meet with my aid as far as it can be rendered in private walks of life; for hence forward my mind shall be unbent; & I will endeavor to glide gently down the stream of life till I come to that abyss, from whence no traveller is permitted to return.[43]

Washington thanked Lafayette for his role in bringing victory, saying "the peace is to be ascribed . . . [to] the armada wch. was preparing at Cadiz, and in which you were to have acted a distinguished part." Lafayette's concerns about slavery evidently pleased the general. "The scheme, my dear Marqs. which you propose as a precedent to encourage the emancipation of the black people of this country from that state of Bondage in wch. they are held, is a striking evidence of the benevolence of your heart. I shall be happy to join you in so laudable a work; but will defer going into detail of the business, till I have the pleasure of seeing you."[44]

Lafayette arrived in Madrid on February 15, 1783, dressed conspicuously—and defiantly—in his American major general's uniform, his magnificent ceremonial sword at his side. He knew that no one at the Spanish court would dare ignore or insult him as they had Jay and Carmichael. Even if they were inclined to refuse an audience to an American major general, they would not do so to an intimate of Versailles ministers, whom the French monarch, a nephew of the Spanish king, had personally appointed maréchal de camp. He prepared his visit carefully, sending letters to Carmichael in Madrid and to Vergennes in Paris, which he knew the Spanish secret police would intercept. "I expect Spain is going to act by you with propriety," he wrote to Carmichael, "but should they hesitate to treat you as a public servant of the United States, then, however, disagreeable is the taste

. . . France may stand a mediator & thro' that generous & common friend, we may come to the wished for connection with the Court of Spain."[45]

After reporting to the French ambassador in Madrid, Lafayette conferred with Carmichael before presenting himself to King Charles III, who peppered him with questions about Yorktown and Cornwallis, and about America generally. "They fear the loss of their colonies," Lafayette wrote to Secretary Livingston, "and the success of our Revolution appears to be an encouragement to this fear. Upon this subject their King has odd notions, as he has indeed upon everything. I gave a description of America and of each of the States, of which [Spanish Foreign Minister] Count de Florida Blanca appeared to know very little." Lafayette assured King Charles that America wanted nothing but prosperous commercial ties to Spain, and that Spain would benefit with long-lasting peace in her American colonies. Then, with Carmichael and the French ambassador ever-present at his side, he visited key members of the Spanish cabinet, introducing Carmichael "in the most public manner as the representative of the country which he serves"[46] and threatening to embarrass Spain by asking France to mediate the growing antipathy—and the several territorial disputes—between Spain and the United States.

After two weeks of intense pressure and thinly veiled threats, Lafayette convinced the Spanish foreign minister to accept Carmichael's credentials and present him to the king. "I have now the pleasure to inform you," Carmichael finally wrote to Livingston, "that the court of Spain has at length thought proper to receive me formally as the chargé d'affaires of the United States." He attributed his success to Lafayette's "zeal and ardor which ever influenced him when the interests of the United States were in question. . . . It is the happiest circumstance of my life that the man whose services I was instrumental in procuring to my country should be the one to whom I owe my first public appearance at the court of Spain."[47] Recognition of American independence removed all immediate threat of a Spanish invasion and forced Spain to negotiate fishing and navigation rights and fix formal boundaries between the United States and Spanish territories in Florida and along the Mississippi.

Ironically, John Adams exploded with rage when he learned of Lafayette's diplomatic triumph and sent a bitter letter to James Warren, the new president of Congress and an old political ally from Massachusetts: "It is my duty to unbosom myself to someone whose discretion I can rely. . . . We are at peace, but not out of danger. That there have been dangerous designs against our real Independence if not against our Union and Confederation, is past a doubt in my Mind—and we have cause to fear that such designs may be revived in various shapes." Referring to the de Broglie plot, Adams asked, "If the Maréchal had been that Commander-in-Chief, as was proposed, what would have been the Situation of your Army & Country? In whose power should we have been?" Then Adams turned to his real concern:

> The Marquis de la Fayette is an amiable nobleman, & has great merit. I enjoy his friendship, & wish continuance of it. But I will conceal nothing from you. . . . The instruction of Congress to their foreign ministers to consult with him was very ill judged. It was lowering themselves & their servants. There is no American minister, who would not have been always ready & willing to consult with him; but to enjoin it & make it a duty was an Humiliation, that would astonish all the World, if it was known. Your ministers will never be respected, never have any influence, while you depress them in this manner. . . . It may be said that he is a convenient go-between. I say this for this very reason, it should have been avoided. There ought to be no go-between. Your ministers should confer directly with the Ministers of other powers; and if they chuse at any time to make use of a third person, they ought to chuse him. . . .
>
> He is connected with a family of great influence in France. He rises fast in the French army. He may be soon in the Ministry. This mongrel character of French Patriot & American Patriot cannot exist long—And if hereafter it should be seriously the politicks of the French Court to break our Union, imagination cannot conceive a more proper instrument for the purpose than the Marquis. . . .
>
> I know the Confederation of our States to be a brittle vessel. I know it will be an object of jealousy to France. Severe strokes will be aimed at it, & if we are not upon our guard to ward them off, it will be broken.[48]

The Adams attack shocked and hurt Lafayette, who had shown Adams nothing but the deepest respect and courtesies. Lafayette's wife and her family had offered Adams the warmest hospitality from the moment he arrived in Paris five years earlier. Lafayette had given him personal letters of introduction to the most influential men in the realm; Adrienne had invited him to dine at her father's home on the rue Saint-Honoré and meet her entire family and other prominent noblemen and ladies; and he had always expressed nothing but warmth in his correspondence with Lafayette. Franklin and his grandson tried to console the sensitive Lafayette. Franklin even sent Foreign Affairs Secretary Livingston a warning that Adams's suspicions bordered on delusion: "The instances he supposes of their [French] ill will to us . . . I take to be as imaginary as I know his fancies to be that Count de Vergennes and myself are continually plotting against him. . . . I am persuaded, however, that he means well for his country, is always an honest man, often a wise one, but sometimes and in some things absolutely out of his senses."[49]

There is nothing to explain Adams's unwarranted attacks except his well-known moodiness and his loneliness for his family and his beloved New

England. "The first wish of my soul is to go home,"[50] he admitted, deploring the "laughers, weepers, cursers and flatterers" of Europe's gilded palaces. He even fell out with Franklin; he charged the Pennsylvanian with collusion with French foreign affairs minister Vergennes and called him "obsequious . . . . selfish . . . and eaten with all the passions which prey upon old age unprincipled."[51]

Lafayette was quick to recover from wounds—emotional as well as physical—and he not only forgave Adams, he ensured that Adrienne was first to welcome Abigail Adams and the Adams children to Paris when they arrived the following year.

When Lafayette returned to Paris from Spain, he learned that crop failures in his native Auvergne had produced widespread famine in that province. Acting on the authority granted by her husband, Adrienne ordered the Lafayette granaries in Chavaniac to release enough grain for the peasants to survive the winter. In addition, she acted to reduce long-term impoverishment by instructing the district governor to establish a spinning and weaving mill, and a school to teach local women to spin raw wool from their husbands' flocks and weave it into cloth. Adrienne reasoned that sheepherders would reap more profits from finished goods than from raw commodities.

Lafayette was astonished at her acumen. "You have rendered the country an enormous service, sweetheart," he wrote, after arriving at Chavaniac, "and I have to tell you that I consult the memorandum with your proposal every day. I hope to raise thirty thousand francs [then a synonym for livres, and, therefore, the equivalent of $300,000 in today's currency] for your manufactury, which promises to be of enormous benefit."[52]

Lafayette's return to Chavaniac marked the first time he had set foot in his boyhood home in the ten years since he began training for knighthood. One of the two aunts who had raised him had died, as had his grandmother and his beloved cousin Marie—the little girl who had been a sister to him. Only his aunt Charlotte, alone and aging, survived—and she all but collapsed from emotion at their reunion. "I got here just before nightfall," he wrote to Adrienne. "The first moment was terrible for my aunt, her cries, her anguish were terrifying. Finally, little by little, she pulled herself together and, despite abundant tears, she has cheered up immensely since my arrival. She has changed and aged terribly, but she has regained a little strength now and spends the day out of her bedroom and comes to the table to eat. Since my arrival, the house is full of people, and she keeps busy receiving them and doing the honors."[53]

The sight and sounds of starving peasants at the château gates stunned him. Some were the boyhood friends he had led through the forest on imaginary quests; they had learned of their seigneur's return—their lord and still master, under French feudal laws. When he appeared, many fell to their knees; some pleaded for food, others for clothing, still others for money; many begged for his intercession to prevent their eviction from their hovels for nonpayment of rents and taxes during the famine. He pledged to help and returned into the château, where obsequious vassals and local officials crowded the reception rooms to pay homage to the Conqueror of Cornwallis. But the constant wailing of peasants grew too much to bear. Learning that his own granaries were stocked to overflowing with wheat and rye, he ordered the overseers of his estates to distribute their contents to the peasants. When they advised him to sell his grain to distributors—that high prices had made it *the best time to sell* his grain—he retorted sternly, "No! Now is the best time to give it away!"[54] Amid cries of *"Vive Lafayette!"* he opened his granaries and distributed more than twelve hundred bushels of rye and eighteen hundred bushels of wheat to the poor, free of charge. He then called together local officials from the communities within his domain to determine the causes of the crop failures and the subsequent famine.

"He was deeply moved by the plight of the people,"[55] according to one local official.

The responsibility for the peasants' plight, he found, lay with the *ferme* to which his estates belonged. *Ferme* carries the double meaning of a commercial "firm," or company, and a "farm," and in eighteenth-century France *la ferme*—in the sense of "the company"—was an all-powerful, government-licensed monopoly that controlled the production, distribution, and sale of every essential product grown or made in France. The *ferme* protected its members in each province by imposing duties on all goods entering a province from other provinces or foreign nations, whether for sale in the province or simply passing through to another province or country. In effect, every product was taxed and retaxed and taxed again innumerable times, depending on its destination and the number of provincial borders it crossed to get to market from its point of origin. For the privilege of establishing and retaining its monopoly, the *ferme* paid royalties to the king and high officials, so that all shared in the wealth the *ferme* generated. Indeed, the king, his ministers, and participating monopolists—some of them aristocrats, others bourgeois—depended on the *ferme*'s ability to create artificial market shortages and high prices to bathe them all in luxury—even as it pushed the ordinary man toward bankruptcy and starvation. In the autumn of 1782, poor crops had sent prices soaring in the Auvergne, and, instead of easing shortages by distributing surplus stocks from its granaries, the *ferme* withheld grain and seed from market throughout the winter. By spring, seeds were so scarce and priced so high that poor farmers had no choice but to sell their lands to richer landlords of the *ferme* at desperation prices.

Outraged by the *ferme*'s assault on impoverished peasants, Lafayette proclaimed his solution: "I will . . . build public granaries to serve as seed banks for grain—and to which I shall contribute my own grain."[56] In effect, he forced the overseers of his vast estate to withdraw his granaries from the monopoly, not only sacrificing his and their profits, but undermining the power of the *ferme* to maintain high prices, artificial shortages, and famine. For the first time, Lafayette recognized that Auvergnats, his people by blood—living in the shadows of his own castle—needed his help as much as Americans, his people by adoption.

His quick, decisive action ended local grain shortages and famine and earned him the immediate acclaim of Auvergnats, who now saw him as a popular social and political leader instead of just another absentee lord of the manor. After five days at Chavaniac, Lafayette visited neighboring towns in Auvergne before returning to Paris. Town after town greeted him with cries of *"Vive Lafayette!"*; brass bands, government officials, judges in red robes and police in dress uniforms paraded to honor his visit. Not just the Conqueror of Cornwallis, he was now the *Frappeur de la Ferme*[57]—the Foiler of the *Ferme*, who had spanked the monopolists.

After he returned to Paris, the king awarded him France's highest military honor—the Cross of St. Louis. His father-in-law, the duc d'Ayen, was one of six living members of the Noailles family who held the cross, and the king gave the duke the honor of inducting his son-in-law into the Order of the Cross, which Louis XIV had created in 1693 for French military men who distinguished themselves by their virtue, merit, and outstanding services to France.[58] His induction set off another flurry of public adulation. "All that Xenophon said of his young Athenian [Alcibiades] would pass for fabulous, if la Fayette had not achieved it," proclaimed a Paris literary magazine.[59] The editor of a new edition of *Plutarch's Lives* dedicated it to Lafayette, "a young hero whose modesty equals his courage and wisdom."[60] He compared Lafayette's career to that of Scipio Africanus, the Roman general who crushed Hannibal and conquered Carthage. A Lafayette cult emerged in Paris, with pamphlets describing mythological adventures of the "unsullied hero of purest motives and rarest wisdom, defying evil men and cruel times in the cause of truth and reason."[61]

Still officially charged by Congress to further American interests in Europe, Lafayette used his enormous personal influence to champion American trade. Freed of mercantile ties to Britain, American merchants could, for the first time, sell their goods anywhere in the world without first sending them to England for taxation by the British government prior to resale. The problem was to get other nations to buy American goods. Most nations were no different from England: they too maintained impenetrable trade barriers to protect their own industries, and France was no exception. The French government taxed American goods at the port of entry, and the *ferme*, in turn, taxed the goods as they crossed every provincial boundary, thus pricing

American products—tobacco, lumber, cloth, and tools—out of the French market.

Before leaving for Chavaniac, Lafayette had asked the French government to declare certain ports free for unrestricted entry of American goods into France. "I cannot repeat too often," he wrote to Foreign Minister Vergennes, "that after a great war and a beautiful peace, it would be ridiculous to lose the fruit of so much blood and treasure, and that only to please one class of people [the *ferme*] who please no one. After having taught England some lessons, let us learn the ones that she now gives us and try to make the Americans feel as well treated by their friends as by their enemies and not force them to give preference to the latter."[62] To the finance minister, Lafayette wrote that France could recapture the costs of the war by trading with the United States, but warned that "we have lost time in obtaining that goal, and at a time when the English are making up for their errors, I think it is important for us to reduce the barriers to our trade for Americans . . . it is up to us to capture almost all the American trade . . . [but] our own trade barriers are threatening us with loss of most of the largest part of that trade."[63]

By the time Lafayette returned to Paris from Chavaniac, his victory over the *ferme* in Auvergne and his letters to the ministry had earned him a new reputation as a champion of free trade—a role he eagerly embraced. Determined to prevent French monopolists from impoverishing American farmers as they had Auvergnat farmers, he found a friendly ally in Vergennes—not because the foreign minister shared Lafayette's sense of social responsibility, but because trade with America had, from the first, been one of the cornerstones of his policy for undermining British commerce and restoring French commercial and military power in the world. Although Vergennes declared Bayonne and Dunkerque free ports for American goods, Lafayette wanted more. Using the minister's own logic, he suggested that French trade with America would improve faster by opening Lorient and Marseilles and making the entire coast of France accessible to American goods to facilitate distribution into the French heartland. By now Vergennes knew the foolishness of arguing with his zealous young friend over American interests; he opened the four ports to American trade.

Believing his work complete, Lafayette did what he had never done before: he took his wife for a summer's vacation of two idyllic weeks of play, rest, and contemplation at Chavaniac—their first conjugal visit to his birthplace. Adrienne met her husband's beloved *tante* Charlotte, with whom she had maintained a warm, regular correspondence. He guided Adrienne through his maze of boyhood memories, along his secret forest paths; he showed her how to pick edible mushrooms and berries, placed sweet wild blackberries between her lips, introduced her to villagers he had known as a boy.

She met and charmed the peasants who lived on Lafayette lands. Like them and all Auvergnats, she was deeply religious, attended daily mass and Sunday services, and won the admiration of both peasantry and priests. She visited the temporary home of the weaving school she had established and gave the director another 6,000 livres to speed its completion and sustain its maintenance.

While Adrienne attended mass one morning, her Gilbert[64] wrote to George Washington that his conduct of the war had been highly praised throughout all Europe:

> Never did a man exist who so honourably stood in the opinions of mankind, and your name, if possible, will become still greater in posterity. Every thing that is great, and every thing that is good were not hitherto united in one man. Never did one man live whom the soldier, Statesman, Patriot, and Philosopher could equally admire, and never was a revolution brought about, that in its motives, its conduct, and its consequences could so well immortalize its glorious chief. I am proud of you, my dear general, your glory makes me feel as if it was my own—and while the world is gaping at you, I am pleased to think, and to tell, the qualities of your heart do render you still more valuable than any thing you have done.
>
> Adieu, my dear General, Mde. de Lafayette joins with me in Presenting our Best Respects to Mrs. Washington. She loves You With all Her Heart. . . . Adieu, adieu, My dear General, Do often remember your adopted son.[65]

12

Completing the Quest

ON SEPTEMBER 3, 1783, Benjamin Franklin, John Jay, and John Adams strode into the Hôtel d'York,[1] not far from Lafayette's home in Paris, to sign the Treaty of Paris that ended the Revolutionary War. The American signatories invited the tortured former president of Congress, Henry Laurens, whom the British had captured and exchanged for Cornwallis, to share in the historic American triumph. As the Americans and British were signing the Treaty of Paris, French and Spanish diplomats signed a separate treaty with the British at the Palace of Versailles ending their war with Britain and establishing peace in western Europe for the first time in more than forty years.

From his camp in the hills above the Hudson north of New York, a jubilant George Washington wrote to Lafayette that the treaties "will put a period to my military services & carry me back to the walks of private life, & to that relaxation and repose which can not but be grateful to a mind which has been on the stretch for more than eight years."[2]

For France, which lost twenty-five hundred men in the American Revolution, the Treaty of Versailles avenged her humiliating defeat in the Seven Years' War and the galling disgrace of an English commissioner overseeing Dunkerque. He sailed home to England immediately after the signing, and King Louis XVI proclaimed an official holiday— the *Fêtes de la Paix*, or Festival of Peace. After a Te Deum at Nôtre-Dame Cathedral, the court staged a gala ceremony in the front courtyard of the Tuileries Palace in Paris. A huge bonfire lit the square in front of the Hôtel de Ville, or city hall, that evening, and the king ordered gargantuan buffets of food and wine in public squares for all the people of Paris—and orchestras to entertain as they ate, drank, danced, and savored victory over their historical nemesis, England.

In the weeks that followed, the Lafayettes made their magnificent home one of the most important social centers in Paris—a rendezvous for all Americans of note living or visiting the capital during one of the most festive eras the city had ever witnessed or ever would again. Paris was aglow with new theaters and clubs; publishers printed new books and periodicals; the Montgolfier brothers sent the first lighter-than-air balloons soaring over Paris and carried the first passengers across thirty miles of countryside from the Tuileries Gardens behind the royal palace. After winter's chill forced balloon enthusiasts into warmer arenas, Dr. Friedrich Anton Mesmer of Vienna entranced them with demonstrations of his new discovery—"animal magnetism." Before everyone's eyes—including those of the delighted Lafayettes—Mesmer "cured" the sick and crippled by inducing trancelike states that harmonized their "dysharmonized" bodily functions. Lafayette enrolled as a "disciple"—for an initiation fee of 2,500 livres (about $25,000)—and Mesmer gladly shared a few secrets of animal magnetism with him, including a "cure" for Lafayette's devastating seasickness whenever he set foot aboard ship. Polar forces would quickly restore his body's harmony, Mesmer assured him, if he simply embraced the mainmast while facing the North Pole.

Although the advent of peace permitted the French finance minister to reduce government spending, Queen Marie-Antoinette found ingenious new ways to increase it, including a study of the different classes of society within her realm. To examine peasant life, she ordered the construction of a hamlet, which still stands, on the palace grounds at Versailles, complete with flocks of sheep, goats, chickens, ducks, and geese. Workers dug an artificial stream and raised a cluster of thatched-roof houses and a working mill on its banks. Palace designers fashioned colorful peasant dresses for the queen, who strolled the footpaths, parasol in hand, to the applause of her courtiers, poised in equally stunning peasant dresses at the windows of the otherwise empty, uninhabited houses. Peasant life, she concluded, was pleasant indeed, if simple, with none of the hardships portrayed by social reformers such as Lafayette. It was a short carriage ride from her hamlet up the hill to the Petit Trianon, her palatial little marble playhouse, where she often went with a few close friends to escape the bustle of palace life.

The rest of the French aristocracy invented equally entertaining pursuits—masked balls, extravagant dinners, and gala soireés at the theater, opera, or ballet. By comparison, the Lafayettes were staid: even Puritan John Adams commented on their strict repudiation of card playing, gambling, late-night parties, and other fashionable amusements. The Lafayettes "received" every Monday evening; theirs was the most celebrated salon, where illustrious members of French nobility mixed with Americans—Benjamin Franklin and John Adams usually prominent among them. At a time when things

American had become the rage of Paris, Lafayette's home was an American shrine, with a cherished portrait of Washington at its altar and American flags draped conspicuously on walls and furnishings. The wall of his "American" study held a gold-lettered copy of the Declaration of Independence that Franklin's grandson William had obtained for him. It filled but one-half of a double frame: Lafayette said the other half awaited "the declaration of rights in France." Even Adams's cranky face melted into a broad smile when Lafayette pulled his guests to the Declaration—as he always did—to see the Adams and Franklin signatures as the two Americans looked on in feigned modesty.

"The object of my wanting a Declaration of Independence," Lafayette explained, "is . . . when I wish to put myself in [good] spirits, I will look at it, and most voluptuously read it over."[3]

Adrienne proved herself a brilliant hostess. Crowds gathered outside the brightly illuminated Lafayette mansion to watch the luminaries flow in and out: the ever-present Franklin; philanthropist-politician William Wilberforce, the founder of England's Anti-Slavery Society; and twenty-four-year-old William Pitt the Younger, who would become British prime minister before the end of the year. Lafayette enjoyed Pitt's "modesty, nobility, and character, which is as rich as the role for which it destines him to play. . . . Since we won the war, I must admit I take a lot of pleasure in meeting with Englishmen. . . . I thought of the horrors they inflicted on America and their ties to tyranny . . . but now I enjoy them and have no difficulty mingling with them, either as a Frenchman, an American soldier or an ordinary person."[4]

Imitations of American-style *égalité* and *liberté* also became fashionable in Paris. Young noblemen like the vicomte de Noailles, who had soldiered in America, introduced simpler, more relaxed, informal American dress and manners. Queen Marie-Antoinette even received men at her table—something no queen had ever done. As Americans flocked to France on business, French aristocrats vied with each other to invite them to their salons. Introducing *mon ami américain* was not only chic, it was an essential for social success at any formal reception. But it was Lafayette's house that most Americans sought, and he welcomed each as an old friend. "Be pleased to consider my house as being your own," he had written Connecticut banker Jeremiah Wadsworth, who came to sell American tobacco to the French tobacco monopoly. Lafayette immediately agreed to help.[5]

In October, former major Pierre Charles L'Enfant, Lafayette's former aide and military engineer at Albany, appeared at the rue de Bourbon with a packet of letters from Washington—one of them dictated by Martha, who was refurbishing their home at Mount Vernon and needed a staggeringly large amount of new household goods. Prefacing it with apologies "for any liberty I might take with you," Washington explained that, after warring with the English for eight years, "I do not incline to send to England (from whence formerly I had all my Goods) for any thing I can get upon tolerable terms elsewhere." Relying on Lafayette's knowledge of "customs, taste & manner of living in America," he asked his French friend to buy and ship a complete set of

> plated ware. . . . Every thing proper for a tea-table . . . a large tea salver, square or round as shall be most fashionable; to stand on the tea-table for the purpose of holding the Urn, teapot, Coffeepot, Cream pot, china cups & saucers & c[eter]a.
>
> A large tea urn, or receptacle for the water which is to supply the tea pot, *at the table.*
>
> 2 large Tea pots—& stands for Ditto.
>
> 1 Coffee-Pot—& stand.
>
> 1 Cream Pot,
>
> 1 Boat or Tray, for the Teaspoons.
>
> 1 Tea-Chest—such as usually appertains to tea or breakfast tables—the inner part of which, to have three departments—two for tea's of different kinds—the other for Sugar. . . .
>
>   Also,
>
> Two large Salvers, sufficient to hold twelve common wine glasses, each.
>
> Two smaller-size Do. for 6 wine glasses, each.
>
> Two bread baskets—middle size.
>
> A Sett of Casters—to hold oil, Vinegar, Mustard, &c.
>
> A Cross or Stand for the centre of the Dining table.
>
> 12 Salts, with glasses in them.
>
> Eight Bottle sliders.[6]
>
> Six large Goblets, for Porter. Twelve Candlesticks.
>
> Three pair of snuffers, & Stands for them.[7]

In addition to Washington's shopping list, L'Enfant brought Lafayette designs for a new American medal. Secretary of War Henry Knox and a group of retired officers had founded the Society of Cincinnati, a fraternal organization to raise funds for Revolutionary War widows and orphans. They named it after Lucas Quinctius Cincinnatus, the Roman who left his farm in 485 B.C. to lead Rome to victory over the Aequians and, as Washington would do, rejected subsequent military and political power and returned to his farm. Perpetually hereditary to the oldest direct or collateral male heir, membership was open to all officers with three years' service in the Revolution who paid an enrollment fee equivalent to one month's military pay. The society elected George Washington its first member and president, and, because America had no mint, Knox sent L'Enfant to Paris to have medals struck at the French mint[8] and to ask Lafayette to organize and head a French branch. Because "we consider you as an American and therefore one of us,"[9] the American branch inducted Lafayette into its membership with Washington and asked L'Enfant to present the first medal and certificate to Lafayette.

When he was not shopping for Martha Washington, Lafayette threw himself into the task of organizing the French branch of the Society of Cincinnati. His immediate friends and former comrades in arms eagerly enrolled—d'Estaing, Rochambeau, de Grasse, the vicomte de Noailles, the comte de Ségur, Gimat, and others. But Lafayette soon discovered that the society provoked as much rage as respect. Poor veterans could not afford membership, and many political leaders—Americans as well as French—feared that hereditary membership would produce an elite military aristocracy that could subvert civilian government. In the United States, Jefferson and Samuel Adams railed against it, and John Adams wrote an angry letter to Lafayette from Holland that "the introduction into America of so great an innovation as an order of chivalry . . . [is] against the spirit of our governments and the genius of our people."[10] Lafayette unilaterally abandoned enrollment fees and assured Adams, "My principles ever have been against heredity."[11] He then wrote to Washington: "Most of the Americans here are indecently violent against our Association . . . Jay, Adams, and all the others. . . . I am as ready as any man to renounce it. You will be my compass, my dear General, because at this distance I cannot judge. In case . . . you find that heredity will injure our democratic institutions, I join with you by proxy in voting against it." With Lafayette's letter in hand, Washington cast his vote and Lafayette's with the majority of American delegates to abolish heredity in the society.

Along with the crates of housewares, Lafayette sent the Washingtons innumerable personal gifts, ranging from French hunting dogs and European plants to a tender portrait of the three Lafayette children—and the first glimpse Washington had of his godson and namesake.

When Martha was not standing over him dictating her list of needs, Washington always wrote thoughtfully and warmly—often poetically—to the young man who remained a son to him:

> At length my Dear Marquis I am become a private citizen on the banks of the Potomac & under the shadow of my own Vine & my own Fig-tree, free from the bustle of a camp & the busy scenes of public life, I am solacing myself with those tranquil enjoyments, of which the Soldier who is ever in pursuit of fame—the Statesman whose watchful days & sleepless nights are spent in devising schemes to promote the welfare of his own—perhaps the

A portrait of the Lafayette children that Lafayette sent to George
and Martha Washington shows Anastasie, left, and Virginie, right.
In the center is George-Washington Lafayette, Washington's godson
and Lafayette's only son, standing by a bust of his father. The Washingtons hung the portrait above the mantel in their living room at
Mount Vernon, along with a cherished portrait of Lafayette. (*From
the author's collection.*)

ruin of other countries, as if this Globe was insufficient for us all—& the
Courtier who is always watching the countenance of his Prince, in hopes of
catching a gracious smile, can have little conception. I am not only retired
from all public employments, but I am retiring within myself; & shall be
able to view the solitary walk, & tread the paths of private life with heart-
felt satisfaction. Envious of none, I am determined to be pleased with all,
& this my dear friend, being the order for my march, I will move gently
down the stream of life, until I sleep with my Fathers.[12]

Washington went on to describe the British evacuation of New York the
previous November—"the American troops took possession of it the same
day & delivered it over to the civil authority of the state . . . the harbour of
New York was finally cleared of the British flag about the 5h. or 6h. of
Decemr." Thus ended the great and decisive "battle" of New York in which
Lafayette had so wanted to participate—without a shot fired. Washington

told Lafayette of going to Philadelphia and thereafter to Annapolis, "where Congress were then, and are now sitting, I did present them my Commission, & made them my last bow—& on the Eve of Christmas entered these doors, an older man by near nine years, than when I left them. . . .

"Come with Madame la Fayette," he urged Lafayette, "& view me in my domestic walks. I have often told you; & I repeat it again, that no man could receive you in them with more friendship & affection that I should do; in which Mrs. Washington would cordially join me. We unite in respectful compliments to your Lady, & best wishes for your little flock. With every sentiment of esteem, admiration & love, I am, my dr. Marqs., your most affectionate friend."[13]

Lafayette eagerly accepted Washington's invitation, asking his "dear general . . . to present dutiful affectionate compliments to Mrs. Washington and . . . tell her that I hope soon to thank her for a dish of tea at Mount Vernon. Yes, my dear general, before the month of June is over you will see a vessel coming up Pottowmack, and out of that vessel will your friend jump with a panting heart and all the feelings of perfect happiness. . . . Adieu, my dear General, accept with your usual goodness the affectionate tribute of a heart so entirely devoted to you that no words can ever express the respect, the love and all the sentiments which you know it is glowing for you, and that make me untill my last breath your obedient servant and affectionate friend."[14] Lafayette renewed his appeal to Washington and Martha to accompany him to France on the return voyage. Adrienne, too, wrote to Washington and invited him and Martha to come to Paris.

By the time Washington received Lafayette's and Adrienne's invitations, however, he and Martha had adopted two of her grandchildren, who were left orphaned by the death of their father—Martha's son by her first marriage. He sent a touching reply to Adrienne: "Mrs. Washington is highly honoured by . . . your polite invitation to Paris; but she is far too advanced in life, and is too much immersed in the care of her little progeny, to cross the Atlantic. This, my dear Marchioness . . . is not the case with you. You have youth . . . and must have a curiosity to see the country, young, rude, and uncultivated as it is, for the liberties of which your husband has fought, bled, and acquired much glory, where every boy admires, every body loves him. Come, then, let me entreat it, and call my cottage your home; for your own doors do not open to you with more readiness than mine would. You will see the plain manner in which we live, and meet the rustic civility; and you shall taste the simplicity of rural life. It will diversify the scene, and may give you higher relish for the gayeties of the court, when you return to Versailles."[15]

Despite the social triumphs of American businessmen in France, commercial success proved more elusive. Establishment of free ports did not loosen the monopoly of the *ferme*, which made internal markets all but impregnable to foreign goods that competed with French goods. The *ferme* not only refused to buy American products such as tobacco, it priced French products such as brandy so high that American merchants could not afford to trade for it. American merchants turned to Franklin for help, and he, in turn, appealed to Lafayette, who took the problem to the new finance minister, Charles-Alexandre de Calonne. Calonne, however, had close ties to the *ferme* and rejected Lafayette's appeal, pledging to protect French industry by strengthening *ferme* control of trade. The resilient Lafayette adopted a daring new strategy learned from essayist Tom Paine: he published a public manifesto exposing the methods used by the *ferme* to drive French market prices higher. Assailing state protection of the *ferme*, he called for establishment of open markets and free competition:

> Our present system has driven American trade away. The ferme can do nothing but impede trade. . . . France has lost the tobacco trade . . . one particular tobacco ship waited in France for nine months, during which Messieurs les Fermiers Généraux [the *ferme's* governors] would neither buy the cargo nor permit it to go to Marseilles, where the Italians wanted to buy it. . . . Good tobacco currently sells in Philadelphia for 50 to 60 shillings [100 shillings = one livre] a hundredweight. When it arrives in France, the various duties bring the cost to 54 livres. . . . These abuses have long restricted our trade, afflicted our citizens, and . . . offset the advantages we have over other nations. . . . These vexations lead to smuggling and cheating, and for a foreigner ignorant of our customs and language, they are even more intolerable.[16]

Lafayette proposed a radically new approach to foreign trade:

> Looking at France and America, we see on the one side raw materials and on the other manufactured goods, which means a very profitable exchange for France. . . . If we avoid ruining the trade, our broadcloth, our silks of every kinds, our linens and fashionable clothing, etc. will find a considerable American market that with care can be further enlarged. . . . While we return their furs to them manufactured into hats, muffs, etc., use their excellent iron, and import their lumber (as the British did before) for the construction of ships, to which we add our own sails, rigging, and so forth, we should also see that there is a profitable market in France for their indigo, rice, and tobacco.
>
> Here, then is a new source of wealth to revive our productions and our manufactures. It would be stupid to dry up this channel of commerce, since it is much easier to improve it.[17]

Lafayette's *Observations* had their desired effect. An embarrassed Calonne wrote to Lafayette from Versailles, sending the king's pledge of "absolute" duty-free entry for American goods: "The Americans will find all the facilities they need, especially at Dunkerque, to sell their leaf tobacco, rice, wood, and other merchandise, as well as to buy things of use to them such as linens, spirits, woolens, &ca. &ca. We are even thinking of building special warehouses and outlets for American merchants that would be made available to them at special low rates. I have given Orders to the *fermiers généraux* to give preferential treatment and prices to American tobacco, and to give American trade advantages available to no other nation." He pledged that "the Government will not suffer [American traders] to experience any kind of vexation. . . . I am going to examine immediately how far customs and duties hurt commerce." To the delight of American merchants, Calonne abolished export taxes on French brandies bound for America.[18]

Lafayette's pamphlet—and Calonne's responses—seemed a spectacular diplomatic and commercial triumph that won praises from American merchants. Washington sent his congratulations, and Congress passed a resolution expressing "the high sense which Congress entertain of his important services to the commerce of France and the United States."[19]

To Lafayette's dismay—and that of American merchants—the French government proved infuriatingly disingenuous. Although Calonne removed government tariffs, he said he had no power to remove other trade barriers, such as piloting fees, anchorage fees, docking fees, loading and unloading fees, and storage fees. Nor could he remove internal duties levied by the *ferme* in each province, town, and privileged area in France on goods traveling overland—even goods bound for another country. Lafayette was as infuriated as his merchant friends and returned to Versailles to confront Calonne, who threw up his hands, saying he could do nothing, that most fees and duties were feudal rights dating back to the Middle Ages. Even more infuriating was his obsequious insistence that, despite his inaction, "His Majesty is at all times prepared to offer the proofs of friendship, based on equity and his sense of justice, that must reign between France and the United States."[20] It was clear that Calonne and the king had placed the interests of friends in the *ferme* above those of the United States and that liberalization of trade between the United States and France would take years to achieve. In the meantime, American merchants would have to establish new trade ties elsewhere.

With trade talks adjourned for the summer, Lafayette prepared for the trip to America he had planned at the announcement of peace with England. His mission to Spain had deprived him of the final salutes of his troops and fellow officers in America—and of Washington's emotional farewell to his officers at Fraunces Tavern in New York the previous December. John Marshall, Washington's friend and fellow Virginian, had described the scene: "'With a heart full of love and gratitude,' Washington had said, lifting a glass to toast them, 'I now take leave of you; I most devoutly wish that your latter days may be as prosperous and happy as your former ones have been glorious and honorable.' Having drunk, he added, 'I cannot come to each of you to take my leave, but shall be obliged if each of you will come and take me by the hand.' General Knox, being nearest, turned to him. Washington, incapable of utterance, grasped his hand, and embraced him. In the same affectionate manner he took leave of each succeeding officer. The tear of manly sensibility was in every eye; and not a word was articulated to interrupt the dignified silence, and the tenderness of the scene."[21]

Lafayette, too, had wanted to embrace their victory. In every letter to Washington, he never failed to ask his "dear general" to "present my best compliments to my friends in the Army," and they, in turn, never failed to reciprocate. Henry Knox, who had named Lafayette godfather to his son, pledged to relive "the pleasures of your friendship with the ardor of a lover, and my Harry Your Godson, shall be taught the same sensations."[22]

"The dissolution of the army," Lafayette lamented to Washington, "has not been heard of by me without a sigh. How happy I have been at the head quarters of that army! How affectionately received in every tent I had a mind to visit! My most fortunate days have been spent with that army—and now that it is [no] more, my heart shall ever reverence and cherish its memory. God grant our brother officers may be treated as they deserve."[23]

Lafayette's return took on the character of a pilgrimage: "To my great satisfaction," he wrote Washington, "my departure is fixed upon the tenth of next month [June]. My course will be straight to Pottowmack."[24]

It was not easy to leave Adrienne and the children. Between the gala soirées and visits to Versailles, he had found time, as never before, for some quiet afternoons and evenings at home with Adrienne and the children. He continually instructed them in English and taught them to venerate the godlike Washington. "My little family," he once told Washington, "are taught before all to revere and to love George Washington." Now, he would have to leave them and risk his life once more on the treacherous Atlantic crossing.[25] The separation caused him "inexpressible heartache," and, at a stagecoach stop the following day, he hired a courier to take a note to Adrienne: "While we're changing horses, I wanted to send you a word, I wanted to tell you again how deeply I regret leaving you; never was my separation from you this painful, my sweetheart, and while this absence will not be as long, without the idea of great public service or glory to sustain me a little, there is no consolation for my sadness. This far from America, I cannot yet feel the pleasure of seeing my friends again, only the pain of leaving behind those I love most. The more time I spend with you, sweetheart, the dearer you become to me, the more I revel in the happiness of our being as one, of being loved by you; but the pain of leaving you also grows worse. . . . Adieu, my sweetheart, it is so sweet to tell you that I love you, so painful to say adieu. . . . I embrace you, my darling, and I hope you know how much I love you."[26]

Lafayette left with a young aide, the chevalier de Caraman, on *Le Courrier de l'Europe*, the first ship in history to provide regular passenger service between France and the United States. The new service was another of the many by-products of peace, which ended state-sponsored privateering and unleashed a tide of transatlantic travel. The safety of the seas notwithstanding, the roll of the ship had its usual effect on the French knight, reducing him to a heaving mass of blubber. He reeled out of his cabin and staggered topside to apply Mesmer's cure for seasickness at the mainmast—only to find the mast too thick to embrace—and coated with tar. "Hugging it," he complained to Adrienne, "is absolutely impossible without getting tarred from head to foot."[27]

While Lafayette's ship lurched westward, an eastward-bound vessel was carrying former Virginia governor Thomas Jefferson to France to help Franklin and Adams expand American commerce in Europe. After more than a month at sea, both Jefferson and Lafayette reached their destinations, with Lafayette, ironically, setting foot on New York Island for the first time, although he had spent months across the Hudson River with his Light Division.

Contrary to his expectations, Lafayette found the United States far from united. The Articles of Confederation had left Congress impotent and the states all but sovereign, independent nations. What started as a league of friendship had become a league of enemies. Instead of warring with England, they were warring with each other, over boundaries, trade, and rights to immigrate into one state from another. They banned many of each other's products and priced others out of local markets with high duties. Eight states had armies, two had fired against each other, and Pennsylvania, Delaware, and Maryland were on the verge of war over navigation rights in Chesapeake Bay. Nor were leaders of different states welcome within the borders of other states to discuss mutual problems and resolve conflicts. There was one exception: Lafayette, who had pledged his life, his fortune, and his sacred honor to every state. He belonged to the nation, and his arrival set off a deluge of nonstop revelry across America, interrupted only on Sundays, when piety kept Americans in church or at home. Every village, city, and state sought to rally around his mystical presence and the ethereal spirit of nationhood he represented.

On the morning of August 5, 1784, Lafayette conquered New York as he had not been able to do during the war. Cannons boomed, church bells rang, bands blared, and thousands cheered as his open carriage displayed him to the city, escorted by a smartly dressed horsetroop, their swords drawn in honor of their former general. Flags and bunting flew from houses and buildings; men, women, and children squeezed through every window to see him, cheer him, and cry out to him by the only name they had ever known: "Mar-quis, Mar-quis, Mar-quis." That evening, according to the French consul in New York, about a hundred former comrades in arms staged a banquet for him at the Masonic lodge, as "the flag of America, unfurled on the roof of the house, heralded . . . the joy in our hearts as well as the solemnity of the occasion that was being celebrated."[28]

The following day, General Horatio Gates, whom Lafayette had once suspected of masterminding the Conway Cabal, took him on a tour of the city's defenses. Thousands cheered their every step. "The Marquis has an old head upon young shoulders," Gates commented,[29] recognizing that the Marquis had matured well beyond his twenty-seven years. He had been an adolescent when he first set foot on American soil; seven years later, he returned an experienced and skilled military leader, diplomat, and statesman—with a receding hairline and expanding paunch to prove it.

After two days of continuous celebration, he left for New Jersey and the road south to Philadelphia, Baltimore, and Mount Vernon. Ten miles outside Philadelphia, a huge cortège of former officers joined the Pennsylvania militia, the City Troop of Horse, and a crowd of city, state, and national officials to escort him into Philadelphia. As in New York, cannons boomed, church bells tolled, and huge crowds cheered hysterically.

"What a thrill it was to see so many of my former soldiers in the crowd," he wrote Adrienne, who was spending the summer at Chavaniac with the children, her mother, and his aunt Charlotte. "Every step I take in this country, sweetheart, brings me new joys. The nation is happy, peaceful, prosperous; the houses I saw burnt are now rebuilt; abandoned properties are now occupied; everything seems to be on the way to complete recovery; I can only hope that my presence here will be useful in promoting the domestic interests of the United States [and] the union that must reign between them—in short, a federal union."[30]

When the cortège arrived in Philadelphia, the legislature named a county in southwest Pennsylvania Fayette County—adjacent to Washington and Greene Counties. Lafayette responded with a plea for a "federal union" to preserve "sacred friendship between the states, which is so necessary . . . [for] free government."[31] A huge dinner celebration followed. As church bells continued pealing and darkness fell, the people of the city honored him by setting every window in the city aglow with candlelight until ten that evening. "Not even for General Washington was more done," the startled French ambassador François Barbé de Marbois wrote to Foreign Minister Vergennes.

The following day, "Mad" Anthony Wayne and the officers of the Pennsylvania Line who had served with Lafayette in Virginia sponsored a banquet. After embracing his French comrade, Wayne toasted him "in behalf of the line [with] all the warmth of affection arising from the intercourse of the field, and while we look back on the scenes of distress freedom had to encounter, we can never forget, that when destitute of foreign friends, you generously stepped forth, the advocate of our rights—the noble example you gave by early bleeding in our infant cause . . . endears you to us as a soldier."[32] Always moved to the verge of tears at such ceremonies, the emotional Frenchman called Wayne and the others "my dear brother officers" and assured them, "that I early enlisted with you in the cause of liberty shall be the pride and satisfaction of my life."[33]

On August 14, he left for Baltimore, and after two days of festivities there, he pressed on to Mount Vernon. Three days later, after a separation of three years, he embraced his "adoptive father" once again.

"Though I do not know if my letter will reach you, my sweetheart, I had to write you of my arrival at Mount Vernon and of the joy I felt at seeing my dear general again; you know me too well for me to have to describe my emotions. . . . I found him on his farm, where our meeting was deeply moving and equally joyful for us both."[34] Martha was equally effusive in embracing their young visitor and showing him the portraits he had sent of Adrienne and himself and their children, hanging in the most prominent place in the living room, above the mantel.

After their emotional reunion, Lafayette gave the Washingtons a beautiful little note in the carefully crafted handwriting of a child just learning her penmanship. "Dear Washington," it began. "I hope that papa whill come back so[o]n here. I am very sorry for the loss of him, but I am verry glade [glad] for you self. I wich [wish] you a werry good health and I am whith great respect, Dear Sir, your most obedient servent, anastasie la fayette."

Lafayette also brought Washington a precious gift from Adrienne—a Masonic apron she herself had embroidered. For the rest of his life, Washington would wear Adrienne's treasured apron at every Masonic and appropriate public function, including his laying of the cornerstone at the United States Capitol in the new federal city of Washington, in September, 1793.[35]

Lafayette spent the next ten emotion-filled days in the bosom of the Washington family—and a large one it was, overflowing with children, large and small. The Washingtons adored children; Martha's widowed daughter-in-law had left them two of her four to raise until she remarried, and she, her second husband, and all four of her children were roaming and romping through the mansion when Lafayette arrived. He embraced them all, particularly Martha's fat little grandson, George Washington Parke Custis, whom Lafayette called "Squire Tub." George Augustine Washington, the general's nephew and Lafayette's aide in the Virginia campaign, was also at Mount Vernon with his fiancée, and each day, legions of other Washington relatives and friends—and all their children—trooped happily in and out of the great home, filling it and the surrounding lawns and gardens with a continuum of happy shrieks and roars of laughter.

"Washington, in retirement," Lafayette wrote to Adrienne,

> is even greater than he was during the Revolution. His simplicity is truly sublime, and he is as deeply involved in the details of managing his lands and home as if he had always been here. . . . To give you an idea of how we spend our time, after lunch, the general and I chat for a while, and, after thoroughly discussing the past, the state of things today and the outlook for the future, he retires to take care of business and gives me things to read that were written during my absence; then we go down to dinner with Mrs. Washington and neighbors; the table conversation turns to events of the war and anecdotes we like to remember. After tea, we resume our private conversations and spend the rest of the evening with the family. There, sweetheart, is how we spend our time; we often speak of you, our children and everything else that has to do with the family.[36]

Martha kept the table overflowing with hams and peach brandy that captivated Lafayette's palate. "There are two of Mrs. Washington's grandsons here," Lafayette wrote to Adrienne,

> as you know she was married once before. The general has adopted them and loves them deeply; it was quite funny when I arrived to see the curious looks on those two small faces who had heard nothing but talk of me the entire day and wanted to see if I looked like my portrait. The general loved reading your letter and that of Anastasie, and I've been charged with sending you the most loving regards of the entire family, and Mrs. Washington told me today that, with both of them so old, you must not deprive them of the joy of receiving you and our little family; I made a solemn vow, sweetheart, to bring you with me on the next trip; Mount Vernon stands on the most beautiful site; it is as if the Pottowmack was created for it. The house is most beautiful and the countryside is charming.[37]

A brilliant horticulturalist and agriculturalist, Washington took Lafayette on his daily ride across his farms at dawn, to give his managers directions for the day. After they returned to the house and ate breakfast, Washington guided Lafayette through his gardens, orchards, and greenhouse, pointing out rare species and questioning Lafayette about varieties of unusual plants in Europe that he might add to his gardens. Always ready to emulate his idol,

Lafayette quickly developed a new interest in horticulture, writing to Adrienne, "I have discovered here a climbing plant that stays green all year and would make a fine showing on the two walls of our terrace. When it reaches you, I beg that you will have it planted at the foot of the two walls. I am also sending something which in summer will cover them with beautiful red flowers."[38]

On November 28, Washington accompanied Lafayette and his aide, de Caraman, as far as Alexandria, before leaving to inspect lands he owned west of the Alleghenies. They said their farewells in a tavern, where Lafayette "got a little tipsy," but shed none of his usual tears, because they had planned another reunion before he returned to France. He and de Caraman continued to Annapolis and then Baltimore. Both cities fêted him with the usual parades, banquets, and accolades. Baltimore held a dinner and formal ball for three hundred at City Hall, where he renewed his acquaintance with James Madison, by then as fervent an advocate of union as Lafayette. The two had met in 1781, when Lafayette was returning to France and Madison was a Virginia delegate in Congress. Six years older than Lafayette, Madison was born of a wealthy planter and had graduated from the College of New Jersey (now Princeton). Like Lafayette, he was an avid student of political philosophy, was fluent in Latin, and spoke French well. They decided to continue north together.

During four days of more revelry in New York, the city designated Lafayette "a freeman and citizen of the City of New York" and unleashed a national frenzy to designate the marquis a "citizen" of every place he visited. By coincidence, when Lafayette was in New York, Congress appointed three commissioners to negotiate peace with the Six (Indian) Nations at a powwow by Lake Oneida in northern New York, and they asked Lafayette to help. The English in Canada had fomented hostilities between Indians and Americans, who were streaming westward through Indian territory to farm the rich Ohio Valley. The Six Nations had once been allies of the French and were themselves divided over white migration, with four tribes demanding war and two favoring peaceful trade. As an Iroquois Indian by adoption who had embraced the American cause, Lafayette represented a bond between Americans, French, and Indians.

"These savages still . . . speak of the French nation with great reverence," Ambassador de Marbois explained, "even though their relations with us ended more than twenty years ago. They love [alcoholic] spirits passionately, but they say that the French were their true fathers because the French refused them this poison that the British furnished them in abundance."[39]

Intrigued by the expedition and increasingly fond of Lafayette, Madison decided to join Lafayette, de Caraman, and the French ambassador on the two-hundred-mile trek. A comfortable boat carried them the first one hundred twenty miles up the Hudson River past Albany to the mouth of the Mohawk River, but the carriage that was to take them the rest of the way broke apart on the rough roads and forced them to continue on horseback through the bitter cold. Only Lafayette had soldiered through the miserable winters of the Revolutionary War, and only he had known to bring a thick cloak—and line it with layers of newspapers to insulate himself from the cold. Lafayette "appears to be impervious to heat, cold, drought, moisture and intemperance of the weather," wrote the shivering de Marbois. The "barbarous and savage" last leg of the journey made the little band "force their horses through the narrow woods, following as best as we could a footpath made for the savages, who always go on foot. The streams form a continuous boggy swamp into which we sank at every step. Trees of immense height and girth fall from old age . . . make the paths difficult for people on horseback. . . . We were lost for a time, but our guides soon found the way again. The trees serve them for compasses. They know which is the south side by the bark, which is brown and more moss-covered on that side than on the north."[40]

A white flag flew over the council hall at Oneida Castle when they arrived. "There we found the chiefs and warriors of the nations assembled," de Marbois recounted. "They received us with the hospitality that the savages show toward all those who are not their enemies. . . . After the usual compliments, they brought us a large salmon that they had just caught. We had lots of milk, butter, fruit, and honey."[41] Two hours of dancing followed, made all the eerier for de Marbois by the curious dress of the chiefs—old French, English, and German uniforms. All were treasured gifts, however, that the chiefs reserved for special occasions.

"Here I am in the country of the savages, surrounded by Hurons and Iroquois," Lafayette wrote to Adrienne effusively. Unlike his terrified companions, he felt like a tourist on a glorious adventure.[42] In a second letter, he quipped that, because of his receding hairline, "I will not lose my scalp, because you cannot lose what you don't have."[43]

Lafayette amazed the trembling French ambassador: "Mr. de la Fayette has their confidence and their devotion to an extraordinary degree," he wrote in his diary. "Those who have seen him before have a great urge to see him again. They have communicated their enthusiasms to their friends, and they seem proud to wear around their necks some trinket that he once gave them."[44]

On October 3, commissioner Oliver Wolcott of Connecticut[45] introduced Lafayette to the powwow by his Iroquois name, Kayewla: "He is a great man among the French, one of the head warriors of the great Onondio [Louis XVI], and as you all know, a general in the American army and a headman among us, who comes with his friends to pay you a visit and give you the advice of a father."[46]

"I thank the great spirit," Lafayette proclaimed, "for bringing me to this place to bring me back to my children, who now gather around this fire to smoke the pipe of peace and friendship together. If you remember the voice of Kayewla, remember, too, his counsel and the necklaces that he often sent you. . . . I now say to you, the American cause is just; it is your cause. . . . Be wiser than the white man, keep the peace among yourselves . . . trade with the Americans . . . such trade will become for you a sign of a new alliance."[47]

After he finished, Mohawk chief Ocksicanechiou stood and addressed Lafayette: "My father, we have heard your words and rejoice that you have visited your children to give them your wise advice. . . . You have done us much good . . . we sense that your words are those of truth. . . . They will strengthen the chain of friendship that we hope will live forever."[48] With that, he placed a necklace of peace around Lafayette—a necklace that French general Montcalm, whom the British defeated at Quebec, had given him as a symbol of French friendship, twenty-five years earlier. Lafayette displayed it to the assembled chiefs, then removed it and placed it back on the chief's neck. Lafayette's gesture awed the entire gathering. "He was the only conspicuous figure there," Madison wrote of Lafayette. "The commissioners were eclipsed. All of them probably felt it. [Arthur] Lee complained to me."[49]

The good feelings that Lafayette engendered climaxed with his offering to take Peter Otisquette, a half-French Oneida boy, to France to educate him to lead his nation and negotiate shrewdly with white nations. Although Otisquette's family agreed, they preferred postponing his departure for a year, and an Onondaga family sent their twelve-year-old boy, Kayenlaha, with him instead.

Lafayette's party left the next day, but the conference continued for nearly three weeks. The goodwill he established produced a treaty in which the Americans recognized Indian sovereignty in western New York, except at Forts Oswego and Niagara, and the Indian nations granted Americans sovereignty over lands between Lake Erie and the Ohio River.

After an easy boat trip down the Mohawk and Hudson Rivers, Madison and Lafayette parted reluctantly. They had grown close, with Lafayette confiding to Madison that his "three hobby horses are the alliance between France and the United States, the union of the latter and the manumission of the slaves." Madison wrote to his close friend Jefferson that Lafayette's concern for the slaves "does him real honor, as it is a proof of his humanity."[50]

Lafayette renewed his American tour with a stop at Hartford, where the assembly declared him and his family honorary citizens. He sent an overdue letter to Jefferson, who was a widower and had taken his oldest daughter, twelve-year-old Patsy, with him to Paris. "When I heard of your going to France, I heartily lamented I could not have the honour to receive you there. . . . My house, dear sir, my family, and any thing that is mine are entirely at your disposal, and I beg you will come and see Mde de Lafayette as you would act by your brother's wife. Her knowledge of the country may be of some use to Miss Jefferson whom she will be happy to attend in every thing that may be agreeable to her. Indeed my dear sir, I would be very angry with either you or she did not consider my house as a second home."[51]

Lafayette wrote to Adrienne, appointing her "mother, chaperone, and anything else you can think of" to Patsy Jefferson. "I beg you to take them under your wing and to do all you can for them. . . . The father, an admirable, cultivated, and charming man overwhelmed me with kindnesses when he was governor of Virginia during the war, and I very much hope that he may like France well enough to replace Mr. Franklin."[52]

From Hartford, Lafayette went to Boston, where his old comrade, General Henry Knox, the commander of the American artillery, waited at the edge of the city with a smartly uniformed military escort and fife and drum corps. America was celebrating the third anniversary of the victory at Yorktown, and a huge crowd formed behind the Conqueror of Cornwallis. Aware of the importance of symbolism, Lafayette left his carriage and mounted a tall white horse for the triumphant ride through the city where the Revolution began. Church bells rang and harbor cannons boomed the traditional thirteen salvos as he rode through the main streets of Boston before the cheering crowds.

The bells rang until dark and resumed their song at dawn the next day and the following one, as Lafayette rode and tramped good-naturedly in an endless succession of parades, presentations, and banquets. Boston's newspapers carried poems eulogizing him; Governor John Hancock hosted a banquet in his honor, and city merchants sponsored an even bigger one—for five hundred guests, in Faneuil Hall. The state assembly made him a citizen of the state, and Harvard College awarded him a doctorate, which he accepted, appropriately, in Latin.

While in Boston, he was the target of requests for endless special favors. Independence had ended duty-free entry of American goods into England, which now taxed American products as foreign goods. Nantucket whalers asked Lafayette to help them gain duty-free entry for whale oil into France. Boston merchants asked for similar privileges for furs and lumber. He pledged to help them all.

After a week in Boston, Lafayette went to Providence for more parades, salutes, and receptions and a visit with Nathanael Greene. At a banquet with members of the General Assembly, he toasted unity among the states:

"May these rising states unite in every measure, as they have united in their struggles."[53] Fortunately, he gave his toast early; by the end of the evening, the sixty assemblymen and their guests had absorbed fifty-one bottles of Madeira, thirty-two bottles of claret, nine bottles of punch, and thirty-two bowls of rum punch—an average of a bottle and one-half (then five pints) of wine and a half-bottle of rum each.

Lafayette traveled two more weeks through New England. Then, with his faithful companion de Caraman and the bewildered twelve-year-old Indian boy, he boarded the French frigate Nymphe in Boston harbor and began a restful sail to Virginia and a belated reunion with Washington, who was to meet him in Richmond. After two weeks, the Nymphe put into Yorktown, where the twenty-seven-year-old Lafayette disembarked and took a nostalgic stroll along the little street he had traveled three years earlier—a lifetime earlier—as a victorious American major general.

After an hour of quiet contemplation, Lafayette resumed his frenetic pace, with a banquet at Williamsburg and a huge reception at Richmond, where he once again embraced his "dear general." Arm in arm, they entered Trower's Tavern to the cheers of the state's leading citizens, including Governor-elect Patrick Henry, who announced he would name his next son Fayette. Virginians quipped that Henry's seventeen children and sixty grandchildren made him, not Washington, the father of his country.

By unanimous vote, the Virginia House of Delegates declared Lafayette a citizen of Virginia and commissioned two busts each of Washington and Lafayette, one pair for the city of Richmond and the second pair for Paris. For three days, Richmond erupted with fireworks, cannon fire, illuminations, feasting, and balls to celebrate the nation's two great heroes, together once again, as they had been at Yorktown. When Lafayette chanced upon a Richmond slave who had served him as a spy in the Virginia campaign, Lafayette gave him a letter attesting to his "essential service to me while I had the honour to command in this state. His intelligence from the ennemy's [sic] camp were industriously collected and most faithfully delivered. He perfectly acquitted himself with some important commissions I gave him and appears to me entitled to every reward his situation can admit of."[54] Lafayette's testimonial won the slave his freedom—and a pension. He adopted the name James Armistead Lafayette, his middle name being that of his former Virginia owner.

On November 22, Lafayette and Washington left Richmond for Mount Vernon, arriving there after two days of intimate camaraderie and conversation. They talked of their families, homes, and gardens, but touched on political and social issues—especially the need for a strong federal union under a constitution that promotes "a way of life that guarantees personal freedom, the enjoyment of private property, and equal justice for individuals."[55]

Lafayette with James Armistead Lafayette, a former slave who served
as a spy for Lafayette during the Virginia campaign. Lafayette's letter
of praise and recommendation to the Virginia legislature won James
his freedom and a pension. (*Réunion des Musées Nationaux.*)

Four days in the intimacy of Washington's family ended in torrents of
tearful farewells—to the endearing little Squire Tub and his sisters, their
mother and stepfather; to George Augustine Washington, the general's
nephew; to the beloved Martha Washington—and to all the other relatives,
friends, and neighbors who came to say good-bye. Washington could not
bring himself to do the same and chose to accompany Lafayette, de Caraman, and Kayenlaha to New York, where they were to sail to France. They

arrived in Annapolis the next day to the usual clangs, booms, and clatter of church bells, cannons, and fireworks—the governor's welcome, the General Assembly speeches, and the governor's ball. By unanimous resolution, the Maryland General Assembly voted that Lafayette "and his heirs male for ever, shall be, and they and each of them are hereby deemed, adjudged, and taken to be, natural born citizens of this state, and shall henceforth be entitled to all the immunities, rights and privileges, of natural born citizens thereof."[56]

Washington's unexpected presence made the festivities more boisterous and so tired him that he decided to forego visiting Philadelphia and New York, where more exhausting celebrations awaited. And so, on December 1, 1784, Lafayette and Washington embraced each other and parted. Neither could speak; Washington pressed a letter into Lafayette's hand. It was for Adrienne: "The pleasure I received in once more embracing my friend could only have been increased by your presence. . . . The Marquis returns to you with all the warmth and ardour of a newly inspired lover. We restore him to you in good health with wreaths of love and respect from every part of the Union." He sent his thanks to Anastasie for her letter—and "a kiss."[57]

The two soldiers mounted separate carriages that rumbled along together to the outskirts of Annapolis and a fork in the road, where, as each peered out to wave at the other, Washington's carriage turned south and Lafayette's rolled off in the opposite direction.

Two weeks later, Lafayette said farewell to Congress. Most members were old friends—President Richard Henry Lee, Virginia's James Monroe, New York's Alexander Hamilton, and others—who greeted him with unrestrained cheers and applause. His speech was short, reiterating his love for the United States and liberty and his hopes for a strong federal union. He had traveled nearly two thousand miles, visited ten states, and addressed the legislatures in six of them. "In unbounded wishes to America, Sir, I am happy to observe the prevailing disposition of the people to strengthen the confederation," he told Congress. "May this immense temple of freedom ever stand a lesson to oppressors, an example to the oppressed, a sanctuary for the rights of mankind! and may these happy United States attain that complete splendor and prosperity that will illustrate the blessings of their government, and for ages to come rejoice the departed souls of its founders."[58] As a parting gift, Congress presented him one of the standards surrendered by Cornwallis at Yorktown.

When Lafayette reached New York, the *Nymphe* had run aground and repairs delayed his departure for a week. General Greene and Henry Knox had come to see him off, and the three spent long hours together reminiscing with Alexander Hamilton. Lafayette urged Greene, Hamilton, and Knox to send their boys to him in Paris for several years of European education.

He promised that he, in turn, would send his own boy, George-Washington, to them. All agreed, with Lafayette saying he wanted his son educated at Harvard. When other former officers learned of the plan, they asked Lafayette to take fourteen-year-old John Edwards Caldwell, the orphan of a Continental Army chaplain, to France to complete his education, and he agreed.

On December 21, 1784, New York governor George Clinton, French consul Jean de Crèvecoeur,[59] and a large crowd of dignitaries escorted Lafayette on a lavishly decorated barge to the frigate *Nymphe*. Greene, Hamilton, and Knox took turns embracing him, and, with Clinton, the American, on one side, and the Frenchman Crèvecoeur on the other, Lafayette boarded. The French ship saluted the American flag with thirteen cannon blasts, and the battery responded in kind. The bewildered Indian boy, already unnerved by the stares he provoked, shuddered at the cannon roars; his newfound companion, the orphaned chaplain's son, comforted him.

Before parting, Governor Clinton slipped a letter into Lafayette's hand. It was from Washington, who had written it on his return to Mount Vernon:

> In the moment of our separation upon the road as I travelled, & every hour since—I felt all that love, respect & attachment for you, with which length of years, close connexion and your merits, have inspired me. I often asked myself as our carriages distended, whether that was the last sight I ever should have of you? And tho' I wished to say no—my fears answered yes. I called to mind the days of my youth, & found they had long since fled to return no more; that I was now descending the hill, I had been fifty-two years climbing—& that tho' I was blessed with a good constitution, I was of a short-lived family—and might soon expect to be entombed in the dreary mansions of my father's. These things darkened the shades & gave gloom to the picture, consequently to my prospects of seeing you again: but I will not repine. I have had my day. . . .
>
> It is unnecessary, I persuade myself to repeat to you my D[ea]r. Marqs. the sincerity of my regards and friendship—nor have I the words which could express my affection for you, were I to attempt it. My fervent prayers are offered for your safe & pleasant passage—happy meeting with Madame la Fayette & family, & the completion of every wish of your heart—in all of which Mrs. Washington joins me. . . .
>
> With every sentimt. wch. is propitious & endearing—I am &c. &c. &c.
>
> G. Washington[60]

The *Nymphe* did not leave its mooring until the following day, and Lafayette had time to send Washington a hurried note of protest:

No, my dear General, our recent separation will not be a last adieu. My soul revolts at this idea, and, if for an instant, I could entertain such an idea, in truth it would make me miserable. I realize that you will never come to France. I cannot hope to have the inexpressible pleasure to embrace you in my house, to receive you in a family where your name is adored; but I will return, again and often, under the roof of Mt. Vernon; we will talk of old times. It is my firm intention to visit from time to time my friends on this side of the Atlantic, and the best loved of all friends I have ever had, or ever shall have anywhere. . . . Adieu, Adieu, my dear General, it is with inexpressible pain that I feel I am going to be separated from you by the Atlantic. Everything that admiration, respect, gratitude, friendship, and filial love can inspire, is combined in my affectionate heart to devote me most tenderly to you. In your friendship I find a delight which words cannot express. Adieu, my dear General; it is not without emotion that I write this word, altho' I know I shall visit you again. Be attentive to your health. Let me hear from you every month. Adieu, Adieu.[61]

But Lafayette was wrong, and Washington was right. They had said their last adieux. Lafayette would never see his beloved general again.

Part Two

The Worst of Times

13

The Notables
and the "Not Ables"

HAVING CHANGED THE COURSE of history in the new world, the marquis de Lafayette sailed back to France in January 1785 determined to do the same in the old. Americans and Frenchmen sensed it: Washington, Franklin, and Jefferson knew it; the king of France and other European monarchs feared it. And with good reason. Lafayette was obsessed with re-creating the America he loved in the France he loved, with sweeping social reforms and republican self-government. He had already proved his abilities to influence people and events in war and set out to do the same in peace. Although no longer an American major general, he was nonetheless a powerful French maréchal de camp, who was not only the Conqueror of Cornwallis but commander of the legendary Noailles regiment. He was an influential statesman, with easy, direct access to the king and the king's cabinet; he was an influential diplomat—America's friend at court in Versailles and the representative of vast American commercial interests in France; and he had immense popularity in France, not just as the Hero of Two Worlds, but as a lord who had ended the famine in Auvergne by giving away his own grain to hungry peasants and, in one province at least, breaking the monopoly of the hated *ferme*— "the firm"—which fixed prices, controlled supplies, and created famine.

Lafayette's monthlong voyage home from America was calm. He spent mornings on board ship teaching Latin, French, and French history to his two wards, the twelve-year-old Onondaga Indian, Kayenlaha, and the fourteen-year-old orphan, John Edwards Caldwell, whose ambition was to become a doctor. Though surprised by the additions to her household, Adrienne immediately embraced the two children. Unlike other European parents, Adrienne and Gilbert did not keep their children at a distance with stone-faced tutors and governesses. They adored their children openly—embraced them spontaneously and showed them off to all their guests, no matter how distinguished. Even the venerable Franklin had to listen patiently and force a smile as seven-year-old Anastasie and five-year-old George sang children's songs in English—and Kayenlaha performed Indian dances with only a few feathers to cover the most sensitive parts of his body.[1] At St. Jean de Crève-coeur's recommendation, Lafayette enrolled young Caldwell with de Crève-coeur's own two sons in the exclusive Pension Lemoyne,[2] an outstanding boarding school across the road from Thomas Jefferson's house on the Champs Elysées,[3] which allowed boys to go home on Sundays and holidays. To Lafayette's astonishment, however, the Benedictine teaching brothers balked at his insistence that the Protestant boy be excused from daily Catholic services. Only Lafayette's illustrious name and ties to the court extracted the school's reluctant assent "to ensure [Caldwell's] perseverance in the religion of his father."[4]

After the excitement of his return abated, Lafayette sent his servants scurrying through Paris with packets of letters from Americans to friends in Paris. There was one from Washington to Franklin; many from Boston to the Adamses; and a distressing letter from Richmond he had to send to Jefferson, with a personal note of condolence: Jefferson's youngest daughter, two-year-old Lucy Elizabeth, had died from whooping cough the previous October. The unwholesome winter dampness of Paris had already laid Jefferson low, and the news of his daughter's death added severe melancholia to his respiratory problems and prolonged his confinement until March. Adrienne had helped the widower Jefferson enroll his older daughter, Patsy, in school the previous autumn, and she and Lafayette looked in on her regularly while her father ailed.

With Lafayette home, Adrienne resumed the Monday evening American dinners, where American officials and merchants mixed with—and sought concessions from—French officials, merchants, and bankers. The Hôtel de Lafayette was open to all Americans, with Lafayette assuming the role of resident godfather to Americans in France: He bailed some out of prison, paid their debts, gave them enough money to return home, and helped them get jobs. "I thought I was in America instead of Paris," said one of the French officers who had served in the American revolution and frequented the Lafayette home. "There were so many English and Americans there, and he speaks English as well as he speaks French. Instead of a runner, he has an American savage dressed in his native costume. The savage always calls him 'father.'[5] Everything in his house is simple. Even his little girls, as young as they are, speak English as well as they speak French. They played and laughed in English with the Americans. . . . I admired the simplicity of so distinguished a young man in comparison to so many young people with far more advantages than he who have done nothing with their lives."[6]

As before, Franklin and Adams remained fixtures at the rue de Bourbon. To Lafayette's immense pleasure, Adams now wore a smile and no longer came alone. Abigail Adams had arrived the previous August with their twenty-year-old daughter, "Nabby," and Adrienne had won their friendship by inviting them and seventeen-year-old Quincy to the rue de Bourbon.

Although Lafayette had looked forward to Jefferson visiting, the Virginian remained overwhelmed with grief and refused to dine out. His spirits did not revive until seven-year-old Polly, his other surviving daughter, arrived from Virginia to join Patsy and made the family as whole as possible. As spring stretched the daylight hours and the sun's rays dispersed the last, dismal winter mists, Jefferson resumed his habitual five-mile walks, strolling down the Champs Elysées to the place Louis XV and, more and more, across the Seine to the rue de Bourbon to drop in for a chat with his old friend Lafayette. Late in March, Adrienne, who remained one of the queen's confidantes, added to Jefferson's cheer with an invitation from the king to join the Lafayettes and the Adams family at Nôtre-Dame Cathedral, to hear a Te Deum sung in thanks for the birth of a second prince.

A few weeks later, Congress appointed Jefferson to succeed Franklin as minister plenipotentiary in France and named Adams America's first ambassador to Great Britain. The New Englander's usually sour face beamed with joy at the prospects of settling in England. Apart from his dislike of France and everything French, Adams had grown "disgusted" with his and Franklin's "inutility"[7] in obtaining treaties of amity and commerce with European nations. Adams had negotiated one with the United Netherlands in 1782, and Franklin one with Sweden the following year. With Jefferson's arrival, however, Adams had hoped to obtain treaties with twenty or more European nations, but they had failed—largely because negotiating a trade agreement with America meant negotiating thirteen agreements—one with each sovereign state. As representatives of Congress, they had no authority to negotiate a single, blanket agreement for all states. Making matters worse was the failure of France to fulfill its treaty of amity and commerce by absorbing American fish, tobacco, rice, lumber, furs, and other products that England used to buy before the Revolution. Although her treaty dated back to 1778, France and the *ferme* monopoly had still not removed the trade barriers and duties that protected French markets from competition.

After his return from America, Lafayette immediately mounted what he had told Madison were his three political "hobby horses"—strengthening the alliance between France and the United States, promoting the union of the American states, and manumission of slaves. The first would not be possible

French queen Marie-Antoinette with her newborn prince and two older children, the princess on the left and the dauphin, or heir to the throne, on the right—so named because the oldest prince—the crown prince—was automatically prince of Dauphiné province, much as the English crown prince is automatically Prince of Wales. (*Réunion des Musées Nationaux.*)

without the second, and he began peppering his political friends in America with letters urging them to form a more perfect union—eight letters on March 16 alone: to Nathanael Greene, asking that "Congress assume powers to regulate trade"[8]; to Elbridge Gerry of Massachusetts, citing "the necessity to strengthen the Federal union, to make commercial regulations"[9]; to President of Congress Richard Henry Lee, to "attend to the confederation, to union and harmony, to every regulation that can give security to the commerce, energy to the government, faith to the public creditors."[10]

Unlike Adams, Jefferson was eager for Lafayette's help in penetrating the ostensibly impenetrable French trade barriers. Jefferson knew and trusted Lafayette. As former Virginia governor, he was grateful to Lafayette for driving the British from his state, and he was personally grateful for the solicitude both Lafayettes had shown for him and his daughters in Paris. Lafayette proved himself every bit as skilled a tactician at the negotiating table as he had been on the battlefield, winning inconspicuous minor skirmishes, one by one, until they added up to victory in the war. Knowing he could not tear down the entire French tariff wall blocking entry of American whale oil, Lafayette punctured a small hole in the wall by turning to the powerful contractor who supplied oil for lighting Paris street lamps. The contractor agreed to buy one thousand tons of inexpensive American whale oil and had enough friends in the finance ministry to win a tariff exemption for the one shipment. After setting the precedent, it was not difficult to win subsequent exemptions, and, by mid-May, the contractor was reselling American whale oil throughout France and agreed to buy four hundred thousand tons of American whale oil over the next six years, all of it to flow into France free of import duties and taxes.

Nantucket whalers were so elated they resolved "in corporation assembled" that each would contribute the milk from one of his cows for twenty-four hours, pool the total, and make a five-hundred-pound cheese to be "transmitted to the Marquis de Lafayette as a feeble, but not less sincere, testimonial of the affection and gratitude of the inhabitants of Nantucket."[11] In Paris, Jefferson and Franklin were ecstatic over Lafayette's success in opening the first chink in the hitherto impenetrable wall of French trade barriers. Even Adams expressed admiration; author-adventurer John Ledyard wrote, "He has planted a tree in America and sits under it at Versailles."[12]

In May 1785, "Quincy" Adams was about to turn eighteen, and his parents sent him back to Massachusetts to attend Harvard. Lafayette took advantage of his departure to give him seven French hounds to deliver to George Washington, along with a letter describing French discrimination against Protestants. Each time the Caldwell boy came home, he bore tales of efforts at school to proselytize him, and Lafayette invariably stormed unto the director's office to demand that the school respect the boy's religion. The weekly conflict infuriated Lafayette; almost all of his American friends were Protestants, and, while Catholic himself, he was a passionate Freemason and had nothing but admiration for the simplicity and democracy of American Protestantism.

"Protestants in France are under intolerable despotism," Lafayette railed to Washington. "Marriages are not legal among them. Their wills have no force by law. Their children are to be bastards. Their parsons to be hanged. I have put it into my head to be a leader in that affair, and to have their situation changed."[13] Establishing freedom of religion in France, he surmised, would be "a work of time, and of some danger to me. . . . Don't answer me," he told Washington. "But when in the course of the fall or winter you will hear something . . . I wanted you to know I had a hand in it."[14]

France had officially outlawed Protestantism a century earlier, when Louis XIV revoked the Edict of Nantes, a doctrine that had established religious tolerance. Its revocation sent two hundred thousand French Protestants fleeing to Holland and Prussia, although hundreds of thousands remained in France and continued to practice clandestinely, many in southern hill towns such as Nîmes. On the pretense of encouraging trade with America,

Lafayette traveled to Nîmes, where he met secretly with Protestant leaders. After listening to their grievances and tales of persecution, Lafayette pledged to champion their cause at Versailles. "The hero of America has become my hero," wrote Jean-Paul Rabaut-St. Etienne, one of the persecuted leaders.[15]

Both Adrienne and her mother, the duchesse d'Ayen, joined Lafayette's crusade for equal rights for Protestants. "My mother shared his beliefs," said Adrienne's daughter Virginie, "and received with great warmth the Protestant ministers that came to our door because of his work. My mother's tolerance was based on the basic principles of her own religion. She believed it a heinous crime to interfere with liberties that God granted to all men."[16]

When Lafayette returned to Paris, Jefferson commissioned Jean-Antoine Houdon, France's most celebrated sculptor, to sculpt busts of Washington and Lafayette for the Richmond and Paris city halls. He had already sculpted magnificent heads of Franklin, Diderot, Rousseau, and Voltaire, and, after making a plaster life mask of Lafayette, he sailed off to America to sculpt Washington at Mount Vernon. Lafayette gave him a letter of introduction, along with a set of dinner plates Adrienne had found for Martha. No ship plied the Atlantic between France and the United States without carrying gifts from the Lafayettes to the Washingtons and vice versa. The two couples seemed bent on personally building trade between their two nations by themselves, with Martha sending Adrienne a variety of seeds and plants, ranging from ginseng to corn, and Lafayette sending hounds and two Spanish jackasses to Mount Vernon—the last, actually, the gift of the king of Spain. Each letter heralded another exchange of gifts—French pheasants and red partridges from Lafayette; wild ducks and hams from Washington—although "the poor ducks were dead on arrival at Le Havre." Lafayette asked Washington to send mockingbirds, which were unknown in France, and Washington asked for nightingales, which were unknown in America. Even the children joined in the flow of goods, with Lafayette sending Washington's granddaughters French dolls, complete with dressing tables and delicate handmade accessories that made French dolls the envy of children throughout the Western world.[17]

With diplomatic activity at its usual summer standstill in Versailles, Lafayette acted to enhance his standing as a military and political leader by accepting Frederick the Great's invitation to join Europe's highest-ranking officers at the legendary summer maneuvers of the Prussian army, then considered the best-trained, best-disciplined troops in Europe. Cornwallis would be there, with King George III's second son, the duke of York, and other military leaders from Britain, France, Russia, and Sweden. Frederick's incongruous invitation to the sworn enemy of despotism and champion of republicanism reflected the Prussian leader's eagerness to appear an enlightened ruler before the world—and to establish a link to America's unbounded wealth. Lafayette said his last good-byes to Franklin and his grandson before they returned to America, and he left for Potsdam and three weeks of lavish banquets and balls at the court of Frederick the Great.

"Despite all I had heard about him," Lafayette wrote to Washington, "I was stunned by his clothes and appearance—like an old, dirty, decrepit corporal, covered with Spanish snuff, his head bent to one side onto his shoulder and his fingers almost dislocated by gout [arthritis]." Three weeks later, however, the seventy-three-year-old monarch metamorphosed into the great military commander he had once been: "When he is at the head of his army, I was surprised by the fire and occasional calmness in the most magnificent eyes I ever saw, which gave his face an expression at once captivating and brutal."[18]

The maneuvers were an overwhelming experience—and a revelation—for Lafayette, who had never seen, let alone commanded, an army of more than 10,000 men. Out on the vast plain, an army of thirty-one battalions—30,000 men—and seventy-five cavalry squadrons, 100 horsemen per squadron, passed in review with a precision that left Lafayette and Frederick's other guests agasp. Then, the battalions and squadrons broke off into various maneuvers that ended in sham battles.

"Nothing can compare to the magnificence of the Prussian troops, to the discipline that reigns in all ranks," Lafayette wrote Washington. "It is a fine tuned machine. . . . With every imaginable situation in war and every appropriate reaction inculcated in their heads, they respond like machines. . . . This entire journey was very useful for my military education." His experiences in the American bush, however, left him mocking European infantry tactics: "Nothing could be more ridiculous: two lines coming up within six yards of one another, and firing in one another's faces till they had no ammunition left."[19]

Each day's maneuvers ended with an elaborate, three-hour banquet. Frederick, who had but a year to live, sat at the head of the table with his nephew, Crown Prince Frederick William, who would later revel in punishing Lafayette for his republican views. Frederick the Great sat Lafayette between the duke of York and Lord Cornwallis and deliberately directed all his questions to the French general—largely about the United States and the Revolutionary War. Cornwallis found the dinners offensive: "My reception . . . was not flattering; there was a most marked preference for La Fayette."[20] When Lafayette predicted that the United States would never entertain an aristocracy or a king, Frederick responded, "Monsieur, I knew a young man who, after having visited countries where liberty and equality reigned, got it into his head to establish all that in his own country. Do you know what happened to him?"

"No, Sire," Lafayette replied.

"Monsieur," the king grinned, "he was hanged."[21]

From Germany, Lafayette went to Vienna, where Marie-Antoinette's brother Joseph II reigned as king of Germany and emperor of the Holy Roman Empire. He was as eager as Frederick to appear an enlightened ruler and establish a link to the New World by receiving the liberal friend of Washington as his guest. Although Lafayette got on well with Joseph, Lafayette's republican views alienated Archduke Francis, who would succeed Joseph as emperor seven years later and, like his Prussian counterpart, retaliate cruelly against the Frenchman. Lafayette took a long route home to France through Bohemia and Saxony, to watch more military exercises near Prague, Dresden, Potsdam, and Magdeburg. "Every where I went, my dear general, I had the pleasure to hear your name uttered with respect and enthusiasm," he wrote to Washington after his return to France. "Every conversation about America began with your praises, which, as your friend, your disciple and your adoptive son, filled my heart with pride. I only wish that other feelings about America had been as satisfying. . . . I often was mortified to hear that the lack of Congressional powers and lack of union between the states will render the confederation insignificant. . . . [Americans] will lose the respect of the world if they do not strengthen the confederation and do not give Congress sufficient power to regulate commerce, pay the debt . . . establish a well organized militia, and, in one sentence, put into effect the measures which you have recommended. I shall give Congress my honest opinion on this subject and I shall write to all my friends across the Atlantic as well."[22]

When Lafayette returned to Paris, he resumed his role as America's trade negotiator. When Nathanael Greene wrote for help selling timber from lands he had bought on Cumberland Island, Georgia, Lafayette sold the minister of the navy on the advantages of high-quality American timber in shipbuilding. Greene received an order for one thousand cubic feet of oak. Lafayette convinced a major French fur merchant to buy 400,000 livres of American furs from a group of former comrades in arms in Boston. Jefferson enlisted Lafayette's aid in opening French markets to American tobacco, Virginia's (and the Jefferson plantation's) most important export. The *ferme*'s duties doubled the price of American tobacco and priced it out of French markets. "It is contrary to the spirit of trade," Jefferson complained, "to carry a commodity to any market where but one person is allowed to buy it, and where, of course, that person fixes the prices." He suggested reducing the *ferme*'s markup to 5 percent, which, he predicted, would so stimulate trade that the *ferme* and the king, as well as American planters and merchants, would reap more revenues. Although Lafayette made little headway on the tobacco issue, he used his all but daily assaults at Versailles to win concessions in other areas, using tactics similar to those he learned in the

Virginia campaign—attacking the tobacco issue and retreating after winning a concession on books; resuming the assault on the *ferme* over tobacco, but withdrawing when he won a concession on paper . . . then shrubs, trees, and seeds. He amazed Jefferson with the number of concessions he extracted from the French government—all without a sou of remuneration. Calling Lafayette "my most powerful auxiliary and advocate," Jefferson told Madison, "his zeal is unbounded and his weight with those in power, great. His education having been merely military, commerce was an unknown field to him. But his good sense enabling him to comprehend perfectly whatever is explained to him, his agency has been very efficacious."[23] Indeed, Lafayette's success in breaching French tariff walls increased American exports to France by one million livres. Years later, Jefferson would toast Lafayette at a dinner in Charlottesville and recall their days together in Paris, when Lafayette had made "our cause his own. His influence and connections were great. All doors of all departments were open to him at all times; to me only formally and at appointed times. In truth, I only held the nail, he drove it in."[24]

Lafayette's constant presence at Versailles not only strengthened the alliance between France and the United States, it strengthened Lafayette's ties to the king, who sought to add luster to his dull image with Lafayette at his side. Louis was only slightly older than Lafayette, but they had attended riding school together, and shared common interests in history, geography, political science, and military strategy. Despite Lafayette's radical ideas for social reform, Louis XVI enjoyed his company and invited him constantly to dine and play cards at all his palaces—Versailles, Marly, the Tuileries, Fontainebleau, and Compiègne. Whenever Lafayette broached issues of social reform such as religious toleration for Protestants and manumission, the indecisive king simply sighed and said nothing. The king invited Lafayette to spend three days with him, inaugurating a huge new engineering project to expand the port at Cherbourg. Not only was Lafayette on the royal barge in the harbor, he rode back to Paris with the king in the royal coach—a conspicuous honor usually reserved for heads of state, but one which Louis gladly proffered to "the friend of Washington." Louis considered Lafayette his personal link to the New World and gave Lafayette three Maltese donkeys and some pheasants and partridges from the royal aviary to send to Washington as a personal gift. Although the birds "drooped and died," Washington interbred the donkeys with the Spanish asses Lafayette had sent earlier and produced a new breed of draft and carriage animal he named Compound.[25]

With the king unwilling to respond on the abolition issue, Lafayette acted on his own. He purchased a 125,000-livre sugarcane plantation, worked by slaves, in Cayenne, French Guyana, and, as he explained to Henry Knox, began "the experiment for enfranchising our Negro brethren. God grant that it may be propagated."[26] Lafayette sent a young engineer–social scientist to take charge of La Belle Gabrielle, as the plantation was called, and to established a program of education and gradual emancipation. He forbade the sale of any slaves, paid each slave according to his production, introduced literacy programs and schooling for the children, and applied rules and punishment equally to blacks and whites. Adrienne and her mother, the duchesse d'Ayen, both embraced the project, with Adrienne arranging for seminarians in Cayenne to educate the slaves and their children.

"My mother had a deep need to propagate good and was horrified by all injustice," Virginie explained. "She was thrilled by my father's decision to work for abolition of the slave trade. When he bought La Belle Gabrielle, her zealous belief in just and liberal ideas made her search ardently for means to put those ideas into immediate practice. My father gave her a large part of the responsibility for the enterprise, in which she believed education was the primary need."[27] In the years that followed, Lafayette added lands to the plantation and ordered his superintendent to acquire more slaves to emancipate. Adrienne remained in constant touch with the seminarians to improve education. "If only we still had her correspondence," her daughter lamented. "We would see the good work she had started and that she planned continuing."[28]

Lafayette's Cayenne project moved Washington to write, "The goodness of your heart displays itself in all circumstances, and I am never surprised when you give new proofs of it; your acquisition of a plantation in Cayenne, with a view to emancipating the slaves, is a generous and noble proof of your humanity. God grant that a similar spirit will animate all the people of this country! but I despair of ever seeing that happen. A few petitions for the abolition of slavery were presented to the last session of the [Virginia] assembly, but they barely obtained a reading. Sudden emancipation would bring many evils, I believe; but certainly it could be, it should be accomplished gradually and by legislative authority."[29]

In September 1786, Houdon returned from America and completed the busts of Washington and Lafayette for Jefferson to present as gifts from the state of Virginia to the city of Paris. Before the ceremony, Jefferson fell and broke his wrist, and William Short, a Jefferson protégé from Virginia who served as secretary of the American legation, presented the statues, crowned in laurel wreaths, for placement among the busts of French kings and other great men in the Grande Salle of the Hôtel de Ville, or city hall. As the illustrious audience cheered, Adrienne heard Short hail her husband as a "Knight of liberty" and "hero of two worlds."[30]

With the presentation of the busts, Lafayette's popularity and acclaim in France reached their peak. A poet extolled him as "modest in the midst of success, noble and great without pride, gentle and good without weakness," exhibiting "the valor of Achilles to the composure of Nestor."[31] Artists, too, celebrated the "hero of the New World," with French and American artists alike producing idealized portraits that seldom looked anything like him. Even the most despotic rulers sought to meet the "friend of Washington" and establish at least a tenuous tie to those who controlled the New World's vast riches. The Russian czarina Catherine the Great invited Lafayette to visit her capital at St. Petersburg in the new year and accompany her and Emperor Joseph to the Crimea.

Just before Christmas, however, a summons from the king forced Lafayette to cancel the Russian trip. At the urging of Finance Minister Calonne, Louis XVI called an Assemblée des Notables—an assembly of the most illustrious members of the realm—to recommend solutions to the nation's fiscal crisis. The national debt and annual deficits had soared uncontrollably and all but emptied the French treasury. Calonne proposed huge cuts in government spending—first, by limiting royal access to state funds, and second, by enacting sweeping tax reforms. Instead of taxing the poorest of the French, with the least to contribute, Calonne recommended taxing the wealthiest classes—hitherto exempt from most taxes. He asked for a property tax of 2 percent to 5 percent on all lands and a stamp tax on legal documents, wills, ships' papers, bills of sale, insurance, university degrees, wine containers, newspapers, almanacs, pamphlets, playing cards, and dice. He proposed eliminating taxes on peasants, which, he said, added little to the treasury and, in fact, drove workers off the land into misery, reduced annual crops, and contributed to food shortages and famine. He asked for an end to the hated *gabelle,* or salt tax, which made it too costly for the poor to preserve meat, and the corvée, which forced peasants to work on public roads one day a week without pay. By paying peasants to work on the roads and leaving the money they earned from field labor in their pockets, Calonne said the government would raise productivity, increase crops, end famine, and reduce homelessness and poverty.

Calonne also called for the creation of a single, common French market, free of provincial trade barriers and duties. Without barriers and duties, the *ferme* would be unable to create artificial shortages that drove up prices and produced famine and discontent throughout the realm. In the political sector, Calonne suggested the establishment of provincial assemblies to relieve Versailles of the responsibility—and costs—of dealing with regional problems that could be handled more effectively, efficiently, and at less cost at the local level.

Although dear to Lafayette's republican heart, Calonne's proposals were nothing short of a social, political, and economic revolution—far too radical for the king to promulgate by decree without setting off a rebellion by aristocrats, most of them high-ranking military officers with large army divisions under their command. Rebellious aristocrats had almost toppled Louis XIV in the early seventeenth century, and Louis XVI knew he would have to move cautiously. Calonne warned him that the nation's economy was too close to collapse for unobtrusive, piecemeal reforms. Immediate change was the only solution. The king hoped that by convening the nation's "notables" he could flatter them into approving Calonne's program as a patriotic duty, although it would cost them the most.

Lafayette hailed Calonne—and the king—as "patriotic" and "noble"— deserving of the nation's "gratitude and good will." He envisioned the Assemblée des Notables as a French equivalent of the American Continental Congress, which, after all, had also been an assembly of the most privileged, illustrious men. Except for Sam Adams, who had been born to but had lost his family's wealth, the fifty-six American "notables" who met at Philadelphia in 1774 ranged from rich to incredibly so: there had been five northern farmers, seven southern planters, thirty lawyers, eleven merchants, one builder, and one wharf owner. Even Lafayette's beloved hero George Washington owned sixty thousand acres and was arguably the richest planter in the south.

The French king named 144 notables: seven princes of the blood, including his two brothers; thirty-six noblemen, including Lafayette; thirty-seven magistrates; twelve government officials; twelve provincial representatives; twenty-six municipal representatives; and fourteen prelates. "The choice of members in the assembly," Lafayette told Washington, "was based on their morality, talents and importance."[32] What Lafayette conveniently overlooked in his eagerness to embrace the French Assembly was that eleven signatories of the American Declaration of Independence—one-fifth of the signers—had been Freemasons devoted to republican self-government and social reform. Moreover, almost all signatories were Protestants—heirs to more than one hundred fifty years of self-rule in congregations that not only formed the seats of government in most communities but also dispensed compulsory public education in many states and, in the north, propagated near-universal literacy among poor and rich alike.

The French notables were universally Roman Catholic, rooted in centuries of centralized, absolute rule by priests and divinely appointed kings— unused to and untrained in self-government in a nation more than 75 percent illiterate. Apart from Lafayette, there were but a handful of Freemasons dedicated to social reform, and, unlike American "notables" at Philadelphia, French *notables* did not gather in Versailles to pledge their lives, fortunes, and sacred honor, but to preserve the first and enhance the second. And of the few with honor, none held it too sacred to sell at the right price.

On February 22, the clarion calls of the king's heralds signaled the opening of the historic Assembly in the Salles des Menus Plaisirs.[33] Apart

The king's speech from the throne to the Assemblée des Notables—the Assembly of Notables—on February 22, 1787, to reform the French fiscal system. (*Réunion des Musées Nationaux.*)

from the notables themselves, ambassadors from other nations, including America's Thomas Jefferson, witnessed the pomp and ceremony as the king mounted the throne in his splendid blue velvet robe, bordered in snow-white ermine; his long, broad cape trailed behind, inlaid with gold and white fleurs-de-lys—the emblem of the House of Bourbon. Atop the king's fat, pasty countenance, the great jewel-encrusted crown of Saint-Louis balanced unsteadily as he began muttering in a bored, barely audible monotone the words that would ultimately be his death sentence. He urged the Assembly to help him reform the realm socially, economically, and politically by approving equitable taxation, freedom of commerce, relief for the indigent, and establishment of provincial assemblies to manage local affairs. After Calonne had echoed the king's words, the Assembly dissolved into seven committees, or bureaux, each chaired by a prince of the blood. The king's youngest brother, the comte d'Artois, chaired Lafayette's bureau.

At first, all went reasonably well. For six weeks, the bureaux feigned interest in tax reform and the plight of peasants, and, when they reconvened in full assembly, they agreed to recommend that the king abolish the hated salt tax, end internal trade barriers for grain, and cut peasant income taxes from 20 percent to 10 percent. They even approved establishing provincial assemblies to give each province more autonomy. But they angrily rejected property taxes and other levies that would have affected them and the rest of the aristocracy—and were essential for ending the national fiscal crisis.

As Talleyrand, the powerful bishop of Autun, put it, "They found glory in opposition."[34] Lafayette was equally annoyed. He told Washington that most of the "notables" were "not ables" who belonged to "a bigoted party" of anti-Protestants and "wicked people" who opposed reform.[35]

The debate soon spilled out of the assembly halls into the streets, where ambitious rabble-rousers harangued hungry crowds with demands for redress. Once grist for the conversational mills of privileged literates, the ideas of the philosophes—Locke, Voltaire, Rousseau, and the like—echoed through the streets. For the first time, thoughts of liberty, equity, and representation penetrated the minds of commoners, who had always believed unquestioningly that God alone had ordained their place in the French political, social, and economic system. Fiery young orators spurred them on—mostly ambitious young lawyers such as Maximilien Robespierre and Georges-Jacques Danton, commoners whose education taught them to envy those born to wealth and power. Mobs of illiterates who had never before thought of politics, let alone voiced opinions, called for the king's head, Calonne's head—anyone's head. All called for destruction of the barrières, or ring of customs posts the ferme had erected around Paris to tax incoming foodstuffs, wine, and firewood. The mobs grew into small armies of 10,000 and 20,000 that marched to Versailles to demand change. The press joined the fracas. "Caricatures, placards, bon mots have been indulged by all ranks of people," Jefferson wrote to Adams. "The King long in the habit of drowning his cares in wine, plunges deeper and deeper; the Queen cries but sins on."[36]

"When Calonne assembled the notables," explained political writer Antoine Rivarol, "he opened the eyes of the people to the defects of the government's leaders as well as the defects in the fiscal situation. The nation could not find a single great statesman in that assembly, and it lost confidence in government forever."[37]

As the split widened between Assembly "not ables" and street mobs, Lafayette asserted himself, assuming leadership of a progressive "American" faction, as it grew to be called. He attacked the ferme for blocking free trade, but had little impact. He proposed civil rights for Protestants, but the comte d'Artois ruled him out of order in mid-sentence, saying the proposal was beyond the scope of the Assembly's agenda.

Outside, the crowds continued growing.

In the midst of the whirlwind, a notorious adventurer and propagandist, the comte de Mirabeau, published a pamphlet[38] with sensational charges that some notables with ties to the court had made fortunes buying inexpensive properties with knowledge in advance that they could resell them to the court at outrageously high profits. The pamphlet was an ill-disguised attack on the queen and her brother-in-law, the comte d'Artois, who had used state funds to buy the Château de Saint-Cloud, west of Paris, from their cousin, the duc d'Orléans, for 1.5 million livres ($15 million in today's currency).

Although the queen blamed the affair on Finance Minister Calonne, Lafayette demanded "a serious examination" of the charges. "I question why ministers of finance would recommend royal purchases of lands that he can-not possibly use. . . . I might also ask why they are buying more property for the king, when most people agree he should be selling the surplus lands he already owns." The comte d'Artois interrupted, calling Lafayette's language too strong, but the intrepid French knight fancied himself another Patrick Henry, in the Virginia House of Burgesses:

"My sense of patriotism is alarmed and demands a full inquiry," he cried. "The millions being dissipated come from taxes, which cannot be justified except to meet the real needs of the state. The millions abandoned to plun-der and greed are the fruit of sweat, tears and blood of the people, and the number of people sacrificed to misery to amass the sums so carelessly wasted shames the sense of justice and goodness that we know to be the natural sentiments of his majesty."[39]

To the dismay of the red-faced comte d'Artois, Lafayette demanded the arrest of speculators who profited from advance knowledge of government land purchases. The notables endorsed Lafayette's call for an inquiry, which the embarrassed count had to request from his royal older brother.

The assault on speculators raised Lafayette to unofficial leadership of reform-minded progressives outside the Assembly, and, to encourage the growth of his following, Lafayette published and distributed his speech in pamphlet form, sending the first copy to Washington. Adrienne wrote to Lafayette's aunt at Chavaniac: "News of the Assembly is still brilliant, my dear aunt . . . and it will come as no surprise to you that the particular Notable in whom you take a personal interest is acquitting himself well."[40]

Lafayette's performance at the Assembly provoked personal attacks against him in anonymously written pro-Royalist pamphlets and letters that floated on the streets of Paris each day. "Monsieur de Calonne went to find the king and demand that I be imprisoned in the Bastille," Lafayette wrote to Washington. "The King and family and the great men about court, some friends excepted, don't forgive me the liberties I have taken, and the success it had among other classes of the people."[41]

By early May, the Assembly had been meeting for more than two months, six days a week, every day but Sunday, often from early morning until late at night, trading accusations on the causes of government deficits, without agreeing on any major reforms. When one Assembly member blamed the French deficit on America's failure to pay its debts, Lafayette leaped to his feet to defend his adopted land, assailing the French government and declar-ing the *ferme's* barriers to American products as the sole reason for Amer-ica's inability to settle its debts.

He then launched a devastating attack on the court for reaping "a cruel harvest" by taxing the poor. Such taxes, he maintained, collected little in comparison to "the profligacy and luxury of the court and the upper classes of society. But let us follow those millions into the country cottages, and we will see the last hope of sustenance for widows and orphans, the final burden that forces the farmer to abandon his plow or the family of honest craftsmen to turn to begging."[42] Waste, inefficiency, and corruption, he charged, had increased annual government spending 50 percent since the end of the Seven Years' War. He demanded sharp reductions in royal spending, which accounted for nearly 15 percent of the annual government budget. He urged cuts in royal household budgets, the sale of unused royal buildings and lodges "for which the king pays but never enjoys," the closing of nonproductive government bureaus, and an end to royal sinecures. He called for the closing of state prisons and the release of political prisoners and smugglers, whose only crime, he said, was to defy the *ferme* monopoly to appease their children's hunger. An increasingly active ally in his political life, Adrienne led a group of Lafayette supporters on a tour of prisons and sent him a report that he cited in the assembly. "The king's heart," he told the notables, "would disavow these prisons as well as the laws of the kingdom that sent prisoners there, if he fully understood their uselessness and danger."[43]

Then, in a final declamation that resounded beyond the gates of Versailles, across France, and the entire continent, Lafayette echoed Rousseau's words: "The rights of the nation outweigh the needs of the government. However great the love of the people for the king, it would be dangerous to think that [the people's] resources are inexhaustible . . . to cite my province alone, I can assure the king that the inequalities of taxation is forcing farmers to abandon their plows, craftsmen to leave their shops and depriving the most industrious citizens of so much of their earnings that they have little choice but move to other countries or turn to begging, and in that part of the kingdom, it would be impossible to raise taxes without increasing misery and despair.

"Now is the moment," he cried out. "I appeal to each of your hearts . . . we can no longer avoid facing the enormous public catastrophe that is about to overrun our unhappy land. We can only pray that the crisis created by wasteful luxury and mindless court profligacy will impress those of us who can abolish those evils more than it impresses its innocent victims.

"It seems to me," he declared, "that the time has come for us to beseech his majesty . . . to convoke a National Assembly."[44]

The words *Assemblée nationale* reverberated eerily across the room, off one wall, then another. One by one, the notables gasped and turned to each other in dismay, hoping no one outside the hall had heard the dreaded words. At first, the comte d'Artois assumed that Lafayette had simply misspoken and had meant to convoke the Estates General. The impasse at the Assembly of Notables had provoked several similar, earlier calls. The Estates General had last met in 1614 and brought together representatives of the three estates: the nobility, the clergy, and the "Third Estate" of privileged commoners—professionals, bankers, and bourgeois business and property owners.

But no, that was not what Lafayette meant. The Estates General gave each estate one collective vote, invariably allowing the combined votes of noblemen and clergy to defeat the Third Estate, which represented nearly ten times the voting population of the other two estates combined. A national assembly would give *each member* a vote, commoner, clergyman, and nobleman alike—a violation of Roman Catholic belief in the divinely ordained "order of things," which placed the nobility and clergy above the common man. A national assembly would strip the aristocracy and the church of their authority and deliver national sovereignty to commoners.

"What, Monsieur!" the comte demanded again. "You demand the convocation of the Estates General?"

"Yes, Monseigneur," Lafayette replied, but corrected him, "and even more than that."

"You want me to write what you have said and take it to the king?"

"Yes, Monseigneur."[45]

A long silence followed; the echoes of Lafayette's words—*more than that: a national assembly*—crackled like sparks, about to ignite the fuel of revolutionary ideas that had spilled from the hall onto the streets. Assembly president Loménie de Brienne, the archbishop of Toulouse, warned King Louis that Lafayette was "the most dangerous man of them all."[46]

14

"I Reign in Paris"

ON MAY 25, 1787, the Constitutional Convention convened in Philadelphia to create a new nation; on the same day in Versailles, the Assemblée des Notables dissolved in indecision and propelled an old nation toward destruction. Ironically, the king, whose inertia, uncertainty, and disinterest had encouraged assembly inaction, thanked the Assembly for doing nothing, and the Assembly president, Archbishop de Brienne, predicted, "The present crisis will become the starting point of a new splendor." As both would soon realize in prison cells, the crisis was the starting point of a new stygian darkness.

Ever-jubilant for small victories in a great war, Lafayette predicted "good effects of this Assembly. . . . On the last day of our session," he boasted to John Jay, "I had the joy of making two motions that received unanimous approval: one in favor of our Protestant citizens, the other to revise the criminal code."[1] Although the king vetoed Lafayette's proposal to revise the criminal code, he approved some of Lafayette's proposals for Protestant rights by legalizing Protestant marriages, legitimizing Protestant children, and granting Protestants the right to own property. Although he limited Protestant worship to the privacy of their homes, he allowed them to establish Protestant cemeteries. Jefferson assailed the king's concessions as too restrictive, but Lafayette was elated and invited Protestant pastors from Nîmes to his home in Paris to celebrate. "The spirit of liberty is gaining ground in this country," he exulted in a letter to Washington. "Liberal ideas are growing from one end of the country to the other."[2]

The king also yielded on the issue of provincial assemblies, but insisted on appointing half the members of each assembly himself. They, in turn, would "elect" the other members to ensure indirect royal control of the entire assembly.

The failure of the Assembly of Notables to raise taxes sent the French economy into free fall, and, by midsummer, the treasury was empty. The king ordered the new provincial assemblies to convene and do what the Assembly of Notables had failed to do: tax themselves to pay for his family's lavish spending. Appointed a representative of the noble order at the Auvergne assembly, Lafayette went to the provincial capital, Clermont-Ferrand, in August, where, as in every other province, the assembly rejected all new taxes—without commensurate reforms in royal spending. "No reforms, no taxes," became their rallying cry. The Dauphiné, the inherited province of the crown prince, followed suit, and Brittany's assembly not only rejected new taxes, it sent twelve noblemen to Versailles to demand spending reforms at the palace. The king promptly imprisoned them in the Bastille. When Lafayette protested, the queen told him that as an Auvergnat he had no business involving himself in the affairs of Brittany. "But I am a Breton, madame," he snapped, reminding the queen of his mother's birthright—"just as your majesty is a Hapsburg."[3] The quick-tempered queen demanded that her husband strip the insolent Lafayette of his rank of maréchal de camp—and the king complied.

"They honor me more than I deserve," Lafayette scoffed, and retired from the active military to devote himself to politics.

Provincial dissent over taxes increased restlessness in Paris, where the slogan "No reforms, no taxes" took on new but insidious opposite meanings for reformers and anarchists. Though all shouted the same words in unison, reformers opposed one without the other; anarchists opposed both and shouted for an end to all government. Pamphlets variously assailed and mocked *l'Autrichienne*, Queen Marie-Antoinette, as "Madame Déficit". Crowds routinely hissed and hooted her and her brother-in-law, the comte d'Artois, when either appeared in public. "But what harm have I done them," the queen protested at the hissing that greeted her at the Paris opera one evening.[4]

"The fiscal problems in France remain unsolved," Lafayette explained to Washington. "We have to cover an enormous deficit with new taxes, but the nation is reluctant to pay for what it has not voted. The notions of liberty have propagated rapidly since the American Revolution. The Assembly of Notables set fire to combustible materials. A war of words has erupted in the press. . . . The people hoot at the Comte d'Artois and burn several ministers in effigy. . . . The discontent has become so widespread that the queen no longer dares come to Paris for fear of being mistreated. The events of the last six months have at least impressed everyone that the king no longer has the right to tax the nation . . . unless such taxes have been stipulated by a national assembly."[5]

Lafayette rejoined the Auvergne assembly for the autumn term, but three months of debate produced the same results as the summer session: no reforms, no taxes. When he returned to Paris in December, he found his and Adrienne's names excluded from the list of invitations to the queen's dinners, balls, and other festivities. For Adrienne, the opportunity to stay home was a welcome one. Besides her own children, an endless parade of American children continued to march through her door—all part of Lafayette's impulsive offer to Greene, Knox, and Hamilton for international student exchanges. Just as the Caldwell boy prepared to return home, Peter Otisquette, another Indian boy, arrived, and after he and Kayenlaha left, George Washington Greene, Nathanael Greene's son—another of George Washington's many godsons—appeared at the door. A year earlier, Nathanael Greene had died prematurely at forty-four, but his widow, Caty, had taken advantage of Lafayette's promise to give the boy a chance to study in France.

"No affair in my life can be more capital," Lafayette wrote to Caty Greene, "no task more pleasing than the one I owe your confidence and that of the good and great man of whose friendship I was proud and happy."[6] As he had done with Caldwell, Lafayette enrolled young Greene at the prestigious Pension Lemoyne, where he could visit Jefferson, across the road, or easily walk down the Champs Elysées to the Pont Royal and cross the Seine to Lafayette's home. Thus, the boy had two families in Paris, although only one—the Lafayettes—paid for his education.[7]

In the autumn of 1787, a letter from Washington enclosed a copy of the new American Constitution: "I don't have to tell you that I read the newly proposed constitution with care and unbounded interest," Lafayette replied. "I admired it greatly and found the different methods of electing the two houses of congress well conceived. . . . For the sake of America, the human race, and your own renown, I beg you, my dear general, do not refuse the responsibility of the presidency during the first few years. You alone can make this political machine operate successfully."[8]

With a copy of the American Constitution in his possession, Lafayette added the word "constitution" to his political rhetoric and helped organize "a constitutional club." What began as a "Society of Thirty," however, quickly mushroomed into a large, albeit informal, political party of progressive social and political thinkers, variously called "the Americans" or "Fayettistes." Members included the marquis de Condorcet, a prominent mathematician who championed abolition; the duc de La Rochefoucauld, a champion of the poor; and comte César de La Tour-Maubourg, a French general and fellow Auvergnat from Le Puy, not far from Chavaniac. Accomplished commoners and clergymen also joined—the astronomer Jean-Sylvain Bailly; the club-footed bishop of Auton, better known as Talleyrand; and Abbé

Sieyès, the chancellor of Chartres, who was working on an inflammatory pamphlet called *Essai sur les privilèges*—"Essay on Privileges." To Lafayette's distress, the grotesque giant the comte de Mirabeau also joined the group. A violent ex-convict, Mirabeau exuded seductive oratory that veiled his hideously pockmarked, leonine face and even more hideous soul that reveled in all kinds of debauchery, including adultery, rape, and pedophilia. From the first, Lafayette despised him, but would have no choice but to deal with him as a power from the huge southern province of Provence.

Although not officially a member, Jefferson was an active and welcome participant. An almost diurnal guest at the rue de Bourbon, Jefferson became Lafayette's closest friend. Fluent in French by now, Jefferson mixed easily with the Society of Thirty, whom he called the "real patriots" of France because of their spiritual ties to America. "This party," he said, "comprehended all the honesty of the kingdom . . . the men of letters, the easy bourgeois, the young nobility . . . who were able to keep up the public fermentation at the exact point which borders on resistance, without entering on it."[9]

In February, Lafayette returned to the Auvergne assembly, where the newfound freedom of debate unleashed an old and bitter rivalry between northern and southern factions. Within a month, the assembly ignored its mission to solve the national fiscal crisis and voted to split the Auvergne into two new provinces. By spring, separatist political movements developed in virtually every province, and, in the months that followed, riots erupted in cities across France that fractured the provinces into smaller semiautonomous entities. Across the Atlantic, meanwhile, the autonomous states in the fractious American confederation agreed to cede much of their autonomy to a new national union.

"In the middle of our troubles [in France]," Lafayette wrote to Washington, "it is a great consolation to me to rejoice over the success of my adopted nation. . . . Permit me once more, my dear general, to plead with you not to refuse the presidency; the constitution as written answers many prayers; but unless I am strongly mistaken, there are certain points that would pose a danger if the United States did not have the good fortune to have their guardian angel to weigh the advantages and disadvantages of each article, determine the degree of power to give the government, limit the powers that could be abused and, finally, indicate what still needs to be done to attain that perfection which the new constitution has come closer to reaching than any other form of government past or present."[10]

Ironically, as Lafayette urged Washington to seize America's reins of government, Washington sent Lafayette paternal advice to move cautiously in France. "I do not like the situation of affairs in France," he warned. "Little more irritation would be necessary to blow up the spark of discontent into a flame that might not easily be quenched. . . . Let it not, my dear

Marquis, be considered as a derogation from the good opinion that I entertain of your prudence when I caution you, as an individual desirous of sig-
nalizing yourself in the cause of your country and freedom, against running
into extremes and prejudicing your cause."[11]

On September 23, 1788, the political forces swirling about him eroded
what little remained (or ever existed) of Louis XVI's will, and he summoned
the Estates General to meet the following spring, for the first time in 174
years, to restore order to France's tangled political, social, and economic
affairs. The king appointed half the members of the first two estates, with
the remainder of the two estates elected by their peers—fellow noblemen in
the First Estate and fellow clergy in the Second. Although commoners
elected members of the Third Estate, electors had to be at least twenty-five
years old and pay so high a poll tax that it disenfranchised almost the entire
commoner population, including peasants, craftsmen, shopkeepers, and
laborers. Of the 610 members of the Third Estate, 25 percent were lawyers,
and nearly 20 percent were industrialists, merchants, and bankers. Fewer
than 10 percent were agriculturists. Intensifying popular distrust was the
Estates General unit rule, which gave each estate a single collective vote
and, therefore, allowed the nobility and clergy, with one vote each, to
ignore the interests of the Third Estate, which represented 90 percent of the
voting population but had only one vote.

On the advice of his ministers, the king recalled the Assembly of Notables in November 1787 to reassess Estates General voting rules. Lafayette
proposed giving the Third Estate at least two votes, to prevent the nobility
and clergy from dominating the proceedings, but the Assembly turned him
down, two to one. "Today," Lafayette noted to a friend after his defeat, "is
the anniversary of Lord Cornwallis' defeat. Today also ended a campaign of
my own that I will remember with pleasure. You are right to think that the
court thinks so ill of me. . . . My conscience and the confidence of the public are my two supports."[12]

Early in 1789, the palace announced it would print paper money to pay
half the crown's debt. The result was economic disaster. The *ferme* doubled
its duties on food; prices soared; markets crashed; vendors refused paper currency; and textile producers closed their doors, laying off more than two
hundred thousand workers across France—more than fifty thousand in Normandy alone and eighty thousand in Paris. Making matters worse, two suc-
cessive years of drought and a freak hailstorm in the Paris region had decimated harvests and produced food shortages that sent prices 60 percent
higher. Food riots erupted in the Dauphiné, Provence, Languedoc, and Brittany. Mobs of peasants and impoverished workers raided church-owned granaries, wheat convoys, and bakeries in every town and city. Mobs swarmed
through the streets; thieves broke into homes—including Jefferson's—to

steal anything made of gold or silver to trade for food. Pamphleteers flooded Paris with leaflets accusing Versailles and the aristocracy of starving the nation into submission and emasculating the Estates General before it even met by retaining the unit rule.

As France reeled violently amid demands for popular rule, the United States walked calmly and firmly toward that end. In September 1788, the Congress of the American Confederation met for the last time, setting the site of the new government in New York and fixing early 1789 for conven-ing the First Congress and balloting by presidential electors. In December, Maryland ceded ten square miles of land along the Potomac River as a site for a new federal city. Many of Lafayette's old friends in America won elec-tion to the First Congress in routine fashion—except for the peg-legged New York lawyer, Gouverneur Morris, whose campaign for a powerful chief executive earned him the displeasure of constituents. Ironically, it was he who had composed the final draft of the Constitution. Forty days after his electoral defeat, he arrived at Le Havre, braving tempest-tossed winter seas to begin a new life in Europe as a representative for American business interests. Toward the end of February, he limped up to Lafayette's door on the rue de Bourbon, with Jefferson at his side.[13] Morris spoke French bril-liantly, was a good friend of Washington, and had high hopes of replacing Jefferson, who had already applied for leave to return to America. The two Americans stayed to dinner, and Lafayette's older daughter, Anastasie, sang from memory a song that Morris himself had written. Morris had brought a letter to Lafayette from George Washington, addressing Lafayette's pleas for Washington to assume the United States presidency.

"Your feelings approach those of my other friends more than my own," Washington replied. "In truth, the difficulties seem to me to multiply and grow larger as the time approaches for me to give a definitive response. In the event circumstances dictate my acceptance, my dear Sir, I will accept the burden with such reluctance and so deep a distrust of my abilities as to render the world incredulous." Washington predicted that the new con-gress would be the finest ever assembled in the world. "Only understanding, honesty, industry and frugality are needed to make us a great and happy people."[14]

Shortly after Morris's visit, Lafayette set off again on the bone-shattering ride to Auvergne—this time to stand for election as a member of the Estates General. Morris predicted that Lafayette's efforts to introduce American-style republicanism in France would result either in "Tyranny" or "Anarchy."[15]

"In effect Time is needful to bring forward Slaves to the Enjoyment of Liberty," he warned. "Time. Time. Education. But what is Education? It is not Learning. It is more the Effect of Society on the Habits and Principles of each Individual, forming him at an early Period of Life to act afterwards the part of a good Citizen. . . . Progress towards Freedom must be slow and can only be compleated in the Course of several Generations."[16]

Lafayette ignored his friend's warnings and pressed on with his revolution. At first, he considered running for election as a member of the Third Estate, but concluded that the majority of that order already shared his views and that he would have a greater impact among the conservative nobility by winning them over to social, political, and economic reform.

"Monsieur de La Fayette is since returned from his political Campaign in Auvergne crowned with success," Morris wrote to Washington:

> He had to contend with the Prejudices and the Interests of his Order, and with the Influence of the Queen and Princes . . . but he was too able for his Opponents. He played the Orator with as much *Eclat* as ever. He acted the Soldier and is at this Moment as much envied and hated as his Heart could wish. He is also much beloved by the Nation for he stands forward as one of the principal Champions for her Rights. . . . We have I think every Reason to wish that the Patriots may be successful. . . . The Leaders here are our Friends. Many of them have imbibed their Principles in America and all have been fired by our example. Their opponents are by no Means rejoiced at the Success of our Revolution.[17]

Morris warned, however, that widespread "depravity" among delegates to the Estates General had put Lafayette's constitutional revolution in jeopardy:

> An hundred Anecdotes and an hundred thousand Examples are required to shew the extreme Rottenness of every Member. . . . There is one fatal principle which pervades all Ranks. It is a perfect Indifference to the Violation of Engagements. Inconsistency is so mingled in the Blood, Marrow and every Essence of this People that when a Man of high Rank and Importance laughs today at what he seriously asserted Yesterday, it is considered as the natural Order of Things. The great Mass of the common People have no Religion but their Priests, no Law but their Superiors, no Moral but their Interest. These are the Creatures who, led by drunken Curates, are now in the high Road *à la liberté* and the first Use they make of it is to form Insurrections everywhere for the Want of Bread. We have had a little Riot here yesterday and I am told some Men have been killed.[18]

The day after Morris penned his letter, George Washington took the oath of office in New York as the first popularly elected president in the United States—and, indeed, the world. A few weeks later, his protégé Lafayette took his seat in the French Estates General in Versailles, among noblemen bent on preserving despotic rule by the aristocracy. By the time the Estates General convened, the continuing drought and spreading famine and unemployment had produced some four hundred riots across France and blanketed

Gouverneur Morris, of New York, a former New York delegate in the Continental Congress and the Constitutional Convention, penned the final wording of the United States Constitution but, because of his strong federalist views, failed to win election to the First Congress. He came to Paris on business, but ultimately replaced Jefferson as American ambassador. (*Library of Congress.*)

the land with universal distrust of anything remotely associated with the king, including the Estates General—and with good reason. Almost every member of the Estates General had his own private agenda. Together, members brought more than fifty thousand petitions to debate—almost all unrelated to famine, unemployment, or reform of the realm.

On May 4, King Louis XVI led the official opening procession, surrounded by his two brothers and the younger prince. The crown prince, or dauphin, lay in bed, gravely ill. Queen Marie-Antoinette followed with the two princesses and, behind them, members of the court and government ministers. The nobility, including Lafayette, followed, in gold jackets, with flamboyant, Henry IV–style wide-brimmed hats from the sixteenth century. All carried swords, the symbols of knighthood and fealty to the king. The clergy followed in red or violet capes. Because of its inferior social status, the Third Estate of commoners was barred from the procession and entered the hall through a side door—wearing black.

"The procession is very magnificent," Gouverneur Morris extolled in his diary. "Neither the King nor Queen appear too well pleased. The former is repeatedly saluted as he passes along with the 'Vive le Roi' but the latter meets not a single acclamation. She looks, however, with contempt on the scene in which she acts a part and seems to say, for the present: 'I submit but I shall have my turn.'"[19]

After the appropriate prayers, the bishop of Nancy preached a sermon while the king nodded off and fell asleep. The next day did not begin auspiciously. The king rose to address the assembly, then realized he had forgotten the manuscript of his speech and sat down nervously while an aide raced back to the royal apartments to retrieve it. A few minutes later, he delivered his meaningless welcome, then deferred to his finance minister, who outlined the needs of the nation and relayed the king's order for each of the estates to begin debate the following day in three separate chambers.

Abbé Sieyès, however, demanded that all orders meet as one and abandon the unit rule in favor of a head count—a change that would automatically have given the Third Estate control of the entire assemblage. "There cannot be one will as long as we permit three orders," he declared, echoing Rousseau's *Le Contrat Social*. "At best, the three orders might agree. But they will never constitute *one* nation, *one* representation, and *one* common will."[20] Lafayette stunned the members of his order by agreeing. Although the Third Estate voted for the change, Sieyès was unable to capture a majority of the clergy's votes and Lafayette rallied only 46 of the 234 noblemen to his side. Many of those who voted against him dropped angry hints of retaliation for his disloyalty to his order. "I begin to worry about you," Jefferson told him. "Your principles are decidedly with the *Tiers Etat*, but your instructions are against it."[21]

"I smother in our chamber," he replied. "The mephitic odors of their prejudices are not good for my lungs."[22]

On June 4, the dauphin, or crown prince, died, and the king retired to his hunting lodge in the Marly Forest to mourn. His departure left conservative ultra-royalists—the so-called "court party"—without direction. With each passing day, Fayettistes won new converts among the clergy, and, on June 17, Abbé Sieyès proclaimed a majority of his order ready to vote with the Third Estate. "Considering that we now represent ninety-six percent of the nation," he moved that they declare themselves a "National Assembly." They agreed, and ended five centuries of rule by the nobility and clergy. They elected the commoner-scientist Bailly as their first president. Although the voting represented a social and political revolution, it was far from national in character, as Sieyès pretended. The Assembly barely represented 10 percent, let alone 96 percent, of the nation, but the vote did force the two, tiny controlling minorities of nobles and clerics to share some of their power with a slightly larger minority of privileged commoners. The nobles and clerics did not cede power graciously, however.

The following day, when members of the new National Assembly went to enter the great hall to begin deliberations, a ring of troops barred the doors. While they stood in the rain, the members of the nobility and the clergy who had voted against change took their seats inside and pronounced all resolutions of the National Assembly null and void. Outside, the members of the National Assembly moved to the royal tennis court, where President Bailly declared, "Considering that the National Assembly has been called to prepare a constitution, restore public order, and uphold the principles of monarchy, nothing will impede the continuation of its deliberations. Regardless of the site it is forced to use and wherever its members assemble, it remains the National Assembly." The members then took the "Oath of the Tennis Court," pledging not to separate. On June 22, the Assembly, with the entire Third Estate, 150 members of the clergy, and 2 noblemen, met in the Church of Saint-Louis in Versailles. Lafayette remained home, putting the finishing touches on a document he and Jefferson had written: "The First European Declaration of the Rights of Man and Citizens," which became the *Première Déclaration européenne des droits de l'homme et des citoyens*.[23]

On June 23, the king emerged from his isolation at Marly, appeared at the church, and ordered the National Assembly "to separate immediately and return tomorrow morning to the chambers assigned to your order to resume your deliberations."[24] The Assembly sat paralyzed in silence, agasp at their king's pompous waddle down the aisle and out the church door. The two nobles in the Assembly and several clergymen stood and obediently followed the king, but Bailly sprang to his feet: "A nation assembled does not accept orders," he cried angrily. The ambitious Mirabeau struggled to raise his huge frame and outshine Bailly: "We are here by the authority of the people; only the authority of bayonets can remove us."[25] The delegates cheered both challenges to royal authority and added a challenge of their own by declaring the inviolability of the Assembly and declaring an end to a millennium of absolute royal rule in France. The following day, the majority of the clergy joined the Third Estate, and, a day later, forty-seven nobles, including Lafayette, took their places in the Assembly.

"This day will be celebrated in our annals," declared Bailly, a man as optimistic and idealistic as Lafayette. "It makes the family complete. It ends forever the divisions which have mutually afflicted us. . . . The National Assembly will now concern itself, without distraction or rest, with the regeneration of the realm and the public welfare."[26]

The cynical Gouverneur Morris saw things more clearly: "The nobles deeply feel their situation," he wrote to Foreign Affairs Secretary John Jay. "The king after siding with them was frightened into an abandonment of them. He acts from terror only. The soldiery in this city . . . declare they will not act against the people."[27] Morris said that after a group of drunken soldiers were jailed, a mob marched to demand their release and "soldiers on guard unfixed their bayonets and joined the mob. A party of dragoons, ordered to disperse the riot, thought it better to drink with the rioters. The soldiers, with others confined in the same prison, were then paraded in triumph to the Palais Royal,[28] which is now the Liberty Pole of this city, and there they celebrated as usual their joy. Probably this evening some other prisons will be opened, for *Liberté* is now the general cry and *Autorité* is a name, not a real existence . . . the sword has slipped out of the monarch's hands."[29]

As anarchy spread across Paris, 30,000 troops massed in and about Versailles to protect the king. The rest of the regular army in Metz—200,000 men—were on alert, awaiting the king's order to march into Paris, but, according to Morris, "all my information [is] that he will never bring his army to act against the people."[30]

On July 7, the National Assembly declared itself a National Constituent Assembly—in effect, a constitutional convention—and three days later Lafayette proposed his "Declaration of the Rights of Man" as a preamble to the nation's first constitution. Jefferson's contributions gave many provisions a familiar ring.

"All men are created free and equal," declared the first article, which also abolished all social classes and distinctions. "All men are born with certain inalienable rights," read the second, "including life, liberty, property, and the pursuit of happiness, the right to work, the right to hold and express opinions and religious beliefs, and the right to defend their persons, their lives and their honor." Article three restricted "the exercise of natural rights" to those which did not interfere with the rights of others. Subsequent articles imposed separation of legislative, executive, and judicial branches of government, open government, impartiality of judges, and "clear, precise and uniform laws for all citizens." It called for legislative consent for all government spending and gave "succeeding generations" the right to change the constitution, to adapt to social and economic change.[31]

Lafayette called the document a "profession of faith, fruit of my past, pledge of my future . . . at the same time, a manifesto and an ultimatum."[32] Jefferson also hailed it and, like Lafayette, misread the character of the French people and their leaders. "I think it probable," he predicted in a letter to his Virginia protégé James Monroe, "this country will, within two or three years, be in the enjoyment of a tolerably free constitution, and that without its having cost them a drop of blood."[33] Morris scoffed at both men, saying it failed to draw a line between liberty and license. He read it at Jefferson's house, where he, the Lafayettes, and a large party of Americans had celebrated July 4.

"Our American example has done them good," Morris admitted, "but like all novelties, liberty runs away with their discretion, if they have any.

They want an American Constitution with the exception of a king instead of a president, without reflecting that they have not American citizens to support that Constitution. . . . Different constitutions of government are necessary to different societies. . . . A democracy [in France]? Can that last? I think not. I am sure not, unless the whole people are changed."[34]

As Washington had warned him it might, Lafayette's declaration of human rights proved the additional "irritation" that Washington had said he feared would "blow up the spark of discontent into a flame that might not easily be quenched."[35] Street-corner orators shouted the provisions of Lafayette's bill of rights to illiterates whom priests had always cowed into believing God had ordained them inferior. Lafayette's document told them they were born equal to priests, noblemen, and kings, and, like beasts unleashed, they interpreted liberty as license and pursuit of happiness as plunder. Pamphleteers added to the frenzy with charges that the Court had conspired with the nobility to withhold grain and starve the people. The presence of troops and cavalry at every bridge and along the major streets provoked still more rumors; a *grande peur*—a "great fear"—swept across France that the nobility had hired an army of foreign brigands to wreak vengeance on farmers and shopkeepers.

On Sunday, July 12, thousands of Parisians poured from their churches and milled about the streets and squares. Orators harangued them at every street corner, denouncing priests as purveyors of the king's lies. In the gardens of the Palais Royal, a huge crowd gathered under the plain trees, hypnotized by the echoing voice of Georges-Jacques Danton, an ugly but nonetheless glib lawyer who thrilled as he watched his words seduce the great mass before him. Suddenly the cry "To arms!" rang out. As some raced for refuge under nearby arcades, the rest of the mob sprang like a great beast of prey out the gates onto the rue Saint-Honoré, hungering for bread and thirsting for blood. Shots rang out near the Tuileries, where palace guards raked the crowd with fire. By day's end, anarchy raged in the streets. The mob burned and demolished forty of the fifty-four hated customs posts, or *barrières*, that the *ferme* had built to collect taxes on foodstuffs entering Paris. Brigands took advantage of the surging mob to loot shops and homes in their path. Ordered by officers to fire on the mobs, army regulars—themselves commoners—refused, and, when several of their sergeants were jailed for disobedience, the mob and the soldiers smashed through the prison gates and released them and all other prisoners.

"The little City of Paris is in as fine a tumult as any one could wish," Morris lamented in his diary. "They are getting arms wherever they can find any. Seize sixty barrils of powder in a boat on the Seine. Break into the Monastery of St. Lazar and find a store of grain which the holy brotherhood had laid in. Immediately it is put into carts and sent to market, and on every cart a friar. The Gardemeuble du Roy[36] is attacked and the Arms are delivered to prevent worse consequences."[37]

To try to restore order, some four hundred electors of the Paris Third Estate formed an ad hoc government at the Hôtel de Ville—the city hall—and organized a "citizen's militia"—a Corps Bourgeois—to patrol the streets and protect property, but it had little effect.

On the evening of July 13, rumors reached the floor of the National Assembly at Versailles that the king had acceded to the queen's demand that troops seize the building and arrest the deputies. The deputies voted to remain in session throughout the night and, the next morning, took up the question of adopting Lafayette's bill of rights. The debate continued past noon and, after a recess for a midday meal, dragged on through the afternoon. Suddenly, at six, the door of the chamber burst open; Lafayette's brother-in-law, the vicomte de Noailles, ran down the aisle, whispered to the chair, then shouted the news that a mob in Paris had seized the medieval Bastille fortress-prison.[38] The mob had run amok all day, searching for arms and powder. More than seven thousand had stormed the Hôtel des Invalides and seized thirty thousand muskets, but, finding little powder, they cried out, "To the Bastille," where they knew they could find a large supply. While the prison governor tried to negotiate, part of the crowd broke into the inner courtyards, and he ordered his troops to fire. Ninety-eight besiegers fell dead and seventy-three others lay wounded. Two detachments of French guards who had joined the insurrection brought up five cannon stolen from the Invalides and blasted through the outer walls. After setting free the only prisoners they could find—four forgers, a libertine, and two madmen—they massacred six of the prison's defenders and seized the prison governor, dragging him through the streets to the Hôtel de Ville before hanging his torn body by the neck from a lamppost.

As the mob's lust for blood intensified, the provost of merchants—the nearest equivalent to a mayor in Paris—accidentally wandered into their midst. Before he could breathe a whisper of protest, they had butchered him, severing his head from his lifeless body and impaling it on the end of a pike to display along the line of march. As an afterthought, they cut down the body of the prison warden and used his head as a similar trophy, with many in the mob reaching over one another to dip their fingers in the blood of their victims and smear their faces with it.

The following morning, a horror-stricken assembly at Versailles assigned Lafayette to head a delegation to implore the king to cooperate with them in restoring order. Before Lafayette could leave the hall, his cousin the duc de Liancourt, the grand master of the wardrobe, appeared and announced the king's imminent arrival. The night before, as he learned of the rioting in Paris, the king is said to have asked Liancourt, "Then is it a full-blown riot?"

Paris mobs storm the Bastille on July 14, 1789, and seize the prison governor, whom they dragged through the streets to hang from a lamppost by city hall a short time later. (*Réunion des Musées Nationaux.*)

"No, Sire," Liancourt replied, "It is a full-blown revolution."[39]

At eleven o'clock in the morning, July 15, 1789, the king entered the National Assembly and addressed them for the first time as "Members of the National Assembly"—in effect, tacitly recognizing their authority and ending thirteen centuries of absolute monarchic rule in France. He asked their help in restoring order in Paris, pledging, in turn, that he would henceforth maintain "free and direct communication" with the Assembly. To avoid further provocation, he ordered his troops to stand down, and he agreed to abolish corvée road-labor, to abolish torture, to reform the criminal code, and to give the Assembly power over taxation and government spending. He called on them to meet regularly as a legislature akin to the British Parliament, with rights to enact legislation, with the consent of the king.

The assembly responded with thunderous applause, and, as they escorted him back to the palace cheering *"Vive le roi!"*, a crowd fell in behind to join in acclaiming their king's wisdom and grace. They refused to leave until the king and queen and their three children appeared on a balcony to acknowledge their cheers. By early afternoon a train of forty carriages, with Lafayette

and Bailly in the lead, raced off to Paris with the news of the king's concessions. Couriers had galloped ahead, and huge crowds gathered along the way
to cheer as Lafayette and the others drove by. The city's electors escorted
them to the City Hall, where Bailly read the king's concession speech. The
electors declared Paris an autonomous commune and voted Lafayette commanding general and military leader of the new government. Elated by the
prospects of organizing and commanding an American-style citizen's militia,
he drew his sword, the symbol of his knighthood and fealty to the king, and,
to thunderous cheers, raised it high in fealty to La Nation!

"Vive le Roi; vive la Nation!" he cried.

"Vive le Roi! Vive la Nation!" they echoed, before beginning a singsong
chant, "La-fa-yette, La-fa-yette, La-fa-yette . . ." One elector crowned the
Houdon bust of Lafayette with a laurel wreath, then held it high above his
head and marched it around the room to the rhythms of "La-fa-yette, La-
fa-yette."[40] When the chorus moderated, an elector called out Bailly's name
and moved to name him civil leader of the new government. The electors
roared their approval, conferring on him the title of "mayor of Paris,"
which they believed more republican than "provost of merchants"—and
somewhat less likely to cost him his head. After the cheering subsided, the
entire throng strode across the river to Nôtre-Dame Cathedral for a
Te Deum.

News of the Paris uprising set off similar revolts throughout the provinces, where hungry peasants joined with the bourgeoisie to replace old
authorities with new assemblies of electors, who pledged to reduce the price
of bread. Mobs in Lille, Rouen, Cherbourg, Dijon, and Rennes mimicked
Paris, with regular army troops deserting to join their civilian countrymen in
seizing power, razing prisons and châteaux, and burning manorial registers
that validated the identities of the local nobility and the properties they
owned. Behind them, they left a trail of rubble and smoldering ruins where
the centuries-old heritage of the French nation had stood. There were few
exceptions to the reign of destruction. In Lyon, royalists resisted and took
control of city government in the name of the king, and in Toulouse, a curious mix of royalists and revolutionaries took joint command. In Aix-en-
Provence, a military junta seized power.

In Paris, Lafayette prepared to return to Versailles to resume his work in
the Assembly, but the electors pleaded with him to remain to assume his
duties as military leader and restore order. "Only I seem to be able to control
the behavior of the people," he wrote to a friend. "A mob of forty thousand
people gather, the ferment builds to a peak until I appear on the scene, and,
with a word from me, they disperse."[41]

The following morning, he carefully pulled together all the symbols of
power he could find. He sent a servant to fetch a tall, stately white horse at

the military academy, while he squeezed into his frayed French general's uniform and nine-year-old George-Washington helped him attach his sheathed sword and other military trappings. As a mounted troop waited in the courtyard, Anastasie, Virginie, and George kissed him good-bye; then Adrienne gave her husband a long embrace before saying adieu and watching him step into the courtyard to mount the great white horse.

"Not once in those days," Virginie wrote, "did she see him leave the house without the feeling that she might be saying her adieux to him for the last time."[42]

As Lafayette trotted along the river Seine and approached the city hall, a huge crowd filled the square in front and blocked his way. What, he demanded, was going on? "Nothing," cried an onlooker, "only an abbé they're about to hang." Infuriated, Lafayette drove his huge white horse—appropriately named Jean Leblanc[43]—into the sea of people, parting it as Moses had parted the Sea of Reeds, until he reached the hapless priest and led him into the safety of the city hall. Throughout the day, he ran out onto the steps of the city hall to demand release of innocent men the mob was about to hang or butcher. The ugly, street-corner agitator Danton resurfaced as a self-appointed captain in the bourgeois guard and dragged a terrified man before the crowd to execute, claiming he was the assistant governor of the Bastille. Apprised of the imminent hanging, Lafayette raced out and identified the man as a city councilman—an elector—whom the council had appointed temporary governor of the Bastille. He demanded his release, ordered Danton to return the elector's sword, and escorted him up the steps into city hall. The red-faced Danton would never forgive Lafayette for the public humiliation.

"I have already saved the lives of six people about to be hanged in different sections of the city," Lafayette wrote. "The people are insane, drunk with power; they will not listen to me forever. As I write . . . eighty thousand people have surrounded the Hôtel de Ville and cry out that we are lying to them, that the troops are not withdrawing, that the king must come. . . . The minute I am gone, they lose their minds. My situation is unlike anyone else's. I reign in Paris, but I reign over an angry population aroused by evil conspirators."[44]

15

Guardian Angel

THE DAY AFTER the Paris mob stormed the Bastille, Lafayette took nominal command of the Bourgeois Guard—a French equivalent to America's citizen's militias. Unlike Americans, who returned in peace to their fields and families, the citizen-militiamen of France roamed the streets in drunken, disorganized bands, looting shops and homes and assaulting anyone who displeased them, for whatever reason. Most had nowhere to go—France had no frontier wilderness for the landless to settle, plant, or hunt, to sustain themselves and their families. The king, the aristocracy, and the clergy owned all French lands, forests, and streams, and none but they could hunt, fish, or even set foot on their properties without permission.

As Lafayette administered the oath of allegiance to his new "army," he recognized that "I may seem to be their chief but I am far from being their master."[1] He established a semblance of administrative control by renaming it the National Guard of Paris and appointing a hierarchy of officers in each district to clear the streets of brigands, vagrants, and homeless, to restore the normal flow of traffic, and to encourage business to return to normal. To quash rumors that the aristocracy planned to starve Paris into submission, he ordered military convoys to escort shipments of flour duty-free into the city's poorest neighborhoods. To end disorders in and around the Bastille, he ordered it razed, to remove an irritating symbol of royal oppression from the streetscape. As wreckers began demolition, he salvaged a key to the main gate of what he called the "fortress of despotism,"[2] to send to George Washington.

On July 17, only three days after the fall of the Bastille, King Louis XVI sought to reestablish a semblance of royal authority in Paris by going to the city to reconcile himself with Lafayette and Bailly—and the constitutionalists who had seized the reins of city government. They, at least, did not seek his head. Recognizing the city's semiautonomous status, the king left his personal guard—the legendary Black Musketeers to which Lafayette had once belonged—at the city gates, and his carriage entered without a military escort. About four hundred deputies from the National Assembly at Versailles, however, had come with the king to show their support and descended from their own carriages to form a line of march on each flank of the king's carriage. Lafayette was there to receive and reassure him "with a few respectful words." Bailly gave Louis the keys to the city: "These are the same that were presented to Henry IV,"[3] the astronomer-mayor told the king. "This is the most beautiful day of the monarchy. It is the occasion of an eternal alliance of monarch and people."[4]

A small troop of elite militia led the way through the city, with Lafayette behind them, his sword drawn, in front of the royal carriage on his great white horse, Jean Leblanc. About 100,000 motley-looking members of the new National Guard of Paris lined the route, according to Jefferson, two and three deep, "armed with guns, pistols, swords, pikes, pruning hooks, scythes, and whatever they could lay hold of."[5] An hour later the procession arrived at city hall, and, in a ceremony fraught with symbolism, Lafayette watched Bailly, the commoner mayor, stand *above the king* on the city hall step, and reach down to hand the monarch a red and blue revolutionary cockade—"the distinctive mark of Frenchmen."[6] The king accepted the humiliating symbol of rebellion, removed his hat before the commoner mayor, and pinned the insignia to its brim. To the cries of *"Vive le roi!"* he then followed Bailly up the steps of city hall, beneath an "arch of steel" formed by the swords of the city's assemblymen. Once in the Grande Salle, the king issued a timid declaration affirming the city's status as a self-governing commune, with Bailly as mayor and Lafayette as commanding general. As he left, the frightened king took his old friend Lafayette aside and, as a gesture of reconciliation, said, "I have been looking for you to tell you that I confirm your nomination to the post of commandant general of the Paris Guard."[7] That night, the king's youngest brother, the comte d'Artois, fled the country with six other princes of the blood and six of the king's ministers.

Although Lafayette restored order in the center of the city, anarchy gripped the rest of Paris. Thousands of brigands, vagabonds, army deserters, and other lawless elements pinned the red and blue cockades of the revolution on themselves and masqueraded as militiamen. Mob disorder flowed in and out of alleyways and streets, advancing and receding unpredictably like a giant amoeba, its jellylike mass oozing in one direction before contracting and reemerging, unpredictably, on a new course. Gouverneur Morris bore witness to its grisly appearance outside his club in the Palais Royal: "After dinner . . . under the arcade of the Palais Royal waiting for my carriage . . .

This painting, entitled *La Voute d'Acier*—The Arch of Steel—
by Jean-Paul Laurens, shows King Louis XVI accepting the revolutionary cockade from Bailly, the first mayor of Paris, at the steps of
the Paris Hôtel de Ville, on July 17, 1789. Lafayette, commander
in chief of the Paris National Guard, looks on at the right, before
escorting Louis under the arch of steel formed by swords of the
Paris electors on the staircase of the Hôtel de Ville. The painting was
significant for depicting the king *below* the commoner mayor, in a
position of obeisance, his hat doffed, looking up and reaching for the
symbolic revolutionary cockade as a gift from the people. (*Réunion des
Musées Nationaux.*)

the Head and Body of Mr. de Foulon are introduced in Triumph. The Head
on a Pike, the Body dragged naked on the Earth. After, this horrible exhibi-
tion is carried thro the different streets. His crime is to have accepted a place
in the ministry. This mutilated form of an old man of seventy-five is shewn
to Bertier, his son in law, the intendant [comptroller] of Paris, and afterwards he also is put to death and cut to pieces, the populace carrying about
the mangled fragments with a savage joy. Gracious God, what a People!"[8]

Morris had witnessed only part of the savagery, which had started earlier that afternoon. Street-corner agitators had spread rumors that Foulon, a financier the king appointed to the finance ministry, had speculated in grain during the winter bread shortages and *boasted*—rather than simply stated fearfully—that Parisians "will be lucky if we give them hay to eat."[9] As he rode through the city, the mob dragged him from his carriage to the city hall square to hang him. Lafayette raced out to stop the outrage: "You want to kill this man without a judgment," he cried out to the mob. "That is an injustice which dishonors you and me and will tarnish all my efforts for liberty, if I were so weak as to permit it. I will not permit it. I will not save him if he is guilty, but I want him . . . tried by a judge before a tribunal according to law. I demand respect for the law, without which there is no liberty, without which I would not have supported the revolution in the New World and without which I will not support the revolution here."[10]

Lafayette's eloquence calmed the frenzy long enough to enable him to escort Foulon into the Hôtel de Ville, but minutes later the mob broke into the building and dragged the old man out to a lamppost to hang. Foulon's body was still convulsing when another mob seized his son-in-law, Bertier de Sauvigny, trying to flee Paris. They dragged him to the city hall square to watch the dreaded Jourdan Coupe-Tête[11] cut his father-in-law's lifeless form from the lamppost, sever its head, and plant it on a pike to show the terrified Bertier. Suddenly Coupe-Tête's vicious knife went to work again, and, as the hysterical mob screamed encouragement, he butchered Bertier alive, piece by piece. A few minutes later, a dragoon raced into the city hall assembly room with a large, bloody piece of meat in his hand and proclaimed, "Here is Bertier's heart!" Another man followed with the dead man's severed head, and still others marched in with Foulon's head and heart on pikes. Coupe-Tête led them all to the Palais Royal, where Gouverneur Morris saw the grisly trophies and uttered his final judgment: "Gracious God, what a people."

From his window at the Hôtel de Ville, Lafayette could see the leering face of the ambitious agitator, Danton, in the mob below, goading it to greater slaughter. Lafayette was helpless to restore law and order. In the days that followed, the madness spread beyond the gates of Paris, with riots breaking out across Alsace in eastern France, in Normandy to the west, and in Burgundy to the south. Revolutionary fervor spread north across French borders to Liège, in the Austrian-occupied Netherlands, where rebels proclaimed a Belgian republic. For the first time, Lafayette understood Gouverneur Morris's warnings that it was easier to begin a revolution and unleash people's passions than to control either. Lafayette had not envisaged the revolution he now saw evolving before him, and it disgusted him, as nothing in the American Revolution had ever done.

"I was called to military command of the capital by the people, on condition of their complete and universal confidence in me," he told the Paris

Assembly. "I have continually told the people that I would defend their interests to my dying breath so long as they heeded my advice. . . . The people have not heeded me, and, as I stated from the beginning, the day when I no longer have the confidence they promised to give me, I shall abandon my position because I can no longer be useful."[12]

His resignation stunned the Paris assembly, which had founded its collective hopes for stability on his heroic stature and military skills. They shouted and pleaded with him not to resign; the old curé of the church of Saint-Etienne-du-Mont, where Sainte Géneviève, the patron saint of Paris, was buried, fell at Lafayette's feet, begging him to retain command and pledging to obey his every order. Lafayette raised the old curé to his feet, and, before he could respond, the assembly voiced a unanimous resolution: "We, the electors of all the districts in the city of Paris, reflecting the unanimous acclamation of all the citizens of Paris and our entire confidence in the virtues, talents and patriotism of Monsieur de La Fayette, again proclaim him general of the National Guard of Paris and promise, in our own names and those of our armed brothers in our districts . . . submission and obedience to all his orders, so that his zeal . . . can complete to perfection the great work of public liberty."[13]

In effect, the assembly appointed Lafayette military dictator of Paris—even offering him a salary of 120,000 livres and an additional 100,000 livres as an entertainment fund. As he and Washington had done in the American Revolution, he emphatically refused all compensation: "When so many citizens suffer, and so many expenditures are necessary, it is repugnant to me to augment them unnecessarily. My fortune is sufficient for the state in which I live, and my time does not permit official entertaining."[14]

Armed with new powers—and the unanimous support of law-abiding citizens—he tightened control of the National Guard and imposed tough law-enforcement procedures on the streets. He named friends from the corps of French officers at Yorktown to impose order and discipline in the guard. Only those who swore allegiance to "nation, king, law and the Commune of Paris" would remain. Ever aware of the symbolism he had used to build the esprit de corps in his Virginians, he presented each guardsman with an ornate certificate of recognition after he took his oath. He issued magnificent new uniforms that he designed himself, combining the red and blue colors of the revolutionary cockade with the white color of the Bourbon flag. Their vests and breeches were white and their blue tunics carried tall red collars and silver epaulettes. By August 9, Lafayette and his officers had organized and trained an elite corps of just under 50,000 men, or what he described as "six superb divisions [about 8,000 men each] composed of sixty battalions,"[15] with one battalion for each district. They seized all the arms they could find and arrested suspects for every type of crime, ranging from pickpocketing to inciting riot with propaganda leaflets. To augment the guard's efforts, Lafayette and Mayor Bailly issued a decree ordering gun manufacturers, dealers, and owners to turn all weapons over to military commanders in their districts.

With relative calm restored, Lafayette plunged into a whirlwind of political activity at Versailles, as well as in Paris, "to end the revolution," as he put it, and build a constitutional monarchy based on the American republic. "Only after the beginning of the American era," he argued, "did the question arise of defining . . . the rights that nature imparted to every man, rights so inherent to his being that society as a whole has no right to deprive him of them."[16] Lafayette seemed to be everywhere, day and night: the Paris city hall, the Assembly in Versailles or the palace, trotting along forest roads, or down the narrow streets of the city's massive slums. In the National Assembly, he voted with the centrist majority to abolish feudal rights; to tax the nobility and clergy; to abolish serfdom and declare all serfs free; and to abolish the church's right to tithe the people, a universal tax that deprived even the poorest of 10 percent of their earnings.

Declaring that "the feudal régime has been entirely destroyed," the Assembly began debating a new constitution, including the shape of the legislative assembly and veto powers of the king, who would serve as chief executive under a new constitutional monarchy. True to his beliefs in all things American, Lafayette favored two chambers in the legislative assembly, with members of both chambers popularly elected. Other proponents of republican government, however, favored a single chamber, while conservatives called for an English-style bicameral legislature, with a nonelective House of Lords. Debate over the king's legislative veto powers caused the most furor, with leftist extremists arguing against any royal veto powers and ultraroyalists demanding absolute royal veto power. Moderates proposed temporary, "suspensive" veto powers, giving the king the right to suspend temporarily legislation he opposed, while the Assembly worked out a compromise that satisfied his objections.

Four parties emerged in the Assembly during the debates. The ultraroyalists, or Court party, favored restoration of an absolute monarchy. The Orléanists were populists seeking to replace Louis XVI with his cousin, the duc d'Orléans. The duke had courted the Third Estate by discarding his title and becoming a commoner under the name "Philippe Egalité"—"Philip the Equal." The republican "Fayettistes" formed a third party that favored a constitutional monarchy with Louis at its helm. A radical lawyer, Maximilien Robespierre, led the fourth party of left-wing extremists who favored overthrow of the monarchy. Described as an "imbecile fanatic" by many Assembly members, Robespierre favored limiting the terms of Assembly members to one session and called for obedient submission of all citizens to a dictatorship of the "common will," which he refused to define, presumably until he himself assumed power.

When Lafayette was not in the National Assembly in Versailles, he was in Paris, often in his office at the Hôtel de Ville, issuing administrative orders, listening to citizen complaints, hearing appeals from aristocrats for passports to flee the city, and shifting troops from one district to another to cope with the continual outbreaks of rioting and looting. Sometimes he left his office to gallop across the city to calm and disperse mobs himself and prevent hangings. He plunged fearlessly into crowds, shaking hands, calling out to command their silence. At just over six feet tall, he towered over his relatively short countrymen, and his stately presence—especially on Jean Leblanc—invariably calmed them while his troops worked their way through the mob, slowly, unobtrusively, forming columns that sliced it in half, then eased along subsidiary paths that eventually dispersed it into small, ineffectual groups who had little choice but to return to their homes.

Lafayette's National Guard of Paris became a model for other towns and cities. Leaders from other provinces sought his counsel in organizing their own American-style citizen's militias, founded on Lafayette's conviction that men with roots in their communities will fight selflessly to preserve them. Almost every community established a local National Guard, with many asking Lafayette to merge them into a national organization and assume overall command himself. Gradually, Paris and the rest of France rested easier: the insurrection, if not the revolution, seemed at an end. Lafayette used the constant threat that he would resign to ramrod ever more stringent decrees through the city assembly. In mid-August, it banned "seditious gatherings" and allowed Lafayette's troops to prevent idlers from gathering around street-corner orators and expanding into a mob. The decree made him the most popular figure in France—the nation's unelected but acknowledged leader. He had given the nation a bill of rights, restored peace in the streets, and made the nation safe for ordinary citizens to go about their business and move about freely and securely.

His family shared in his glory, with Adrienne making appropriate public appearances at civic ceremonies and leading efforts to provide for the poor. "She believed so deeply my father's principles and was convinced of his power to do good and prevent evil," her daughter Virginie recalled, "that she displayed incredible strength in facing the many dangers to which she was exposed. . . . She accepted all the demands made by each of the districts of Paris—sixty in all—to appear at ceremonies for various patriotic causes."[17] When one guard unit sought to make ten-year-old George-Washington Lafayette an honorary second lieutenant, his father turned the honor into theater: "Gentlemen," he proclaimed to the assembled militiamen, "my son is no longer mine; he belongs to you and to our nation"[18]—and the troops roared as the little boy stepped forward and stood at attention in his snappy-looking new uniform of a fusilier in the Paris guards.

Lafayette nevertheless rejected every suggestion that he assume government leadership, either as regent for the king or civilian *stathoudérat* ("stateholder"). "I shall decline no burden, no danger," he declared, "provided that the moment calm is restored, I shall again become a private citizen."[19] He would never explain why his emulation of America's George Washington did not extend to his assumption of executive powers in his native land.

At the end of his exhausting day as military commander of Paris, Lafayette returned home to the rue de Bourbon, hoping always to spend a quiet evening with his wife and children, but invariably faced by a gauntlet of political allies or American friends in the entrance hall. "My father's table was open to all," said Virginie. "My mother charmed all her guests with her hospitality, but deep in her heart she was suffering. She saw my father at the head of a revolution whose outcome no one could foretell. No one was more terrified than she by the dangers facing those she loved; but she rose above herself and her fears and, with my father, remained devoted to fighting evil."[20]

To reduce risks to his family, Lafayette often held discussions on the new constitution in the safety of the American legation at Jefferson's house, often debating from four o'clock in the afternoon until ten at night. Jefferson called the discussions "truly worthy of being placed in parallel with the finest dialogues of antiquity . . . by Xenophon, by Plato and Cicero." Although Jefferson was reluctant to participate at times, Lafayette assured him he would be "useful in moderating the warmer spirits and promoting a wholesome and practical reformation."[21] Gouverneur Morris also received "requests to throw some thoughts together respecting the constitution."[22]

On August 26, the National Assembly approved Lafayette's Declaration of the Rights of Man and the Citizen, or bill of rights, but not before Mirabeau and Abbé Sieyès had expanded it from nine to seventeen provisions and eroded Lafayette's foundation for liberty into a foundation for both license and dictatorship. Gone were Lafayette's definitions of individual responsibility, along with his provisions for universal suffrage, the abolition of slavery, gender equality, and free trade. Added to the original proposal were unrestricted freedoms of religion and the press, along with a universal right to resist "oppression," which the document left to each individual to define. Despite the changes, the document reinforced Lafayette's ill-conceived belief that the French revolution had ended and that his nation was on a firm course toward establishing republican government under a constitutional monarchy.

The Assembly's progress on constitutional issues, however, did nothing to address the national economic collapse, and the beast that was the Paris mob refused to lie still and wait. Camille Desmoulins, a failed lawyer who loved cafés more than courtrooms, habitually harangued the crowd in the gardens of the Palais Royal. Secretly financed by the duc d'Orléans, Desmoulins spouted slander against the king, the king's ministers, the National Assembly—indeed, anyone or anything that came into his besotted mind. "We don't take him seriously," Robespierre said of Desmoulins, who had been a classmate in high school. "He has too much imagination to have any common sense."[23] Common sense or not, Desmoulins grew as addicted as Danton to the orgiastic pleasure of seducing the great beast of the mob with outrageous oratory that sent it heaving and snapping at each provocative phrase the orator tossed to it like a scrap of meat. The more outrageous, the more the beast heaved and snapped—and the more he thrilled at his power. In a fierce attack on the National Assembly, he charged that a "suspensive veto" would give the king power to "suspend" opponents from the gallows.[24] The crowd erupted in fury, but Lafayette rushed to the scene with the Paris National Guard to quell the disturbance before it could issue onto nearby streets. Desmoulins stirred the crowd the following night with an attack on the constitution; again Lafayette's guardsmen struck quickly and sent the mob scrambling home.

In the days that followed, central Paris remained relatively calm, but two areas on the city's periphery festered with misery and discontent— Montmartre, to the north, where twenty thousand emaciated, unemployed peasants had migrated from the drought-stricken countryside to seek non-existent manufacturing jobs they assumed the city could offer. The second social sore stretched across the eastern industrial suburb of Faubourg Saint-Antoine, where hunger and despair gripped fifty thousand unemployed workers and other "heroes of the Bastille." With the drought extending into its third year, millers had little wheat to make flour, and bread prices climbed 60 percent. The Paris assembly decreed free trade in grain and subsidized purchases for the poor, but there simply was not enough bread to feed everyone.

"Paris is in danger of hourly insurrection for the want of bread," Jefferson warned, in a report to Secretary of Foreign Affairs John Jay. "The patience of . . . people . . . is worn thread-bare . . . civil war is much talked of and expected."[25] It was Jefferson's last report from Paris. After an emotional farewell dinner with Lafayette, he left for the United States to join George Washington's administration as first United States secretary of state.

Far from producing poetic paeans to liberty, freedom of the press flushed the filth of malcontents such as Mirabeau, Desmoulins, Robespierre, and Danton onto the streets of Paris. In the midst of bread shortages, they released a flood of leaflets and pamphlets to inflame public passions with accounts of the royal family—and the National Assembly—basking in luxury at Versailles

Georges-Jacques Danton, the glib, rabble-rousing lawyer whose appeals to the mob sparked the first widespread rioting in Paris that marked the beginning of the French Revolution. (*Réunion des Musées Nationaux.*)

The psychotic Jean-Paul Marat, a foul, ill-kempt Swiss dwarf, incited Paris mobs to mass murder with inflammatory editorials in a daily leaflet. (*Réunion des Musées Nationaux.*)

Maximilien Robespierre, a lawyer who led the extreme, left-wing radicals in the French constitutional assembly and whom many described as an "imbecile fanatic." (*Réunion des Musées Nationaux.*)

while Parisians starved. They demanded that the king and the National Assembly move into Paris to share the city's misery. In mid-September, an even more venomous tongue spewed poison into the propaganda stream. Jean-Paul Marat was a foul, ill-kempt, Swiss dwarf[26] who had failed as a physician and turned to scientific research that earned him nothing but public ridicule from Voltaire and other philosophes and scientists. Paranoid fantasies followed and metamorphosed into a psychotic fascination with killing that got him arrested for inciting murder.

"This fanatic filled me with disgust when I saw him the first time," wrote René Levasseur, a Jacobin member of the National Assembly. "He reminded me of a hideous insect. His clothes were sloppy, his face discolored . . . his eyes yellowed, his skin scaly with eczema; his lower lip swollen, as if filled with venom ready to spit. . . . He was a bitter man who tolerated no opposition; he believed he was a misunderstood genius."[27]

The promise of unfettered freedom of the press emboldened the "hideous insect" to publish a daily leaflet, L'Ami du Peuple—The Friend of the People. "Weary of the persecution I suffered for so long at the hands of the Academy of Sciences," Marat ranted in an editorial, "I embrace with ardor the opportunity of punishing my oppressors and achieving my rightful position in life. . . . A year ago, five or six hundred heads would have been enough to render you free and happy," he told his readers. "Today, it will take ten thousand. In a few months, you will produce a miracle and chop off one hundred thousand heads."[28]

Increasingly repelled by the orators in the gardens of the Palais Royal by his club, Morris mocked them. "These are the modern Athenians," Morris said of the French. "Alone learned, alone wise, alone polite, and the rest of Mankind Barbarians."[29]

As the hunger worsened in Paris, the fiery words of Marat and other propagandists reignited the insurrection that Lafayette had quelled. District after district declared itself independent; Danton, Desmoulins, Robespierre were everywhere, like hydras' heads, appearing before crowds to cry, "Aux armes!"—"To arms." Lafayette and his troops raced from district to district to the point of exhaustion, dispersing crowds, breaking up riots, pursuing agitators. Events controlled his every waking minute; the most powerful man in France was, in effect, powerless. "This man is very much below the business he has undertaken," Morris noted in despair, "and if the sea runs high he will be unable to hold the helm."[30]

On October 1, a regiment of Black Musketeers, summoned from Flanders by the queen to protect the royal family, trotted through the gates of the palace in Versailles. At the queen's lavish welcoming banquet that evening, officers tore off their revolutionary tricolor cockades, trampled them underfoot, and, after pinning on the white cockade of the Bourbon kings, fell to their knees with religious fervor to pay homage to Marie-Antoinette. The following day, the king, bolstered by the presence of loyal troops, rejected the Declaration of the Rights of Man in adamant tones that reflected his wife's scorn for republicanism as much as his own. On October 4, news of the queen's banquet and the king's veto sparked rioting across Paris; at the Palais Royal, Danton and Desmoulins competed with each other for the crowd's attention, each screaming invectives to avenge the insult to the cockade and the French people. The next morning, Marat's *L'Ami du Peuple* called for insurrection, and, after finding bakeries empty, without a crumb for their children, thousands of mothers from the famine-stricken industrial suburb of Faubourg Saint-Antoine marched to city hall to demand help from Lafayette and Bailly.

It was not yet eight o'clock and city hall was still closed. As the women waited for Lafayette and Bailly, the huge bell in the city hall spire rang out suddenly, mysteriously. Usually reserved for emergencies, the tocsin echoed menacingly across the rooftops. Gangs of men armed with pikes streamed from nearby streets into the plaza and smashed their way into the Hôtel de Ville to loot its gilded halls, while the mass of women set off in two great columns toward Versailles, to demand redress from the National Assembly and raid the palace bakery. "Let's fetch the baker, the baker's wife, and the baker's apprentice," they chanted (or so tradition has it), referring to the king, the queen, and the four-year-old dauphin—the crown prince. The citizen soldiers of Lafayette's National Guard, many of them husbands and sons of the protesters, joined the march to protect the women from assault by the king's troops at Versailles. Thousands more civilians joined as the throng moved up the Champs Elysées and streamed out of Paris, with guns, pikes, scythes, and other curious weapons—and at least three National Guard cannons.

"This liberty is the Devil when we know not what to do with it," Morris commented, saying the French were not adapted to the enjoyment of freedom.[31]

When Lafayette finally appeared at city hall, a group of grenadiers from six of his most elite companies awaited and demanded that he lead them to Versailles to "wipe out the Bodyguard and the Flanders regiment that trampled on the National cockade. . . . *Mon général*, the king is tricking us all, including you," a grenadier lieutenant pleaded. "We must remove him; his son will be king; you will be regent; all will be well. . . . General, we must go to Versailles. All the people want us to."[32]

Lafayette reminded them of their oaths to king and country and argued against their project, but gangs of armed men gathered about them and soon filled the square, chanting "*A Versailles! A Versailles!*"—"To Versailles!" In the background, the notorious Jourdan Coupe-Tête leaned nonchalantly against a lamppost, his black beard hiding all expression, his swift, sharp knife hidden within the black shroud that draped over his ghoulish form. A cold autumn rain began to fall; Lafayette pledged to end the food crisis and went into the city hall to write orders for the National Guard to scour the countryside, seize all wheat, and bring it to Paris. An hour later, he emerged and mounted his white horse to lead his men to the wheat fields. Unnerved by the vicious mob around them, however, his troops had grown impatient—and wet.

"A Versailles! A Versailles!" demanded the unrelenting mob. His troops joined the chant and crowded about his horse. "It is not for La Fayette to command the people," a voice shouted, "it is for the people to command him!"[33] A prisoner of his own army, he had little choice but accede to their demands or face mutiny and, possibly, a useless death at the nearby lamppost, where the implacable Coupe-Tête and his blade awaited. Moreover, he heard a new and more dangerous voice ring out for the first time—the anarchists crying, "A bas la nation!"—"Down with the nation; down with France!"[34] He knew that if his grenadiers joined the anarchists at Versailles, the royal family and the National Assembly were doomed.

Lafayette agreed to lead his guardsmen to Versailles but demanded that they reaffirm their oaths to protect the king, the royal family, and the palace from the mob and contain the disorder. Although they warned they would not fire "on women begging for bread,"[35] Lafayette agreed and sent word to the Paris Assembly that he was obeying the will of the people and leaving for Versailles. In a face-saving pretense that it retained authority over the military, the Assembly issued an official decree that "ordered the commandant general to go to Versailles . . . to prevent disorder" and to "request the king" to come to live "in his ancestral home in Paris."[36]

After renewing their oaths of loyalty to king and country, the grenadiers let their general pass, then reined their horses into formation behind him and, at five in the afternoon, rode smartly off the square into the driving rain to begin the twelve-mile trot to Versailles. A huge mob, including Coupe-Tête, followed on foot, some of them raising an occasional cry of "Vive Lafayette!" At the rear, behind the anarchists, a mob of brigands trailed to pillage homes and churches along the way and perhaps the palace itself. Behind them, other National Guard units fell into place. By the time they reached the Champs-Elysées, the cold autumn rain had drenched the entire procession, and the shouts, silenced by chills and shivers, gave way to the sounds of twenty thousand sloshing feet. Lafayette saw the lights in Jefferson's former home as he rode up the hill to Chaillot wondering how to convert an obviously humiliating defeat into victory—as he had done so long ago at Barren Hill. He wondered what Washington would have done. Neither of his friends was there to advise him. By mid-evening he reached the Pont de Sèvres over the Seine, about halfway to Versailles—and crossed, calling it his own "Rubicon."[37]

"Lafayette has marched by compulsion," Morris recounted, "guarded by his own troops who suspect and threaten him. Dreadful situation, obliged to do what he abhors or suffer an ignominious death, with the certainty that the sacrifice of his life will not prevent the mischief."[38]

It was midnight when Lafayette reached Versailles; a troop of king's officers intercepted him with a message that the king "regarded his approach with pleasure and had just accepted *his* Declaration of the Rights of Man."[39] There would be no armed conflict with the mob. Relieved at the king's cession, Lafayette led his army of troops and tramps in an unearthly torchlight parade down the broad avenue de Paris through the center of Versailles toward the palace gates. Some provocative shots rang out from the darkness beyond, but the mob was too weary to respond. A few hundred yards from the palace, the steady slosh of the marchers slowed and fell silent as Lafayette stopped before the National Assembly hall. It was a shambles. Earlier in the day, the mob of women had overrun it, demanding bread. Many still lay sleeping on the benches and floors.

Lafayette went to the palace gates. Inside the Cour Royale, or royal courtyard, the Black Musketeers, his old regiment of ceremonial bodyguards when he was a boy, stood ready to fire. Earlier in the day they had used rifle butts to repel the howling women who tried to breach the tall grillwork around the palace courtyard. The king had forbidden them to fire on women and ordered the palace bakery to send all its bread to the hungry mob.

"Here comes Cromwell!" a voice rang out, as Lafayette approached.

"Monsieur," Lafayette fired back, "Cromwell would not have come here alone."[40]

The king had left orders to admit Lafayette, who proceeded to the monarch's apartment, "covered with mud from head to foot," to reaffirm his oath of allegiance and present the mob's two demands: food and the transfer of the king and his government to Paris. With his brother the comte de Provence at his side, the king agreed to the first demand, but deferred deciding on the transfer to Paris. It was three in the morning; they were all too exhausted to debate. Lafayette accepted the king's one concession and went across the road to sleep at the Noailles mansion, the Versailles home of Adrienne's grandfather. He had spent twenty exhausting hours without food or rest; he was encrusted with mud and filth. A servant brought him food and wine; another dressed his hair until he announced, "Good morning! I am falling asleep . . ." and collapsed.[41]

At 6:00 A.M., an aide's cry awakened him; a mob had smashed through the palace gate, reached the Cour de Marbre, the innermost marble courtyard of the palace, and fallen upon the Black Musketeers, the adolescent royal bodyguards, who continued observing the previous day's orders not to fire. As some attackers streaked up the staircase to the queen's apartments, others dragged the captured bodyguards to Jourdan Coupe-Tête, who quickly dispatched two of the helpless boy-soldiers and impaled their severed heads on pikes as trophies, then smeared their blood on his beard and hands to excite the people's lust. Upstairs, the queen's bodyguards shouldered shut the doors to her apartments against the surging mob, allowing her to escape through a secret passageway to the king's apartments, before they, too, fell to the mob.

Lafayette raced out of the Noailles mansion, his knight's blood aboil. He leaped on the first horse he found. Brandishing his sword, he charged furiously through the palace gates into the mob, and, at the sight of the two musketeers' heads on pikes, drove his great horse into the rioters, his grenadiers following at his flanks. The terrified rioters fell back before the advancing horses, racing off with their grisly trophies on the road to Paris—along with golden candelabra, silver-threaded tapestries, and any other palace treasures they could carry. Lafayette demanded Coupe-Tête's arrest, but it was too late. His black shroud had vanished. Lafayette spurred his horse up the hill to the entrance of the royal apartments, where the mob was about to disembowel a bevy of royal bodyguards. "Fortunately, Lafayette arrived in time," sobbed one of the guardsmen afterwards. "He saved our lives."[42]

After ordering guardsmen to present bayonets to the crowd, Lafayette raced up the stairs to the king's apartments. Terrified courtiers, ministers, deputies, and servants cringed in every corner, beneath tables, behind sofas. At the door of the king's apartment, a court official uttered the last gasp of the ancien régime at the onrushing figure of the marquis de La Fayette: "Monsieur," he called out, "the king accords you the right to enter his cabinet."[43] Before he reached mid-sentence, Lafayette had penetrated the king's salon, where he found the king and queen unharmed, along with their three terrified children and the king's sister, brother, and aunts. He also found his sad old friend from Newport, the comte d'Estaing, whom the king had appointed commander of the Royal Guard. Lafayette assured them all he would see to their safety. It was 8:00 A.M.

Two hours later, with the angry crowd still milling about below, Lafayette convinced Louis to yield to the crowd's demands that he go to Paris. Lafayette then stepped onto the balcony and "angrily assailed the crowd" for invading the sanctity of the royal residence and attacking the royal bodyguard. Louis followed him, with his wife and children, and announced that they would all go to Paris. After they stepped inside, the crowd called for Marie-Antoinette's head, and Lafayette asked the unpopular queen: "Madame, what do you intend to do?"

"I know the fate that awaits me," she said calmly. "I am ready to die at the feet of my king and in the arms of my children."

"Come with me, Madame," Lafayette replied.

"What! Haven't you seen the gestures they've made at me?"

"Yes, Madame, but let us go," and they stepped onto the balcony "above a sea of faces that roared their anger at the Austrian." Lafayette could not make himself heard, and he decided on a decisive, though potentially dangerous gesture: he kissed the queen's hand. The crowd fell silent, shocked at first, then gradually began to cry out, "*Vive le général! Vive la reine!*"—"Long live the general! Long live the queen!"[44]

For the moment, the royal family was safe. Across the courtyard, however, the queen could see the mob continuing to brutalize the royal guard. "Now that you have saved us," she pleaded, "what can you do for our guardsmen?"

"Bring me one," he ordered.

Ever aware of the power of symbols, Lafayette led the youngest, lowest ranked Black Musketeer he could find onto the balcony. Lafayette's majestic figure and stage presence silenced the crowd. In his grandest, most theatrical manner, he turned to the young officer, gave him his own tricolor cockade to replace the white Bourbon cockade on his hat, and embraced the boy. The crowd roared its approval, and Lafayette's National Guardsmen, until then reluctant to risk their own lives defending the royal guard, rushed to their sides, gave each their tricolor cockades, and turned against the crowd with raised bayonets to defend the musketeers. The grateful king responded by giving Lafayette command of the royal musketeers and all troops in the surrounding province of Ile de France.[45]

Lafayette's next task was complex—leading a mixed throng of sixty thousand people to Paris, twelve miles away. Half had come to Versailles to slaughter the other half. Lafayette invested the order of march with symbolism, coaxing the mob to march first as a victorious army and lead the court and flour wagons to Paris. At one o'clock that afternoon, with the mob on its way, the royals were ready to leave. Half the National Guard were to march in front to buffer the royal family from the tail end of the mob. Behind the guardsmen a long train of wagons would follow, filled with flour from palace bins—a gift to the hungry people of Paris from the royal family. The royals would follow the flour wagons, with Lafayette and d'Estaing on horseback on either side as formal escorts. Behind the royal coaches, a long line of carriages would transfer the government from Versailles to Paris, rolling throughout the night and into the next day with courtiers, ministers, servants, and the rest of the huge population that worked and lived in what was the equivalent of a capital city. Lafayette assigned squads of trustworthy soldiers to remain at Versailles to protect what would soon be an empty palace but was nonetheless the most brilliant architectural jewel in France and home of the nation's greatest artistic treasures.

On October 6, 1789, at one o'clock in the afternoon, King Louis XVI and his family quit Versailles for the last time and began a humiliating, terrifying, six-hour ride to Paris, essentially as prisoners of the mob. Along the way, crowds of leering peasants hurled insults and clods of mud at the magnificent gold carriage as it passed. The comte d'Estaing tried to calm the queen, urging her to trust Lafayette and pointing out that the boys in the royal guards were marching arm in arm with national guardsmen—all of them now sworn to protect the royal family. Lafayette sent word to mayor Bailly of the cavalcade's approach, and Bailly was at the city gates to greet the royal family when they arrived. He thanked the king for bringing flour to Paris to relieve the famine. Under the new protocol of the revolution, the city Assembly, he said, awaited his immediate visit to the Hôtel de Ville. Louis expressed his "pleasure and confidence to be among the citizens of my good city of Paris."[46]

As the cavalcade resumed, the queen asked Lafayette if she and her exhausted children might abandon the line of march at the Tuileries Palace. Seeing the restless crowds in the streets ahead, he advised against it, fearing they might misinterpret her disappearance as a rejection of her royal obligations.

A double column of guardsmen stood between the Paris mob and the royal family as its soiled carriage rolled past the palace to the city hall, where the king and queen climbed the stairs to the Grande Salle to receive greetings from the Paris Assembly. Amid cries of "Vive le roi!" Mayor Bailly addressed the royal couple, citing the king's expression of "pleasure" in returning to Paris.

"Pleasure and confidence," the queen interrupted to correct him.

"Pleasure and confidence," echoed the king.

The royal couple's spontaneous humor—and Bailly's immediate bow to them—sent waves of laughter and cheers through the assembly. "Gentlemen," Bailly turned to his audience, "the words of the queen must surely make you happier than if I had not erred." The assemblymen responded with shouts of "Vive la reine!"[47] Louis and Marie-Antoinette stepped out onto the balcony overlooking the square to wave to the huge crowd below. As the cheers of "Vive le roi!" rang out, Lafayette felt a grateful hand clasp his own. It was that of the king's sister, Madame Elizabeth. Later, after Lafayette escorted the royal family safely into the Tuileries Palace, the king's aunt, Madame Adelaide, embraced him, crying, "I owe you more than my life, Monsieur; I owe you the life of my poor nephew the king."[48] William Short, the American chargé d'affaires after Jefferson returned to America, reported that Lafayette's success in saving the royal family "acquired for him from all parties the appellation of the guardian angel of the day."[49]

16

Prisoners of the Mob

IT WAS 9:30 AT NIGHT when Lafayette bade the king and queen goodnight at the Tuileries Palace and left for home on the rue de Bourbon. Although it was only a short ride across the Seine, he had journeyed across a lifetime of history in the few days since he had last seen Adrienne and the children. The centuries-old Bourbon monarchy had all but disintegrated, along with Lafayette's fantasy of a constitutional monarchy in France. Louis XVI and his queen were, in effect, prisoners in the Tuileries Palace, with Lafayette their chief jailer, and little more than a prisoner himself. Troops ringed the palace, ostensibly to protect the royal family from the mob; in reality, they were there to prevent the royal family's escape to Austrian territory, where Emperor Joseph II awaited the safe arrival of his sister Marie-Antoinette and her husband to send his powerful army into France and crush the revolution.

On October 10, the National Assembly ended Louis XVI's reign as King of France and Navarre and redesignated him King of the French; *La Nation*—the ethereal, undefined "popular will"—was supreme, with the king a mere executive—the "first functionary" of government. Like the king, the Assembly abandoned Versailles and reconvened in Paris, in what had been the king's manège, a huge indoor riding arena and stable by the Tuileries Gardens across the royal riding path from the Noailles mansion.[1]

With riots still breaking out unpredictably in some Paris neighborhoods, the Assembly imposed martial law and reaffirmed Lafayette's dictatorial powers to crush any remnants of disorder by hanging anyone who provoked sedition or rebellion—in word or deed. His new powers did not come a moment too soon. "There has been hanged a baker this morning by the populace," Morris reported, "and all Paris is under arms. The poor baker was beheaded

257

according to custom and carried in triumph thro the streets. He had been all night at work for the purpose of supplying the greatest possible quantity of bread this morning. His wife is said to have died with horror when they presented her husband's head stuck on a pole. Surely it is not in the usual order of divine providence to leave such abominations unpunished. Paris is perhaps as wicked a spot as exists. Incest, murder, bestiality, fraud, rapine, oppression, baseness, cruelty; and yet this is the city which has stepped forward in the sacred cause of liberty. The pressure of incumbent despotism removed, every bad passion exerts its peculiar energy. How the conflict will terminate, heaven knows. Badly I fear, that is to say in slavery."[2]

Lafayette was as appalled as Morris at the baker's beheading. "All is lost," he warned his officers, "if the service [the Guard] continues to conduct itself in this way. We are the only soldiers of the revolution, the only defenders of the royal family, the national assembly and the national treasure. All of France, all of Europe have their eyes on us. Any attack on these sacred institutions can dishonor us forever. . . . I ask you, therefore, Gentlemen, in the name of our country, that you bind your citizen troops closer to me than ever by asking them to swear to sacrifice all personal interests to duty."[3] Still the master of symbolism, he painted routine police service as a holy crusade and, within days of his plea, his men had identified, tried, and hanged two leaders of the mob that decapitated the baker.

Lafayette used his powers under martial law to attack the causes of the insurrection: he ordered troops to empty all granaries in the nearby countryside and establish a free flow of grain and firewood into Paris. As its belly filled with food and wine, as fires warmed its hovels, the beast that was Paris settled into an uneasy slumber, confident that Lafayette would see to its future needs.

When the National Assembly met to write a constitution and establish a new government, Lafayette emerged as the logical choice for Assembly president, but he rejected the suggestion. Although he retained his Assembly seat, policing the city left him little time to fill its responsibilities, let alone those of the presidency. "All I want for the nation is liberty, order and a good constitution," he explained. "I believe that is what the nation wants as well, and I hope we will reach our goal. . . . My present job is to ensure public tranquillity, and, in my role as a member of the National Assembly, to help strengthen our liberties and to protect the king and queen from all the conspiracies against them."[4]

His absence, however, created a devastating leadership vacuum in an assemblage with no experience in sacrificing personal interests for the greater good. Morris explained the Assembly to Washington: "One large half of the time is spent hallowing and bawling. . . . Such as intend to hold forth write their names on a tablet . . . and are heard in the order that their names are written down, if the others will hear them, which very often they refuse to do but keep up a continual uproar till the orator leaves the pulpit. . . . Our friend La Fayette has given in to measures as to the Constitution which he does not heartily approve, and he heartily approves many things which experience will demonstrate to be injurious. He left America, you know, when his education was but half-finished. What he learnt there he knows well, but he did not learn to be a government maker."[5]

By the end of the year, Lafayette's failure to assume Assembly leadership allowed his opponents to warp the democratic structure he and Jefferson had fashioned in their Declaration of the Rights of Man. Like the two orders that had preceded it to power, the Third Estate promoted its own interests, replacing royal despotism with parliamentary despotism. Although Lafayette tried to remain optimistic, a tint of anxiety shaded his New Year's greeting to Washington in January 1790:

> My dear general,
>
> How often I miss your wise counsels and friendly support. We have advanced the revolution without running the ship of state onto the reefs of the aristocracy and the factions. In the midst of ceaseless opposition by partisans of the past and ambitious men, we are marching forward towards a reasonable conclusion. Although what used to exist has been destroyed, a new political structure is rising in its place; without being perfect, it is enough to assure liberty. The result will, I hope, be a happy one for my country and for humanity. We can see the seeds of liberty in other parts of Europe; I shall encourage their development by every means in my power.
>
> Adieu, my dear general; please send my tender respects to Mrs. Washington; remember me to Hamilton, Harrison, Knox and all our friends.[6]

Adrienne could not conceal her pride over her husband's towering presence in French affairs. "Monsieur," she wrote to Washington, "In the midst of the agitations of our revolution, I never cease to share in Monsieur de Lafayette's happiness at having followed in your footsteps, in having found in your example and your lessons a means of serving his country, and in picturing the satisfaction with which you will learn of his success."[7]

Though pleased by Adrienne's optimism, Washington was less sanguine about the French Revolution. "The revolution which has been effected in France," he wrote to Morris, "is of too great a magnitude to be effected in so short a space, and with the loss of so little blood. . . . The licentiousness of the people on the one hand, and sanguinary punishments on the other, will . . . contribute not a little to the overthrow of their object."[8]

Morris agreed: "The King is in effect a prisoner at Paris and obeys entirely the National Assembly, this Assembly may be divided into three parts. One called the Aristocrats. . . . Another has no name, but which consists of all sorts of people, really friends to a good free government. The third is composed of what are called here the *Enragés*, that is the Madmen. These are the most numerous. . . . They have already unhinged every thing."[9]

Without Lafayette to lead them, the "friends to a good free government" in the Assembly fell silent, and by early 1790 the "madmen," led by Robespierre, Danton, and Marat, systematically destroyed all hopes for republican government by abandoning its mission to write a constitution and usurping the powers of a supreme governing council—a politburo that revoked the king's authority, abolished provincial assemblies, abolished the Roman Catholic Church, outlawed dissent as treasonous, and ruthlessly punished all opposition to its decrees. To ensure political control over the nation, it established a new, centrally controlled, pyramidal administrative system that fractured France into 83 departments, successively subdivided into 547 districts, 4,732 cantons and 43,360 communes, each with a federal prosecutor—a commissar—as watchdog over local officials and responsible only to the Assembly in Paris.

The Assembly nationalized the lands of king, church, and émigré noblemen who had left the country, and it eliminated private property rights, granting everyone the right to hunt, fish, and trespass on anyone else's lands. It chopped the feudal properties it seized into relatively small, individual freeholds to sell at auction—ostensibly to redistribute to peasants, workers, craftsmen, and shopkeepers and to give them the right to vote that came with property ownership. By *auctioning* the land, however, Assembly madmen—Robespierre, Danton, and company—prevented the very redistribution it claimed to favor. Eighty percent of the French population could not afford bids high enough to buy any land at auction; successful bidders were usually members of the assembly, their families, and friends. The American Congress, in contrast, "opened the fertile plains of the Ohio to the poor, the needy & the oppressed of the Earth," Washington wrote to Lafayette. "Any one therefore who is heavy laden or who wants to cultivate may repair thither & abound."[10]

In abolishing Roman Catholicism, the French Assembly stripped the pope of all authority in France and created a new state church, with clerics mere civil servants, salaried by the state and elected by the people in each parish. To assume office, clerics had to swear allegiance to *La Nation*; refusal was tantamount to treason, subject to loss of pension, eviction from their homes, and up to two years' imprisonment. The Assembly banned ecclesiastical dress outside church.

To reduce the staggering national debt, the Assembly seized religious artifacts in church and cathedral treasuries and melted them into gold and silver bullion, destroying centuries of religious artworks. It then floated 400 million livres (about $4 billion in today's currency) of hybrid bonds called *assignats*, backed by the value of nationalized church and royal lands that the government would sell at auction whenever it needed to redeem the bonds.[11]

The French National Assembly's actions provoked immediate, widespread class warfare that would grow to unimaginable savagery over the next two years. Workers surged through city streets and alleyways, stripping every unguarded mansion of its treasures; outside the cities, peasant mobs burned and looted stately homes and castles, destroying centuries of great French art. Only the kindliest, most beloved landowners, like Lafayette's aunt Charlotte at Chavaniac, were spared the horrors, humiliations, and flames of the mobs' torches. The class war spread to the military, where rank-and-file soldiers—mostly commoners ineligible for promotion into officers' ranks—assaulted their aristocrat officers. Thousands of French officers fled to Spain, Germany—anywhere—to escape the agony of execution by their men—often disembowelment by bayonet thrusts.

Adding to the savagery of class warfare were the brutalities of religious conflict. The schism in the French Catholic church cut across class lines. Eighty of the eighty-eight bishops in France and more than half the priests—some twenty thousand—refused to take secular vows to the constitution, as did one hundred fifty of the two hundred fifty clerics in the National Assembly. The creation of a French national church effectively created two French churches—an illegal, underground church led by devout Roman Catholic *refusés* and a revolutionary Gallican church of *jureurs*, or secular "swearers" to the constitution. Parishioners split accordingly—often into armed camps in the same village or neighboring communities. Bands of *refusés* assaulted *jureurs* as religious heretics; *jureurs* attacked *refusés* for political heresy and treason.

Pope Pius VI and the College of Cardinals condemned the assembly's actions and rejected the new Gallican church. Within weeks, thousands of royalists and devout Catholics took up arms against Gallican revolutionaries in southern France. Leaflets decried revolutionaries for spiriting the French to the gates of Hell. In Nîmes, Catholic antirevolutionaries massacred Protestants, and revolutionaries in the nearby papal enclave of Avignon attacked Roman Catholics and sacked churches. The religious civil war spread into every household, provoking flight by some, defiance by others, and terror in all. The Lafayette home was no different: shortly after the first communion of Lafayette's younger daughter, Virginie, her grandfather the duc d'Ayen packed up as many of his things as he could carry from the sumptuous Hôtel de Noailles in Paris and fled to Lausanne, Switzerland. Adrienne's sister Pauline and her husband and family fled to exile in England.

Adrienne, on the other hand, refused to abandon her home or beliefs and defied the new religious laws. Unlike her husband, she was a fiercely devout Roman Catholic and refused to take the civil oath the Gallican priest administered to prorevolution parishioners at her church of Saint-Sulpice in Paris. "Instead," her daughter Virginie recalled, "she went regularly to churches and chapels where the persecuted clergy had taken refuge and continued to preach [Roman Catholic orthodoxy]. She constantly welcomed into our home *refusés* priests and their parishioners who were fleeing persecution and asked our protection; she encouraged them to continue preaching and to fight for the freedom to practice their religion. My father did not for a moment consider interfering with her, but you can imagine how painful it was for my mother to realize how much her actions were eroding his popularity." Adrienne refused to waver from her devotion, however, and, when Lafayette invited the new Gallican bishop of Paris to dinner at the rue de Bourbon, "she refused to receive him as a clergyman," Virginie wrote. "She dined out, although it caused a frightful stir."[12]

The religious schism reached into the Tuileries Palace as well. The king—a devout Roman Catholic—had pledged to accept the constitution as soon as the Assembly completed it, but in doing so he had not anticipated that it would outlaw the Roman Catholic Church. He turned for advice to his only sworn protector among the revolutionaries:

"Sire," Lafayette replied. "Your majesty has deigned to assure me of his confidence and his disposition to follow my counsel. . . . I swear to Your Majesty that . . . the last drop of my blood will prove to you my fidelity . . . my ardent love for my country and the most loyal feelings for Your Majesty."[13] The king said he was "fully reassured" by Lafayette's "loyalty of character and his attachment to my person."[14]

The queen was less certain: "I am quite sure that Monsieur de La Fayette wishes to save us," she declared, "but who is going to save us from Monsieur de La Fayette?"[15]

Despite the mounting horrors of religious civil war, Lafayette clung desperately to his dream of establishing republican government in France. "There is ample material to criticize and libel," he admitted to Washington, but he insisted that "we have made . . . more changes in ten months than even the most presumptuous patriots could have hoped for. . . . Reports about our anarchy, our internal disturbances, are vastly exaggerated. In the end, this revolution, as in America, needs just a bit more action by the government to strengthen liberty and make it flourish throughout the world."[16]

As summer approached with the constitution still unfinished, impatience and unrest continued spreading. The fanatic Robespierre took advantage of Lafayette's distaste for political leadership and won election to the presidency of the Jacobin club, a powerful political organization founded, ironically, by constitutional moderates like Lafayette and Bailly.[17] With

Rousseau's *Social Contract* as his bible, Robespierre converted the Jacobins into a radical leftist group that preached the sovereignty of *La Nation*, which Robespierre defined as "infallible, with unlimited authority, regardless of the consequences, no matter how extreme these may be."[18] Appalled by the Jacobin shift to extremism, Lafayette left the Jacobins and formed a new "Club of 1789" with centrists eager to finish writing the constitution and allow the nation to elect a new government. "The Revolution has been accomplished," Lafayette thundered in the National Assembly; "nothing remains but to establish its constitution."[19]

But Assembly Jacobins invented endless numbers of issues to keep it mired in acrimonious debate—none of them constitutional issues. In a debate over capital punishment, Dr. Joseph Ignace Guillotin, a professor of anatomy at the Paris University Medical School, proposed a more humane method of execution than the ax or wheel. The wheel often left criminals dismembered but not dead, while the executioner's ax frequently missed its mark and embedded in the chest or skull. Guillotin proposed an invention of Dr. Antoine Louis—the "Louison," a device that severed heads at the neck swiftly, cleanly, and accurately; the criminal, according to Guillotin, would feel nothing but "a gentle caress."[20] The assembly approved the instrument but renamed it the Guillotine, despite Guillotin's furious protests.

Adding to the histrionics in the National Assembly were the demands of a new, more radical group called the *Société des amis des droits de l'homme et du citoyen* (Society of the Friends of the Rights of Man and the Citizen), which demanded that the Assembly scrap previously approved provisions of the constitution and begin again. Organized by Danton, Marat, and Desmoulins in the Cordelier[21] convent at Saint-Germain des Près, the "Cordeliers" demanded abolition of all titles. Lafayette stunned the Assembly by rising to support them, saying their proposal had "something of the American character, precious fruit of the New World that must serve in large measure to reinvigorate the old."[22] Although weary of Lafayette's constant references to America, the majority voted with the Cordeliers, and the marquis de La Fayette forever after called himself Lafayette. His bitter enemy, Danton, further reduced his rank by scornfully referring to him by his patronymic name, Motier.

With the National Assembly unable or unwilling to finish its constitution, Lafayette and Bailly acted on their own to move the nation toward self-government. They asked the local Paris Assembly, where they had a controlling influence, to organize a *Fête de la Fédération*—a Festival of Federation—to celebrate the first anniversary of the storming of the Bastille on July 14. They would ask the national guard—the citizen soldiers across France—to elect delegations of about one hundred fifty members from each of the eighty-three French departments to represent them in Paris—to demonstrate how quickly and smoothly the rest of the nation could act if the National Assembly would only finish its work.

From its inception, the *Fête* was a brilliant social, economic, and political stratagem—a Lafayette masterpiece of symbolism. Preparations for the *Fête* absorbed tens of thousands of the restless unemployed who wandered the streets aimlessly in the heavy summer sun and found their only joy in the camaraderie of a riotous mob. They now thronged to the huge Champs de Mars—a vast parade ground that stretched from the Ecole Militaire—the officers' training school—to the Seine River. For weeks, the mob dug with picks and shovels and moved the dirt in wheelbarrows to the edge of the esplanade. Bands played to lighten their labor; women and children brought them food and drink; actors and singers entertained them when they rested. To the cheers and applause of the gigantic throng, Lafayette rode in on his white horse every day or two, dismounted, and picked up a shovel to dig alongside the laborers for a few hours. Gradually, they transformed the entire esplanade into a gigantic stadium, with huge, sloped "grandstands" of earth along both lengths. At one end of the field, in front of the Ecole Militaire, they built a tribune draped in scarlet for the king's throne; at the other end, by the Seine River, they constructed a magnificent Arch of Triumph, fraught with symbolism, including a platform at its top for members of the National Assembly—the people's representatives. In the center of the stadium, they fashioned the Nation's Altar, from which to celebrate Gallican mass and administer the oath of allegiance to the nation.

As June turned to July, departmental guard units streamed toward the capital along the roads of France—by foot, donkey, horse and carriage; citizens joined them—peasants and noblemen alike. They toasted each other and the new spirit of brotherhood at every roadside tavern, inviting others to join them with the words that became a national slogan: *"Lafayette dit: Vienne qui voudra!"*—"Lafayette says, come whoever wants to!"[23]

In Paris, the envious Mirabeau predicted that Lafayette would use the *Fête* to seize power. "He will make himself generalissimo, have himself named to the generalship, then receive the dictatorship from those who say they represent the nation."[24] On July 10, fourteen thousand citizen soldiers from everywhere in France assembled in the square in front of the Hôtel de Ville—the *elected* representatives of three million citizen soldiers from eighty-three departments. By acclamation, they proclaimed themselves the Assembly of the Federation and Lafayette their president. The next day he led a delegation of guardsmen to the National Assembly, where he called upon them to finish writing the constitution. As elected commander of three million citizen soldiers, he did not need to threaten; they understood.

"The national guard has come to pay you their respect and recognition," he declared. "The nation, which is still seeking its freedom, has charged you with giving it a constitution. But it has waited in vain. . . . Finish your work, gentlemen, and determine the number of amendments needed in a basic French constitution; our patience is growing thin for a constitutional code for our first legislature. . . . The rights of man have been declared; the sovereignty of the people has been recognized; powers have been delegated. . . . The people are indebted to you for the glory of freedom under the constitution, but they await a finality that cannot come without a plan for organizing the government and then a government."[25]

From the king's former riding ring, they marched across the Tuileries Gardens to the palace, where Lafayette presented his deputation to the king: "We wish to venerate your majesty with the most beautiful of all titles, that of chief of the French and king of a free people. Rejoice, Sire, in the prize of your virtues; let this expression of genuine homage, which despotism could never elicit, be the glory and recompense of a citizen king."[26]

Lafayette called the king's response "noble and touching: 'Tell your fellow citizens that I would have liked to tell them all what I am telling you here; tell them that their king is their father, their brother, their friend; that he can only be happy when they are happy . . . when they are free . . . when they prosper.'"[27] Before leaving, the guardsmen from the provinces asked to be presented to the queen, whom they had never seen. She emerged with the dauphin, now five, in her arms, and, as she passed each of the men, each kissed the little boy's hand.

The next day dawned a dismal gray, with light rain falling intermittently. A cheerful crowd of 160,000 blanketed the sloped mounds that rimmed the Champ de Mars, and at least that many covered the grassy plain beyond. They had come from all parts of France; many had camped there all night to ensure their witnessing the historic ceremony. Lafayette had drawn the order of march in the procession, with the king, queen, and dauphin entering from the south to take their seats at the same time that members of the National Assembly entered from the north to take their seats atop the Triumphal Arch, at a level superior to that of the royal family. Then Lafayette and his legendary white horse, Jean Leblanc, led the parade of guardsmen through the Arch of Triumph, with a troop from each of the eighty-three departments marching its banner to the National Altar. Troops from the regular army and navy followed, until detachments from every department and the entire military surrounded the altar, among them an inconspicuous young Corsican officer, Napoléon Bonaparte.

"The spectacle of that day . . . was really sublime and magnificent," American chargé d'affaires William Short wrote to Morris, who was in London on a diplomatic mission for Washington. "The most perfect order & harmony reigned as well then, as at the illuminations & bal[l]s of the Sunday following."[28] Once the troops were in position, two hundred priests, each wearing the revolution's secular red, white, and blue sash, climbed the steps to the altar, followed by Talleyrand, the papal-turned-Gallican bishop of Autun, who changed political—and religious—colors quicker than a chameleon. As smoke poured from great urns at each corner of the altar, Talleyrand blessed the regimental flags and celebrated mass—all the while whispering to his acolyte, "Don't do anything to make me laugh."[29]

After the prayers, Lafayette trotted majestically across the stadium to the king's throne, and, as he had as a young Black Musketeer, asked the king's orders. He then rode back to the center of the stadium, dismounted, and ascended the altar stairs. After a dramatic pause for silence, his voice boomed out: "We swear to be forever faithful to nation, law and king, to protect persons and property . . . and to remain united with all Frenchmen by unbreakable bonds of brotherhood."[30] Lafayette then raised his hands in admonition, and more than 300,000 people thundered as one, "*Je le jure!*"— "I so do swear!"[31] The president of the National Assembly repeated the oath from the triumphal arch, then the king from his throne. The queen then rose to present the crown prince—the dauphin, their next king—to the cheering throng. As the artillery fired salvo after salvo of celebratory fire, the crowd shouted "*Vive l'Assemblée nationale!*"; "*Vive le Roi!*"; and "*Vive Lafayette!*" Atop the altar, Lafayette turned and pointed toward the triumphal arch, where a small troop marched in bearing a flag never before seen in Europe. As the crowd quieted, Lafayette snapped to attention and saluted: the flag bearer was John Paul Jones, with Tom Paine at his side, carrying the first American flag with the Stars and Stripes ever displayed outside the United States. For Lafayette, the flag symbolized the fulfillment of his dream to unite his native and his adoptive lands under the banner of liberty.

"I think this will have produced a good effect," Short wrote Morris. "The demagogues of the assembly never remained more silent or more quiet. . . . The Marquis de La Fayette seemed to have taken full possession of the *fédérés*—his popular manners pleased them beyond measure & of course they approved his principles. When I left Paris he was adored by them—that moment may be regarded as the zenith of his influence. He made no use of it, except to prevent ill."[32]

When Lafayette descended from the altar, a swarm of guardsmen and men from the regular army all but crushed him in their eagerness to embrace him. "Some kissed his face, others his hands, the less fortunate his uniform," wrote a journalist at the scene. "After great effort, he mounted his horse. He had hardly seated himself in his saddle that they started kissing him again, his legs, his boots, the harness of his horse and, finally, the horse itself."[33]

View of the *Fête de la Fédération* on the Champ de Mars, on July 14, 1790, the first anniversary of the attack on the Bastille prison. Previously a parade ground for the Ecole Militaire, seen at rear, the area was transformed into a huge stadium by an army of laborers who built the earthen viewing areas by digging and transferring the surface soil. The Eiffel Tower now stands at the near end, by the Seine River, in the area of the triumphal arch. (*Réunion des Musées Nationaux.*)

An officer said, "Mounted on his white horse . . . he seemed to be in command of all France," while another witness declared, "You are watching Monsieur de La Fayette galloping into the centuries yet to come."[34]

Although he rode off the Champ de Mars wreathed in public adulation, he left the king and queen—especially the vengeful queen—humiliated by the insignificant role he had given them. Equally humiliated were radical Assembly demagogues from both ends of the political spectrum—the royalists on the right and the "madmen," as Morris called them, on the left. Lafayette had ignored them all. Mirabeau pouted that Lafayette was a modern-day Caesar: "It is useless to point out to what degree the king was compromised,"[35] he wrote to the king, "and to what degree the *Fête* served to make him [Lafayette] the man of the Federation, the unique man, the man of the provinces."[36]

While Mirabeau and Lafayette's other enemies fumed and fussed, Paris and the visiting citizen soldiers continued celebrating *Lafayette et liberté.*

Each night, dazzling displays of fireworks exploded in the skies over Paris, while gigantic torches bathed the city streets and public buildings in multi-colored illuminations; thousands flocked to two huge balls on the Champs-Elysées and on the square where the Bastille had stood a year earlier. The entire city metamorphosed into a carnival-*cum*-ballroom, with clowns, acro-bats, and other entertainers jowling, jumping, and juggling on every corner, and small orchestras serenading crowds of clumsy, drunken dancers in every street and square—all without a single incident of violence. The people adored Lafayette and his vision of a new and stable *Nation*, with liberty and prosperity guaranteed by a constitution—and the three-million-man national guard under his command. Street-corner agitators and *coupe-têtes* stayed dis-creetly out of sight, although the disturbing strains of "Ça ira, ça ira" echoed occasionally from dark alleys and drew anxious glances from merrymakers within earshot:

> Ah! ça ira, ça ira, ça ira!
> Les aristocrates à la lanterne,
> Ah! ça ira, ça ira, ça ira!
> Les aristocrates on les pendra.[37]

After a week's revelry, Lafayette stunned friends and enemies alike by rejecting the post of national commander, saying that control of the guard in more than one department would concentrate too much power in the hands of one man and risk replacing royal autocracy with a military autoc-racy. Just as he had rejected political power in the National Assembly, he now rejected military power, believing that the French were as able as Americans to govern themselves without an autocrat; that the citizen sol-diers of the National Guard—like those in America's state militias—would return peacefully to their homes and farms.

"The time will come perhaps," William Short wrote to Gouverneur Morris, "when he will repent having not seized that opportunity. . . . It would have been easy for him to have engaged the assembly to have fixed the epoch of the elections for the next legislature. I fear now that nothing but some crisis which I do not foresee will engage them to do it. It is natu-ral enough to suppose that any body of men whatever who concentrate in themselves all sorts of power—who suppose themselves authorized to pro-long their existence indefinitely—& who are exempt from all punishment for crimes unless caught in *flagrant délit* will not be readily disposed to descend from such an height."[38]

Lafayette, of course, was simply following the chivalric example of his "beloved general" in America by ceding military control of the nation to civil governance. "I hope our work will finish at the end of the year," he wrote to Washington, "and your friend . . . will rejoice in abandoning all power and political duties to become a simple citizen in a free constitutional monarchy."[39]

On July 20, he gathered the fourteen thousand citizen soldiers together to send them home to their provinces. Still clinging to his fantasy of an American Utopia in France, he cried out:

> As we leave each other, I will not speak to you of my deep and everlasting thanks to you nor my devotion to the people and the protection of their rights, to which I have devoted my life. Certain of your trust and confidence, I will talk to you of our duty. We must, gentlemen, repeat that word—duty—as brothers who are separating but who, once separated, will continue to act as one, tied by the same belief, knowing that the slightest infraction will be felt by every member of this great family. Let our love of liberty, gentlemen, be our guide. That word says it all: love of order, respect for law and for morality; with liberty, all property is inviolate; the lives of the innocent are sacred, man is innocent until proved guilty under the law; with liberty, there are universal guarantees and all prosper. But let us not forget, gentlemen that liberty is based on strict principles that fear license as much as tyranny.[40]

What Lafayette seemed unable—or unwilling—to recognize was that France feared neither license nor tyranny; indeed, it had lived with and known little else for thirteen centuries and embraced them both.

A month later, he heard from Washington: "I am happy, my excellent Friend, to see that, in the midst of the frightful tempests that have beset your political vessel, you have been able, by your talent and your courage, to steer it until now on so sure a course through so many reefs; and rejoice that your young king seems so well disposed to assent to the rights of the nation. Not for an instant have my wishes diminished for your success in so hazardous and important an enterprise; but often the articles we receive from English newspapers fill us with more fear than hope. How much all those involved in this daring journey will owe to their principal pilot when the ship reaches port and finds peace, liberty and glory! That is where it is headed, and I hope it will soon reach it."[41]

Sadly, the ship had already veered sharply from that course—not just in France, but elsewhere in Europe. As Morris put it to Washington, "The French disease, in other words, Revolt, [is spreading to] Hungary, parts of Germany, Italy and Savoy, with France and Flanders already in different stages of that disease. Poland is constitutionally afflicted with it. In Sweden and Holland slight circumstances would bring it forward."[42] Across Europe, rebels hailed—and monarchs damned—Lafayette for having carried the disease from America and released it on their continent. Both rebels and monarchs would soon punish him harshly for doing so.

The *Fête de la Confédération* marked the peak of Lafayette's popularity and influence in France. As Morris had warned him, France had no American citizens to support a Constitution, and without them, both Lafayette and his dream of constitutional rule were doomed. In rejecting political and military power, Lafayette's political ineptitude was matched only by that of the king, who was a past master of the art—"a creature who," Morris said, "eats and drinks and sleeps well and laughs and is as merry a grig as lives. . . . Poor man, he little thinks how unstable is his situation."[43] The king missed an opportunity to build popular support after the ceremonies at the Champ de Mars. After the unanimous cry of "*Vive le roi,*" almost every delegation of the National Guards approached him with enthusiastic pleas for him to visit their provinces—something no king had ever done. Even Lafayette was taken aback when the king refused.

The "madmen" surged into the leadership vacuum that Lafayette and the king created. Cordeliers flocked to the streets with leaflets assailing Lafayette as "the vile tool of a despot." The scabrous Marat spent much of his time immersed in a bathtub full of cool water to relieve the maddening itch that was rotting his skin, but he used the time resourcefully. He wrote leaflets assailing Lafayette as "a greedy courtier," "vile panderer to despotism," and "a mortal enemy of the nation," and he issued a poisonous pamphlet detailing Lafayette's fictitious adulterous adventures, *The Nights of Love of General Motier and the Beautiful Antoinette, Written by Her Little Spaniel.*[44]

Robespierre's Jacobins added to the disorder, dispatching agents across France to organize revolutionary clubs and infiltrate local government and police. At the time of the *Fête de la Fédération*, in July 1790, the Jacobins had but 152 clubs in France—less than two in each of the 83 departments. Within a year, they had more than one thousand, with members influencing every area of French life, including the National Assembly. The Jacobins also organized clubs in the military to intensify rebellion among rank and file commoners against high-born officers. Sailors in the French fleet mutinied in Brest, and in eastern France, three regiments of regular troops rebelled in the city of Nancy. The commanding general, Lafayette's cousin the marquis de Bouillé, crushed the mutiny, executing twenty soldiers and sentencing forty others to life imprisonment at hard labor. After Lafayette called his cousin "the savior of the public cause," a Jacobin mob gathered near the National Assembly to protest the "massacres of Nancy" and shout "*A bas Lafayette!*"—"Down with Lafayette!" Riots erupted across Paris again. As soon as he snuffed out one, Jacobins and Cordeliers staged others that kept him galloping about the city in a tragically hopeless race to stem the course of history. Mirabeau warned the king: "Popular outbreaks are the ruin of Monsieur de La Fayette. He will one day fire on the people. By that act alone, he will deal himself a mortal wound."[45]

In despair, Lafayette turned to the wellspring of his chivalric idealism: "My dear general," he wrote in March 1791. "Whatever hope I may have had of overcoming the problems of our revolution, I continue to be bounced about in an ocean of dissatisfaction and commotion of every kind; I am attacked with equal animus from every direction . . . by all the adversaries of my doctrine of liberty and equality."[46]

For the moment, Washington could offer little comfort. As president of the United States, he could not risk having spies intercept a letter of advice on the internal affairs of another sovereign nation. In reiterating his "deepest affection and esteem," Washington told Lafayette, "Our nation (and it is really yours as well) is making rapid progress towards stable politics and social happiness. The laws of the United States, adapted to all the needs of the public good, are writted with wisdom, moderation and accepted with joy. . . . I hope ardently for the same in the country that is the immediate object of your patriotic attachment; the distance that separates us and the delicate nature of the subject has always made us [me] suspend our opinions of your affairs." After transmitting his and Martha's best regards, Washington noted that his nephew, "Your former aide-de-camp, George Augustine Washington, has a second son, whom he named for you."[47]

With Lafayette's prestige eroding, Jacobins forced the National Assembly to ignore his ultimatum to finish writing a constitution. Its every decree heaped more misery on workers, shopkeepers, and the lower classes. Still facing national bankruptcy, the Assembly flooded the nation with worthless paper money—more than 1 billion livres. Prices and unemployment soared. Life under the Third Estate grew as intolerable as it had been under the king, the aristocracy, and the *ferme*.

"This unhappy country presents to our moral view a mighty ruin," Morris wrote to Washington. "Like the remnants of antient [sic] magnificence, we admire the architecture of the Temple while we detest the false god to whom it was dedicated. Daws and ravens and the birds of night now build their nests in its niches. The sovereign, humbled to the level of a beggar's pity, without resources, without authority, without a friend. The assembly at once master and a slave, new in power, wild in theory, raw in practice. It engrosses all functions tho incapable of exercising any, and has taken from this fierce ferocious people every restraint of religion and of respect. Such a state of things cannot last."[48]

On Easter Sunday in the spring of 1791, the royal family sought to leave the Tuileries Palace to celebrate mass in their little château retreat in Saint-Cloud, a forest southwest of Paris. Suspicious that the family might flee to the Austrians, the Paris National Guard prevented their carriage from leaving the Tuileries Palace gates. Sent for by the king, Lafayette dashed into the palace enclave on Jean Leblanc and ordered his troops to let the king's family pass. They refused. A mob formed and threatened to storm the palace. Lafayette relented, and escorted the royal family back into their palace prison. Two days later, he resigned his command, leaving a terrified king fearing for his life and that of his family—and Washington fearing for Lafayette's life: "I received your letter, my dear Marquis, and I thank you for its details, but I must tell you that I have often predicted, with much anxiety, the dangers you face. . . . Your letters are far from comforting for an old friend. But I understand that for someone whose love of country engages him in dangerous enterprises and is guided by pure and just motives such as yours, preservation of life is of secondary consideration." Washington had just returned from a three-month tour of the American south, where he noted the "flourishing" industry and economy and what he called "the happy disposition of the people":

> The attachment of all classes of citizens to the government seems a happy presage . . . for their future. . . . While wars and civil discord are raging in almost all the nations of Europe, peace and tranquillity reign among us. This contrast between the United States and Europe is too striking not to be noticed by even the most superficial observer. . . . But we do not wish to remain the only people tasting the sweetness of good government founded on equality. We earnestly wish that your country will find calm and happiness and that all Europe will be delivered of its commotions and uneasiness.
>
> Your friends in America often show, by their anxiety for your safety, how much they care for you. Knox, Jay, Hamilton and Jefferson send their affectionate greetings to you, but none of them with greater sincerity and attachment than your affectionate servant. . . .
>
> G. Washington.[49]

Within hours of Lafayette's resignation, commanders of each of his battalions all but overran his home to plead with him—many on bended knees—to resume his command. Mayor Bailly arrived to second their requests. Adrienne received them politely but, in embarrassed tones, said there was little she could do to change the general's mind. In truth, she was "overflowing with joy at the thought of my father's returning to private life," daughter Virginie recalled. "Her joy lasted only four days." After insisting that they sign oaths to obey the law, he rescinded his resignation and led a delegation of officers to the palace to apologize to the king, while Adrienne "resumed her painful pursuit of worrying about my father's safety."[50]

Lafayette purged the Guard of militiamen and officers who refused to sign the oath, but in doing so he only weakened his own force while the dissenters joined the growing army of Jacobins. In mid-May, the Assembly created a special "High Court" to judge crimes against the state, and, a month later, the Jacobin leader, Robespierre, won election as chief public prosecutor. With the Jacobin noose tightening around the government and Lafayette evidently powerless to protect the royal family from mobs, King Louis and his brother the comte de Provence decided to flee Paris with the royal family. A corps of French regulars loyal to the king awaited at Metz, under the command of the marquis de Bouillé, Lafayette's cousin who had crushed the troop rebellion in Nancy. Just across the border in the Netherlands, the Austrian army of Marie-Antoinette's brother, Emperor Joseph II, offered further protection.

Rumors that the royal family intended to flee had circulated for months, but Lafayette had obtained—and had accepted—the king's word that he would remain in Paris. At midnight on June 20, two identical carriages rolled into the courtyard of the Tuileries Palace. The king and queen, their three children, and the king's sister slipped quietly into one, while the king's brother the comte de Provence and his wife climbed into the other. The two vehicles rolled out the gates and sped off in different directions—one to the northeast, toward Metz; the other almost due north toward Mons, in Belgium. It was after five o'clock the next morning before their absence was discovered and an aide aroused Lafayette. Distraught by the king's deception, he dispatched National Guardsmen in every direction to catch the king's carriage, then went to the National Assembly to explain the king's disappearance as best he could before rejoining the search for the royal carriages. Crowds on every street screamed at him angrily, with cries of "Traitor" replacing the accustomed *vivats*.

Danton showered Paris streets with leaflets accusing Lafayette of planning the king's escape. Then he strode to the well of the National Assembly, pointed an accusatory finger at Lafayette's empty seat, and thundered:

And you, Monsieur Lafayette; you who recently guaranteed the person of the king in this assembly on pain of losing your head, are you here to pay your debt? You swore that the king would not leave. Either you sold out your country or you are stupid for having made a promise for a person whom you could not trust. Even in the most favorable circumstance, you have shown yourself incapable of leading us. I want to believe that you are only guilty of honest errors. But if it is true that the liberty of this nation depends on but one man, it deserves to be enslaved. France can be free without you. Your power weighs heavily on all eighty-three departments. Your reputation flies from one pole to the other. Do you really want to be great? Become a simple citizen again and stop helping the French people.[51]

The Cordeliers distributed thousands of copies of Danton's speech across France. Not to be outdone, Marat demanded Lafayette's and Bailly's heads, and the National Guard broke up a mob marching toward Lafayette's home, led by a man with a pike, intent on gratifying Marat's demand. On the evening of June 22, the comte de Provence crossed the border safely into Belgium and the protection of the Austrian army, but his brother the king was less fortunate. The French National Guard caught the royal family's carriage in Varennes, more than 150 miles northeast of Paris and less than 70 miles from safety and salvation at Metz. Three days later, Lafayette and the National Guard led the royal carriage back into Paris through a howling mob surrounding the Tuileries Palace, demanding royal heads to adorn their pikes—along with that of Lafayette. After settling into his apartment, the king admitted Lafayette, who still believed stubbornly that his countrymen were as capable as Americans of governing themselves under a constitution.

"Sire," he told the king, "your majesty knows my loyalty to the crown; but I must tell you that if the crown separates itself from the people, I will remain at the side of the people." He then read the king the National Assembly decrees, placing the king, the queen, and the rest of the royal family under twenty-four-hour guard and delivering the terrified little six-year-old dauphin to "a special military guard under direct orders of the Commanding General and a guardian to be named by the National Assembly." The Assembly ordered all who had accompanied the royal family arrested for questioning. After reading the decrees, Lafayette asked whether the king had any orders before he left. "It seems to me," Louis XVI replied to his old friend, "that I am more subject to your orders than you are to mine."[52]

The king, however, had totally misjudged his own situation and that of Lafayette. If the king was, as he believed, a prisoner of Lafayette, Lafayette, in turn, was now a prisoner of the mob. Indeed, the capture of the royal family in Varennes effectively ended Lafayette's chances to introduce American-style democracy and individual liberty in France. The age of knighthood and chivalry he had sought to prolong faded into the pages of history and fiction, along with his importance and influence on the world stage. At the age of thirty-four, he was obsolete and descending inexorably toward tragic oblivion in his native land. The "madmen" took control of French streets and filled them with hysterical rioters demanding whatever they were told to demand—not even knowing the meaning of the words and phrases they chanted. Desmoulins demanded the establishment of a popular republic; Danton a regency under Philippe Egalité. The ugly dwarf Marat sought a dictatorship—his own—and a crowd of equally misshapen idolaters shrieked their approval. Robespierre agreed, but wanted the job himself and sniffed about indecisively to determine the direction of the political winds before setting his own course. And as rioters slaughtered each other in the streets, Lafayette continued his futile pleas for the constitutional rule of law, which the vast majority of Frenchmen neither wanted nor understood.

"How I wish I could travel to your side of the Atlantic," he wrote plaintively to Washington, "but we are not in a state of peace that would allow my absence. The émigrés hover over our frontiers, intriguing with every despotic government; our armies are made up of aristocratic officers and undisciplined soldiers; the license of the multitude is not easily repressed; the capital [city], which sets the standard for the nation is tossed about by the different parties. The assembly is exhausted. . . . I continue to face attack by factions and conspiracies—you can see that the effect of my resignation was to restore the strength of law a bit. If I only received adequate support for the suppression of license, the people would soon learn the meaning of the word liberty."[53]

Lafayette's letter so frightened Washington that he replied immediately, canceling presidential appointments to pen four pages urging caution on "the adopted son" he so dearly cherished: "The deep interest I take in all your affairs is causing me continual anxiety for your safety. . . . I hope deeply that the affairs of your nation will soon permit you to retire from the excessive tribulations to which you have lately been exposed."[54]

As anxious as Washington was for Lafayette's safety, Marie-Antoinette's brother, the Austrian emperor, was even more anxious for the safety of his sister, and he issued the so-called Padua Circular calling for joint action by Europe's monarchies to "vindicate the liberty and honor of the most Christian King and his family and to limit the dangerous extremes of the French revolution."[55] Robespierre pounced on the Padua Circular as an opportunity to seize power. He issued an address to the French people and bullyragged the National Assembly to call 100,000 volunteers to man the frontiers with Germany against an Austrian invasion.

On the second anniversary of the storming of the Bastille, Robespierre's Jacobins ordered their followers to the Champs de Mars to sign a petition at the Nation's Altar to overthrow the king and declare France a republic. They found two derelicts sleeping under the Altar, assumed they were spies, and chopped off their heads. After implanting their trophies on pikes, part of the crowd began marching off toward the Bastille, singing "Ça ira." Lafayette rode into the arena on his white horse with the remnants of his National Guard to restore order. A year earlier, his entrance had evoked cheers; now it provoked nothing but eerie silence and sullen looks.

A shot rang out.

Guardsmen charged into the mob and seized the would-be assassin. Mayor Bailly trotted into the arena with more troops and proclaimed martial law. The mob responded with a hail of stones and another shot that felled a dragoon. The troops returned fire and sent the Jacobins toppling to the ground—men, women, and children; one hundred fell dead and at least as many wounded. As terrified survivors scattered, two Jacobins hiding behind the arena gates assassinated a pair of soldiers trotting past. Another group of Jacobins set out for the rue de Bourbon to assault Lafayette's home.

"Kill his wife and take him her head!" the rioters chanted as they surged through the gates. Inside, the Lafayette children cowered. "I remember the horrible shouts we heard," Virginie wrote afterwards. She was nine at the time. "I remember the terror of everyone in the house; but above all the terrifying shouts and cries. And I remember my mother's reassuring voice. . . . She took us in her arms to comfort us, then, in the face of imminent danger, she calmly took the steps needed to protect us. She doubled the guard and ordered them into the courtyard to battle the mob at the front of the house. Some of the rioters were already climbing over the garden wall on the side of the house, however. Fortunately, a cavalry troop happened by and dispersed them. . . . It is impossible to describe my mother's anxiety for my father while he remained at the Champ de Mars, exposed to the rage of the furious multitude."[56]

The slaughter on the Champ de Mars and the subsequent declaration of martial law sent Jacobin and Cordelier leaders fleeing to avoid arrest: Desmoulins and Robespierre went into hiding; Danton fled to London. Marat went underground. Without demagogues to lead it, the Paris mob dispersed into small gangs that did little but roam the streets and parks of the city aimlessly, bullying anyone who accidentally walked into their midst and could afford the ransom for safe passage. Lafayette returned to his seat in the Assembly, where, in the absence of delaying tactics by radicals, a majority approved a finished constitution by the end of summer. It was a patchwork of provisions that promised everything to everyone but guaranteed nothing to anyone—a formula for oligarchy and anarchy. On September 13, 1791, the king went through the formality of approving the document, and at the end of September, the Constitutional Assembly adjourned for the last time—but not before granting amnesty to all rioters imprisoned in the three years since the Assembly of Notables had met. The amnesty released the Jacobin mob onto the streets to await its next call to action.

On October 1, 1791, the first elected legislature under the French constitution—a caricature of America's First Congress—met for its initial session, and, for one brief moment, Lafayette's dream of constitutional rule in France seemed close to reality. A week later, Lafayette fulfilled his pledge to return to private life—as Washington had done after the American Revolution. He resigned from the National Guard, turned command of the military to the civilian mayor, and bade his troops farewell. They, in turn, presented him with a sword forged from the locks of the Bastille. "You may be sure," Mayor Bailly declared, "that we shall never forget the hero of Two Worlds."

17

The Most Hated Man in Europe

TEN YEARS TO THE DAY after Cornwallis surrendered at Yorktown, two splendid carriages overflowing with flowers struggled up the hill to the Château de Chavaniac. Lafayette was home. After fourteen years of revolution in two worlds, he had returned to his birthplace as a private citizen— to the cheers of his neighbors and childhood playmates and the tears of his aging aunt Charlotte. He and Adrienne pulled into the castle gates in the lead carriage; their two daughters, fourteen-year-old Anastasie and nine-year-old Virginie, followed in the second vehicle with their governess. Their ten-day trip from Paris had seemed an eternity. Cheering crowds stopped them in every town and village, crowding about their carriages, good-naturedly refusing to let them pass until he stepped out to address them; until he introduced his wife and daughters; until the mayor had filled their arms with flowers and given them keys to the city and other municipal mementos. The excitement delighted the girls, but Adrienne was exhausted after the frightening events in Paris and remained fraught with anxiety until a few days later, when Félix Frestel arrived safely with eleven-year-old George-Washington in tow. Frestel was principal of the Collège de Plessis, Lafayette's old secondary school, and the Lafayettes had retained him to tutor their son privately until the boy was old enough to enroll in class. A month after George arrived, Adrienne's mother, the duchesse d'Ayen, came to Chavaniac to add still more gaiety to the family reunion.

Lafayette seemed content to settle into the quiet life of a country gentleman—the George Washington of Chavaniac. "After fifteen years of revolution," he wrote to the American President, "I am profiting from a new and agreeable life of calm in the mountains where I was born. I have a fine plantation here, a former feudal estate transformed into a farm and directed by an English gardener I brought over to teach me agriculture. I am happy living among neighbors who are no longer vassals, and I have given my family the first peaceful weeks they have enjoyed for a long time."[1]

And in another letter, he added, "I rejoice in this total change. I love my aunt . . . I was so happy to see her again; she is very well and did not think I would ever come back to Chavaniac until she saw me here, settled into the house. . . . I have as much pleasure in complete rest as I ever did in the fifteen years of action . . . and success. I am left with but one last role—as a farmer."[2]

In Paris, Jacobins rejoiced almost as much as Lafayette in his new role—and took full advantage of his absence to further roil the already turbulent political waters of national politics. It was not long, however, before ripples from the political maelstrom in Paris lapped at the edges of Lafayette's fields at Chavaniac. To Adrienne's consternation, a delegation from nearby Brioude, the capital city of southern Auvergne, arrived at Chavaniac to announce that moderates in the departmental assembly had blocked an attempted Jacobin takeover by electing Lafayette president. As Adrienne held her breath anxiously, her husband thanked his fellow Auvergnats, but declined the honor. No sooner had the Brioude delegates left, however, than another delegation arrived—this one from Paris; Bailly had resigned as mayor, discouraged by Jacobin street riots and overwhelmed by the double burden of administering the city and commanding Lafayette's National Guard.

Without Lafayette's strong presence, Paris constitutionalists seemed helpless to prevent Jacobin infiltration into every area of public life. Gangs of Jacobin thugs menaced newly elected moderates as they entered and left the National Assembly. Despite a two-thirds majority, the gentlemanly constitutionalists sat paralyzed with fear, unable to cope with the bedlam the Jacobin minority created about them, pounding fists, stamping feet, shouting insults, or chanting them in unison. The Jacobins ignored national bankruptcy and famine to extend their power into the lives and thoughts of every man, woman, and child in France. Their first official act struck the words *Sire (Sieur)*, *Madam (Madame)*, and *Majesty (Majesté)* from the French language. The new law required people to address each other as *citoyen* and *citoyenne* ("citizen" and "citizenness") instead of *Monsieur* and *Madame*—or face denunciation and arrest as enemies of the state. Moderate political leaders desperately sought Lafayette's return to Paris to run for mayor, but he declined. Zealous friends entered his name in absentia, without his consent, and although Adrienne was delighted when he lost, the Jacobins seized the reins of government, and within weeks a "Committee of Insurrection," headed by the savage Danton, took control of the National Guard, which policed the city.

Jacobin control in Paris emboldened revolutionaries and brigands elsewhere in France to sack chateaux, churches, and rectories. Aristocrats fled in panic—westward to London, north to Brussels, and eastward to the Rhine—especially to Coblenz, where the king's brothers had established a pseudo French court as an emigré capital and center for counterrevolutionary activities. Bloodied clerical *refusés* and their parishioners went into hiding. In Paris, mobs plundered shops and food convoys. Violence became an integral part of daily life—a vocation for some, an avocation for others. Jacobins encouraged *le petit peuple*—the ordinary "little people"—to join in the daily slaughter by distributing more than ten thousand pikes to those without guns. "The pike has become a sacred symbol," Robespierre chortled contentedly.[3]

In Avignon, the grisly Jourdan Coupe-Tête resurfaced and led a band of cutthroats on an arson spree that gutted the area's châteaux and turned thousands of acres of church-owned lands into an inferno just before the grain and grape harvests. Not content with his handiwork, Coupe-Tête and his men broke into Avignon's grim Prison de la Glacière—the "ice-house" prison—and, during two unimaginably bloody days on October 16 and 17, 1791, systematically butchered dozens of imprisoned Catholic priests and parishioners in their cells—many of them women and children jailed for refusing to foresake their oaths to the Roman Catholic Church. In Paris, the Jacobins intimidated the National Assembly to grant full amnesty to Coupe-Tête and make preaching by *refusés* priests an act of treason, subject to summary execution.

"Their new Constitution is good for nothing," Morris raged to Washington in one of his first reports as the new American ambassador to France. "The truth is that instead of seeking the public good by doing what was right, each sought his own advantage. . . . The Assembly . . . commits every day new follies, and if this unhappy country be not plunged anew into the horrors of despotism it is not their fault. . . . They have lately made a master stroke to that effect. They have resolved to attack their neighbors. . . . America in the worst of times was much better because at least the criminal law was executed, not to mention the mildness of our manners."[4]

With the economy in shambles and hunger and anarchy engulfing the nation, war did, indeed, seem a logical answer to the nation's problems by channeling popular furor and energy in a struggle against imagined enemies beyond the nation's borders. Early in 1792, the Assembly warned Austria that France would declare war if the Austrians did not disperse the French emigré regiments in Coblenz and elsewhere in its territory. The Assembly ordered three armies of 50,000 men each to mass along the northern and eastern frontiers, with the sixty-seven-year-old Rochambeau in command of the Army of the North on the left flank, and General Nicolas Luckner on the right flank commanding the Army of the Rhine. Aware that Lafayette had captured one-third of the votes in the Paris election without even showing his face, Lafayette's enemies forced the Assembly to appoint him commander of the Army of the Center—not to honor him, but to send him to war and keep him too busy to meddle in French politics. To his family's deep distress, Lafayette had no choice but ride out of the gates of Chavaniac on Christmas Day, 1791. It would be years before any of them would ever see him again.

Like the other two French armies, Lafayette's army was in total disarray. One-third of its officers—all of them noblemen—had fled across the border to join the emigrés. Jacobins had infiltrated the rank and file and encouraged disobedience, anarchy, and desertion. Instead of 50,000 troops, Lafayette found fewer than 25,000—many of them peasant volunteers for whom military service offered prospects of food and plunder. "Their army is undisciplined to a degree you can hardly conceive," Morris reported to Washington. "Already great numbers desert. . . . Their *Gardes Nationales* who have turned out as volunteers are in many instances . . . corrupted scum . . . [with] every vice and every disease which can render them the scourge of their friends and the scoff of their foes."[5]

Lafayette, however, tried to remain optimistic: "Do not believe, my dear general, the exaggerated reports you may receive, above all those that come from England. Liberty and equality will be saved in France, that is certain. . . ."[6] As Lafayette would soon learn, Morris had a far better grasp of French affairs than he.

On April 28, France declared war against Austria and Prussia and sent Rochambeau and Lafayette, the heroes of Yorktown, northward to seize Belgium from the Austrians. The invasion was disastrous: facing disciplined lines of more than 150,000 Austrian, Prussian, and Hessian troops and 20,000 French emigrés, the French troops fled in panic. When French general Théobald Dillon ordered his fleeing soldiers to turn and face the enemy, they slaughtered him and kept running. Old Rochambeau quit in disgust and was arrested and imprisoned as a traitor. His aide since Yorktown, Lafayette's brother-in-law the vicomte de Noailles, fled to England in the belief that his wife, Adrienne's sister Louise, was safely in Switzerland with their three children and the rest of the Noailles family. After the Army of the North surrendered to the Austrians, the king of Prussia ordered the allied armies to march on Paris to rescue the royal family. The National Assembly declared an emergency, stripped the nation of voting rights, and declared itself an absolute ruling body in perpetuity, with members to serve indefinitely and no longer subject to popular vote. It ordered the deportation of all *refusé* priests, French-born or not. In the first—and last—courageous act of his reign, the king used his constitutional right to veto the decrees.

When Lafayette heard of the king's stand, he decided the time had come to act against the Jacobins with a strong declaration of support for the king: "Continue, Sire, to exercise the authority that the national will has delegated to you to defend constitutional principles against all enemies. . . . In so doing, you will find that all the friends of liberty and all good Frenchmen will rally around your throne to defend it against rebel plots and factions. And I, Sire, will continue zealously to serve the cause to which I have devoted my entire life, with loyalty to the oath I took to the nation, the law and the king."[7] At the same time, he sent a long, scathing address to the Assembly denouncing Jacobin intrigues:

> In the belief that . . . the Constitution is the law governing the legislature, I blame you, Gentlemen, for the powerful efforts to divert you from the course you have promised to follow. I will let nothing deprive me of the right as a free man to perform my duty as a citizen . . . I have great respect for the representatives of the people, but I have greater respect for the people, for whom the Constitution is the ultimate declaration of their will. . . . Can you deny that . . . the Jacobin faction is causing all the disorder? I accuse them openly. Organized like a separate empire in the city, with branches across the country; directed by a handful of leaders blinded by ambition, this sect has formed a separate nation amidst the French people, usurping their powers and subjugating their representatives, eulogizing the crimes of Jourdan [Coupe-Tête]. . . . I denounce them. . . . They would overturn our laws; they rejoice in disorder; they rise up against public authority that the people have established.

Lafayette demanded that the Assembly crush the Jacobins, calling it "a sect that has usurped the people's sovereignty, tyrannized citizens . . . I implore the National Assembly to arrest and punish the leaders of violence for high treason against the nation." If the Assembly failed to restore constitutional law, he threatened to march into Paris with his army to do the job for them.[8]

His declaration came too late, however. The Jacobins already ruled Paris, and they now moved swiftly and mercilessly to destroy Lafayette and the last semblances of constitutional law. "*A bas Lafayette!*" ("Down with Lafayette!"), they roared in the Assembly; "Lafayette is a scoundrel!" Desmoulins cried out. Danton leaped to his feet and shouted, "Lafayette has left no doubt that he is behind the coalition of European tyrants." Finally Robespierre stood and signaled for silence: "Lafayette is the most dangerous enemy of France," he declared. "Smite Lafayette, and the nation is saved!"[9]

On June 20, Robespierre led a Jacobin mob into the Assembly. As terror-stricken moderates sat silently, the thugs marched about the hall for three long hours, crying, "The people have awakened. Blood will flow on the Tree of Liberty and make it flower."[10] At a signal from Robespierre, they left as suddenly as they had entered and streamed across the Tuileries Gardens into the royal palace. The National Guard had fled, and, as he had at Versailles, the king ordered his guards not to fire on the people—"his children," he called them naively. The mob surged into the palace and found the king alone and unguarded—"humbled to the level of a beggar's pity, without resources, without authority, without a friend,"[11] as Morris had once described him. A group of toughs milled about him menacingly as others hopped down the cellar stairs to pillage the wine stores. Some returned with wine, sat him down, and spent the next few hours drinking, smoking, and mocking the king. A quartet of toughs found Queen Marie-Antoinette and the king's sister, Madame Elizabeth, and forced them to sit beside the king. As the grimacing thugs blew smoke defiantly into the faces of the helpless royal trio, others forcibly slipped the red bonnet of the revolution onto the king's head and made him drink wine, clink glasses with them, and repeatedly toast *La Nation* until he all but passed out and slumped silently in his chair, ready for death.

When Lafayette learned of the mob's outrages, he concluded that the enemies within were a greater threat to the nation than foreign armies; he rode into Paris at top speed and, in full uniform, strode onto the floor of the Assembly, apparently ready to proclaim military rule:

> Gentlemen, it is as a citizen that I have the honor of speaking to you; but the opinion I shall express is that of all Frenchmen who love their country, their liberty, their tranquillity and the laws of the land. . . . It is time to guaranty the Constitution against attempts to undermine it and to assure the independence and dignity of the National Assembly and the king; it is time to crush the hopes of evil citizens . . . who seek to plunge the people of this nation into shameful, intolerable slavery.
>
> I beg the National Assembly, first, to find and punish the leaders and instigators of the violence of June 20 for treason; second, to destroy the sect that is threatening the sovereignty of this nation and is tyrannizing its citizens—and has left no doubt in its public statements of its responsibility for these atrocities; third and last, I beg of you, in my own name and those of all honest people in the kingdom, to take effective measures to ensure respect for all constitutional authorities, particularly your own and that of the king—and thus give the army the assurance of protection against internal attacks on the Constitution while its brave soldiers shed their blood to defend our borders.[12]

Lafayette's blunt words left the Assembly members "gaping," according to Gouverneur Morris. Without waiting for replies, Lafayette marched out of the hall and across the Tuileries Gardens to the palace to commiserate with the royal family. Marie-Antoinette's cold eyes reiterated her old disdain, but the king and his sister, Madame Elizabeth, all but wept as he once again pledged his friendship and personal protection. Lafayette then rode home across the Pont du Carousel to the rue de Bourbon for what would be his last night in his "American" home. Loyal guardsmen had surrounded it to protect it against looters, and a skeleton staff had maintained the interior, but only ghostly echoes resounded within; his wife and children remained in Chavaniac and most of his friends and relatives were in exile.

The next day, Lafayette went to a reception at the palace, where Morris, the American ambassador, awaited him. Morris had heard from Caty Greene, who, in Lafayette's absence, feared for her son's safety and asked that sixteen-year-old George Washington Greene return home to America immediately. Morris and Lafayette renewed their debate over the French constitution, which the American called "that wretched piece of paper. I tell him . . . that I presume that he has lived long enough in the present style to see that a popular government is good for nothing in France."[13] Lafayette, however, insisted that two-thirds of the Assembly "despised the Jacobins, and even the Jacobin minority included some deputies who voted with them because of fear."[14] Lafayette said he would use the citizen militia he had once commanded—the Paris National Guard—to reimpose constitutional rule. Learning that the king was to review the guard the following day, he would accompany the king and, after the review, address the men, rekindle their loyalty, and lead them on an assault of Jacobin headquarters. The king agreed enthusiastically, but, before dawn the next morning, the Jacobin mayor learned of the plan and, as commander of the guard, canceled the review.

In another of his incredible failures to seize the reins of government, Lafayette decided against trying to rally the guard and rode back to the frontier to bring his regular army troops back to Paris. In doing so however, he ceded control of Paris to the Jacobins and left the Assembly and the royal family defenseless. Robespierre proclaimed Lafayette a traitor at a Jacobin rally near the Palais Royal and demanded his execution. As a horrified Morris looked on from the entrance of his club, the mob responded by burning Lafayette's effigy. "I verily believe," he wrote to Jefferson, "that if Mr. de La Fayette were to appear just now in Paris unattended by his army he would be torn to pieces. Thank God we have no [rabble] in America and I hope the education and manners will long prevent that evil."[15]

Fearing for the French king's safety, the duke of Brunswick, who commanded the coalition of Prussian, Austrian, and French émigré armies, warned he would raze Paris and exact "an exemplary and never to be forgotten vengeance" on its people if the Jacobins mistreated the royal family.[16] Jacobins in the Assembly responded with a call for military volunteers: "Citizens!

The Fatherland is in danger!"[17] As panic spread through the streets, men of all ages rushed to enlist. A ragtag force of 600 guardsmen arrived from Marseilles, singing a stirring anthem originally written for the Army of the North but renamed "La Marseillaise" and reworded with a sadistic call to soak the people's standards in their enemies' blood. For the next month, the drunken Marseilles guardsmen raged through the streets of Paris, chanting their anthem, brutalizing bystanders, and waving flags soaked in the blood of their victims.

On August 10, Robespierre's Jacobins demanded the king's abdication and sent thousands of insurrectionists to the Tuileries Palace, where they broke through gates and slaughtered the king's guards. As he had done before, the king had ordered them not to fire on the people, and, for their loyalty, they suffered unimaginable butchery, as the mob disemboweled them, one by one, and planted their heads on pikes to parade through the palace, until six hundred guards and two hundred servants lay butchered. The horror-stricken royal family fled across the gardens to the National Assembly and asked for its protection. Members of the mob followed the royals into the Assembly hall, waving their grisly trophies in the faces of terrified deputies.

To save themselves from massacre, Assembly members suspended the king's royal powers and ordered him and his family placed under house arrest in the Palais de Luxembourg, once the home of Henry IV's queen, Marie de Médicis—and of Lafayette and his mother when he first came to Paris as a boy. Yielding to Jacobin threats, the Assembly suspended the constitution and created a new all-powerful "executive council," headed by Danton as minister of justice. It then voted to dissolve itself and ordered new elections, with universal suffrage, to select a permanent "Convention" with absolute powers to govern France indefinitely as a people's dictatorship.

The removal of Louis XVI from the throne automatically severed diplomatic relations with all foreign nations. Their ties were to him; like other monarchs who ruled by divine right, he had been the state—"L'état c'est moi."[18] His removal ended the missions of foreign ambassadors accredited to him and the missions of his ambassadors abroad. Between August 13 and 17, England, the Netherlands, Denmark, Prussia, Poland, Russia, the Swiss Confederation, and Spain—where the king's cousin Charles IV ruled—severed relations with France, setting the stage for a world war that would last eighteen years.

On August 13, Danton ordered the royal family transferred from the Palais du Luxembourg to a grim prison in the *donjon* of the Temple—the huge twelfth-century fortification of the Knights Templar.[19] The next day, he ordered Lafayette's arrest. Lafayette ordered his troops to assemble and prepare to march against the Paris revolutionaries and free the king. Once

A Jacobin thug waves the head of a victim at the president of the French National Assembly. The Jacobin mob slaughtered six hundred palace guards and two hundred servants. (*Réunion des Musées Nationaux.*)

again, he acted too late: Jacobins had infiltrated his forces, and, when he ordered his assembled troops to repeat their oath to the Constitution, two battalions refused. He ordered their arrest, but, to his dismay, not a soldier or an officer responded.

Facing mass mutiny, Lafayette saw but two courses of action open to him. He could return to Paris to face certain—and useless—execution on the guillotine. Prosecutor Robespierre had accused "Motier-La Fayette, heretofore general of the Army of the North, of rebellion against the law, of conspiracy against liberty and of treason against the nation."[20] Trial was not an option for treason—only summary application of Dr. Guillotin's unforgiving blade. His other option was flight. He could forsake his native land, which had rejected the Rights of Man, and settle in a land that embraced those rights—his adopted land: America. "What safety is there," he pondered, "in a country where Robespierre is a sage, Danton an honest man, and Marat a God?"[21]

He wrote to Adrienne:

Whatever fate may hold in store for me, my sweetheart, you know my soul too well not to know the agony I suffered in leaving the land to which I have dedicated my life—a land that might have been free and was worthy to be so if selfish interests had not corrupted the public interest. . . . Outlawed in my own land for having served her with courage, I have been forced to flee into enemy territory from France, which I had defended with so much love. To the very last minute, I fought for the Constitution I swore to uphold. . . . I became the object of attacks from every direction until it became demonstrably clear that . . . I was to die for no justifiable purpose. . . . I shall go to England, where I want my entire family to join me. I hope my aunt can make the journey as well. . . . I make no excuses for having brought ruin to my family—either to the children or to you; but no one among you would have wanted me to owe my fortune to conduct contrary to my conscience. Come join me in England; let us resettle in America, where we will find the liberty that no longer exists in France; and my tender love will find ways to console you for the happiness you may lose. Adieu, my sweetheart.[22]

On the evening of August 19, Lafayette led fifty-three officers and men on horseback through the rain across the frontier into Austrian-occupied Belgium—among them the ever-loyal La Colombe, who had sailed with him aboard the *Victoire* to South Carolina in 1777 and fought with him from Brandywine to Yorktown. With him, too, was a trusted military aide, Jean-Xavier Bureaux de Pusy, and Général le comte César de La Tour-Maubourg, his fellow Auvergnat from Le Puy and Fayettiste political ally in the National Assembly.

Lafayette's flight provoked consternation among Paris Jacobins, who smashed their way into the Hôtel de Ville, shattered the Houdon busts of Lafayette and Bailly, and ripped out the bas-relief with Lafayette's profile from the outer wall of the building. A Jacobin deputy in the Convention demanded that Lafayette's house on the rue de Bourbon be leveled, and Robespierre ordered Adrienne and the Lafayette children in Chavaniac seized as hostages until the Austrians returned Lafayette to French authorities and the guillotine. Morris reported to Secretary of State Jefferson: "He and his friends had nothing to hope for . . . his circle is compleated. He has spent his fortune on a Revolution and is now crush'd by the wheel he put in motion. He lasted longer than I expected."[23] Calling Lafayette "the most hated man in Europe," he explained that European monarchs reviled Lafayette as much as Robespierre's Jacobins—the first, for starting the revolution and threatening their God-given absolute powers; the second for demanding constitutional restrictions on the absolute powers they had usurped.

The Austrians escorted Lafayette and his companions to Nivelle, just south of Brussels, where Lafayette requested passports to proceed to England; the Austrians refused, addressing him in mocking tones as "Citizen Motier." Lafayette immediately wrote to the duke of Saxe-Teschen, the uncle of the

Austrian emperor, demanding a reason for his detention—and he wrote to William Short, who had been appointed American ambassador to Holland after Morris took over the Paris embassy:

> My dear friend,
>
> You have been acquainted with the atrocious events which have taken place in Paris, when the Jacobin faction on the 10th of August overthrew the Constitution, enslaved both the Convention and the king, the one by terror, the other by destitution and confinement, and gave signal for pillage and massacre.
>
> I raised an opposition to Jacobin tyranny; but you know the weakness of our *honnêtes gens* [honest folks]; I was abandoned. . . . Nothing was left for me but to leave France. However, we have been stopped on our road and detained by an Austrian detachment, which is absolutely contrary to the *droits des gens* [rights of non-combatants]. . . . You will greatly oblige me, my friend, by leaving for Brussels as soon as this letter reaches you, and by insisting on seeing me. I am an American citizen, and an American officer. I am no longer in the service of France. In demanding my release, you will be acting within your rights, and I have no doubt of your immediate arrival. God bless you.[24]

Lafayette also wrote to his old Fayettiste ally, the philanthropist duc de La Rochefoucauld: "If I regain my liberty," he told the duc, "I shall become once more purely American, and finding again in that happy land an enlightened people, friends of liberty, observers of the law, grateful for the happiness that I had to be useful to them. I shall relate to my great friend Washington and all my other companions from the American revolution, how, despite my efforts, the French revolution was defiled by criminals, thwarted by plotters and destroyed by the vilest of men using corruption and ignorance as instruments of destruction."[25] La Rochefoucauld never read Lafayette's letter. Before it arrived, a Jacobin mob pulled him from his family's carriage along a road near Paris and, as his wife and mother watched in horror, severed his head from his body before taking the two women off to prison—and the guillotine.

The murder of Lafayette's friend began a period of unrestrained and unpredictable mob pillage and butchery that destroyed much of the nation's most treasured art and furnishings and left more than three thousand dead—many of them defenseless priests and aristocrats in their prison cells, but just as many innocent passersby who happened along the wrong street or alley at the wrong time. The September Massacres, as historians called the savagery, began on Sunday, September 2, after the bloodthirsty Marat warned Parisians that the departure of volunteers to fight the Prussians would "leave our families at the mercy of priests and aristocrats who may break out of prison and kill them all." Morris summarized the mob's response in his diary:

> Sunday 2d—This afternoon they announce the murder of priests who had been shut up in the Carmes [a Carmelite monastery]. They then go to the Abbaye and murder the prisoners there.
>
> Monday 3d.—The murdering continues all day. I am told there are about eight hundred men concerned in it.
>
> Tuesday 4.—The Murders continue.
>
> Thursday 6.—There is nothing new this day. The murders continue. . . .[26]

On September 10, Morris wrote to Secretary of State Jefferson:

> We have had one week of uncheck'd murders in which some thousands have perished in this city. It began with between two and three hundred of the clergy who had been shut up because they would not take the oath prescribed by law and which they said was contrary to their conscience. *These Executors of speedy Justice* went to the Abbaye where the persons were confin'd. . . . These were dispatch'd also, and afterwards they visited the other prisons. All those who were confin'd either on the accusation or suspicion of crimes, were destroy'd. Madame de Lamballe [a friend of Queen Marie-Antoinette] was I believe the only woman killed and she was beheaded and disemboweled, the head and entrails paraded on pikes thro' the streets, and the body dragg'd after them. They continu'd I am told in the neighborhood of the Temple until the Queen look'd out at this horrid spectacle.[27]

In addition to the slaughter of innocents, the mobs smashed their way into churches, mansions, and monuments. In their search for treasure, they shattered the magnificent sarcophagi of the kings and queens of France in the Basilica of Saint-Denis, destroying some of the world's most treasured funerary art and scattering the ashes, dust, and bones of Clovis, Charlemagne, Saint-Louis, Francis I, Catherine de Médicis, and other French monarchs onto the parvis outside the church.

Even as Morris penned his letter to Jefferson, the terrifying chorus of "La Marseillaise" echoed along the narrow winding street of Chavaniac leading up to Lafayette's château. Adrienne ordered a governess to flee with ten-year-old Virginie to a nearby farmer's house, while the tutor Frestel rushed thirteen-year-old George-Washington into the woods to the rear and up to a hillside hut of a friendly abbé. Fifteen-year-old Anastasie hid in a secret cubby in one of the towers. Adrienne had just hidden a few of Lafayette's papers and his ceremonial swords when Jacobin guardsmen marched into the château. As their commander read the order for her arrest—"The woman Lafayette is to be arrested, together with her children."[28]—grinning Jacobin thugs dumped the contents of armoires and *écritoires* and snatched up treasured family papers and letters "as evidence" to send her husband to the guillotine.

"Whose portraits are these?" one of the thugs asked the maid. "Famous aristocrats?"

"They are good men who are no longer with us," she replied defiantly, "and if they were here, things would not be going this badly."[29] The man almost ran her through, but relented and satisfied his fury by slashing the canvases.

As the commander led Adrienne to the door, Lafayette's seventy-three-year-old aunt Charlotte appeared, balancing herself unsteadily on a rustic cane, and shrilled her determination to accompany her niece. The commander obliged. Then Anastasie emerged from her hiding place and refused to leave her mother's side. The three women climbed into the carriage. "If your father knew you were here," Adrienne scolded her daughter gently, "he would be very worried—but also very proud of you."[30]

Whatever anxieties Adrienne harbored when she climbed into her carriage at Chavaniac, she stepped out of the carriage at Le Puy, twenty-five miles away, tall, steady, and strong, her head held high and haughty, her jaw set firmly—a study in controlled fury and unyielding courage. The ragged-looking peasant guards stepped back, puzzled, somewhat frightened. She had been raised in and about the court of France and knew how to carry herself in regal fashion, how to intimidate her social inferiors with a single icy glance. She used every wile at her command as she marched into the council hall and demanded copies of all letters seized at Chavaniac and the right to read each letter aloud to the town council, to force members to hear every word of what the Jacobins charged was "evidence" against her husband. When a councilman suggested that the letters might prove painful for her, she replied, "On the contrary, Monsieur!"—she refused to call him "citizen."

"On the contrary, Monsieur. The sentiments in them sustain me and are my consolation."[31]

The councilmen had never confronted such a woman and dared not oppose her. After her reading disclosed no evidence of any crime, she denounced her imprisonment as unjustifiable and demanded the right to remain at the chateau in Chavaniac on parole until specific charges against her arrived from Paris. The council agreed and permitted her to return to the Lafayette homestead with Anastasie and Aunt Charlotte—and six guards.

"Gentlemen," Adrienne turned on them angrily. "I renounce my parole if you put guards at my door. I am not shocked that you do not believe I am an honest woman . . . but you cannot strip me of my belief in my own integrity, and I shall not accept parole at the point of bayonets."[32] Taken aback once again by this unusual woman, the council relented and let her live at Chavaniac without guards.

She did not, however, return to a normal life. The Paris Jacobins had declared her husband an émigré and ordered his assets confiscated; the state not only owned Chavaniac, it controlled the family's income-producing properties elsewhere in France—even the plantation in Guyana where the Lafayettes were educating slaves they had bought and freed. Without income, Adrienne and her family would have to live off the land. According to government records, Adrienne lodged a formal protest "against the enormous injustice of applying the laws governing émigrés to one who is at this very moment a prisoner of the enemies of France."[33] The Jacobins ignored her protest, with one government representative saying he "should like to tear out the entrails of Lafayette" and execute not only Adrienne but her children, whom he called "serpents that the Republic was warming in its bosom."[34]

Lafayette, meanwhile, languished in chains in a Prussian prison. Of the original fifty-three soldiers who had fled with him, the Austrians had released some and sent others to prison in Antwerp. But the king of Prussia—the nephew of Frederick the Great, who had dined with Lafayette during the great summer maneuvers seven years earlier—ordered Lafayette and three other officers imprisoned indefinitely. In a curt note to Lafayette, the duke of Saxe-Teschen explained the king's reasoning:

"We have not arrested you as a prisoner of war or a citizen or an émigré," the duke scolded. "As it is you who fomented the revolution that overturned France, as it is you who put your king in irons, deprived him of all his rights and legitimate powers and kept him in captivity, as it is you who were the principle instrument of all the disgraces that overwhelmed that unfortunate monarch, it is only too just that those who are working to reestablish his dignity should hold you until the moment when your master, having recovered his liberty and his sovereignty, can, according to his sense of justice or clemency, dictate your fate."[35]

After hearing from Lafayette, Ambassador Short wrote to Morris and to Thomas Pinckney,[36] the American ambassador in London, who had been South Carolina governor and had known Lafayette during the Revolutionary War. The three ambassadors were equally distressed and began a furious, three-way correspondence that only exposed their impotence with nations like Prussia and Austria, which had yet to establish formal relations with the United States. "I search in vain some foundation whereon to establish a right to demand his liberation," Pinckney wrote to Short. "It will afford me real pleasure to find that Mr. Morris or you upon more mature reflexion have discovered any plan to which my concurrence can add efficacy. . . . A claim of the rights as an American citizen to a person in the Marquis's circumstances appears to me to be claiming nothing."[37]

Morris agreed: "The enemy may consider him as a prisoner of war, as a deserter, or as a spy," he said. "I do not exactly see how America could claim him." Moreover, Morris warned, if America did claim him as a citizen and the Prussians turned him over, the United States government would be bound under American law "to put him to death for having attack'd a neutral power, or else by the very act of acquitting him declare war against those who had taken him.

"These are points of such magnitude," Morris concluded, "that I do not feel myself competent to decide them on behalf of my country . . . until I receive express orders from the President of the United States. . . . I rather think that my interference would prove offensive and do more harm than good to Monsieur de La Fayette."[38]

As the impotent American diplomats discussed his fate, leaders of the coalition of countries against France determined that "Lafayette's existence is incompatible with the security of the governments of Europe" and that he should be held in maximum security. On September 18, Prussian authorities transferred him and the three other prisoners to Wesel, a fortress prison just across the German border from Holland, north of Dusseldorf. Ignoring his protests that he was an American citizen, guards dumped him unceremoniously into a small, dark dungeon cell by himself, with a board for his bed on the damp, dirty floor, with nothing to read and no writing instruments. Silent jailers stood beyond the door, each working two-hour shifts, noting his every move. At first, he fought off the vermin and rats that wandered through his cell, but the noxious prison food, inadequate water, and accumulating filth soon sapped his energy and spirit, and he surrendered to illness and fever.

William Short grew alarmed: "The treatment of M[r]. de la Fayette & his companions of misfortune at Wesel is cruel & rigorous in the extreme," Short wrote to Morris in Paris, but Morris was helpless.[39] A month later, Short wrote again: "As to our fellow citizen in confinement, I can only tell you that the most impenetrable secrecy has been observed. . . . It is certain that he is the individual of all France that both the Austrians & Prussians hate the most cordially—the desire of revenge & determination to punish made them commit the most flagrant act of injustice. . . . It has been reported that our fellow citizen has lost his reason & is in a state of insanity."[40] Although the prison doctor at Wesel urged that Lafayette be transferred to cleaner quarters and given access to fresh air, the king of Prussia refused. He suggested that Lafayette could earn more comfort only by providing military information about France—to which Lafayette replied softly, "Your king is very impertinent; even if I am his prisoner, I will suffer no insults from him."[41]

"Poor Lafayette," Morris consoled Washington, who had sent him a letter to forward to Lafayette. "Your letter for him must remain with me yet some time. His enemies here are as virulent as ever."[42]

With no way of knowing her husband's fate, Adrienne grew fearful for the survival of George-Washington—the only person who could inherit and bequeath his father's fabled name to future generations. The tutor Frestel descended from his mountain hideaway late one night and slipped into the château to report on young Lafayette's health and discuss his future. Adrienne and Frestel agreed on a plan for Frestel to obtain a false license and passport as a merchant and go to the fair at the port city of Bordeaux with George, who would feign the role of his apprentice. They would then book passage to England and seek help in getting to America from Thomas Pinckney. She gave Frestel a letter for Washington, George's godfather:

"In this abyss of misery, the thought of owing to the United States and to Washington the life and liberty of La Fayette causes a ray of hope to shine in my heart. I expect everything from the kindness of the people in whose land he helped to form a model of that liberty of which he is now the victim."[43] She begged Washington to use his influence to obtain Lafayette's release, then sealed the envelope and gave it to Frestel. "My mother refused to see my brother again," Virginie wrote later, "for fear she would not have the strength to separate herself from him and let him go."[44] Within a few days, however, Frestel reappeared at Chavaniac after midnight, saying he had been unable to obtain the necessary papers to travel to the Bordeaux fair. Frestel and George returned to Chavaniac for the winter.

On September 20, the ragtag army of undisciplined French Jacobins charged like madmen into the Prussian lines at Valmy, about forty miles west of Verdun, howling "*Vive la Nation!*" hysterically, leaping over the bodies of their fallen comrades into the steady hail of musket balls and bayonet thrusts. Ignoring death, they materialized from every direction; peasants with picks charged from every farmhouse and village door to join them—some behind the Prussian lines, many on their flanks. Unlike the disciplined, well-fed, uniformed armies of Louis XIV, the French revolutionary armies of 1792 mixed professionals with ill-clothed irregulars, untrained peasants, and workers—all of them ravenous for food, drink, and plunder. Jacobin agents had infiltrated every hamlet, town, and city, pledging a policy of *La guerre aux châteaux; la paix aux chaumières*—"War on castles; peace with cottages."[45] The Jacobins invited the poor, the disaffected, and the homeless to crusade against the aristocracy and the Roman Catholic clergy—and they did, with a fury that had accumulated during centuries of deprivation. The French army became the world's largest pirate army since the French crusades.

Rather than risk slaughter for a king and cause not their own, Prussian regulars pulled back from the insanity to the natural defenses of the Rhine River. The retreat sacrificed the unprotected plains of the western Rhineland to marauding French hordes. Within a month the French had recaptured northern and eastern France and overrun the German Palatinate, including the historic cathedral cities of Mainz and Worms, on the west bank of the Rhine. In the south and southeast, they swept through Savoy, seizing the capital city of Chambéry and the Mediterranean port of Nice.

In Paris, some moderates in the new Convention united with radicals in self-congratulatory embraces and arrogant pronouncements of French invincibility. The moderates were led by Girondin merchants from the Bordeaux region along the huge Gironde estuary in southwestern France. Commoners all, they had profited handsomely from the Revolution by buying auctioned lands of the church and aristocracy at distress prices. Many learned the language of radicals, while the radicals stroked their egos and fed their greed for profits with promises of wealth, all the while dipping into their pockets and assuring them that radicalism in the name of France was the highest form of patriotism—that "one cannot make an omelet without breaking eggs."[46] On the opening day of the Convention, moderate Girondins eagerly jumped into the revolutionary frying pan and voted with Robespierre radicals to decree "royalty abolished in France" and proclaim France "a republic."[47]

As French forces piled victory upon victory, thousands of hungry, unemployed peasant volunteers joined the army to profit from plunder in foreign territory. The French treasury also profited. As they had done in France, French Jacobins seized the assets of the aristocracy and church treasuries in conquered lands, melted gold and silver relics into bullion, and sold lands at auction. Far from bankrupting France as some moderates had feared, the war was solving the nation's fiscal as well as social crises.

After the army overran Monaco and Belgium, the Convention proclaimed the unity of all French-speaking peoples in Europe and called for worldwide revolution, pledging "fraternity and aid to all peoples seeking to recover their liberty. . . . We will not be satisfied until Europe—all Europe—is afire."[48] In December 1792, French forces massed along the northern Belgian border with Holland, while the French navy sailed into Naples harbor to begin conquest of the Italian peninsula, the Vatican, and the Mediterranean world. The Convention proclaimed that "all of Europe, including Moscow, will become Gallicized, Jacobinized, communized."[49] Declaring a new French era for the world, the Convention decreed a new "republican calendar" to replace the Christian calendar: what had been September 22, 1792 anno Domini retroactively became Day One of mankind's "Year I of Equality."[50]

The French military victories came at a steep price for King Louis XVI and his family, who lost their value as hostages. With his forces retreating, the duke of Brunswick could no longer demand their release in exchange for sparing Paris. Indeed, their continued existence became a dangerous symbol of resistance to Jacobin rule. On December 3, Robespierre demanded the trial and execution of the king for high political crimes. Assuming that Lafayette still held some symbolic value for French revolutionaries, Prussian authorities retaliated—chaining him and his friends, La Tour-Maubourg and Bureaux de Pusy, in an open peasant's cart for transport deep into Prussian-held Saxony through crowds of taunting villagers. On December 31, 1792, Prussian soldiers marched them into a subterranean dungeon in the fortress at Magdeburg, three hundred miles from the French border. The guards led the prisoners to separate cells, each "three paces wide by five and one-half."[51] Only a thin gray beam of light pierced the thick, wet outer wall, through a slit too high and narrow to imagine that a sky or world might lay beyond. The only hint of life on earth tumbled meaninglessly through the iron grating in the ceiling of his cell, in unintelligible, mumbled German whispers from two guards who kept a constant watch on him from above.

Adrienne's sister Louise, the vicomtesse de Noailles, was in Paris caring for her ailing grandfather and appealed to Ambassador Morris for help in ameliorating Lafayette's prison conditions. The Jacobins had confiscated the family's assets; they had no money to send to the prison to pay for Lafayette's food, and he was evidently dying from the verminous gruel that the prison served without charge and the harsh conditions. Morris acted swiftly, using his own funds to establish open-ended credit at a Dutch bank "to supply the sums needful for him . . . no moment is to be lost in administering relief."[52] After he learned that Adrienne Lafayette and the children were also without funds, Morris placed 100,000 livres of his own money in another Dutch account, impervious to Jacobins, for her to pay Lafayette's outstanding debts and her family's expenses. Adrienne appealed to Washington, who contributed 2,000 livres of his own to the Dutch account, pretending that it was a repayment of some personal debt to Lafayette when he had visited America.

"If I ever see and am reunited with my husband again, it will be thanks only to your goodness and that of the United States," Adrienne answered Washington. "I can do nothing for him; I can neither receive a word from him nor write to him. That is the situation I now suffer."[53] Washington was as helpless as Adrienne. As president of the United States, he could not take any public action to free Lafayette without risking diplomatic conflict with France, which remained a United States ally, and he had no influence whatever with either Austria or Prussia, which had no diplomatic ties to the United States.

As cruel and undeserved as it was, Lafayette's confinement far from France actually saved his life by sparing him a cart ride to the guillotine. The king was not as fortunate. On January 15, 1793, the French Convention voted 707 to 0 that the king was guilty of conspiring against public liberty. The next day, moderates tried to replace the lid of civilization on the Revolution, but failed. The Convention condemned the king to death, 361 to 360. Moderates tried, but failed again, to reverse the vote. Some urged holding him in prison for trial after the war; others suggested sending the royal family to exile in America. In this second group was Tom Paine, whose tracts titled *The Rights of Man* had won him honorary French citizenship and a seat in the revolutionary Convention. Robespierre silenced them all. He sent Paine to prison and threatened other dissenters with the same fate or worse. On the morning of January 21, Louis XVI climbed the steps to the guillotine in the Place de la Révolution, now the Place de la Concorde. The blade fell at 10:22.

"The late King of this Country has been publicly executed," American ambassador Morris reported to Secretary of State Thomas Jefferson. "He died in a manner becoming his Dignity. Mounting the scaffold he express'd anew his forgiveness of those who persecuted him and a prayer that his deluded people might be benefited by his death. On the scaffold he attempted to speak but the commanding officer . . . ordered the drums to beat."[54]

After displaying the king's head to the frenzied cheers of the mob, the executioner and his assistants tossed the king's head and then his body into a corpse-filled cart, and guardsmen made a path for it through the crowd toward the Madeleine Cemetery about a half-mile away, where a gaping trench, its floor lined with the previous day's grisly deposits, awaited the new arrivals.[55]

The beheading of the king outraged the civilized world. In Germany, the French king's brothers proclaimed Louis's still-imprisoned seven-year-old son, Louis-Charles de France, the new king. By the end of March 1793, a huge European coalition had formed to crush the French revolution and prevent its spread into neighboring countries. In Europe, only Turkey, Scandinavia, Russia, and Switzerland did not take up arms against France. England, Holland, Spain, the Italian states, and the Papacy's Swiss Guards joined the Austrians and Prussians. Foreign armies poured into France: the Spanish along the Mediterranean in the southwest, the Prussians across the Rhineland in the east, and the Austrians from the north. Far more threatening, the powerful British army landed in Toulon and was preparing to cross the Channel and invade Normandy and Brittany to support royalist counterrevolutionaries. France had but one ally left in the world: the United States. President Washington, however, issued a proclamation of neutrality, declaring that the United States was at peace with Great Britain and France. With America's

The executioner displays King Louis XVI's head from the scaffolding of the guillotine on the place de la Révolution, now the place de la Concorde, in Paris, on January 21, 1793. (*Réunion des Musées Nationaux.*)

wounds from its own revolution still healing, the United States could not afford any distraction on the road to economic recovery.

Jacobin leaders were furious. Early in April, they dispatched a new ambassador, "Citizen" Edmond Charles Genêt, to the United States with instructions to foment a Jacobin uprising in America. "French agents," explained Noah Webster, the editor of the New York newspaper *American Minerva*, "spread pamphlets and other papers tending to alienate the minds of people from the government of their country and . . . labored zealously to effect a revolution in the United States and overthrow the government."[56]

While his agents provoked street riots, Genêt commissioned privateers to prey on British and Spanish vessels along the U.S. coast and organized American militias in Georgia and Louisiana to attack the Spanish. President Washington denounced him for infringing on U.S. sovereignty, but the cheering mobs convinced Genêt that a Jacobin uprising was in his grasp, and he sailed to New York to lead American Jacobins in seizing the capital and overthrowing the president.

As Genêt sailed for New York, invading armies in France sent French revolutionary forces reeling, and, by early June, counterrevolutions against the Jacobins had erupted in more than sixty departments. The Revolution was in danger, and, with the Coalition growing more confident of victory, the king of Prussia eased the cruel conditions in Lafayette's prison. He permitted the transfer of American funds in Holland to the Magdeburg prison to buy Lafayette books and better food. One of the guards took Lafayette for an hour's walk in the prison garden each day, and his health and spirit improved—especially after Thomas Pinckney induced the Prussian ambassador in London to forward a portion of a letter from Adrienne that said she and the children were alive and well at Chavaniac. With the letter came a pen, ink, and paper for a brief reply under the watchful eyes of Prussian decoding experts.

"It was more than I dared hope, my sweetheart, that the five dearest people in my life would still be together in the safety of Chavaniac," Lafayette wrote:

> I had envisioned you in far more difficult, far sadder circumstances, but I know that you will find solace in knowing that your tenderness and love are the happiest memories of my life, my consolations in solitary confinement and the wellspring of my everlasting joy in the future, if I am allowed to return to my family.
>
> My health is fair . . . they pull me out of my hole an hour each day to let me breath fresh air; I have some books, and, although my ability to read fast has now become a disadvantage, I have found materials in English, French, and Latin that I can use in imaginary discussions with the dead—inasmuch as they have sequestered me from the living. . . . That is about all the news from the underground prison that I am allowed to disclose to you.
>
> Adieu, my sweetheart; I beg you all not to succumb to torment over me, but to think only of our reunion. I find it impossible to believe that my star will extinguish as long as my poor old aunt has miraculously survived these latest shocks. From the bottom of my heart, I send all my love to her, as well as Anastasie, George, Virginie and Monsieur Frestel, who is now a member of our family as well.
>
> Adieu, Adieu, I embrace you and love you with all my heart and soul.[57]

18

The Prisoners of Olmütz

THE BLOODY CONVERSION from constitutional monarchy to republic required a new constitution, but, with enemy armies and counterrevolutionaries threatening, Robespierre cut short the Convention debate by sending a mob of eighty thousand Jacobin thugs to surround the meeting hall and drag twenty-nine recalcitrant Girondin delegates to prison. The remaining delegates immediately approved a constitution that Robespierre had written, creating a "people's republic" with universal suffrage. Its preamble bore Lafayette's title—*Déclaration des Droits de l'Homme et du Citoyen* ("Declaration of the Rights of Man and the Citizen")—but left no doubt about the identity of its new author, which appeared in bold-faced capitals under the title and on the signature line at the bottom. He even claimed it as his own literary property in fine type elsewhere.

After a mock referendum sustained the new constitution by 1.8 million votes to 3,000 (5 million abstained), Robespierre suspended it for the duration of the Revolution and seized all powers for a Jacobin triumvirate: Danton, Marat, and, of course, himself. They, in turn, delegated administrative authority to two twelve-member committees: an administrative Committee for Public Safety and a Committee for General Security, a precursor of the twentieth-century Soviet Comintern, with a network of armed "vigilance committees" in every town and city to remove and arrest officials who veered from the Robespierre party line.

The counterrevolutionaries did not retreat, however. In mid-July, royalist Charlotte Corday stabbed Marat to death in his habitual lair—the bathtub. The assassination infuriated Robespierre and Danton, who turned to terror to destroy their enemies. Jacobin thugs burst into the queen's cell at the Temple Prison and tore her shrieking eight-year-old boy-king from her arms. It was the last time his mother or anyone other than his abductors would ever see him, alive or dead.[1]

The Convention facilitated the spread of the Terror by redefining the word "suspect" so broadly that police could arrest anyone for any reason. They herded hundreds of thousands of "suspects" into prisons to languish until revolutionary tribunals condemned them to death in mock trials that barred cross-examination or defense responses.

"Suspects," Robespierre shouted, "must be run to earth in their burrows by day and by night."[2]

Accordingly, the Committee of Public Safety in Paris ordered the 136 remaining Girondin deputies of the Convention imprisoned, tried, and executed, while vigilance committees elsewhere in France imprisoned almost 500,000 men, women, and children suspected of opposing the Revolution. The committees executed more than 40,000—17,000 on the guillotine and the rest with bullets, knives, nooses, or garrotes in their streets, shops, homes, and beds—dumping their victims in nameless mass graves.

Inevitably, the excesses of the Jacobin Revolution produced revulsion in the United States and turned public opinion against France. As harsh as they once had seemed, the English appeared quite civilized next to the French Jacobins. "The people of this country are deceived," editor Noah Webster warned in the weekly New York *Herald*. "They believe the French to be fighting for liberty. This opinion is not well founded. They began the revolution with honest views of acquiring their rights, but they have overleaped this limit and are contending for plunder and empire."[3]

Appalled by French ambassador Genêt's attempt to foment a Jacobin revolution in America, Congress and the president demanded that France recall him. Fearful the Americans might abrogate their treaty and join the British war against France, Robespierre dispatched a new ambassador with orders to arrest Genêt and return him for trial and execution in France. Ironically, Genêt appealed for mercy to the man he had defamed, George Washington, who granted the Frenchman political asylum.[4]

Although Genêt escaped the guillotine, few in high places were as fortunate. Queen Marie-Antoinette went to her death in October. As her horrified sister-in-law, Madame Elizabeth, looked on helplessly, Jacobin soldiers led the beautiful queen from her cell, out the prison gate, to a cart and the jeers of an angry crowd. She held her head high, looked ahead implacably, almost beatifically, as the cart worked its way through the shrieking mob to the instrument of death. The queen's head fell on October 16, 1793; as they had done with her husband nine months earlier, the attendants threw her head and corpse into a cart with other guillotine victims and carried it to the huge burying pit in the Madeleine Cemetery to rot anonymously with thousands of other innocents.

A few days after the queen's death, the guillotine left the duc d'Orléans "shortened by a head,"[5] as his executioner quipped, despite his having embraced the revolution by changing his name to Philippe Egalité—"Philip the Equal"—and voting enthusiastically in the Convention earlier in the year to execute his cousin, Louis XVI. On October 31, the guillotine claimed twenty liberal deputies of the Convention, and ten days later, the last of the great Paris Fayettistes, former mayor Jean Sylvain Bailly, paid his last respects to the bloody blade.

Early in November, the vigilance committee from the nearby city of Brioude arrived at Chavaniac and, as Adrienne watched in horror, burned all papers, documents, and other materials "in any way tainted with the spirit of feudalism," including precious deeds, baptismal certificates, and portraits of Lafayette's forebears—all evidence that an aristocracy had ever existed or owned the château and lands. The next morning, as her children sobbed hysterically, a cart took Adrienne and the village priest away to prison in Brioude, to await transfer to Paris and the guillotine. Almost at the same moment, another cart in Paris was carrying a group of women to prison in the Palais du Luxembourg to await execution. Among them were Adrienne's grandmother, mother, and sister—the old duchesse de Noailles; the duchesse d'Ayen; and Louise, the vicomtesse de Noailles. They had all come to Paris from their haven in Switzerland to tend to the dying old duc de Noailles. After his death, the Jacobins had refused to allow them to return to Switzerland.

With vigilance committees controlling most of France, resistance to the revolution collapsed. Regular army troops crushed the counterrevolutions in most of western France, and Colonel Napoléon Bonaparte's artillery pushed the British out to sea at Toulon and ended the counterrevolution in the south. Robespierre exacted retribution in the fanatically stubborn, devoutly Catholic Vendée province in western France by ordering a mass slaughter of thousands—men, women, and children. "One saw nothing but cadavers everywhere," a survivor reported, "among them women whom the soldiers had stripped, raped and killed."[6] Although severely crippled, the Vendéens continued guerrilla activities for another decade.

As the internal rebellion subsided, the French army returned to the nation's borders to repel external enemies. Within weeks, they recaptured and reannexed Belgium, overran Holland, retook and reannexed Savoy, and pushed the Spaniards beyond the Pyrenées, seizing Catalonia in eastern Spain and San Sebastiàn in the west.

In contrast to French prisons, Lafayette's dungeon cell in Magdeburg at least provided sanctuary from the guillotine, if not unending monotony and solitude. He described himself "encircled by ditches, ramparts, guards, double sentries and palisades . . . in a quadruple gated, barred, chained, locked,

grated, narrow, moist, subterranean dungeon . . . doomed to moral and bodily decay."[7]

By early 1794, the French armies neared the German border, and the
Prussians moved him to Neisse, deep in Prussia near Poland, five hundred
miles from France. Lafayette believed his captors were planning his secret
execution—that he would simply disappear and no one would know where
or when. He found a sliver of wood, moistened it, and dipped it in soot to
write his last words: "Adieu, then, my dear wife, my children, my aunt . . .
whom I shall cherish to my last breath."[8]

The dungeon at Neisse was but a temporary stop, however. Lafayette
had become an embarrassment to the Prussian king, Frederick William II,
who, like his uncle, Frederick the Great, was eager to appear an enlightened
despot and had even promulgated a new code of laws that left suspects innocent until proved guilty. The Prussian courts had never charged Lafayette
with a crime; the government had simply held him and the other French
officers as a courtesy to its Austrian ally, and Frederick William insisted that
the Austrians take responsibility for the prisoners. In the spring, the Austrians took the French officers to Olmütz, Moravia, now the western part of
the Czech Republic.

In comparison to Prussian prison cells, the cells at Olmütz were chambers of horrors. The prison was in a part of the city wall over the Morawa
River, which carried the city sewerage and filled the prison above it with a
suffocating stench and swarms of disease-carrying mosquitoes and flies.
Lafayette, La Tour-Maubourg, and Bureaux de Pusy were each chained in
solitary confinement, unaware of the other's presence, forbidden to talk, in
rags, and with no personal possessions. Identified by numbers and never
hearing their names, they ate with their fingers from filth-encrusted pots,
breathed the foul fumes of their own wastes, and were not allowed to bathe.

As Lafayette arrived at Olmütz, a similar vehicle was taking Adrienne—
"*la femme Lafayette,*" as the Jacobins called her—to prison in Paris. Her
guards spared her the discomfort of riding in chains. Frestel barely had time
to bring the children to wave tearful good-byes and give their mother her
last glimpse of her babies. "*Trouvez votre père! Trouvez votre père!,*" she cried
out to them. "Find your father; go to your father."[9] Frestel rushed the children back to the château and the care of their great-aunt, then hurried back
to the Paris road to follow Adrienne's cart and track her whereabouts. A few
days later, her cart lumbered down the rue Saint-Antoine in the east end of
Paris and into a small street to the Hôtel de La Force, once the palatial
mansion of her friends, the duc and duchesse de La Force. Thick iron grills
encased its windows; Jacobins had stripped its wall paneling, gilded ceilings,
parquet floors, and sumptuous tapestries. Its splendid furnishings and paintings
had vanished; only naked stone encased the rooms where Europe's aristocracy

This idealized engraving shows Lafayette being enchained at Olmütz prison. In fact, Lafayette was barely recognizable—thin and only barely covered by rags; his hair (and wig) had fallen out, and oozing sores covered his skin. (*Collection Viollet, Roger-Viollet, Paris.*)

had once sat enthralled by the incredible pianistic skills of the little Austrian boy Wolfgang Amadeus Mozart.

After Adrienne entered the Hôtel de La Force prison, Frestel went to see American ambassador Morris, who immediately limped over to the Tuileries Palace to demand her release. He met a cold reception. His earlier protests of French treaty violations against America and his outspoken criticisms of Jacobin excesses had infuriated the leaders of the revolution and left him unwelcome. Undaunted, he stormed through the palace, excoriating the government for imprisoning Adrienne without formal charges and leaving no doubt about America's attachment to the family of General Lafayette; the execution of Adrienne Lafayette, Morris warned, would turn Americans against France. Morris's unrelenting criticisms led the government to declare him persona non grata but left Robespierre well aware of Lafayette's exalted status as "Friend of Washington." To avoid creating a martyr who might add the United States to the long list of nations warring against France, Robespierre ordered the tribunal to leave Adrienne in prison, but omit her name from the daily lists of those sent to the tribunal for condemnation to death.

While Adrienne languished in prison, Paris guillotines chopped almost nonstop during the day. Growing ever more paranoid, Robespierre turned *La Terreur* into *La Grande Terreur*, converting almost every mansion in Paris into a prison and supplementing the guillotine on the place de la Révolution with killing machines on the place de la Bastille and the place du Trône (now the place de la Nation), on the east edge of Paris near Vincennes. Each of the blades lopped off twenty or more heads a day, accommodating "clients" from every segment of the social and political spectrum: the abolitionist Malesherbes; the scientist Lavoisier; and King Louis XVI's younger sister, the gentle and harmless Madame Elizabeth. The comte d'Estaing, who led the French fleet at Newport, went under the knife for protesting the execution of Marie-Antoinette. "The gods are thirsty," Desmoulins grinned.[10]

The guillotine even claimed Jourdan Coupe-Tête, the butcher of Versailles and Avignon, who cut off one head too many to save his own. Only renowned foreign prisoners, such as Tom Paine, and a few, select French "friends of America," such as Adrienne de Lafayette and the comte de Rochambeau, escaped the call to the guillotine—largely to avoid provoking the American government, which, on paper, remained a French ally.

As Robespierre's paranoia became the target of Paris satirists, he closed all theaters and made the steady chop-chop-chop of the guillotines the only entertainment in town—a precursor of the short plays of violence, horror, and sadism that became popular a century later at the Théâtre du Grand Guignol. Enterprising innkeepers turned the Terror into a profitable enterprise by setting up outdoor cafés on nearby embankments to sell food and drink to spectators while they watched the performances.

As prison space grew scarcer, Desmoulins had the temerity to urge the release of women and children. "They have been given the name of suspects," he declared, "but this is a term completely foreign to the spirit of justice."[11] Desmoulins's forbearance infuriated Robespierre: "The Terror *is* Justice," he thundered, "prompt, severe, inflexible."[12] He then arrested Desmoulins and Danton, and, in April 1794, they and their followers climbed the steps of death on the guillotine and left the insane Robespierre the uncontested leader of the Revolution. Terrified members of the Convention elected him president and, at his command, unanimously passed a decree ending even mock trials for suspects, because they slowed the journey to the guillotine. In the next thirty days, the guillotines of Paris alone claimed more than 1,250 victims, an average of more than thirty a day.

Early in July, a judge convicted Adrienne's grandmother, mother, and sister of "planning to dissolve the National Convention and assassinate the members of the Committee of Public Safety."[13] The family priest followed the cart to the guillotine at the place du Trône (or "place du Trône renverse"—"Square of the Overturned Throne"—as the Jacobins called it by then) and managed to get close enough to give them absolution before watching them die. The old lady was first; the duchesse d'Ayen was tenth—quickly, like all the others. Death was precise and mechanical: three executioner's assistants seized the duchesse by the arms, while others strapped her upright against a hinged vertical plank, face forward, ripped the clothing off the back of her neck, and stepped back quickly to avoid the splatter of blood.

The huge crowd of onlookers fell silent.

Thud; thud; thud. The sounds resounded across the square.

Thud: the hinged plank with its body slammed to the horizontal, positioning the victim's neck beneath the blade.

Thud: the neckpiece dropped and pinned the head firmly in place.

Thud: the blade struck home, and the head fell softly into the basket beneath a spray of blood as the crowd roared its approval.

The assistants moved swiftly, releasing the corpse and dropping it into a cart at the base of the scaffold, where street peddlers pounced like hyenas to its side and stripped off shoes and other salable items of clothing with professional efficiency and speed. After holding high the severed head by its hair to display it to the cheering crowd, the executioner tossed it into the cart and turned to clean the blade of his instrument.

By the end of July, Robespierre's paranoia reached proportions that grew intolerable for even his most loyal supporters. After accusing his own Jacobin clubs of plotting against him, he demanded the immediate arrest and execution of the entire Convention—every member. It was one demand too many. By then the number of widows and orphans had reached staggering proportions; the very women who had marched to Versailles to demand the king's head on a pike, and the Jacobins who had led them, turned against Robespierre. Tens of thousands of suspects came out of hiding to join them. As the mob outside cried "*A bas Robespierre!*" Convention delegates summoned up the courage to defy him and demand that he name those he suspected of treason; he refused, and the following day the once-timid Convention staged a coup, abolishing his Committee of Public Safety and ordering his arrest and that of his terrorist confederates. That evening, July 23, 1794, a pistol shot blew off half his jaw; some said he had attempted suicide, but a guard claimed he had shot Robespierre trying to escape. The source of the shot was immaterial. With his head swathed in blood-soaked bandages, Robespierre lay in agony for but one night; the guillotine put him out of his misery the following day, with nineteen of his closest political allies, including his brother. While a mob watched in silent disbelief, seventy-one more Robespierristes followed him to the same fate the following day in a bloody finale to the Terror. The final toll would remain unmatched in the civilized world until the twentieth century. In only two years, the French sent one million of their own men, women, and children to prison. In a nation of twenty-six million, about two hundred thousand are *known* to have died; untold thousands of others—many of them simply nameless, homeless, jobless peasants and workers—were killed summarily without knowing why and dumped into mass graves. Ironically, the "popular" revolution claimed far more commoners than aristocrats: 28 percent of the dead were peasants and 31 percent were craftsmen. Only 2 percent were clergymen. The guillotine alone killed nearly seventeen thousand; police and soldiers killed the others, often in counterrevolutionary uprisings in the provinces.

"You must give thanks to God, who has saved my life," Adrienne wrote to console her children after learning that the guillotine had claimed her mother, sister, and grandmother.

After Robespierre's death, moderates moved into seats of power, and, during the ensuing months, they outlawed Jacobin clubs, abolished vigilance committees, restored economic and commercial freedom, and released several hundred thousand imprisoned "suspects" from prison, including General Rochambeau and other badly needed military leaders.[14] The new government also released most political prisoners, including seventy-three surviving Girondins and all but a relative handful of aristocrats and others deemed enemies of the state. While former suspects danced in the streets to celebrate the end of the Terror, Adrienne, to her dismay, remained imprisoned for reasons she still did not and could not understand.

Fortunately, a new American ambassador had arrived in Paris: James Monroe, the former Continental army captain who had kept watch over the wounded Lafayette after the Battle of Brandywine. Although Monroe won the release of Tom Paine and a few American citizens, Adrienne could not claim United States citizenship under the reorganized American government, which had stripped the states of control over citizenship. In France, moreover, she remained the wife of a French deserter. Monroe did not want to make a diplomatic misstep that could prolong her detention. Instead of making a formal demand that French authorities could reject, he adopted a subtle approach to embarrass the government into releasing her: he sent his wife to visit Adrienne in prison.

"As soon as she [Mrs. Monroe] entered the street," Monroe wrote, "the public attention was drawn to [her carriage], and at the prison gate the crowd gathered round it. Inquiry was made, whose carriage was it? The answer given was, that of the American minister. Who is in it? His wife. What brought her here? To see Madame LaFayette. . . . On hearing that the wife of the American Minister had called with the most friendly motives to see her, she became frantic, and in that state they met. The scene was most affecting. The sensibility of all the beholders was deeply excited. The report of the interview spread through Paris and had the happiest effect." A few days later, Monroe joined his wife and the two made frequent visits to Adrienne together, always with armfuls of provisions that drew the attention of public and press—and embarrassed the Committee of Public Safety, which had no explanation for her continuing incarceration. "Informal communications took place in consequence between Mr. Monroe and the members of the Committee, and the liberation of Madame LaFayette soon followed."[15]

The end of the Terror also encouraged Lafayette's friends and supporters in Europe, England, and America to demand his release from the inhuman conditions of Olmütz. In London, a group of exiled Fayettistes organized a plan for his escape. Justus-Erich Bollmann, a young German doctor, agreed to go to the Inn of the Three Swans at Olmütz. He learned that the prison doctor had ordered guards to take Lafayette on a carriage ride into the countryside for his health every other day. By an incredible coincidence, a twenty-one-year-old American student from South Carolina was also at the inn—Francis Huger, son of Major Benjamin Huger, Lafayette's host when he first landed in South Carolina, more than seventeen years earlier. Young Huger eagerly joined the Bollmann plot and, on November 8, a sunny Saturday morning, the two trotted up to Lafayette's carriage, leaped from their saddles, subdued the guard, and shouted breathlessly to Lafayette to mount one of the horses and "Go-t'Hoff, Go-t'Hoff; we will follow." The carriage driver bounded forward to seek help and was well down the road, leaving Lafayette's two rescuers with but one horse to make their escape. Knowing he had less to fear than the German doctor if captured by the Austrians, Huger sent Bollmann off to Hoff, a small post on the German border, where a carriage was waiting to take them to safety in Germany. When Bollmann arrived, however, Lafayette was nowhere to be found. Lafayette had misunderstood the Huger-Bollmann chorus—"Go t'Hoff"—to mean "Go off; go off." So he raced "off," following the main road and missing the small lane that turned "to Hoff." Soldiers caught and arrested all three conspirators and threw them in irons in solitary dungeon cells at Olmütz. Believing they were part of an international political plot, the humiliated prison commander confronted Lafayette angrily and pledged that the two young men "will be hanged before your window, and I shall take pleasure in serving them as hangman." They were, in fact, sentenced to six months of hard labor and released.[16]

On January 22, 1795, after sixteen months' imprisonment without formal charges or trial, Adrienne Lafayette walked out the prison gates in Paris, firmly resolved to flee with her family to America's tranquil shores and escape forever the madness and savagery of France. She determined to smuggle George to his godfather in America immediately, to isolate him from his father's enemies. She would then go to Austria with her daughters and remain with Lafayette until his release permitted them to join their son. She went directly to the Monroe house on the rue de Clichy and asked his help in getting passports for her and the children. Six days later, Frestel arrived with fourteen-year-old George-Washington Lafayette, and a few weeks later, Monroe obtained government counterstamps on their passports for them to go to America, with the boy traveling as "George Motier." Adrienne gave Frestel a letter for President Washington written in French, which she hoped the American president would be able to read and understand:

> *Monsieur,*
>
> *Je vous envoie mon fils avec une confiance . . .*
>
> [Sir, I send you my son. . . . It is with deep and sincere confidence that I entrust this dear child to the protection of the United States (which he has long regarded as his second country and which I have long regarded as our sanctuary), and to the particular protection of their president, whose feelings towards the boy's father I well know.
>
> [The bearer of this letter, sir, has, during our troubles, been our support, our resource, our consolation, my son's guide. I want him to continue in that role. . . . I want them to remain inseparable until the day we have the joy of reuniting in the land of liberty. I owe my own life and those of my children to this man's generous attention. . . .
>
> [My wish is for my son to live in obscurity in America; that he resume the studies that three years of misfortune have interrupted, and that far from lands that might crush his spirit or arouse his violent indignation, he can work to fulfill the responsibilities of a citizen of the United States. . . .
>
> [I will say nothing here about my own circumstances, nor those of one for whom I feel far greater concern than I do for myself. I leave it to the friend who will present this letter to you to express the feelings of a heart which has suffered too much to be conscious of anything but gratitude, of which I owe much to Mr. Monroe. . . .
>
> [I beg you, Monsieur Washington, to accept my deepest sense of obligation, confidence, respect and devotion.]

As she had done since her husband's imprisonment, she signed it defiantly "Noailles Lafayette," to display proudly the two old noble names she bore.[17]

After a heartbreaking separation from her son, Adrienne went to Chavaniac to find her daughters and Lafayette's elderly aunt. To ensure her aunt a safe haven, she again drew, albeit reluctantly, on the Morris account to repurchase the château from the government. "It is true," she wrote to the American, "that this is a tiny obligation in comparison to the one I owe you for my very life, but permit me to acknowledge both debts, which I will always remember with feelings of warmth and gratitude."[18]

When Adrienne returned to Paris, the business and financial leaders who had survived the Robespierre massacres had seized the reins of government and written a new constitution that replaced Robespierre's "people's republic" with a "bourgeois republic." They restricted voting to taxpaying business and property owners and replaced the Declaration of the Rights of Man and the Citizen with a "Declaration of Rights *and Duties* of Citizens." The phrase "men are born free with equal rights" was missing. As one delegate explained, "If you say that all men are equal in rights you incite to revolt."[19] The constitution created a bicameral legislature—a Council of Five Hundred (les Cinq-Cents), or lower house, and a Council of Elders (les Anciens), or upper house—and it vested executive powers in a Directory of five members, each elected for five years by the legislature.

After returning to Paris with her daughters, Adrienne took advantage of the unsettled conditions in government to convince appropriate bureaucrats that neither she nor her mother had been emigrées—indeed that neither had ever left France. As such, she insisted, she was entitled as her mother's heir to recover ownership of La Grange, one of her mother's properties in Brie, about seventy-five miles east of Paris, with a once-magnificent château that dated back to the Crusades. Cannonballs from the Hundred Years' War lay embedded in its black, impregnable walls, and its enormous round towers looked over the nearby Yères and Ivron Rivers. Ten centuries of war and five years of revolution had left its interiors bare and its exterior in sad disrepair, but Adrienne saw it as a possible source of capital if property values increased and perhaps a harbor for the family if they ever returned to France.

On September 1, 1795, Monroe gave Adrienne an American passport bearing the name of Mrs. Motier of Hartford, Connecticut—the only American community that had indeed decreed her husband and his *entire* family citizens, not just his male heirs. She and the girls went to Dunkerque and boarded an American packet to Hamburg, Germany, and, a week later, stepped off, into the crushing embraces of Adrienne's sister Pauline and her beloved aunt, the comtesse de Tessé. The countess had fled France with enough jewelry, currency, and negotiable securities to acquire property in nearby Altona as a sanctuary for family friends and relatives. After only a few days rest, however, Adrienne shocked them all by announcing, "I am going to Olmütz."

On October 3, less than a month after leaving Paris, Adrienne and the girls were in Vienna, where her late grandfather, the marquis de Noailles, had once served as ambassador. One of his friends arranged for a private audience for her with Emperor Frederick II.

"We were with her," her daughter Virginie recalled. "She was received politely and asked permission only to share my father's prison cell. 'I consent,' the emperor replied, 'but as for his liberty, that will be impossible; my hands are tied.'" Fearful of finding Lafayette languishing in inhuman conditions, she asked the emperor's permission to write to him directly to ameliorate her husband's prison life. "I consent," the emperor said again. "But you will find Monsieur Lafayette well nourished, well treated. Your presence will add to his comfort. In addition, you will be pleased with the [prison] commandant. In our prisons we give our prisoners numbers, but every one knows your husband's name quite well."[20]

On the morning of October 15, Adrienne's carriage approached the forbidding towers of the Olmütz city wall and the prison entrance. An hour later, Lafayette heard bolts clanking, doors creaking and slamming; suddenly the door of his cell opened and there stood his wife and two daughters, as if in a dream. He had no warning they would come. Suddenly their arms enveloped his emaciated, nearly lifeless, and all but naked body. Behind them, the doors slammed shut and the four Lafayettes huddled together on the cold, damp floor, together again for the first time in more than three years. The emotion of the moment—and the stench of the sewerage flowing beneath his window, his cell pot, his own putrescence—all but overpowered them.

While they lay entangled in each other's arms, the guards searched the baggage of the new arrivals and confiscated everything of value—their purses and money, of course, and even the silver forks Adrienne had brought for their meals. Like Lafayette, the women learned to eat foul food with their fingers, all the while inhaling the suffocating fumes from the sewerage flowing below their window and the cell pots they used to relieve themselves. Too often, they heard the "horrible music"[21] of prisoners shrieking under the pain of flogging. As night fell, the guards reentered the cell and led the girls away to be locked in a separate, adjacent cell, where they shared a single wooden pallet for their rest while their mother lay on a similar device, cradling the skeletal remains of her knight in her arms.

Each day's routine was the same, Adrienne wrote to her aunt:

> They bring us breakfast at eight, after which they lock me up with my daughters until noon. We all meet for dinner, and except for two interruptions by the jailers coming for our dinner plates and bringing our supper later, they leave us together until eight o'clock, when my daughters are

returned to their cage. . . . We have more to eat than we need, but the food is indescribably filthy. . . . Each time they use keys . . . they go through the most ridiculous precautions. . . . While an officer who dares not speak to us without witnesses watches a fat corporal with a bunch of keys unlock our doors, the whole guard is drawn up in the passage and they can all see into our rooms when the doors are opened. You would laugh to see our two girls . . . one blushing to the tips of her ears, the other making a face that is sometimes proud, sometimes comic, as they pass beneath the crossed swords and into our room—the door to which is immediately locked. What is not pleasant is that the small courtyard beyond the passage is the scene of all-too-frequent floggings. . . . We can hear the whole horrible procedure.[22]

Overwhelmed by the satanic surroundings, Adrienne asked to see the prison commander, who, the emperor had assured her, "would please me. The guards told me he was forbidden to have contact with me, but that I might write to him. I asked three things: 1st, to attend mass on Sundays with my daughters, 2nd to have a soldier's wife clean their cell, 3rd, to be cared for by Monsieur de Lafayette's two servants from the army [who were still imprisoned]. He never replied; I asked to write to the emperor; they refused, but said my requests to the commander had been sent to the proper authorities in Vienna."[23] More than two months later, two days after Christmas, Adrienne received a reply from the Austrian minister of war: "I am not in a position to defer to your requests, despite my desire to do so. I can only remind you that you consented to share your husband's fate, and it will not now be possible to alter your situation."[24] She wrote again and again and received nothing but the same curt reply: "The Council of War and I cannot defer to any demands by prisoners of state."[25]

The guards did, however, let Adrienne and the girls keep their books, and they gave them writing materials—a tactical error that would let them describe their plight to the rest of the world. Adrienne, of course, gave the girls daily school lessons and religious instruction; Lafayette read to them and lectured on the United States and other favorite topics. They kept active in other ways: Adrienne and Virginie replaced the rags that barely covered Lafayette's skeletal torso with clothes they made from parts of their skirts, and Anastasie fashioned a pair of shoes for him from Adrienne's corset. And they all wrote and wrote. He made notes for political tracts and paeans to American liberty and republican government. Adrienne wrote a touching biography of her mother, the duchesse d'Ayen, and Virginie followed her mother's example by writing an equally moving biography of Adrienne.[26] Adrienne coaxed the prison commander to let her write to specific family members, whom she had to identify with each letter to obtain approval. He read every word she wrote. He rejected a letter to her son, to prevent a description of Olmütz from reaching America and embarrassing the Austrian government. Europeans accepted the horrors of prison dungeons with far more equanimity than Americans, who had not yet built such institutions and considered public humiliation in the stocks harsh enough punishment for most crimes. So Adrienne wrote instead to her sister Pauline and to her aunt, the comtesse de Tessé, and they, in turn, forwarded descriptions of the Prisoners of Olmütz to increasingly noisy Fayettistes in England, France, and the United States who demanded the Lafayettes' release.

The Lafayettes received occasional news from the outside world. In a severely censored letter from Pauline, Adrienne learned that her son had arrived safely in Boston in September. What she did not know was that her son's arrival plunged his godfather, the American president, into a potentially embarrassing political and diplomatic situation that posed dangers to the Lafayette family. Earlier that summer, the American Senate had ratified a treaty with Britain expanding trade and giving America's former oppressor most-favored-nation trade status. The treaty infuriated the French government, which saw it as an abrogation of their own treaty of amity and commerce with the United States. In Paris, the French foreign minister threatened to seize American ships bound to and from Britain, and Washington recalled American ambassador Monroe, who had been instrumental in obtaining Adrienne's release from prison. If, in addition, Washington publicly offered sanctuary to Lafayette's son in the American capital, the French government would almost certainly interpret it as a direct insult and a hostile act.

In addition to the diplomatic hazards in Philadelphia, there were health hazards. The capital was at the epicenter of the worst yellow fever epidemic in American history; it had killed as much as 10 percent of the population from New York to Norfolk, Virginia, but had spared Boston and most of New England. Washington decided to leave the boy in New England until the government recessed later in the year and he could move to Mount Vernon with little or no fanfare. To fulfill Adrienne's wish that George "resume his studies . . . in obscurity," Washington asked Massachusetts senator George Cabot to enroll young Lafayette incognito at Harvard College, "the expense of which as also of every other means for his support, I will pay." In a letter marked "private and confidential," Washington gave Cabot

> the most unequivocal assurance of my standing in the place and becoming to him a father, friend, protector and supporter . . . my friendship for his father has increased in the ratio of his misfortune . . . [but] for prudential motives, as they may relate to himself, his mother and friends, whom he has left behind, and to my official character, it would be best not to make these sentiments public; and of course it would be ineligible that he should

come to the seat of government where all the foreign characters (particularly those of his own nation) are residents, until it is seen what opinion will be excited by his arrival. . . . Let me in a few words declare that I *will be his friend,* but the manner of becoming so considering the obnoxious light in which his father is viewed by the French Government, and my own situation as the Executive of the United States requires more time to consider in all its relations.[27]

Washington also wrote to his godson: "To begin to fulfill my role of father, I advise you to apply yourself seriously to your studies. Your youth should be usefully employed, in order that you may deserve in all respects to be considered as the worthy son of your illustrious father."[28]

By the time Lafayette began his studies, Bollman and Huger had arrived in America, met with Washington, and described the abortive Lafayette escape and the horrors of Olmütz prison. By then, the saga of Adrienne's devotion to her husband, the injustice of his imprisonment, and the atrocity of two little girls languishing in prison had become the stuff of legend. *The Prisoners of Olmütz, or Conjugal Devotion* played to packed theaters in Paris and London; newspapers published epic poems such as "The Captivity of La Fayette":

> Within this gloomy prison, the prototype of Hell,
> For [three] [four] [five]* years bowed beneath the weight of chains,
> Forgotten in the world of man, the world of nature,
> Here in the depths where light scarce penetrates,
> Thus am I forced relentlessly to suffer pains
> And die piecemeal, before the eyes of my oppressor.[29]

The Lafayettes became the subject of heated debates in the French legislature, the British Parliament, and the American Congress. Because of the American policy of neutrality, Congress rejected a resolution declaring the American government's "ardent wish for his deliverance."[30] In London, Prime Minister Pitt, who had dined at Lafayette's house in Paris a decade earlier, refused to debate the issue and asked a political aide to reply: "Those who start revolutions will always be, in my eyes, the object of an irresistible reprobation. I take delight in seeing them drink to the dregs the cup of human bitterness that they have prepared for the lips of others."[31]

Early in 1796, three months of foul air, water, and food took its toll on Adrienne's health: she developed a fever; her arms and legs swelled; painful

---

*The number changed annually.

blisters punctuated the swellings. The prison doctor urged her to seek help from specialists in Vienna, and she wrote to the emperor for permission. In the seven weeks that followed, her fever worsened. Irritated by the harsh wooden pallet, her blisters erupted one by one and amalgamated into large, oozing ulcerations. The prison commander refused her the comforts of a chair or mattress, offering only straw, which he knew would intensify her pain and, he hoped, allow him to rid the prison of her embarrassing presence. In April, the emperor agreed to let her come to Vienna for medical help, but, he warned, once she left her prison cell, he would not allow her to return.

"The price of my health care," she replied defiantly, "is not acceptable. I have not forgotten that while we faced death—I from Robespierre's tyranny, Monsieur de Lafayette from the moral and physical sufferings of his imprisonment—his children and I were unable to obtain any news about him nor was he able to learn whether we were still even alive. I will not again expose myself to such horrors by another separation.

"Whatever the state of my health and the discomfort for my daughters, we will share every moment of this imprisonment with full appreciation for His Majesty's kindness."[32] And, as usual, she signed her letter with the aristocratic signature "Noailles Lafayette." As Lafayette would later write of her with pride, "What a brave, but foolish heart to remain almost the only woman in France compromised by her name who refused to change it."[33]

Adrienne's illness worsened, with swelling and edema depriving her of motion in both arms. Fever plunged her into long periods of restless sleep. When she awoke and saw her husband and daughters hovering about her anxiously, a smile inevitably crossed her face. "Despite her suffering," Virginie recalled, "she seemed happier than she had ever been. It is hard for me to describe how happy she was. To understand, you have to recognize the fear she had lived with for so long—during the frequent separations and endless adventures that took my father away from home into great danger. She had spent the previous three horrible years almost without hope of ever finding him again. Now her lifelong dream was fulfilled. Each day, she saw the influence of her presence on my father's health and all the comfort her presence provided him. She was surprised to recover her ability to feel so happy and even felt somewhat guilty knowing that it came at the expense of keeping my father prisoner."[34]

Adrienne's illness—and her bold refusal to abandon her husband—raised the level of worldwide debate over the Prisoners of Olmütz to fever pitch. Even President Washington, the apostle of American neutrality, abandoned diplomatic discretion. He was in the last year of his second term as president and planned to retire. Dispensing with diplomatic caution, he sent a personal note instructing Pinckney in London "to make known to the

Austrian Ambassador" the American president's desire to see his friend Lafayette set free. "I need hardly mention how much my sensibility has been hurt by the treatment this Gentleman has met with; or how anxious I am to see him liberated therefrom."[35] In May, he ignored the lack of formal diplomatic relations with Austria and sent a personal, handwritten letter to the Austrian emperor:

> It will readily occur to your Majesty that occasions may sometimes exist, on which official considerations would constrain the Chief of a Nation to be silent and passive, in relation to objects which affect his sensibility, and claim his interposition, as a man. Finding myself precisely in this situation at present, I take the liberty of writing this *private* letter to Your Majesty, being persuaded that my motives will also be my apology for it.
>
> In common with the People of this Country, I retain a strong and cordial sense of the services rendered to them by the Marquis de la Fayette; and my friendship for him has been constant and sincere. It is natural therefore that I should sympathize with him and his family in their misfortunes, and endeavor to mitigate the calamities which they experience, among which his present confinement is not the least distressing.
>
> I forbear to enlarge on this delicate subject. Permit me only to submit to your majesty's consideration whether his long imprisonment and the confiscation of his Estate and the indigence and dispersion of his family— and the painful anxieties incident to all these circumstances, do not form an assemblage of sufferings, which recommend him to the mediation of Humanity? Allow me, Sir! on this occasion to be its organ; and to ask that he may be permitted to come to this country, on such conditions and under such restrictions, as your Majesty may think it expedient to prescribe.[36]

A torrent of letters flowed to Vienna, from England as well as America, from political leaders, men and women of letters, and ordinary citizens, but, like Washington's letter, they had no effect—and Adrienne's health continued to deteriorate by the day. "Because of the condition of my blood and the excessively unsanitary conditions of this prison," she wrote to Robert Parish, the American consul at Hamburg, "my arms have been for some time unbelievably swollen, and my fingers incapable of movement. . . . My skin is peeling. . . . The pain, the impossibility of my closing my hands, and the spasms in my whole nervous system make my life more than a little disagreeable."[37]

Under increasing pressure from the American public, Congress instructed Gouverneur Morris to go to Vienna to negotiate Lafayette's release. He reached Vienna in September, but waited three months before the Austrian chancellor granted him an interview, prefacing it with a disdainful statement that Morris had no standing at court. Austria, he grumbled, would not negotiate with a nation with which it had no diplomatic ties and which was an ally of France, with whom Austria was at war. He did, however, admit that Lafayette's situation had become an embarrassment—and noted that England was Austria's ally. "If England were to ask us for Lafayette," he declared, "we would be all too happy to rid ourselves of him."[38] Knowing that Adrienne's condition was worsening, Morris rushed word to London Fayettistes, who forced a vote in Parliament—but lost, 132 to 52.

The saga of the Prisoners of Olmütz continued into the new year— behind the dungeon walls in Austria and in the pages of periodicals in the world beyond. Fayettistes were gaining more influence in the French legislature and in the salons of power. "We must return La Fayette to France and to the Republic," Madame de Staël, the renowned French author, wrote to a member of the Directory. "I guarantee that he will be the best citizen—after you, of course."[39] In May 1797, the Directory yielded, deciding it could enhance its own popular support by freeing the Prisoners of Olmütz. It instructed Napoléon Bonaparte, commander in chief of the French army in Italy, to demand Lafayette's release in peace discussions then under way between Austria and France. Napoléon's army had humiliated Austrian forces in Italy, seized Venice, and encamped seventy miles away from Vienna, poised to capture the capital and crush the rest of Austria. "Obtain, as a condition, if you can, the freedom of La Fayette, Bureaux de Pusy and La Tour-Maubourg," said the order to Bonaparte. "The national honor is at stake in their release from prison, where they are held only because they started the [French] Revolution."[40]

The French demand was nothing short of blackmail. Napoléon was not a man to be denied. With each conquest, he exacted reparations that covered French military costs and not only enriched France but stripped the nations he conquered of their wealth. Envisioning a French guillotine in the courtyard of the magnificent Schönbrunn Palace and all its art transferred to the Louvre in Paris, the Austrian emperor sued for peace. On July 24, an Austrian officer arrived at Olmütz from Vienna and entered Lafayette's cell with a court decree: "Because Monsieur de Lafayette is regarded as author of a new doctrine whose principles are incompatible with the tranquillity of the Austrian monarch, His Majesty the emperor and king owes it to reasons of state not to restore his freedom until he pledges not to return to Austrian territory without special permission of the emperor."[41]

Lafayette all but laughed: "The emperor does me honor by treating me as one power to another and by believing that as a simple individual I am so strong a threat to a vast monarchy with so many armies and devoted subjects." Lafayette rejected the emperor's terms, saying he had been arrested and imprisoned illegally. "I have no wish ever again to set foot in the court of the emperor or in his country even with his permission, but I owe it to my principles to refuse to recognize that the Austrian government has any right over me." Moreover, he demanded that the Austrians release his comrades La Tour-Maubourg and Bureaux de Pusy and their aides.[42]

Lafayette's intransigence was ill-timed and almost cost him, his family, and his friends years of additional imprisonment. A royalist counterrevolution had broken out again in France, and Napoléon pulled a division of troops from the Austrian front and returned to France to crush internal dissent. His emissary broke off negotiations for Lafayette's release to await further instructions. Before returning to Austria, Napoléon helped stage a coup d'état that replaced the Directory with a three-man junta that added political powers to Napoléon's military powers. At Napoléon's suggestion, the "New Directory" decreed five years of universal compulsory military service for all twenty-year-old men in France. The decree not only expanded the army and gave Napoléon free rein to conquer foreign lands, it removed the most rebellious elements from the streets of French cities and scattered them across the face of Europe, where they could no longer threaten the French government.[43]

When negotiations resumed for Lafayette's release, the new French régime made it clear he was no more welcome in France than in Austria. His fervor for constitutional, republican rule threatened the New Directory as much as it had the Austrian emperor. Napoléon himself saw Lafayette as a threat to his own growing popularity. The French and the Austrians soon agreed that the solution lay in exiling Lafayette from Europe in America. They opened negotiations with Robert Parish, the American consul at Hamburg, then an independent city state with commercial ties to the United States and an important funnel for American trade to midcontinent countries like Prussia and Austria with no formal relations with the United States. Gouverneur Morris was in Hamburg on business and helped Parish negotiate America's agreement to receive "the entire caravan of La Fayettes, wife, children and their companions" at the consulate and assure their departure within twelve days—presumably to America.[44]

On September 19, 1797, five years and a month after the Austrians had taken Lafayette prisoner and twenty-three months after Adrienne, Anastasie, and Virginie had joined him, an Austrian major led the Lafayette family and their friends out of Olmütz on the road to Hamburg, four hundred miles to the northwest. Crowds hailed them along the way with cheers, flowers, and expressions of sympathy. Messengers intercepted them with pleas from Paris Fayettistes to return and seize power from the Directory. "I might have exploited popular enthusiasm, the devotion of the National Guard and all that for my own profit," he recalled, but he was unwilling to violate his principles by seizing power unconstitutionally.[45]

Two weeks later, the caravan reached the banks of the Elbe River, across from Hamburg. To his and his family's amazement, American ships clogged the harbor, with flags flying high in his honor. An American captain invited them to dine on board, and it was late afternoon before American sailors rowed them from the ship to the Hamburg side of the river. Robert Parish stood in front of a cheering crowd to greet them and lead them to the con-sulate, where the two Lafayettes collapsed on a sofa and sobbed uncontrol-lably. The French knight seemed a broken man. When he finally found the strength to stand, he embraced Parish and sobbed, "My friend, my dearest friend, my deliverer! See the work of your generosity. My poor, poor wife." Prison life had eroded Adrienne's beauty and aristocratic bearing. She had not yet turned forty, but her hair had grayed, the hauteur of her cheeks and forehead had collapsed; her once-graceful alabaster limbs had swollen out of shape into thick, scarlet, scabrous appendages. Moved to tears himself, Parish retreated to his study and sent word to Morris, who came with the Austrian minister to effect the official transfer of the prisoners to American custody.[46]

The Lafayettes had little rest during the few days permitted them in Hamburg. Lafayette, Maubourg, and Pusy visited the French consul, who offered them Foreign Minister Talleyrand's promise of passports to France if they pledged allegiance to the New Directory. Once a member of Lafayette's liberal Society of Thirty, the wily chameleon had survived the Terror by fleeing to America, where he made a small fortune speculating in finance before returning to France to serve Napoléon. Lafayette and the others sent a dutiful message of thanks to Napoléon:

> Citizen general,
>
> The prisoners of Olmütz, fortunate in owing their deliverance to the benevolence of their nation and to your irresistible military strength, rejoiced, while in captivity, in the knowledge that their liberty and their lives were tied to the victories of the Republic and to your personal glory. Today, they rejoice in the homage they wish to pay to their liberator.[47]

After signing the letter with the others, Lafayette remained true to his principles, however, and refused to swear allegiance to the new government, which had come to power by unconstitutional means. Infuriated by Lafa-yette's rejection, Talleyrand ordered Lafayette's lands in Brittany, hitherto untouched, sold at public auction. At forty-one, Lafayette was not only deeply in debt, but the sale of his last properties left him a pauper, without income, without property, and without a country.

After nearly two weeks, Adrienne was still too weak and ill to voyage to America, and the Lafayette caravan crossed into Denmark, where, fifty miles to the north, Adrienne's aunt, the comtesse de Tessé, had purchased a large estate at Witmold, on the north shore of Lake Ploën. Adrienne's sister Pauline and her husband, who had fled to England during the Terror, had joined the countess and were waiting when the Lafayettes arrived—as were surviving members of the La Tour-Maubourg and Bureaux de Pusy families. To Adrienne's distress, one surviving member of the Noailles family was absent: her father, the duc d'Ayen—now the duc de Noailles, since his father's death. Still in exile in Switzerland, he sent his daughter a clumsy, almost distant letter that only added to her pain when he explained the reason for his absence: he had remarried. The new duchesse de Noailles sent a note welcoming Adrienne back from prison and expressing hope that her father's remarriage would not pain her. Too devout a Roman Catholic to countenance her father's remarriage—and too devoted to her mother—Adrienne was devastated and replied in uncharacteristically bitter tones:

"You must have foreseen, my dear Papa, how torn my heart would be on receiving your letter . . . it is by making myself one with my mother that I maintain my strength. There is no circumstance in my life which brings me closer to her than in sending my every wish for your happiness." In a postscript, she added these words to her father's new wife: "Duchess, you have well judged the deep and painful impression made upon my heart by your letter and by my father's, an impression which will remain as ineffaceable as my regrets."[48] Adrienne and her father would never see each other again.

During the ensuing days, the families shared hours of joyful rest and play—and too many hours of tear-filled tales of family tragedies during the Terror. After a month, the Lafayettes had regained enough strength to move into a place of their own, with more spacious quarters for themselves and the girls, and a quiet study for Lafayette in which he could add his memoirs to those of previous generations of the world's fallen, forgotten heroes. Adrienne remained weak and ill, however. Her daughters tried to comfort her, but she spent much of the day praying and weeping softly at the constant vision of her grandmother, mother, and sister riding the wooden cart to their deaths.

After a sober holiday celebration, bitter January winds from the Baltic Sea whirled about the gray stone château; eddies of mist sped by, metamorphosing into ghastly specters of relatives and friends in the grips of the Terror. Lake Ploën froze into a thick, impenetrable black block and reduced the once-joyous landscape into a silent congregation of dark, leafless trees, mourning autumns past and patiently awaiting future springs.

Then, in February, a blinding burst of sunshine exploded through the mournful winter shroud:

It was George; George had returned from America.

After the riot of embraces and kisses had subsided, George handed his father a letter:

Mount Vernon, 8 October 1797.

My dear Marquis,

This letter will, I hope, be presented to you by your son, who is worthy in every way to be your son and that of your amiable Lady. . . . The conduct of your son since he set foot on American soil has been exemplary and has earned him the trust of all who have had the pleasure of knowing him. . . . He can tell you better than I how I felt about your sufferings. . . . I hasten to congratulate you, and you may rest assured that no one does so with a deeper or more ardent affection than I. Every act of your life gives you the right to rejoice over the liberty you have recovered as well as restoration of the confidence of your nation, and if the possession of these gifts cannot recompense you entirely for the wrongs you have suffered, they will at least ease the painful memory. . . .

Mr. Frestel has been a real mentor for George; a father could not have been more attentive to an adored son, and he richly deserves the highest praise for his virtue, his good judgment and his prudence. . . . Your son and he carry with them the wishes and a sense of loss of our family [and] all who know them.

Rest assured that at no time have you ranked higher in the esteem of this nation. . . . If pleasant memories or circumstances bring you back to visit America with your Lady and your daughters, none of its inhabitants will receive you with more respect and affection than Mrs. Washington and myself; our hearts are filled with affection and admiration for you and them.[49]

19

Resurrection

LAFAYETTE HAD NOT SEEN his son for six years. George had just turned nineteen, the same age as Lafayette when he first sailed for America. George had spent two and a half years in America, with his tutor, the faithful Félix Frestel, always at his side—initially at Cambridge, then a few weeks with Alexander Hamilton in New York, before going to the Washingtons in Mount Vernon after the president's retirement. On his return to France, George first went to Paris, where he found only the blackened stone shell of his beautiful boyhood home on the rue de Bourbon. His father's supporters arranged an audience to plead with Napoléon to end his father's exile, but Napoléon had left to inspect the troops, and his wife, Joséphine, received the handsome young man instead. Recognizing the advantages of cloaking her husband's ambitions in Fayettiste republicanism, she received the boy with much fanfare, declaring, "Your father and my husband must make common cause."[1]

George's arrival in Holstein revived the spirits of all three exiled families. "At last, my dear aunt, our wonderful George is with us," Lafayette wrote to Aunt Charlotte at Chavaniac, "and I can assure you we are more than pleased with him. He is perfect physically: tall, with a noble and charming face. His temperament is all that we could wish. He has the same kind heart that you remember, and his mind is far more mature than is usual for his age."[2] Virginie was as excited as her parents. "My brother is grown so tall," she wrote to Aunt Charlotte, "that when he arrived we could scarcely recognize him, but we have found all those qualities in him that we always knew. He is just as good a brother as he was at Chavaniac. He is so like Papa that people in the streets can see immediately that he is his son."[3]

When the first birds and buds of spring returned in 1798, Charles de La Tour-Maubourg, one of two younger brothers of Lafayette's fellow prisoner at Olmütz, asked for twenty-year-old Anastasie's hand. Except for Lafayette and Adrienne, members of the two families seemed shocked: the Revolution had made paupers of the two youngsters; he had no assets or income to support her; she had no dowry. The comtesse de Tessé argued that it would be the first such marriage since Adam and Eve.

Lafayette and Adrienne, however, were overjoyed. "When I think of the horrible situation of my children not long ago," said Adrienne, "when I see all three of them about me and I am about to adopt a fourth after my own heart, I cannot thank God enough."[4]

Early in May, Charles and Anastasie were married at Witmold; the comtesse de Tessé provided a trousseau and the wedding feast. Adrienne all but collapsed with fever on the morning of the wedding; ugly abscesses reappeared on her arms and legs and made it impossible for her to walk. She refused to postpone the wedding, however, and George and Charles carried her into the elegant grand salon at Witmold and placed her on a couch to watch the ceremony.

Spring air and sunshine—and the joy she saw in Anastasie's face—improved Adrienne's health, although residual edema in her legs left her limping noticeably. Though less than sound physically, she was sound enough mentally to recognize that her family could not remain in exile indefinitely without income, living off the goodness of her aunt. With Lafayette barred from France, America seemed their only refuge. "The Americans still owe Gilbert the land he refused to accept at the end of the war," Adrienne explained to Aunt Charlotte. "He agrees that it would be only reasonable now to take the gift then offered."[5] The Lafayettes, however, did not have "enough money to keep the family six months [in America],"[6] and she said that as soon as she was well she would go to Paris to reclaim and sell as much as possible of the Noailles properties to raise cash for the trip and subsequent expenses.

To prepare their way in America, Lafayette wrote to his friend Alexander Hamilton, who had served as Washington's secretary of treasury and had since become New York's foremost attorney and most powerful political leader. Hamilton's reply was devastating. The United States and France, Hamilton explained, were in an undeclared war with each other. President John Adams had recalled Washington from retirement to his former post as commander in chief of American armed forces and appointed Hamilton inspector general to lead the army in the field. Congress created a standing army of fifteen thousand men to repel a French invasion; it had strengthened state militias and created a new Navy department to build three frigates and arm all merchant ships. Hamilton wrote that among "the sad results of the Revolution, I was most disappointed by the disputes that developed between our two nations and that seem to portend a complete rupture in relations. . . . I never believed that France could become a republic, and I am convinced the longer the effort continued, the more miseries it would bring." He assured Lafayette that "my friendship for you will survive all revolutions" and that "no one believes more than I how much our nation should love you," but concluded, "In the present state of our affairs with France, I cannot insist that you come here."[7]

Hamilton's letter left Lafayette without a plan for his family's future. Adrienne had left for Paris with Virginie, Anastasie, and Charles, to raise funds for their voyage. Isolated as he was in Holstein, he could not be aware of the depth of American furor toward France, and his years in prison left him living in an earlier world when French and American interests were one. The undeclared war had started after the Directory sent French privateers to prey on American ships in retaliation for the refusal of the United States to join France at war with Britain. French agents in the United States once again provoked anti-British riots, and the French ambassador violated diplomatic protocol by actively campaigning against the election of President Adams, who reiterated Washington's policy of neutrality and supported trade with Britain. After his election, Adams sent emissaries to Paris to negotiate an end to French depredations, but Foreign Minister Talleyrand sent three agents—known infamously as agents X, Y, and Z—to demand a bribe of 50,000 livres as his personal price for negotiating. The Americans angrily rebuffed the demand, Talleyrand threatened war, and America, led by Adams and his Federalist Party, accepted the challenge.

"The friendship of France," wrote New York's Federalist editor, Noah Webster, "is to be dreaded by the citizens of the United States as the most dangerous mischief. Her *enmity* alone can save us from ruin . . . instead of respecting the rights of other nations, the French government has invaded, conquered, and annexed to France the little helpless republic of Geneva. She has conquered a part of the Swiss cantons . . . Holland is enslaved . . . , Genoa. . . . Venice has been annihilated—divided and sold!!! So much for her promised respect which France was to pay to the 'independence of other nations,' as far as it respects Europe. The people of America . . . do not wish for friendly intercourse with a nation which practices such cowardly acts on our national happiness."[8]

After receiving Hamilton's letter, Lafayette appealed to Washington: "I have the impression that [Hamilton] fears that the unfortunate discord between the two republics will create some difficulties for me. . . . You know too well, my dear general, that my affection for America, my sense of duty to her, make America's shores the only appropriate place for me to retire."[9] He pleaded with Washington to intervene personally in the Franco-American dispute, saying he was convinced that the French government wanted nothing but peace with its old ally.

When Adrienne and the others reached the French border, authorities refused them entry because of Charles's status as an émigré. Charles and Anastasie turned back to Utrecht, Holland, to find lodgings, while Adrienne and Virginie continued to Paris with the added burden of getting her son-in-law's name scratched from the émigré list. With limited funds and no family left in the French capital, Adrienne was alone with her daughter in a city that the Noailles family had all but ruled only a few years earlier. She turned to her former personal maid, the devoted Marie-Josèphe Beauchet, who had written and offered "a very comfortable room where . . . you will find a warm fire, a comfortable bed. Madame, allow me to beg you, in the name of all those feelings which attach me so closely to you to take up your residence with us. . . . You will find in me an eager waiting maid, a cook with whom you will find no fault, and a secretary of intelligence who is eager to serve you . . . and you will be close at hand to the Directory."[10] It was an offer that reflected the love Adrienne inspired in others and one that Adrienne could not afford to refuse. Her former maid had done well for herself, had married a well-placed civil servant, and lived in a small house on the rue de l'Université, a pleasant street not far from where the Lafayettes had lived before the Jacobin destruction.

Adrienne set about her tasks the following morning, with sixteen-year-old Virginie at her side. Her weighty, edematous legs moved slowly over the uneven paving stones, each painful limp shunting her from side to side as she made her way to ministry after ministry, up and down endless flights of stairs, waiting hours on hallway benches for the chance to ask, argue with, beg, or bribe faceless clerks and officials to recover her rightful inheritance. But the answer was always the same: a shrug of regret and another form to fill for submission to another clerk at another ministry, across another courtyard, up another staircase to another hallway bench. The futile exercise continued until the end of the year—and, ironically, actually helped her rebuild strength and recover her health, if not her lands.

In January, Lafayette received a letter from Washington that was even more discouraging than Hamilton's. By then, Congress had formally repealed all its treaties with France, and the two nations had stepped up their

Almost two years of prison aged
Adrienne de Lafayette prematurely,
graying her hair and leaving her
arms so swollen that she could
barely raise them. After months of
rest in Scandinavia, she improved
enough to go to Paris to try to
recover the family's properties that
the Jacobins had confiscated during
the revolution. (*From the author's
collection.*)

undeclared naval war to all-out naval hostilities. Washington tried to explain
the American position:

> While [French] agents constantly uttered the word peace and pretended
> that they did not want to involve us in their quarrel with Great Britain,
> they took steps here which would inevitably lead to war. . . . They were
> guilty of violating treaties, international law and all the rules of justice and
> decency. But they fooled only themselves . . . for once the citizens of this
> country recognized the nature of the quarrel [with France], they rose up as
> one, they offered their services, their lives, their fortunes to defend the
> government they had chosen. . . . They have pledged, if the French should
> try to invade . . . to repel such an attack.
>   You mentioned that the Directory is disposed to resolve our differ-
> ences. . . . If that is the case, let them prove so with deeds! Simple words
> will have no effect at present. . . . The tactic of France . . . has been to
> assume that those who work for peace acted because of ties to Great
> Britain. You can rest assured that this assertion rests on no foundation and
> has no other goal but to excite public clamor against men of peace. . . .
> Once harmony is restored with France, no one would receive you with
> more open arms and more ardent affection than I. But it would be less than
> honest and altogether contrary to the friendship that I have for you to
> say that I want you to arrive before then . . . the scenes you would witness,

the role you might be forced to play . . . would place you in an untenable position. . . .

I hope Madame de Lafayette will succeed on her voyage to France, and that she will return in a better state of health. Please accept my congratulations on the marriage of your older daughter. Give them both and Virginia my most affectionate regards. I have written to George; Mrs. Washington joins me, as would the rest of the family if they were here. We wish you all the blessings that this life can offer, in compensation for your sufferings.

I would add what you already know, that it is with the most sincere friendship and the warmest esteem, that I remain, etc.

"G. Washington."[11]

Lafayette was crestfallen; Washington's letter shattered his dream of becoming an American in the land whose liberty he had helped assure. The two nations he loved most—his native land and his adopted land—had both rejected him. Overwhelmed by loneliness, he longed for Adrienne and his daughters. Anastasie was expecting her first child in February, and Charles had leased a country house at Vianen, not far from Utrecht. With the help of a member of the Directory who had been a Fayettiste, Adrienne was able to get Lafayette a passport to Holland, and the family reunited at Vianen a few weeks before Anastasie gave birth to twin girls—Lafayette's first grandchildren.

In May, Lafayette accepted the inevitable and replied to Washington: "Your opinion, my dear general, is as it has always been for me, an immense influence. I know your paternal heart cannot wait to embrace me, and yet you turn me away from the voyage that would give us both so much pleasure."[12] In fact, the undeclared war between the United States and France had intensified—as had the wars, both undeclared and declared, between France and just about every other nation in the Atlantic, European, and Mediterranean worlds. Although the American navy had fought the French to a stalemate by trading victories in the Caribbean and Atlantic, other nations were less fortunate. The French had swept down the Italian peninsula through Rome and Naples, while the French fleet in the Mediterranean had seized Malta from the British and carried Napoléon's armies into Egypt.

Adrienne returned to Paris, this time with George, who, she believed, might intimidate government clerks more than Virginie. With Anastasie still nursing her twins, Lafayette had little to do but plant a cottage garden and relive the past. He had not realized how dependent he had grown on Adrienne in prison: "I am sad and all alone," he wrote to her, "and even though this separation is no different from last year it takes less to make me feel pained. I am already impatient to see you and impatient for our reunion. . . .

I hope it will not be three months before you return. . . . Adieu, my darling Adrienne, my heart longs for you, worships you, and loves you tenderly."[13]

Without George to prod him, Lafayette lost patience with his *Mémoires*—struggling to remember what he may have said or written, never certain, and, in the end, always writing the same, long, tiresome paean for American liberty. Even he now realized that the ruthless advance of French forces was as unrelated to the rights of man and the French Revolution he had fostered as the French crusades had been to Christianity at the beginning of the millennium. Napoléon and the French armies were enslaving every conquered people, converting each nation into vassal states and looting their treasure. Boatloads of gold, silver, jewelry, tapestries, statuary, paintings, and other stolen treasure sailed into French harbors from all parts of the Mediterranean. Paris became the greatest repository of stolen European, Egyptian, and Middle Eastern art in the world.

By mid-1799, Adrienne had become so adept at law—and in bureaucratic thinking—that she reacquired full ownership of La Grange, along with a French passport and restoration of citizenship for her son-in-law, Charles de La Tour-Maubourg, and his brother Victor. George returned to Vianen to look after his father, whose loneliness for his wife had turned to despondency: "I was thinking very sadly but tenderly of you the day before yesterday, my dear Adrienne, when suddenly George entered my room. . . . When will we see the entire family together again?

"George and I have spent the time since yesterday planning a farm for you; either in the beautiful Shenandoah Valley, in the back country of the state of Virginia, not far from *Federal-City* and Mount Vernon, or in the beautiful prairies of New England, within reach of Boston, for which you know my predilection."[14]

On September 6, 1799, Lafayette turned forty-two, and two weeks later reminded Adrienne, "It is two years today, dear Adrienne, since we left the prison to which you came, bringing me consolation and life. . . . How can we arrange our spending the winter together?"[15]

Unfortunately, the recovery of her title to La Grange did not end Adrienne's work in Paris; she still faced the task of removing her husband's name from the list of émigrés, restoring his citizenship and titles to his lands. In mid-October Bonaparte returned to France with another shipload of looted art. All Paris turned out to cheer his arrival, and, while he bathed buoyantly in adulation, Adrienne stepped forward smartly and offered to add to his laurels by personally presenting the collective praises of the Prisoners of Olmütz if he would grant her an audience to do so. It was an offer he could not resist. Now a master politician, Adrienne arrived with seventeen-year-old Virginie dressed to perfection as a picture of abused innocence. After presenting her compliments, Adrienne elicited the pronouncement she had sought: "Your husband's life," Bonaparte declared, "is bound to the preservation of the republic."[16]

Adrienne sent Lafayette an urgent message to dispatch an obsequious letter to Napoléon—immediately! Ironically, it was she who now commanded the family's struggles: she managed the family's finances; she, not Lafayette, was in touch with the world's political and social realities. "Here is my letter for Bonaparte," he answered obediently. "I have followed your advice about making it short."

"My love of liberty and our nation," Lafayette wrote to Bonaparte, "would have been enough to fill me with joy and hope at your arrival in France. To my concern for the public good, I add an enthusiastic and profound appreciation for my liberator. The welcome that you gave the prisoners of Olmütz has been reported to me by her whose life I owe to you; I rejoice in my obligations to you, Citizen General, and in the happy conviction that to applaud your glory and hope for your success is a civic duty as well as an act of attachment and gratitude."[17]

Although he followed Adrienne's advice to the letter, he still lived in the past, with visions of a France that would never be: "Meanwhile, my darling Adrienne," he asked pathetically, "what should I do . . . to lend my influence . . . to reestablish the doctrine of liberty?"[18]

Adrienne's sense of timing could not have been better. On November 9, ten days after she delivered her husband's letter to Bonaparte, the Corsican staged another coup d'état, suspending the constitution, dismissing the legislature, and establishing dictatorial rule under a three-man, Roman-style Consulate, with himself as First Consul. Of the previous government, only the political chameleon Talleyrand remained at his post as foreign affairs minister. The quick-thinking Adrienne took advantage of the confusion in other ministries, however, to obtain a passport with an assumed name for her husband and sent a family friend racing north to Holland with instructions to return to France immediately.

"A couple of hours later I was on my way," Lafayette wrote in his memoirs.[19]

After he arrived in Paris, Adrienne urged him to notify Bonaparte and Talleyrand. Bonaparte flew into a rage, and Talleyrand demanded that Lafayette return to Holland immediately, but Adrienne believed the two were simply posing. She recognized it would be too impolitic even for Bonaparte to discard the political benefits as "liberator of the Prisoners of Olmütz" by expelling Lafayette—especially while trying to consolidate his control of a shaky new government that had seized power illegally. To solidify his own political foundation, Napoléon needed, above all, to reconcile the feuding political factions that divided France—royalists, Jacobins, and Fayettiste republicans. All could still organize enough street riots to threaten almost any government. Adrienne offered Bonaparte a diplomatic solution he could not refuse. Lafayette would pledge his support to Bonaparte, then disappear from public life and retire to obscurity as a gentleman farmer at the Noailles family's Château de La Grange, in the isolated countryside of Brie, seventy-five miles east of Paris.

Bonaparte saluted Adrienne's astonishing political skills and courage before dictating terms to her. "I am proud to know you, Madame," he told her. "You have a great deal of character and intelligence. But you may not fully understand the situation. The arrival of Monsieur de La Fayette embarrasses me. . . . You may not understand me, Madame, but General La Fayette, finding himself no longer in the center of things, will understand me. . . . I implore him, therefore, to avoid all political activities. I rely on his patriotism."[20] Bonaparte agreed to let Lafayette stay in France, but he would remain so illegally, still officially an émigré in exile, without French citizenship, and subject to summary arrest. If Lafayette refrained from all political activities, however, Napoléon pledged eventually to restore his citizenship. Adrienne understood completely and hustled her husband off to the obscurity of Brie.

With Lafayette's embarrassing presence removed, Napoléon moved swiftly to consolidate his power. Under his direction, the Consulate replaced the previous, meaningless French constitutions with a new, meaningless constitution—much shorter than the others, but nevertheless labeled "constitution." It omitted the rights of man, liberty, equality, and fraternity. Although it created a bicameral legislature of sorts, it gave the First Consul exclusive legislative and executive powers: only he could initiate laws; only he could nominate ministers, generals, civil servants, and judges. In December 1799, a staged plebiscite approved Bonaparte's new Consulate and constitution and officially ended the French Revolution. In effect, it set the French political clock back a century to the era of Louis XIV, creating a military dictatorship where a monarchical dictatorship had once reigned, but it restored peace and personal security to the nation for the first time in more than a decade, and, if the plebiscite was any indication, the vast majority approved. With bayonets at every polling station, they had little choice.

True to Adrienne's word to Bonaparte, Lafayette retired to a life of obscurity as an illegal émigré in exile at La Grange, where he spent the winter supervising repairs and redecoration while Adrienne analyzed the family's financial situation. He had little choice. Even when he received the devastating news that his mentor, Washington, had died, he had to remain in seclusion at La Grange, while Napoléon led a lavish memorial service at the Invalides in Paris. Not only did Napoléon not invite "the friend of Washington," he omitted all mention of Lafayette's name. Washington did not forget Lafayette, however. In his will, he bequeathed him "a pair of finely-wrought steel pistols, taken from the enemy in the revolutionary war."[21]

True to his word to Adrienne, Bonaparte quietly and without fanfare removed Lafayette's name from the list of émigrés and restored his French citizenship on March 1, 1800—as he did for Lafayette's friends Bureaux de Pusy and La Tour-Maubourg and all members of the original Assemblée nationale of 1789. That summer, Adrienne took Virginie to try to recover Lafayette's lands in Brittany, while he took advantage of his freedom as a citizen to visit his beloved old aunt Charlotte at Chavaniac for the first time in nine years. Both journeys were essential to the family's economic survival. Adrienne had done a careful analysis of the family's finances: they were about 200,000 livres in debt, including the moneys they owed Morris. A return to productivity of the lands at La Grange would earn them only 10,000 livres a year from farming and livestock. Timber sales from adjacent forests would yield another 5,000 livres but still leave them with only 10 percent of Lafayette's earnings when he married Adrienne and not nearly enough to support the family and repay the family's debts. They had to recover the lands in Brittany and restore productivity at Chavaniac.

At the end of the summer the Lafayettes gathered at La Grange. Once again, Adrienne had proved herself an astonishing negotiator. She had recovered the titles to all her husband's lands in Brittany and sold the least productive properties for a total of 61,200 livres, with which she immediately reduced the family debts. She then contracted with tenant farmers to pay the Lafayettes monthly rents totaling 4,800 livres and raised the total family income to about 20,000 livres a month.

On September 30, the United States and France agreed to a new treaty that restored commercial and diplomatic relations. The First Consul's older brother, Joseph Bonaparte, who spoke fluent English and helped negotiate the new treaty, invited Lafayette to a lavish two-day fête he was planning at his château north of Paris to celebrate the reconciliation of the two former allies. Fireworks illuminated the skies, a chorus sang, and the First Consul punctuated the celebration with a toast in memory of "the souls of the Frenchmen and Americans dead on the field of battle for the independence of the New World."[22] In the course of the festivities, Lafayette and Napoléon stood face to face for the second time in their lives. They had not spoken to each other the first time, when Bonaparte was a young officer amid his troops at the 1790 *Fête de la Fédération* in Paris—and Lafayette was commander in chief of the National Guard administering the oath of allegiance to constitutional rule in France. Now their roles had reversed: Bonaparte was commander in chief of France as well as the French military, and Lafayette had little or no official standing as a retired officer. Though Bonaparte was twelve years younger, they found much in common. Like Lafayette, Napoléon was of noble birth, albeit *petite noblesse Corse*—lesser Corsican nobility—but not without influence. Both were superbly educated, and, like Lafayette, Bonaparte was fluent in Latin and thoroughly versed in the works of all the philosophes of the Age of Enlightenment. Both were brilliant military tacticians and insightful leaders who had earned the devotion and unswerving loyalty of their men. Both were charming, skilled diplomats who made friends easily, and both had faced national crises that had carried them to the pinnacles of political power, but unlike Lafayette, Bonaparte eagerly seized power by whatever means he could whenever he had the opportunity.

According to Lafayette, Bonaparte sought to legitimize his dictatorship by offering Lafayette the ambassadorship to America, but Lafayette refused. "I am too American to go to America in the role of a foreigner," he replied.[23] Bonaparte resented Lafayette's "disapproving, if not hostile attitude. No one likes to pass for a tyrant," he grumbled. "General La Fayette seems to designate me as such."[24] Lafayette was quick to answer: "The silence of my retirement is the maximum of my deference; if Bonaparte were willing to serve the cause of liberty, I would be devoted to him. But I can neither approve an arbitrary government, nor associate myself with it."[25]

In fact, Bonaparte had no need to disguise his dictatorship as anything other than what it was. He was unquestioned master of France and becoming master of Europe, with no need of Lafayette at his side. In the ensuing two years, Bonaparte extended French conquests beyond those of Louis XIV; they rivaled those of even the Roman Empire, stretching from the huge Louisiana Territory and the Caribbean islands of North America across the face of Europe and over the Mediterranean to Malta and Egypt. Napoléon planned to convert his military conquests into a new, common European Union, with France at its center, providing a common language, culture, military establishment, legal system, economy, and currency. He made French mandatory in schools, introduced the new *franc* as a common currency, and integrated the elite military units of Prussia and Austria into a Grande Armée. He reorganized European industry into a new "Continental System," with France as the continent's primary manufacturer and the rest of Europe relegated to raw materials production and a market for finished French goods. Raw materials were to flow into France for conversion by French manufacturers into finished goods that France would then sell throughout Europe and the world. In a referendum during the summer of 1802, 3,658,000 Frenchmen voted to make Bonaparte "Consul for life," with Lafayette among the tiny minority of 9,000 who dared vote nay. Two years later, Napoléon emulated Charlemagne and brought the pope from Rome to Nôtre-Dame Cathedral in Paris, took the crown from the pope's hands, and crowned himself emperor. "What a mummery," said one of his generals. "Nothing is missing but the hundred thousand men who sacrificed themselves to do away with all this."[26]

Napoléon Bonaparte, who crowned himself emperor of France, tried to legitimize his dictatorship by offering Lafayette the ambassador-ship to America. Lafayette refused. (*Réunion des Musées Nationaux.*)

After celebrating the restoration of diplomatic and commercial ties to America at Joseph Bonaparte's estate, Lafayette returned to La Grange, determined to re-create Mount Vernon and wait for his nation to recall him to service—as America had eventually recalled Washington. During the following year, Lafayette studied the latest techniques in agriculture and animal husbandry. He proved as brilliant and passionate as Washington in the practical application of agricultural theory, and he made the fields of La Grange the most productive and profitable in the region. He was equally gifted with livestock, carefully selecting a few Spanish merino rams and ewes and developing the largest, most productive and profitable herd of merino sheep in France—and the only one near Paris. His more than seven hundred animals produced the finest wool then available and commanded the highest prices. Meanwhile, he hired an architect to renovate the château, adding a magnificent library for himself in one of the towers and apartments for each of his children, their spouses or future spouses, and their offspring, and for Madame de Tessé and her husband. He added a room for the tutor, Frestel, of course, and several guest rooms. A landscape architect added terraces and a fish pond in the park adjacent to the château. By the end of 1801, Lafayette had

The magnificent Lafayette Château de La Grange—the "Mount Vernon of France"—about seventy-five miles east of Paris in Brie. (*From the author's collection.*)

transformed La Grange into a French Mount Vernon, including the constant chatter, songs, and laughter of friends, relatives, and children.

Adrienne, meanwhile, continued her supervision of the family's financial affairs, traveling to Paris each month to negotiate with lawyers representing the family's creditors, including Gouverneur Morris, by then a U.S. senator. She also continued badgering government officials to restore the family's titles or obtain compensation for properties and assets seized by Jacobins. Ultimately, she recovered more than 500,000 francs in compensation for government confiscation of Noailles family properties and assets—about $2.5 million in today's currency.

On one of her regular trips to Paris, Adrienne determined to discover where her mother, sister, and grandmother had been buried. She learned that about thirteen hundred heads and bodies from the guillotine at the place du Trône (now the place de la Nation) had been carted to two huge burial pits at nearby Picpus, near the ruined convent of the Augustines. She and her surviving sister launched an enormous letter-writing campaign to surviving relatives of the victims across France and eventually raised enough funds to build the Cimetière de Picpus, complete with a chapel adjacent to the burial pits. Although they never disinterred the dead, engraved plaques on the walls and stelae in the ground attest to their presence. Picpus remains the only private cemetery in France reserved exclusively for direct descendants of the 1,306 victims of the guillotine on the place du Trône—among them the poet André Chénier, whose death was immortalized in the tragic opera by Giordano.

In the spring of 1802, George-Washington Lafayette married Emilie de Tracy, the daughter of Destutt de Tracy, a renowned philosopher who had served in the Constituent Assembly with Lafayette and as a cavalry commander under him at the frontier in 1792, just before Lafayette fled France. Père Carrichon, the priest who had blessed the three Noailles ladies at the guillotine, performed the ceremony. After the wedding, the Lafayette and de Tracy families went south together for a long visit to Chavaniac—"to share our new-found happiness with our old aunt, who still had all her faculties," according to Virginie. "Nothing had been able to destroy her or embitter her."[27]

During their vacation at Chavaniac, Adrienne's sister invited a young guest, the marquis de Lasteyrie du Saillant, who fell in love with Virginie and married her the following year. Although they scheduled the wedding for February 1803, they had to postpone it after Lafayette slipped on the ice near what is now the place de la Concorde in Paris and broke his upper left leg. Concerned passersby carried him to the nearby rue d'Anjou, where Madame de Tessé, Adrienne's aunt, now lived. Two surgeons debated whether to allow it to heal naturally and leave him with a permanent limp or treat it with a racklike machine that had just been invented to stretch broken bones into place gradually, with a turn of several screws each day. Always eager to pioneer new scientific techniques, Lafayette made the disastrous decision to try the machine. After Lafayette endured forty days and nights of excruciating pain, the inventor removed the machine to find that the straps had gripped Lafayette's leg so tightly he had developed gangrene. The gangrene disappeared after two weeks, but he lost almost all movement of his upper leg at the hip. The surgeon never again used his machine.

Lafayette's long confinement provoked some public interest. Old comrades in arms visited regularly, and a range of revolutionaries—some of them old has-beens, others young would-bes—sought his counsel. Through the pain, Lafayette held court as he had at the rue de Bourbon, as guests of all ranks and all nations flocked to see the fallen knight. But his endless discourses on liberty and constitutional rule grew tiresome to all but his immediate family and a few old dreamers like the Polish patriot Tadeusz Kosciuszko, who was a frequent visitor. Both men were vestiges of the past, shunned by those who controlled the present. More than ten years older than Lafayette, Kosciuszko had fought with Greene in the Carolina campaign and returned to Poland to lead an unsuccessful fight for independence. Like Lafayette, his mind remained rooted in the previous century, while his hands worked the soil of his garden in exile on the outskirts of Paris. Like Lafayette, he held fast to a dream of American liberty in his native land—a dream he would never live to see.[28]

An unexpected visit in April lifted Lafayette's and Adrienne's spirits to euphoric levels: James Monroe arrived unexpectedly, having come as the special envoy of President Thomas Jefferson to negotiate the purchase of the Louisiana Territory from France. Napoléon had acquired the territory from Spain in 1800, in hopes of restoring the French empire in North America, but President Jefferson issued a thinly veiled threat of war, and Napoléon agreed to sell it and focus his empire-building efforts in Europe. Monroe had not seen Lafayette in twenty years and Adrienne in nine. Normally austere, he could not resist the enveloping embrace and tears of Adrienne, who could only think of him and his wife as her angelic redeemers. Monroe's visit proved as providential financially for the Lafayettes as it was emotional. Congress had allocated tens of thousands of acres in the Ohio Territory to veterans of the Revolutionary War and assigned Lafayette 11,500 acres on the banks of the Ohio River. Although there was no question of the Lafayettes emigrating, Adrienne asked whether the land could be used to generate income, and Monroe agreed to act as an intermediary to secure a sizable loan against the property at low interest from a London bank, Baring Brothers. The loan allowed the Lafayettes to wipe out all their debts, including the old Morris loan. In effect, they were solvent for the first time since the Jacobin Revolution, with their only obligation secured by their own unneeded property in America. Monroe had once again proved an angelic friend to the Lafayettes.

After Lafayette returned to La Grange, he refused to let his injury prevent him from supervising his farm and gardens. Every morning, his family helped him to a cushioned chaise longue by the window of his library, where he shouted instructions to his foreman and workers through a megaphone.

Late in the year, Lafayette received a letter from President Thomas Jefferson, asking him to become governor of the new territory of Louisiana to ensure a bond between the local French and American populations. "I would prefer your presence to an army of 10,000 men to assure the tranquillity of the country," Jefferson wrote. "The old French inhabitants would immediately attach themselves to you and to the United States. You would annul the efforts of the foreign agitators who are arriving in droves."[29] To make the invitation more attractive, Jefferson decreed a transfer of Lafayette's Ohio land grant to a far more valuable parcel in Louisiana that would guarantee Lafayette immense wealth to complement the fame and power he would obtain as governor of America's largest single territory. Congress had approved the appointment, and Jefferson assured Lafayette that his "great services and established fame" had made him "peculiarly acceptable to the nation at large."[30]

True to form, Lafayette again rejected an opportunity for power. He found all sorts of excuses to postpone his decision. Italy had just rebelled against French rule, he explained to Jefferson, and his son and two sons-in-law had been called to military service. Adrienne and he were responsible for caring for his daughters and their two children, and for George's wife, who had just given birth to a little girl. Moreover, with his son and sons-in-law in the military, he feared, with good reason, that his departure and renunciation of allegiance to France would expose them and the rest of his family to harsh government retaliation—not to mention his own possible arrest and imprisonment if French vessels stopped his ship on the way to America.

He nevertheless did not want to reject forever the chance for asylum in America. After debating for more than six months, he wrote to Jefferson a second time:

> I cannot continue without expressing my deep appreciation to Congress and to you. You, my dear friend, have seen my hopes for French and American liberty; you shared those hopes. The cause of humanity has been victorious and been reaffirmed in America; nothing can stop it anymore, or displace it or tarnish its progress. Here, it is deemed irrevocably lost, but for me to pronounce this sentence and to do so through expatriation goes against my hopeful character. I cannot see how, unless some force placed me in physical constraints, I could abandon even the smallest hope. . . . I tell myself that I, the promoter of the revolution, I must not recognize the impossibility of seeing reestablished, during our lifetime, a just and generous liberty, American liberty.
>
> Now that I have opened my heart to you, will it seem unreasonable to you or ungrateful to defer a decision that will force me to bid a formal adieu to Europe and establish a definitive tie to America.[31]

But Jefferson could no longer wait, and, in fact, Jefferson knew Lafayette so intimately that he had already dismissed the idea of appointing him, recognizing that Lafayette's roots stretched too far and deep in his native land ever to abandon it.

Just as Jefferson reached out to Lafayette, Napoléon made a similar gesture by awarding him the Legion of Honor and an appointment as a Peer of the Realm in the Senate—an honor that carried no responsibilities and was equivalent to a seat in the British House of Lords. "I replied to members of the government and to Bonaparte himself," Lafayette told Jefferson, "that I am determined to live in complete retirement."[32] In fact, Lafayette had other reasons for rejecting the emperor's awards. "I would have accepted eagerly," he confided to a friend in Paris, "under a democratic regime in which a senate seat would have given me the occasional opportunity to serve the principles of liberty and my country."[33] Lafayette's rejection left the sensitive emperor deeply insulted. He retaliated by blocking the army promotions of Lafayette's son and sons-in-law, despite the highest recommendations of their commanders, who cited their gallant service. Indeed, George suffered a minor wound saving the life of his general.

Adrienne was not unhappy with either of Lafayette's decisions, nor did Lafayette have any regrets. Both had tired of political intrigues. Both wanted nothing more than to share each other's love and companionship in the peace and beauty of their magnificent estate at Château de La Grange, surrounded by their children and grandchildren, their relatives and in-laws, and the stream of friends and neighbors that flowed through their huge home. In 1804, Virginie added another granddaughter to the burgeoning Lafayette household—her first child and the Lafayettes' fourth grandchild. With so large a family at La Grange, neither Adrienne nor her knight had any reason to return to Paris; he had no political or military agendae, and she had straightened out the family finances in brilliant fashion to ensure their comfort for the remainder of their lives. Moreover, he had found a calling he loved in agriculture: his innovations in animal husbandry and land management had made La Grange so profitable that he was able to buy adjoining lands and expand his estate without dipping into capital. He priced all produce himself, sending enormous cartloads to market each day. The only sadness that intruded in their lives was the inevitable news that a friend or relative had died. Their brother-in-law the vicomte de Noailles was killed fighting a slave rebellion in Haiti, and not long thereafter, Lafayette learned that he had lost another friend, whom he considered a brother: Alexander Hamilton had died of a bullet wound in a duel with Aaron Burr in New Jersey.

"The deplorable death of my friend Hamilton hurt me deeply," he wrote Jefferson for solace. "I am sure that, regardless of the differences between your two parties, you always admired him and feel his loss as deeply as I."[34]

The Lafayettes kept the gates of La Grange open at all times, and travelers inevitably peeked in to stare at the famous hero who chatted amiably with strangers about America, Indians, Washington, Cornwallis, and other exotic subjects. As his grandmother had done at Chavaniac, he permitted the less fortunate to glean whatever the reapers left in the fields, along with tree trimmings to burn in their ovens and hearths. He routinely forgave poachers who hunted on his property or chopped down trees to heat their homes.

In 1805, Russia and Austria joined Britain in a new coalition against France, but French armies swept northward through Austria and crushed a combined Austro-Russian army at the decisive battle of Austerlitz in Moravia (now the eastern part of the Czech Republic). Two days later Austria sued for peace, and the Russian army limped home to Mother Russia to lick its collective wounds. In 1806, Napoléon destroyed the Prussian army at Iéna and extended the French Empire eastward to Warsaw. With peace apparently at hand, with no chance for promotion, and with their military commitments complete, George-Washington Lafayette and the two Lafayette sons-in-law resigned their commissions. Although Lafayette grumbled at the emperor's pettiness, Adrienne rejoiced to have the boys home safely; she wanted no more knights in the family and reveled in the presence of the three young couples and their children, all of whom made La Grange their permanent home.

"The rest of her precious life was consecrated to us," Virginie recounted. "She felt too deep, too passionate a love for family life to want any other type of existence. Neither the grandeur that she had witnessed nor the fame seen close up provoked as much happiness as her simple existence [at La Grange]. She filled her entire life with love."[35]

Filling one's life with love was not difficult at La Grange: Lafayette had fashioned the estate into a self-contained, self-sufficient community, with ample supplies of every imaginable human need—even entertainment on Sunday evenings, with dancing to an abbé's fiddle and picnics under the trees with neighbors and ever-present guests. Every day saw the justifiably proud Lafayette limp through the sheep pens, cow sheds, and dairy, leading a line of often-famous guests who feigned interest in his lectures on the latest scientific advances in agriculture and animal husbandry as they slogged and slid through ankle-deep animal wastes. The pride and admiration in the faces of his workmen, from the foremen to the youngest shepherd, mirrored that of his loyal foot soldiers in Virginia.

In August 1807, as Lafayette neared his fiftieth birthday, he and George went to visit Aunt Charlotte and inspect the Chavaniac properties. In their absence, Adrienne developed terrible pains and high fever; she began vomiting uncontrollably, unable to retain any food or liquid. Anastasie moved her to Madame de Tessé's house in Paris to be near her doctor. In the days that followed, her fever increased. Lafayette and George raced up from Chavaniac, and the rest of the family came from La Grange. Lafayette refused to leave her bedside.

"Is it not indiscreet for so many of us to be here?" she asked him.

"No, not at all," he smiled. "We are only sixteen to feed." When she pleaded with him to spend some time with the others, he protested, "I have nothing else to do but to care for you."[36]

In the days that followed, the pain increased and she drifted in and out of comatose sleep. "God and my father occupied all her thoughts during those last moments," Virginie recalled. "It is impossible to understand how much she meant to him and he to her, even in the midst of her delirium, in total silence; their faces were portraits of infinite tenderness and devotion.

"On Christmas night, at midnight, in the year 1807, we lost her. She had blessed us all that morning. That evening, her last words to us were,

'I am not suffering.' Then she looked at my father and whispered: 'I am yours entirely.'"—"*Je suis toute à vous.*"[37]

Adrienne's death plunged Lafayette into depression. She was only forty-eight years old; he only fifty. With Washington gone; Greene, Hamilton—all those he loved—gone, he had no one to turn to for solace among his old friends but Jefferson, who had lost his own wife two years before coming to Paris: "Who better than you can sympathize for the loss of a beloved wife? The angel who for thirty-four years has blessed my life was to you an affectionate, grateful friend. Pity me, my dear Jefferson."[38]

In January, he unburdened himself to La Tour-Maubourg, a Masonic brother who had experienced the horrors of Olmütz and whose younger brother had married Anastasie. Day after day he wrote—revealing himself as he had never done before, on more than fifty manuscript pages. "Until now," he admitted, "you have always seen me able to overcome circumstances; today, circumstance is stronger than I. I will never recover.

"For thirty-four years of a marriage in which her love, her goodness, the greatness, the tenderness, the goodness of her soul honored my life, I grew so accustomed to all that she was for me that she became an indistinguishable element of my own existence. . . . I knew I loved her a great deal, that I needed her, but it is only in losing her that I have been able to separate myself from what is left of me for the rest of a life which had once seemed to me so full and will now forever be empty of happiness and comfort."[39]

Lafayette buried Adrienne in a corner of the Picpus cemetery, where, somewhere beneath the earth nearby, lay the martyred bodies of her sister, mother, and grandmother and thirteen hundred other innocents. He returned to La Grange and walled up the entrance to her apartment. It remained as she had left it, untouched for the rest of his life—an inviolable sanctuary, penetrated by only a small, secret door through which he alone disappeared on certain days of the year to be with her.

20

Apotheosis

ADRIENNE'S DEATH left Lafayette's heart and spirit all but broken. He wanted no part of public life, and in the seven years that followed, he seldom wandered from La Grange and the comforting embraces of his children and grandchildren, whose faces mirrored his beloved Adrienne so hauntingly. Life at La Grange settled into a hypnotic routine broken only once, by the loss of his beloved aunt Charlotte, who died in 1811 at Chavaniac, at eighty-two.

When weather permitted, Lafayette threw himself into his agricultural projects. His damaged hip was too stiff and painful to allow him to ride a horse, but he limped about with a cane and traveled about the farm in a small hackney—and developed a noticeable paunch. His farm continued to prosper; many of the animals he bred won prizes. "I have become a pretty good agriculturist," he boasted, "and lame though I am, I husband my strength where walking is concerned, and manage to do and to oversee what is essential."[1] On days too wet or cold for outdoor pursuits, he dictated anecdotes for his *Mémoires* to his son, George, who never left his father's side. And he wrote letters, of course—especially to Jefferson, his last close tie to the glorious American Revolution and the disastrous French Revolution. After two terms as president, Jefferson had followed Washington's example and refused to run for a third term. His Virginia protégé, James Madison, Lafayette's companion in Indian country in 1784, was now president, and Jefferson had retired from public life to Monticello and started a voluminous correspondence with Lafayette. The two shared reminiscences, along with irrational dreams of spreading American liberty in other lands. As he had with Washington, Lafayette exchanged countless gifts—he sent Jefferson a pair of sheepdogs. And the two friends reported regularly to each other, with detailed analyses of events in their respective worlds.

"At this moment," Lafayette reported to Jefferson, "immense continental forces are attacking the Russian Empire. Will [Czar] Alexander fight? Will he negotiate? He runs a risk in either case, of defeat or ensnarement; but if he stretches out the war for a long time by retreating strategically and extending the French line of supply, he could well embarrass his opponent."[2]

"You must have heard by now of the glorious achievements of our little Navy," Jefferson reported back to Lafayette on America's war against the British in 1813. "I do not know if history will ever provide an example of a more brilliant naval engagement than Perry's victory on Lake Erie."[3]

Lafayette's analysis of the Russian campaign proved prescient. The czar followed Lafayette's battle plan, with a strategic retreat that not only extended the French line of supply, it left nothing but scorched earth for the French to conquer. Ashes covered fields where grain and other foodstuffs had grown that might have fed French troops. The retreating Russians burned forests that might have fueled French campfires or repaired French wagons, and they burned every structure that might have sheltered French troops from Russia's vicious snows and arctic weather. The French marched into Moscow on September 14, but the Russians turned it into an inferno that left it useless for winter quarters.

With the invasion of Russia, Napoléon's French empire and his Continental System began to collapse. The "Grande Armée" that tramped across the Russian steppes was the military hallmark of that system, integrating a half-million French, Prussian, and Austrian troops into a single "Great Army"—a *European* army that ruled three-quarters of the continent. What his army had not seized by force, he acquired by marriage, linking Austria's Hapsburg empire to France by divorcing the barren Empress Joséphine in favor of Hapsburg archduchess Marie-Louise, the daughter of the Austrian emperor. A year later, she bore him a son, whom he named Napoléon II and proclaimed king of Rome.

Far from bringing economic union, Napoléon's Continental System had shattered the economies of member states. Funneling raw materials from conquered nations into France for manufacture had undermined manufacturing in satellite nations, produced mass unemployment, and provoked widespread worker unrest. His scheme for cultural and linguistic unity was equally disruptive. The great Italian sculptor Canova and other prominent artists denounced the removal of Italian art to Paris. Beethoven protested by stripping his *Eroica* symphony of its dedication to the French emperor. To silence the mounting criticism, Napoléon censored the press and theater, banned new literary works, and arrested his opponents.

"Your very existence is truly miraculous," one of Napoléon's officers warned Lafayette, but Lafayette simply shrugged, insisting that "living retired with my family on a farm, I have not given my enemy much cause for antagonism . . . although I have nonetheless always been open about my opinion of the famous emperor's 'System' and my deep desire to see it end."[4]

Its end was drawing near. Europe responded to the scheme for linguistic unity by refusing to teach French in schools and speak it in daily life. Tacit protests turned into rebellion in Spain, where guerrilla forces rose against Joseph Bonaparte, whom Napoléon had placed on the Spanish throne. As the guerrillas gained momentum, British forces invaded and linked up with remnants of the Spanish army in a war that ultimately cost France 300,000 troops and huge financial losses that depleted the arms and manpower of the Grande Armée Napoléon led into Russia. In November 1812, the fearsome Russian winter struck prematurely and sent his army reeling back from Moscow through howling blizzards and frigid cold. Russian partisans struck from all sides, decimating the French forces and slowing the retreat of survivors until they starved to death. In the disorder, Prussian and Austrian troops deserted, and, by the end of November, only 10,000 of the more than 450,000 troops who invaded Russia were still fit for combat.

News of the disaster provoked uprisings against French occupation throughout Europe. In May, the Congress of Vienna sent Napoléon an ultimatum, demanding a French pullback behind its natural boundaries of the Rhine, the Alps, and the Pyrenees and the restoration of all pre-Napoleonic monarchies. In June, English and Spanish forces defeated the French, and the English crossed the Pyrenees into southern France, while the Austrian army recaptured parts of northern Italy. When Napoléon failed to respond to the Congress of Vienna's ultimatum, it adjourned, and a coalition of allied forces annihilated what was left of the Grande Armée at the Battle of Leipzig in October. Early in 1814, allied armies invaded France from the north, and, as they approached Paris, the once impotent French legislature made secret overtures for peace. Napoléon's Austrian empress, Louise, fled with her little son, Napoléon II, to Vienna—and to a lover who offered her more attention than her husband did.

Napoléon's minister of foreign affairs, Talleyrand, remained in Paris and changed spots again by deposing Napoléon as emperor and assuming the presidency of a provisional government. Talleyrand invited the heir apparent—the comte de Provence—to return from exile in England and assume the throne as Louis XVIII, succeeding his late nephew, the short-lived boy-king Louis XVII.

In the midst of the turmoil, Adrienne's aunt, the comtesse de Tessé, and her husband fell ill, and Lafayette went to Paris to look after them. Within a few weeks, the count died, and Adrienne's beloved aunt followed him to the grave two weeks later. They bequeathed to Lafayette their town house at No. 8, rue d'Anjou, just off what is now the rue du Faubourg Saint-Honoré, behind the present-day American Embassy.

On March 31, 1814, the allied armies entered Paris, and, as Lafayette watched, a grand carriage bore the horrifyingly fat new king, Louis XVIII, to restore the French monarchy. Napoléon and his shrinking force encamped helplessly forty miles south of Paris at the royal palace of Fontainebleau, where his generals urged him to abdicate. On April 6, he agreed, and, in exchange for averting a savage end to the conflict, the allies granted him sovereignty to the island of Elba, off the western Italian coast opposite Corsica, with the title of emperor, an annual income of 2 million francs and a guard of four hundred volunteers.

With a new French government came the inevitable new constitution. Called the Constitutional Charter, it restored the king's "divine right" as "supreme head of state" and Roman Catholicism as the state religion. The king made certain "gracious concessions" by retaining some rights from older, more liberal constitutions, including equality before the law, freedom from arbitrary arrest, freedom of thought and expression, and freedom of religion. Louis assumed legislative as well as executive powers. Although he alone would initiate new laws, the Charter created a bicameral quasi-legislative body to vote on them. The king would appoint the members of the upper house, or Chamber of Peers, and voters would elect members of the lower house, or Chamber of Deputies, with voting eligibility determined by the amount of taxes they paid to the crown each year. In the end, only about ninety thousand were eligible to vote in a nation of more than 25 million. Although Lafayette railed at the regressive voting restrictions, most of France was content with the Charter. More than half the French population was illiterate, and 75 percent lived in small villages where, for centuries, agriculture was their sole pursuit and the priest's word their only law. Only Paris had more than five hundred thousand people; only Lyons and Marseilles more than one hundred thousand, and only five other cities more than fifty thousand.

The king invited Lafayette to his first royal audience, where both Louis and his younger brother the comte d'Artois "received me cordially." At the audience, George introduced him to the young duc d'Orléans, who had inherited his title after his father, Philippe Egalité, died on the guillotine. Like George, the young duke had fled to America for two years, and the two had met when the duke visited the Washingtons at Mount Vernon for a few days.

Although the Restoration in France brought peace to the rest of Europe, it did not pacify the infinite numbers of chronic malcontents endemic to

The obese Louis XVIII, once Lafayette's companion in riding school, acceded to the French throne after Napoléon's abdication in 1814. (*Réunion des Musées Nationaux.*)

France. Bonapartists seethed with bitterness over Napoléon's military humiliation in Russia. Demobilization left hundreds of thousands of former soldiers unemployed, as did the end of Napoléon's Continental System, which had made France the economic hub of Europe. Adding to social discontent was the wave of angry émigrés who streamed back into France demanding the restoration of their former properties from equally angry peasants who had worked the land as their own for twenty years or more. Wisely, Lafayette retreated to the quiet isolation of La Grange to focus on farming instead of politics.

Napoléon, on the other hand, saw the rising discontent as an opportunity to return to power. After six months, he sailed back to France and landed in Cannes on March 1, 1815. With a detachment of only several hundred guards, he marched northward toward Paris through the fierce snows of the Alps,[5] gradually gathering a huge army of unemployed workers, former soldiers, and malcontents along the way; although the king sent troops to arrest him, they rallied around their former leader and joined the enormous throng tramping across France. Three weeks later, the march reached the gates of Paris, where the entire population, it seemed, hailed Napoléon's return—not, ironically, as the former emperor and the conqueror of Europe, but as the leader of a new revolution against the Bourbon monarchy. Sensing popular sentiment, he donned the revolutionary cockade of 1789 rather than the trappings of the empire.

King Louis XVIII fled to Ghent, Belgium, and Napoléon once again moved into the royal apartments in the Tuileries Palace, but his hold on the palace—and, indeed, on France—was tenuous. The right favored restoration of the monarchy; the left favored revolution, war, and anarchy. Napoléon's only hope, Lafayette explained, lay in "making himself a constitutionalist. His mind and his character are like opposing currents; he is a strange mixture of imperialist, terrorist, and liberal, but public opinion is stronger than he, and he has a prodigious talent: he submits to everything that he cannot dominate."[6]

On April 19, a courier arrived at La Grange with a message from Joseph Bonaparte, begging Lafayette to come to Paris immediately. Napoléon had asked centrist leaders to establish a new French government. They had already amended the constitutional charter, which Bonaparte agreed to submit to a national plebiscite; he also called for new national elections for the lower house. Napoléon wanted to appoint Lafayette leader of the House of Peers—and, in effect, leader of the entire National Assembly. Although Lafayette felt a surge of excitement at his recall to leadership, he remained true to his principles and refused to serve a usurper.

"If my fellow citizens call me," Lafayette declared, "I will not reject their confidence, but I will not reenter political life by the peerage or any other favor of the emperor."[7] Napoléon was furious. "Everyone in the world has learned his lesson," he railed, "with the single exception of Lafayette. He has not yielded a jot. You see him calm. Well, let me tell you, he is ready to begin again."[8]

Early in May, Bonaparte dusted off the Fayettiste symbols of the revolution and staged a huge pageant on the Champ de Mars in front of his old school, the Ecole Militaire. As Lafayette had done twenty-five years earlier, Napoléon swore to support the new constitution and proclaimed peace with the nation's European neighbors. On May 10, the department that included La Grange elected Lafayette as its representative to the national legislature—the Chamber of Deputies, or lower house—and George won election at Chavaniac. On June 4, the Chamber of Deputies elected its leaders—all young men, although they paid homage to the old republican by selecting Lafayette as third vice president.

Despite Bonaparte's efforts to establish a peaceful, constitutional regime, the allies feared him and French lust for power too much not to act. They declared France in violation of the Congress of Vienna accords and massed their troops in Belgium, on the northern French border. On June 12, Napoléon led his 180,000-man army from Paris to engage them. Eight days later, he returned, disheveled, physically exhausted. He had met his Waterloo. On

June 18, 1820, an allied force of more than 200,000 British, Dutch, German, Saxon, and Prussian troops had outmaneuvered, outgunned, and all but overrun the French armies, which fled in panic back to France. With allied forces pouring into northern France, Napoléon demanded that the Chamber of Deputies vote him emergency dictatorial powers and dissolve. When Lafayette protested, Napoléon's brother Lucien accused him of disloyalty.

"That is a slanderous accusation," Lafayette thundered. "What gives the previous speaker [Lucien Bonaparte] the right to accuse this nation of being disloyal for failing to persevere in following the Emperor? The nation has followed him in the sands of Egypt, and in the steppes of Russia, on fifty fields of battle, in his reverses as in his successes . . . and for having thus followed him we now mourn over the blood of three million Frenchmen!"[9] That evening, Lafayette made a motion "that we all go to the Emperor and say to him that . . . his abdication has become necessary to save the nation." The Chamber agreed, but Bonaparte rejected their demand. Lafayette responded by threatening, "If the Emperor does not send in his abdication within an hour, I will propose to the Chamber that he be dethroned."[10]

On June 22, 1815, four days after Waterloo, Napoléon ended his "Hundred Days" by abdicating in favor of his son, Napoléon II. Lafayette arranged passage to America for the fallen Corsican, but when Napoléon reached Rochefort, a British squadron prevented his ship from leaving port. Napoleon appealed for safe passage to the British government, which granted it to him on a British vessel that carried him to the forsaken island of Saint Helena, off the west African coast in the southern Atlantic. He died five years later, on May 5, 1821, three months short of his fifty-second birthday. His older brother, Joseph Bonaparte, was more fortunate: he sailed to America and settled in Bordentown, New Jersey, in a Georgian mansion, whose interior he transformed into a French-Empire showpiece.

After naming Napoléon II emperor, the Chamber of Deputies elected a five-man directory to assume executive power, bypassing Lafayette as a relic, out of touch with the times. They did, however, appoint him to a peace mission, with the hopeless task of negotiating a halt to the Allied march on Paris. The allies laughed at the French appeal and sent their troops swarming into the capital to hoist the white flag of the Bourbon monarchy above the Tuileries Palace. When Lafayette returned with George to his house on the rue d'Anjou, the entire Lafayette clan was there waiting. Prussian troops had overrun Brie, and high-level Prussian officers had commandeered the château at La Grange as their headquarters.

In drawing up the peace accords, the allied powers resolved to teach their incorrigibly arrogant French foe to leave its neighbors alone and live within its own borders. As reparations, they extracted not only the costs of the twenty-five-year global upheaval unleashed by the French Revolution but also many of the costs of the perennial havoc the French had wreaked on Europe during the millennium since Charlemagne's Franks had ravaged the continent. To crush any French ambitions for territorial expansion, the allies sent more than one million soldiers to occupy two-thirds of France—sixty-one of the eighty-three departments—for at least five years, and more, if necessary. The allied-imposed Second Restoration returned Louis XVIII to the throne as a puppet king and stripped the boy Napoléon II of his title and all imperial claims.[11]

With only slightly more than ninety thousand privileged men permitted to vote, the first parliamentary elections returned a fanatically ultra-Royalist Chamber of Deputies, which ruthlessly sheared the Constitutional Charter of individual rights. It permitted the imprisonment of suspects without trial, imposed harsh punishment of authors for criticizing the regime, subjected antigovernment demonstrators to trial by courts-martial, and allowed for the exile or execution of military leaders who supported Napoléon during the Hundred Days. The second Restoration set off a new round of internecine French savagery. During the White Terror—so named for the color of the Bourbon monarchy's flag—mobs of royalists and former émigrés dragged Jacobins, Bonapartists, and republicans from their homes, beating and killing untold thousands, especially in royalist provinces in the south and west. Although allied troops eventually ended the slaughter, the White Terror silenced the voices of French extremists on the left—and brought peace to Europe for the first time in seventy-five years. The intervention of British friends in the allied high command restored La Grange to Lafayette in the autumn of 1815, and he returned to private life.

Three years of startling economic gains followed and produced such surprising political and social stability in France that the allies believed the French had, at last, learned the advantages of peace at home and abroad. They withdrew their troops two years early, in 1818 instead of 1820, and the government eased restrictions on individual rights and the press. At La Grange, Lafayette's flock of merino sheep multiplied to more than one thousand head; his dairy herd grew to fifty cows; and his more than five thousand apple trees yielded a delicious cider that became the staple beverage in the region and one of the most sought-after ciders in France.

La Grange became a vastly profitable enterprise that kept Lafayette riding about in his trap each day from six or seven o'clock in the morning until three in the afternoon. He awoke with the sun, at five in summer—usually after seven hours of restful sleep. He spent an hour in bed reading and sometimes writing, then sat, or, if the pain in his joints permitted, knelt to talk silently to Adrienne for a quarter hour, holding before him the miniature portrait of her when she was fourteen. Inscribed on the frame were her dying words, *"Je suis toute à vous"*—"I am yours entirely." In it, also, was a lock of her hair. By seven o'clock, he was ready to tour his "plantation," as he liked to call it. With George hovering always at his side, he took a short respite for a mid-morning breakfast—often in one of the help's cottages, sitting with his men, whose reverence for him increased accordingly.

His return from the fields took him into his study, where George helped him with his *Mémoires* and his voluminous correspondence. At six each evening, the courtyard bell sounded dinner, and as many as thirty people poured into the huge dining room—his children and grandchildren, of course, and an endless procession of guests. Lafayette sat in the middle of the long board, with Virginie and Anastasie opposite as hostesses, and the various grandchildren climbing over each other to sit near their grandfather. George always sat at his father's side, growing more amazed each day as he gained new insights into the man he called Papa. George's faithful former tutor, Frestel, brought the total number of family members at the table each night to a dozen, but guests arrived continually to swell the number to unpredictable levels. Lafayette's in-laws, the Tracys, La Tour-Maubourgs, and Lasteyries, visited regularly, as did his old friends the Ségurs, retired generals like de Broglie, and an endless parade of illustrious guests, many from America for whom a visit to La Grange was a patriotic duty. Worldly men like Jeremy Bentham, the British philosopher, came to discuss political science with the author of the French "Rights of Man," and less worldly, would-be revolutionaries traveled from all parts of Europe to learn how to overthrow autocratic monarchs in their lands. He fed them not only respect, which few of his generation ever offered, but money—and, of course, the fine food, drink, and lodging that he lavished on every visitor to La Grange.

In 1817, crops failed on neighboring farms and threatened Brie with famine. Lafayette opened the gates of La Grange, often feeding soup and bread to seven hundred people a day—and giving each a sou. When his foreman told him his granaries could not feed all the neighbors *and* the huge Lafayette household, Lafayette moved the household to Chavaniac and instructed his foreman at La Grange to continue feeding the hungry in Brie. In 1818, the grateful people of his department elected him to the national assembly—to the annoyance of King Louis XVIII and the allied monarchs, who feared he would rekindle the flames of revolution. Their fears were not ill founded.

With the threat of retaliation by allied forces removed, growing numbers of young liberals, republicans, and Freemasons spoke out in opposition to the royal régime. The Indépendants, as they called themselves, needed only a leader to carry their banner in the Chamber of Deputies. Who better than the legendary hero of two worlds, the friend of Washington? Lafayette's knight's blood flowed warm again as the new generation rallied about him, and he raised his rhetorical flag of American liberty in the French assembly,

demanding freedom of the press, sanctity of the individual, personal liberties, and—heresy of all heresies in a monarchy—the right of all taxpayers to
vote. His son had never before seen his father in full armor, charging passionately into the face of the enemy.

The steady stream of liberal rhetoric, however, soon tempted French
extremists to test the political waters in the hopes of provoking another revolution. In 1820, a fanatic assassinated the king's nephew, who was second
in line to inherit the throne. The government reimposed censorship and
arrest without trial, and it introduced so-called plural voting, which gave
the wealthiest of the privileged two votes instead of one and all but blocked
the election of young Indépendants. The sixty-one-year-old Lafayette, with
thirty-nine-year-old George at his side, retaliated by organizing the young
liberals about him into a new political club, Les Amis de la Liberté de la
Presse—the Friends of the Liberty of the Press. On May 15, Les Amis sent
thousands of students swarming through Paris streets demanding restoration
of individual liberty and freedom of the press and repeal of plural voting. Six
hundred students armed themselves and formed barricades; the cavalry
charged, broke through the barricades, cracked student skulls, and dragged
nine conspirators off to prison. Lafayette called on Parliament "to return to
the national, constitutional and peaceable path—the path of good will," but
royalists booed and cursed him.

"When civil war breaks out," a royalist replied to Lafayette, "its blood is
on the head of those who have provoked it. The previous speaker [Lafayette]
knows that better than any one. He has learned . . . with death in his soul
and the blush of shame on his cheeks, that he who excited furious mobs is
obliged to follow them and almost to lead them."[12]

Revitalized, Lafayette could not resist parrying, "It seems to me the aristocracy is getting angry—like women who get angry with the artist who
paints their portrait."[13]

Lafayette's remarks had little effect on the overwhelmingly royalist
majority in the French Chamber, but it drew ever-growing numbers of young
revolutionaries to his door on the rue d'Anjou—from Italy, Greece, Spain,
Portugal, even Brazil. "The ideas of liberty are fermenting everywhere," he
wrote to James Monroe, who had succeeded Madison to the American presidency, "and France is participating a great deal. Revolution and counterrevolution are face to face. This new generation is enlightened and generous—intellectually superior to the Jacobins and Bonapartists. I am sure
today's young will support the right to pure liberty."[14]

The ferment he described had started in Italy among the Carbonari, a
secret society of young men whose antimonarchist beliefs and methods
spread through Europe like a virulent fever.[15] As it worked its way into
France, its leaders sought a figurehead whom they described as "a gentleman

of olden days who fought for the mere beauty of the cause, the pleasure of combat and to oblige a friend."[16] They enlisted Lafayette, who, excited by their youthful fervor, readily offered them his money as well as his voice, and, without Adrienne's firm hands on the family purse strings, Lafayette dipped far too carelessly—and too deeply—into his capital to finance their cause.

In the autumn of 1821, the Charbonniers, as they were called in France, organized a plot to overthrow Louis XVIII. The king posted spies outside La Grange to track Charbonnier leaders, and the police were able to smash the coup before plotters had fired a shot. Police swept across France, arresting thousands. Although they considered arresting Lafayette and George, the king's advisors feared repercussions if they imprisoned the legendary Prisoner of Olmütz. The government silenced the press, and, in the election of 1823, the royalists silenced Lafayette by using plural voting to defeat his bid for reelection. When the new royalist-dominated Chamber met in February 1824, it extended its right to remain seated from five to seven years. At sixty-six, Lafayette had again failed in his quest to bring American liberty to France.

On his desk, however, was a letter from President Monroe with a resolution from Congress inviting him to visit the United States as "the Nation's Guest." The timing could not have been better—for both men. Lafayette's political life seemed at an end, and, after forty years, he longed "to see for himself the fruit borne on the tree of liberty" he had helped plant in America.[17] Monroe, on the other hand, had just issued a fierce warning to European powers to stay clear of American waters north and south. He enjoined them from colonizing any more lands in the Americas or attempting to export monarchy to independent American nations. The president believed that the presence of Lafayette—the last living major general of the American Revolution—as "the Nation's Guest," on the approaching golden anniversary of independence from the British monarchy, would serve as symbolic reinforcement of his new Monroe Doctrine.

Monroe's invitation not only insulted King Louis XVIII, it convinced some members of his court that America was plotting to seize the French West Indies and appoint Lafayette governor. The king made Lafayette's departure as unpleasant as possible by ordering troops on horseback to disperse the crowd that gathered with the American consul at quayside to see him off at Le Havre. Although Congress had offered to bring him to America aboard a navy frigate, he deemed it undemocratic to use such a vessel for his personal use and booked passage on an American merchantman with George, his secretary August Lavasseur, and his valet.

In contrast to the disagreeable scene at Le Havre, dozens of ships jammed New York Harbor, their masts and stays aflutter with flags and ensigns. Guns boomed and church bells pealed from all directions, and tens of thousands lined the shores to cheer him as his ship passed by. Thirty thousand greeted him on lower Manhattan when he landed; fifty thousand more awaited on Broadway to see the huge procession that would escort him up to City Hall. At the foot of the gangway, a group of veterans in patched-up, ill-fitting old uniforms stood as straight as their crooked old limbs allowed. As he passed before them, each snapped out his name and company, and the battle where he had served with the marquis: "Monmouth, sir"; "Barren Hill, sir"; "Brandywine, sir" . . . It was all too much for the old man, and he burst into tears. He turned to his son for solace. More than forty years had passed; he felt helpless for a moment—old and lame, without his sword or rifle, without his general's uniform, without his youth.

But the cannon booms, the pealing church bells, and the cheering crowds revived him, and he climbed into the mayor's magnificent open carriage to begin the procession. The "Guards of Lafayette"—young, elite volunteers—stood in smart parade dress to lead the way; each wore a broad bandoleer marked "Welcome La Fayette." The procession up Broadway to City Hall—normally a twenty-minute walk—took two hours. Horse guards led the way, troops marched, bands played, flags and bunting blanketed the buildings. Storms of flower petals rained from every window and rooftop. The mayor and other dignitaries welcomed him to City Hall, where he stood for two more hours shaking hands until his own were raw. As darkness enveloped the city, fireworks lit the sky, and spectacular illuminations set the city's public buildings aglow. Lafayette was guest of honor at a spectacular "Lafayette Ball" that evening on Castle Island, an otherwise forbidding fortress at the southern tip of New York Island (Manhattan). Hundreds of workers and artists had transformed it into what newspapers described as "a fairy zone . . . such as we read of in oriental tales,"[18] surrounded by thirty-foot-tall scrims illuminated from the rear. One bore a huge portrait of Lafayette, another a breathtaking view of the château at La Grange. Adjustable lighting changed the shading and colors of the château each hour to simulate a full day there, from dawn to dusk. A third transparency showed Lafayette and Washington standing in a red, white, and blue "Temple of Liberty." Musicians composed waltzes and marches to honor him, and five thousand guests came to what was, for the moment, unquestionably the most elaborate formal banquet and ball ever staged in America.

New York celebrated Lafayette's presence for four days and nights, almost continuously. Americans had never seen anything like it. He spent two hours each afternoon greeting the public at City Hall—trying to shake every hand in the endless line. Some waited all night to see him. They came from every walk of life: weeping veterans hobbled up to kiss his hand and ask, "Sir, do you remember . . . ?" (And he always said he did.) Women brought their babies for him to bless; fathers led their sons into the past, into American history, to touch the hand of a Founding Father. It was a mystical experience they would relate to their heirs through generations to come. Lafayette had materialized from a distant age, the last leader and hero at the nation's defining moment. They knew they and the world would never see his kind again.

After four exhausting days and nights, he and his party left on what they hoped would be a tranquil carriage ride through the New England countryside to Boston, with restful stops at quiet wayside inns. But crowds lined every inch of the route. At the approach to every town and village, militiamen, cavalrymen, and fife-and-drum corps waited to escort him into town—by torchlight if necessary. They waited in the hot sun and driving rain; they waited through the night and lit the town with bonfires to greet him. Regardless of the hour, church bells tolled his arrival, and militiamen fired thirteen-shot salutes from the town cannon or their own muskets. The pastor of every church welcomed him with a prayer and the mayor of every town with a speech; then, after a reverential silence, Lafayette limped front and center to address the townspeople.

> My obligations to the United States, ladies and gentlemen, far surpass the services I was able to render. These date back to the time when I had the good fortune to be adopted by the United States as one of her young sol-diers, as a beloved son. The approbation of the American people . . . is the greatest reward I can receive. I have stood strong and held my head high whenever, in their name, I have proclaimed the American principles of lib-erty, equality and social order. I have devoted myself to these principles since I was a boy, and they will remain a sacred obligation to me until I take my final breath. . . . The greatness and prosperity of the United States are spreading the light of civilization across the world—a civilization based on liberty and resistance to oppression, with political institutions based on the rights of man and republican principles of government by the people.[19]

His message could not have come at a better time in America's history, and it generated a patriotic fervor that swept the nation. Lafayette had arrived ten years after America's victory over Britain in the War of 1812. President Monroe's election two years later had set off an "Era of Good Feeling," with a vast westward expansion that added six states to the Union and six stars to the flag, and produced unprecedented economic development that enriched every home and transformed the nation into the most prosperous on earth. The land was awash in optimism as it approached the fiftieth anniversary of independence; Americans were enjoying, as never before, the fruits of freedom that Lafayette and the other Founding Fathers had won for them. Besides venerating him for his role in the Revolution, they venerated him as a mis-sionary of America's republican principles—a heroic opponent of tyranny who had suffered the worst cruelties in the Old World for his love of the New World. His visit not only revived American patriotism, it reminded Americans of their good fortune as the only people on earth with the freedom to govern themselves and their nation. In celebrating Lafayette, they were celebrating themselves and their nation as they had never done before and would never again do in their lifetimes.

"Sir, America loves you," proclaimed the mayor of a small town that welcomed him on his way to Boston.

"Sir," Lafayette replied, "I truly love America." And so he did.[20]

The two-day trip to Boston took four days, with Lafayette sometimes spending what was left of each night in a hotel or public lodging house, but just as often as the guest of prominent citizens and political and military leaders. It was two o'clock in the morning when he reached the outskirts of Boston, where Governor William Eustis of Massachusetts awaited with a procession of torch-lit carriages—and an explosion of rockets—to welcome Lafayette to his country home for the night. After only two hours' sleep, cannon booms and the blare of a band startled Lafayette from his sleep. On the lawn outside his window he saw the Lafayette Light Infantry in parade dress, complete with their distinctive red and black plumes.

"My brave Light Infantry!" he cried out to George. "That is exactly how their uniforms looked. What courage! How I loved them!" An imaginative commander of a company of riflemen had reproduced the old uniforms and arranged the surprise.[21]

It took Lafayette's procession two hours to weave its way through the crowds that clogged the two-mile route to Boston. They passed through a succession of twenty-four triumphal arches—one for each state—built of wood frames, covered with stretched canvas, painted to look like granite blocks. Almost 75,000 packed Boston's narrow streets as Lafayette proceeded, amid the thunder of booming cannons and clapping church bells, to the State House to address the legislature. He spent three weeks in the Boston area, visiting Massachusetts coastal towns and Portsmouth, New Hampshire—and sharing Sunday dinner with the eighty-nine-year-old John Adams in Quincy. In the most important of the many Masonic receptions, he was elevated to the thirty-third degree and named Honorary Grand Master of the Supreme Council of the Northern United States before two thousand brother Masons, who invited him to return the following June 17 to lay the cornerstone of the Bunker Hill Monument.

"Liberty, brotherhood and goodwill to man are the symbols of Freemasonry," he responded. "May the practice of these principles forever earn us the esteem of humanity's friends and reproof of its enemies."[22]

Every city tried to outdo the previous city's celebration. Learning of Boston's extravagant festivities, New York outdid its own first reception when

Triumphal arches sprouted along Lafayette's parade route in every
city—thirteen in Philadelphia, twenty in Boston. Made of canvas
stretched over a wooden framework and painted to look like stone,
they stood thirty to forty feet high and forty to fifty feet across. The
arch shown here stood in New Orleans to welcome Lafayette in
1825. (*From the author's collection.*)

Lafayette returned by staging an even larger and grander formal ball at Castle
Garden. And in its determination to surpass both New York and Boston,
Philadelphia added huge floats to its procession, one for every trade—and
twenty thousand marchers, who tramped beneath thirteen elaborate triumphal arches, one for each of the original states.

Lafayette's visit actually saved Independence Hall and generated the
first effort in America to restore and preserve historic sites for future gener-

ations. The hall had stood empty and rotting in the twenty-five years since Congress had moved to Washington City, but the prospect of Lafayette's visit forced Philadelphia to restore it, to provide Lafayette with a place to greet the public. Lafayette received visitors in the room in which the Founding Fathers—many of them his friends—had signed the Declaration of Independence. In addition to encouraging the preservation of historic sites, Lafayette's visit generated a surge of monument construction—until then, not a customary public art form in the United States. As a Mason, he laid the cornerstones for monuments to Revolutionary War heroes in almost every city he visited—to his old friend "Baron" de Kalb in Camden, South Carolina; to Pulaski in Savanna, Georgia; and to his beloved Nathanael Greene, also in Savannah. Lafayette's tour generated a vast expansion in various arts and crafts. The communities he visited commissioned artists to paint his portrait for their municipal buildings, schools, and Masonic lodges—and to reproduce them in various sizes for books or souvenirs to sell to the public. A huge and altogether new souvenir industry emerged, with hundreds of artists and craftsmen working day and night to meet the demand for mementos of his visit. They produced medallions, scarves, handkerchiefs, sashes, gloves, fans, bowls, jugs, plates, furniture—many of fine quality—bearing his name and image. Writers, poets, and songsmiths produced stories, poems, and songs about him, including "Companion of Washington," "Prisoner of Olmütz," "The Nation's Guest," and the popular "Lafayette March."

What began as a four-month tour would stretch into a thirteen-month triumphal procession over six thousand miles, through all twenty-four states, from New Hampshire to South Carolina, across the south to New Orleans and up the Mississippi by steamboat to St. Louis. Crowds of fifty thousand to one hundred thousand turned out to see and cheer him in every city; even small towns drew throngs of ten thousand or more from miles around. From St. Louis, he traveled through Tennessee, Kentucky, Ohio, and western Pennsylvania, then up to Buffalo and Niagara Falls, before returning east.

Lafayette made several detours on his travels. One was on the way from New York to Philadelphia, to visit and reminisce with Joseph Bonaparte at the latter's astonishing re-creation of a French château at Bordentown, New Jersey. And, on the way from Philadelphia to Washington City, he stopped to show his son the scenes of his heroics at Brandywine. Despite his denials, Americans insisted on believing that his limp came from his wound at Brandywine. After an emotional reunion with President Monroe, Lafayette went to an even more emotional—and tearful—visit to Mount Vernon and the tombs of George and Martha Washington. The Washingtons and Custises he had known as children forty years earlier gathered about him with their own children and grandchildren. Martha's grandson, the playwright George Washington Custis, presented him with a ring containing a lock of Washington's hair, which is now on display at Chavaniac.

In Washington City, as it was called then, the simplicity of "the presidential palace" and the president's blue suit stunned Lafayette's secretary, Lavasseur, who expected "those puerile ornaments which so many simple ninnies wear in the ante-chambers of the palaces of Europe."[23] Not a sentinel or guard was in sight when they walked to the entrance of the white Georgian mansion; a lone servant let them in and showed them to the Cabinet Room. Monroe had hoped Lafayette would sleep at the Executive Mansion, but "the people of Washington claim you; they say you are the guest of the nation, and that they only have a right to entertain you." Although the arrangements committee had prepared a lavish suite at a hotel, the president promised Lafayette, "Your plate will always be laid at my table, and I hope that whenever you have no other engagement you will dine with me."[24] They came for breakfast the following morning and to a formal dinner that evening with cabinet members, the justices of the Supreme Court, and high-ranking naval and military officers.

On October 19 Lafayette reached the ruins of Yorktown for the celebration of the anniversary of Cornwallis's surrender—at George Washington's actual tent. At the dinner and ball that evening, he paid tribute to his "brothers" Hamilton and Laurens and his "adoptive father," Washington. From Yorktown, he went to Richmond and then to Monticello for a reunion with the enfeebled, eighty-one-year-old Thomas Jefferson. Jefferson hobbled down the steps of the entrance to greet his old friend; the two embraced and cried. At sunset, they rejoiced at the unexpected arrival of the seventy-four-year-old James Madison. Madison wrote that he found Lafayette "much increased in bulk," while Lafayette wrote that he found Jefferson "much aged." The next day, the three friends drove to Charlottesville to see Jefferson's magnum opus, the University of Virginia, the great secular institution that Jefferson had founded and which he ranked with the Declaration of Independence and Virginia's statute of religious freedom as his three greatest achievements. He had designed its buildings and lawns and created its innovative curriculum—by far the broadest in America, with instruction in every area of science and mathematics, five modern and three ancient languages, the arts and letters, political science, law, economics, history, and international affairs—but, purposely, no religion.

When one university dignitary expressed surprise at Lafayette's command of English, he snapped back, "And why would I not speak English? I am an American, after all—just back from a long visit to Europe."[25]

Lafayette spent ten days with Jefferson before leaving for Montpelier and four days with Madison and his wife, Dolley. After Lafayette left, Jefferson had to replenish almost all the red wines in his cellar.

Although Lafayette was inundated with more than four hundred invitations to visit the rest of the south and west, the approaching winter would make most roads impassable, and he postponed the rest of his tour until spring. He spent December, January, and February in the nation's capital, witnessing the climax of the most contentious presidential election Americans had ever witnessed—with four candidates, whose vicious rhetoric raised sectional differences to levels that threatened Congress with political schisms not seen since pre-Union days during the Confederation. General Andrew Jackson of Tennessee, the hero of the Battle of New Orleans, won the popular vote, but neither he nor any one of the other three candidates—Secretary of State John Quincy Adams of Massachusetts, Secretary of War John C. Calhoun of South Carolina, and Speaker of the House Henry Clay of Kentucky—won a majority of electoral votes on December 1. The House of Representatives would have to select the president.

Again, Lafayette's presence proved fortuitous for the nation. The four candidates had little choice but to put aside their differences to celebrate their nation's independence and Lafayette's heroism when he arrived to address a joint session of Congress on December 10. As he entered the great hall, two thousand people rose as one to cheer the great knight. The feuding presidential candidates rose with them, as did the justices of the Supreme Court, leaders of the army and navy, and the entire diplomatic corps, with one exception: the French ambassador was absent.

Three days after his speech, President Monroe asked Congress to compensate "the Nation's Guest" for his services and sacrifices to the nation. Although the arrangements committee was paying all his expenses on his current tour, he had spent half his fortune on the American Revolution, lost the rest in the French Revolution, and had spent much of the capital that Adrienne had recovered to finance the abortive revolution of the Charbonniers. He would have to live thereafter on the volatile proceeds of his farm. Thomas Jefferson and James Madison both supported the proposal, and Congress granted him $200,000 in government bonds yielding 6 percent annually and redeemable in ten years. It also awarded him a township of about thirty-six square miles of unsold public lands in Florida, on the southern Georgia border near Tallahassee, which it named La Grange Township.

On New Year's Day, Congress gave a banquet in Lafayette's honor; the four feuding candidates were there. The president, who would soon retire after eight years, broke with tradition and also attended, and the dinner began with Henry Clay's toast to Monroe. After a portrait of Lafayette was presented to the Congress, Clay raised his glass to Lafayette: "To the great apostle of liberty whom the persecutions of tyranny could not defeat, whom the love of riches could not influence, whom popular applause could never seduce. He was always the same, in the shackles of Olmütz, in his various labors on the summits of power and glory."[26]

Lafayette stood to reply with a toast "to the perpetual union of the United States. It has always saved us in times of storm; one day it will save the world."[27] His prescient words embarrassed the candidates into softening the tones of their bitter rhetoric. On February 9, 1825, the House of Representatives elected John Quincy Adams president. Some Jackson supporters had threatened violence, and foreign diplomats were gleefully predicting the collapse of the American republic, but at President Monroe's reception for the president-elect at the Executive Mansion, Andrew Jackson appeared and stepped forward, his hand outstretched, to congratulate John Quincy Adams and pledge his loyal support. Lafayette beamed with satisfaction as he watched the promise of American liberty and republican self-government fulfilled. The French knight was content: liberty in America was secure.

In March, he began touring southern and western states, spending a few days each in the major cities of North and South Carolina, Georgia, Mississippi, and Louisiana. The governors greeted him in every state capital, and Masonic lodges sponsored banquets in every town. He all but exploded with pride in North Carolina, where he visited the first American town named in his honor—Fayetteville. In the years that followed his visit, Americans would rename more than six hundred villages, towns, cities, counties, mountains, lakes, rivers, educational institutions, and other landmarks for him or his château at La Grange.

His trip across the south exhausted the old knight. The bumpy, rutted roads and primitive wagon trails sent his carriage or stagecoach lurching unpredictably and left him ill, often too shaken to eat or sleep. In contrast, the two-week steamboat ride up the Mississippi from New Orleans was a delight. The *Natchez* was a luxuriously appointed boat, its lounge an ornate hotel lobby with rich oriental rugs, oil paintings, and chandeliers. It carried a famous New Orleans chef, an orchestra, and a large staff of maids and butlers that saw to the passengers' every need. The magnificent river journey had completely rejuvenated him by the time he reached St. Louis at the end of April. He all but fainted, however, at the governor's banquet when a young man approached, looking every bit like the ghost of the young Alexander Hamilton. It was Hamilton's son.

From St. Louis, the *Natchez* steamed to the Ohio and up to the mouth of the Cumberland River, where the Lafayette party switched to a smaller steamboat for the trip to Nashville, Tennessee. General Andrew Jackson, the hero of New Orleans, greeted the Hero of Two Worlds in full parade dress, with the Tennessee militia. Lafayette spent three days at Jackson's "Hermitage" mansion, with Jackson showing him every inch of his huge farm and discussing the latest agricultural techniques.

Two days after Lafayette resumed his trip upriver, an enormous jolt awakened him at midnight. The boat had run aground and was sinking. George and Lavasseur rushed into Lafayette's cabin, led him topside to the rail, and lowered him carefully into a lifeboat—a job made difficult because of his stiff leg. After rowing him to the Kentucky shore, they helped the captain and crew evacuate the ship before its hull sank into the Ohio River mud. Although everyone aboard escaped uninjured, all their possessions were lost—including (much to his relief) more than six hundred unanswered letters Lafayette had accumulated during his American tour. They spent the rest of the night huddled around huge bonfires, and early the next morning, another steamboat, bound for New Orleans, stopped to rescue them. When the owner learned Lafayette's identity, he put about and took the stranded passengers to Louisville, Kentucky.

From Kentucky, the Lafayette troupe went to Indiana, Ohio, western Pennsylvania—with a special visit to Fayette County—and up to Buffalo and Niagara Falls, where the chief of the Senecas greeted him. He returned east to Albany on the amazing new New York State Barge Canal—then one of the wonders of the world—and he arrived in Boston in time to celebrate the fiftieth anniversary of the Battle of Bunker Hill. Two hundred thousand lined the roads as the procession began, led by eight open carriages, each carrying five veterans of the Battle of Bunker Hill—forty in all. Seven thousand troops marched behind them in parade dress. Lafayette followed in a huge open carriage drawn by six splendid white horses. George and Lavasseur followed in a second carriage, while a third carriage carried the day's principal orator, the golden-tongued Massachusetts representative Daniel Webster. Fifteen thousand waited in the wooden amphitheater built around the crest of the hill, where the city's Order of Masons awaited. As Right Worshipful Grand Master, Lafayette took the silver trowel and laid the cornerstone. A pastor, a veteran of Bunker Hill, gave the benediction; then a huge choir exploded into "Old Hundred":

> O is not this a holy spot?
> 'Tis the high place of Freedom's birth;
> God of Our Fathers! Is it not
> The holiest spot of all the earth?[28]

Tears streamed down Lafayette's face as Webster began his address, directing the first part to the veterans of Bunker Hill before turning to Lafayette:

> You are connected with both hemispheres and with two generations. Heaven saw fit to ordain that the electric spark of liberty should be conducted, through you, from the New World to the Old; and we, who are now here to perform this duty of patriotism, have all of us long ago received it in charge from our fathers to cherish your name and your virtues.[29]

After Webster finished, the choir exploded into song, praising God and America; the cannons boomed, church bells pealed; and, as participants prepared to leave, Lafayette asked for a canvas sack and carefully troweled it full of soil from Bunker Hill to carry back to France. After the huge banquet that followed, Lafayette wrote to his children in La Grange "of the most beautiful patriotic fête ever celebrated. Nothing can compare to it except the *Fédération* of '90. . . . Nothing can describe the effect of that republican prayer pronounced before an immense multitude. . . . I stood up at the head of all the other Revolutionary soldiers. . . . We sat down at a table with four thousand others, where I said that after celebrating the fiftieth anniversary of freedom in the American hemisphere, the toast of the next such anniversary will be to Europe's freedom."[30]

Before leaving Boston, Lafayette returned to Quincy to say farewell to John Adams, then went off to Maine and Vermont to fulfill his pledge to visit all twenty-four states. He laid the cornerstone of the University of Vermont at Burlington, then took the midnight steamboat down Lake Champlain, and another down the Hudson from Albany to New York, where he arrived on July 4. He laid the cornerstone of the public library in Brooklyn, where heaps of stones blocked the view of a group of children. Some of the men lifted them up to see, and Lafayette swept one six-year-old boy into his arms, kissed his cheek, and set him down to watch as he laid the cornerstone. The boy's name was Walter Whitman.

Lafayette spent ten days in New York, returned to Philadelphia, revisited the Germantown and Brandywine battlefields, and went for a month's stay at the White House in Washington as President John Quincy Adams's personal guest. They were old friends: Lafayette had known the president when Adams was a winsome boy of fifteen living with his father in Paris and called simply Quincy. Adams allowed his aging friend to rest after his long trip; he scheduled no receptions or banquets and went along with Lafayette when the latter wanted to revisit his three old friends in Virginia—Monroe, Jefferson, and Madison. All knew it was the last time they would ever see each other. Thomas Jefferson died ten months later, on July 4, 1826, as did the president's father, John Adams, on the very same day, in Quincy, Massachusetts.

John Quincy Adams insisted on Lafayette's remaining at the White House for an official celebration of the Frenchman's sixty-eighth birthday on September 6. Although presidents never offered toasts, Adams broke with protocol and raised his glass "to the 22nd of February and the 6th of September, the birthday of Washington and the birthday of Lafayette." Lafayette responded, "To the 4th of July, the birthday of liberty."[31]

Washington City declared a holiday the following morning to say goodbye to the last living general of the Revolutionary War. A huge, silent crowd encircled the White House; the president and the members of the cabinet all awaited Lafayette's appearance. Finally he arrived, and the president, his voice trembling, said farewell on behalf of the American people:

"We shall look upon you always as belonging to us, during the whole of our life, as belonging to our children after us. You are ours by more than patriotic self-devotion with which you flew to the aid of our fathers at the crisis of our fate; ours by that unshaken gratitude for your services which is a precious portion of our inheritance; ours by that tie of love, stronger than death, which has linked your name for endless ages of time with the name of Washington. . . . Speaking in the name of the whole people of the United States, and at a loss only for language to give utterance to that feeling of attachment with which the heart of the nation beats as the heart of one man, I bid you a reluctant and affectionate farewell."[32]

An eternity passed before Lafayette finally brought his emotions under control long enough to reply: "God bless you, Sir; and all who surround you. God bless the American people, each of their states and the federal government. Accept this patriotic farewell of a heart that will overflow with gratitude until the moment it ceases to beat."[33]

Lafayette broke into sobs and embraced Quincy, then limped into an anteroom with George to recover his composure before returning to his carriage for his last ride on American soil. A line of militiamen stood at attention on either side of the drive as his carriage rolled out the drive. The president remained in the peristyle waving good-bye until Lafayette's carriage disappeared into the mass of humanity along the route to the quay on the Potomac. The cannons boomed their customary twenty-four-salvos—one for each state—but instead of provoking the usual cheers, the shots echoed eerily across an all but silent city. The thousands who watched his carriage pass stood silent, in mourning, their children perched on their shoulders clutching small American flags in their tiny hands, their voices too choked with tears to sustain more than an occasional hoarse "Good-bye, marquis" or a sad "A-doo, marquis, a-doo." They were mourning not only the passing of the man but the end of the most glorious age in American history—an age of heroes; an age of chivalry that gave them a new nation unlike any in history, with liberties that ordinary people had never before enjoyed.

The Custis and Washington families waited at quayside to say good-bye, and a column of Lafayette's own Virginia militia stood at the ready as he and George walked to the boat. Thick crowds lined both banks of the river waving and calling "A-doo" as his steamboat carried him downstream to board America's newest frigate, the *Brandywine*, which the president and Congress had commissioned to take him back to France.

Twenty-four days later, the speedy new ship approached Le Havre, fired a salute, and received an answering salute—to the immense relief of all aboard who had anticipated an unpleasant reception by French authorities. A friendly crowd waited at quayside to greet Lafayette, and, as he was about to disembark, the officers aboard the *Brandywine* struck the national ensign and presented it to him. "Here, General, take it," said the ship's commander. "We could not confide it to more glorious hands."[34]

The next day, Lafayette left for Paris; when he reached Rouen—about halfway to the capital—a crowd of well-wishers gathered outside his inn to serenade him while he and his son dined. When he appeared on the balcony to thank them, troops charged from all sides, swords drawn, slashing and clubbing at the men, women, and children in the crowd, wounding dozens and arresting others. Lafayette and his son thought of the America they had left and despaired for their native land.

21

Les Adieux

F AT K ING L OUIS XVIII DIED while Lafayette was in America, and his younger brother, the comte d'Artois, succeeded to the throne as Charles X. Charles's years of exile during the Terror and the Empire had transformed the once profligate playboy into a vengeful tyrant, intent on recovering absolute rule. The French were bristling under his ever-tightening restrictions when Lafayette returned to La Grange. The people of Brie built a triumphal arch to welcome his return, proclaiming him *L'Ami du Peuple*—The People's Friend. In the spring of 1827, they elected him to the Chamber of Deputies, and, a month later, police arrested an editor for publishing one of Lafayette's fiery speeches attacking the royal regime. "If the words are blamable," Lafayette protested to the police magistrate, "the responsibility falls on me, and if they need explanation no one more than I should be called to give that explanation."[1]

Fearing worldwide condemnation if he silenced the Prisoner of Olmütz, the king silenced all the voices in the Chamber by dissolving it and calling for new elections and a new, more accommodating Chamber. But the people of Brie returned Lafayette to the new Chamber the following year, and his Tuesday evening salon at his house in the rue d'Anjou became the most important liberal institution in Paris—as it had been on Monday evenings in the rue de Bourbon. Once again, his dining table overflowed with food and drink. In Adrienne's place, Virginie and Anastasie took turns as hostess, while George tried his best to bar the door to spies, bores, and spongers. As in the rue de Bourbon, his salons attracted prominent Americans, from whom he learned that his old friend, the retired president James Monroe,

King Charles X in his coronation robes after his acces-
sion to the French throne in
1824, on the death of his
older brother, Louis XVIII.
(*Réunion des Musées Nationaux.*)

was in dire financial straits. Monroe had saved Adrienne's life when he was
an American envoy in Paris, and, as president, he had coaxed Congress into
giving Lafayette title to an entire Florida township and enough government
bonds to wipe out his debts from the Charbonnier fiasco. Monroe's financial
problems stemmed from his carelessness as an envoy in Europe, where he
had paid his expenses with his own money and failed to demand immediate
reimbursement from public funds.

"My dear Monroe," Lafayette wrote eagerly, "permit your earliest, your
best and your most obliged friend to be plain with you. It is probable that,
to give you time and facilities for your arrangements, a mortgage might be of
some use. The sale of one-half of my Florida property is full enough to meet
my family settlement. . . . You remember that in similar embarrassment I
have formerly accepted your intervention. It gives me right to reciprocity."[2]

Charles X tried suppressing criticism of his reign by tightening sanctions
on the press and all forms of entertainment. The censorship grew intolerable, with police charging even into a crowd of operagoers emerging from a

performance of Rossini's *Guillaume Tell* (*William Tell*)—the story of Swiss rebellion against the Austrian empire. Rioting ensued, and, after the elections in the spring of 1830, Charles opened the Chamber of Deputies with a warning to Lafayette and other liberals: "Should subversive activities present my government with any obstacles, I will find the power to remove them. I am resolved to maintain public order."[3] The Chamber immediately rebuked the king, saying that the Constitutional Charter required "that your government's political views and the wishes of your subjects be in unity. . . . This unity does not exist."[4]

Infuriated by the rebuke, the king dissolved the Chamber a second time and ordered new elections, but subjected periodicals to prepublication censorship to prevent publicity for liberals. When the election of July 12 failed to change the political complexion of the new Chamber—indeed, Lafayette won reelection by the largest margin ever—the incorrigible king dissolved the Chamber a third time, even before it had a chance to meet—and provoked another French Revolution. Antiroyalists poured into the streets and raised barricades with toppled trees, paving stones, and old furniture—on the Place de la Bastille, along the rue Saint-Antoine, in side streets, and on the quays. After a bloody battle at river's edge, a mob seized the Hôtel de Ville, as its forebears had done in 1789. King Charles tried to halt the flood of antigovernment leaflets by ordering printing presses to shut down, but the mechanics and printers refused to obey and spilled into the streets to join workers, shopkeepers, and students at the barricades. When he learned of the insurrection, the seventy-three-year-old Lafayette raced into Paris from La Grange. A crowd of military-school cadets filled the rue d'Anjou in front of his door at four the next morning to ask his instructions. As dawn spilled across Paris, the church bells rang out as they had in 1789. King Charles fled to his country château at Rambouillet, thirty miles southwest of Paris, but before leaving he ordered royal troops to attack the barricades. The revolutionaries, however, had seized the army's water supplies. By mid-afternoon, the thirsty troops fell back exhausted in the stifling August heat, but not without leaving a trail of dead and wounded as a bloody reminder of their might.

When Lafayette appeared for a meeting of deputies the next morning, the sight of the brave old veteran limping from his carriage evoked cheers from onlookers. Suddenly, the spontaneous cry of "*Vive Lafayette! Vive la liberté!*" spread through the streets and across the barricades. The vision of the legendary knight captured the imagination of the young, inspiring them to battle on, battle harder, but Lafayette's presence so terrified the royal commanding general that he ordered Lafayette's immediate arrest. When he heard the general's order, Lafayette shouted angrily to his fellow deputies, "Let us rather *order* [the general] in the name of the law to cease firing on the people.

"These events, Messieurs," he barked, "can no longer be confined within the limits of strict legality. This is a revolution. A provisional government is necessary, and should be formed immediately." When the other deputies hesitated, Lafayette lost patience: "Already, Messieurs, my name is placed, by the confidence of the people and with my consent, at the head of the insurrection. I ardently desire the approval of my colleagues, but if you do not reach a decision by tomorrow, I shall consider myself at liberty to act alone, and in my own name. Tomorrow I will establish my headquarters at Paris."[5]

That evening, Lafayette limped up to the barricades and embraced soldiers, former Charbonniers, workers, students. For two days they had fought without direction, but when the legendary hero suddenly emerged from their nation's past, they eagerly raised him to leadership. On the third day, the fighting renewed on all fronts until midday, when the royal troops retreated, at first in orderly fashion, then, fearful of possible massacres, in full flight up the Champs-Elysées and out of Paris. The deputies charged Lafayette with bringing the revolution under control to forestall the madness and excesses of 1789. They resanctioned the National Guard and named him commander, and, as he had in 1789, he donned the uniform of a French general and ordered his citizen's militia to restore calm to the city.

"My duty commands me to respond to the public confidence and to devote myself to the common defense," he told the deputies. "My conduct at seventy-three will be what it was at thirty-two." Outside, the chants of the crowd grew more insistent: "*Vive Lafayette! Vive la liberté!*" As he had in '89, he led the procession to the Hôtel de Ville—limping on foot now instead of riding his stately white horse, but nonetheless a knight triumphant. And as their parents had done in '89, the people of Paris cheered him wildly as he passed—from the rooftops, from every window, and along the streets and squares. History repeated itself eerily as he climbed the steps into the Hôtel de Ville and up the grand staircase. When a guardsman offered to show him the way to the Grande Salle, he laughed, assuring the young man he knew the building well. As he reached the council chamber, he saw the broken fragments of the busts of Louis XVIII and Charles X— smashed by the mob, much as an earlier mob had smashed the busts of him and Bailly. Shreds of white Bourbon flags with the fleur de lys lay about the room. He ordered the revolutionary tricolor raised over the Hôtel de Ville and proclaimed an end to the "Three Glorious Days," as the Revolution of 1830 has been called ever since.

"My dear fellow citizens and brave comrades," he told the crowd below, "the confidence of the people of Paris calls me once more to command public forces. I have accepted with devotion and with joy the powers confided to me, and, as in 1789, I feel strengthened by the approbation of my honorable colleagues assembled today in Paris. I will make no profession of faith.

My sentiments are known. The conduct of the people of Paris during these last few days renders me prouder than ever to lead them. . . . Liberty shall triumph or we will perish together. *"Vive la liberté! Vive la patrie!"*[6]

On October 29, 1830, France invested Lafayette "with a veritable moral and political dictatorship, the title to which was written in no decree," according to one deputy, "but was imposed upon him in such a way that no one dreamed of contesting it."[7] At seventy-three, it was the second time in his life that he had reigned in Paris—the second time in his life that he neared the completion of his quest to bring liberty and constitutional government to his native land.

His second reign would last but a day.

True to character, he refused to retain power unconstitutionally. From the moment he seized the reins of power, they seemed to slip out of his hands—as they had in 1789. As it did then, near hysteria reigned in the Grande Salle at the Hôtel de Ville. Crowds of unsolicited advisors, mostly young liberals and Charbonniers, milled about, shouting demands for reform. Couriers raced in and out with reports of emergencies: royal troops were at the top of the Champs Elysées preparing a counterattack; brigands were looting the national mint at the Hôtel de la Monnaie; mobs were stripping shops of bread and food. And outside the city hall—the constant, irritating chanting continued: *"Vive la République! Vive Lafayette! Vive la République!"*

A courier arrived from the king pledging to repeal recent decrees and recall the Chamber of Deputies, but Lafayette dismissed him: "It is too late," he said. "Reconciliation is impossible; the royal family has ceased to reign. The Bourbons are finished. The people have already revoked the king's decrees themselves. As a delegate of the people I can have nothing to do with the representative of the fallen monarchy."[8] The Charbonniers cheered, urged him to proclaim a republic, but he rejected their demand, saying that only the people could proclaim a republic, by popular referendum.

Conservative bankers, merchants, and powerful landowners in the Chamber of Deputies were already acting to forestall that possibility—to preserve their economic and political power and protect their assets. Lafayette's republic would mean sharing political power with the unpropertied. Moreover, they argued, the establishment of a republic would violate the Peace of 1815, which had restored the Bourbon monarchy. Europe's monarchs might invade France again if the nation abolished the monarchy and proclaimed a republic. Accordingly, the deputies restructured the executive branch of government, creating a powerful new Lieutenant General of the Realm—a *stathoudérat* ("stateholder")—to replace the king as chief executive—but they named a royal to fill the post: the duc d'Orléans, a direct descendant of Louis XIII, whose Orléanist veins carried blood as pure as that of his Bourbon cousin, King Charles. The selection of another royal

to head the state sent shock waves across the barricades; republicans threatened renewed civil war.

At midnight on July 30, the duc d'Orléans acted to forestall such a possibility by sending a messenger to the Hôtel de Ville with a request to meet
with Lafayette the following morning. Lafayette knew he would have to
decide before then whether to proclaim a republic based on the American
constitution or allow the duc d'Orléans to assume the throne. Either choice
risked civil war. "If we establish a monarchy, the duc d'Orléans will be king,"
an aide counseled him, "and if we establish a republic, you will be president.
Do you want the responsibility of governing a republic?"[9] His thoughts
turned back to 1793 and the ease with which Jacobin terrorists had seized
and perverted the First French Republic. Lafayette consulted with American
ambassador William C. Rives. "What will our friends in the United States
say," he asked, "if they learn that we have proclaimed the republic?" The
American minced no words: "They will say that forty years of experience
have been lost on the French."[10]

Although he regretted disappointing the idealistic young men he had
embraced in the Charbonniers, Lafayette's decision proved less painful than
he had anticipated. He had, after all, championed constitutional monarchy
under Louis XVI, after the Revolution of 1789, and the duc d'Orléans was a
far more appropriate candidate as constitutional monarch—affable, dressed
in modest bourgeois suits, and as comfortable speaking English as Lafayette.
He had spent two years in exile in Philadelphia during the Terror and had
met Washington at Mount Vernon—when young George-Washington Lafayette was there. The duke was fifty-seven and carried a comfortable paunch,
but he had seen his share of military campaigns in the regular army and
before that had even served in Lafayette's National Guard. And he had suffered the cruel loss of his father to the guillotine. He had witnessed the horrors of the Terror and the beauties of American democracy. He had much in
common with Lafayette, and each genuinely liked the other. Lafayette
invited the duke to come to the Hôtel de Ville the following day, much as
Louis XVI had done in July 1789. As then, Lafayette waited at the foot of
the steps to greet the monarch, who arrived on horseback instead of in a
gilded carriage and shook hands in an eager, democratic way. "Messieurs,"
the duke told the crowd of onlookers, "I am simply an old National Guardsmen come to visit his former general."[11]

The comment provoked a few cheerful cries of *"Vive le duc,"* as well as
unpleasant shouts of *"Pas de Bourbons!"*—"No Bourbons!" Lafayette led the
duke up the grand staircase to the Grande Salle, where, together with republican leaders, Lafayette had drawn up a historic seven-point *Programme de
l'Hôtel de Ville* to which the duke would have to agree in order to win republican support and prevent civil war: (1) Sovereignty of the "nation"—that is,

Lafayette (right) hands the duc d'Orléans (left, with sash), soon to be the "citizen" king Louis-Philippe I, the *Programme de l'Hôtel de Ville*, a doctrine of basic constitutional rights. (*Réunion des Musées Nationaux.*)

the people—over the head of state and the constitution; (2) Abolition of hereditary peerage; (3) Complete reform of the judiciary; (4) Municipal and communal elections based on widest possible public participation, with no property qualifications; (5) Popular election of lower-level judiciary; (6) Reform of privileges and monopolies that restrict industry and free commerce; (7) All the foregoing adopted provisionally and prior to submission [in a popular referendum] to the nation, which has the sole power to establish the system of government that it prefers.

"You know that I am a republican," Lafayette told the duke, as the latter read the document, "and I see the Constitution of the United States as the most perfect document in existence."[12]

"I think as you do," replied the duke. "It is impossible to have spent two years in America and not be that opinion. But do you believe that, given the French situation and French thinking, it would be wise to adopt it in France?"[13]

"No," Lafayette agreed. "What the French people need today is a popular throne, wrapped in republican institutions—but entirely republican."[14]

"That is exactly what I believe," the duke replied—and Lafayette took him at his word, shook his hand, and, as one knight to another, never questioned the duke's honor by asking for his signature on the historic document. Witnessing the handshake was Lafayette's old friend the comte de Ségur.

After the duc d'Orléans expressed his concurrence, Lafayette waved the document containing the *Programme* before his political supporters, declaring that "constitutional monarchy is the best form of republic."[15] He issued a proclamation urging regular army troops and officers to serve the new government and called on all citizens to remember that the duke was "one of the young patriots of '89." Outside the Hôtel de Ville, the antiroyalist cries had reached thunderous proportions. Both men had seen the *coupe-têtes* of '89 and realized the need for quick action. Lafayette seized a large tricolor flag—the flag of the Revolution—pressed it into the duke's hand, and led him onto the balcony, where he embraced him with both arms and kissed him on both cheeks—a gesture that writers across France described as "the republican kiss, with which the Hero of Two Worlds created a king."[16] On August 2, Charles X abdicated and fled to exile in England. Five days later, the Chamber of Deputies elected the duc d'Orléans king, with Lafayette voting aye.

After the vote, the Chamber revised the Constitutional Charter, transferring all legislative powers from the executive to the legislature, breaking all government ties to the Roman Catholic Church, abolishing in perpetuity all censorship, and abolishing the extraordinary courts that could sentence enemies of the state without trial. The tricolor replaced the white Bourbon flag as the national emblem, and the new monarch would take the throne as "King of the French" instead of "King of France" and swear to observe the Constitutional Charter before doing so. The new king took the name Louis-Philippe I, which united the names of the Bourbon and Orléans royal houses,[17] but he called himself a "citizen king" and continued living in his own "modest" palace, the Palais-Royal, instead of moving into the royal Palais des Tuileries. He wore ordinary bourgeois clothes, with the only distinguishing element a button bearing the emblem "Live free or die."

"It is really to you, General, that we are indebted for all this," the new queen told Lafayette after the coronation, and the new king sent him a note that evening: "I cannot retire, *mon cher Général*, without thanking you for your good efforts today, and for the success that you have obtained." And he signed it "Your affectionate [friend], Louis-Philippe."[18]

"There is the king we needed," Lafayette declared in response. "There is the most republican solution that we were able to find."[19]

Lafayette's happy pronouncement set Paris ablaze with festivities. While the worst elements of the mob slithered away into dark alleys, the rest of France hailed Lafayette as hero of the Revolution. On August 15, the City of Paris held a banquet for three hundred guests in his honor and presented him with two small cannons that remain at La Grange. The great author

Henri Beyle, who wrote under the pen name Stendhal, called Lafayette "admirable . . . the anchor of our liberty."[20] America, too, hailed Lafayette's triumph, with President Jackson proclaiming it a triumph for American liberty. New Orleans sent its flag to the City of Paris, and Baltimore sent its flag to Lafayette, who was still a citizen of that city and the state of Maryland.

Louis-Philippe tried basking in the aura of Lafayette's popularity: he named Lafayette Commander of the National Guard of the Realm, and his oldest son immediately enlisted and placed himself under Lafayette's direct command. On August 29, Lafayette restaged the huge *Fête de la Fédération* of 1790, with three hundred thousand spectators lining the banks of the Champs de Mars as four squadrons of mounted guards escorted the new king across the arena to join Lafayette at a tent in front of the Ecole Militaire. The king then distributed flags to each of the battalions, and, as they had in 1790, the troops listened to Lafayette intone the oath of allegiance to the nation. Then, in one thunderous voice, the entire throng cried out, as their parents had in 1790, *"Je le jure!"*—"I so do swear."

In the days and weeks that followed, Louis-Philippe renamed the former place de la Révolution the place de la Concorde,[21] to symbolize the unity and peace that would henceforth reign among the French—for a few weeks at least. A month later, the natural division between conservatives and liberals in the Chamber of Deputies widened into an unbridgeable divide. Lafayette seized the leadership of the minority liberal wing, demanding more reforms each time he spoke: abolition of the House of Peers and the peerage, abolition of slavery, universal suffrage, and French military support for revolutions against autocratic rule in other nations. In September and early October 1830, the revolution in France inspired the Belgians to drive out the Dutch and declare independence; the Poles rebelled against Russian rule; Spanish rebels were in arms against the harsh rule of King Ferdinand; and Italians up and down the Italian boot were in arms against the petty tyrants who ruled the peninsula's mosaic of autonomous duchies. Even Germans had taken to the streets with cries of *"Hoch Lafayette!"*

In the Chamber of Deputies, Lafayette moved that French troops support Belgian independence. He organized a committee to help Polish rebels, and he induced Louis-Philippe to finance the rebellion in Spain—much to the annoyance of Europe's other monarchs, who sent ministers to a London conference to restore the 1815 military coalition against France and stop the disease of French revolution from spreading through Europe again. "When the masses rise up, provoked by troublemakers like Lafayette," wrote an Austrian minister to the retired Talleyrand, "who can stop them?"[22]

Americans, on the other hand, hailed his every move, with delegations from every major city in the United States flocking to Paris to pay tribute. "This evening," he said at a dinner for a delegation of Philadelphians and French army officers, "I find all the sentiments of my life fused here, the grandsons of my companions in America, the sons of my comrades of '89 and my new brothers in arms of the Revolution of 1830." He then asked the guests to fill their glasses and stand:

"To the memory of Washington!"[23]

In the Chamber of Deputies, however, conservatives held a majority, and they acted to protect their own interests: they restored protective tariffs and banned certain imports to prevent foreign competition; they banned all worker organizations to prevent strikes; and they restricted voting to tax-paying property owners—about two hundred thousand men, in a nation whose population had mushroomed to thirty-five million.

Lafayette's continuing demands for reform and freedom—elsewhere in Europe as well as in France—not only provoked the enmity of Europe's other monarchs, they gradually alienated Louis-Philippe by relegating him to the shadows of the French political stage, while Lafayette stood front and center in the limelight. Other European monarchs mocked Louis-Philippe as a puppet-king manipulated by the dangerous revolutionary, Lafayette, while French conservatives called Lafayette the unelected "Mayor of the Palace" and joined cartoonists in unmerciful mockery of the king as "a pear"—*une poire*—a double entendre that reflected the shape of his body—a bulbous torso and an undersized head—as well as his brain ("pear" being a synonym in French slang for *simpleton*).

On Christmas Eve, the Chamber's conservative majority staged a political coup d'état to rid the government of republican influences. It stripped Lafayette of all authority by abolishing the post of Commander of the National Guard of the Realm and converted the National Guard into a national police force under the minister of the interior. As a sop to republicans, the president of the chamber proposed naming Lafayette Honorary Commander, but Lafayette refused, saying that "such nominal titles do not befit a free people or me."[24]

The upper echelon of Lafayette's officers immediately resigned in anger, and liberals in the Chamber denounced the dismissal with equal fury. Only Lafayette himself seemed calm—indeed, he seemed relieved by his ouster. When one of his generals asked him to organize resistance to the Chamber's actions, Lafayette replied, "No, no . . . I know where I stand. It is time for me to retire. I know I hover over the Palais-Royal like a nightmare; not for the king and his family . . . but those around him. Do you think I did not hear [Minister] Viennet tell the king when he saw me enter, 'Here comes the mayor of the palace?' There is no doubt I was useful in bringing him to power . . . on his promise to support the *Programme de l'Hôtel de Ville.* Everyone seems to have forgotten that promise, but I still insist strongly on holding him to it—and that is what the court cannot forgive. . . . From all this I conclude that I have become a bother . . . but I cannot change my convictions."[25]

In the days that followed, Louis-Philippe issued a proclamation regretting Lafayette's retirement, and Lafayette said his farewells to fellow officers in the Paris National Guard and the National Guard of the Realm. In a thinly veiled rebuke to the Chamber of Deputies, however, he announced that his retirement from the military did not mean retirement from politics. Indeed, he converted his seat in the Chamber into the most visible pulpit of ultraliberal ideas in Europe and a rallying point for parliamentary opposition to the increasingly conservative French government. He spoke eloquently on what he called the source of all divisions in Europe—the conflict between two guiding principles: the sovereign rights of peoples and the divine right of kings; between liberty and equality on the one hand and despotism and privilege on the other. He openly encouraged revolution, independence, and human rights in Ireland, Greece, Poland, Italy, and the colonies of South America. In England and the United States, liberal voices echoed his cries for liberty.

By early spring, the anti-French coalition of European monarchs convinced Louis-Philippe that Lafayette's inflammatory rhetoric risked igniting another general war. Conservatives at home warned the king that street demonstrations in Paris for rebels in other lands could easily metamorphose into rebellion and elevate Lafayette to power. Already seething with anger over the proliferation of "pear" and "puppet" posters—and Lafayette's daily accusations that the king had broken his pledge to support the *Programme de l'Hôtel de Ville*—Louis-Philippe broke with Lafayette. He denied he had ever discussed the *Programme* and all but accused Lafayette of lying. To placate his fellow monarchs, he moved out of his home and into the royal Palais des Tuileries and made overtures for closer court-to-court relations—a move that brought immediate praise from the anti-French coalition and an increase in French foreign trade. After a futile protest to the king, Lafayette left the royal Palais des Tuileries for the last time.

"*Adieu l'Amérique*," sneered one of the king's aides as he watched the old knight leave.[26]

Lafayette returned to tend his estate at La Grange for the summer. His neighbors not only reelected him to the Chamber of Deputies, they voted him mayor of the village at La Grange and elected him to the General Council of the *département*, or county—two posts he had not sought. By the time he returned to the Chamber in the autumn, the Russians had crushed the Polish revolution. He nevertheless renewed his calls for French subsidies for revolutions against other despots, for the abolition of slavery, for the abolition of the Chamber of Peers, and for the abolition of property rights as a voting qualification. Conservatives had heard it all before and had tired of him, but they could not ignore him. He remained the unquestioned—and apparently eternal—leader of the opposition and the almost universal hero of the young. They had read of his legendary exploits in their history texts, knew him as the living symbol of liberty in America, and saw his heroic life as proof that they could realize their own ideals. There he stood beside them, returned to life from the past, from America, to lead them into the future. What they *could* not understand, however, and what he *would* not understand, is that the future in France would only repeat the past.

Late in 1831, the untitled bourgeois barons of business who ruled France in the Chamber of Deputies veered onto the path of their aristocratic predecessors. After silk workers in Lyons won a guarantee of a minimum wage from the city's chief administrator, or prefect, factory owners refused to pay it. The workers rioted and seized the plants and the city's public buildings. The Paris government dismissed the prefect and ordered regular army troops to crush the worker revolt and impose martial law, including a ban on singing "La Marseillaise." Lafayette protested in vain. The following year, he proposed laws to provide political asylum for refugees fleeing despotic regimes. The Chamber rejected his proposal.

In early 1832, a cholera epidemic that had started in India and swept through Asia Minor and eastern Europe reached France. A month later, more than a thousand Parisians and many times that number elsewhere in France were dead. Lafayette sent George back to La Grange to help Anastasie and Virginie cope with the needs of the family and the villagers, while he remained in Paris to help the government deal with the emergency.

In mid-May, the disease killed the prime minister, who also held dual powers as minister of the interior, with control of the French national police force. Despite Lafayette's cries of outrage, Louis-Philippe assumed the two posts himself, thus accumulating sweeping new powers not granted him under the Constitutional Charter. Two weeks later, he used his police powers with frightening enthusiasm after the epidemic claimed General Maximilien Lamarque, a revered hero of the Napoleonic Wars and an outspoken liberal in the Chamber of Deputies.

One hundred thousand soldiers and veterans from all parts of France engulfed the church of the Madeleine in Paris to escort their dead leader to the cemetery. The cortège stretched for two miles through the narrow streets, with Lafayette and other former maréchals de camp as pallbearers. They stopped at the Place de la Bastille for eulogies, and, one after the other, the solemn voices droned on, until Lafayette rose to recount his vivid memories of the two revolutions of 1789 and 1830. Cries of "*Vive la République!*" and "*Vive Lafayette!*" interrupted him. He tried in vain to recapture the crowd's attention. "Do not spoil this day," he shouted. But red Jacobin flags sprouted, one by one; the crowd swayed, rustled, and finally dissolved into whirlpools of turmoil, seized anew by the French disease of riot and revolution. Police on horseback charged from nearby alleyways, driving their terrified animals into the melee, their sabers flashing, slashing and beating at the swell of humanity about them. The swirl of savagery sucked men, boys, and women to the ground in pools of blood, many trampled to death by fleeing celebrants. Barricades rose at the openings of the alleys and streets off the square. George managed to hustle his father from the fracas, and they made their way safely through back streets to the calm of the little rue d'Anjou.

The battle at the Bastille raged for two days and two nights, until Louis-Philippe ordered the artillery to blast the barricades with cannon fire. The king himself mounted his horse and led troops down the rue Saint-Antoine in the heart of the workers' district, to beat back the crowds. After two days of fighting, the troops backed the last of the insurrectionists into the Saint-Merry monastery, in the shadow of the Hôtel de Ville. At the citizen-king's order, cannons leveled the walls, annihilated its defenders, and ended the insurrection.

The Lamarque funeral riots left Lafayette in despair—aghast at the inability of either French leaders or the French people to govern themselves under a republican constitution. Conservatives and liberals blamed him for the insurrection and its outcome: the former charged that his inflammatory oratory had provoked the uprising, the latter that he fled the fighting instead of leading the insurrection and overthrowing Louis-Philippe. The king blamed everyone. He dissolved the assembly and imposed martial law.

Exhausted and suffering increasingly from joint pains, Lafayette returned to La Grange for the summer to tend his prize livestock and orchards. He resigned as mayor of the village and from the general council, saying that his differences with the king might have harsh economic repercussions on his neighbors. "Today," he explained, "arbitrary government has replaced the engagements of the Charter for what can, without opposition, last fifteen days, fifteen months or fifteen years, as in the two preceding régimes."[27] In contrast to the horrors of epidemic and insurrection in Paris, La Grange was a utopia for him, as he was surrounded by his huge, loving family—Anastasie, Virginie, and George, their spouses, thirteen grandchildren, and an expanding brood of great-grandchildren. Along with a few in-laws and their children, they numbered more than thirty at the long table for each meal—and often many more if visitors from America or some other country arrived. The gentle summer sun and constant laughter of children rejuvenated the old knight; his beautiful animals won four blue ribbons at the annual livestock show, while his apple and pear orchards yielded record crops for the local villagers to press into cider and eau de vie before the huge harvest celebration that Lafayette sponsored for them on the château grounds.

"I have become, within the limits of our canton, a pretty good agriculturist," he still boasted, "and lame though I am, I gather my strength where walking is concerned, and manage well enough to do and oversee what is essential."[28]

The seventy-five-year-old Lafayette in the park outside his château of La Grange, east of Paris. "Lame though I am," he said, "I husband my strength where walking is concerned." (*From the author's collection.*)

In November, he returned to the Chamber of Deputies in Paris to continue his futile attacks on the government. As he had done during the Empire and the Restoration, he politely refused all invitations to the Palais des Tuileries and gleefully accepted invitations by Masonic lodges or visiting Americans to dinners in his honor, where he could preach the gospel of liberty to the converted. James Fenimore Cooper gave just such a dinner and presented Lafayette with tributes from the New York National Guard and from the state of North Carolina.[29]

Louis-Philippe banned political meetings and reintroduced censorship of the press—in part to eradicate the infuriating pear and puppet cartoons. While ever-larger pears appeared mysteriously on every wall each morning, Lafayette and other opponents developed a simple way around the ban on political meetings: they held banquets. There was no law against a group of friends gathering to eat veal and drink wine—and make a long toast that might include an expression of hope for changes in government policies.

The regime was impervious to changes that might expand individual liberties, however. Fearful that Lafayette was plotting to overthrow the government, the king posted a squad of police at the gates of La Grange. In March 1833, it marched into the château and arrested a refugee who had served as a government minister in the short-lived Republic of Poland.

Lafayette's protests were of no avail, as were his renewed demands for a law to grant asylum in France to political refugees. Louis-Philippe, on the other hand, granted full amnesty to all surviving Bonapartistes.

Tired and discouraged after a fruitless spring session of the Chamber, Lafayette returned for a summer's reinvigoration at La Grange in the warmth of his huge, adoring family. He had little inclination to return to the Chamber for the autumn session. At seventy-six, his eyesight and hearing were failing, his stiff hip joint made walking painful, and all his friends were dead. To some, he remained a living legend, but he felt like a rusty relic and postponed his return to Paris until after Christmas. On January 3, 1834, he made what would be his last appearance in the Chamber's political arena. He claimed (incorrectly) that journals were misquoting him as having said that the constitutional monarchy created in the Revolution of 1830 was the best of republics. "No, Messieurs, it would not have befitted a man who declared himself *a disciple of the American school*—a friend and associate of Washington, Franklin and Jefferson—to say that the amalgam that we fashioned and which we then thought to be in the interest and the will of the nation was *the best of republics.* . . . Above all, a republic must render justice to that part of the population that has thus far been ignored in the legislation of basic rights—to that part of the population that is suffering. . . . Messieurs, true republicanism is the sovereignty of the people; it is the natural and inalienable rights that even an entire nation has no right to violate."[30]

A month later, he insisted on attending the funeral of a fallen deputy; the chill February drizzle cut through to his skin as he marched the long miles to the grave site, where he stood stoically even as tremors racked his aged body. George rushed him home, where he collapsed. Doctors treated him day and night, and, after three weeks, he recovered enough to walk about the house and resume writing letters.

"My dear friend," he wrote to James Fenimore Cooper, who had promised to keep him abreast of American affairs after Cooper left Paris. "I have always found that distance, far from weakening, seems to reanimate all the more my feeling of American pride. You have probably learned from various French newspapers of the precarious state of liberty and tranquillity in this country. . . . A handful of malcontents took up arms in Paris last night and this morning, and they were defeated by overwhelmingly superior forces, but not without spilling some blood. . . . It seems the government is preparing new, oppressive laws."[31]

On the morning of May 9, 1834, an open carriage carried him to the Bois de Boulogne under a magnificent blue sky, but by midday a thunderstorm swept in with a near-arctic gale that left him drenched, trembling from the cold, and near collapse with fever and pain when he got home. Crowds gathered outside and stood silent vigil, day and night. Lafayette's doctor issued daily bulletins to the press. George and other members of his family sat by his bed twenty-four hours a day. He slept most of the time, although he experienced occasional bursts of energy and abandoned his bed to sit in a chair and read a newspaper. When the doctor walked into his room one afternoon, Lafayette startled him by thrusting a Swiss newspaper into his hands and snarling, "*La Gazette de Suisse* has just killed me, and you pretend to know nothing about it? Well, then, I will tell you more: to kill me legally, they have even consulted the celebrated Doctor [name omitted], whom I hardly even know. That should give you great confidence in the newspapers."[32]

When his condition failed to improve, the doctor urged calling in consultants. "What for?" Lafayette protested, and the doctor explained, "As long as there is a single possibility for ending your illness . . . we must find it . . . we are responsible to your family, your friends and all the French people. You are their father."

"Yes," Lafayette muttered, "I am their father so long as they do not have to heed a word that I say to them."[33]

At four in the morning of May 20, 1834, United States major general Gilbert du Motier de La Fayette, maréchal de camp, awakened and grasped the locket that held the portrait of young Adrienne with its inscription, "*Je suis toute à vous,*" on the frame. The great knight pressed it to his lips, closed his eyes, and died.

"General Lafayette was taken from his family and his country on May 20," said the terse announcement on the card that George-Washington Lafayette sent to his father's friends around the world. "In accordance with his last wishes, his coffin was placed in the Picpus Cemetery, where his lifelong partner already rests and where the same tomb will reunite them."[34]

When the news reached America, the nation went into mourning. Every city in the land held memorial services, and the Lafayette Guards, with their distinctive red and black plumes, marched at half-step through Boston for one last time. In Washington, President Andrew Jackson ordered the same military honors for Lafayette that President John Adams had ordered for George Washington thirty-five years earlier. The nation lowered its flags to half-staff, and every military post and navy ship fired a twenty-four-gun salute at daybreak the next morning and a single cannon shot every half hour thereafter throughout the day until sunset. Every officer in the army and navy wore black crepe brassards for six months. Congress passed a joint resolution expressing the sorrow of its members and the people of the United States to George-Washington Lafayette and the members of his family. It ordered both chambers draped in black bunting for the remainder of the session and asked its members, as well as all Americans, to dress in mourning for thirty days. Massachusetts representative John Quincy

Adams, the former president,[35] gave the official eulogy at a joint session of Congress, attended by the president and his cabinet, the members of the United States Supreme Court, and the entire diplomatic corps.

"Pronounce him one of the first men of his age," Adams exclaimed, "and you have yet not done him justice. . . . Turn back your eyes upon the records of time; summon from the creation of the world to this day the mighty dead of every age and every clime—and where, among the race of merely mortal men, shall one be found, who, as the benefactor of his kind, shall claim to take precedence of Lafayette?"[36]

Newspapers across the nation reprinted his oration, and Congress voted to print fifty thousand copies for distribution to schools, libraries, and the general public throughout the United States. Hundreds of cities and towns across America that hadn't done so during or after his visit in 1824 renamed themselves or their schools or streets Lafayette, Fayette, or Lagrange.

In France, King Louis-Philippe deemed the fallen knight as much a menace in death as he had been in life and banned all official recognition of Lafayette's passing. With the memory still fresh of the riots at General Lamarque's funeral, the president of the Chamber of Deputies limited his recognition to one sentence: "The name of general Lafayette will forever be celebrated in our history as one of the principal founders of the constitutional monarchy, which he greeted, along with us, with acclamation and good wishes."[37] To prevent street demonstrations, Louis-Philippe ordered a military funeral that barred public participation. A liberal newspaper mocked the "pear king" in an editorial: "Hide yourselves, Parisians! The funeral of an honest man and a true friend of liberty is passing by."[38]

Lafayette's valet walked behind the hearse carrying a velvet cushion bearing his master's sword and epaulets. George-Washington Lafayette and the rest of the family and friends followed, then a deputation from the Chamber of Deputies, and behind them three thousand members of the disbanded National Guard, all unarmed. At every major cross-street, armed cavalrymen and artillery stood at the ready to prevent crowds from forming. "It would have taken a pitched battle to approach Lafayette's coffin," wrote the editor of the liberal newspaper *National*. "No one dared approach; indeed, the spirit of Lafayette must have been indignant. The true friend of the people of Paris was separated from the public by bayonets and sabers."[39]

Another journalist published this description. "The French army imprisoned him in a bier the way the Austrian army imprisoned him in a state prison. The hearse was surrounded by a battalion whose bayonets still dripped with French blood and kept the people from rendering homage to their liberator. The terrifying precautions and insulting deployment of troops transformed the capital into a city at war in the midst of a public calamity. The cemetery that awaited the remains of the defender of liberty was placed in a

The grave of Lafayette (right) and his wife, Adrienne de Noailles, lies covered with soil from Bunker Hill, in the cemetery of Picpus, in eastern Paris near the place de la Nation. (*Roger-Viollet.*)

state of siege. A mourning public faced a force of artillery larger than would be deployed against a foreign invasion. Not a single minister or government official appeared in the official escort."[40]

Citizen-King Louis-Philippe did not utter a word about the death of the knight who had placed him on the throne.

The cortège crossed the place du Trône, where a guillotine had slaughtered Adrienne's mother, grandmother, and sister forty years earlier. About one hundred yards away lay Picpus Cemetery, where Lafayette would rejoin Adrienne, after a separation of twenty-seven years. After lowering his father beside his mother, George-Washington Lafayette covered his father's coffin with the dirt they had carried back from Bunker Hill, thus fulfilling Lafayette's wish to be buried in American as well as French soil.

Eighty-three years later, when General John Pershing's American Expeditionary Force helped liberate France in 1917, he sent his aide Colonel Charles E. Stanton to the Picpus cemetery to replant the American flag above Lafayette's grave. In a stirring ceremony on America's July 4th Independence Day, Stanton saluted the French knight who had helped free the United States: "Lafayette, we are here."[41]

Epilogue

The fruitful Lafayette line continued to multiply, with the number of his direct descendants now in the hundreds. None, however, can lay agnatic claim to his surname, which disappeared when George-Washington Lafayette's two sons died without male issue. None of the descendants of Anastasie, Virginie, or George-Washington Lafayette are agnates born with the Lafayette family name, but they have not allowed his name to disappear. They have simply tacked their great ancestor's name onto their own to produce a large current generation of hyphenated Lafayettes who adopted the pre-Revolution spelling La Fayette. These include Geneviève and Michel Aubert-La Fayette and their children, and Gilbert Bureaux de Pusy-La Fayette, who carries the great knight's first and last names and the name of Lafayette's aide, Bureaux de Pusy, who went to prison at Olmütz.

George-Washington Lafayette spent the years immediately following his father's death organizing Lafayette's letters, speeches, and papers and compiling his *Mémoires, Correspondence et Manuscrits du Général Lafayette, publiés par sa famille*, which was published in six volumes in Paris in 1837–1838, and simultaneously in two much larger volumes in Brussels. He retained his seat in the Chamber of Deputies until the summer of 1849, remaining a loyal member of the ultraliberal minority his father had organized to oppose the restrictive dicta of King Louis-Philippe. He lived to see the third French revolution of his life in 1848, when a clumsy government effort to prevent a republican rally in Paris provoked a clash between troops and demonstrators that exploded into full-scale insurrection and forced Louis-Philippe to abdicate. After moderates proclaimed the Second French Republic in February, 1848, George-Washington Lafayette won reelection to his old seat in the Chamber of Deputies, but he failed to win the following year. He died in November 1849, never having attained the celebrity of his father.

Lafayette descendants continued to live in the château at La Grange, which is now the property of the estate of the late marquis René de Chambrun, a direct descendant. Although he no longer admits visitors, the marquis

381

permitted the compilation and photo reproduction of all materials relevant to Lafayette by the U.S. Library of Congress and the Cornell University Library, Ithaca, New York, where they remain available to researchers. Although Lafayette's descendants still owned the château at Chavaniac at the beginning of World War I, they had not lived in it for decades, and it fell into disrepair. In 1916, they sold it to an American philanthropic organization, which transformed it into a renowned children's institution that housed, fed, and educated almost twenty-five thousand abandoned war orphans from France, Poland, Russia, Armenia, and other war-ravaged lands after World War I. Despite their generosity, a cynical French writer grumbled, "One can only imagine the reaction of American public opinion at the announcement of the purchase of Mount Vernon by a French association!"[1]

After World War II, the Lafayette Fund began the long task of restoring the château. Part is now a conference center, but the principal rooms hold period furnishings and works of art that have made the château one of the most remarkable, if least known, museums in France. As visitors go from room to room, a stirring, brilliantly produced self-guided tour uses hidden speakers and projectors to carry visitors back in time to Lafayette's birth, his marriage and wedding feast, and other important events of his life in America as well as France.

The impact of Lafayette's attempt to introduce American liberty in France remains one of the most curious—and most tragic—phenomena in western history. In the two centuries that followed, the French staged five revolutions, established five republics, and submitted—often enthusiastically—to despotic rule under three monarchs, two emperors, and one fascist dictator. In contrast to the single document that guided American government during those same two centuries, France has written more than a dozen constitutions and embarked on foreign military adventures that slaughtered millions across the face of Europe, West Africa, Indochina, and even Mexico. When Lafayette introduced American liberty to France, he unwittingly infected his people with an incurable passion for license and lust for world conquest—what the rest of Europe labeled the "French disease" during the French Revolution and under Napoléon I. Not long after Lafayette's death, Louis-Philippe would send French armies to North Africa, and thirty years after Lafayette's death, Napoléon III expanded the Second Empire across the face of Europe into the Russian Crimea, and even sent 30,000 French troops to Mexico in a vain attempt to reestablish the French empire in North America. Even the crushing defeat by the Prussians in 1871 did not subdue French lust for foreign conquest. By 1900, the Third Republic had established a colonial empire in northern and western Africa and in Indochina—an empire larger than the one she had lost in the eighteenth century. Though not solely responsible, French colonial expansionism helped provoke World War I and the unnecessary slaughter of more than five million troops. And still France expanded her empire—into Lebanon and Syria. Even after her disgrace in World War II, France sent 100,000 more troops to their death in a futile nine-year war to retain her colonies in Indochina—and then repeated the savagery in Algeria, again losing 100,000 troops before finally granting independence to all her colonies in the 1960s. Only in the ensuing decades did she, for the first time in five centuries, forego foreign wars of aggression and confine herself to her own borders.

England's Lord Acton argued that Lafayette taught the French the Americans' "theory of revolution, not their theory of government—their cutting, not their sewing." But, as historian Susan Dunn points out, "The cutting—whether colonial war or regicide, whether declaration of independence or tennis court oath—is the easy part. The art is in the sewing."[2]

Notes

Preface

1. John Quincy Adams, *Oration on the Life of Lafayette*, 82 (Published by an Act of Congress, December 1834).

2. Lloyd Kramer, *Lafayette in Two Worlds* (Chapel Hill: University of North Carolina Press, 1996), 4.

3. Kramer, 5.

4. John Stuart Mill, "Death of Lafayette," published in *Monthly Repository*, 22 May 1834, cited in Kramer, 19.

5. Brand Whitlock, *La Fayette* (New York: D. Appleton, 1929), II:283.

6. Ibid.

Chapter 1. The Young Knight

1. The original spelling of the name Lafayette was indeed *La Fayette*, the name of the hamlet that surrounded the family's castle. Thus, the earliest known lord of the castle and hamlet was *Pons, de La Fayette*, or *Pons, lord of* [the vassalage] *La Fayette*. The occasional use of a lowercase *l*—as in *la Fayette*—is incorrect, because it implies that the full name of the town was Fayette, when, in fact, it was a corrupted abbreviation of *Villa Faya*. The better-known modern spelling as a single word, *Lafayette*, was Lafayette's own doing during the American Revolutionary War, to simplify his signature on hastily written orders and messages to his superior officers. He adopted the spelling permanently—and dropped the *de* that preceded it—when he abandoned his noble title and became *Citizen Lafayette* at the beginning of the French Revolution. In this book, I have used the single-word spelling in my own, original text, but left it as it appeared when citing original documents.

2. Henri Doniol, *Histoire de la Participation de la France à l'Etablissement des Etats-Unis d'Amérique* (Paris: Imprimerie Nationale, 1886, 5 vols.), I:651–652.

3. Etienne Charavay, *Le Général La Fayette, 1757–1834, Notice Biographique* (Paris: Société de la Révolution Française, 1898), 534. [The Lafayette quotation is from Appendix I, which is a fragment of a never-completed *Autobiographie de La Fayette par lui-même*, unrelated to and not included in Lafayette's multivolume autobiography *Mémoires, Correspondence et Manuscrits du Général Lafayette publiés par sa famille*, cited below.]

4. La Fayette to Mme. de Pougens, 11 Pluviose, an 6* (January 30, 1798), in Henry Mosnier, *Le Château de Chavaniac—Lafayette. Description-Histoire-Souvenirs* (Le Puy, 1883), facsimile at end. [*In October 1793, the French revolutionary Convention decreed a new revolutionary calendar that represented not only a rupture with the political past but also with the religious past. For details, see chapter 17, n. 50.]

5. Charavay, 532.

6. At one point, the Lafayette fiefdom stretched from what is now the city of Clermont-Ferrand in northern Auvergne to the city of Le Puy-en-Velay to the south.

7. Originally any infantryman armed with a musket, *mousquetaire* came to designate a member of the king's elite household cavalry after Henri IV organized a company of noblemen armed with lightweight, short-barreled carbines. His son, Louis XIII, replaced carbines with muskets in 1622, thus creating the first company of king's musketeers. Cardinal Mazarin dissolved the group during the regency in 1646, but Louis XIV re-created it in 1657 under the name Gray Musketeers, because of the uniformly gray coats of the horses. In 1663, Louis organized a second company, the Black Musketeers, who rode only black horses and later rode to international fame in the novels of Aléxandre Dumas. Made up exclusively of noblemen, the two companies—each with 250 men, and their squires and valets—were quartered at Versailles, rode behind the king in military processions, and were at his side, day and night, when he went to war. (*Encyclopaedia Universalis—Thesaurus Index*, Paris, 1989.)

8. Vercingetorix (d. 46 B.C.) was chief of the Gallic tribe of the Arverni, who rebelled against Roman rule in 52 B.C., just as Julius Caesar had all but subjugated Gaul. Named leader of the Gauls, Vercingetorix used guerrilla warfare to harass Caesar's supply lines and did battle on rocky, mountainous terrain that was unfavorable to the Romans. He successfully held the Arvernian hill-fort of Gregovia against an assault by Caesar. Vercingetorix followed up this victory by an attack on the Roman army that failed and forced him to retreat with 80,000 troops to the fortress of Alesia, where Caesar's 60,000-man force laid siege and forced its surrender. Caesar captured Vercingetorix, took him to Rome in chains, and exhibited him in triumphal parades before executing him six years later.

9. Charavay, 531.

10. The Franks were a group of Germanic tribes who overran the native Gauls and eventually gave France its first king, Clovis I (c. 466–511).

11. Jean Tulard, Jean-François Fayard, Alfred Fierro, *Histoire et Dictionnaire de la Révolution Française, 1789–1799* (Paris: Editions Robert Laffont, S.A., 1987, 1998), 19.

12. *Chavaniac Lafayette: Le Manoir des deux mondes*, Hadelin Donnet (Paris: le cherche midi editeur, 1990), 58.

13. Ibid.

14. The word *abbé*—literally an *abbot*—referred, in fact, to anyone wearing an ecclesiastical dress. It thus included scholars or lettered men who, in the absence of formal schools, served as private tutors to the rural nobility.

15. *Mémoires, Correspondence et Manuscrits du Général Lafayette, publiés par sa famille* (Bruxelles: Sociètè Belge de Librairie, Etc., Hauman, Cattoir et Compagnie, 1837, 2 vols.), 1:12. [Note: Three identical French-language editions of *Mémoires* were published simultaneously, a six-volume edition in Paris, the large two-volume Brussels edition (with double columns to the page) cited here, and a twelve-volume edition also published in Brussels. All carry identical, detailed indexes listing complete contents in chronological order, making it easy to find any item in one edition on the appropriate page in the oth-

ers. For purposes of this book, I found the two-volume edition handier for both research and travel than the more cumbersome six-volume edition.]

16. Ibid.

17. Paul Pialoux, *Lafayette: Trois Révolutions pour la Liberté* (Brioude-Haute Loire: Edition Watel, 1989), 27.

18. The palace had once been the home of Marie de Médicis (b. 1573, Florence, Italy—d. 1642, Cologne, Germany), daughter of Francesco de' Medici, grand duke of Tuscany, and Joanna of Austria. Shortly after French king Henry IV divorced his wife, Margaret, he married Marie de Médicis and made her his queen (October 1600) to obtain a large dowry that would help him pay his debts. In 1601 Marie gave birth to the future Louis XIII, and during the following eight years she bore the king five more children. She built the Luxembourg Palace and its vast, stunning gardens, and from 1622 to 1624 commissioned the Flemish artist Peter Paul Rubens to decorate its galleries with twenty-one paintings that portrayed the greatest events of her life and rank among his finest work. The paintings now hang in a special gallery in the Louvre Museum, and the Luxembourg Palace, which had been converted into apartments when Mme. de La Fayette moved to Paris, became a prison during the French Revolution. Later restored, it now houses the French Senate. Although the palace is closed to the public except by special arrangement, the gardens and park rank among the most beautiful in Paris and are by far the most popular and most frequented.

19. Except for its spelling, the French *collège* was and remains a secondary school and bears no relationship to the American college. Originally, the English word *college* (cf. *collegial, collegiality*) referred to any building used for educational or religious purposes, and the first colleges in America—Harvard, Yale, and so forth—were, indeed, founded as divinity schools to train Puritan ministers.

20. Now called the Lycée Louis le Grand (Louis the Great [Louis XIV] High School), the school still stands on its original site and is the equivalent of an American "magnet" high school, a public school open only to those with the highest scores on a series of competitive examinations—in effect, limiting its student body to the most intellectually gifted children in Paris. The school, across the rue Saint-Jacques from the Sorbonne, has interior gardens that rank among the most beautiful in Paris, but they are not open to the public.

21. Ibid.

22. The *livre*, literally *pound*, was the unit of French currency, as the franc is today. Officially called the *livre tournois* because it was minted in the city of Tours, the livre was a gold coin that was subdivided into twenty *sols*, or coins, which later came to be called *sous*. The purchasing power of the eighteenth-century livre was equal to about one-tenth of a modern U.S. dollar. (Source: 1999–2000 Britannica.com Inc.)

23. Charavay, 535.

24. The House of Bourbon was the ruling royal family of France. The quotation was that of John Adams, in Charles Francis Adams, ed., *The Works of John Adams* (Boston, 1851), III:149–150.

25. Originally signifying a type of carbine whose barrel seemed to spit fire like a dragon, *dragoon* (*dragon*, in French) was later applied to a heavily armed mounted soldier carrying such weaponry.

26. In the Middle Ages, each feudal estate had its own army, which the lord equipped and financed himself, and which was bound to serve the king at the latter's request. The practice continued into the late eighteenth century, with many regiments in

the king's army still under the patronage—and often the command—of nobles such as the duc d'Ayen.

　　27. Most of the huge Hôtel de Noailles was destroyed during the many revolutions that raged in Paris during the eighteenth and nineteenth centuries. The front and rear façades of the central portion of the once palatial structure, however, still stand and are incorporated in the Saint James & Albany Hotel on the rue de Rivoli. Visitors may view the rear façade from the open-air tea garden in the central courtyard. The front façade is visible from the gateway on the rue Saint-Honoré. Prior to the French Revolution, the Hôtel de Noailles was one of the social centers of Paris, far more than the seldom-used Palais des Tuileries across the park. In addition to hosting balls there, the d'Ayens hosted major concerts by such luminaries as Austria's renowned boy pianist Wolfgang Amadeus Mozart, who stayed at the Hôtel de Noailles with his father, Leopold, for at least a week. One musicologist claims that Wolfgang composed two *Noailles Sonatas* for piano during his visit, but I have been unable to substantiate the claim in either the Köchel listings or *The New Grove Dictionary of Music and Musicians*.

　　The nearby Tuileries Palace, which Communards destroyed in the riots of 1871, stretched north to south across the Tuileries Gardens, connecting each of two pavilions that are now incorporated into the ends of the projecting arms of the Louvre Palace. Louis XIV had virtually abandoned it in favor of Versailles, which became the seat of most royal social and diplomatic functions and relegated the Tuileries Palace to a pied-à-terre in town, when, after attending a late-evening social function, the royal family was too tired for the trip back to the country.

　　28. *Vie de Madame de Lafayette par Mme. de Lasteyrie, sa Fille, précédée d'une Notice sur sa Mère Mme. la Duchesse d'Ayen, 1737–1807* (Paris: Léon Techener Fils, 1868), 43. [Henceforth referred to as "Lasteyrie."]

　　29. Ibid., 12.

　　30. Ibid., 43–44.

　　31. Ibid., 45–46.

　　32. Ibid., 48.

　　33. A French *académie* was a school at the university level, offering, in addition to the standard academic curriculum, a range of training (dancing, fencing, riding, etc.) to finish every aspect of the nobleman's education and produce a "compleat" courtier.

　　34. Ibid.

　　35. Brand Whitlock, *La Fayette* (New York: D. Appleton, 1929, 2 vols.), I:18.

　　36. Comte Louis-Philippe de Ségur, *Mémoires ou souvenirs et anecdotes* (Paris, 1824–1826, 3 vols.), I:109.

　　37. *Mémoires*, 11–12.

　　38. Stanley J. Idzerda, ed., *Lafayette in the Age of the American Revolution, Selected Letters and Papers, 1776–1790* (Ithaca, New York: Cornell University Press, 1977–1983, 5 vols.), I:389. This citation is one of many not included in Lafayette's published *Mémoires*, which his son, George-Washington de Lafayette, edited and expurgated after his father's death. As Idzerda explains, Lafayette's son eliminated many passages from his father's original documents and letters to avoid tarnishing his father's reputation and embarrassing surviving family members. Although there is no reason to doubt the authenticity of this particular citation—or, indeed, Idzerda's scholarship—many works were published during Lafayette's lifetime and after his death for the sole purpose of defaming him, for reasons that will become clear in Part II of this book.

39. From fewer than a dozen lodges in 1740, the Freemasons in France had expanded to more than 550 lodges, with one hundred thousand members, by the mid-1770s—60 of them in Paris and 68 in the French Royal Army.

40. *Mémoires*, 12.

41. Although there is some controversy over the identity of the lodge they joined, the most convincing evidence—from archival research at the central Grande Orient lodge in Paris—indicates it was Le Contrat Social, a particularly liberal lodge with an appropriate Rousseauvian name. Reference: "L'Initiation du Général Lafayette," *Le Symbolisme, Organe Mensuel d'Inititation à la Philsophie du Grand Art de la Construction Universelle* (Paris: Direction et Administration, 1923), 246.

42. Abbé Raynal's seminal work was published in 1773 bearing the forbidding title *Histoire philosophique et politique des établissements du Commerce des Européens dans les deux Indes* (Paris, 1773).

43. Raynal, *Histoire philosophique . . .* , 242 ff.

Chapter 2. The Quest

1. Doniol, I:244. Vergennes detailed his proposal in what remains one of the most important documents in American history. Entitled *Réflexions*, it was the first policy paper on French intervention in the American Revolution. For the entire text of Vergennes' *Réflexions*, see Doniol, I:243–249.

2. Ibid. After winning approval for his scheme, Vergennes turned to famed playwright Caron de Beaumarchais (1732–1799), the assumed name of Pierre-Augustin Caron, to head his secret new enterprise. Celebrated as a carefree bon vivant, Beaumarchais had long lived a double life as an unlikely and effective government spy. A master of intrigue, he was as addicted to participating in adventure, espionage, and speculation as he was to writing about them. Indeed, he was every bit as cunning and resourceful as Figaro, the fictional valet hero in his popular comedy, *Le Barbier de Séville (The Barber of Seville)*, which had opened the 1775 Paris theater season. Backed by credits of 2 million livres (about $20 million in modern currency)—half from the king and half from the king's uncle, Charles III of Spain—Beaumarchais established a company in the Spanish West Indies called Hortalès et Cie. to sell surplus French and Spanish arms, ammunition, and other war materiel to the Americans. Deane proved no match for the wily playwright, who sold the American surplus cannons, field pieces, muskets, mortars, powder, cannon and balls, tools, clothing, tents, and blankets worth less than 2 million livres for American whale oil, tobacco, and other products worth three times that amount. He pocketed a small fortune, earned his royal backers a return of twice their original investment, helped reduce the French national debt, and unloaded huge stocks of obsolete French arms and ammunitions. He described his shipments in a letter to Congress, of February 28, 1777: "Gentlemen, I have the honor to fit out for the service of Congress, by the way of Hispaniola, the ship *Amelia*, loaded with field and ordinance pieces, powder and leaden pigs. . . . This is the fourth ship I have addressed to you since December last; the other three have steered their course towards your eastern ports . . . the *Amphitrite* of 480 tons . . . loaded with cannons, muskets, tents, intrenching tools, tin, powder, clothing, etc. . . . the *Seine* . . . of 350 tons, loaded with muskets, tents, mortars, powder, tin, cannons, musket balls, etc. . . . the *Mercury*, of 317 tons . . . loaded with one

hundred tons of powder, 12,000 muskets, the remainder in cloth, linen, caps, shoes, stockings, blankets, and other necessary articles for the clothing of the troops."

Beaumarchais wrote *Le Mariage de Figaro* (*The Marriage of Figaro*), the decidedly antiaristocratic sequel to *Le Barbier de Séville*, in 1785, and Mozart transformed it into the opera *Le Nozze di Figaro*, which opened the following year. It was not until 1816 that the Italian composer Gioacchino Rossini converted *Le Barbier de Séville* into the popular opera *Il barbiere di Siviglia*. Beaumarchais's life rivaled that of the scheming barber Figaro. The son of a watchmaker, he started out as an inventor, but legal actions over patents for one of his inventions provoked him to study law, and his brilliant arguments won him acclaim among jurists and the French court. The secretary for foreign affairs began sending Beaumarchais on secret royal missions to England and Germany as early as 1773, and despite his growing popularity as a dramatist, he suffered so many losses from financial speculation that he gladly accepted the Vergennes assignment to establish a company to trade arms and war materiel to the American colonists in exchange for American products. The conspicuous wealth he accumulated in the venture led to his imprisonment by French revolutionaries in 1792, but the intervention of a well-connected former mistress led to his release, and he died of natural causes.

3. *Mémoires*, I:13.

4. "Le Stathoudérat du Comte de Broglie," in Doniol, II:50–97.

5. Comte de Vergennes, *Mémoire* [memorandum] to Louis XVI, April 18, 1778, in Flassan, VI:140; Doniol, I:244, from *Etats-Unis, Mémoires et Documents, 1765 à 1778*, Archives, French Ministry of Foreign Affairs, quai d'Orsay, Paris.

6. Friedrich Kapp, *The Life of John Kalb, major-general in the Revolutionary army* (New York, 1870), 94–95 [originally published as *Leben des amerikanischen Generals, Johann Kalb* (Stuttgart, 1862)], as cited in Edwin S. Corwin, *French Policy and the American Alliance of 1778* (Gloucester, Mass.: Peter Smith, 1969), 90–91.

7. Ibid.

8. "Deane to the Committee of Secret Correspondence, Paris, December 6, 1776," Francis Wharton, *The Revolutionary Diplomatic Correspondence of the United States* (Washington, D.C.: Government Printing Office, 1889, 6 vols.), II:218.

9. "Deane to the committee of secret [Congressional] correspondence, Paris, November 6, 1776," Wharton, II:191.

10. Jared Sparks, *The Writings of George Washington* (Boston: Tappan and Dennet, 1834, 12 vols.), V:446.

11. *Mémoires*, I:13.

12. Ibid.

13. "Deane to the Committee of Secret Correspondence, Paris, December 6, 1776," Wharton, II:220–221.

14. Doniol, II:375.

15. M. Dubois-Martin, secretary to the comte de Broglie to Kalb, December 8, 1776, in Charlemagne Tower, Jr., *The Marquis de La Fayatte in the American Revolution, with some account of the Attitude of France toward the War of Independence* (Philadelphia: J. B. Lippincott, 1895, 2 vols.), I:28.

16. William A. Duer, ed., *Memoirs, Correspondence and Manuscripts of General Lafayette, Published by His Family* (New York: Saunders and Otley Ann Street and Conduit Street London, 1837 [only vol. I published of the eight originally anticipated]), 9–10.

17. Mercy-Argenteau [ambassador at Versailles] to Maria Theresa [Austrian Empress and mother of Marie-Antoinette], February 15, 1777, A. Arneth and A. Geffroy, ed.,

Correspondence secrète entre Marie-Thérèse et Mercy-Argenteau (Paris, 1874–1875, 3 vols.), III:20, in Louis Gottschalk, *Lafayette Comes to America* (Chicago: University of Chicago Press, 1935), 117.

18. William Petty, 1st Marquis of Lansdowne and 2d Earl of Shelburne (1737–1805), had opposed the Stamp Act of 1764 and, as secretary of state under Pitt (1766–1768), was dismissed for attempting to effect a reconciliation with the colonies. From 1768 to 1782, he led the unsuccessful parliamentary opposition to the government's policies in the American colonies.

19. *Mémoires*, I:13–14.

20. L. to duc d'Ayen, March 9, 1777, *Mémoires*, I:37–38. [Although Lafayette dated the letter "*Londres, 9 mars 1777*," he only started the letter in London and did not finish it until he arrived in Paris. He did not arrange for its delivery until March 17, the morning after he had left for Bordeaux.]

21. Lasteyrie, 55–57. [Years later, a book of letters turned up, all in the handwriting of Adrienne de Lafayette, and including her reconstruction, based on her recollection, of letters she had received from her husband during his voyage to America. Included among those from his first voyage was a short, undated one that she entitled, cryptically, "First letter, at the moment of his departure, of which I had known nothing." A part of the Dean Collection of Lafayette manuscripts at Cornell University, Ithaca, New York, it has never been cited as an authentic document by any respected historian or Lafayette biographer in the 170 years since his death. Indeed, there is no way to authenticate it as having been originally the product of Lafayette's pen, because it is not in his handwriting. Eager to assure his stature in history as a virtuous as well as a courageous man, Lafayette and his family purged some disagreeable elements of his life from his autobiography, manuscripts, and letters. It is not unreasonable to assume that after the French Revolution as he and his family tried to reconstruct their personal papers from memory, they may have invented some letters and documents that had not been there before the revolution, to shed a warmer light on his otherwise thoughtless acts. Certainly, a farewell letter to his wife would make Lafayette seem less the thoughtless adolescent than he surely was. There is, however, no evidence—not even a brief mention—that he ever wrote his wife before his abrupt departure to America—not in his original autobiography, nor in hers, both of which are careful to note and cite the letter he wrote to his father-in-law, the duc d'Ayen. There is much evidence, however, to indicate that it was not his work but hers. It is undated; it is in her handwriting; and the language, wording, and punctuation are not consistent with his writing. It is more the language of an adolescent girl than that of the nineteen-year-old Lafayette. "I am too guilty, to justify myself, I am punished too cruelly not to be worthy of [your] pardon. If I had known my sacrifices would make me feel so horrible, I would not now be the most miserable of men. . . . [Your father] will explain my blunders. . . . " [and so on]. Nowhere does Lafayette ever refer to his adventure as *une folie*—a blunder. Indeed, in his letter to his father-in-law, who considered it a blunder, Lafayette writes of it as "a unique opportunity to distinguish myself and learn my craft [as a soldier]. To his wife, he writes of it as "striving for glory" as a "defender of liberty."

[A second letter, also in Adrienne's handwriting, allegedly sent by Lafayette from San Sebastiàn on April 19, is equally inconsistent, maintaining that he had wanted to spend a fortnight with Adrienne before leaving and that an unknown "they" had refused. He goes on to whine (again, inconsistent with his personality and all his other letters to his wife) that the world had misunderstood him and "since they tear me away from you, since they force me not to see you for a year, since they only want to destroy my pride. . . ." Again, no mention of this letter can be found in the mountains of manuscripts and letters of that period, including her own memoirs, which state categorically that her mother "informed me herself of his cruel departure" and that "the first news" she received from her husband about his trip "arrived on the first of August, a month after I had given birth."]

22. Doniol, II:395.

23. "Lord Stormont to his government," undated citation in Lasteyrie, *Vie de Madame* . . . , n. 197–198.

24. *Mémoires*, I:13–14.

25. Kalb to Mme. Kalb, April 1, 1777, in Doniol, II:386.

26. Ibid.

27. Deane to Vergennes, April 5, 1777 (with two enclosures), *Deane papers*, II:38–40, in Gottschalk, *Lafayette Comes* . . . , 111, 112 n.

28. S. Deane to M. Gérard, April 2, 1777, Doniol, II:392.

29. S. Deane "To His Excellency Count de Vergennes," Paris, April 5, 1777, in Doniol, II:393.

30. Marquis de Noailles to comte de Maurepas, April 8, 1777, in Doniol, II:396–397.

31. Stormont to Weymouth, April 9, 1777, in Gottschalk, *Lafayette Comes* . . . , 117.

32. Vergennes to Marquis de Noailles, April 15, 1777, in Doniol, II:400–401.

33. Vergennes to Marquis de Noailles, April 11, 1777, in Doniol, II:402.

34. *Mémoires*, I:14. [Note: Historians continue to debate whether Maurepas—and more especially Vergennes, the author of the imperialistic *Réflexions* policy—did, indeed, give Lafayette tacit permission to join the Americans by *not* fulfilling the duc d'Ayen's request that the king issue a lettre de cachet for Lafayette's arrest. As with the original de Broglie scheme, there is no documentary evidence to link Vergennes directly to Lafayette's "escape" from France, but there is much indirect evidence—primarily the virtual impossibility of such an escape in a totalitarian state if the head of government does not look the other way, as many historians contend. Once again, as in the de Broglie affair, Vergennes had nothing to lose by letting Lafayette leave France. If Lafayette's adventure failed, Vergennes could produce a backdated lettre de cachet and claim to have done his best to prevent his escape from France; if Lafayette succeeded, he could (as he would) anoint Lafayette a national hero and claim partial credit for the young man's success. Princeton University professor of politics Edward S. Corwin (*French Policy*, 92, op. cit.) concurred that it would have been "easy . . . to disavow LaFayette . . . ; if he succeeded, France would reap the fruits of success."

35. Duer, 13.

36. Ibid., 85–92.

37. Ibid, June 15, 1777, in Tower, I:171.

Chapter 3. First Blood

1. *Mémoires*, I:13.

2. Sparks, *Writings*, V:450, cited in *Mémoires*, I:13, n. 1.

3. Ibid.

4. Lasteyrie, 57.

5. Maurepas to the marquis de Noailles, May 2, 1777, Doniol, II:411.

6. *Questions sur les mesures à prendre pour se précautionner contre l'Angleterre,* Vergennes to the Ministerial Council, April 1777, in Doniol, II:409–410.

7. "Franklin and Deane to Committee of Secret Correspondence, Paris, April 9, 1777," Wharton, II:286–290.

8. Washington to the President of Congress, February 20, 1777, Sparks, *Writings,* IV:327.

9. Washington to Richard Henry Lee, May 17, 1777, Sparks, *Writings,* IV:423.

10. "Franklin and Deane to Committee of Foreign Affairs, Paris, May 25, 1777," Wharton, II:324.

11. *"Diary of the Chevalier Du Buysson,* one of the officers who had gone to America with the Marquis de La Fayette," in Doniol, III:215–216.

12. Ibid.

13. John Rutledge (1739–1800) had been a delegate to the Stamp Act Congress of 1765 and to the first and second Continental Congress. He would later be elected governor of South Carolina and serve courageously against the British. After the Revolution, he served in the Constitutional Convention and was later appointed to the U.S. Supreme Court by George Washington.

14. *Mémoires,* I:13. [The clever William Moultrie (1730–1805) built an unconventional fort of sand and palmetto logs on Sullivan's Island at the entrance to Charleston Bay. Instead of splintering, the soft, spongy logs and sand absorbed the British cannon balls, which actually strengthened the walls. After a full day's bombardment on June 28, 1776, the British abandoned their attack and withdrew, delaying for about two years their plans to establish a foothold in the southern colonies. Moultrie would later become a two-term governor of the state, from 1785 to 1787 and from 1792 to 1794.]

15. L to Adrienne de La Fayette, June 19, 1777, *Mémoires,* I:40–42.

16. *Mémoires,* I:40–42.

17. Lasteyrie, 58.

18. *Diary of Chevalier Du Buysson,* in Doniol, III:215–216.

19. L to Adrienne de La Fayette, Petersburg, July 17, 1777, *Mémoires,* I:42.

20. *Mémoires,* I:1.

21. *Diary of Chevalier Du Buysson,* in Doniol, III:215–216.

22. L to Adrienne, Annapolis, July 23, 1777, *Mémoires,* I:42–43.

23. *Diary of Chevalier Du Buysson,* in Doniol, III:218.

24. Ibid.

25. Washington to Gouverneur Morris, July 24, 1778, John. C. Fitzpatrick, *The Writings of George Washington* (U.S. Congress, Washington, D.C., 1931–1944, 39 vols.), XII:226–227.

26. Greene to [Adams?], May 28, 1777, G. W. Greene, *The Life of Nathanael Greene, Major-General in the Army of the Revolution* (New York, 1871, 3 vols.), I:417.

27. *Diary of Chevalier Du Buysson,* in Doniol, III: 219.

28. Ibid., 219–220.

29. *Journals of the Continental Congress, 1774–1789,* iii, 303, cited in Tower, I:184.

30. Padover, Saul K., ed., *The Washington Papers* (Norwalk, Conn.: The Easton Press, 1955), 1.

31. Ibid.

32. *Mémoires,* I:16.

33. Padover, 11.

34. *Mémoires*, I:16n, citing Sparks, *Writings*, V: Appendix No. 1.

35. L to The Honorable Mr. Hancock, president of Congress, Philadelphia, August 13, 1777, cited in Tower, I:184–185.

36. *Mémoires*, I:16.

37. Ibid.

38. William Alexander Lord Stirling (1726–1783) was one of the few generals in the American army who may have had a legitimate claim to a title—besides Lafayette, of course. A brilliant military engineer, he claimed direct descent from Sir William Alexander, a favorite of James I, who had given him an enormous land grant in Canada, including the whole of Nova Scotia and most of New Brunswick. The peerage became extinct with the death of the fifth earl in 1739. Lord Stirling's father, James, came to America in 1715 and became a lawyer in New York City. William Alexander obtained a fine education, showed gifts in mathematics, and became a successful New York merchant. In 1762, he went to England to lay claim to his title, but the House of Lords rejected it. William returned to America the following year and, ignoring the House of Lords, assumed the title for the rest of his life. Perhaps the Continental army's most skilled engineer, he built fortifications at Fort Lee, New Jersey; Washington Heights on New York Island; and in Brooklyn Heights, where his work still bears the name Fort Stirling.

39. Tower, I:221, citing Saffell, *Records of the Revolutionary War*, 333–336.

40. *Mémoires*, I:16.

41. Comte Guillaume-Matthieu Dumas to Committee of Foreign Affairs, August 22, 1777, Wharton, II:377–378.

42. Kalb to John Hancock, August [?], 1777, cited in Tower, I:186–187.

43. *Journals of Congress*, September 8, 1777, III:377, cited in Tower, I:187–188.

44. Kapp, *Kalb*, 127, cited in Tower, I:190.

45. *Mémoires*, I:17.

46. Ibid.

47. L to Adrienne de Lafayette, October 1, 1777, *Mémoires*, I:44.

Chapter 4. Boy General

1. Lasteyrie, 60.

2. L to Madame de Lafayette, Philadelphia, September 12, 1777, *Mémoires*, I:43.

3. Sparks, *Writings*, V:59.

4. Ferling, John, *John Adams, A Life* (New York: Henry Holt, 1992), 126.

5. Idzerda, II:111–112.

6. *Mémoires*, I:18.

7. Ibid.

8. L to Madame de Lafayette, October 1, 1777, in *Mémoires*, I:43–45.

9. Ibid.

10. Washington to R. H. Lee, October 17, 1777, Fitzpatrick, *Writings*, IX:388.

11. Etienne Taillemite, *La Fayette* (Paris: Librairie Arthème Fayard, 1989), 46.

12. De Ségur, *Mémoires*, I:110–111.

13. L to George Washington, October 14, 1777, Idzerda, I:121–123.

14. L to Madame de Lafayette, Whitemarsh, November 6, 1777, *Mémoires*, I:46–47. His beautifully poetic last line to his wife reads, "*Adieu, Adieu; qu'il me serait doux de vous*

embrasser à présent, de vous dire moi-même: Je t'aime plus que je n'ai jamais aimé, et c'est pour toute ma vie."

15. Greene to Mrs. Greene, November 20, 1777, G. W. Greene, I:514.

16. Greene to George Washington, November 26, 1777, ibid., I:528.

17. L to George Washington, Haddonfield, November 26, 1777 [original, in English], Duer, 120–123.

18. Sparks, *Writings*, V:170.

19. Journals of Congress, 1st December, 1777, in Tower, 254.

20. L to duc d'Ayen, Camp Gulph, Pennsylvania, December 16, 1777, *Mémoires*, I: 30–35.

21. Ibid.

22. Idzerda, I:457–458.

23. L to John Adams, Headquarters [Valley Forge], January 9, 1778, Wharton, II:468.

24. John Adams to L, Braintree, February 3, 1778, Wharton, II:486–487.

25. Franklin, Deane, and Lee to the Committee of Foreign Affairs, Paris, December 18, 1777, Wharton, 2:452–455.

26. *Mémoires*, I:21; Duer, 34–36.

27. Ibid.

28. L to Madame de Lafayette, January 6, 1778, *Mémoires*, I:36–37.

29. Ibid.

30. L to Madame de Lafayette, January 6, 1778, *Mémoires*, I:56–57.

Chapter 5. An American Winter

1. Although the American dollar we know had not yet been coined or printed, the term *dollar*—derived from the Dutch coin the *daaler* and the German *taler*—had long been current in Dutch and German settlements in New York and Philadelphia—and it had acquired the generic meaning of virtually any common monetary unit. When Lafayette came to America, the coin, or "dollar," with the widest circulation was the *peso de ocho*, or so-called Spanish dollar, which Americans misconstrued as meaning "piece of eight," instead of "weight of eight." The *peso de ocho* was divided into eight *reals*, which were minted in Spain, and which Americans called *bits*—again, misconstruing the word *peso*. The colloquial term *bit* carried over into the development of the dollar, which was first divided into "eight bits," with the 25-cent coin, or quarter, called "two bits."

2. *Mémoires*, I:22.

3. L to Washington, January 5, 1778, cited in Louis Gottschalk, *Lafayette Joins the American Army* (Chicago: University of Chicago Press, 1937), 110.

4. L to George Washington, December 30, 1777, Valley Forge, Duer, 134–139.

5. George Washington to L, December 31, 1777, Valley Forge, Duer, 139–140.

6. *Mémoires*, I:18.

7. L to Robert Morris, January 9 [1778], in Gottschalk, *Lafayette Joins . . .* , 109.

8. Kalb to Laurens, January 7, 1778, Kapp, 137.

9. L to Madame de Lafayette, January 6, 1778, *Mémoires*, I:56–57.

10. *Mémoires*, I:33.

11. Ibid.

12. Pierre Charles l'Enfant (1754–1825) was later promoted to major, served in the southern army, and remained in the United States after the Revolution to become an

American citizen and start a career as an architect. In 1787, he planned and supervised the conversion of New York's old city hall into Federal Hall, the temporary seat of the new federal government. In 1791, President George Washington invited l'Enfant to lay out plans for a new national capital along the Potomac. Although construction began almost immediately, he was dismissed for his imperious attitude in February 1791, and his plan was abandoned for more than a century. In 1901, when the city's haphazard growth could no longer meet governmental needs, the l'Enfant plan, with its central system of parks, malls, and radiating avenues, was revived.

13. *Mémoires*, I:22.

14. *Instructions for the Marquis de La Fayette, Major-General in the Army of the United States, commanding an expedition to Canada*, Department of State, Papers of the Old Congress (Vol. I:18), cited in Tower, I:272–274.

15. Ibid.

16. L to Gates, February 7, 1778, Valley Forge, Pennsylvania, Gottschalk, *Lafayette Joins* . . . , 130–131.

17. *Mémoires*, I:59.

18. L to Washington, February 9, 1778, Hemingtown [Flemmingtown], Duer, 153–154.

19. L to Washington, Albany, February 19, 1778, Duer, 154–158.

20. Ibid.

21. L to Henry Laurens, Albany, February 19, 1778, Idzerda, 295–297.

22. Ibid.

23. George Washington to L, Head Quarters [Valley Forge], March 10, 1778, Duer, 161–162.

24. Ibid., February 23, 1778, Duer, 158–161.

25. Jared Sparks, *The Life of Washington* (Boston: Tappan and Dennet, 1843), 256. [Sparks completed this work, and it was first printed by Metcalf, Keith, and Nichols, Printers to the University, in Cambridge, Massachusetts, in 1839, five years after Lafayette's death.]

26. L to Gates, March 11, 1778, in Tower, I:288.

27. *Mémoires*, I:23.

28. Fragment of a Letter [from L] to the President of Congress, Albany, March 20, 1778, Duer, 163–164.

29. W. C. Ford, ed., *Journals of the Continental Congress, 1774–1789* (34 vols.), X:217 (March 2, 1778).

30. Henry Laurens to L, March 4, 1778, Louis Gottschalk, *Lafayette Joins the American Army* (Chicago: University of Chicago Press, 1937), 150.

31. L to Henry Laurens, March 12, 1778, Gottschalk, *Lafayette Joins* . . . , 151.

32. Laurens to L, March 24, 1778, Gottschalk, *Lafayette Joins* . . . , 161.

33. Thomas Conway (1735–1800?) recovered from his wound and returned to France, regaining his position as a colonel in the French army. After fighting in Flanders and India, he was appointed governor general of French India in 1787. He returned to France at the outbreak of the Revolution, and, in 1793, he was exiled as a royalist. He disappeared from public life and is believed to have died around 1800.

34. L to Madame de Lafayette, Valley Forge camp, in Pennsylvania, April 14, 1777.

35. *Mémoires*, I:24.

36. The French word *étranger* can mean either "stranger" or "foreigner."

37. Kazimierz [English: Casimir] Pulaski (1747–1779) had fought gallantly, but lost, against Russian, Prussian, and Austrian invaders, who carved up Poland in 1770–1772. He fled to Turkey, then France, before getting a commission from Franklin and Deane to serve in America. He fought at Brandywine and was appointed brigadier general in charge of the Continental army cavalry. After refusing to serve under Wayne, he resigned, but Lafayette won his reinstatement, with orders to organize the so-called Pulaski Legion. The term "legion," however, was a figurative one, referring to a mixed battalion of infantrymen and cavalrymen numbering in the hundreds. The literal meaning of "legion" refers to units of 3,000 to 6,000 foot soldiers in the Roman army.

38. L to George Washington, Havre, France, October 7, 1779, Duer, 310.

39. Franklin and Deane to the President of Congress, Passy, February 8, 1778, Wharton II:490–491.

40. *Mémoires*, I:34.

41. Ibid.

42. L to Henry Laurens, May 1, 1778, Gottschalk, *Lafayette Joins* . . . , 176.

43. L to Madame de Lafayette, Valley Forge camp, June 16, 1778, *Mémoires*, I:67.

44. Sparks, *Life*, 267–268.

45. Ibid.

46. Robert Morris to George Washington, May 9, 1778, York, Pennsylvania, Sparks, *Writings*, V:357 n.

47. *Mémoires*, I:33.

Chapter 6. The Alliance

1. Lasteyrie, 61.

2. Sparks, *Writings*, V:360.

3. Duer, 172.

4. *Mémoires*, I:34.

5. Ibid., I:25.

6. Ibid., I:34.

7. Ibid.

8. *Mémoires*, I:25.

9. Ibid.

10. Bruce Lancaster, *From Lexington to Liberty, The Story of the American Revolution* (Garden City, N.Y.: Doubleday, 1955), 349.

11. Tower, I:384.

12. *Mémoires*, I:26.

13. Duer, 54.

14. Ibid.

15. Journals of Congress, December 5, 1778.

16. Equivalent to the twentieth-century battleship, the ship of the line evolved from the galleon, a slow three- or four-masted vessel that had a high superstructure on its stern and usually carried heavy guns along two decks. The cumbersome vessels engaged in chaotic or ship-to-ship combat, with one ship firing and ramming, and its men boarding, a single enemy ship. In the eighteenth century, designers streamlined the galleons, ridding them of the ungainly superstructure aft and reducing the number of masts to three. Most were about 200 feet (60 m) long, displaced 1,200 to 2,000 tons, and had

crews of 600 to 800 men. Their armament stood along three decks, with a bottom-deck battery of thirty cannons firing balls of 32 to 48 pounds; the middle-deck battery of thirty guns firing balls of about 24 pounds; and the upper battery consisting of thirty or more 12-pounders. In line-of-battle warfare, ships lined up in single file at regular intervals of about one hundred or more yards bow to stern, for distances that stretched as much as twelve miles (nineteen km), with all ships in the line firing their guns broadside at the ships in the enemy line. The tactic relied entirely on firing power to destroy enemy ships and permitted a single admiral to command an entire fleet.

The frigate was equivalent to today's cruiser. A three-masted vessel, it carried thirty to forty 12-pounders on a single gun deck and additional guns on the stern and forecastle. Frigates were too small and not powerful enough to engage in line-of-battle warfare with ships of the line, but, because of their greater speed, they served as scouts or as escorts protecting merchant convoys from privateers and enemy raiders, and they cruised the seas as raiders.

17. Doniol, III:243.

18. Tower, I:439.

19. Corvettes were small, fast, three-masted vessels smaller than frigates, with only about twenty guns on their top decks. They were most often used as dispatchers among ships of a battle fleet and as armed escorts for merchant fleets.

20. Thomas C. Amory, *The Military Services and Life of Major-General John Sullivan, of the American Revolutionary Army* (Boston, 1868), 74.

21. John Laurens to Henry Laurens, August 22, 1778, in Gottschalk, *Lafayette Joins . . .* , 249.

22. *Mémoires*, I:78.

23. Official Report of the comte d'Estaing to the Secretary of the French Navy, Doniol, III:374–382.

24. Greene, II:117.

25. Tower, I:474–475.

26. Tower, I:478.

27. L to Washington, Newport, August 25, 1778, Duer, 186–194.

28. Washington to L, White Plains, September [1], 1778, Duer, 195–196.

29. Washington to d'Estaing, Head Quarters, September 11, 1778, Sparks, *Writings*, VI:57.

30. Tower, I:494.

31. Sparks, *Writings*, VI:44.

32. Ibid.

33. Tower, I:486–487.

34. Greene to d'Estaing, Boston, September 23, 1778, Doniol, III:392–393.

35. L to Washington, September 1, 1778, Duer, 199–202.

36. Sullivan to Congress, August 31, 1778, in Tower, I:490.

37. Ibid.

38. *Mémoires . . .* , I:80–82.

39. Harlow Giles Unger, *John Hancock: Merchant King and American Patriot* (New York: John Wiley & Sons, 2000), 277.

40. Washington to L, September 25, 1778, Duer, 223–227.

41. Doniol, III:422.

42. Doniol, III:417–418.

43. Duer, 234–236.

44. *Mémoires*, I:29. [Gottschalk disputes Lafayette's recollection, insisting that Washington's camp lay about twenty-two miles away. "It was obviously improbable that Washington went every day tearfully to ask the doctor how Lafayette was, as the *Mémoires* assert that he did. That would have meant a ride of . . . about five or six hours on horseback every day for several weeks."—*Lafayette Joins* . . . , 304, n. 4.]

45. Duer, 64.

46. Washington to Henry Laurens, November 14, 1778, Sparks, *Life,* 289.

47. Doniol, III:464–466.

48. Mémoires, I:29.

49. Washington to Franklin, Philadelphia, December 28, 1778, Gottschalk, *Lafayette Joins* . . . , 313.

50. Duer, 243–244.

51. Duer, 244–245.

Chapter 7. Return to Royal Favor

1. *Mémoires*, I:29.

2. Ibid.

3. Ibid., 91.

4. Lasteyrie, 63.

5. Ibid.

6. Ibid.

7. André Maurois, *Adrienne, or The Life of the Marquise de La Fayette,* translated by Gerard Hopkins (New York: McGraw-Hill, 1961), 75.

8. Charles-Augustin Sainte-Beuve (1804–1869), cited in Maurois, 76, from unidentified source.

9. John Adams to L, Passy, February 21, 1779, in Idzerda, 234–236.

10. Dragoons were heavily armed cavalrymen who carried a type of carbine or short musket that belched fire like a dragon with each discharge and earned the name "dragoon."

11. L to Louis XVI, February 19, 1779, Idzerda, 439–440.

12. Rochon de Chabannes, in Louis Gottschalk, *Lafayette and the Close of the American Revolution* (Chicago: University of Chicago Press, 1942), 77.

13. *Mémoires*, I:30.

14. Franklin to L, Passy, March 22, 1779, Warren, III:91–92.

15. *Mémoires*, I:31.

16. Franklin to John Paul Jones, April 27, 1779, Gottschalk, *Lafayette and the Close of* . . . , 13–14.

17. L to John Paul Jones, April 27, 1779; Jones to L, May 1, 1779, Gottschalk, *Lafayette and the Close of* . . . , 14.

18. Duer, 278–282.

19. L to Jones, May 22, 1779, Gottschalk, *Lafayette and the Close of* . . . , 18.

20. L to Vergennes, St.-Jean-d'Angely, June 10, 1779, Doniol, IV:291.

21. Duer, 286–290.

22. Duer, 290–296.

23. Duer, 296.

24. François Métra et al., *Correspondance secrète, politique et littéraire* (London, 1787–1790, 18 vols.), VIII:139, in Maurois, 79.

25. L to Vergennes, Le Havre, July 30, 1779, *Mémoires*, I:108.

26. "Dr. Franklin to the Marquis de Lafayette, Passy, August 24, 1799," Duer, 303.

27. L to Washington, Havre, October 7, 1779, Duer, 310–314.

28. Attributed. Aboard the *Bonhomme Richard*, September 23, 1779. (Source: *Bartlett's Famous Quotations*.)

29. General Lincoln to the president of Congress, Charlestown, October 22, 1779, Doniol, IV:265.

30. Washington to L, West Point, September 30, 1779, Duer, 304–309.

31. Ibid, except paragraph beginning, "But to conclude . . . " which does not appear in Duer, but is cited in Idzerda, II:317–318, and Fitzpatrick, *Writings*, XVI:368–376. In compiling Lafayette's letters and manuscripts for publication, his son expurgated almost all suggestive passages.

32. Gottschalk, *Lafayette and the Close of . . .* , 81, citing Percy Noel (tr.), "Our Revolutionary Forefathers: the journal of François, marquis de Barbé-Marbois [secretary to La Luzerne]," *Atlantic Monthly*, CXLII (1928), 156.

33. Adrienne to L, December 24, 1779, Idzerda, II:465–466.

34. L to Franklin, December 24, 1779, Idzerda, II:341.

35. L to Maurepas, Paris, January 25, 1780, Idzerda, II:466–470.

36. L to Vergennes, Versailles, February 2, 1780, *Mémoires*, I:114–115.

37. *Instructions remises à M. de La Fayette, le 5 mars 1780*, Doniol, IV:314–318.

38. John Adams to Laurens, Paris, February 27, 1780, Wharton, III:524–526.

39. Franklin to Washington, Passy, March 5, 1780, Wharton, III:537–538.

40. Franklin to Huntington, President of Congress, Passy, March 4, 1780, Wharton, III:534–537.

41. Maurois, 82.

42. Lasteyrie, 201.

43. L to Adrienne, Etampes, March 6, 1780, Maurois, 83.

44. Duer, 318.

Chapter 8. The Traitor and the Spy

1. Washington to L, Morristown, May 1780, Duer, 320–321.

2. Lancaster, 380.

3. Lancaster, 380–381.

4. Sparks, *Writings*, VII:50.

5. L to Adrienne, *Water Bury sur la Route de Boston au Camp*, May 6, 1780, Idzerda, III:429–431.

6. Ibid.

7. *Mémoires*, I:92.

8. Ibid., I:93.

9. Sparks, *Writings*, VII:50.

10. L to James Bowdoin, Morristown, May 30, 1780, Idzerda, III:43.

11. L to Samuel Adams, Head Quarters at Morristown, May 30, 1780, Idzerda, III:41–43.

12. L to Joseph Reed, Head Quarters at Morristown, May 31, 1780, Idzerda, III:43–45.

13. L to George Clinton, Morristown, May 31, 1780, Idzerda, III:45.

14. L to Mrs. Reed, June 25, 1780, Gottschalk, *Lafayette and the Close of* . . . , 91.

15. Washington to Rochambeau, July 16, 1780, Fitzpatrick, *Writings*, XIX:185–187.

16. *Mémoires*, I:123.

17. Ibid., I:123–124.

18. Ibid.

19. Ibid., I:124–125.

20. Ibid., I:125–126.

21. Ibid., I:126.

22. The number of troops in eighteenth-century military units differed from today's units, with only 2,000 to 5,000 troops in an eighteenth-century division—the equivalent of today's brigade and far below the 7,000 to 20,000 troops that make up the modern division.

23. James Thacher, *A military journal during the American Revolutionary War* (Boston, 1823), 286–287, cited in Gottschalk, *Lafayette at the Close* . . . , 156–157.

24. Ibid, I:93.

25. Doniol, IV:404–407.

26. L to Adrienne, near Fort Lee, October 7, 1780, *Mémoires*, I:128–129.

27. *Mémoires*, I:127.

28. Ibid.

29. Tower, II:166–168, from M. Ernouf, "Le Complot d'Arnold (1780), raconté par Lafayette," *Revue de la Révolution*, Tome 5, Année 1885.

30. John André's remains were eventually returned to Britain and now lie in London's Westminster Abbey.

31. *Mémoires*, I:129 and Idzerda, III:506.

Chapter 9. Ride to Glory

1. Henry ("Light-Horse Harry") Lee (1756–1818) was born in Virginia and educated at the College of New Jersey (now Princeton). He had already won a dramatic victory in August 1779, when his "legion" stormed and captured the British fort at Paulus Hook (now Jersey City), New Jersey. He joined Greene in the South Carolina campaign, before rejoining Lafayette in the siege of Yorktown. After the Revolutionary War, he served in the Virginia legislature and the Continental Congress before becoming a three-term governor of his native state. The father of Robert E. Lee, he wrote and delivered the famous Congressional eulogy in December 1799, after Washington's death, calling his former commander in chief "First in war, first in peace, and first in the hearts of his countrymen."

2. Marquis de Chastellux, *Travels in North America, in the Years 1780, 1781, and 1782* (London, 1787, 2 vols.), II:12 ff., cited in Tower, II:182–183.

3. L to Washington, October 30, 1780, Duer, 358–362.

4. Washington to L, October 30, 1780, Duer, 362–363.

5. Ironically, the end of the revolution saw American military leaders adopt a similar attitude toward snipers. Although each war saw their return to battle, the peace that followed invariably relegated them to the ranks of cowards who refused to "stand up and fight like men," and few, except Sergeant Alvin York in World War I, ever received

battlefield decorations. Not until World War II, when massive forces of Japanese snipers forced the U.S. Army Infantry to retaliate with similar forces, were sniper scouts finally recognized universally for their heroism in action. Sniper scouts have remained an integral part of the infantry since then, playing essential roles in both Korea and Vietnam. The specific origin of the phrase "stand up and fight like a man" is unclear.

6. Derived from the Spanish word *guerra*, or "war" (*guerrilla* = little war), the term did not appear until the Peninsular War (1808–1814) in Spain, when the British army applied the lessons learned in South Carolina to support an uprising by the Spanish and Portuguese against Napoléon's forces in the Iberian Peninsula. But guerrilla warfare itself, if not its name, originated as an effective weapon of modern revolution with Nathanael Greene's campaign in South Carolina, in which small, mobile forces used snipers and unconventional warfare to defeat a larger, more powerful conventional army. The campaign remains a focus of careful study and emulation for military leaders everywhere. Both China's Mao Tse Tung and North Vietnam's Ho Chi Minh were familiar with the South Carolina campaign and the tactics of Francis Marion and Daniel Morgan.

7. Greene to L, December 29, 1780, Idzerda, III:274–276.

8. Benjamin Franklin founded the American Philosophical Society in 1743 for "ingenious and curious men" committed to establishing a national system of public education as essential to the success of democracy. Franklin remained president until his death in 1790, when Thomas Jefferson succeeded him to that office.

9. Chastellux, *Travels* . . . , II:12 ff., in Tower, II:183.

10. The capture of Laurens was particularly frightening for America and, of course, for the Laurens family. If the Americans won the war and the British recognized American independence, the British would have to treat Laurens as a prisoner of war and exchange him for a comparable British prisoner. If the British crushed the revolution, however, they had every intention of treating him as a rebel and hanging him for treason, as they would have done with every other American "founding father."

11. L to marquis de Castries, New Windsor, January 30, 1781, Idzerda, III:294–301.

12. L to comte de Vergennes, New Windsor, January 30, 1781, *Mémoires*, I:135–138.

13. L to Adrienne, New Windsor, February 2, 1781, Ibid., I:138–139.

14. Ibid.

15. Ibid.

16. Ibid.

17. John Buchanan, *The Road to Guilford Courthouse: The American Revolution in the Carolinas* (New York: John Wiley & Sons, 1997), 325.

18. Ibid.

19. Instructions from Washington to L, New Windsor, February 20, 1781, Idzerda, III:334–336.

20. L to Washington, Williams Burg, March 26, 1781, Idzerda, III:417–418.

21. Comte de Vergennes, *Mémoire* [memorandum] to Louis XVI, April 18, 1778, in Flassan, VI:140.

22. L to Alexander Hamilton, April 10, 1781, Idzerda, IV:16.

23. Washington to L, New Windsor, April 6, 1781, Duer, 395–396.

24. L to Washington, Elk, April 10, 1781, Idzerda, IV:19–24.

25. L to Chevalier de La Luzerne, Elk, April 10, 1781, Idzerda, IV:453–454.

26. Ibid.

27. George Washington to Noah Webster, July 14, 1788, Harlow Giles Unger, *Noah Webster: The Life and Times of an American Patriot* (New York: John Wiley & Sons, 1998), 149.

28. Washington to L, New Windsor, April 11, 1781.

29. L to Washington, Susquehanna Ferry, April 14, 1781, Idzerda, IV:30–32.

30. Ibid.

31. L to Washington, Baltimore, April 18, 1781, Duer, 403–406.

32. Ibid.

33. *Mémoires*, Duer, 259–260.

34. L to Washington, Baltimore, April 18, 1781, Duer, 403–406.

35. Washington to L, New Windsor, May 5, 1781, Idzerda, IV:86.

36. Doniol, IV:613.

Chapter 10. "The Play Is Over"

1. *Mémoires*, I:93.

2. Jefferson to von Steuben, March 10, 1781, Dumas Malone, *Jefferson the Virginian* (Boston: Little, Brown and Company, 1948), 346.

3. Malone, *Jefferson the Virginian*, 101.

4. Jefferson to Lafayette, March 10, 1781, and May 14, 1781, Malone, *Jefferson the Virginian*, 345 and 350.

5. *Mémoires*, Duer, 405n.

6. L to Washington, Camp Wilton on Jas. River, May 17, 1781, Idzerda, IV:108–109.

7. L to Greene, Camp Wilton on the James River, May 18, 1781, Idzerda, IV:110–114.

8. *Mémoires*, I:95–96.

9. Washington to L, New Windsor, May 31, 1781, Tower, II:340.

10. Tower, II:340.

11. L to George Weedon, Wilton, May 15, 1781, Idzerda, IV:104–106.

12. L to Anthony Wayne, Camp Wilton, May 15, 1781, Idzerda, IV:102–103.

13. Anthony Wayne to L, Yorktown [Pennsylvania], May 20, 1781, Idzerda, IV:116–117.

14. Von Steuben to L, Forks James River, May 30, 1781, Idzerda, IV:147.

15. L to Washington, Richmond, May 24, 1781, Duer, 416–418.

16. L to Hamilton, Richmond, May 23, 1781, Duer, 515–517.

17. Washington to L, New Windsor, May 31, 1781, Idzerda, IV:153–156.

18. Washington to L, New Windsor, June 4, 1781, Idzerda, IV:168.

19. Rochambeau to de Grasse, June 11, 1781, Tower, II:399.

20. *Mémoires*, I:96.

21. Cornwallis to Clinton, May 26, 1781, Tower, II:238.

22. *Mémoires*, I:97. [Gottschalk (*Lafayette and the Close . . .* , p. 431) claims never to have found the quotation during his search of "the several available collections of Cornwallis' correspondence," but he reports Sir Henry Clinton having written to Lord George Germain, English secretary of state for the colonies, on June 9, 1781, saying that Cornwallis had written that "the boy could not escape him."]

23. L to Washington, Richmond, May 24, 1781, Duer, 416–418.

24. Lasteyrie, 75.

25. *Mémoires*, I:96.

26. L to Anthony Wayne, Forks of the Chickahominy, May 27, 1781, Tower, II:321–322.

27. Ibid., Gold Mine Creek, Southana [South Anna] River, May 29, 1781, Idzerda, IV:141–142.

28. The letter is, apparently, lost, but Lafayette refers to it in his replies to Greene.

29. Bowers, 279.

30. The French occupation of many German-speaking areas east of France created a tendency among some German noblemen to Frenchify their names.

31. L to Washington, Camp, June 28, 1781, Duer, 418–420.

32. *Mémoires*, Duer, 435n. ff.

33. Sparks, *Life*, 334.

34. Tower, II:347.

35. L to Washington, July 20, 1781, Duer, 421–422.

36. Ibid.

37. Abbé Claude Robin [chaplain to Comte de Rochambeau], *Nouveau voyage dans l'Amérique septentrionale en l'année 1781, etc.* (Philadelphia and Paris, 1782), 71–72, in Gottschalk, *Lafayette and the Close* . . . , 271.

38. Wayne to Washington, July 8, 1781, Gottschalk, *Lafayette and the Close* . . . , 266.

39. L to Greene, Ambler's Plantation opposite James Island, July 8, 1781, Idzerda, IV:236–239.

40. Washington to L, Peekskill, New York, June 29, 1781, Idzerda, IV:219–220.

41. Washington to L, July 30, 1781, Sparks, *Life*, 337.

42. Tower, II:370.

43. L to Washington, Malvan Hill, July 20, 1781, Duer, 421–422.

44. Duer, 428n–429n.

45. L to Washington, Ambler's Plantation, July 20, 1781, Duer, 422–423.

46. Ibid., 423–424.

47. Ibid., August 6, 1781, 425–426.

48. L to Washington, Forks of York River, August 21, 1781, Duer, 427–430.

49. L to Adrienne, Camp, between the branches of the York River, August 24, 1781, *Mémoires*, I:154–155.

50. L to Washington, Malvan Hill, July 31, 1781, Duer, 425.

51. Ibid.

52. L to Washington, Mattapony River, August 24, 1781, Idzerda, IV:349–351.

53. Tower, II:431.

54. Ibid.

55. *Mémoires*, I:98.

56. Ibid., I:136n. ff.

57. Washington to L, Philadelphia, September 7, 1781, Idzerda, IV:390–391.

58. Tower, II:447.

59. *Mémoires*, I:99.

60. Ibid., 451.

61. Ibid., 454.

62. Ibid., 456.

63. Henry Lee, *Memoirs of the war in the southern department of the United States* (Philadelphia, 1812, 2 vols.), II:361.

64. L to comte de Maurepas, Camp near York, October 20, 1781, Duer, 445.

Chapter 11. Conqueror of Cornwallis

1. L to Adrienne, on board *La Ville de Paris*, October 22, 1781.

2. Comte de Vergennes to L, Versailles, December 1, 1781, Idzerda, 487–488.

3. Marquis de Ségur to L, December 5, 1781, *Mémoires*, I:160.

4. Ibid.

5. Washington to L, Mount Vernon, November 15, 1781.

6. Gottschalk, *Lafayette and the Close* . . . , 336, from *Atlantic* [magazine], I (1824), 400.

7. L to Samuel Cooper, Camp York, Virginia, October 26, 1781, Idzerda, IV:429–432.

8. Tower, II:462–463.

9. Congress to king of France, November 29, 1781, Wharton, IV:858.

10. L to John Hanson, President of Congress, November 25, 1781, Gottschalk, *Lafayette and the Close* . . . , 339.

11. Noailles to Molly Robinson, December 14, 1781, Gottschalk, *Lafayette and the Close* . . . , 343.

12. L to Washington, *Alliance*, off Boston, December 21, 1781, Duer, 448–449.

13. Although the British government gave Arnold a small pension, the English scorned him as a traitor. He died in London on June 14, 1801, deeply embittered, at the age of sixty.

14. L to Washington, *Mémoires*, I:168–169.

15. Lasteyrie, 203.

16. Gottschalk, *Lafayette and the Close* . . . , 349, from an entry on January 22, 1782, in an "unpublished journal of the book dealer Hardy," entitled "Mes loisirs," in the *Bibliothèque Nationale*, Paris.

17. Lasteyrie, 203–204, 425.

18. L to Washington, Versailles, January 30, 1782, Idzerda, V:8–10.

19. Franklin to Livingston, Passy, March 4, 1782, Wharton, V:214–217.

20. Washington to L, Philadelphia, January 4, 1782, Idzerda, V:2.

21. L to Livingston, St. Germain, June 25, 1782, Idzerda, V:45.

22. L to Vergennes, undated citation in Taillemite, 98.

23. L to Franklin, February 25, 1782, Idzerda, V:15.

24. Comte de Ségur to L, Rochefort, July 7, 1782, Idzerda, V:367.

25. L to Livingston, Paris, March 30, 1782, Gottschalk, *Lafayette and the Close* . . . , 357–358.

26. Gottschalk, *Lafayette and the Close* . . . , 364.

27. L to Livingston, Paris, March 30, 1782, Idzerda, V:20–21.

28. Gottschalk, *Lafayette and the Close* . . . , 358.

29. Ibid., 363.

30. L to Livingston, Paris, March 30, 1782, Idzerda, V:20–21.

31. L to Vergennes, Paris, March 20, 1782, Wharton, V:266–267.

32. L to Adams, Paris, May 7, 1782, Idzerda, V:36–37.

33. L to Washington, Paris, June 29, 1782, Idzerda, V:49–51.

34. Now the seat of the Assemblée nationale—the French equivalent to the U.S. House of Representatives—the Palais Bourbon was built in 1722 for Louis XIV's illegitimate daughter, the duchesse de Bourbon. Napoléon added a neo-Grecian portico with twelve Corinthian columns and a massive frieze to mirror the Madeleine (now a church) at the end of the rue Royale, across the Seine and the place de la Concorde. In 1830, the interior was altered to accommodate the amphitheater for the legislature.

35. L to Washington, October 24, 1782, Idzerda, V:64–65.

36. Mémoires, I:163.

37. Washington to L., Verplanks, New York, October, 1782, Idzerda, V:62–64.

38. Jay to Robert Livingston, November 17, 1782, Wharton, VI, 48.

39. L. H. Butterfield, ed., Diary and Autobiography of John Adams (Cambridge, Mass., 1961, 4 vols.), III:303.

40. L to Washington, March 2, 1783, Gottschalk, Lafayette and the Close . . . , 407.

41. L to Washington, Cadiz, February 5, 1783, Idzerda, V:90–93.

42. Ibid.

43. Washington to L, Newburgh, April 5, 1783, Idzerda, V:119–121.

44. Ibid.

45. L to William Carmichael, Cadiz, January 20, 1783, Wharton, VI:222–223.

46. L to Livingston, Bordeaux, March 2, 1783, Wharton, 6:268–270.

47. Carmichael to Livingston, Madrid, February 21, 1783, Wharton, 6:259–260.

48. Adams to James Warren, Paris, April 16, 1783, Idzerda, V:121–124.

49. Franklin to Livingston, Passy, July 22, 1783, Wharton, 6:582.

50. From a letter without addressee and apparently never sent, dated April 9, 1784, in The Hague, and cited in Page Smith, John Adams (Garden City, N.Y.: Doubleday, 1962, 2 vols.), I:570.

51. Smith, I:569.

52. L to Adrienne, Chavaniac, March 27, 1783, Idzerda, V:377–378.

53. Ibid.

54. Charavay, 97, from Doniol, Une correspondence administrative sous Louis XVI, épisode de la jeunesse de La Fayette, dans les Séances et travaux de l'Académie des Sciences morales et politiques (1875), CIV:49.

55. Ibid., letter from Gueyffier, sub-governor of Brioude, to the intendant of Auvergne, March 27, 1783.

56. L to Adrienne, Chavaniac, March 27, 1783, ut supra.

57. Literally, striker of the ferme.

58. Ironically, French legend elevated Louis IX (1214–1270)—"Saint-Louis"—to undeserved status—indeed, sainthood—for his role as leader of the Seventh Crusade. At best, he was a military blunderer, who arrogantly underestimated the strength and intelligence of his foes. In Egypt, he confidently charged ashore and raced toward Cairo, only to have Egyptian defenders open their swollen irrigation canals. Thousands of French Crusaders drowned, while the rest of the force found itself trapped with their king on an isolated sandbar, far from their ships. After plague killed thousands more, the French king paid a huge ransom for his and his decimated army's release. He sailed off to Palestine, where, after four years, he had to show something for his costly adventure and claimed to have recovered the Crown of Thorns, which now lies in the treasury of the

Cathedral of Nôtre-Dame, in Paris, and is displayed to the public each year on Good Friday in the Sainte-Chapelle, Saint-Louis's own private chapel on the Ile de la Cité. Determined to crush the Moslem infidel, he returned with his armies to North Africa toward the end of his life but died of the plague in Tunis. His army returned home in defeat with his body, whose remains were placed with those of previous French kings in the royal crypt at Saint-Denis Basilica (now cathedral), on the northern outskirts of Paris.

59. L'année littéraire (1783), IV, 278, cited in Louis Gottschalk, Lafayette Between the American and the French Revolution (1783–1789) (Chicago: University of Chicago Press, 1950), 14.

60. Ibid., II, 66–68.

61. Metra, XIV, 296, cited in Gottschalk, Lafayette Between . . . , 21.

62. L to Vergennes, Paris, March 19, 1783, Mémoires, I:183.

63. L to Fleury, Paris, March 19, 1783, Idzerda, V:375–376.

64. Pronounced Jeel-bear.

65. L to Washington, Chavaniac in the province of Auvergne, July 22, 1783, Idzerda, V:145–147.

Chapter 12. Completing the Quest

1. What was once the Hôtel d'York still stands, albeit renovated out of all recognition, at 56 rue Jacob, on the Left Bank in Paris, where a marble plaque to the left of the entrance reads:

EN CE BATIMENT

JADIS HOTEL D'YORK

LE 3 SEPTEMBRE 1783

DAVID HARTLEY,

AU NOM DU ROI D'ANGLETERRE

BENJAMIN FRANKLIN,

JOHN JAY, JOHN ADAMS

AU NOM DES ETATS-UNIS D'AMERIQUE

ONT SIGNE LE TRAITE DEFINITIF DE PAIX

RECONNAISSANT L'INDEPENDENCE

DES ETATS-UNIS

("In this building, once the Hôtel d'York, on 3 September 1783, David Hartley, in the name of the king of England Benjamin Franklin, John Jay, John Adams in the name of the United States of America signed the final treaty of peace recognizing the independence of the United States").

2. Washington to L, Newburgh, June 15, 1783, Idzerda, V:135–136.

3. L to William Temple Franklin, Paris, November 19, 1783, Idzerda, V:165.

4. Unsigned manuscript—no addressee and dated only "Paris, Tuesday morning," Idzerda, V:382.

5. L to Jeremiah Wadsworth, September 28, 1783, Idzerda, V:154–155.

6. Bottle coasters.

7. Washington to L, Princeton, October 30, 1783, Idzerda, V:159–162.

8. The original French mint—the Hôtel de la Monnaie—was built from 1768 to 1774, on the quai de Conti, on the Paris Left Bank. It is now one of the world's finest

currency museums, with specimens dating back to Charlemagne, and, though too inefficient to produce coins, it continues to produce commemorative medals, many for sale to the public.

9. Knox to L, Westpoint, June 16, 1783, Idzerda, V:137.

10. Adams to L, The Hague, March 28, 1784, Gottschalk, *Lafayette Between* . . . , 64.

11. L to John Adams, Lorient, June 25, 1784, Idzerda, V:227.

12. Washington to L, February 1, 1784.

13. Ibid.

14. L to Washington, March 9, 1784, Gottschalk, *Lafayette Between* . . . , 65.

15. Washington to Adrienne, Mount Vernon, April 4, 1784, Padover, 84–85.

16. "Observations on the Commerce between France and the United States," Idzerda, V:382–389.

17. Ibid.

18. Calonne to L, Versailles, January 9, 1784.

19. Ford, ed., *Journals* . . . , 26:332–333.

20. Calonne to L, Paris, June 16, 1784, Idzerda, V:396–397.

21. John Marshall, *Life of Washington* (Philadelphia, 1804–1807, 5 vols.), II:57.

22. Henry Knox to L, Westpoint, June 16, 1783, Idzerda, V:137.

23. L to Washington, Paris, January 10, 1784, Idzerda, V:191–193.

24. L to Washington, May 14, 1784, Idzerda, V:216–218.

25. Although both the Washingtons had invited Adrienne to visit Mount Vernon with her husband, there was no question of both Lafayette parents risking their lives on the North Atlantic passage while their children were so young. Virginie was not yet two, George-Washington was only four and a half, and Anastasie was seven.

26. L to Adrienne, June 20, 1784, La Flèche, Idzerda, V:398.

27. L to Adrienne, June 28, 1784, aboard the *Courrier de New York*, Idzerda, V:400.

28. J. Hector St. John de Crèvecoeur, *Letters from an American Farmer and Sketches of Eighteenth-Century America* (London, Davies and Davis, 1782), rewritten, expanded, and republished in Paris (1784) as *Lettres d'un cultivateur américain* . . . , in three volumes, from which this quote, in III:317–318. *See also* n. 58.

29. Gottschalk, *Lafayette Between* . . . , 85.

30. L to Adrienne, Philadelphia, August 13, 1784, Idzerda, V:401–403.

31. *Maryland Gazette*, August 26, 1784.

32. "Address of the Committee of Officers of the Late Pennsylvania Line, with Lafayette's Reply," *Pennsylvania Journal*, August 14, 1784.

33. Ibid.

34. L to Adrienne, Philadelphia, August 13, 1784, Idzerda, V:401–403.

35. Author's note: Although there is no dispute over Adrienne de Lafayette's having embroidered a Masonic apron for George Washington, who did treasure it, Gottschalk maintains that "the chances . . . are nil that it was presented to Washington by Lafayette in 1784." His basis for this argument is that he could find "no supporting primary testimony." However, he offers no supporting primary testimony that it was *not* presented at that time nor any evidence that it was presented at any time other than in 1784, by Lafayette, as most nineteenth-century sources—including some who knew Lafayette—insist.

36. L to Adrienne, Mount Vernon, August 20, 1784, Idzerda, V:403–404.

37. Ibid.

38. L to Adrienne, Church's Tavern, October 10, 1784, Maurois, 123.

39. E. P. Chase, ed., *Our Revolutionary forefathers: the letters of François, marquis Barbé de Marbois* (New York, 1929), 185–193.

40. Ibid.

41. Ibid.

42. L to Adrienne, October 4, 1784, Idzerda, V:416–417.

43. Gottschalk, *Lafayette Between* . . . , 112.

44. Barbé de Marbois, op. cit.

45. A signer of the Declaration of Independence who had commanded the Connecticut militia, Wolcott (1726–1797) was a delegate to Congress from Connecticut and would later become governor of that state.

46. Ibid.

47. *Mémoires*, I:193.

48. Ibid.

49. Madison to Thomas Jefferson, Philadelphia, October 17, 1784, Idzerda, V:271–274.

50. Madison to Jefferson, Philadelphia, October 17, 1784, Idzerda, V:273–274.

51. L to Jefferson, Hartford, October 11, 1784, Idzerda, V:266–267.

52. L to Adrienne, undated, Maurois, 122.

53. Gottschalk, *Lafayette Between* . . . , 120–121.

54. *Recommendation for James,* "Done Under My Hand, Richmond, November 21st 1784," in Idzerda, V:278–279.

55. Padover, 11.

56. Gottschalk, *Lafayette Between* . . . , 145.

57. Maurois, 124.

58. L's "Address to the Continental Congress," Trenton, December 11, 1784, Ford, XXVII, 684 (December 13, 1784).

59. Michel-Guillaume-Jean de Crèvecoeur (1735–1813) was born in Caen, in Normandy, France, and emigrated to Canada as a mapmaker in the French and Indian War. He settled on a farm in Orange Country, New York, in 1769, but conflicting loyalties at the beginning of the Revolution sent him fleeing to London, where he wrote the immensely popular *Letters from an American Farmer,* signed "J. Hector St. Jean." His vivid descriptions of farming on the American frontier remain a classic. The French government appointed him consul to three American states in 1783; he returned to his farm, found his house burned, his wife dead, and his children missing. He recovered his children and became a popular figure in America, becoming friends with Franklin and Jefferson and maintaining a regular correspondence with Washington.

60. Washington to L, Mount Vernon, December 8, 1784, Idzerda, V:279–280.

61. *Mémoires*, I:198.

Chapter 13. The Notables and the "Not Ables"

1. It is not clear what formal education Kayenlaha received in Paris. Upon his arrival, Lafayette said, he planned to make the boy "a favourite servant"—a status somewhat akin to a court jester, with freer rein than ordinary servants.

2. A pension differed somewhat from the traditional boarding school in that it was an urban institution, and children routinely went home on Sundays and holidays, for family events, and when they were ill and needed special care.

3. Jefferson's house, the Hôtel de Langeac, stood at what is now the corner of the Champs-Elysées and the rue de Berri, then the rue Neuve de Berri. According to Jefferson biographer Dumas Malone, it was "capacious—it had a basement, ground floor, mezzanine and first floor . . . extensive grounds . . . separated by a dry moat from the Champs-Elysées." It stood just inside the gate, on the Paris side, from Chaillot, then a village contiguous to Paris, stretching down through the heavily wooded slopes to the Seine River—across from where the Eiffel Tower now stands. The Champs-Elysées was a wide, graveled avenue, with trees on either side, running from the Chaillot gate to the place Louis XV (now the place de la Concorde). It was a popular holiday area for riding on horseback or in coaches. Behind the rows of trees stood magnificent mansions akin to Jefferson's, with lovely garden expanses. Jefferson loved gardening, and the Indian corn he planted in his garden was the first in France. Dumas Malone, Jefferson and the Rights of Man (Boston: Little, Brown, 1951), 20.

4. Gottschalk, Lafayette Between . . . , 162.

5. There is no precise information about the two Indian boys who went to live with the Lafayettes in Paris. Peter Otisquette, the Oneida Indian boy, arrived in Paris at the end of 1785 and, according to the best estimates, remained for about three years—until late 1788, when he and Kayenlaha, the Onondaga boy, sailed home to America together.

6. Xavier de Schonberg, January 14, 1787, in Charavay, 137.

7. Adams to Jay, Paris, April 13, 1785, Malone, Jefferson and the Rights . . . , 21.

8. L to Nathanael Greene, Paris, March 16, 1785, Idzerda, V:302–304.

9. L to Elbridge Gerry, Paris, March 16, 1785. Gottschalk, Lafayette Between . . . , 158.

10. L to Richard Henry Lee, Paris, March 16, 1785, Idzerda, V:306–308.

11. New Plymouth Gazette, September 19, 1786.

12. Gottschalk, Lafayette Between . . . , 267. [Ledyard won international fame by traveling with Captain James Cook on the latter's third voyage to the Pacific and publishing A Journal of Captain Cook's Last Voyage, in 1783.]

13. L to Washington, Paris, May 11, 1785, Idzerda, V:322–323.

14. Ibid.

15. Rabaut-St. Etienne to L, June 22, 1785, Anon., "Les promoteurs de l'édit de 1787 qui a restitué l'état civile aux Protestants de France: correspondence de Lafayette, Paul Rabaut, Rabaut-Saint-Etienne de Poitevin (1785–1788)," Bulletin de la Societé de l'Histoire du Protestantisme français, III (1855), 333, cited in Gottschalk, Lafayette Between . . . , 179.

16. Lasteyrie, 209–210.

17. Whitlock, I:299–300.

18. L to Washington, Paris, February 8, 1786, Mémoires, I:203.

19. L to Washington, Paris, February 8, 1786, Mémoires, I:203–207.

20. Cornwallis to Alexander Ross, October 5, 1785, in Charles Ross, ed., Correspondence of Charles, first marquis Cornwallis (London, 1859), I:212, cited in Gottschalk, Lafayette Between . . . , 186.

21. Charavay, 122.

22. L to Washington, Paris, February 8, 1786, Mémoires, I:203–207.

23. Jefferson to Madison, January 30, 1787, Gottschalk, *Lafayette Between* . . . , 203.

24. Malone, *Jefferson and the Rights* . . . , 46.

25. George Washington Parke Custis, *Recollections*, 455–456, cited in Gottschalk, *Lafayette Between* . . . , 272.

26. L to Henry Knox, Chavaniac, June 12, 1785, Idzerda, V:329.

27. Lasteyrie, 207–208.

28. Ibid.

29. Washington to L, Mount Vernon, June 8, 1786, *Mémoires*, I:209–210.

30. A Virginian, Short had studied law with James Monroe under Jefferson's tutelage at the College of William and Mary, Williamsburg, Virginia, in 1780.

31. *Journal Encyclopédique*, 1787, II:82–83, cited in Gottschalk, *Lafayette Between* . . . , 252.

32. L to Washington, Paris, May 5, 1787, *Mémoires*, I:225.

33. Literally, the "pocket-money room," the Salle des Menus Plaisirs was a large, all-purpose game and recreation room that could be used for any of a wide range of activities, according to the king's wishes.

34. Taillemite, 145.

35. L to George Washington, Paris, February 7, 1787, *Mémoires*, I:224–225.

36. Jefferson to Adams, August 30, 1787, Smith, II:720.

37. Antoine Rivarol, dit le Comte de, *Mémoires* (Paris, 1824), 91.

38. Unsigned, undated. *Dénonciation de l'agiotage au roi et à l'Assemblée des Notables*.

39. *Mémoires*, I:213–220.

40. Adrienne Lafayette to comtesse de Chavaniac, Paris, March 17, 1878. Maurois, 137.

41. L to George Washington, May 5, 1787, *Mémoires*, I:225–226.

42. *Mémoires*, I:213–220.

43. Ibid.

44. Ibid.

45. Ibid., I:218.

46. Whitlock, I:311.

Chapter 14. "I Reign in Paris"

1. L to John Jay, Paris, May 3, 1787, *Mémoires*, I:226–227.

2. L to Washington, Paris, August 3, 1787, *Mémoires*, I:227–228.

3. Cloquet, 15.

4. Maurois, 147.

5. L to Washington, Paris, October 9, 1787, *Mémoires*, I:228–229.

6. L to Mrs. Nathanael Greene, Paris, September 5, 1788, cited in Gottschalk, *Lafayette Between* . . . , 405.

7. Except for Caldwell, the education Lafayette lavished on his various wards proved of little value. Although Lafayette found Greene "a very hopeful youth," he drowned in a hunting accident shortly after his return home to America a year later. And while Otisquette "astonished those who met him" by the knowledge he had acquired of French, English, and music, he turned to drink and reverted to barbarism after his return

to his tribal home in America, and he died within a few years.—Gottschalk, *Lafayette Between* . . . , 405.

8. L to Washington, Paris, January 1, 1788, *Mémoires*, I:232.

9. Jefferson to Dr. Richard Price, January 8, 1789, in Malone, *Jefferson and the Rights* . . . , 194–195.

10. L to Washington, Paris, May 25, 1788, *Mémoires*, I:235–236.

11. Washington to L, June 19, 1788, Fitzpatrick, *Writings*, XXIX:524.

12. Unidentified manuscript scrap, L to [?], [Versailles?].

13. In 1780, Morris lost control of the horse pulling his carriage, and as the runaway animal dashed ahead wildly, with the carriage whipping from side to side and threatening to roll over, Morris jumped to safety and broke his leg—suffering a compound fracture that required immediate amputation.

14. Washington to L, January 29, 1789, *Mémoires*, I:210.

15. Beatrix Cary Davenport, ed., *A Diary of the French Revolution By Gouverneur Morris (1752–1816), Minister to France during the Terror* (Boston: Houghton Mifflin Company, 1939, 2 vols.), I:13.

16. Ibid., I:xxiii.

17. Morris to Washington, Paris, April 29, 1789, in Davenport, I:59–62.

18. Ibid.

19. Davenport, I:66.

20. Emmanuel Sièyes, *Qu'est-ce que le tiers état?*, in Susan Dunn, *Sister Revolutions: French Lightning, American Light* (New York: Farrar, Straus and Giroux, 1999), 61.

21. Charavay, 170.

22. Ibid.

23. Although Lafayette's original "Rights of Man" remains the heart of the current French Bill of Rights, subsequent drafts—including one by the notorious Robespierre—expanded the nine original provisions to seventeen and left the originals observed on paper more than in practice.

24. Jean Tulard, Jean-François Fayard, Alfred Fierro, *Histoire et Dictionnaire de la Révolution Française, 1789–1799* (Paris: Editions Robert Laffont, S.A., 1987, 1998), 37.

25. Ibid.

26. Louis Gottschalk and Margaret Maddox, *Lafayette in the French Revolution* (Chicago: University of Chicago Press, 1969), 70.

27. Morris to John Jay, Paris, July 1, 1789, Davenport, I:129–131.

28. The Palais Royal in Paris was never the royal palace its name implies. Built by and for Cardinal Richelieu, it became the temporary residence of the young future king, Louis XIV, and his mother, Anne of Austria, during the regency of his uncle Philippe d'Orléans. Now the site of the Conseil Constitutionel, a French equivalent of the American Supreme Court, the Palais was acquired from Richelieu by the Orléans family, and, in the years preceding the French Revolution, the duc d'Orléans refurbished the palais itself, then built an enormous rectangular residential complex, three and four stories tall, stretching about one hundred meters to the north, with an arcade of shops, gambling dens, and houses of prostitution along its base—and a shaded, columned walkway around the central gardens. Burned and restored several times in the nineteenth and twentieth centuries, the Palais Royal has seen chic boutiques and restaurants replace the gambling dens and brothels.

29. Morris to John Jay, Paris, July 1, 1789, Davenport, I:129–131.

30. Ibid.

31. Taillemite, 173–174.

32. *Mémoires*, I:417.

33. Jefferson to Monroe, August 9, 1788, Malone, *Jefferson and the Rights* . . . , 193.

34. Morris to William Carmichael [Madrid], Paris, July 4, 1789, Davenport, I:134–138.

35. Washington to L, June 19, 1788, Fitzpatrick, *Writings*, XXIX:524.

36. Now the Ministry of the Navy, the Gardemeuble du Roy is the huge, columned, neo-Grecian building that still stands on the northeast corner of the place de la Concorde where it meets the rue Royale. It was originally built as a warehouse for the king's huge collection of furniture and furnishings, from which he could draw as needed to replace materials in one of his many palaces.

37. Davenport, I:145–147.

38. A medieval fortress on the east edge of Paris, the Bastille did not become a prison until the seventeenth century, when Louis XIV converted it into a place of detention for important persons charged with miscellaneous offenses. Surrounded by a moat more than eighty feet wide, its eight one-hundred-foot-high towers and walls became a symbol of oppression that was visible across the city and the nearby countryside. Charles V ordered its construction in 1370 as a fortified gate and added a fortification, or *bastide* (the name Bastille is a corruption of *bastide*), to protect approaches to the wall around Paris.

39. Whitlock, I:329.

40. [Bertrand Barère de Vieuzac], *Le Point du jour, ou résultat de ce qui s'est passé aux Etats-généraux*, 27 avril-17 juin 1789 (Paris, 1790), 210; *Gazette de Leide, supplément*, July 28, 1789.

41. *Mémoires*, I:274.

42. Lasteyrie, 216.

43. "John the White" or, figuratively, "the clean" or "the pure."

44. *Mémoires*, I:274.

Chapter 15. Guardian Angel

1. Gottschalk and Maddox, 123.

2. L to Washington, Paris, March 17, 1790, *Mémoires*, I:323.

3. Henry IV (1553–1610), the first Bourbon king of France, reigned from 1589 to 1610 and restored stability after the religious wars in which Roman Catholics slaughtered tens of thousands of Protestants. As the Seine "ran red with blood" at the Massacre of Saint Bartholomew's Day, Henry converted to Roman Catholicism to save his own life.

4. Gottschalk and Maddox, 127.

5. Jefferson to Madison, July 22, 1789, in Gottschalk and Maddox, 127.

6. *Gazette de Leide*, July 28, 1789.

7. *Mémoires*, 253, n3.

8. Davenport, I:158–159.

9. *Mémoires*, I:238.

10. *Mémoires*, I:258.

11. Matthieu Jouve Jourdan (1749–1794), better known as Jourdan Coupe-Tête (Jourdan the Head-Cutter), started out as a butcher, but, in the face of chronic meat

shortages, became a farrier before opening a cabaret at the outbreak of the Revolution. The sadistic horrors he perpetrated during the Revolution made him a French folk hero whose name parents cited to elicit obedience from recalcitrant children. He was born near Le Puy, not far from Lafayette's own birthplace in the Auvergne, and he would die on the guillotine during the period known as the Terror, in 1794, just two months before Robespierre.—*Le Petit Robert des Noms Propres* (Paris: Dictionnaires Le Robert, 1994), 1088; Tulard et al., 903–904.

12. *Mémoires*, I:260.
13. Charavay, 181.
14. *Mémoires*, I:264.
15. Ibid.
16. Ibid, I:268–269.
17. Lasteyrie, 215.
18. Gottschalk and Maddox, 193.
19. *Mémoires*, I:276.
20. Lasteyrie, 215.
21. Whitlock, I:348.
22. Davenport, I:161.
23. Tulard et al., 761.
24. Whitlock, I:345.
25. Jefferson to Jay, September 23, 1789, in Gottschalk and Maddox, 287.
26. Marat (1743–1793) apparently stood 5′1″, but his mannerisms and posture made him seem shorter and provoked his many critics and enemies to refer to him as "the dwarf."—Tulard et al., 969–971.
27. *Mémoires* of René Levasseur, in Tulard et al., 970.
28. Tulard et al., 969–971.
29. Davenport, I:242.
30. Ibid., I:223.
31. Davenport, I:242 [Monday, October 5, 1789].
32. *Mémoires*, I:282.
33. Whitlock, I:355.
34. *Mémoires*, I:282.
35. Gottschalk and Maddux, 332.
36. Ibid.
37. *Mémoires*, I:282. [When Julius Caesar crossed the Rubicon "river" into Italy to war against Pompey, "crossing the Rubicon" became a metaphor for making an irrevocable, life-changing decision—although the Rubicon was, and remains, more of a gully than a river.]
38. Davenport, I:242 [Monday, October 5, 1789].
39. *Mémoires*, I:282.
40. Ibid.
41. There is some question of how many minutes or hours Lafayette slept, because his *Mémoires* contain two different descriptions of the critical events of October 5 and 6. The first is his own recollection, written in 1829; the other a reconstruction by his son, culled from notes Lafayette had planned to publish in 1814. In either case, he could not have slept more than three hours, and he may have slept far less.
42. Corporal Bérard, of the Noailles Company, in Charavay, 190n.

43. *Mémoires*, I:283.
44. Ibid.
45. Ibid.
46. Ibid., I:284.
47. Ibid.
48. Ibid.
49. Short to Jay, October 9, 1789, in Gottschalk and Maddox, 385.

Chapter 16. Prisoners of the Mob

1. The royal manège, or indoor riding facility, was a huge rectangular building that stretched from west to east on what is now the rue de Rivoli, at the intersection of the rue de Castiglione. The building was torn down in 1801, when Napoléon I ordered the construction of the rue de Rivoli as the new, wider, central east-west thoroughfare across the city, to replace the old, narrow rue Saint–Honoré, between the place de la Révolution (now the place de la Concorde) and the place de la Bastille.

2. October 21, 1789, Davenport, I:252.

3. *Mémoires*, I:298.

4. Taillemitte, 220.

5. Davenport, I:382, Morris to Washington, Paris, January 24, 1790.

6. *Mémoires*, I:320–321.

7. Sparks, I:322.

8. Davenport, I:373 (Washington to Morris, New York, October 13, 1789, delivered in Paris 21 January 1790).

9. Ibid., I:376–377, Morris to Washington, Paris, January 22, 1790.

10. Washington to L, Mount Vernon, July 25, 1785, Idzerda, V:336–340.

11. The issue had a total value of about $4 billion in today's currency. Each assignat had a face value of 1,000 livres ($10,000), yielding annual interest of 5 percent—far too high for the average Frenchman, but well within reach of Assembly members, who could not only buy the bonds but vote to declare them in default and, therefore, claim huge parcels of valuable church land at no additional cost.

12. Lasteyrie, 217–221.

13. *Mémoires*, I:523–526.

14. Whitlock, I:385.

15. Maurier, 181.

16. L to Washington, Paris, March 17, 1790, *Mémoires*, I:322–323.

17. Founded in 1789 after the Assembly moved from Versailles to Paris, the Jacobin club's actual name was the *Société des amis de la Constitution*—"Society of the Friends of the Constitution." It held its meetings in the refectory of the Jacobin Monastery, a Dominican monastery founded in 1217 in Paris on the rue Saint-Jacques, hence the sobriquet *Jacobins*. In 1613, the Dominicans moved their monastery to a site just off the rue Saint-Honoré to what is now the place du Marché Saint-Honoré, only a few steps away from where the Constituent Assembly of 1789 convened. Although the Dominican brothers renamed it the Couvent de l'Annunciation, they retained the Jacobin sobriquet that members of the political club eventually adopted. Political activists tended to meet in religious sites because of the sanctuary they provided from political arrest.

18. *Le Petit Robert . . .* , 1774.

19. *Mémoires*, 1:305.

20. Anecdotal, French Ministry of Culture.

21. The Franciscan friars, or "gray monks," as they were also called, earned the sobriquet of *cordeliers* from the thick ropes of braided strands they used as belts for their long gray robes.

22. Whitlock, 1:390.

23. Ibid., 393.

24. Taillemite, 237.

25. *Mémoires*, 1:335–336.

26. Ibid., 1:336.

27. Ibid.

28. William Short to Morris, July 27, 1790, Davenport, 1:565.

29. Tulard et al., 1109.

30. *Mémoires*, 1:337.

31. Ibid.

32. William Short to Morris, July 27, 1790, Davenport, 1:565–566.

33. [no author cited] *Histoire authentique et suivie de la Révolution de France* (Londres: 1792, 2 vols.), 1:702, in Charavay, 234.

34. Charavay, 235.

35. Ibid., 236.

36. Ibid., 238.

37. Arguably, "*Ça ira*" can be translated as "All will be well"; "We'll be all right"; "We'll succeed," etc.; thus:

> All will be well, will be well, will be well;
> The aristocrats to the lamppost [to be hung];
> All will be well, will be well, will be well;
> The aristocrats, we'll hang them all.

. . . or thereabouts.

38. William Short to Morris, July 27, 1790, Davenport, 1:565.

39. L to Washington, Paris, August 28, 1790, *Mémoires*, 1:384.

40. *Mémoires*, 1:338.

41. Washington to L, New York, August 11, 1790. Ibid., 1:382–383.

42. Morris to Washington, August 16, 1790, Davenport, 1:574.

43. Morris to Washington, January 24, 1790, Davenport, 1:384.

44. *Soirées amoureuses du général Motier et de la belle Antoinette, par le petit épagneul de l'Autrichienne* (unsigned, dated 1790; 32 pp., 8 vols.), cited in Charavay, 252, and probably written by Marat, who habitually called Lafayette "Motier."

45. Charavay, 247.

46. L to Washington, Paris, March 7, 1791, *Mémoires*, 1:394.

47. *Mémoires*, 1:393. [The newborn's full name was George Fayette Washington.]

48. Davenport, II:68–69.

49. Washington to L, Philadelphia, July 28, 1791, *Mémoires*, 1:398–399.

50. Lasteyrie, 223.

51. Danton, June 21, 1791, Proceedings of *La Societé de Jacobins*, in Charavay, 269–270.

52. Charavay, 272.

53. L to Washington, Paris, June 6, 1791, *Mémoires*, I:397–398.
54. Washington to L, Philadelphia, September 10, 1791, *Mémoires*, I:400.
55. A. Goodwin, "Reform and Revolution in France: October 1789–February 1793," *The New Cambridge Modern History* (Cambridge: The Cambridge University Press, 1965), VIII:692.
56. Lasteyrie, 226.

Chapter 17. The Most Hated Man in Europe

1. L to Washington, Chavaniac [undated], extracted from references contained in a second letter dated January 22, 1792, *Mémoires*, I:481.
2. *Mémoires*, I:400–401.
3. Tulard et al., 95.
4. Morris to Washington, Paris, December 27, 1791, Davenport, II:332–333.
5. Morris to Washington, Paris, December 27, 1791, Davenport, II:334.
6. L to Washington, Paris, March 15, 1792, *Mémoires*, I:483.
7. L to Louis XVI, June 16, 1792, *Mémoires*, I:489.
8. L to the Legislative Assembly, June 16, 1792, and read on June 18, *Mémoires*, I:450–452.
9. Whitlock, I:455.
10. Quotation attributed to the "head of the delegation of rioters." Tulard et al., 95.
11. Morris's description of the king in a letter to Washington, November 22, 1790, Davenport, II:68.
12. *Mémoires*, I:435.
13. Davenport, II:457.
14. Ibid.
15. Morris to Jefferson, Paris, August 1, 1792, Davenport, II:483.
16. Whitlock, I:466–467.
17. A. Goodwin, "Reform and Revolution in France: October 1789–February 1793," *The New Cambridge Modern History* (Cambridge: The Cambridge University Press, 1965), VIII:704.
18. "I am the state." [Remark attributed to Louis XIV before the Estates General in 1651—*Bartlett's Familiar Quotations*, 281:3.]
19. The Knights Templar were a French religious military order founded in 1119 to protect Christian pilgrims bound for the Holy Land. After the loss of Palestine, they returned to Europe, where their involvement in power struggles between the Pope and various French kings led to the order's demise and the execution of many of its members. Its last grand master, Jacques de Molay, was executed in 1314, and the order's assets were seized by the church and state. Nothing remains of the fortress in Paris, which was built in 1139 and covered most of the land now bounded by the rue du Temple, rue Vendôme, rue Beranger, rue Picardie, and rue de Bretagne in the third arrondissement, just behind the huge Pompidou Center. The *donjon* prison was built in 1265 and demolished in 1809–1810. Section by section, the rest of the fortress was leveled over the next forty years.
20. Whitlock, I:475.
21. Whitlock, II:38.
22. L to Madame de Lafayette, Rochefort, August 21, 1792, *Mémoires*, I:498–499.

23. Morris to Jefferson, Paris, August 22, 1792, Davenport, II:531.

24. L to William Short, Nivelle, August 26, 1792, Charavay, 582.

25. L to Monsieur de la Rochefoucauld, Nivelle, August 26, 1792, *Mémoires*, I:499–501.

26. Davenport, II:541.

27. Davenport, II:540.

28. Maurois, 219.

29. Lasteyrie, 238.

30. Lasteyrie, 240.

31. Whitlock, II:18; Maurois, 221.

32. Ibid., 253–254.

33. Maurois, 239.

34. Solon Reynaud to Frestel [undated], Maurois, 243; Whitlock, II.

35. Charavay, 340–341.

36. Born in Charleston, South Carolina, Pinckney (1750–1828) was educated at Westminster School and Oxford University before taking a year of training at the military academy in Caen, France. Admitted to the bar in England, he returned home to fight in the Revolution. He was wounded and captured at Camden, taken to Philadelphia, and freed after an exchange of prisoners.

37. Thomas Pinckney to William Short, London, September 14, 1792.

38. Morris to Short, Paris, September 12, 1792, Davenport, II:556–557.

39. Short to Morris, November 13, 1792, Davenport, II:560.

40. Short to Morris, The Hague, December 7, 1792, Davenport, II:560.

41. Whitlock, II:14.

42. Morris to Washington, Paris, October 23, 1792, Davenport, II:565.

43. Whitlock, II:21.

44. Lasteyrie, 264.

45. A. Goodwin, "Reform and Revolution in France: October 1789–February 1793," *The New Cambridge Modern History* (Cambridge: Cambridge University Press, 1965), VIII:711.

46. *On ne saurait faire une omelette sans casser les oeufs*—French proverb from the French Revolution of 1789, of unknown origin. —*Bartlett's Familiar Quotations*, 786:19.

47. Tulard et al., 348.

48. Ibid., 348–350.

49. Proclamation of Cordelier leader Pierre Gaspard Chaumette, in the Convention, November 16, 1792. Tulard et al., 349.

50. The French revolutionary, or "republican," calendar, as they called it, began on the autumnal equinox, September 22, 1792. Each year was divided into twelve months of thirty days each, with a five-day holiday period added at the end of each year and a sixth day added in leap years. Instead of weeks, every month was divided into "*décades*" of ten days each. The names of the months were *vendémiaire, brumaire, frimaire, nivôse, pluviôse, ventôse, germinal, floréal, prairial, messidor, thermidore,* and *fructidore,* with each name derived from the weather or farming activity typical of the period (e.g., *ventôse* = wind time; *germinal* = planting time, etc.). Individual days were renamed for seeds, trees, flowers, fruits, animals, or tools, instead of saints or Christian festivals. Invented by Danton's friend, the self-styled poet Philippe-François Fabré d'Eglantine, the calendar remained

in effect for thirteen years, until January 1, 1806, when Napoléon ordered a return to the Gregorian calendar used by the rest of the western world. D'Eglantine went to the guillotine with Danton on 15 *germinal* of Year II (April 5, 1794).

51. *Mémoires*, II:80.

52. Davenport, II:561.

53. Adrienne Lafayette to Washington, March 13, 1793, Charavay, 345.

54. Morris to Jefferson, Paris, January 25, 1793, Davenport, 601–602.

55. Nothing remains of the Cimetière de la Madeleine, which blanketed an area in the present-day 8th Arrondissement of Paris, stretching from what is now the rue des Mathurins, across the Boulevard Haussmann to the Gare St.-Lazare railway station. During the Restoration, the brothers of King Louis XVI, namely, King Louis XVIII and his successor, King Charles X, undertook the impossible task of recovering their brother's remains; they transferred some skeletal parts they claimed were those of the late king and his wife to graves in the Basilica of Saint-Denis, north of Paris, which houses the sarcophaguses of almost all the kings of France, including Clovis, Charlemagne, Saint-Louis, and Francis I. After the reburial, Charles X built a large, churchlike memorial that still stands over the part of the Madeleine Cemetery where the Jacobins dumped King Louis's corpse. Called L'Expiatoire Louis XVI, it is surrounded by a small park on the corner of the Boulevard Haussman and the rue Pasquier, but it is open to visitors by appointment only and closed to the general public to prevent gatherings by royalist cults.

56. *American Minerva*, December 8, 1793, cited in Unger, *Noah Webster*, 180.

57. L to Adrienne, Magdebourg, October 2, 1793, *Mémoires*, II:83.

Chapter 18. The Prisoners of Olmütz

1. Louis-Charles de France (1785–1795?) was proclaimed King Louis XVII in absentia in Germany by his uncles (the future Louis XVIII and Charles X) and the royalist emigrés, after his father's execution on January 21, 1793. With France at war with Austria and Prussia, the boy was a valuable pawn in negotiations between the French revolutionary government and its enemies. On July 3, 1793, he was taken from his mother and allegedly put under the surveillance of a cobbler, Antoine Simon. Marie-Antoinette was guillotined on October 16, 1793, and in January 1794 Louis was sent back to the Temple Prison, where the harsh conditions of his confinement rapidly undermined his health, and he died soon after. An inquest insisted that Louis had succumbed to scrofula (tuberculosis of the lymph glands), but so much secrecy surrounded the last months of his life that the truth remains hidden by rumors. Some contend that he did not die and escaped from the Temple. Others claim he was poisoned, while still others say he met the usual fate of prisoners—decapitation and disappearance into a mass grave with other nameless prisoners. During the decades that followed his disappearance, more than thirty persons claimed to be Louis XVII. After his abduction from his mother's cell, French government apologists for the Revolution concocted a variety of tales regarding his fate. The most charming placed him in the care of "Simon," a kindly, loving shoemaker, who raised the boy as a patriotic commoner, singing songs of the Revolution until his death from tuberculosis at the age of twelve. No trace of his body or documentary evidence of his fate after his abduction from his mother's cell or how he met his death has ever been found.

2. Tulard et al., 175.

3. [New York] Herald, March 4, 1797. Unger, Noah Webster, 186.

4. On the following July 4, Genêt marched in the Independence Day parade in New York City beside Governor George Clinton. A month later, he married Clinton's daughter, Cornelia, whose dowry they used to buy a farm in Jamaica, on "longisland." He settled down to the life of "an American cultivator," became an American citizen, and disappeared from public life. He died on his farm on Bastille Day, July 14, 1834, at the age of seventy-one. One of his great-great-grandsons, Edmond Charles Clinton Genet, was the first American aviator killed in World War I, in the skies over France with the Lafayette Escadrille, a group of American flyers who volunteered to fight with the Allies before the United States entered the war.

5. Maurois, 243.

6. Tulard et al., 153.

7. Mémoires, II:80.

8. Ibid., II:85.

9. Whitlock, II:31.

10. Maurois, 244.

11. Tulard et al., 761.

12. Maurois, 244. [D'Estaing's remains were eventually transferred to the Eglise Saint-Roch, on the rue Saint-Honoré, almost across the street from the Noailles mansion. A plaque on a column near the altar, placed there by the Society of the Cincinnati, commemorates his presence and his contributions to the American War of Independence.]

13. Ibid., 253.

14. At 69, Rochambeau (1725–1807) was too old to return to war after his ordeal in prison. He later received the Legion of Honor and a handsome pension from Napoléon.

15. James Monroe, Autobiography of James Monroe (Syracuse, N.Y.: Syracuse University Press, 1959, Stuart Gerry Brown, ed.), 70–71.

16. Whitlock, II:50.

17. Lasteyrie, 338–343.

18. Taillemite, 370.

19. C. W. Crawley, ed., "War and Peace in an Age of Upheaval, 1793–1830," The New Cambridge Modern History (Cambridge: Cambridge University Press, 1965), IX:286.

20. Lasteyrie, 353–354.

21. "De Madame de Lafayette à Madame de Tessé, Olmütz, le 10 mai 1796," Mémoires . . . , II:96.

22. Ibid.

23. Mémoires, II:92.

24. Lasteyrie, 365.

25. Ibid.

26. The two biographies were later published in the previously cited, single-volume work, Vie de Madame de Lafayette par Mme. de Lasteyrie, sa Fille, précédée d'une Notice sur sa Mère Mme. la Duchesse d'Ayen, 1737–1807 (Paris: Léon Techener Fils, 1868).

27. Washington to Senator George Cabot, September 7, 1795, Fitzpatrick, Writings, II:288.

28. Whitlock, II:69.

29. *The Captivity of La Fayette, a Heroic Epistle, with Characters and Historical Notes Not Yet Known to the Public, on the Illustrious Prisoners of Olmütz, in Moravia*, by Charles d'Agrain, cited in Maurois, 302–303.

30. Whitlock, II:70.

31. Ibid., 70–71.

32. Lasteyrie, 377–379.

33. *Mémoires*, II:230.

34. Lasteyrie, 372–373.

35. Whitlock, II:70; Maurois, 299.

36. Washington to the emperor of Germany, May 15, 1796, Lafayette Papers, Pierpont Morgan Library, New York.

37. Maurois, 300.

38. Ibid.

39. Charavay, 359.

40. Ibid., 360.

41. *Mémoires*, II:97.

42. Ibid.

43. Compulsory universal military service remained a basic French institution until 2001.

44. Whitlock, II:78.

45. Whitlock, II:81.

46. Ibid., II: 82–83.

47. Charavay, 365.

48. Maurois, 325.

49. *Mémoires*, II:123–124. [On October 6 after his release from prison, Lafayette wrote to Washington, but that letter has been lost.]

Chapter 19. Resurrection

1. Whitlock, 91.

2. Maurois, 335–336.

3. Ibid., 336.

4. Lasteyrie, 396–397.

5. Ibid., 337.

6. Whitlock, 96.

7. *Mémoires*, II:134–135.

8. *New York Spectator*, November 16, 1798, in Unger, *Noah Webster*, 234.

9. L to Washington, August 20, 1798, *Mémoires*, II:140–142.

10. Marie-Josèphe Beauchet to Adrienne, Paris, December 18, 1797, in Maurois, 329–331.

11. Washington to L, December 25, 1798, *Mémoires*, II:142–144.

12. L to Washington, Vianen, May 9, 1799, *Mémoires*, II:155–156.

13. L to Adrienne, Vianen, August 5, 1799, *Mémoires*, II:158.

14. L to Adrienne, Vianen, August 5, 1799, *Mémoires*, II:163.

15. L to Adrienne, Vianen, September 19, 1799, II:169.

16. Maurois, 370.

17. L to Général Bonaparte, Utrecht, 9 brumaire an VIII (October 30, 1799), *Mémoires*, II:188.

18. L to Adrienne, Vianen, October 30, 1799, *Mémoires*, II:187.

19. *Mémoires*, II:191.

20. Lasteyrie, 403–404, and *Mémoires*, II:191–192.

21. Sparks, *Life*, 552. [Lafayette would bequeath Washington's pistols to Andrew Jackson, who, in turn, bequeathed them to George-Washington Lafayette. They remained in the Lafayette family until 1958, when they were sold to a private collector. In 1983, they were sold at auction in Paris for the equivalent of nearly $38,000. In 2001 they fetched about $1 million in auction in New York.]

22. Whitlock, II:113.

23. *Mémoires*, II:197.

24. Whitlock, II:115.

25. *Mémoires*, II:197.

26. Ibid., 301.

27. Lasteyrie, 408.

28. Thaddeus Kosciusko (1746–1817) would move to Switzerland in 1816, and, after his death there, his remains were taken to the cathedral in Krakow, Poland. For his service in the American Revolution, Congress had granted him lands in the Ohio territory, and, influenced by Lafayette, he bequeathed proceeds from the sale of those lands to found the Colored School at Newark, New Jersey, one of the first educational institutions for black students established in the United States.

29. *Mémoires*, II:224.

30. Dumas Malone, *Jefferson the President: First Term, 1801–1805* (Boston: Little, Brown, 1970), 357.

31. L to Jefferson, La Grange, October 8, 1804, *Mémoires*, II:224–226.

32. L to Jefferson, La Grange, October 8, 1804, *Mémoires*, II:226.

33. *Mémoires*, II:196.

34. L to Jefferson, La Grange, October 8, 1804, *Mémoires*, II:226.

35. Lasteyrie, 406–407.

36. Lasteyrie, 414–416.

37. Ibid.

38. Whitlock, II:144 [source not identified].

39. Lasteyrie, 417. [In Lasteyrie, 417–459, Lafayette's daughter Virginie included far more (though by no means all) of his letter to La Tour-Maubourg than his son, George-Washington Lafayette, included in the compilation of Lafayette's *Mémoires*, where it appears in II:229–231, and represents, at most, about ten manuscript pages.]

Chapter 20. Apotheosis

1. Maurois, 464 [source unidentified].

2. L to Jefferson, La Grange, July 4, 1812, *Mémoires*, II:233.

3. Jefferson to L, Monticello, November 3, 1813, *Mémoires*, II:234.

4. *Mémoires*, II:239.

5. The route he followed remains today the route de Napoléon, a particularly beautiful, albeit narrow and treacherous, north-south road across the French Alps that carries travelers back in time, far from modern, multilane *autoroutes*.

6. *Mémoires*, II:300.

7. Ibid.

8. Charavay, 394.

9. Ibid., II:285.

10. *Mémoires*, II:286.

11. By then, Napoléon II was living in Austria with his maternal grandfather, Austrian emperor Francis II, who had changed his grandson's name to the duke of Reichstadt. Raised as an Austrian, speaking German, and forbidden to utter a word of French, he entered an Austrian military academy, became an officer in the Austrian army, and died of tuberculosis at the age of twenty-one. As a gesture of unity with the collaborationist French government, Hitler transferred Napoléon II's ashes to the Hotêl des Invalides in Paris in 1940 to lay near his father's tomb.

12. Whitlock, II:192–193.

13. Ibid, 198.

14. L to Monroe, Paris, July 20, 1820, *Mémoires*, II:345–346.

15. The Carbonari (Ital., "charcoal burners") originated in Naples during the Napoleonic period to overthrow French rule. Meeting by firelight in the mountains, they organized themselves in cells of twenty men each, often not knowing each other's real names and never knowing anyone from other cells. Each cell sent an elected leader to a central committee, which determined overall policy and action. In 1820, the Carbonari led an unsuccessful attempt to overthrow the King of Naples.

16. Whitlock, II:194.

17. Mayor of Baltimore to the City Council, July 24, 1824, in Anne C. Loveland, "Lafayette's Farewell Tour," *Lafayette, Hero of Two Worlds: The Art and Pageantry of His Farewell Tour of America, 1824–1825*, Essays by Stanley J. Idzerda, Anne C. Loveland, and Marc H. Miller (Flushing, New York: The Queens Museum, 1989), 89.

18. "The Fete at Castle Garden," *The Port Folio*, XVIII (Oct. 1824), 324, cited in Marc H. Miller, "Lafayette's Farewell Tour and American Art," *Lafayette, Hero of Two Worlds . . .* , 112.

19. Charavay, 441.

20. Whitlock, II:218.

21. Ibid., 222.

22. Charavay, 439.

23. Ibid., 233.

24. Ibid.

25. Ibid., 224.

26. Whitlock, II:247.

27. Ibid., 248.

28. Whitlock, II:273. [The title "Old Hundred" refers to Psalm C (Psalm 100)—*All people that on earth do dwell*—in the "old" Anglo-German Psalter, which was replaced by a newer version of the Psalter in 1696. The hymn's melody, which is also used for the doxology and other hymns in Protestant churches, was composed by Loys Bourgeois and first appeared in the German Psalter of 1551. "Old Hundred" was one of the most popular hymns in American churches, and, as with "Yankee Doodle," new verses were often written and sung to its melody on special occasions, as in the verse cited by Whitworth for the Bunker Hill ceremonies. W. H. Havergal, *History of the Old Hundredth Psalm Tune* (New York, 1854); Stanley Sadie, ed., *The New Grove Dictionary of Music and Musicians* (London: Macmillan, 1980), 13:529.].

29. Ibid., II:174.

30. *Mémoires*, II:390.
31. Whitlock, II:282.
32. Ibid., 283.
33. Ibid., II:393–394.
34. Whitlock, II:287.

Chapter 21. *Les Adieux*

1. *Mémoires*, II:403.
2. Morgan, 437.
3. Taillemite, 483.
4. Ibid.
5. Whitlock, II:317.
6. *Mémoires*, II:456.
7. Odilon Barrot, cited in Whitlock, II:327.
8. Whitlock, II:330.
9. Charavay, 473.
10. Whitlock, II:333.
11. Ibid., 335.
12. *Mémoires*, II:463.
13. Ibid.
14. Ibid.
15. Charavay, 477.
16. Chateaubriand, cited in Charavay, 474.
17. The House of Bourbon originated with Adhémar, who became baron of Bourbon (now Bourbon-Archambault), in the central-French province of Bourbonnais, about fifty miles north of Vichy. The first Bourbon king was Henry IV of Navarre, whose grandson was Louis XIV. It was Louis XIV's younger brother, Philippe I, the duc d'Orléans, who founded the collateral branch of the Bourbons known as the House of Orléans. Louis-Philippe I was his great-grandson.
18. Letter from the king to L, August 29, 1830, *Mémoires*, II:469.
19. Whitlock, II:343.
20. Ibid., 346.
21. Louis-Philippe's choice of name for the place was actually the second time it had carried the name place de la Concorde. In 1795, the Directory gave it that name after it ordered the guillotine removed, but it retained its old name, the place de la Révolution, in everyday parlance until 1830.
22. Charavay, 495.
23. Whitlock, II:351–352.
24. Letter to the king from L, December 25, 1830, *Mémoires*, II:492.
25. *Histoire et Mémoires par le Général comte de Ségur*, VII:372, cited in Charavay, 486–487.
26. Whitlock, II:381.
27. Charavay, 498–500.
28. Maurois, 464.
29. Already recognized by Americans as their nation's foremost writer, Cooper (and his literary works) gained such world renown that, in 1826, he traveled to Europe with

his family and remained seven years. After spending two years in Paris, he moved to Switzerland and then Italy, returning to France only after the Revolution of 1830 had ended. Outspoken in defending American democracy against European critics, he quite naturally became fast friends with Lafayette during his stays in Paris, and they began a warm correspondence after Cooper returned to the United States.

30. *Mémoires*, II:586.

31. L to Monsieur Fenimore Cooper, Paris, April 14, 1834, *Mémoires*, II:587.

32. Cloquet, 294.

33. Ibid., 295.

34. *Mémoires*, II:589, written by George-Washington Lafayette.

35. Andrew Jackson defeated Adams in the latter's bid for reelection in 1828. Adams won election to the House of Representatives, however, in 1830 and was serving his ninth consecutive term when he died in office, in 1848. His brilliant speeches in the House earned him the sobriquet "Old Man Eloquent."

36. John Quincy Adams, *Oration on the Life of Lafayette*, 82 (Published by an Act of Congress, December, 1834).

37. Charavay, 513.

38. From the *National*, May 21, 1834, cited in Whitlock, II:412.

39. From the *National*, May 23, 1834, cited in Charavay, 516.

40. Ibid., 516–517.

41. Charles E. Stanton (1859–1933), July 4, 1917, in *Bartlett's Familiar Quotations*, 580:16. Although the quotation is often attributed to Pershing himself, he set the record straight in his Pulitzer Prize–winning autobiography, *My Experiences in the World War* (1931), denying ever having said "anything so splendid." The American flag continues to fly above Lafayette's grave and is replaced with a new one every year on July 4 by the American ambassador to France and the highest ranking American officer in France.

Epilogue

1. Donnet, 100.

2. Dunn, 19.

Selected Bibliography of Principal Sources

[Author's note: *Lafayette's remarkable life story attracted some of the most renowned nineteenth-century intellects, whose credentials, in my opinion, deserve recognition. I have therefore added short biographical information about some of the most illustrious authors whose works served as primary sources for this book.*]

Primary Sources

Etienne Charavay, *Le Général La Fayette, 1757–1834, Notice Biographique* (Paris: Société de la Révolution Francaise, 1898). [*An important French archivist at the end of the nineteenth century, Charavay's is universally acknowledged as the definitive, broad-based biography of Lafayette.*]

Jules Cloquet, *Souvenirs sur la Vie Privée du Général Lafayette* (Paris: A. Et W. Galignani et Cie., 1836). [*Cloquet was Lafayette's personal physician in the last years of his life.*]

Edward S. Corwin, *French Policy and the American Alliance of 1778* (Princeton, N.J.: Princeton University Press, 1916, reprinted, 1969).

Beatrix Cary Davenport, ed., *A Diary of the French Revolution By Gouverneur Morris (1752–1816), Minister to France during the Terror* (Boston: Houghton Mifflin, 1939, 2 vols.).

Henri Doniol, *Histoire de la Participation de la France à l'Etablissement des Etats-Unis d'Amérique* (Paris: Imprimerie Nationale, 1886, 5 vols., quarto). [*Doniol (1818–1906) was born in the Auvergne, not far from Lafayette's birthplace, and became a renowned lawyer and, subsequently, the prefect, or chief executive officer, of various departments in central France, before changing careers to become a historian and a prolific author of historical works and works of political science. In 1882, he was named head of the French National Printing Bureau, and the National Assembly commissioned him to collate the thousands of documents in the archives of the Foreign Ministry relating to French Government participation in the American Revolutionary War. His is the definitive exposition of French government policy and the motivation for that policy during the last half of the eighteenth century.*]

William A. Duer, ed., *Memoirs, Correspondence and Manuscripts of General Lafayette, Published by his Family* (New York: Saunders and Otley Ann Street and Conduit Street

London, 1837. [*Duer (1780–1858) was a renowned New York City jurist and educator who oversaw New York public schools before becoming a state supreme court justice in 1822. In 1824, he became president of Columbia College, and, when illness forced his retirement in 1847, he turned to writing biographies of the patriots he had known as a boy when his father (William Duer, 1747–1799) was a member of the Continental Congress. In addition to translating the Lafayette Mémoires, Duer wrote an original biography of Continental army general William Alexander, Earl of Stirling.*]

John C. Fitzpatrick, *The Writings of George Washington* (Washington, 1931–1944, 39 vols.). [*Commissioned by Congress.*]

Louis Gottschalk, *Lafayette Comes to America* (Chicago: University of Chicago Press, 1935).

———, *Lafayette Joins the American Army* (Chicago: University of Chicago Press, 1937).

———, *Lafayette and the Close of the American Revolution* (Chicago: University of Chicago Press, 1942).

———, *Lafayette Between the American and the French Revolution (1783–1789)* (Chicago: University of Chicago Press, 1950).

Louis Gottschalk and Margaret Maddox, *Lafayette in the French Revolution* (Chicago: University of Chicago Press, 1969).

Stanley J. Idzerda, ed., *Lafayette in the Age of the American Revolution, Selected Letters and Papers, 1776–1790* (Ithaca, New York: Cornell University Press, 1977–1983, 5 vols.).

Lafayette, Hero of Two Worlds: The Art and Pageantry of His Farewell Tour of America, 1824–1825, Essays by Stanley J. Idzerda, Anne C. Loveland, and Marc H. Miller (Flushing, New York: The Queens Museum, 1989).

George-Washington Lafayette [*Gilbert Motier, Marquis de Lafayette*], *Mémoires, Correspondence et Manuscrits du Général Lafayette, publiés par sa famille*, Paris: H. Fournier, aîné, 6 vols., 1837; Bruxelles: Société Belge de Librairie, Etc., Hauman, Cattoir et Compagnie, 2 vols., 1837.

Mme. de Lasteyrie, *Vie de Madame de Lafayette par Mme. de Lasteyrie, sa Fille, précédée d'une Notice sur sa Mère Mme. la Duchesse d'Ayen, 1737–1807* (Paris: Léon Techener Fils, 1868).

Dumas Malone, *Jefferson and the Rights of Man* (Boston: Little, Brown, 1951).

André Maurois, *Adrienne, The Life of the Marquise de La Fayette* (New York: McGraw-Hill, 1961). [*Best known outside France for his romantic novels, Maurois (1885–1967) was a prolific biographer—of Disraeli, Shelley, Victor Hugo, Proust, and Balzac, in addition to Adrienne de Lafayette.*]

Gouverneur Morris, *A Diary of the French Revolution By Gouverneur Morris (1752–1816), Minister to France during the Terror* (Boston: Houghton Mifflin, 1939, Beatrix Cary Davenport, ed., 2 vols.).

Paul, Pialoux, *Lafayette: Trois Révolutions pour la Liberté* (Brioude: Editions Watel, 1989).

Nathan Schachner, *Thomas Jefferson: A Biography* (New York: Appleton-Century-Crofts, 1951, 2 vols.).

Page Smith, *John Adams* (New York: Doubleday, 1962, 2 vols.).

Jared Sparks, *The Life of Washington* (Boston: Tappan and Dennet, 1843), 256. [Sparks completed this work, and it was first printed in Cambridge, Massachusetts, in 1839, five years after Lafayette's death, by Metcalf, Keith, and Nichols, Printers to the University].

————, *The Writings of George Washington*, 12 vols. (Boston, Tappan and Dennet, 1834–1837). *[Jared Sparks (1789–1866) was a renowned American educator, author, historian, and theologian, whose historical works ranked with the poetry of Longfellow, the essays of Emerson, and novels of Alcott among the most influential, early-nineteenth-century American literary works. A graduate of Harvard, with a B.A. and an M.A., he became president of the college in 1849. In addition to his works on Washington, his many significant historical works include* The Works of Benjamin Franklin *and* The Library of American Biography *(25 vols.)].*

Etienne Taillemite, *La Fayette* (Paris: Librairie Arthème Fayard, 1989).

Charlemagne Tower, Jr., LL.D, *The Marquis de La Fayette in the American Revolution, with some account of the Attitude of France toward the War of Independence* (Philadelphia: J. B. Lippincott, 1895, 2 vols.). *[A Harvard graduate, Tower (1848–1923) was the son of an industrial magnate with extensive interest in the Minnesota iron ore fields. After receiving a law degree, he practiced law in Philadelphia before becoming president of Minnesota Iron Company. The family sold their business interests in 1887, and Tower became vice president and trustee of the University of Pennsylvania and wrote what historians agree is the definitive study of Lafayette in the American Revolution. When McKinley became president, Tower's wealth, erudition, and conservative political views made him a logical candidate for the diplomatic corps, which sent him to Vienna, St. Petersburg, and Berlin during a twelve-year career that ended in 1912.]*

Jean Tulard, Jean-François Fayard, Alfred Fierro, *Histoire et Dictionnaire de la Révolution Française, 1789–1799* (Paris: Editions Robert Laffont, S.A., 1987, 1998).

Francis Wharton, *The Revolutionary Diplomatic Correspondence of the United States, Edited under Direction of Congress, with preliminary index, and notes historical and legal. Published in conformity with Act of Congress of August 13, 1888.* (Washington: Government Printing Office, 1889, 6 vols.). *[A lawyer, clergyman, teacher, government official, author, and editor, Wharton (1820–1889) graduated from Yale University, won success as a lawyer in Philadelphia, and gained a formidable reputation for his works on criminal law. After the death of his wife in 1854, he turned to religious work for twenty years, before returning to the law and building a reputation in international law. After he became chief of the legal division of the U.S. Department of State in 1885, Congress entrusted him with compiling the definitive three-volume* Digest of the International Law of the United States, *to which the eight-volume* Revolutionary Correspondence *was a supplement. When meshed with the equivalent Doniol work from the archives of the French foreign ministry, Wharton's work provides an almost minute-by-minute description and understanding of the entire American Revolutionary War.]*

Brand Whitlock, *La Fayette* (New York: D. Appleton, 1929, 2 vols.). *[A prolific writer, political reformer, and diplomat, the Ohio-born Whitlock (1869–1934) had been a journalist and a lawyer before serving four terms as reform mayor of Toledo at the beginning of the twentieth century. After he had rid the city of graft, broken a local ice monopoly, and improved the lot of working men and women, the democratic administration rewarded him with an appointment as minister to Belgium at the outbreak of World War I. By that time, he had already published eight books, including one well-received novel. In Belgium, he worked tirelessly to organize food distribution among the civilian population of Belgium and the occupied zone of France. After the war, Belgium overwhelmed him with honors, and the U.S. government raised him to the rank of ambassador. He resigned in 1922 and spent the rest of his life in Europe—mostly in Brussels and the French Riviera—as a writer, "vacillating," as he put it, between fiction and nonfiction. In the last decade of his life he wrote two more novels, an autobiography, and his epic two-volume biography of Lafayette.]*

Additional Historical Works and Secondary Sources

Charles Francis Adams, ed., *The Works of John Adams* (Boston, 1851).

John R. Alden, *A History of the American Revolution* (New York: Alfred A. Knopf, 1969).

Harry Ammon, *The Genet Mission* (New York: W. W. Norton, 1973).

————, *James Monroe* (Newtown, Conn.: American Political Biography Press, 1971).

Thomas C. Amory, *The military services and life of Major-General John Sullivan, of the American Revolutionary Army* (Boston, 1868).

Helen Augur, *The Secret War of Independence* (New York: Duell, Sloan and Pearce, 1955).

Olivier Bernier, *Lafayette, Hero of Two Worlds* (New York: E. P. Dutton, 1983).

Soulange Bodin, *La Diplomatie de Louis XV et le Pacte de Famille* (Paris, 1894).

Claude G. Bowers, *The Young Jefferson* (Boston: Houghton Mifflin, 1945).

Edgar Ewing Brandon, ed., *Lafayette, Guest of the Nation: A Contemporary Account of the Triumphal Tour of General Lafayette Through the United States in 1824–25, as Reported by the Local Newspapers* (Oxford, Ohio: 1950–1957, 3 vols.)

John Buchanan, *The Road to Guilford Courthouse: The American Revolution in the Carolinas* (New York: John Wiley & Sons, 1997).

L. H. Butterfield, ed., *Diary and Autobiography of John Adams* (Cambridge, Mass., 1961, 4 vols.).

E. P. Chase, ed., *Our Revolutionary forefathers: the letters of François, marquis Barbé de Marbois* (New York, 1929).

Marquis de Chastellux, *Travels in North America, in the Years 1780, 1781, and 1782* (London, 1787, 2 vols.).

[Marquis de] Condorcet, *Mémoires sur la Révolution française extraits de sa correspondance et de celle de ses amis* (Paris, 1824, 2 vols.).

W. P. Cresson, *James Monroe* (Chapel Hill: University of North Carolina Press, 1946).

J. Hector St. John de Crèvecoeur, *Letters from an American Farmer and Sketches of Eighteenth-Century America* (London, Davies and Davis, 1782), rewritten, expanded, and republished in Paris (1784) as *Lettres d'un cultivateur américain . . .* , (Paris, 1784).

Henri Doniol, *Une correspondence administrative sous Louis XVI, épisode de la jeunesse de La Fayette*, dans les *Séances et travaux de l'Académie des Sciences morales et politiques* (1875).

————, *La Fayette dans la Révolution, Années d'Amérique, Années de Pouvoir et Années de Geole la Veille du Consulat, 1775–1799* (Paris: Librairie Armand Colin, 1904).

Hadelin Donnet, *Chavaniac Lafayette: Le Manoir des deux mondes* (Paris: le cherche midi editeur, 1990).

François Ribadeau Dumas, *La destinée secrète de La Fayette ou le messianisme révolutionaire* (Paris: Editions Robert Laffont, 1972).

Susan Dunn, *Sister Revolutions: French Lightning, American Light* (New York: Farrar, Straus and Giroux, 1999).

Harold Underwood Faulkner and Tyler Kepner, *America, Its History and People* (New York: Harper & Brothers, 1942).

John Ferling, *John Adams, A Life* (New York: Henry Holt, 1992).

Alfred Fierro, *Dictionnaire du Paris disparu* (Paris: Editions Parigramme. CPL, 1998).

John C. Fitzpatrick, ed., *The Writings of Washington* (Washington, D.C.: U.S. Congress, 39 vols.).

M. de Flassan, *Histoire générale et raisonnée de la Diplomatie française depuis la Fondation de la Monarchie jusqu'à la Fin du Règne de Louis XVI* (Paris, 1811, 7 vols.).

W. C. Ford, ed., *Journals of the Continental Congress, 1774–1789*, 34 vols.

G. W. Greene, *The Life of Nathanael Greene, Major-General in the Army of the Revolution* (New York, 1871, 3 vols.).

Stuart W. Jackson, *Lafayette, A Bibliography* (New York: Burt Franklin, 1930).

Daniel Jouve, Alice Jouve, Alvin Grossman, *Paris: Birthplace of the U.S.A.: A Walking Guide for the American Patriot* (Paris: Gründ, 1995).

Friedrich Kapp, *The Life of John Kalb, major-general in the Revolutionary Army* (New York, 1870), translated from *Leben des amerikanischen Generals Johann Kalb* (Stuttgart, 1862).

Lloyd Kramer, *Lafayette in Two Worlds: Public Cultures & Personal Identities in an Age of Revolutions* (Chapel Hill: University of North Carolina Press, 1996).

Bruce Lancaster, *From Lexington to Liberty, The Story of the American Revolution* (Garden City, New York: Doubleday, 1955).

André Lebey, *La Fayette, ou Le Militant Franc-Maçon* (Paris: Librairie Mercure, 1937).

Dumas Malone, *Jefferson the Virginian* (Boston: Little, Brown, 1948).

——— , *Jefferson and the Ordeal of Liberty* (Boston: Little, Brown, 1962).

——— , *Jefferson the President: First Term, 1801–1805* (Boston: Little, Brown, 1970).

——— , *Jefferson, the Sage of Monticello* (Boston: Little, Brown, 1977).

John Marshall, *Life of Washington* (Philadelphia, 1804–1807, 5 vols.)

[Masonic Publications] "L'Initiation du Général Lafayette," *Le Symbolisme, Organe Mensuel d'Inititation à la Philosophie du Grand Art de la Construction Universelle* (Paris: Direction et Administration, 1923).

David McCullough, *John Adams* (New York: Simon & Schuster, 2001).

François Métra et al., *Correspondance secrète, politique et littéraire* (London, 1787–1790, 18 vols.).

Meade Minnigerode, *Jefferson—Friend of France* (New York: G. P. Putnam's Sons, 1928).

James Monroe, *Autobiography of James Monroe* (Syracuse, N.Y.: Syracuse University Press, 1959, Stuart Gerry Brown, ed.).

——— , *The Writings of James Monroe, 1778–1831* (Washington: United States Congress, 1849, 7 volumes, edited by Stanislaus Murray Hamilton).

George Morgan, *The Life of James Monroe* (Boston: Small, Maynard, 1921).

Richard B. Morris, ed., *Encyclopedia of American History* (New York: Harper & Brothers, 1953).

Henry Mosnier, *Le Château de Chavaniac—Lafayette. Description-Histoire-Souvenirs* (Le Puy, 1883).

Saul K. Padover, ed., *The Washington Papers* (Norwalk, Connecticut: Easton Press, 1955).

Paul Pialoux, *Lafayette: Trois Révolutions pour la Liberté* (Brioude-Haute Loire: Edition Watel, 1989).

Abbé Guillaume Raynal, *Histoire philosophique et politique des établissements du Commerce des Européens dans les deux Indes* (Paris, 1773).

Abbé Claude Robin [chaplain to Comte de Rochambeau], *Nouveau voyage dans l'Amérique septentrionale en l'année 1781, etc.* (Philadelphia and Paris, 1782).

Comte de Ségur, *Mémoires, ou Souvenirs et Anecdotes* (Paris: Alexis Eymery, 1824–1826, 3 vols.).

James Thacher, *A military journal during the American Revolutionary War* (Boston, 1823).

Jules Thomas, *Correspondence Inédite de Lafayette, 1793–1801* (Paris: Librairie Ch. Delagrave, 1903).

Lyon G. Tyler, *Letters and Times of the Tylers* (Richmond, 1884, 2 vols.).

Harlow Giles Unger, *John Hancock, Merchant King and American Patriot* (New York: John Wiley & Sons, 2000).

————, *Noah Webster: The Life and Times of an American Patriot* (New York: John Wiley & Sons, 1998).

Periodicals

American Minerva
Boston Magazine
Bulletin de la Societé de l'Histoire du Protestantism français
Gazette de Leyde
The [New York] Herald
Journal de Lyon
Mercure de France
National [France]
New Plymouth Gazette
New York Spectator
Pennsylvania Journal
Revue Rétrospective

Reference Works

Bartlett's Famous Quotations
Dictionnaire de Biographie Française
Dictionary of American Biographies
Dictionary of National Biographies
Encyclopedia of American Education
Encyclopedia Britannica, 10th Ed.
Encyclopedia Universalis
Funk & Wagnall's New Encyclopedia
The New Cambridge Modern History
Le Petit Robert des Noms Propres
Webster's American Biographies
Webster's New Biographical Dictionary

Index

Printed in the United States
91869LV00004B/17/A